A Hero and a Spy
The Revolutionary War Correspondence of Benedict Arnold

Russell M. Lea

HERITAGE BOOKS
2008

HERITAGE BOOKS
AN IMPRINT OF HERITAGE BOOKS, INC.

Books, CDs, and more—Worldwide

For our listing of thousands of titles see our website
at
www.HeritageBooks.com

Published 2008 by
HERITAGE BOOKS, INC.
Publishing Division
100 Railroad Ave. #104
Westminster, Maryland 21157

International Standard Book Numbers
Paperbound: 978-0-7884-3811-0
Clothbound: 978-0-7884-7677-8

This book is humbly dedicated
to the loving memory of my Mother and Father.

Acknowledgements

I wish to thank the following groups and individuals that were instrumental in assisting me to complete this work.

Steven Rosenthal of SR Consultants;
Carl Settlemyer and the Washington Area lawyers for the Arts;
Corinne Will and the staff at Heritage Books;
Suzanne Christoff, Alan Aimone, and the staff of the USMA Library;
Suzanne Brahm and the staff of the Highland Falls Library;
The staff of the New York Public Library;
The staff of the New York Historical Society;
The staff of the New York State Library;
The staff of The Library of Congress;
The staff of The National Archives;
Katherine Ludwig, Greg Johnson, and the staff of the David Library;
The staff of the Westchester Historical Society;
The staff of the Army Historical Foundation;
The staff of The Historical Society of Pennsylvania;
The staff of Stony Point Battlefield State Historic Site;
The staff of Fort Ticonderoga;
The staff of the Skenesborough Museum at Whitehall;
The staff of Saratoga National Historic Park;
The Rangers of the National Park Service;
David and Cathy Lilburnes of Antipodean Books, Maps, & Prints;
Sara Mosha and the Historical Society of the Tarrytowns;
Dr. Jennifer Bryant, Gary LaValley, and the staff of the Nimitz Library – USNA;
The staff of the Armel-Leftwich Visitors Center – USNA;
The Quarrie Family and the North Castle Historical Society;
Jeff and Susan Wells of Stone Wells Bed & Breakfast;
Rod Bulley of Haverstraw, New York.

Cover image courtesy of Library of Congress Prints and Photographs Division – Catalog number LCUSZ62-56169

Introduction

In reflection of the 225th anniversary of the Revolutionary War, one battle is set apart from all others, for rather than being a battle of cannons, it was a battle of character. Although the word "character" may hold a variety of descriptions such as; the possession of good qualities, human values, ethics, integrity, and moral strength; one who strives to be a man of character, can only head in one direction, the right way. There is no gray area here, nor is there any excuse for the lack of it. Benedict Arnold was headed in the right direction initially, but as fate intervened, he was overcome by greed; the inordinate desire to fill one's ego and pocket. With a sense of boundless ambition and reckless impatience, he betrayed his country in a way as never before or since.

America owes its thanks to many heroes of the Revolution including Arnold, who, from the very beginning of our country's fight for freedom, valiantly performs his duty in honor of his country by pursuing life, liberty, and those who threaten it. He recaptures Fort Ticonderoga from the British; leads an Army through the wilderness of Maine; takes a bullet while attacking Quebec; stops the enemy's naval forces at Valcour Island; repels 2,000 British regulars with only 500 Militiamen at Ridgefield; and takes another bullet while defeating enemy land forces at Saratoga. Two of these engagements stopped the British from attacking Albany, gaining control of the Hudson Valley, and dividing New England from the rest of the country. His battlefield exploits allowed Washington to view him as his best fighting General. He is a true patriot to say the least, but, in his quest for glory, he initiates some political battles along the way. When Congress delays his reimbursements and promotion, Arnold sees the powers that be as much of an enemy as the British. At his moment of greatest vulnerability when he is injured, broke, insulted, and tired of the war, the British present him with a proposal to finish the game to their advantage. Driven by power, greed, and an overbearing ego, he accepts an offer that he cannot refuse; pay and recognition for his services. Determined to win the war by hook or by crook, he chooses the latter and forever changes the original meaning of his name; honor. His strategy is simple and straightforward; give the British a victory where he had defeated them before, but there is one factor that he fails to consider; the mercy of the Almighty.

I discovered the life of this amazing individual while doing research for two trivia books that I wrote on the history of West Point for its bicentennial; W. P. Bicentrivia and The Long Green Line. This is the true story of seven attempts to bring down one Nation under God and its outcome saved the states, for had the British succeeded in capturing West Point, America would have lost its War of Independence. Over 100 of Arnold's letters have been included to gain a complete understanding of his life's journey that would eventually drive him to become **A Hero and a Spy**. Read the book. See the sights. Feel the history.

Contents

I
New Haven

Dating back as early as **1100** from Monmouthshire, Wales, the name Arnold held a history that was considered highly respectable for centuries, and so it should, for it is derived from an old English term meaning, honor. The first member of the Arnold family to venture to the New World was William, born in Leamington, England in **1587**; he crossed the pond to settle in Providence, Rhode Island in **1636**. About seventeen years later in **1653**, one of his three sons, Benedict, had moved to Newport and later served three separate terms as Governor of the colony from between **1663** until his death in **1678**. His son, Benedict II, moderately followed in his footsteps by serving as a member of the Assembly in **1695**. The grandson of William, Benedict III, served as a merchant ship captain, buying goods from England and the West Indies and selling them in New England. In order to enhance his business, he moved to the popular shipping port of Norwich, Connecticut in **1730**. On **November 8, 1733**, he married Hannah Waterman, the young, attractive, devout Puritan widow of his employer, Absalom King. Of the six children that she would eventually bear, the first son, Benedict IV, would die in his youth along with three other children. One daughter named Hannah would live on to carry her mother's good name and another son, Benedict V, would live on to crucify his father's.

Born on the harsh winter day of **January 14th, 1741**, Benedict Arnold grew up to become a restless youth, biding his time in reckless adventures, attracting the attention of his peers, and soon evolving into a natural born leader. Along with having strong sporting skills in fencing, boxing, running, and leaping, he was quite a marksman with the pistol and musket as well, which paved much of his later success in battle. When Benedict was eleven, his mother enrolled him in the Canterbury Academy boarding school just fifteen miles to the north in order to gain an education that would instill the discipline in him that would lead him to military greatness. During summers, he would sail with his father until his trade business was devoured by the effects of the war and eventually drove him to drown his misery in the Jamaican rum that he imported. In a letter dated **August 12, 1753**, his mother pleads that he not follow the ways of his father when she writes, *'Pray, my dear son, whatever you neglect, don't neglect your precious soul, which once lost can never be regained.'* [5] Another letter sent

1

the following spring emphasizes his mother's undying spiritual integrity of the Puritan faith.

To Benedict Arnold

Norwich, April 12th, 1754

Dear Child

I received yours of the 1st instant, and was glad to hear that you were well. Pray, my dear, let your first concern be to make your peace with God, as it is of all concerns of the greatest importance. Keep a steady watch over your thoughts, words, and actions. Be dutiful to superiors, obliging to equals, and affable to inferiors, if any such there be. Always choose that your companions be your betters, that by their good examples you may learn.

From your affectionate mother,

Hannah Arnold

P. S. I have sent you 50s. Use it prudently, as you are accountable to God and your Father. Your Father and Aunt join me in love and service to Mr. Cogswell and Lady, and yourself. Your sister is from home. Your Father puts on twenty more. [5]

After just two years at Canterbury, his mother became overwhelmed with his father's debts and could no longer afford to pay for his schooling. Back at home and restless at heart, Benedict spent some time with the Mohegan Indian Chief Benjamin Uncas, who taught him the warrior ways of fishing, hunting, horseback riding, and canoe handling. Feeling the pressure of having his family fortune and reputation slip away, Benedict strove to prove his own self worth in order to make up for his father's failure. It was then that he began to show signs of the bold, fearless, and daunting man of action that would some day benefit him on the battlefield. Although he also revealed a side of him that was aggressive, impatient, and defiant.

When Benedict was fourteen, his father was arrested for debts that he could not pay and his mother was forced to send him to a relative, where he would serve as an apprentice to a chemist until the age of twenty-one. Dr. Daniel Lathrop, a graduate from Yale, was trained as a physician in London and returned to America to become the only apothecary between New York and Boston, thus making him a very wealthy man. Living in the Lathrop's riverfront mansion, Benedict returned to the world of wealth and trade that was previously taken from him by his father's drinking and debt. It was Lathrop who taught young Benedict the art of being a shrewd businessman, but it was the French and Indian War that allowed him to discover his call to arms.

In **early 1757**, Lathrop gave Benedict permission to defend his country after Indians supporting the French threatened New England by invading Fort William Henry near Lake George in upstate New York. The Norwich troops that he was marching with were turned back after one week after not seeing any action, nevertheless Benedict found the Army much more exciting than an apothecary. A year later, he made his way west and crossed the border into New York, where no one knew him as a servant. There he signed up with Captain Reuben Lockwood's company of Westchester militia on **March 30, 1758** to attack the French-held Fort Ticonderoga, at the intersection of Lakes George and Champlain in upstate New York. When his mother found out about his illegal enlistment, she was clearly distraught and arranged to have an influential friend of the family bring Benedict back to his apprenticeship, for she was bound by a legal agreement to have him remain in service until he was twenty-one. A year later, he escaped again and was brought back from a bounty hunter who answered an ad in the *New York Gazette* placed by Dr. Lathrop, who offered forty shillings for Benedict's return. He was more successful on his third attempt and made it all the way up to Albany, where he impressed his comrades with his marksmanship, athletic ability, and discipline.

When he had learned that his mother was gravely ill with yellow fever, he did not wait to get permission to leave, but appointed himself absent without leave to visit her. When British recruiters came through town, his mother hid him with the help of sympathetic neighbors in order to save him from inevitable death as a deserter. Benedict's courage shone later that summer when his mother died on **August 15, 1758** as he publicly arranged for her funeral and for the care of his sister and father. On her headstone she was remembered as 'a pattern of piety, patience, and virtue.' When he was advertised as a deserter in May of 1759, he returned to his militia unit without punishment, but never got to see any of the engagements during his year away from the Army, which included the British victory of Canada. Back home, his father drank more than ever and was arrested for public drunkenness. Dr. Lathrop had put up 300 pounds to keep him out of debtor's prison and taken back a mortgage on the Arnold's house to keep the family from losing it.

After his father passed away in **1761**, Dr. Lathrop helped Benedict set up his own merchant's shop the following year in nearby New Haven, the fastest growing seaport on Long Island Sound and the third largest town in Connecticut. From there he traveled to London and stocked up on the latest European goods from medicines, to ladies cosmetics, to textbooks. On one trip back to Norwich to visit his beloved sister, Hannah, Benedict learned that a Frenchman was pursuing her in courtship. Although the war had ended in **1763**, his hatred for the French had not. Upon hearing that his sister was dating a Frenchman, he confronted the man and forbade him to see her again. When the man reappeared, Benedict fired a warning shot at him from a distance, but the round was close enough to reiterate Benedict's message loud and clear, which the man heard this time and was never seen again. Shortly afterwards, he paid off the mortgage held by Dr. Lathrop, moved his sister to New Haven, sold his father's house, and bought a forty ton sloop, which he aptly named *Fortune*. While his sister minded the store in New Haven, Benedict set sail to expand his enterprising talent as a trader in Canada and the West Indies.

His newfound success did not last for long for the end of the war gave birth to a trade tax by the British government in order to pay for the defense of the American colonies. The war bill amounted to a staggering 122 million pounds with an annual interest rate of 4.4 million pounds and an additional 7 million pounds just to maintain the new colonies. Parliament started the collection process with the Sugar Act of **1764**, which required all iron, hides, whale fins, raw silk, and salt from the colonies to be shipped to England first before being traded anywhere else. The first application of taxation without representation on the colonies was the enactment of the Stamp Act in **1765**. This collected a tax on all paper items embossed with the royal stamp, such as: newspapers, almanacs, pamphlets, insurance policies, legal documents, shipping invoices, and playing cards. Everyone soon felt the impact and was soon in debt with everyone else. This loss in profit forced Benedict and many others to secretly protest the Stamp Act by smuggling goods aboard their ships and selling them off later. When Benedict's ship, the *Fortune*, sailed into New Haven in **January of 1766**, a sailor who served aboard named Peter Boles demanded his wages from Benedict. When Benedict informed him that he could not pay him, Boles paid a visit to the customs house on the **24**th with the intention of reporting him as a smuggler. There he learned that the collector was not available, but made an inquiry to his

4

assistant, Mr. Sanford, what share of a cargo would be paid to an informer if it was seized by customs. Sanford inquired what kind of cargo was to be considered, but Boles was only willing to trust the collector with his information and vowed to return the next day to meet with him. On Monday the 29th, Benedict learned of Boles meeting, hunted him down, and "gave him a little chastisement." [80] After Benedict's interrogation, Boles confessed in writing, promised to leave New Haven, and never return. Hours later, Benedict, having discovered that Boles was hiding inside the home of John Beecher, gathered a gang of sailors, broke into Beecher's house, dragged Boles out to the green, tied him to a whipping post, and gave him forty lashes with a small cord. Once done, the sailors ran him out of town for good. Two members of the grand jury named John Wise and Tilley Blakeslee ordered the justice of the peace, Roger Sherman, to put Benedict on trial for public violence. Although a crowd in support of Benedict marched through the streets protesting the jury members' witch hunt, a trial was ordered by Sherman, the jury members won the case, and Benedict paid a fifty shilling fine. Shortly afterwards, Benedict realized that "if you can't beat 'em, join 'em" and became a member of the Sons of Liberty, which openly protested the Stamp Act and brought about its repeal in **March of 1766**.

On **February 22, 1767** Benedict married Margaret Mansfield, the daughter of Samuel, who served as the High Sheriff of the county. Although Benedict spent much of his time at sea to pay off his debts, he was home long enough to father three sons named Benedict VI, Richard, and Henry and built a grand home for them overlooking the harbor in New Haven. Although the recent Stamp Act had been repealed, it was also replaced with the Quartering Act, which required all colonies with garrisoned British troops to furnish them with supplies and imposed additional restrictions on colonial trade. When colonists objected to this decision without their consideration, British regulars were sent to dispel those who publicly displayed their dissention. In Boston, a mob of 60 people, armed only with snowballs, protested the presence of the soldiers, who panicked and opened fire on the crowd, killing five citizens in what was to be called "The Boston Massacre" on Monday **March 5, 1770**. Benedict was on a shipping expedition in the West Indies when he heard the news and wrote home with the reaction on **June 9th**.

To Douglas, Esquire, New Haven

St. George's Key, 9th June, 1770

Dear Sir

I am now in a corner of the world whence you can expect no news of consequence, yet was very much shocked the other day on hearing the accounts of the most wanton, cruel, and inhumane murders committed in Boston by the soldiers. Good God! Are the Americans all asleep; and tamely yielding up their liberties, or are they all turned philosophers, that they do not take immediate vengeance on such miscreants; I am afraid of the latter and that we shall all soon see ourselves as poor and as much oppressed as ever a heathen philosopher was.

With greatest Esteem, Dear Sir, your sincere Friend,

B. Arnold [56]

Although violence was quelled following the incident, the bitterness was not and Parliament introduced the Tea Act on **May 10, 1773**, which allowed the British owned, East India Tea Company to be the exclusive importer of tea into the colonies and do so at a cheaper price, the only catch was that they had to impose a tax. This Act of Parliament among others with a similar motive to tax the colonies without representation were aptly named "The Intolerable Acts" by the Americans, because they just weren't going to stand for this $#!+ (rubbish). The Colonists made their point clear on **December 16**[th] when the Massachusetts radical, Samuel Adams organized a thousand men disguised as Mohawk Indians to board three E. I. T. C. ships and hold a "party" by dumping 342 chests of leaves valued at $90,000 into Boston Harbor. Born in Braintree, Massachusetts in 1722, Adams was a second cousin to John Adams, who attended the Boston Latin School before graduating from Harvard and later working with his father in the family brewery although living a sober, righteous, and godly life. Inspired by the theories of John Locke, he entered politics and became one of the most incendiary characters of the rebellion. He ardently protested the proposals and passages of acts to tax the colonies and founded the first Committee of Correspondence, which established official contact between towns and cities. His contemporaries would later consider him as the "Father of the Revolution." Seeing that the Americans were acting like bratty children to their mother country, Parliament decided to discipline them by closing the Port of Boston on **June 1**[st], **1774**. Benedict traveled to Philadelphia in support of another one of the many organizational ideas originated by Samuel Adams, the first Continental Congress, which met for the first time on **September 5**[th]. Many of the preliminary meetings were held as breakfast, lunch, and dinner meetings at the homes of the Philadelphia elite. Among these many homes, Benedict had paid a visit to a particular one owned by a British Judge named Edward Shippen. Born as a Presbyterian in Philadelphia back in '29, Shippen had studied law here and in London at the Middle Temple before passing the bar and holding several local offices in Philadelphia. He was also the proud father of three beautiful daughters, to whom Benedict had been introduced. Little did he know at the time that the youngest of the three, Peggy, age fourteen, would become his wife within four years and remain loyal to him for better or for worse.

In **February of 1775**, a Massachusetts attorney named John Brown had volunteered to travel to Montreal as a representative of the Boston Committee of Correspondence in order to establish a reliable means of communication with the inhabitants of Canada and gain an understanding of their political opinion in regards to the American rebellion. Brown was a graduate from Yale who served as a King's attorney, a member of the Pittsfield, Massachusetts Committee of Correspondence and the Provincial Congress. Reporting on an opportunity he discovered while enroute to Canada, Brown wrote a letter to Samuel Adams and Joseph Warren on **March 29th**, suggesting an assault on the now British held Fort Ticonderoga, located on the western heights overlooking Lake Champlain in upstate New York. Long before the installation of the New York State Thruway, Lake Champlain, stretching 125 miles from north to south and spanning breadths as wide as 14 miles and as narrow as 14 yards, was *the* key way to getting around the Hudson and St. Lawrence River valleys.

To Mr. Samuel Adams, Dr. J. Warren
Committee of Correspondence in Boston
Montreal, March 29, 1775
Gentlemen
Immediately after the reception of your letters and pamphlets, I went to Albany to find the state of the lakes and established a correspondence with Dr. Joseph Young... I have the pleasure and satisfaction to inform you that, through the industry and exertions of our friends in Canada, our enemies are not at present able to raise ten men for administration. The weapons that have been used by our friends to thwart the constant endeavors of friends of Government (so called) have been chiefly in terror...

7

One thing I must mention, to be kept as a profound secret. The fort at Ticonderoga must be seized as soon as possible, should hostilities be committed by the King's troops. The people on New Hampshire Grants have engaged to do this business and in my opinion they are the most proper persons for the job. This will effectually curb this Province, and all the troops that may be sent here.

As the messenger to carry this letter has been waiting some time with impatience,
I must conclude, by subscribing myself, gentlemen,
your most obedient humble servant,
J. Brown [25]

Previously on Monday the 6th, Dr. Joseph Warren delivered an oration at the request of the inhabitants of the Town of Boston, to commemorate the bloody tragedy of the 5th of March 1770.

My ever honored fellow citizens
It is not without the most humiliating conviction of my want of ability that I now appear before you; but the sense I have of the obligation I am under to obey the calls of my Country at all times...
That personal freedom is the natural right of every man, and that property, or an exclusive right to dispose of what he honestly acquired by his own labor, necessarily arises therefrom, are truths which common sense has placed beyond the reach of contradiction; and no man, or body of men, can, without being guilty of flagrant injustice, claim a right to dispose of the persons or acquisitions of any other man, or body of men, unless it can be proved that such a right has arisen from some compact between the parties, in which it has been explicitly and freely granted...
Our fathers having nobly resolved never to wear the yoke of despotism, and seeing the European world, through indolence and cowardice, falling prey to tyranny, bravely threw themselves upon the bosom of the ocean, determined to find a place in which they might enjoy their freedom, or perish in the attempt. Approving Heaven beheld the favorite ark dancing upon the waves and graciously preserved it, until the chosen families were brought in safety to the western regions. They found the land swarming with savages, who threatened death with every kind of torture; but savages, and death with torture, were far less terrible than slavery. Nothing was so much the object than abhorrence as a tyrant's power; they knew that it was more safe to dwell with man, in his unpolished state, than in a

8

Country where arbitrary power prevails. Even anarchy itself, that bugbear held up by the tools of power, (though truly to be depreciated,) is infinitely less dangerous than arbitrary Government. Anarchy can be but of short duration; for when men are at liberty to pursue that course which is most conducive to their own happiness, they will soon come into it; and, from the rudest state of nature, order and good government must soon arise. But tyranny, when once established, entails its curse on a Nation to the latest period of time, unless some daring genius, inspired by Heaven, shall, unappalled by danger, bravely form and execute the arduous design of restoring liberty and life to his enslaved, murdered Country...

The attempt of the British Parliament to raise a revenue from America, and our denial of their right to do it, have excited an almost universal inquiry into the rights of mankind in general, and of British subjects in particular; the necessary result of which must be such a liberality of sentiment, and such a jealousy of those in power, as will, better than an adamantine wall, secure us against the future approaches of despotism...

The mutilation of our Charter has made every Colony jealous for its own; for this, if once submitted to by us, would set on float the property and Government of every British settlement upon the Continent. If Charters are not deemed sacred, how miserably precarious is everything founded upon them?

Even the sending troops to put these Acts into execution is not without advantage to us. The exactness and beauty of their discipline inspire our youth with ardor in the pursuit of military knowledge. Charles the Invincible taught Peter the Great the Art of War. The battle of Pultowa convinced Charles of the proficiency Peter had made.

Our Country is in danger, but not to be despaired of. Our enemies are numerous and powerful, but we have many friends determined to be free, and Heaven and earth will aid the resolution. On you depend the fortunes of America. You are to decide the important question, on which rest the happiness and liberty of millions yet unborn. Act worthy of yourselves – the faltering tongue of hoary age calls on you to support your country. The lisping infant raises its suppliant hands, imploring defense against the monster slavery. Your fathers look from their celestial seats with smiling approbation on their sons, who boldly stand forth in the cause of virtue; but sternly frown upon the inhuman miscreant who, to secure the loaves and fishes to himself, would breed a serpent to destroy his children...

Having redeemed your Country and secured the blessings to future generations, who, fired by your example, shall emulate your virtues, and learn from you the Heavenly art of making millions happy, with heart-felt joy – with transports all your own, you cry, the glorious work is done! then drop the mantle to some young Elisha, and take your seats with kindred spirits in your native skies. [25]

A similar incident followed in the early morning hours of **April 19th**. Under the orders from England, British General Thomas Gage dispatched seven hundred light infantrymen towards Lexington, Massachusetts to confiscate munitions that were stored by the colonists in an effort to prevent a war, not start one. Born in Sussex, England in 1721, Gage attended Westminster School along with John Burgoyne and George Germain and grew up to be a tall, slender, and bright-eyed model of a man who turned up his prominent, aristocratic nose at Roman Catholics and Indians. Aside from that, he was charming, courteous, dignified, friendly, gallant, and well spoken. With a brave heart and a political mind, he rose through the ranks during the French and Indian War, bearing many a battle scars for himself while maintaining a strict sense of discipline among his men. His accomplishments eventually garnered him the authority to raise the first regiment of light infantry in the history of the British Army, the hand of a Jersey girl, and the position of Military Governor of Boston. Knowing the hearts and minds of the inhabitants, not to mention the expectations of his in-laws, his goal as Governor was to bring about a *resolution*, not a Revolution. He had tried his diplomatic best to negotiate a peaceful settlement between "Mother E" and her colonies, but mother's patience had just run out.

Leading the redcoats to Lexington was a Scotsman by the name of Major John Pitcairn of the Royal Marines, who had also bestowed the respect of the inhabitants and his soldiers. As they reached their objective at first light, they sighted fourteen minutemen under the command of Captain John Parker, who was a local farmer, mechanic, town official, and veteran of the French and Indian War. It was Parker who gave the most memorable orders of the day, "Stand your ground! Don't fire unless fired upon. But if they mean to have a war, let it begin here." [19] Pitcairn, a strict disciplinarian, called out at a distance of thirty paces for the Americans to disarm and desist. Parker measured up the situation, saw the strength and rigidity of the British, and begrudgingly retracted his previous order, telling the men to disperse, but not to lay down their arms. One by one they dispersed, muskets in hand. Pitcairn repeated his order to disarm, but was again ignored. Suddenly out of nowhere, a shot rang out, a "shot heard round the world." Pitcairn, who hadn't seen where the shot had come from, assumed that it was from the Americans and gave the order to "fire." [19] The men hesitated in confusion, because they didn't think the shot came from the Americans. Pitcairn grew impatient and repeated his order to fire, which the troops did, but fired above their heads as a warning shot. Pitcairn, now angered, then ordered his troops to "fire at them." [19] The order was followed by a murderous volley that struck down eight minutemen in the back as they fled and injuring another ten. The dead and wounded were moved to safety and the munitions to nearby Concord, where the British continued their search, but were once again unsuccessful. When they put a few wagons and barrels of flour to the torch, the minutemen opened fire from behind walls, fences, and houses causing 273 casualties among the invaders. When a British relief force made a counterattack at Lexington, none including women and children were spared from the carnage of gunfire and torching of homes that were suspected of housing snipers. In a sermon delivered in the Church of Lexington by Reverend Jonas Clark on the one-year anniversary of the event that acted as the blasting cap to the Revolution, the American account claims that the British fired first.

April 19, 1776

Between the hours of twelve and one, on the morning of the nineteenth of April, we received intelligence by express from the Honorable Joseph Warren, Esq., at Boston, "that a large body of the King's troops (supposed to be a brigade of about 12 or 15 hundred) were embarked in boats from Boston, and gone over to land on Lechmere's Point (so called) in Cambridge; and that it was shrewdly suspected that they were ordered to seize and destroy the stores belonging to the colony, then deposited at Concord."...

Accordingly, about half an hour after four o'clock, alarm guns were fired, and the drums beat to arms, and the militia were collecting together. Some, to the number of about 50 or 60, or possibly more were on the parade, others were coming towards us. In the mean time, the troops having thus stolen a march upon us and, to prevent any intelligence of their approach, having seized and held prisoners several persons whom they met unarmed upon the road, seemed to come determined for murder and bloodshed – and that whether provoked to it or not! When within about half a quarter of a mile of the Meeting House, they halted and the command was given to prime and load; which being done, they marched on till they came up to the east end of said Meeting House, in sight of our militia (collecting as aforesaid) who were about 12 or 13 rods distant.

Immediately upon their appearing so suddenly and so nigh, Capt. Parker, who commanded the militia company, ordered the men to disperse and take care of themselves, and not to fire. Upon this, our men dispersed – but many of them not so speedily as they might have done, not having the most distant idea of such brutal barbarity and more than savage cruelty from the troops of a British King, as they immediately experienced! For, no sooner did they come in sight of our company, but one of them, supposed to be an officer of rank, was heard to say to the troops, "Damn them! we will have them!" upon which the troops shouted aloud, huzza'd, and rushed furiously towards our men.

About the same time, three officers (supposed to be Col. Smith, Major Pitcairn and another officer) advanced on horse back to the front of the body, and coming within 5 or 6 rods of the militia, one of them cried out, Ye villains, ye rebels disperse! Damn you, disperse! – or words to that effect. One of them (whether the same or not is not easily determined) said, "Lay down your arms! Damn you, why don't you lay down your arms?" the second of these officers, about this time, fired a pistol towards the militia as they were dispersing. The foremost, who was within a few yards of our men, brandishing his sword and then pointing towards them, with a loud voice said to the troops, "Fire! By God, fire!" – which was instantly followed by a discharge of arms from the said troops, succeeded by a very heavy and close fire upon our party, dispersing, so long as any of them were within reach. Eight were left dead upon the ground! Ten were wounded. The rest of the company, through divine goodness, were (to a miracle) preserved unhurt in this murderous action!...[20]

A British account by Lieutenant John Barker of the King's Own claims that the Americans fired first.

1775, April 19th. Last night between 10 an 11 o'clock, all the Grenadiers and Light Infantry of the Army, making about 600 men (under the command of Lt. Col. Smith of the 10th and Major Pitcairn of the Marines), embarked and were landed upon the opposite shore on Cambridge Marsh; few but the commanding officers knew what expedition we were going upon. After getting over the marsh, where we were wet up to the knees, we were halted in a dirty road and stood there two o'clock in the morning, waiting for provisions to be brought *from the boats and to be divided, and which most of the men threw away, having carried some with 'em. At 2 o'clock we began our march by wading through a very long ford up to our middles. After going a few miles we took 3 or 4 people who were going off to give intelligence.*

About 5 miles on this side of a town called Lexington, which lay in our road, we heard there were some hundreds of people collected together intending to oppose us and stop our going on. At 5 o'clock we arrived there and saw a number of people, I believe between 2 and 3 hundred, formed in a common in the middle of the town. We still continued advancing, keeping prepared against an attack though without intending to attack them; but on our coming near them they fired one or two shots, upon which our men without any orders rushed in upon them, fired and put 'em to flight. Several of them were killed, we could not tell how many because they were got behind walls and into the woods. We had a man of the 10th Light Infantry wounded, nobody else hurt. We then formed on the common, but with some difficulty, the men were so wild they could hear no orders... [20]

On the morning of the **20th**, Captain Benedict Arnold of the Governor's Guards, a militia company composed of the most spirited and active young men of the city, led his men to the meeting place of the town's leaders at Hunt's Tavern and requested the keys to the town's powder magazine. From inside the tavern, Colonel David Wooster was selected to go out and speak to him. Born in Stratford, Connecticut in 1710, Wooster was a Yale graduate and veteran of the French and Indian War. Addressing Arnold, he proclaimed, "This is colony property. We cannot give it up without regular orders from those in authority." [63] "Regular orders be damned," Benedict barked, "our friends and neighbors are being mowed down by redcoats. Give us the powder or we will take it!" [63] When Wooster repeated his appeal, Benedict threatened to break down the door and break out the powder before declaring, "None but almighty God shall prevent my marching!" [63] Wooster surrendered the keys, giving Benedict his first military victory. He and his men marched out of the town carrying their state flag emblazoned with the motto, '*Qui transtulit sustinet,*' meaning, 'He who brought us hither will support us.'

II
Ticonderoga

On the **30th of April 1775**, Arnold wrote to Joseph Warren, now President of the Provincial Congress of Massachusetts, and responded to his request based on John Brown's earlier suggestion.

To the Honorable Joseph Warren
and the Honorable Committee of Safety
Cambridge, April 30, 1775

Gentlemen
You have desired me to state the number of cannon etc. at Ticonderoga. I have certain information that there are at Ticonderoga eighty pieces of heavy cannon, twenty brass guns from four to eighteen pounders, and ten to twelve large mortars. At Skenesborough on the south bay, there are three or four brass cannon. The fort is in a ruinous condition and has not more than fifty men at the most. There are large numbers of small arms and considerable stores and a sloop of seventy or eighty tons on the lake. The place could not hold out an hour against a vigorous onset.
Your most obedient servant,
Benedict Arnold [48]

Warren then relayed the intentions of the Massachusetts Committee to Alexander McDougall of the New York Committee. After immigrating to America from Scotland as a boy, McDougall delivered milk from his father's farm in New York City, getting to know the streets and the people who lived on them. As a rugged and muscular young man he worked on board several merchant ships before serving on two privateers during the French and Indian War. Although primarily self-educated, the combination of his work experience through the years along with his methodical mind, honest principles, and negotiating talents allowed him to later become a successful merchant when he returned home. When the Crown had made its proposition of taxation without representation, he authored an address of protest entitled, "A Son of Liberty to the Betrayed Inhabitants of the Colony." [86] He was arrested for this on charges of libel and imprisoned for over one year, becoming the first martyr in the patriot cause. Turning his words into action, he held his own New York Tea Party by spilling the contents of the *London* into the East River. His strong position on the American cause brought him to preside over the meeting in the Fields, (now New York City Hall

Park), which brought about a non-importation resolution and the decision to send delegates from New York to the Continental Congress. On the very same day as Warren's letter to him, McDougall was appointed Colonel of militia in the 1st New York Regiment.

To Alexander McDougall, Esq.

Cambridge, April 30, 1775

Gentlemen

It has been proposed to us to take possession of the fortress at Ticonderoga. We have a just sense of the importance of the fortification and the usefulness of those fine cannon, mortars, and field pieces, which are there; but we would not, even upon this emergency, infringe upon the rights of our sister Colony, New York. But we have desired the gentleman who carries this letter to represent the matter to you, that you may give such orders as are agreeable to you.

We are, with the greatest respect, your most obedient servants,

Joseph Warren, Chairman [48]

Impressed by his leadership potential, the Massachusetts Committee of Safety promoted Arnold to the rank of Colonel on **May 3rd** and issued orders for him to take Ticonderoga back from the British as directed by a letter from Dr. Benjamin Church, written by William Cooper. Educated at the Boston Latin School and graduating from Harvard, Church traveled to England where he served as a surgeon in the Royal Navy and studied medicine at the London Medical College. After returning to America, he was a staunch supporter of the patriot movement and became a delegate to the Massachusetts Provincial Congress, yet at the same time he was secretly providing military intelligence to Royal Governor Thomas Gage.

To Benedict Arnold, Esquire, Commander of a body of troops on an expedition to subdue and take possession of the Fort of Ticonderoga, &c.

In Committee of Safety, Cambridge, May 3, 1775

Sir

Confiding in your judgement, fidelity, and valor, we do, by these presents, constitute and appoint you Colonel and Commander-in-Chief over a body of men not exceeding four hundred. Proceed with all expedition to the western part of this and the neighboring colonies, where you are directed to enlist those men and with them forthwith to march to the Fort at Ticonderoga and use your endeavors to reduce the same, taking possession of the cannon and stores upon the lake. You are to bring back with you such of the cannon, mortars, stores, &c., as you shall judge may be serviceable to the Army here, leaving behind what may be necessary to secure that post with a sufficient garrison. You are to procure suitable provisions and stores for the Army and draw upon the Committee of Safety for the same and to act in every urgency according to your best skill and discretion for the public interest, for which this shall be your sufficient warrant.

Benjamin Church, Chairman Com. of Safety
Wm. Cooper, Secretary [25]

Coincidentally, an extract of a letter from a gentleman in Pittsfield, Massachusetts to an officer at Cambridge, dated Monday the 4th, shows similar orders from Connecticut given to Colonel Ethan Allen, who acted on them along with John Brown. After serving in the French and Indian War, Allen was selected to head an armed force called the "Green Mountain Boys" that was raised to protect holders of land granted by New Hampshire and disputed by New York, which eventually became Vermont. Being an animated, opinionated, boastful, and egotistical backwoods philosopher, he authored a piece on the issue. Wielding a strong physique, this frontier rebel held a courageous and impulsive manner that made him more inclined to force rather than reason.

I have the pleasure to acquaint you that a number of gentlemen from Connecticut went from this place last Tuesday morning (the 28th), having been joined by Colonel Easton, Captain Dickinson, and Mr. Brown, with forty soldiers, on an expedition against Ticonderoga and Crown Point, expecting to be reinforced by a thousand men from the grants above here, a post having previously taken his departure to inform Colonel Ethan Allen of the design and desiring him to hold his Green Mountain Boys in actual readiness. The expedition has been carried on with the utmost secrecy, as they are in hopes of taking those forts by surprise. We expect they will reach those forts by Saturday next or Lord's Day at farthest. The plan was concerted at Hartford last Saturday (April 25), by the Governor and Council; Colonel Hancock, and Mr. Adams, and others from our province being present. Three hundred pounds were drawn immediately out of the treasury for the aforesaid purpose, and committed to those gentlemen that were here. We earnestly pray for success to this important expedition, as the taking those places would afford us a key to all Canada. Should success attend this expedition, we expect a strong reinforcement will be sent from the western part of Connecticut to keep those forts, and to repair and fortify them well.

We have had much work here of late with the tories; a dark plot has been discovered of sending names down to General Gage; in consequence of which, and the critical situation of this town, we have been obliged to act with vigor, and have sent Mr. Jones and Mr. Graves to Northampton Jail, where they now lie in close confinement, and have sent a hue and a cry after Major Stoddard and Mr. Little, who have fled to New York for shelter. We hope it will not be too long before they are taken into custody and committed to close confinement. Our tories are the worst in the province; all the effect the late and present operations have had upon them is, they are mute and pensive, and secretly wish for more prosperous days to toryism.

As to your important questions, Sir, you have the fervent prayers of all good men that success may attend them. I hope God will inspire you with wisdom from above in all your deliberations, and your soldiers with courage and fortitude, and that Boston will be speedily delivered into your hands, the General thereof, and all the King's troops, that the den of thieves, that nest of robbers, that asylum for traitors and murderers, may be broke up, and never another red coat from England set foot on these shores. [25]

Arnold raced towards Castleton, Vermont, where a council had gathered on the evening of the 8th, but he was too late, for they had already marched without him to the fort. Forging ahead, he met up with Allen in the area of the fort and presented his orders from Massachusetts. Unfortunately the decision as to who was to command was decided by eighty-three of Allen's "Green Mountain Boys" from Vermont, who laughed at Arnold's demand to command to command troops that he didn't raise. When he insisted upon taking command, some of the men threatened to go home before following orders from anyone except Allen. Arnold was angry, but outnumbered and was able to negotiate a joint command in which he would lead the men from Massachusetts and Connecticut while Allen led the troops from Vermont. In order to transport troops across the lake, a company of men under orders from Allen captured vessels and the area of Skenesborough at the southern tip of Lake Champlain on the 9th. Skenesborough had been named after the fifty-year-old Lieutenant Governor of Ticonderoga and Crown Point, Philip Skene, who had been born in London and had served in the area during the French and

Indian War before establishing prosperous foundries, sawmills, and shipyards in the town.

At the first hint of dawn on the **10th**, the formation marched up the slope to the base of the east curtain wall, through a portal and tunnel, then up a set of stone steps that led to the parade ground. A sentry sighted the invaders, raised his musket, took aim at the first in line, and pulled the trigger, only to hear the hollow click of the hammer falling, but not firing. The only thing left to do was to turn and run into the bombproof on the north side of the parade ground. The men immediately went to work on securing the muskets that were neatly stacked outside the barracks and the forty British soldiers sleeping inside.

Arnold and Allen, accompanied by a few men, charged across the courtyard, where they were confronted by a second sentry, who attempted to keep them at bay, but was smacked down by the flat of Allen's sword. Allen demanded to know the whereabouts of the commander's quarters, which the cowering sentry revealed by pointing to a set of stairs that led up to the second story of the western barrack. With Arnold hot on his heels, Allen rushed up the steps and bellowed, "Come out, you old rat!" [31] A Lieutenant Jocelyn Feltham appeared at the top of the stairs and attempted to hold a conversation with Allen and Arnold in an effort to stall enough time for the cavalry to arrive, but all troops had already been seized. Allen displayed his lack of patience by pointing his sword at Feltham and shouting threats of no quarter, he declared that he had orders from the state of Connecticut along with Arnold, who had similar orders from the state of Massachusetts. As Allen's men shouted in support of their leader, the commanding officer, Captain William Delaplace and his wife appeared in the doorway and asked under what authority were they acting on. In a bold voice, Allen declared, "In the name of the Great Jehovah and the Continental Congress." [31] Seeing that none of his men were present and assumed their capture, Delaplace surrendered. As the morning light illuminated the fort, more men from nearby Vermont arrived and joined their fellow statesmen in a wild looting spree after discovering ninety gallons of spirits in a rum cellar. On the **11th**, Allen acknowledged Arnold's presence in his report to Abraham Yates of the Albany Committee, but didn't acknowledge his share of the command. Yates was a born and raised Whig in Albany who attended the Dutch Reformed Church, and worked as a surveyor, lawyer, land speculator, and financier. In public service he held positions as sheriff, member of the Common Council, and Committee of Correspondence. Allen had also warned Yates that Sir Guy Carleton, the Governor of Canada, would not let the American's keep the fort if he could help it. Carleton was a caring man who had fought with distinction in order to gain Canada during the French and Indian War and had pushed for the passage of the Quebec Act. This work of legislation established the citizens the right to a common language, civil law, religion, and government in the form of a Commonwealth.

To Abraham Yates, Chairman of the Committee, Albany
Ticonderoga, May 11, 1775
Gentlemen
    I have the inexpressible satisfaction to acquaint you that at daybreak of the tenth instant, pursuant to my directions from sundry leading gentlemen of Massachusetts Bay and Connecticut, I took the fortress of Ticonderoga, with about one hundred and thirty Green Mountain Boys. Colonel Easton with about forty valiant soldiers, distinguished themselves in the action. Colonel Arnold entered the fortress with me side by side. The guard was so surprised that contrary to expectation, they did not fire on us, but fled with precipitancy. We immediately entered the fortress and took the garrison prisoners, without bloodshed or any opposition. They consisted of one captain, a lieutenant, and forty-two men.
    Little more need be said. You know Governor Carleton of Canada will exert himself to retake it; and as your county is nearer to any other part of the Colonies, and as your inhabitants have thoroughly manifested their zeal in the cause of their country, I expect immediate assistance from you both in men and provisions. You cannot exert yourselves too much in so glorious a cause. The number of men need be more at first till the other Colonies can have time to muster. I am apprehensive of a sudden and quiet attack. Pray be quick to our relief and send us five hundred men immediately – fail not.
From your friend and humble servant,
Ethan Allen, Commander of Ticonderoga [25]

    A similar report by Allen was sent to the Massachusetts Congress, but fails to recognize their orders to Arnold or even mention his name.

To the Honorable Congress of the Province of the Massachusetts Bay, or Council of War

Ticonderoga, May 11, 1775

Gentlemen
I have to inform you with pleasure unfelt before, that on break of day on the tenth of May, 1775, by the order of the General Assembly of the Colony of Connecticut, took the Fortress of Ticonderoga by storm. The soldiery was composed of about one hundred Green Mountain Boys and near fifty veteran soldiers from the Province of the Massachusetts Bay. The latter was under the command of Colonel James Easton, who behaved with great zeal and fortitude, not only in council, but also in the assault. The soldiery behaved with such resistless fury, that they so terrified the King's Troops that they dare not fire on their assailants, and our soldiery was agreeably disappointed. The soldiery behaved with uncommon intensity when they leaped into the Fort; and it must be confessed that the Colonel has greatly contributed to the taking of that Fortress, as well as John Brown, Esq., Attorney at Law, who was also an able counselor and was personally in the attack. I expect the colonies will maintain this Fort. As to the cannon and warlike stores, I hope they may serve the cause of liberty instead of tyranny, and I humbly implore your assistance in immediately assisting the Government of Connecticut in establishing a garrison in the reduced premises. Colonel Easton will inform you at large.

From, gentlemen, your most obedient humble servant,
Ethan Allen [25]

A detailed narrative from Allen made it into the newspapers with an acknowledgement to Colonel Seth Warner, a fellow Vermonter from Bennington, but failed to mention Arnold at all.

While I was wishing for an opportunity to signalize myself in my country's behalf, directions were privately sent to me from the then Colony of Connecticut to raise the Green Mountain Boys, and, if possible, with them to surprise and take the fortress of Ticonderoga. This enterprise I cheerfully undertook; and, after first guarding all the several passes that led thither, to cut off all intelligence between the garrison and the country, made a forced march from Bennington, and arrived at the lake opposite to Ticonderoga on the evening of the ninth day of May, 1775, with two hundred and thirty valiant Green Mountain Boys and it was with the utmost difficulty that I procured boats to cross the lake. However, I landed eighty-three men near the garrison, and sent the boats back for the rear guard, commanded by Colonel Seth Warner, but the day began to dawn, and I found myself

21

under a necessity to attack the fort before the rear could cross the lake, and, as it was viewed hazardous, I harangued the officers and soldiers in the manner following:

"Friends and fellow soldiers: you have for a number of years past, been a scourge and terror to arbitrary power. Your valor has been famed abroad and acknowledged, as appears by the advice and orders to me, from the General Assembly of Connecticut, to surprise and take the garrison now before us. I now propose to advance before you, and, in person, conduct you through the wicked gate; for we must this morning either quit our pretensions to valor or possess ourselves of this fortress in a few minutes; and, inasmuch as it is a desperate attempt, which none but the bravest of men dare undertake, I do not urge it on any contrary to his will. You that will undertake voluntarily, poise your firelocks."

The men being, at this time, drawn up in three ranks, each poised his firelock. I ordered them to face to the right: and at the head of the center file marched them immediately to the wicked gate aforesaid, where I found a sentry posted, who instantly snapped his fuse at me: I ran immediately towards him, and he retreated through the covered way into the parade within the garrison, gave a halloo, and ran under a bombproof. My party, who followed me into the fort, I formed on the parade in such a manner as to face the two barracks, which faced each other.

The garrison being asleep, except the sentries, we gave three huzzahs, which greatly surprised them. One of the sentries made a pass at one of my officers with a charged bayonet and slightly wounded him. My first thought was to kill him with my sword; but, in an instant, I altered the design and fury of the blow to a slight cut on the side of the head; upon which he dropped his gun and asked quarter, which I readily granted him and demanded of him the place where commanding officer kept. He showed me a pair of stairs in the front of a barrack on the west part of the garrison, which led up to a second story in said barrack, to which I immediately repaired and ordered the commander, Captain Delaplace, to come forth instantly or I would sacrifice the whole garrison; at which the captain came immediately to the door, with his breeches in hand, when I ordered him to deliver me the fort instantly:

He asked me by what authority I demanded it.

I answered him, "In the name of the great Jehovah and the Continental Congress."

The authority of the Congress being very little known at that time, he began to speak again; but I interrupted him, and, with my drawn sword over his head, again demanded an immediate surrender of the garrison; with which he then complied, and ordered his men to be forthwith paraded without arms, as he had given up the garrison. In the meantime some of my officers had given orders, and in consequence thereof, sundry of the barrack doors were beat down and about one third of the garrison imprisoned, which consisted of the said commander, a Lieutenant Feltham, a conductor of artillery, a gunner, two sergeants, and forty rank and file; about one hundred pieces of cannon, one thirteen inch mortar, and a number of swivels. This surprise was carried out in the gray of the morning on the tenth day of May 1775...

Colonel Warner, with the rear guard, crossed the lake and joined me early in the morning, whom I sent off without loss of time, with about one hundred men, to take possession of Crown Point, which was garrisoned with a sergeant and twelve men; which he took possession of the same day, as also of upwards of one hundred pieces of cannon. [18]

Colonel Ethan Allen

When Arnold refused to release command of the fort to Allen, Mott wrote to his superiors in Massachusetts.

To the Provincial Congress now sitting at Watertown

Ticonderoga, May 11, 1775

Gentlemen

This is to certify that previous to Colonel Benedict Arnold's arrival to the Forts Ticonderoga and Crown Point, a Committee sent from the Colony of Connecticut, furnished with money for the purpose of reducing and garrisoning said Forts, had, with the assistance of seventy-five men from Massachusetts, and one hundred and forty from the New Hampshire Grants, marched within a few miles of Ticonderoga, and this morning, at daybreak, took possession of said Fort, and have given the command thereof into the hands of Colonel Ethan Allen. And said Arnold refuses to give up his command, which causes much difficulty; said Arnold not having enlisted one man, neither do we know that he has or could do it. and as said Committee have raised the men, and are still raising supplies for the purpose of repairing said Forts, taking the armed sloop, and defending this country and said Forts, we think that said Arnold's farther procedure in this matter highly inexpedient, both in regard to expense and defense.

James Easton, Edward Mott

Epap. Bull   Noah Phelps
Committee of War for the Expedition
against Ticonderoga and Crown Point. [48]

Arnold, armed with his orders from the Committee of Safety, sought out the Committee of War in nearby Shoreham, Vermont, which claimed to be the brains behind the raid on Ticonderoga, as Mott explained to his constituents.

To The Honorable Provincial Congress
or the Council of War for the Province of Massachusetts Bay
                                          Shoreham, May 11, 1775
Gentlemen
            I would congratulate you on the surrender of the garrison of
Ticonderoga to the American Forces. The affair was planned and
conducted after the following manner. A number of the principal
gentlemen of the Assembly at Hartford, on Friday, the twenty-eighth
of April, conversing on the distressed condition of the people of
Boston, and the means necessary to relieve them, fell on the scheme to
take that Fortress, that we might have the advantage of the cannon
that were there, to relieve the people of Boston. I told the gentlemen
that in my opinion it might be taken by surprise with a few men if
properly conducted. On which they desired me, if I was willing to
serve my country in that way, to joint Captain Noah Phelps of
Simsbury and Mr. Bernard Romans on that design, and furnished us
with three hundred pounds in cash from the treasury, and desired us
to go forward to the upper towns and search into the situation of said
garrison, and, if I thought proper, to proceed to take possession of the
same. On which we collected to the number of sixteen men in
Connecticut, and proceeded forward till we came to Colonel James
Easton's at Pittsfield, and there consulted with Colonel Easton and
John Brown, Esq., who, after they heard our plan of operation agreed
to join us; and, after informing them that we intended raising our men
on the New Hampshire Grants for the aforesaid purpose, as it would
be difficult to raise and march a number of men through the country
any distance without our plans being discovered. Colonel Easton and
Mr. Brown told us that the people on the Grants were poor and at this
time of year it would be difficult to raise a sufficient number of men
there to take and hold said garrison, where upon Colonel Easton
offered to raise men in his own regiment for the aforesaid purpose, to
join with the Green Mountain Boys. On which I set out with him for
the Town of Jericho, where Colonel Easton raised between forty and

fifty men and proceeded to Bennington, at which place the men arrived the next day. At which place a council of war was called, Colonel Easton being chairman, it was voted that Colonel Ethan Allen should send forward parties to secure the roads to the northward to prevent all intelligence from arriving before us. On Sunday evening, the seventh of this instant, we arrived at Castleton, where, the next day, was held a council of war by a Committee chosen for that purpose, of which Committee I have the honor to be chairman. After debating and consulting on different methods of procedure in order to accomplish our designs, it was concluded and voted that we would proceed in the following manner, viz: That a party of thirty men under the command of Captain Herrick, should, on the next day, in the afternoon, proceed to Skenesborough, and take into custody Major Philip Skene and his party, and take possession of all the boats that they should find there, and in the night proceed up the lake to Shoreham with the remainder of our men, which was about one hundred and forty, who were under the command of Colonel Ethan Allen, and Colonel James Easton was his second, and Captain Seth Warner the third in command; as these three men were the persons who raised the men, they were chosen to command and to rank according to the number of men that each one raised. We also sent off Captain Asa Douglass of Jericho to proceed directly to Panton, and there consult his brother-in-law who lived there, and send down some boats to Shoreham, if possible, to help our people over to the fort. All this was concluded should be done, or attempted on to go in each party, all were preparing for their march, being then within about nine miles of Skenesborough and about twenty-five miles, the way we went, from Ticonderoga.

Colonel Benedict Arnold arrived to us from you with his orders. We were extremely rejoiced to see that you fully agreed with us as to the expediency and importance of taking possession of those garrisons, but were shockingly surprised when Colonel Arnold presumed to contend for the command of those forces that we had raised, who we had assured should go under the command of their own officers, and be paid and maintained by the Colony of Connecticut. But Mr. Arnold, after we had generously told him our whole plan, strenuously contended and insisted that he had a right to command them and all their officers, which bred such a mutiny among the soldiers which had nearly frustrated our whole design, as our men were clubbing their firelocks and marching home, but were prevented by Colonel Allen and Colonel Easton, who told them that he should not take the command of them, and if he had, their pay would be the same as though they were under their command; but they would damn the pay and say that they would not be commanded by any others but those they engaged with; and after the garrison was surrendered, Mr. Arnold again assumed the command of the garrison, although he had not one man there, and demanded it of Colonel Allen, on which we gave Colonel Allen his orders in writing as follows, viz.

'*To Colonel Allen,*
Sir

  Whereas agreeable to the power and authority to us given by the Colony of Connecticut, we have appointed you to take the command of a party of men and reduce and take possession of the garrison at Ticonderoga, and the dependencies thereto belonging, and as you are now in actual possession of the same, you are hereby required to keep the command and possession of the same, for the use of the American Colonies, until you have further orders from the Colony of Connecticut or the Continental Congress.
    Signed, per order of the Committee of War,
    Edward Mott, Chairman of said Committee'

  Colonel James Easton was of great service both in council and action, and in raising men for the above expedition, and appeared to be well qualified to be not only a Colonel of the Militia at home, but to command in the field. And also John Brown, Esq. of Pittsfield, we recommend as an able counselor, and full of spirit and resolution, as well as good conduct; wish they may both be employed in the service of their country equal to their merit.

  I have the pleasure to add that on Wednesday morning last, the tenth of this instant about the break of day, our men entered the gate, till when they were undiscovered, and in the most courageous and intrepid manner darted like lightning upon the guards, so that but two had time to snap their firelocks at us and in a few minutes the fortress with its dependencies were delivered into our hands. There are about forty soldiers taken prisoners of war including officers and excluding those taken at Skenesborough. Not one life lost in these noble acquisitions.

  I am, Gentlemen, in haste, your most obedient humble servant,
    Edward Mott, Chairman of the Committee of War [48]

Arnold then notified the Massachusetts Committee that he had accomplished his mission and maintained command as ordered, but preferred to hand it over to someone else.

To The Committee of Safety, Cambridge

Ticonderoga, May 11, 1775

Gentlemen

I wrote you yesterday that arriving in the vicinity of this place, I found one hundred and fifty men collected at this instance of some gentlemen from Connecticut (designed on the same errand on which I came) headed by Colonel Ethan Allen, and that I had joined them, not thinking proper to wait the arrival of the troops, I had engaged on the road, but to attempt the fort by surprise; that we had taken the fort by four o'clock yesterday morning without opposition, and had made prisoners, one captain, one lieutenant, and forty odd privates and subalterns, and that we found the fort in a most ruinous condition and not worth repairing; that a party of fifty men were gone to Crown Point, and that I intended to follow with as many men to seize the sloop &c., and that I intended to keep possession here until I had farther advice from you. On and before our taking possession here, I had agreed with Colonel Allen to issue further orders jointly, until I could raise a sufficient number of men to relieve his people; on which plan we proceeded when I wrote you yesterday, since which, Colonel Allen, finding he had the ascendancy over his people, positively insisted I should have no command, as I forbid the soldiers plundering and destroying private property. The power is now taken out of my hands, and I am not consulted, nor have I a voice in any matters. There is here at present near one hundred men, who are in the greatest confusion and anarchy, destroying and plundering private property, committing every enormity, and paying no attention to public service. The party I advised were gone to Crown Point are returned, having met with head winds, and that expedition, and taking the sloop, (mounted with six guns,) is entirely laid aside. There is not the least regularity among the troops, but everything is governed by whim and caprice; the soldiers threatening to leave the garrison on the least affront. Most of them must return home soon, as their families are suffering. Under our present situation, I believe one hundred men would retake the fortress and there seems no prospect of things being in a better situation. I have therefore thought proper to send an express, advising you of the state of affairs, not doubting you will take the matter into your serious consideration, and order a number of troops to join those I have coming on here, or that you will appoint some other person to take the command of them and this place, as you shall think most proper. Colonel Allen is a proper man to head his own wild people, but entirely unacquainted with military service; and as I am the only person who has been legally authorized to take possession of this place, I am determined to insist on my right, and think it my duty to remain here against all opposition, until I have further orders. I cannot comply with your orders in regard to the cannon &c., for want of men. I have wrote to the Governor and General Assembly of Connecticut, advising them of my appointment, and giving them an exact detail of matters as they stand at present. I should be extremely glad to be honorably acquitted of my commission, and that a proper person might be appointed in my room. But as I have, in consequence of my orders from you, gentlemen, been the first person who entered and took possession of the fort, I shall keep it at every hazard until I have further advice and orders from you and the General Assembly of Connecticut.

I have the honor to be, your most obedient humble servant,

Benedict Arnold

P. S. It is impossible to advise you haw many cannon are here and at Crown Point, as many of them are buried in the ruins. There is a large number of iron, brass, mortars, &c., lying on the edge of the lake, which, as the lake is high, are covered with water. The confusion we have been in has prevented my getting proper information, further than that there are many cannon, shells, mortars, &c., which may be serviceable to our Army at Cambridge.

B. A. [48]

On the **14**[th], with the help of Bernard Romans, Arnold gave a progress report to the committee along with a follow up request for his replacement. Born in Holland around 1720, Romans studied botany, mathematics, and engineering in England before coming to America as a civil engineer following the start of the French and Indian War. Afterwards he was appointed principal deputy surveyor for the Southern District, exploring the coasts and botany of Florida and publishing his findings. Upon the commencement of the Revolution, he served as a member of the Connecticut Committee to take Ticonderoga, the third difficult personality assigned to do so, but his egocentric contemporaries, Allen and Arnold, had axed his authority.

To the Massachusetts Committee of Safety

Ticonderoga, May 14, 1775

Gentlemen

My last was the 11th instant per express, since which a party of men have seized on Crown Point, in which they took eleven prisoners, found sixty-one pieces of cannon serviceable and fifty-three unfit for service. I ordered a party to Skenesborough to take Major Skene, who have made him prisoner, and seized a small schooner, which is just arrived here. I intend setting out in her directly, with a bateau and fifty men, to take possession of the sloop, which we are advised this morning by the post, is at St. John's, loaded with provisions, &c., waiting a wind for this place. Enclosed is a list of cannon, &c., here, though imperfect, as we have found many pieces not included and some are on the edge of the lake, covered with water. I am, with the assistance of Bernard Romans, making preparation at Fort George, for transporting to Albany those cannon that will be serviceable to our Army at Cambridge. I have about one hundred men here and expect more every minute. Mr. Allen's party is decreasing and the dispute between us subsiding. I am extremely sorry matters have not been transacted with more prudence and judgement; I have done everything in my power and put up with many insults to preserve peace and serve the public. I hope soon to be properly released from this troublesome business, that some more proper person may be appointed in my room.

Till which I am, very respectfully, gentlemen, your most obedient humble servant, Benedict Arnold

P. S. Since writing the above, Mr. Romans concludes going to Albany to forward carriages for the cannon &c. and provisions, which will be soon wanted. I beg leave to observe he has been of great service here and I think him a very spirited, judicious gentleman, who has the service of the country much at heart and hope he will meet proper encouragement.

B. A. [25]

As reported by Warren in Cambridge on the **17th**, the Massachusetts Council endorsed Arnold to take command.

The Committee appointed to consider the account of taking the fortress of Ticonderoga, reported the resolve, and letter to the Assembly of Connecticut, which were accepted, and the letter ordered to be authenticated and sent forward:

To the Honorable Assembly of Connecticut

29

Gentlemen

We have the happiness of presenting our congratulations to you on the reduction of that important fortress, Ticonderoga; we applaud the conduct, both of the officers and soldiers, and are of opinion, that the advantageous situation of that fortress, makes it highly expedient, that it should be repaired and properly garrisoned. In the mean time, as we suppose that there is no necessity for keeping all the cannon there, we should be extremely glad, if all the battery cannon, especially brass cannon, which can be spared from that place, or procured from Crown Point, which, we hope, is, by this time, in the hands of our friends, may be forwarded this way, with all possible expedition, as we have here to contend with an Army furnished with as fine a train of artillery as ever was seen in America; and we are in extreme want of a sufficient number of cannon to fortify those important passes, without which we can neither annoy General Gage, if it should become necessary, nor defend ourselves against him; we, therefore, must, most earnestly, recommend this important matter to your immediate consideration; and we suggest it our opinion, that the appointing Colonel Arnold to take charge of them and bring them down in all possible haste. This may be a means of settling any dispute which may have arisen between him and some other officers which we are always desirous to avoid, and, more especially, at a time when our common danger ought to unite us in the strongest bonds of amity and affection.

We are, Gentlemen, your most obedient humble servants, [48]
Joseph Warren, Chairman

On the same day, Colonel James Easton delivered his version of the attack on Ticonderoga to Watertown, giving himself the credit that Arnold deserved, where it was read and picked up as a story by the *New England Chronicle* newspaper on the **18**[th].

New England Chronicle, Thursday, May 18, 1775
Cambridge, May 18.

Yesterday Colonel James Easton arrived at the Provincial Congress in Watertown from Ticonderoga & brings the glorious news of the taking that place by the American forces, without the loss of one man; of which interesting event we have collected the following particulars, viz.

Last Tuesday night, May 9, about 240 men from Connecticut and this province under Col. Ethan Allen and

Colonel Easton arrived at the Lake near Ticonderoga, 80 of them crossed it, and came to the fort about the dawn of day. The sentry was much surprised at seeing such a body of men and snapped his piece at them; our men, however rushed forward, seized and confined the sentry, pushed through the covered way, and all got safe upon the parade while the garrison were sleeping in their beds. They immediately formed a hollow square and gave three huzzahs, which brought out the garrison; and an inconsiderable skirmish, with cutlasses and bayonets ensued, in which a small number of the enemy received some wounds. The commanding officer soon came forth; Col. Easton clapped him upon the shoulder, told him he was a prisoner, and demanded, IN THE NAME OF AMERICA, an instant surrender of the fort, with all its contents, to the American forces. The officer was in great confusion, and expressed himself to this effect: Damn you, what – what does all this mean? Col. Easton again told him that he and his garrison were prisoners: The officer said that he hoped he would be treated with honor. Colonel Easton replied, he should be treated with much more honor that our people had met with from British troops. The officer then said, he was all submission and immediately ordered his soldiers to deliver up all the arms, in number about 100 stands. As they gave up their arms, the prisoners were secured in the hollow square.

The American forces having thus providentially got possession of this important fortress, found it upwards of one hundred pieces of cannon, several mortars, and a considerable quantity of shot, stores, and some powder.

After this acquisition, a detachment of our troops was dispatched to take possession of Crown Point, where there is a considerable number of cannon. Another detachment was sent to Skenesborough, where they took Major Skene and his family, with a number of soldiers, and several small pieces of cannon.

Colonel Easton met several hundred men from the western parts of this Province on their way to Ticonderoga. They were on the same expedition, not knowing the Fort was taken till they met Colonel Easton. Part of them pursued their march in order to secure and garrison the Fort.

The prisoners to the number of about one hundred, including Negroes, &c., were brought off by John Brown, Esquire. Colonel Allen was left commander of the fort.

The officers and soldiers in this important expedition behaved with the utmost intrepidity and good conduct, and

therefore merit the highest applause of their grateful Country.
[25]

Arnold received his own praise when he led his own men to capture three British ships at St. John's, located on the western shore of the Richelieu River in Canada. He then earned the respect of Allen and his men when he found them in a very hungry condition and fed them as his own. On the **19**[th], Arnold wrote a report of his latest victory to the committee and appointed twenty-year-old Captain Eleazer Oswald from Connecticut as his secretary.

To the Massachusetts Committee of Safety

Crown Point, May 19, 1775

Gentlemen

My last was of the 14th *instant by Mr. Romans via New Haven. I then acquainted you of the occasion of delay in not carrying your orders into execution. The afternoon of the same day, being joined by Captains Brown and Oswald, with fifty men, enlisted on the road, they have taken possession of a small schooner at Skenesboro, we immediately proceeded on our way for St. John's and at eight o'clock P.M., the 17*[th] *instant, arrived within thirty miles of St. John's; the weather proving calm, manned out two small bateaus with thirty-five men, and the next morning, at six o'clock, arrived at St. John's, surprised and took a sergeant and his party of twelve men, the King's sloop of about seventy tons with two brass six-pounders and seven men, without any loss to either side. The captain was gone to Montreal and hourly expected with a large detachment for Ticonderoga, a number of guns and carriages for the sloop, which was just fixed for sailing; add to this, there was a captain of forty men at Chambly, twelve miles distant from St. John's, who was expected there every minute with his party; so that it seemed to be a mere interposition of Providence that we arrived at so fortunate an hour. We took such stores on board as were valuable and the wind proving favorable, in two hours after we arrived, weighed anchor for this place with the sloop and four of the King's bateaus, having destroyed five others; so that there is not left a single bateau for the King's troops, Canadians, or Indians to cross the lake in, if they have any such intention.*

I must, in justice to Colonel Allen, observe that he left Crown Point soon after me for St. John's, with one hundred and fifty men, and on my return met him five leagues this side and supplied him with provisions, his men being in a starving condition. He informed me of

32

his intention of proceeding on to St. John's with eighty or one hundred men and keeping possession there. It appeared to me a wild, impracticable scheme, and provided it could be carried into execution of no consequence, so long as we are masters of the Lake and of that I make no doubt, as I am determined to arm the sloop and schooner immediately.

I wrote you gentlemen in my former letters that I should be extremely glad to be superseded in my command here, as I find it next to impossible to repair the old fort at Ticonderoga and am not qualified to direct in building a new one. I am really of opinion it will be necessary to employ one thousand or fifteen hundred men here this summer, in which I have the pleasure of being joined in sentiment by Mr. Romans, who is esteemed an able engineer. I am making all possible provision for wheel carriages to carry such cannon, &c. to Albany as can be spared here and will be serviceable to our Army at Cambridge.

I must refer you for particulars to the bearer, Captain Jonathan Brown, who has been very active and serviceable and is a prudent, good officer; and I beg leave to observe I have had intimations given me that some persons had determined to apply to you and the Provincial Congress to injure me in your esteem by misrepresenting matters of fact. I know of no other motive they can have, only my refusing them commissions for the very simple reason that I did not think them qualified. However, gentlemen, I have the satisfaction of imagining I am employed by gentlemen of so much candor that my conduct will not be condemned until I have the opportunity of being heard.

I am, with the greatest respect, gentlemen, your most devoted and very humble servant,

Benedict Arnold

P. S. Enclosed is a memorandum of such cannon, &c. as I intend sending to Cambridge, also of such as is here. By a return from Montreal to General Gage, I find there are seven hundred and seventeen men in Canada, of the seventh and twenty-sixth regiments, including seventy, which we have taken prisoners. [48]

B. A.

On the **22nd**, Arnold dispatched a similar report to the Committee of Safety at Albany with an additional request from each for more manpower and gunpowder. On the same day, the Massachusetts Congress wrote to Arnold to note its appreciation to him, its endorsement to the Continental Congress, and its wish to released from the matter.

To Colonel Arnold

Watertown, May 22, 1775

Sir

This Congress have this day received your letter of the eleventh instant, informing the Committee of Safety of the reduction of the fort at Ticonderoga, with its dependencies which was laid before the Congress by said Committee. We applaud the conduct of the troops and esteem it a very valuable acquisition.

We thank you for your exertions in the cause, and considering the situation of this Colony at this time, having a formidable Army in the heart of it, whose motions must be constantly attended to, and as the affairs of that expedition began in the Colony of Connecticut, and the cause being common to us all, we have already wrote to the General Assembly of that Colony to take the whole matter respecting the same under their care and direction, until the advice of the Continental Congress can be had in that behalf, a copy of which letter we now enclose you.

We are, &c.

(Signed by the members of the Massachusetts Congress) [25]

Although no reason is stated, J. Palmer, the committee member assigned to write to Congress, notes Arnold's rank as that of captain instead of colonel, thus demoting him on paper.

To The Honorable President of the Provincial Congress, now sitting at Watertown

In Committee of Safety, Cambridge, May 22, 1775

Sir

This Committee having received from Captain Benedict Arnold, by letter of the 11th of May, instant, information respecting the reduction of Ticonderoga, and the situation of that fortress in many respects, beg leave to lay said letter before the Honorable Congress, that they may proceed thereon in such manner as to them in their wisdom shall seem meet. This Committee apprehend it to be out of their province in any respect, whatever.

We are, with due respect, your Honor's obedient humble servants,

J. Palmer, Chairman [25]

It wasn't until March of 1779 that Allen added an addendum to his initial report in his narrative and acknowledged Arnold's contributions.

... But one thing now remained to be done to make ourselves complete masters of Lake Champlain: This was to possess ourselves of a sloop of war, which was then laying at St. John's; to effect which, it was agreed in a council of war to arm and man out a certain schooner, which lay at South Bay, and that Capt. (now General) Arnold should command her, and that I should command the bateau. The necessary preparations being made, we set sail from Ticonderoga in quest of the sloop, which was much larger and carried more guns and heavier metal than the schooner.

General Arnold, with the schooner sailing faster than the bateaus, arrived at St. John's and by surprise possessed himself of the sloop before I could arrive with the bateau. He also made prisoners of a sergeant and twelve men, who were garrisoned at that place. It is worthy of remark that as soon as General Arnold had secured the prisoners on board and had made preparation for sailing, the wind which but a few hours before was fresh in the south and well served to carry us to St. John's, now shifted and came fresh from the north; and in about one hour's time General Arnold sailed with the prize and schooner for Ticonderoga. When I met him with my party, within a few miles of St. John's, he saluted me with a discharge of cannon, which I returned with a volley of small arms. This being repeated three times, I went on board the sloop with my party, where several loyal Congress healths were drank.

We were now masters of Lake Champlain and the garrisons depending thereon.

Ethan Allen [20]

On the **23rd**, Arnold sent a report to the Massachusetts Committee, stating that Allen and his men had retreated back to Vermont after a number of remaining British troops in the area had made their presence known.

To the Committee of Safety at Cambridge
                                          Crown Point, May 23, 1775
Gentlemen
    My last was of the 19th instant by Captain Jonathan Brown. I then advised you of my taking possession of the King's sloop, &c.; and that, on the 18th instant, on my return from St. John's, Colonel E.

Allen, with about eighty or one hundred men, passed me with intention of making a stand at St. John's; and not being able to dissuade him from so rash a purpose, I supplied them with provisions &c. Yesterday he arrived at Ticonderoga with his party and says that on the evening of the 18th instant, he arrived at St. John's, and hearing a detachment of men on the road from Montreal, laid in ambush for them; but his people being so much fatigued, (when the party was about one mile distant,) thought proper to retreat and crossed the Lake at St. John's, where they continued the night. At dawn next day they were, when asleep, saluted with a discharge of grapeshot from six field pieces and a discharge of small arms from about two hundred regulars. They made a precipitous retreat and left behind them three men. Immediately on this advice I proceeded here with the sloop and schooner, well armed as possible under our circumstances, and eighty men, which, with the part here before, makes near one hundred and fifty men, with whom I am determined to make a stand here to secure the cannon, it being impossible to remove them at present. I am in hourly expectation of two or three hundred men more; most of those here are enlisted. Colonel Allen's men are in general gone home.

As the regulars have good information of our strength and movements, I am apprehensive of their paying us a visit, provided they can get bateaus from Montreal to St. John's. I shall make every possible preparation to give them a warm reception. I have commissioned Captain John Sloan in the sloop and Captain Isaac Matthews in the schooner. I have wrote to New York for a number of gunners and seamen to man the two vessels, being in great want of them. At present obliged to stay on board one of them myself.

As soon as a sufficient number of men arrives, I shall lose no time in carrying your orders into execution in regard to the cannon, &c. This morning, very luckily, an escort of provisions (five barrels of pork and thirty barrels of flour) arrived here as a present from Albany, under the care of Captain Elisha Phelps. The last barrel of our pork being abroach, I have ordered fifty barrels of pork and one hundred of flour from Albany, which I expect soon; prior to which I bought fifteen oxen and thirty barrels of flour, which is all the provisions purchased as yet. The people who have enlisted are promised the same bounty as given in the Massachusetts Bay. A sum of money will be requisite to carry matters into execution. I have one hundred and sixty pounds, found in the sloop; but as it was the captain's property, do not choose to make use of it at present. I have sent to Albany repeatedly for powder and can get none; have only one

*hundred and fifty pounds here, which I brought from Concord. I beg
you will order a quantity to be forwarded here immediately. I have
wrote to Connecticut, but can have no dependence from that quarter,
as it is very scarce there.*

*I hope some gentleman will soon be appointed in my room
here, who is better able to serve the public than I am.*

Interim, I am, gentlemen, your most obedient humble servant,

Benedict Arnold

*P. S. Since writing the above, one of Colonel Allen's party,
who was taken prisoner at St. John's, has made his escape and says,
that on the 19th instant there were four hundred regulars at St, John's,
who expected to be joined by more men and were making all possible
preparation to cross the lake and retake Crown Point and
Ticonderoga. I have sent express to Fort George and Skenesborough
to rally the country. You may depend, gentlemen, that these places
will not be given up unless we are overpowered by numbers or
deserted by Providence, which has hitherto supported us.*

I am yours, &c.,

B. Arnold [48]

In the postscript of a similar letter to the Assembly of
Connecticut, Arnold took it upon himself to order another fifteen
hundred troops.

*P. S. This will be delivered to you, gentlemen, by Captain
Phelps, who has been very serviceable here, whom I must refer you to
for particulars. Mist beg leave to observe, I think it highly necessary
for Connecticut to send here immediately fifteen hundred men at least,
with good arms, ammunition, &c.* [25]

Arnold then sent a final report to Congress, in which he
referred to the above letters. In a petition for the release of his men to
the Connecticut Assembly on the **24th**, Delaplace didn't acknowledge
Arnold or Congress.

*To the Honorable General Assembly of the Governor
and Company of the English Colony of Connecticut,
in New England, in America, now convened at Hartford.*

Hartford, May 24, 1775

*The memorial of William Delaplace, a Captain in His
Majesty's Twenty-sixth Regiment, and commandant of the Fort and
Garrison of Ticonderoga, in behalf of himself and the officers and*

soldiers under his command, beg leave to represent our difficult situation to your Honors and petition for redress.

Your memorialist would represent, that on the morning of the tenth of May instant, the Garrison of the Fortress of Ticonderoga, in the Province of New York, was surprised by a party of armed men under the command of one Ethan Allen, consisting of about one hundred and fifty, who had taken such measures effectually to surprise the same, that very little resistance could be made, and to whom your memorialists were obliged to surrender as prisoners; and overpowered by a superior force, were disarmed, and by said Allen ordered immediately to be sent to Hartford, in the Colony of Connecticut, where your memorialists now are detained as prisoners of war, consisting of officers, forty-seven private soldiers of His Majesty's Troops, besides women and children. That your memorialists being ignorant of any crime by them committed, whereby they should be thus taken and held, are also ignorant by what authority said Allen thus took them, or that they are thus detained in a strange country, and at a distance from the post assigned them; thus not know in what light they are considered by your Honors, consequently not know what part to act; would therefore ask your Honors' interposition and protection, and order that they be set at liberty, to return to the post from whence they were taken, or to join the Regiment to which they belong; or if they are considered in the light of prisoners of war, your Honors would be pleased to signify the same to them, and by whom they are detained, and that your Honors would afford us your favor and protection during the time we shall tarry in this Colony; and your memorialists will ever pray.

William Delaplace
Captain Commandant Ticonderoga Fort [25]

On the **26**[th], Arnold reported to the committee that the British had abandoned their plans to retake the forts.

To the Committee of Safety, Cambridge

Crown Point, May 26, 1775
Gentlemen

My last of the 23rd *instant; I then advised you of the situation of the matters here, since which there has been no alteration. Very few men have arrived. We have fixed the sloop with six carriage and twelve swivel guns; the schooner with four carriage and eight swivels. Both vessels are in good order and tolerably well manned. Eight*

38

gentlemen having arrived from Hartford, who are seamen, I have sent two ten-inch iron mortars and two eight-inch howitzers to Ticonderoga, to be forwarded to Fort George.

You may depend on my sending the cannon from this place as soon as possible. There are three thirteen-inch iron mortars here – beg to know what I shall do with them. I have received large donations of flour, pork, peas, &c., from Albany – near seventy barrels – and I am informed there is a large quantity on the road from that place and a quantity supplied from Connecticut.

The advice I received from Butterfield and communicated in the postscript of my last of the 23rd instant, proves to be premature. I have good intelligence from a bateau immediately from St. John's, which place she left on the 19th instant, that the regulars were returned to Chambly.

I am, with great respect, gentlemen, your obedient servant,

Benedict Arnold [48]

On the same day, Allen sent the Connecticut Assembly a copy of a letter to the Canadian Indians asking for their help in the war against King George III. While growing up, George III was a sluggish, unemotional, and immature boy who developed into a self-disciplined man with a sense of duty yet stubborn and self-righteous when he inherited the throne at age twenty-two. Although he had ended the Seven Years' War with France (French and Indian War) with his proposals in the first Treaty of Paris, he helped to instigate the rebellion of the colonies in America by imposing taxes to pay the bill.

To The Honorable General Assembly

Crown Point, May 26, 1775

Honorable Gentlemen

I here communicate to you a copy of a letter I sent by Mr. Winthrop Hoit and Captain Abraham Ninham, a friendly Stockbridge Indian, to the several tribes of Indians in Canada.

"Headquarters of the Army, Crown Point, May 24, 1775

By advice of council of the officers, I recommend our, trusty and well-beloved friend and brother, Captain Abraham Ninham, of Stockbridge, as our ambassador of peace to our good brother Indians of the four tribes, viz: the Hocnawagoes, the Swagaches, the Canesadaugans, and the Saint Fransawas.

Loving brothers and friends: I have to inform you that George the Third, King of England, has made war with the English Colonies

39

in America, who have ever till now been his good subjects; and sent his Army and killed some of your good friends and brothers at Boston, in the Province of the Massachusetts Bay. Then your good brothers in that province, and in all the colonies of English America, made war with King George, and have begun to kill the men of his Army, and have taken Ticonderoga and Crown Point from him, and all the artillery, and also a great sloop which was at St. John's, and all the boats in the lake, and have raised, and are raising two great armies; one is destined for Boston, and the other for the fortresses and department of Lake Champlain, to fight the King's troops that oppose the colonies from Canada; and as King George's soldiers killed our brothers and friends in a time of peace, I hope, as Indians are good and honest men, you will not fight for King George against your friends in America, as they have done you no wrong, and desire to live with you as brothers. I was always a friend to Indians, and have hunted with them many times, and know how to shoot and ambush like Indians, and am a great hunter.

I want to have your warriors come and see me, and help me fight the King's Regular Troops. You know they stand all close together, rank and file, and my men fight so as Indians do, and I want your warriors to join me and my warriors, like brothers, and ambush the Regulars. If you will, I will give you money, blankets, tomahawks, knives, paint, and anything that there is in the Army, just like brothers; and I will go with you into the woods to scout; and my men and your men will sleep together, and eat and drink together, and fight Regulars, because they first killed our brothers; and will fight against us; therefore I want our brother Indians to help us fight; for I know Indians are good warriors and can fight well in the bush. You know it is good for my warriors and Indians to kill the Regulars, because they first began to kill our brothers in this country without cause.

Ye know my warriors must fight, but if you our brother Indians do not fight on either side, we will still be friends and brothers; and you may come and hunt in our woods, and come with your canoes on the lake, and let us have venison at our forts on the lake, and have rum, bread, and what you want, and be like brothers.

I have sent our friend, Winthrop Hoit, to treat with you on our behalf in friendship; you know him, for he has lived with you, and is your adopted son, and is a good man. Captain Ninham, of Stockbridge will tell you about the whole matter more than I can write. I hope your warriors will come and see me. So I bid all my brother Indians farewell.

Ethan Allen,
Colonel of the Green Mountain Boys"
This, gentlemen, is a copy of the letter I have sent the Indians;
I hope it may have a good effect. I thought it advisable that the
Honorable Assembly should be informed of all our politics.
And am, gentlemen, with the greatest respect,
your most obedient and humble servant,
Ethan Allen [25]

On the **27th**, the Massachusetts Congress wrote to Arnold stating that if someone was to be found guilty of slandering him, then he would have his day in court.

To Colonel Arnold, Ticonderoga
Watertown, May 27, 1775
Sir
We have, this day, with pleasure, received your letter to the Committee of Safety, of the 19th instant by Captain Brown, and return you our hearty thanks for your exertions in the public cause, and fully agree with you that the interposition of Providence, in this and many other instances, is apparent, for which we have the greatest cause for thankfulness.

We are clearly of opinion that keeping Ticonderoga is a matter of great importance and we make no doubt the honorable Continental Congress will take that affair immediately under their wise consideration and give all necessary orders therefore, as we have addressed them most earnestly on the subject.

You inform us that you have had intimations that some persons were determined to apply in order to injure your character. If any such applications should be made here, you may be assured we shall be so candid as not to suffer any impressions to your disadvantage until you shall have opportunity to vindicate your conduct.

We enclose a Resolve of this Congress, appointing and directing Colonel Joseph Henshaw to repair to Hartford and consult with the General Assembly there upon this important matter, by which you will see the resolution this Congress has taken relative hereto.

We would just add that the letter you refer to of the 14th instant by Colonel Romans has not come to hand, so that no order can be taken thereon.
We are, &c.
(Signed by the members of the Massachusetts Congress.) [48]

The enclosed resolution ordered Arnold to report before them and present his financial report in order to be properly relieved.

Resolved, That Col. Joseph Henshaw be appointed and directed to repair to Hartford and inquire whether provision is made by the General Assembly of the Colony of Connecticut, for securing and maintaining the fortress at Ticonderoga and the adjacent posts; and if that Assembly has made provision for that purpose, the said Col. Henshaw proceed directly to Ticonderoga, and acquaint Col. Arnold that it is the order of this Congress that he return and render accounts of his expenses in that expedition, in order that he may be honorably discharged; but if Col. Henshaw shall find that such provision is not made, and the general assembly be not sitting, that he proceed to Ticonderoga and inform Col. Arnold that it is the order of this Congress that he continue there, with such number of forces as said Col. Henshaw shall judge necessary for the purpose. Nevertheless, if the said Col. Henshaw shall find the General Assembly sitting and that they have not made such provision, that he consult with them touching this important matter, and take their proposals, and immediately make report to the Congress of this Colony. 87.

On the **28th**, the Massachusetts Committee revealed to Arnold that the Massachusetts Congress was in fact not informed of his orders to take Ticonderoga.

To Colonel Arnold

Cambridge, May 28, 1775

Sir

The expedition to Ticonderoga, &c., requiring secrecy, the Congress of this Colony was not acquainted with the orders you received from this Committee. It gives us great pleasure to be informed by express, Captain Brown, that the success you have met with is answerable to your spirit in the undertaking. We have now to acquaint you that the Congress have taken up this matter and given the necessary directions respecting these acquisitions. It is, then, Sir, become your duty and is our requirement that you conform yourself to such advice and orders as you shall from time to time receive from that body.

We are, &c. [25]

(Signed by the members of the Massachusetts Committee of Safety.)

On the **29th**, Arnold wrote to Congress to express his concern regarding their proposal to pull the Army out of its most strategic position at Ticonderoga.

To The Honorable Continental Congress
Crown Point, May 29, 1775
Gentlemen
Your resolution of the 18th instant, and recommendation of measures to the City of New York and Albany, in consequence of the taking possession of Ticonderoga and Crown Point, has this moment been delivered me, as commanding officer here, the purpose of which induces me to believe the Committee of Safety of the Massachusetts Bay have not informed you of my appointment or instructions from them, which I have taken the liberty to enclose; and, in consequence, arrived in the neighborhood of Ticonderoga the 9th instant, where I met one Colonel Allen, with about one hundred men raised at the instance of some gentlemen from Connecticut, who agreed we should take a joint command of the troops. The next morning at four o'clock, we surprised the garrison and took them prisoners, the particulars of which you have doubtless heard. Some dispute arising between Colonel Allen and myself, prevented my carrying my orders into execution until the 16th, when, being joined by fifty men of my own regiment and a small schooner taken to Skenesborough, which I immediately armed and sailed for St. John's in quest of the sloop. The 17th, being becalmed within ten leagues of St. John's, I manned out two small bateaus with thirty-five men, and, after rowing all night, at six o'clock next morning landed at St. John's and took a sergeant and his party of twelve men prisoners, the King's sloop of seventy tons, mounted with two brass six-pounders and seven men, and in two hours after left St. John's, having previously taken on board such stores etc., as were valuable. Providence remarkably smiled on us, as a few hours delay would have ruined our design, a party of one hundred and twenty men with six pieces of cannon for the sloop, being on their march from Montreal, at only twenty miles distant; add to this a party of forty men on a march from Chambly, twelve miles distant. Colonel Allen arrived at St. John's the same evening with one hundred men, and being attacked the next morning by the regulars, retreated and left three men behind, two of which are since arrived.

I have armed the sloop with six carriage and twelve swivel guns; the schooner with four carriages and eight swivels. I have sent to Lake George one brass twelve-pounder, six large brass and iron mortars and howitzers, and am making all possible preparation for transporting all the cannon here and as many as can be spared at Ticonderoga to Fort George.

I must beg leave to observe, gentlemen, that the report of Ticonderoga's being abandoned have thrown the inhabitants here into the greatest consternation. There are about five hundred families to the northward of Ticonderoga, who, if it is evacuated, will be left at the mercy of the King's troops and Indians, and who have, part of them, joined the Army and cannot now remain neutral, to whom a removal would be entire ruin, as they have large families and no dependence but a promise crop on the ground. I need not add to this, gentlemen, that Ticonderoga is the key of this extensive country, and if abandoned, leaves a very extensive frontier open to the ravages of the enemy, and to continual alarms, which will probably cost more the expense of repairing and garrisoning it.

I esteemed it my duty, as a servant of the public, to give you the foregoing hints and hope the urgency of the times will be a sufficient apology for the liberty I have taken.

> *I have the honor to be, very respectfully, gentlemen,*
> *your most obedient humble servant,*
> *Benedict Arnold* [25]

Arnold then followed up with a letter to the Massachusetts Committee to express his reaction to the above-mentioned proposal.

The Committee of Safety, Cambridge

> *Crown Point, May 29, 1775*

Gentlemen

I was equally surprised and alarmed this day on receiving advice via Albany that the Continental Congress had recommended the removing all the cannon, stores, &c., at Ticonderoga, to Fort George, and evacuating Ticonderoga entirely, which being the only key of this country, leaves our very extensive frontiers open to the ravages of the enemy; and if put into execution, will be the entire ruin of five hundred families to the northward of Ticonderoga. I have wrote the Congress and given my sentiment very freely, with your instructions to me, as I fancy they have had no intelligence of my appointment or orders.

Colonel Allen has entirely given up the command. I have one hundred and fifty men here and expect in two or three weeks to have my regiment complete and believe they will be joined by a thousand men from Connecticut and New York. I have sent to Lake George six large brass and iron mortars and howitzers, one brass and three iron twelve-pounders, and shall pursue your orders with all the dispatch in my power.

I am, Gentlemen, with great respect,
your most obedient and humble servant,
Benedict Arnold [48]

Maintaining his post until properly relieved, Arnold then submitted a requisition to the New York Congress for tools, materials, and tradesmen.

To the Provincial Congress of New York

Ticonderoga, May 29, 1775

Memorandum of Men, &c, wanted for the ensuing summer, viz:

1,200 men including B. Arnold's regiment of 400 men: 100 men of the train of artillery: 2 surgeons and their mates: 20 men for ten teams: 20 masons and blacksmiths: 2 gun smiths: 10 caulkers: 25 ship carpenters: 25 house carpenters: - the latter may doubtless be found among the privates who enlist, except the master workmen: 600 hatchets: 100 narrow axes: 50 broad axes: 50 pickaxes: 200 spades: 200 wooden shovels, shod: 50 hoes: 100 camp kettles 100 tents with proper equipage: arms, blankets, &c., for the men.
I observe the Committee of New York intend forwarding a number of articles, for which reason I omitted them.

Sundry necessaries for transporting the cannon over Lake George, viz:

To be built on Lake George, 2 flat bottom boats, forty feet long, twelve wide, and four deep, with strong knees, well timbered, and of four-inch oak plank – these may be built at Sparden's, where there is timber and a sawmill:
1 flat bottom boat, of same size and construction, to go between Ticonderoga and the landing or Lake Champlain:
4 gins, the triangles fifteen feet long – the wood may be procured here:
8 falls for the gins, of three and a half-inch white rope, from the best hemp:
1 coil two and a half inch rope, 1 coil two inch rope, 1 coil one and a half inch rope, 100 fathoms each: 40 pounds sewing twine:

10 dozen sail and roll rope needles: 1 dozen palms: 4 pieces raven duck:

10 barrels pitch: 4 barrels tar: 500 pounds oakum:

3 seines, thirty fathoms long, capped twelve feet and arms six feet deep, made of large twine, the meshes one and a half inches wide, which will probably supply the Army with fish, as they are very plenty and good:

1 barrel twenty penny nails: 1 barrel ten penny nails: 1 barrel four penny nails: 2 dozen nail hammers, with other necessary tools for the house and ship carpenters – iron may be supplied from Skenesborough:

steel will be wanted – 4 pair strong wheels, wanted between Lakes George and Champlain, that will carry three tons weight:

4 pair strong wheels wanted at Fort George.

N. B. Common cart wheels will answer (if good) for most of the small cannon: there will probably be wanted at Fort George, 10 good teams of four yoke of oxen each, to bring up provisions &c., and take such cannon and mortars to Albany as may be wanted by our Army at New York or Cambridge: 8 yoke of good oxen will be wanted at Ticonderoga – these may probably be procured in the neighborhood, of which Colonel Webb may inform himself.

Benedict Arnold
Colonel and Commandant at Ticonderoga, &c. [25]

Meanwhile, in the hopes of gaining an ally, Congress extended an olive branch "to the oppressed inhabitants of Canada," asking for their support as a friend against tyranny. [26] On the **31st**, Henshaw relayed his report from the General Assembly to Arnold, confirming that Colonel Benjamin Hinman would be succeeding him.

To Colonel Arnold

Hartford, May 31, 1775

Sir

By Captain Brown I would advise you of my consulting the General Assembly of this Colony respecting the fortress at Ticonderoga. They have ordered Colonel Hinman to take the command there with one thousand men, and four companies raising at Albany, artificers, &c., to repair and defend that post. It is expected you will continue with Colonel Allen and put the place in the best posture of defense you are able and guard against any surprise from the enemy till the successors arrive and you receive further directions from the Congress. I should have proceeded from hence to

Ticonderoga, but some events taking place since my departure from the Congress makes it necessary for me to repair immediately thither.

I am, Sir, your most obedient servant,
Joseph Henshaw [25]

Upon receiving Arnold's letter of the 23rd, Congress in turn reversed their decision and made a commitment to maintain that which they had achieved. Included in the resolution was a request for Governor Jonathan Trumbull to appoint a commander for Ticonderoga and Crown Point. Trumbull was born in Lebanon, Connecticut in 1710 and graduated from Harvard before becoming an exceptional man of commerce dealing directly with Great Britain instead of going through Boston. After studying law, he served as a member of the legislature and speaker of the house. Being devoutly religious with a sobering manner, discriminating prudence, and rigid principles, he also rose to the achieve the honor of county court judge, assistant judge of the superior court, chief justice, deputy governor, and governor. He strove to come to a peaceful resolution with England, believing that strife would only bring about separation, but on the declaration of war, he supported the cause of the colonies one hundred percent.

Wednesday, May 31, 1775
...A letter received from Col. Arnold, dated Crown Point, 23 May, 1775, was laid before the Congress, informing that he had certain intelligence that "on the 19th there were then 400 regulars at St. John's, making all possible preparations to cross the lake and expected to be joined by a number of Indians, with a design of retaking Crown Point and Ticonderoga," and earnestly calling for a reinforcement and supplies. This letter being taken into consideration.

Resolved, That the Governor of Connecticut be requested immediately to send a strong reinforcement to the garrisons of Crown Point and Ticonderoga, and that so many of the cannon and other stores be retained, as may be necessary for the immediate defense of these posts, until further orders from this Congress, and that the Provincial Convention of New York be informed of this resolve, and desired to furnish those troops with provisions and other necessary stores, and to take effectual care that a sufficient number of bateaus be immediately provided for the lakes.

Ordered, That the above resolve be immediately transmitted in a letter by the Pres. to Gov. Trumbull and the Convention of New York.

Ordered, That the President in his letter acquaint Gov. Trumbull, that it is the desire of Congress, that he should appoint a person, in whom he can confide, to command the forces at Crown Point and Ticonderoga. [26]

The Massachusetts Congress gave its due recognition to Arnold on **June 1st**, but revealed that he could only be relieved from duty by the powers that be in Philadelphia.

To Col. Arnold, Ticonderoga
                    Colony of Massachusetts Bay, Watertown, June 1, 1775.
Sir
        This Congress has received yours of 19 & 23rd May ultimo, per Captain Brown and Captain Phelps, a copy of which has been sent to New Hampshire. They highly approve of and take great satisfactions in the acquisitions you have made at Ticonderoga, Crown Point, on the lake, &c. As to the state you are in respecting men, provisions, &c., we have advice from Connecticut and New York that ample preparation is making its way with the greatest dispatch in those two colonies from whence you may depend on being seasonably supplied. They are sorry to meet with repeated requests from you that some gentleman be sent to succeed you in command; they assure you that they place the greatest confidence in your fidelity, knowledge, courage, and good conduct and they desire that you at present dismiss the thought of quitting your important command at Ticonderoga, Crown Point, Lake Champlain, etc., and you are hereby requested to continue your command over the forces raised by this colony posted at those several places, at least until the Colony of New York or Connecticut shall take on them, the maintaining and commanding the same agreeable to an order of the Continental Congress. [48]
                (Signed by the members of the Massachusetts Congress)

The praise that he received from Congress was then echoed in a letter from his sister that truly demonstrated their mother's influence on her.

To Benedict Arnold
                                        New Haven, June, 1775
Dear Brother
        I take this opportunity from Captain Oswald to congratulate you on your late success in reducing Ticonderoga, and making

48

yourself master of the vessels on the lakes. I sincerely wish all your future endeavors to serve your country may be crowned with equal success and pity the fatigue you must unavoidably suffer in the wilderness. But as the cause is undoubtedly a just one, I hope you may have health, strength, fortitude, and valor, for whatever you may be called to. May the broad hand of the Almighty overshadow you; and if called to battle, may the God of Armies cover your head in the day of it. 'Tis Him and Him only, my dear brother, that we can look for safety or success. His power is ever able to shield us from the pestilence that walks in darkness and the arrows that fly by noonday. May a Christian resignation to His will strengthen your hands and fortify your heart. May you seek his aid and rest your whole confidence in Him; and then you will have no fear but that of offending Him; and if we are to meet no more in time, may a wise preparation for eternity secure to us a happy meeting in the realms of bliss, where painful separations are forever excluded. The men who went under your care to Boston give you the praises of a very humane and tender officer. I hope those now with you may meet with an equal degree of tenderness and humanity.

Your affectionate Sister,
Hannah Arnold [5]

With a pass to travel to New York, Feltham wrote an after action report to Gage on the **11th**, in which he acknowledged Arnold's authority and admitted losing the fort to a lack of security.

To His Excellency General Gage

New York, June 11th 1775

Sir

    Capt. Delaplace of the 26th Regiment has given direction to lay before you, in as plain a narrative as I can, the manner of the surprise of the fort of Ticonderoga on the 10th May, with all the circumstances after it that I thought might be of any service in giving your Excellency any light into the affair.

    Capt. Delaplace having in the course of the winter applied to Genl Carleton for a reinforcement, as he had reason to suspect some attack from some circumstances that happened in his neighborhood, Genl Carleton was pleased to order a detachment of a subaltern and 20 men to be sent in two or three separate parties, the first party of which was sent as a crew along with Major Dunbar, who left Canada about the 12th April. I, being the first subaltern on command, was ordered down with 10 men in a few days more to give up to Capt.

Delaplace with Whom Lt. Wadman was to remain, having received orders from the regiment some time before to join there. As he was not arrived when I came, I had orders to wait until he did. I was 12 days there before he came, which was about an hour after the fort was surprised.

I had not lain in the fort on my arrival having left the only tolerable rooms there were for Mr. Wadman if he arrived with his family, but being unwell, had lain in the fort for two or three nights preceding the 10th May, on which morning, about half an hour after three in my sleep, I was awakened by numbers of shrieks, & the words, 'no quarter, no quarter,' from a number of armed rabble. I jumped up about which time I heard the noise continue in the area of the fort. I ran undressed to knock at Capt. Delaplace's door & to receive his orders or wake him; the door was fast the room I lay in being close to Capt. Delaplace's. I stepped back, put on my coat & waist coat & returned to his room, there being no possibility of getting to the men as they were numbers of the rioters on the bastions of the wing of the fort on which the door of my room and back door of Capt. Delaplace's room led, with great difficulty, I got into his room being pursued from which there was a door down by stairs into the area of the fort. I asked Capt. Delaplace, who was now just up, what I should do, & offered to force my way if possible to our men. On opening this door, the bottom of the stairs was filled with the rioters & many were forcing their way up, knowing the commanding officer lived there, as they had broke open the lower rooms where the officers live in winter, and could not find them there. From the top of the stairs I endeavored to make them hear me, but it was impossible, on making a signal not to come up the stairs, they stopped & proclaimed silence among themselves. I then addressed them, but in a style not agreeable to them, I asked them a number of questions, expecting to amuse them till our people fired, which I must certainly own I thought would have been the case. After asking them the most material questions I could think viz by what authority they entered his Majesty's fort, who were the leaders, what their intent, &c., &c., I was informed by one Ethan Allen and one Benedict Arnold that they had a joint command, Arnold informing me he came from instructions received from the Congress at Cambridge, which he afterwards showed me. Mr. Allen told me his orders were from the Province of Connecticut & that he must have immediate possession of the fort and all the effects of George the Third (those were his words). Mr. Allen insisting on this with a drawn sword over my head and numbers of his followers firelocks presented at me, alleging I was commanding

*officer & to give up the fort, and if it was not complied with, or that
there was a single gun fired in the fort, neither man, woman, or child
should be left alive in the fort. Mr. Arnold begged it in a genteel
manner, but without success, it was owing to him they were prevented
getting into Capt. Delaplace's room, after they found I did not
command. Capt. Delaplace now being dressed came out, when after
talking to him some time, they put me back into the room, they placed
two sentry's on me, and took Capt. Delaplace downstairs, they also
placed sentry's at the back door. From the beginning of the noise till
half an hour after this, I never saw a soldier, though I heard a great
noise in their rooms and cannot account otherwise than that they must
have been seized in their beds before I got on the stairs, or at the first
coming in, which must be the case as Allen wounded one of the guard
on his struggling with him in the guard room immediately after his
entrance into the fort. When I did see our men, they were drawn up
without arms, which were all put into one room over which they
placed sentries and allotted one to each soldier. Their strength at first
coming, that is the number they had ferried over in the night,
amounted to about 90, but from their entrance & shouting, they were
constantly landing men till about 10 o'clock, when I suppose there
were about 300, & by the next morning at least another 100, who I
suppose were waiting the event & came now to join in the plunder,
which was most rigidly performed as to liquors, provisions, &c.,
whether belonging to his Majesty or private property...*

I remain your Excellency's most obedient humble servant,
Jocelyn Feltham, Lt. 26th Regt. [28]

In a letter to Congress on the **13**[th], Arnold transmitted the
Indians decision to support the American cause along with the
forewarning of a potential attack from the north. He added that
Carleton hadn't been able to acquire a significant amount of Canadian
support. Although they had given the British their all against France
during the French and Indian War, their neighbors to the south were
no Frenchmen, so most chose to remain neutral.

To The Honorable Continental Congress
now sitting at Philadelphia

Crown Point, June 13, 1775

Gentlemen
*As commanding officer here, I think it my duty to acquaint you
that having sent one Mr. Hoit, an Indian interpreter, to Montreal and
Caughnawaga, to consult with some gentlemen of my acquaintance in*

the former place, and with the Indians in the latter, to know their intentions in the present dispute, he has returned with the agreeable intelligence that the Indians are determined not to assist the King's troops against us. They have made a law, that if any one of their tribe shall take up arms for that purpose, he shall immediately be put to death; this is confirmed by five of their chief men, who are nowhere with their wives and children, and press very hard for our Army to march into Canada, being much disgusted with the regulars. The Stockbridge Indians, whom I lately sent to them with a belt of wampum and speech, confirm the above. My friend in Montreal, a merchant and gentleman of probity, writes that great numbers of the Canadians have expected a visit from us for some time, and are very impatient of our delay, as they are determined to join us whenever we appear in the country with any force to support them. This I am confirmed in by a party of the Canadians, having just returned from a short excursion to the Isle-au-Noix, (Nut Island,) where a number of them offer to join us.

Governor Carleton, by every artifice, has been able to raise only about twenty Canadians and those of the noblesse, who are in expectation of places of profit and honor. He is now at Montreal and has threatened the English merchants, if they will not defend it in case of attack, he will set fire to the city and retreat to Quebec. There are now in Canada, of the seventh and twenty-sixth regiments, only five hundred and fifty effective men, who are quartered in the following manner: At St. John's and Chambly, three hundred; at Montreal, forty; at La Chine, twelve; at Trois Rivieres, forty; at Quebec, one hundred and twenty; and some small parties at outposts. From the foregoing matters of fact, which you may rely are undoubted and from my personal knowledge of the country and disposition of the Canadians, I beg leave to observe that if the Honorable Congress should think proper to take possession of Montreal and Quebec, I am positive two thousand men might very easily effect it; for which purposes I beg leave to recommend the following plan of operations:

The men to embark at Crown Point and proceed in the sloop, schooner, bateaus, &c., to within two miles of St. John's; seventeen hundred men to form a grand division, of which one thousand to proceed directly to Montreal; the other division of seven hundred to cut off the communication between St. John's, Chambly, and Montreal, and the remainder to remain with the shipping to secure our retreat. Who will be able, by a diversion in favor of the main body, until they show themselves off Montreal, whose gates, on our arrival at that place, will be opened by our friends there, in *consequence of a plan for that purpose already entered into by them. Of course Chambly and St. John's must fall into our hands as well as Quebec, unless a number of troops should arrive there before this plan can be carried into execution, the utility of which the Honorable Congress will be the best judge. But I must beg to observe, it appears to me the reduction of those places would discourage the enemies of American liberty, and, in a great degree, frustrate their cruel and unjust plan of operation, and be the means of restoring that solid peace and harmony between Great Britain and her colonies, so essential to the well being of both; at least it will, in my humble opinion, be more advantageous, and attended with less expense, to reduce Quebec and keep possession, where provisions of every kind are plenty and a strong fortress built to our hand, than rebuilding Ticonderoga, as it will entirely deprive Great Britain of the lucrative branch, (the fur trade,) and be an inexhaustible granary in case we are reduced to want, as there are annually shipped from Quebec five hundred thousand bushels of wheat. I hope the urgency of the times and my zeal in the service of my country will apologize for the liberty of giving my sentiments so freely on a subject which the Honorable Congress are doubtless the best judges of, but which they in their hurry may not have paid the attention to which the matter requires. I beg leave to add, that if no person appears who will undertake to carry the plan into execution, (if thought advisable,) I will undertake, and, with the smiles of Heaven, answer for the success of it, provided I am supplied with men, &c., to carry it into execution without loss of time. I must beg leave to refer you to the bearer, Captain Oswald, for particulars, who is entrusted with an imperfect memorandum of such articles as are most wanted.*

I have the honor to be, with the greatest respect, gentlemen, your most devoted humble servant,

Benedict Arnold

P. S. The American Colonies in general are equally in danger from Canada, whether it remain in the hands of Britain, under the present form of its government, or should be restored to the French, which many suspect is intended by the Ministry in England. But should Canada be placed under a free government, agreeable to the English Constitution, like the other colonies, we should forever after be secure from any danger that way, as it would ever remain an English colony, even though by the treachery of the British Ministry it should be given up to France; so that this measure; though at first view it might seem like going beyond our own province to invade the rights of Great Britain, yet a due regard to our own defense, as well as the advantage of the inhabitants of that country, makes it necessary.

B. A. [25]

On the same day, the Massachusetts Congress sent Walter Spooner, Jedediah Foster, and James Sullivan to Ticonderoga with orders to personally audit Arnold's designation of his duties and the fort's practicability. Born in Berwick, Maine, Sullivan had studied law under his brother, John Sullivan, and received an appointment as King's attorney of York County after he was admitted to the bar.

To Walter Spooner, Jedediah Foster, and James Sullivan, Esquires:
June 13, 1775
You are directed to proceed, as soon as may be, to the posts of Ticonderoga and Crown Point, by the road through the new settlements, called the New Hampshire Grants; that you carefully observe the quality of the said road and judge of the feasibleness of transporting provisions by the said road to the waters of Lake Champlain; that you take with you copies of the commission and instructions of the Committee of Safety to Col. Benedict Arnold and inform yourselves as fully as you shall be able, in what manner the said Col. Arnold has executed his said commission and instructions.

That you make and give to the said Arnold, and any men whom he shall, by virtue of the said commission and instructions retain in the service of this colony, such orders as to you shall seem meet: provided always, that you do not authorize the said Arnold to engage and retain in the pay of this Colony, as soldiers, a greater number than that specified in his said commission and instructions, and provided that the said Arnold and his men whom he has retained are free and willing to continue at one or both of the said posts, under the command of such chief officer as is, or shall be appointed by the government of Connecticut; and in case you shall order such number of men to be continued at or near the said posts in the pay of this Colony, as you shall judge it necessary there should be, that you appoint a committee of one or more persons, in the pay of this Colony, to provide supplies for such men, and a commissary to deal out such supplies to them: which committee and commissary you are to appoint in writing under your hands.

And you are to determine and order, respecting the said Arnold's continuing in the commission and pay of this Colony, as to you shall appear most for the general service and safety, after having made yourselves fully acquainted with the spirit, capacity, and

54

conduct of the said Arnold. And in case you shall judge it proper to discharge the said Arnold, that you direct him to return to this Colony and render his account of the disposition of the money, ammunition, and other things which he received at his setting out upon his expedition, and also of the charges he has incurred, and the debts which he has contracted in behalf of this Colony, by virtue of the commission and instructions aforesaid...

You are further directed, when you shall have transacted what you are by the foregoing instructions authorized to do and transact, at the posts abovesaid, by the very first opportunity, to advise the General American Congress thereof, as also of your opinion of the necessity and importance of maintaining the said posts, for the general defense of these Colonies: and when you have made yourselves fully acquainted with the state and condition of the said posts, and the dispositions and establishments which you shall find are made for maintaining of them, if you shall judge that any further provisions are necessary for securing and maintaining them, you are directed, fully and respectfully, to signify your thoughts thereon to the General Congress. You are also directed to advise the General Convention of the Colony of New York and the Governor of the Colony of Connecticut, respectfully, of what you shall order and transact, by virtue of said instructions. [48]

On Wednesday the **14**[th] in Philadelphia, Congress established the United States Army. On Friday the **16**[th], Hinman arrived from Connecticut, but the letters from Congress and Henshaw to announce the change of orders had not been delivered. When Hinman announced to Arnold that he was to turn over the command of Lake Champlain to him, Arnold rebutted him on the grounds that he had received no order from Massachusetts to do so. On the **22**[nd], those orders appeared with the arrival of Spooner, Foster, and Sullivan, who confirmed that Hinman's command was an official appointment from Connecticut's newly appointed Brigadier General, David Wooster of New Haven. Arnold refused to bow down to an officer with less seniority than him, neither would he subject his men who fought so honorably to this type of treatment. These were his men whom he led in battle and paid with his own money. On the **23**[rd], Arnold responded to the appointment of the Spooner Committee by Congress.

To the Honorable President and the Members of the American Congress now sitting at Philadelphia

Ticonderoga, June 23, 1775

May it please your Honors

The Congress of the Colony of the Massachusetts Bay, on the fourteenth day of June last, appointed Walter Spooner, Frederick Foster, and James Sullivan, a committee to repair to the fortresses of Ticonderoga and Crown Point on the Lake Champlain, to inquire into the importance of holding those posts and also the method by which they may be maintained; to establish there in the pay of said colony, so many men to defend the same posts as they should judge necessary, not exceeding four hundred: And the said committee were also by said Congress directed, when they should have made themselves fully acquainted with the situation and importance off said posts, respectfully to signify their thoughts thereon to your Honors.

Wherefore, by order of said committee, I take leave to inform you, that it is the opinion of said committee, such is the importance of these fortresses, that should they once be in the hands of the enemies of America, the Colony of New York, together with the New England Colonies, would be in continual danger of having depredations committed on them by the regular forces who would be possessed of those garrisons; and should the Canadians and savages, who, we hope, are not yet at odds with us, be inclined to take part with the Ministerial Army, the distress of the colonies before mentioned must be extremely great. A garrison at the south end of Lake George, however defensible, could be of little service to the new England Colonies, because the most easy route for an Army from Quebec into New England would be through Lake Champlain to South Bay, from whence they might travel by land through the new settlements of New York into the New England Governments and destroy the frontier towns on their march, drive the farmers from their fields, prevent the large supplies of wheat and other necessaries which may soon be expected from these new settlements, send distress and famine into the bowels of the country, and this all without being on a right line within many miles of the south end of Lake George.

I am also ordered by said committee to signify to your Honors, that it is of the opinion of said committee that the defense of these fortresses must be supported by holding the command of Lake Champlain, which they conceive may be more easily done by having vessels of various constructions, well manned and armed, floating there; for which purpose the committee have stationed four hundred men there, which are all that the embarrassed circumstances of our colony can at present admit of, to cooperate with near a thousand under the command of Colonel Hinman, who is sent to these posts by the Government of Connecticut; but whether the forces now on the

56

lake are sufficient for the purposes aforementioned, your honors will judge.

B. Arnold [25]

That being said, Arnold notified the committee that he would resign, which they accepted, but directed him to remain in command of the area until he was properly relieved. Upon that time he was to present himself to Congress and produce a list of his expenses.

To Colonel Arnold

Crown Point, June 23, 1775

Sir

You have signified to the committee who are appointed and directed by the Provincial Congress of the Massachusetts Bay to inquire into the state of the fortresses at Crown Point, Ticonderoga, &c., and the appendages thereof, your resolution to resign all your command of the said fortresses, and the vessels and stores thereunto belonging, for reasons under your hand expressed.

This is to inform you, that it is the expectation of the Provincial Congress aforesaid, that the chief officer of the Connecticut forces at those stations will command the same for the present; and the committee accordingly expect that you conform yourself to the directions of said Congress in that behalf, and deliver the same to such chief officer of the Connecticut forces, or his order, for which this shall be your authority. The committee expect that you will, as soon as may be, lay an account of your disbursements before the Provincial Congress, agreeable to our instructions, a copy whereof is lodged with you.

By order of the committee.

Walter Spooner, Chairman [48]

On the **24**[th], Arnold responded to the Spooner Committee in writing for the record.

To Messrs. Spooner, Foster, and Sullivan – present

Crown Point, June 24, 1775

Gentlemen

Your instructions of the 14th instant from the Provincial Congress of the Massachusetts Bay, in regard to my conduct here, now being before me, I will answer in course.

In the first place, I observe you are appointed to examine my conduct and in what manner I have executed my commission. I look on this instruction at this juncture as unprecedented, and a very plain intimation that the Congress are dubious of my rectitude or abilities, which is sufficient inducement for me to decline serving them longer.

Secondly, the Congress have authorized you to judge of my spirit, capacity, and conduct, and determine whether I shall continue in commission, and if so, that I shall be under the command of a person appointed by the Colony of Connecticut. In answer to the first part, it appears to me very extraordinary that the Congress should first appoint an officer and afterwards, when he had executed his commission, to appoint a committee to examine if he was fit for his post. I think the examination should have been prior to the commission, and that after executing that commission they should order a younger officer of the same rank to take the command of the fortresses, vessels, &c., conquered, plainly indicates the loss of their confidence, and is a most disgraceful reflection on him and the body of troops he commands, which is a sufficient inducement to resign, not to mention the very great hardship on the private men, who, having served well near two months, are now to be mustered, and if, by sickness or hard labor, they are reduced to the distress of begging their bread until they can get home to their friends.

The last objection I have to make is, that I have so far lost the confidence of the Congress, that they have declined sending me money, as was promised by Captain Brown, to discharge the small and unavoidable debts I have contracted for necessaries for the use of the Army, for which my own credit is at stake, and I am reduced to the necessity of leaving the place with dishonor, or waiting until I can send home and discharge those debts out of my private purse. The latter of which I am determined to do, though I have already advanced one hundred pounds, lawful money, out of my private purse. All which reasons I believe will be thought a sufficient inducement for me to decline holding my commission longer.

I am, Gentlemen, your most humble servant,

Benedict Arnold [25]

Rather than turning his men over to Hinman as a defeated officer would turn over his sword, he disbanded his unit instead, which made many of the men mutinous for fear that they would not be paid. On the **25th**, an unknown eyewitness named Veritas gave his account of the taking of Ticonderoga to the press, giving Arnold credit for the capture.

To John Holt, printer of the New York Journal

Mr. Holt,
 The following erroneous account of the reduction of Ticonderoga was published in Mr. Thomas' Oracle of Liberty the 24ᵗʰ May last, and as the writer of the account which follows it, had no opportunity of seeing it till very lately, he being up at the forts, ever since they were taken, he could not contradict it sooner. I beg therefore you will replenish it in your next journal, together with the account that follows it, which may be depended upon.

I am, yours, &c.

(Here is reprinted the account by Easton, which appeared in the *New England Chronicle* at Cambridge on May 18, 1775.)

 As the above account of the reduction of Ticonderoga, which from its complexion, I suppose originated from that very modest gentleman, Col. Easton himself, is so replete with falsehood, and is so great an imposition on the public, that I think it my duty, in order to undeceive the public, and to do justice to modest merit, to give you a candid detail of the whole matter, for the truth of which I appeal to every officer and private who were present, which is as follows:
 Some gentlemen arrived in the New Hampshire grants from Connecticut, with a design on seizing the fortress of Ticonderoga, were there joined by a number of men, among whom were Col. Allen and Easton, the former, with the assistance of Captain Warner, collected about 150 men, with whom they marched to Castleton, 20 miles from Ticonderoga, where they left Col. Easton and proceeded 10 miles towards Shoreham, the next day Col. Arnold arrived at Castleton from Cambridge, having concerted in similar plan and being commissioned by the Massachusetts Congress to raise a regiment, he proceeded on to the party under the command of Colonel Allen, when Colonel Arnold made known his commission, &c – it was voted by the officers present that he should take a joint command with Col. Allen (Col. Easton not presuming to take any command). When the party had marched to Shoreham, two miles on the Lake below Ticonderoga, where they waited for bateaus to cross the lake, until midnight, and none arriving, Col. Arnold, with much difficulty, persuaded about 40 men to embark with him in a bateau accidentally taken there, and landed half a mile from the fort, and immediately sent back the bateau, which by reason of a violent storm of wind and rain did not return until break of day with a small boat, and near 50 men in both. It was then proposed by some gentlemen to wait open

day and the arrival of the remainder of the men which amounted at that time to near 100; this Col. Arnold strenuously opposed and urged to storm the fort immediately, declaring he would enter it alone if no man had courage to follow him – this had the desired effect, he with Col. Allen headed the party and proceeded directly to the fort – when they came within about 10 yards of the gate, the sentry discovered them and made a precipitate retreat, he was pursued closely by Colonel Arnold, who was the first person that entered the fort, and Col. Allen about 5 yards behind him – this I was an eyewitness of being only a few yards distant. Col Arnold immediately ordered the men to secure the doors of the barracks and went himself with Col. Allen to the commanding officer, Captain Delaplace, and desired him to deliver up his arms, and he might expect to be treated like a gentlemen, which he immediately complied with, as did the whole garrison.

I do not recollect seeing Col. Easton until 9 o'clock and was told he was the last man that entered the fort, and that, not till the soldiers and their arms were secured, he having concealed himself in an old barrack near the redoubt, under the pretence of wiping and drying his gun, which he said got wet in crossing the lake. Since which I have often heard Col. Easton, in a base and cowardly manner abuse Col. Arnold was soon made acquainted with the liberty he had taken with his character, and upon his refusing to give proper satisfaction, I had the pleasure of seeing him heartily kicked by Colonel Arnold, to the great satisfaction of a number of gentlemen present, although Easton was armed with a cutlass and a pair of loaded pistols in his pocket.

I am your humble servant,

Veritas [25]

On **July 3rd**, the residents in the area of Ticonderoga openly expressed their gratitude to Arnold in a letter to him and a notice in the newspaper for his contribution of public service in the defense of their homes.

To Benedict Arnold, Esquire, Colonel of a Massachusetts Regiment and Commander-in-Chief of an expedition to Lake Champlain, for taking the fortresses on said Lake, and the armed vessel thereon, into the possession and protection of the American Army.

Lake Champlain, July 3, 1775

We, the subscribers, the principal inhabitants on the said Lake, in behalf of ourselves and on behalf of all the inhabitants,

60

contiguous thereto, amounting in number to about six hundred families, deeply impressed with a sense of your merit, and the weighty obligations which we lie under to you in your military capacity, think it our duty to address you in this public manner, to testify our gratitude and thankfulness for the uncommon vigilance, vigor, and spirit, with which you have achieved those important conquests, so essentially necessary for our preservation and safety from the threatened and much dreaded incursions of an inveterate enemy.

The humanity and benevolence which you have exercised towards the inhabitants of those parts most immediately affected by the present convulsions, by supplying them with provisions in their distress, render you no less worthy our admiration, then your tenderness and polite treatment of such prisoners as have fallen into your hands entitle you to the most favorable opinion of some of the regular officers, whose grateful sentiments thereon you have already received. So you are likewise, in a peculiar manner, entitled to our warmest thanks, since you have thereby, and by the proofs they have had of your prudence and valor, been the means of keeping our enemy and their scouting parties at a distance from us, to which your vigilance, in constantly employing such a number of boats on the north part of this lake, hath not a little contributed.

The humane and polite manner in which you treated your prisoners, insures to you the applause of all: you have thereby shown your adversaries a bright example of that elevation and generosity of soul, which nothing less than real magnanimity and innate virtue could inspire.

By your vigilance and good conduct, we have been, under Providence, preserved from the incursions and ravages of an enraged enemy, to whose declared vengeance we lay entirely exposed; and therefore we cannot help expressing our sorrow at the approaching period of your removal from us. Convinced of your competency to the undertaking of protecting us, we cannot help lamenting our situation on the thoughts of losing you, being ignorant of the experience or abilities of the gentlemen appointed to succeed you.

We sincerely wish you rewards adequate to your merit, and are, with the utmost gratitude, regard, and esteem, Sir, your most obliged and most obedient servants.

(Signed by a number of the principal inhabitants, on behalf of themselves and the rest.) [25]

On the **4**[th], Arnold responded to the residents of Ticonderoga in appreciation for their support.

To the very respectable inhabitants on Lake Champlain
                                        Crown Point, July 4, 1775
Gentlemen
      *Permit me to return you my most hearty thanks for the polite
and obliging address you have been pleased to present me this day,
which, as it convinces me of your esteem and approbation of my
conduct in a military capacity, is more than an adequate recompense
for the poor services and protection I have been happy enough to
render you, which both duty and humanity required of me. I am much
pleased to have it in my power, in this public manner, to return you
my sincerest thanks for your support, vigilance, and spirited conduct
in the public cause, and cannot help regretting the necessity I am
under of leaving you so soon.*
      *I heartily wish you the protection of that kind Providence
which has so remarkable interposed in your favor heretofore, and beg
leave to assure you I shall, at all times, be happy in hearing of the
welfare of all the inhabitants on Lake Champlain, but of my friends in
particular.*
                *I am, with the greatest respect and esteem, gentlemen,
                        your most obedient humble servant.*
                                        Benedict Arnold [25]

      In a letter to Trumbull on the **6th**, Edward Mott, Chairman for
the Committee of War, translates Hinman's version of Arnold's
refusal to hand over his command to him.

To Governor Trumbull

                                        Albany, July 6, 1775
Honored Sir
      *I arrived here last night, ten o'clock, from Ticonderoga; am
sent express by Colonel Hinman to acquaint the committee at this
place, and also the Provincial Congress at New York, with the
condition of the troops and garrisons at Ticonderoga, Crown Point,
and Fort George; expect to set out from hence for New York
tomorrow; have not as yet waited on the committee here, but write
these lines by Captain Stevens, who will not tarry, but sets out for
home this morning. When I arrived at Ticonderoga, Colonel Hinman
had no command there, as Colonel Arnold refused to let him
command either of the garrisons, but had given the command of
Ticonderoga to Captain Herrick, from whom Colonel Hinman's men
were obliged to take their orders or were not suffered to pass to and*

from the garrison. The same day a committee of three gentlemen from Massachusetts, viz: Mr. Spooner, Colonel Foster, and Colonel Sullivan, returned to Ticonderoga from Crown Point, and informed us that they had been to Colonel Arnold with orders from the Congress requiring him to resign the command to Colonel Hinman, and that he, with his regiment, should come under the command of said Hinman; which said Arnold positively refused; on which said committee discharged Colonel Arnold from their service and desired the privilege to speak with the people who had engaged under Arnold, but were refused. They further informed that Colonel Arnold and some of his people were gone on board the vessels; that they understood they threatened to go to St. John's and deliver the vessels to the regulars, and that Arnold had disbanded all his troops but those that were on board said vessels; that they were treated very ill and threatened, and after they came away in a bateau, they were fired upon with swivel guns and small arms by Arnold's people; and that Colonel Arnold and his men had got both the vessels and were drawn off into the lake. On which I desired Colonel Hinman to let me, with Lieutenant Halsey and Mr. Duer, with some men to row, have a bateau and proceed up the lake and go on board the vessels. We obtained liberty and Colonel Sullivan consented to go with us. We got on board the vessels about eleven o'clock in the morning and he confined three of us on board each vessel; men sat over us with fixed bayonets and so kept us till sometime in the evening when we were dismissed and suffered to return. We reasoned with the people on board the vessels all the while we were there and convinced some of them of their error, who declared they had been deceived by Colonel Arnold. After we returned to the fort, called up Colonel Hinman, who ordered Lieutenant Halsey, with twenty-five men, to return again to the vessels and get what people he could on board to join him, and bring one or both vessels to the fort, which was all settled the next day. Colonel Sullivan was much insulted while we were on board the vessels, chiefly by Mr. Brown, one of Colonel Arnold's captains. Captain Stevens, who is waiting while I write these lines, will not wait longer or you should hear more particulars. I expect you will have a full account from the gentlemen committee after they have laid it before the Congress. Captain Elisha Babcock can give a full account of those matters; he tells me he shall be at Hartford in a few days. Shall give further accounts from New York.

> *I am, Sir, at command,*
> *your Honor's most obedient and humble servant,*
> *Edward Mott* [25]

On that same day, although he was still under investigation, Brown received a promotion to the rank of Major while Arnold's auditors reported back to submit their statement to the Massachusetts Congress, which included an opportunity for Arnold's next command.

Report of the Committee sent to Ticonderoga
Cambridge, July 6, 1775

The committee appointed to proceed to the posts of Ticonderoga and Crown Point, &c., beg leave to report that they proceeded through the new settlements called the New Hampshire Grants and carefully observed the road through the same, and find that there is a good road from Williamstown to the place where the road crosseth the river called Paulet River, which is about fifteen miles from Skenesborough; from thence to the falls at Wood Creek near Major Skene's house, the road is not feasible and is unfit for carriages, but cattle may be driven that way very well.

Your committee, having taken with them the copies of the commission and instructions from the Committee of Safety to Col. Benedict Arnold, and informed themselves, as fully as they were able, in what manner he had executed his said commission and instructions, have found that he was with Col. Allen and others at the time the fort was reduced; but do not find that he had any men under his command at the time of the reduction of those fortresses; but find that he did, afterwards, possess himself of the sloop on the lake. At Saint John's we found the said Arnold, claiming the command of said sloop, and a schooner, which is said to be the property of Major Skene; and also all the posts and fortresses at the south end of Lake Champlain and Lake George, although Col. Hinman was at Ticonderoga, with near a thousand men under his command at several posts.

Your committee informed the said Arnold of their commission, and, at his request, gave him a copy of their instructions; upon reading of which, he seemed greatly disconcerted and declared he would not be second in command to any person whomsoever; and after some time contemplating upon the matter, resigned his post and gave your committee his resignation under his hand, dated the 24th of June; which is submitted, and, at the same time, he ordered his men to be disbanded, which he said were between two and three hundred. Your committee, not finding any men regularly under said Arnold, by reason of his so disbanding them, appointed Col. Hinman, who was the principal commanding officer at these posts of the Connecticut *forces, and endeavored to give the officers and men who had served under said Arnold, an opportunity to reenlist; of whom, numbers enlisted and several of the officers agreed to hold their command under the new appointment...*

Your committee found that as soon as Col. Arnold had disbanded his men, some of them became dissatisfied and mutinous, and many of them signified to the committee that they had been informed they were to be defrauded of their pay for past services. The committee, in order to quiet them, engaged, under their hands, in behalf of the Colony of Massachusetts Bay, that as soon as the rolls should be made up and properly authenticated, they should be paid for their past services, and all those who should engage anew should have the same bounty and wages as is promised to those who serve within said Colony...

Your committee, when they had received Col. Arnold's resignation, directed him to return to Congress and render an account of his proceedings, agreeably to their instructions, a copy of which order is herewith submitted.

Your committee are of opinion, that the maintaining of these posts is of the utmost importance to the security of the Colony of New York and the New England Colonies, which was a sufficient inducement to the committee to continue in the pay of this Colony the number of men before mentioned. The fortresses not being at present tenable, then there must be a sufficient number of men to command the lake and prevent the enemy from landing.

Your committee are of opinion that the best security of these posts in their present state is by armed vessels of various construction, to be kept constantly cruising the lake, and small boats with swivel guns to act as scouts, which will effectually prevent the Army from sudden surprise.

Your committee have, agreeably to their instructions, advised the Hon. American Congress, the Hon. Convention of the Colony of New York, and the Governor of Connecticut, by respectfully signifying to them, their opinion of the importance of the maintaining those posts and the measures for effecting the same.

All which is humbly submitted,
Walter Spooner, by order [48]

On the 11th, as requested by Major General Philip Schuyler, Arnold notified Congress that the Indians had changed their minds and would not ally with us, but rather with the enemy. Schuyler was born in Albany and had married Catherine Van Rensselaer during the time of his service in the French and Indian War. Afterwards he became an established entrepreneur and was appointed as a member of the General Assembly and Colonial Assembly as well as a delegate to the Continental Congress. Aside from his prominent civic duties, he served as a colonel in the militia and was commissioned as one of four major generals at the start of the Revolution, a fitting position for a man of his nature, with piercing eyes and a tall, commanding presence.

To The Honorable Continental Congress

Albany, July 11, 1775

Gentlemen

 General Schuyler has desired me to acquaint you of the state and situation of the Army in the Northern Department. Six days since, when I left Crown Point, there were at that post near three hundred men, without employ, having received no orders to fortify; at Ticonderoga, about six hundred in the same state; at Fort George, upwards of three hundred men; some few employed in building bateaus and on scouting parties. Very little provision at any of the places; none made for the sick, which are daily increasing; only five hundred weight of gunpowder at all the places; and no engineer or gunner at either. Great want of discipline and regularity among the troops. On the other hand, the enemy at St. John's indefatigable in fortifying and collecting timber (supposed) for building a vessel. The disposition of the Canadians and Indians, from the latest accounts, very favorable. A promise has, however, been extorted from the latter to defend Governor Carleton if attacked in Montreal; this of course.

 By giving up the command, I have been prevented receiving regular intelligence as heretofore; the latest near twenty days since.

 I have receive no answer to my letter of the 13th June, by Captain Oswald.

 Can only add, I am, with the greatest respect, gentlemen, your most obedient and very humble servant,

Benedict Arnold

P. S. I had forgot to inform you my regiment is disbanded. [25]

On the way home to straighten out his affairs came the biggest blow of all when he learned that his wife had died suddenly from fever on **June 19th**. She was only thirty.

III
Quebec

On Tuesday, the 1st of **August 1775**, Arnold appeared before the Massachusetts Provincial Congress, who appointed a five-man committee headed by Dr. Benjamin Church, to review his financial statements for settlement. After reading the earlier reports from Easton and Spooner, the committee did not consider Arnold in a respectable light and scrutinized every expenditure. After two and a half weeks, he then met with the Commander-in-Chief, General George Washington in Cambridge and disclosed his plan to head up an expedition through Maine and attack the British military source at Quebec, the capital city and key to Canada. Born in Pope's Creek, Virginia, Washington had lost his father when he was just eleven and grew up as an ambitious youth under his mother's loving guidance and "Sir Matthew Hale's Contemplations", which would shape him for the rest of his life. He became a surveyor as a young man before serving in the French and Indian War as an aide-de-camp. Afterwards he married, worked as a planter, served in the House of Burgesses, 1st and 2nd Continental Congress, and trained local militia. The theory of "dress for success" certainly applied here, as he was the only member to show up in uniform consistently, which complimented his tall, athletic frame, firm disposition, philosophic mind, fearless spirit, and untarnished dignity. It was these striking characteristics that brought about his nomination and appointment as Commander-in-Chief of the Continental Army, serving his first command at Bunker Hill.

Washington had approved Arnold's plan on three conditions; that Arnold present the report requested by the Massachusetts Provincial Congress, that he put himself under Major General Philip Schuyler's command in the attack, and that he treat Canadians as fellow Americans making a common cause against British oppressors. Arnold reported as ordered and was dismayed to be initially denied the 1,000 pounds that he paid out to his men until Washington and Connecticut Congressman Silas Deane intervened to have him paid in full. After graduating from Yale, Deane taught school while he studied law, eventually opening his own practice in the thriving town of Wethersfield, Connecticut. His first marriage was to a widow with a prosperous store, which made him a considerable amount of wealth although she died four years later. His second marriage was to the granddaughter of a former governor of the colony, which strengthened his connections with the Connecticut aristocracy.

Various positions that he held included chairman of a local committee against the Townshend Acts, member of the General Assembly, secretary of the Committee of Correspondence, and Connecticut delegate before being elected to Congress.

Among the senior officers selected for the trek to Quebec were Lieutenant Colonels Christopher Greene, a business man who had served in the Rhode Island legislature before the war; and Roger Enos from the 2nd Connecticut who had served in the French and Indian War. Major Return Jonathan Meigs had been commissioned as a lieutenant in the 6th Connecticut before the war and had marched with them to secure Boston after hearing of the action of Lexington. Simultaneously, Major Timothy Bigelow, a blacksmith from Worchester, Massachusetts had led his company of minutemen to Cambridge. On **August 21st**, Arnold ordered a large quantity of small wooden boats called bateaus to be constructed to carry the men and supplies up to Quebec.

To Captain Colburn

August 21, 1775

Sir

His Excellency General Washington desires you will inform yourself how soon there can be procured or built at Kennebec, two hundred light bateau capable of carrying six or seven men each, with their provisions and baggage (say 100 weight to each man) the boats to be furnished four oars, two paddles, & two setting poles. [18]

I am, &c.,

B. Arnold

Unfortunately, Colburn would not be able to commence construction until **September 6th**, which forced him to build them quickly rather than carefully and would eventually lead the expedition to near disaster. On the **11th**, the rifle companies made their way from Prospect Hill near Cambridge to Newburyport, Massachusetts led by Captains Daniel Morgan from Winchester, Virginia; William Hendricks from Cumberland, Pennsylvania; and Matthew Smith from Lancaster, Pennsylvania. The riflemen maintained the fighting style of Colonial warriors armed with a long rifle, long knife, tomahawk, and small axe while dressed in the silent camouflage of a deerskin hunting shirt, leggings, and moccasins.

Morgan had worked as a farm laborer and teamster prior to the French and Indian War in which he was given 500 lashes as punishment for striking back at an officer. His only other battle scar was one that he received from a shot to the neck by that went through his jaw and took out several teeth. Having been part of the teams before the war, he was an accomplished horseman, while his natural athletic ability made him the fastest runner and his size gave him the advantage in many a drinking brawl. Returning home, this six-foot tall, 200-pound frontiersman settled down to get married, and raise a family on his farm, thus transforming himself into a devout Christian and a mild mannered man of noble bearing, whose wrath was only aroused by the sight of injustice. In a letter to Arnold on the 14th, Washington outlined the rules of engagement, which encompassed morality, prudence, religion, and military strategy.

To Colonel Benedict Arnold,
Commander of the detachment of the Continental Army destined against Quebec

September 14, 1775

Sir

You are intrusted with a command of the utmost consequence to the interest and liberties of America. Upon your conduct and courage and that of the officers and soldiers detached on this expedition, not only the success of the present enterprise, and your honor, but the safety and welfare of the whole continent may depend. I charge you therefore, and the officers and soldiers under your command as you value your own safety and honor and the favor and esteem of your country, that you consider yourselves as marching, not through an enemy's country; but that of our friends and brethren, for such the inhabitants of Canada, and the Indian nations have approved themselves in this unhappy contest between Great Britain and America. That you check by every motive of duty and fear of punishment, every attempt to plunder or insult any of the inhabitants of Canada. Should any American soldier be so base and infamous as to injure any Canadian or Indian, in his person or property, I do most earnestly enjoin you to bring him to such severe and exemplary punishment as the enormity of the crime may require. Should it extend to death itself it will not be disproportional to its guilt at such a time and in such a cause: but I hope and trust that the brave men who have voluntarily engaged in this expedition will be governed by far different views, that order, discipline, and regularity of behavior will be as conspicuous as their courage and valor. I also give it in charge

69

to you to avoid all disrespect to or contempt of the religion of the country and its ceremonies. Prudence, policy, and a true Christian spirit will lead us to look with compassion upon their errors without insulting them. While we are contending for our own liberty, we should be very cautious of violating the rights of conscience in others, ever considering that God alone is the judge of the hearts of men, and to him only in this case, they are answerable. Upon the whole, Sir, I beg you to inculcate upon the officers and soldiers, the necessity of preserving the strictest order during their march through Canada, if they should by their conduct, turn the hearts of our brethren in Canada against us. And on the other hand, the honors and rewards which await them, if by their prudence and good behavior they reconcile the affections of the Canadians and Indians to the great interests of America and convert those favorable dispositions they have shown into a lasting union and affection.

Thus wishing you and the officers and soldiers under your command, all honor safety, and success,

I remain, Sir, your most obedient humble servant,

George Washington [24]

Accompanying the letter was a copy of Arnold's official orders from Washington.

To Colonel Benedict Arnold
By His Excellency George Washington Esqr.
Commander-in-Chief of the Army of the United Colonies of North America.

1st. You are immediately on their march from Cambridge to take command of the detachment from the Continental Army against Quebec & use all possible expedition as the winter season is now advancing and the success of this enterprise (under God) depends wholly upon the spirit with which it is pushed & the favorable disposition of the Canadians and Indians.

2nd. When you come to Newburyport you are to make all possible inquiry what men of war or cruisers there may be on the coast to which this detachment may be exposed on their voyage to Kennebec River – and if you shall find that there is danger of being intercepted you are not to proceed by water, but by land, taking care on the one hand not to be diverted by light & vague reports & on the other not to expose the troops rashly to a danger which by many judicious persons has been deemed very considerable.

3rd. You are by every means in your power to endeavor to discover the real sentiments of the Canadians towards our cause & particularly to this expedition: ever bearing in mind that if they are adverse to it & will not cooperate or at least willingly acquiesce it must fail of success – In this case you are by no means to prosecute the attempt, the expense of the expedition & the disappointment are not to be put in competition with the dangerous consequences which may ensue from irritating them against us and detaching them from that neutrality which they have adopted.

4th. In order to cherish those favorable sentiments to the American cause that they have manifested you are as soon as you arrive in their country to disperse a number of the addresses you will have with you, particularly in those parts where your route shall lay and observe the strictest discipline & good order, by no means suffering any inhabitant to be abused or in any manner injured either in his person or property – punishing with exemplary severity every person who shall transgress & making ample compensation to the party injured.

5th. You are to endeavor on the other hand to conciliate the affections of those people & such Indians as you may meet with by every means in your power – convincing them that we come at the request of many of their principal people, not as robbers or to make war upon them but as the friends and supporters of their liberties as well as ours: And to give efficacy to these sentiments you must carefully inculcate upon the officers and soldiers under your command that not only the good of their country & their honor, but their safety depends upon the treatment of this people.

6th. Check every idea; & crush in its earliest stage every attempt to plunder even those who are known to be enemies to our cause, it will create dreadful apprehensions in our friends and when it is once begun none can tell where it will stop, I therefore again most expressly order that it will be discouraged & punished in every instance without distinction.

7th. Whatever King's stores you shall be so fortunate as to posses yourself of, are to be secured for the Continental use agreeable to the Rules and Regulations of War published by the Honorable Congress. The officers and men may be assured that any extraordinary services performed by them will be suitably rewarded.

8th. Spare neither pains nor expense to gain all possible intelligence on your march to prevent surprises & accidents of every kind - & endeavor if possible to correspond with General Schuyler so that you may act in concert with him. This I think may be done by means of the St. Francois Indians.

9th. In case of a union with General Schuyler, or if he should be in Canada upon your arrival there, you are by no means to consider yourself as upon a separate & independent command but are to put yourself under him & follow his directions. Upon this occasion & all others I recommend most earnestly to avoid al contention about rank – In such a cause every post is honorable in which a man can serve his country.

10th. If Lord Chatham's son should be in Canada & in any way fall in your power you are enjoined to treat him with all possible deference and respect. You cannot err in paying too much honor to the son of so illustrious a character & so true a friend to America. Any other prisoners who may fall into your hands you will treat with as much humanity & kindness as may be consistent with your own safety & the public interest. Be very particular in restraining not only your own troops but the Indians from all acts of cruelty & insult which will disgrace the American Arms - & irritate our fellow subjects against us.

11th. You will be particularly careful to pay the full value for all provisions or other accommodations, which the Canadians may provide for you on your march. By no means press them or any of their cattle into your service, but amply compensate those who voluntarily assist you. For this purpose you are provided with a sum of money in specie, which you will use with much frugality & economy as your necessities & good policy will admit – keeping as exact an account as possible of your disbursements.

12th. You are by every opportunity to inform me of your progress, your prospects & intelligence - & upon any important occurrence to dispatch an express.

13th. As the season is now far advanced you are to make all possible dispatch – but if the unforeseen difficulties should arise or if the weather should become so severe as to render it hazardous to proceed in your own judgement & that of your principal officers (whom you are to consult) – In that case you are to return: giving me as early notice as possible that I may give you such assistance as my be necessary.

14th. As the contempt of the religion of a country by ridiculing any of its ceremonies or affronting its ministries or votaries has ever been deeply resented – You are to be particularly careful to restrain every officer & soldier from such imprudence & folly & to punish every instance of it – On the other hand as far as lays in your power you are to protect & support the free exercise of the religion of the country &

the undisturbed enjoyment of the rights of conscience in religious matters with your utmost influence & authority.

Given under my hand at Headquarters Cambridge, this 14th day of September, One Thousand Seven Hundred Seventy Five.

George Washington [24]

On the same day, Washington wrote out a State of the Union address to our neighbors to the north.

Address to the Inhabitants of Canada

14 September 1775

Friends and Brethren

The unnatural contest between the English Colonies and Great Britain has now risen to such a height that arms alone must decide it. The Colonies, confiding in the justice of their cause and the purity of their intentions, have reluctantly appealed to that being, in whose hands are all human events. He has hitherto smiled upon their virtuous efforts – the hand of tyranny has been arrested in its ravages, and the British arms which have shone with so much splendor in every part of the globe, are now tarnished with disgrace and disappointment. – Generals of approved experience, who boasted of subduing this great continent, find themselves circumscribed within the limits of a single city and its suburbs, suffering all the shame and distress of a siege. While the trueborn Sons of America, animated by the genuine principles of liberty and love of their country, with increasing union, firmness and discipline repel every attack, and despise every danger.

Above all, we rejoice, that our enemies have been deceived with regard to you – They have persuaded themselves, they have even dared to say, that the Canadians were not capable of distinguishing between the blessings of liberty, and the wretchedness of slavery; that gratifying the vanity of a little circle of nobility – would blind the eyes of the people of Canada. – By such artifices they hoped to bend you to their views, but they have been deceived, instead of finding in you that poverty of soul, and baseness of spirit, they see with a chagrin equal to our joy, that you are enlightened, generous, and virtuous – that you will not renounce your own rights, or serve as instruments to deprive your fellow subjects of theirs. – Come then my brethren, unite with us in an indissoluble union, let us run together to the same goal. – We have taken up arms in defense of our liberty, our property, our wives, and our children, we are determined to preserve them or die. We look

73

forward with pleasure to that day not far remote (we Hope) when the inhabitants of America shall have one sentiment and the full enjoyment of the blessings of a free government.

Incited by these motives and encouraged by the advice of many friends of liberty among you, the Grand American Congress have sent an Army into your province, under the command of General Schuyler; not to plunder, but to protect you; to animate and bring forth into action those sentiments of freedom you have disclosed, and which the tools of despotism would extinguish through the whole creation. – To cooperate with this design, and to frustrate those cruel and perfidious schemes, which would deluge our frontiers with the blood of women and children; I have detached Colonel Arnold into your country with a part of the Army under my command – and have enjoined upon him, and I am certain that he will consider himself, and act as in the country of his patrons, and best friends. Necessaries and accommodations of every kind, which you may furnish, he will thankfully receive, and render the full value. – I invite you therefore as friends and brethren, to provide him with such supplies as your country affords; and I pledge myself not only for your safety and security, but for ample compensation. Let no man desert his habitation – let no one flee as before an enemy. The cause of America and of liberty is the cause of every virtuous American citizen; whatever may be his religion or his descent, the United Colonies know no distinction but such as slavery, corruption and arbitrary domination may create. Come then, ye generous citizens, range yourselves under the standard of general liberty – against which all the force and artifice of tyranny will never be able to prevail.

G. Washington [24]

On the **15th**, Washington saw Arnold off on one of the most challenging expeditions in the Army's history. The last contingent of Arnold's troops arrived at Newburyport on the **16th**, where they crammed about nine hundred men and their stores of military supplies onto nine vessels named: *Abigail, Admiral, Britannia, Broad Bay, Conway, Eagle, Hanna, Houghton,* and *Swallow* on the **18th**. In his journal, Private Abner Stocking recalled the **19th** as the day they set sail – straight into danger.

September 19th – This morning we got under way with a pleasant breeze, our drums beating, fifes playing, and colors flying. Many pretty girls stood upon the shore, I suppose weeping for the departure of their sweethearts.

74

At eleven o'clock this day we left the entrance of the harbor and bore away for Kennebec River. In the latter part of the night, there came on a thick fog and our fleet was separated. At break of day we found ourselves in a most dangerous situation, very near a reef of rocks. The rocks indeed appeared on all sides of us, so that we feared we should have been dashed to pieces on some of them. We were brought into this deplorable situation by means of liquor being dealt out too freely to our pilots. Their intemperance much endangered our own lives and the lives of all the officers and soldiers on board; but through the blessing of God we all arrived safe. 82.

Abner Stocking

The ships carefully maneuvered up the Kennebec River by day and anchored each night until they reached Gardiner on the **21st**. Once there, they loaded up the bateaus that Arnold had ordered and continued on to Fort Western, a few miles up the river in Augusta where they regrouped on the **23rd**. On the **24th**, being unfamiliar with the territory, Arnold dispatched two parties of explorers to make their way to Fort Halifax, just south of Waterville. The first consisted of a party of six men and a guide under Lieutenant Archibald Steele to reconnoiter the river. The second was made up of seven men, a guide, and a surveyor led by Lieutenant Church to scout out the Great Carrying Place and other areas that had to be trampled through. A visitor's center and museum for Fort Western can be found on the original site today. On the **25th**, Morgan led the first division, whose task was to landscape the way for three other divisions, which would follow each day afterwards. Following Morgan's departure, Arnold wrote his second progress report to Washington.

To His Excellency General Washington

Fort Western, 25th Sept 1775

My it please your Excellency

My last of the 19th instant from Newburyport, advising of the embarkation of the troops I make no doubt your Excellency received. The same day we left Newbury, and arrived safe in the river next morning except a small vessel which run on the rocks, but is since off without damage and arrived safe. I found the batteaus completed, but many of them smaller than the directions given & very badly built. Of course I have been obliged to order twenty more, to bring on the remainder of the provisions, which will be finished in three days. Many of the vessels were detained in the river by running aground & headwinds, which delayed us a day or two. The 23rd instant I dispatched Lieutenant Steel of Captain Smith's company, with six men in two birch canoes to Chaudiere Pond to reconnoiter & get all the intelligence he possibly could from the Indians, who I find are hunting there.

The same day I dispatched Lieut. Church & seven men with a surveyor & pilot, to take the exact courses & distance to the Dead River so called, a branch of the Kennebec, and yesterday the three companies of rifle men under the command of Capt. Morgan, embarked with forty-five days provisions, as an advanced party to clear the roads over the carrying places. Col. Green and Major Bigelow march today with the second division and Col. Enos the next day with the remainder.

As soon as the whole are embarked I propose taking a birch canoe & joining the advanced party. I have found it necessary to divide the detachment for the convenience of passing the carrying places, at the first of which there are some carriages to be procured I design Chaudiere Pond as a general rendezvous, and from thence to march in a body.

Enclosed is a letter to Mr. Coburn, from a party sent to Quebec, by which your Excellency will see all the intelligence I have received. I have conversed with the party, who saw only one Indian, one Natanis, a native of Norridgewalk, a noted villain and very little credit I am told, is to be given to his information.

The Indians with Higgins set out by land and are not yet arrived. I have engaged a number of good pilots & believe by the best information I can procure, we shall be able to perform the march in twenty days – the distance of about 180 miles.

I intended Col. Green should have gone on with the first division of one company of riflemen & two companies of musketeers – This was objected to by the captains of the rifle companies, who insist on being commanded by no other person than Captain Morgan and myself – This Capt. Morgan tells me was your Excellency's intention, but I was not acquainted with it before I came away, I should be very glad of particular instructions on that head, that I may give satisfaction to the field officers with me. There is at present the greatest harmony among the officers and no accident has happened except the loss of one man, supposed to be willfully shot by a private, who is now taking his trial by court martial.

Major Mifflin could not send money for the batteaus, the commissary has been obliged to pay for them with one hundred pounds I have lent him, out of the pay received for the month of September, and has been obliged to draw an order in favor of the bearer, Mr. John Wood, who has engaged to deliver this to your Excellency. I have promised him his time and expenses paid. I should be glad the manifestos might be forwarded on by him, if not sent, with the last intelligence from General Schuyler, to whom I intend sending one of the Indians as soon as they arrive.

> *I have the honor to be, very respectfully,*
> *your Excellency's most obedient humble servant,*
> *Benedict Arnold*

P.S. Since writing the foregoing I have received a letter from Col. Reed, with the manifesto's, and the court martial have condemned the man who shot the other, to be hanged, which sentence I have approved, but have respited him until your Excellency's pleasure in the matter is known and design sending him back in one of the transports. Enclosed are all the papers relative to the matter with his confession at the gallows before respited.

The first three divisions of my detachment are gone forward – the last goes tomorrow, when I shall join Capt. Morgan as long as possible and am with much respect,

> *Your Excellency's most obedient humble servant,*
> *Benedict Arnold* [25]

As he was the last man to leave Fort Western on the **29**[th], Arnold's journal entry shows him reaching Fort Halifax on the **30**[th].

Saturday Sept 30th 1775. At 6 A.M. crossed the 3-mile falls & at 10 arrived at Fort Halifax where I found Capt Dearborn's & Goodrich's companies just over the falls which are at 60 rods over – Good carrying place. [57]

On **October 2**[nd], Arnold arrived at Norridgewock Falls and directed the troops around the falls for the next seven days. On the **12**[th], he ordered a log cabin to be built to serve as a hospital for the ill and injured at the starting point of the Great Carrying Place, where the men would be taking the bateaus overland to the next waterway. He then wrote to Washington again on the **13**[th], explaining that the trip had not exactly gone according to plan.

To His Excellency George Washington
Second Portage from Kennebec to the Dead River, Oct. 13, 1775
May it please your Excellency

A person going down the river presents the first opportunity I have had of writing to your Excellency since I left Fort Western, since which we have had a very fatiguing time, the men in general not understanding bateaus, have been obliged to wade and haul them more than half way up the river. The last division is just arrived – three divisions are over the first carrying place and as the men are in high spirits I make no doubt of reaching the River Chaudiere in eight or ten days, the greatest difficulty being, I hope, already past. We have now with us about twenty-five days provisions for the whole detachment, consisting of about nine hundred and fifty effective men. I intend making an exact return but must defer it until I come to Chaudiere.

I have ordered the commissary to hire people acquainted with the river & forward on the provisions left behind, (about 100 barrels) to the great carrying place, to secure our retreat – the expense will be considerable, but when set in competition with the lives of liberty of so many brave men I think it trifling and if we succeed the provisions will not be lost. I have had no intelligence from General Schuyler or Canada, and expect none till I reach Chaudiere Pond, where I expect a return of my express and to determine my plan of operation, which as it is to be governed by the circumstances, I can say no more than if we are obliged to return, I believe we shall have a sufficiency of provisions to reach this place, where the supply ordered the commissary to send forward, will enable us to return on our way home so far that your Excellency will be able to relieve us. If we proceed on we shall have a sufficient stock to reach the French inhabitants, (where we can be supplied,) if not Quebec.

I am, with the greatest respect,
your Excellency's most obedient humble servant,
Benedict Arnold
P. S. Your Excellency might possibly think we have been tardy in our march, as we have gained so little, but when you consider the badness & weight of the bateaus and large quantity of provisions etc. we have been obliged to force up against a very rapid stream, where you would have taken the men for amphibious animals, as they were great part of the time under water, add to this the great fatigue in portage, you will think I have pushed the men as fast as they could possibly bear. The officers, volunteers, and privates, in general have acted with the greatest spirit & industry. [57]

B. A.

The pioneering party led by Steele had done as ordered, but almost died of starvation and hypothermia before they met up with Arnold's advance troops on the 17th. When they regrouped, they regained their faith, which was enhanced by Arnold rallying his men as he passed up and down the Dead River in a fast, birch bark canoe that was paddled by Indians. Arnold's own spirit rose when he obtained a map from Samuel Goodwin, who committed himself to the American cause as reflected in a letter to Washington.

To his Excellency George Washington, Esq.

Pownalborough, October 17, 1775

Sir

According to your Excellency's verbal orders, by Colonel Benedict Arnold, I supplied him with a plan of the sea coast, from Cape Elizabeth to Penobscot, and the River Kennebec to the several heads thereof, and the several carrying places to Ammeguntick Pond and Chaudiere River, (which Ammeguntick empties into said Chaudiere River, which Chaudiere empties into the River St. Lawrence, about four miles above Quebec,) and the passes and carrying places to Quebec. I also made several small plans for each department, for their guide; and also gave him a copy of a journal which represented all the quick water and carrying places to and from Quebec, both ways, viz: east and west; the west is the way to go, and the east to come. Sir, if there was a road cut, it would be much easier carrying an Army and provisions, and would shorten the way much; and then you might have a post to pass once a week or ten days.

I think it would be for the general interest for you to have a copy of said plan, &c., and then you would be a judge of what would be best to be done. It hath been a great cost and labor to me to obtain those plans etc., and make them. Sir, if you think it worth your notice and will give orders therefore, I will copy one for you and wait on you with it, and give you the best intelligence I can, as I think I know as much of this country as any one, as I have been travelling, surveying, and settling this part, ever since the year 1750. I would willingly go to lay out a road and see it cleared &c., and do everything necessary, if agreeable, and orders therefore, and you &c., should think it worth while.

But submitting all to your better judgement, I am, Sir, with all due respect, your most obedient, devoted, and very humble servant,

Samuel Goodwin

N. B. Mr. Reuben Colburn informed me you wanted a plan. I thus began it about three weeks before Colonel Arnold arrived, or I could not have got it ready for him.

Please excuse the smallness of the paper, for there is a famine of it here. [25]

On the **19th**, it began to rain. On the **20th**, it began to pour. By the night of the **21st**, it came down in torrents. On the morning of the **22nd**, the men realized that they had been hit by a late season hurricane when they discovered that the river had risen nine feet. Scrambling to save their supplies and equipment, they rushed to a nearby hill to build fires and dry out. Finally on the **23rd**, it subsided to a tolerable rate to allow them to continue on. As Meig's men tried to steer their way through the swift water, one of the bateaus collided with another, overturning it and starting a chain reaction that ended up swamping seven boats, provisions and all. That night, Arnold held a council and concluded to send back the sick and feeble, and forge on with the remainder, for with the lack of food now available, only the strong would survive. On the **24th**, following a message to the commissary Colonel Farnsworth to expect visitors, he dispatched notification of his decision to Enos and Green, who were bringing up the rear.

To Col. Enos
        Dead River, 30 miles from Chaudiere Pond, Oct. 24, 1775
Dear Sir
    The extreme rains and freshets in the river have hindered our proceeding any farther. When I wrote you last, I expected before this to have been at Chaudiere. I then wrote you that we had about 25 days provisions for the whole. We are now reduced to 12 or 15 days and don't expect to reach the pond under four days. We have had a council of war last night, when it was thought best, and ordered to send back all the sick and feeble with three days provisions and directions from you to furnish them until they can reach the commissary or Norridgewock; and on that receipt of this you should proceed with as many of the best men of your division as you can furnish with 15 days provision; and that the remainder whether sick or well, should be immediately sent back to the commissary to whom I wrote to take all possible care of them. I make no doubt you will join with me in this matter as it may be the means of preserving the whole detachment, and of executing our plan without running any great hazard, as fifteen days will doubtless bring us to Canada. I make no doubt you will make all possible expedition.

                               I am, Dear Sir, yours
                                   B. Arnold [57]

Upon receiving the above letter, Enos and Greene held a council themselves on the **25**[th] to decide if they should continue on or not. Greene voted to continue on while Enos, lacking the courage, did not, and led his men on a retreat back to Fort Western on the **26**[th]. Unbeknownst of this, Arnold sent another dispatch to Enos on the **27**[th] with anticipation of meeting him at their predetermined, long awaited, and exhaustive destination.

To Col. Enos

Chaudiere Pond, 27th Oct. 1775

Dear Sir

Forward on the enclosed letter to his Excellency Genl Washington by express. If you have any officer who is not hearty and well, send him; and give orders to take particular care of the sick and those who are returning, as well as of any other matters that are necessary.

I hope to see you in Quebec and am, Dear Sir, your humble servant,

B. Arnold[57]

In his letter to Washington, Arnold noted that things had gone from bad to worse.

To His Excellency General Washington

Chaudiere Pond, 27th Oct. 1775

May it please your Excellency

My last of the 13th instant from the portage of the Dead River, advising your Excellency of our proceeding I make no doubt you have received. I then expected to have reached this place by the 24th instant, but the excessive heavy rains & bad weather have much retarded our march. I have this minute arrived here with seventy men, and met a person, on his return, whom I sent down some time since to the French inhabitants – he informs me they appear very friendly, and by the best information he could get will very gladly receive us: He says they informed him General Schuyler had a battle with the regular troops at or near St. John's, in which the latter lost, in killed or wounded, near 500 men, (This account appears very imperfect) and that there were few or none of the King's troops at Quebec, and no advice of our coming. Three days since I left the principal part of the detachment about eight leagues below the great carrying place, and as our provisions were short by reason of losing a number of loaded bateaus at the falls and rapid waters, I ordered all the sick

81

*and feeble to return, & wrote Colonel Enos & Green, to bring on in
their divisions, no more men than they could furnish with fifteen days
provisions, and send back the remainder to the commissary, as the
roads prove much worse than I expected, and the season may possibly
be severe in a few days. I am determined to set out immediately with
four bateaus & about fifteen men, for Sartigan, which I expect to
reach in three or four days, in order to procure a supply of provisions
and forward back to the detachment the whole of which I don't expect
will reach there in less than eight or ten days. If I find the enemy is
not apprised of our coming, and there is any prospect of surprising
the city, I shall attempt it as soon as I have a proper number of men
up. If I should be disappointed in my prospect that way, I shall await
the arrival of the whole, and endeavor to cut off their communication
with Govr. Carleton, who I am told is at Montreal.*

*Our march has been attended with an amazing Deal of
Fatigue, which the officers and men have borne with cheerfulness. I
have been much deceived in every account of our route, which is
longer, and has been attended with a thousand difficulties I never
apprehended, but if crowned with success and conducive to the public
good, I shall think it trifling.*

*I am with the greatest respect,
your Excellency's most obedient humble servant,
B. Arnold
P. S. As soon as I can get time, shall send your Excellency a
continuation of my journal.*

B. A. [57]

For Arnold, the light at the end of the tunnel came in the form
of snow, which froze the surface of Lake Megantic. Struggling
through the thin ice, he and his men rowed crossed the lake and made
their way up the Chaudiere River towards Point Levi. The rapids
along the Chaudiere allowed Arnold and his men to make good time,
but not with good luck, for two of the bateaus were smashed by rocks
just below the surface, throwing men and materials into the churning
water. The men were able to grab hold of other protruding rocks and
hold on for dear life until their comrades came to their rescue.
Following the recovery, the men gathered on shore to dry out by the
fire once again. After struggling just under 300 miles in just over
thirty days since they left Fort Western, Arnold finally reached the
farming village of Sartigan on the **30th**, where he gathered much
needed food. On the **31st**, as Arnold sent food baskets south to meet
his withered warriors, Morgan's men made their way down the

perilous Chaudiere, which had consumed seven of their bateaus, but fortunately not a man was lost. On **November 1st**, prior to receiving Arnold's care package, twenty-year-old Dr. Isaac Senter of New Hampshire wrote of the Army's shriveled condition in his journal.

Wednesday, Nov. 1st. – Our greatest luxuries now consisted in a little water, stiffened with flour in imitation of shoemaker's paste, which was christened, with the name of "Lillipu." Instead of the diarrhea, which tried our men most shockingly in the former part of our march, the reverse was now the complaint, which continued for many days. We had now arrived as we thought to almost the zenith of distress. Several had been entirely destitute of either meat or bread for many days. These chiefly consisted of those who devoured their provision immediately, and a number who were in the boats. The voracious disposition many of us had now arrived at rendered almost anything admissible. Clean and unclean were forms now little in use. In company was a poor dog that hitherto lived through all the tribulations, became a prey for the sustenance of the assassinators. This poor animal was instantly devoured, without leaving any vestige of the sacrifice. Nor did the shaving soap, pomatum, and even the lip salve, leather of their shoes, cartridge boxes, &c., share any better fate; passed several poor fellows, truly commiserating them. [62]

Isaac Senter

On the **2nd**, Private Abner Stocking also wrote of the trials that each man had to bear followed by the triumph they all felt when they finally reached civilization.

November 2nd. – When we arose this morning many of the company were so weak that they could hardly stand on their legs. When we attempted to march, they reeled out like drunken men, having now been without provisions five days. As I proceeded I passed many sitting, wholly drowned in sorrow, wishfully placing their eyes on every one who passed by them, hoping for some relief. Such pity-asking expressions I never before beheld. My heart was ready to burst and my eyes to overflow with tears when I witnessed distress, which I could not relieve. The circumstances of a young Dutchman and his wife, who followed him through this fatiguing march, particularly excited my sensibility. They appeared to be much interested in each other's welfare and unwilling to be separated, but the husband, exhausted with fatigue and hunger fell victim to the king of terrors. His affectionate wife tarried by him until he died, while the rest of the company proceeded on their way. Having no implements with which she could bury him she covered him with leaves, and then took his gun and other implements and left him with a heavy heart. After travelling 20 miles she came up with us.

Just at evening this day, we met cattle coming up the river, sent to us for our relief. This was the most joyful sight our eyes ever beheld. The French people who drove them informed us that Colonel Arnold had arrived in their settlement two days before with the advance party and had purchased cattle as soon as possible and sent them on.

A cow was immediately killed and cut open in great haste; a small calf being found in her, it was divided up and eaten without further ceremony. I got a little piece of the flesh, which I eat raw with a little oatmeal with cold water and thought I feasted sumptuously. [57]
Abner Stocking

The first of Greene's men arrived at the French settlements on the **3rd** two whole days before Enos and company reached Fort Western on the **5th**. As Enos had put his men before the mission, Arnold took care of his men when the need arose to complete the mission, as revealed in the journal of seventeen-year-old, Pennsylvania Private John Joseph Henry on the **7th**.

November 7th – The Army now formed into more regular and compact order, in the morning pretty early, we proceeded. About noon my disorder had increased so intolerably, that I could not put a foot forward. Seating myself upon a log at the wayside, the troops passed on. In the rear came Arnold on horseback. He knew my name and character, and good-naturedly inquired after my health. Being informed, he dismounted, ran down to the riverside, and hailed the owner of the house, which stood opposite across the water. The good Canadian, in his canoe, quickly arrived. Depositing my gun and accoutrements in the hands of one of our men, who attended upon me, and had been disarmed by losing his rifle in some of the wrecking's above, and Arnold putting two silver dollars in my hands, the Frenchman carried me to his house. Going to bed with a high fever upon me, I lay all this and the following day without tasting food. That had been the cause of the disease, its absence became the cure.
[57]
John Joseph Henry

In order to recoup from his losses, Arnold made a plea with the Indians to join him in his quest.

"Friends and Brethren: - I feel myself very happy in meeting with so many of my brethren from the different quarters of the great country, and more so, as I find we meet as friends, and that we are equally concerned in this expedition. Brothers, we are the children of those people who have now taken up the hatchet against us. More than one hundred years ago we were all as one family. We then differed in our religion, and came over to this great country by consent of the king. Our fathers bought land from the savages and we have grown a great people – even as the stars in the sky. We have planted the ground and by our labor grown rich. Now a new King and his wicked great men want to take our lands and our money without our consent. This we think unjust and all our great men from the River St. Lawrence to the Mississippi met together at Philadelphia, where they all talked together and said a prayer to the king that they would be brothers and fight for him, but would not give up their lands and money. The King would not hear our prayer, but sent a great Army to Boston and endeavored to set our brethren against us in Canada. The King's Army at Boston came out into the fields and houses and killed a great many women and children while they were peaceably at work. The Bostonians sent to their brethren in the country, who came in unto their relief and in six days, raised an Army of fifty thousand men, which drove the King's troops on board their ships and killed or wounded fifteen hundred of their men. Since that time they dare not come out of Boston. Now we hear the French and Indians in Canada have sent to us that the King's troops oppress them and make them pay a great price for their rum, etc. and press them to take up arms against the Bostonians, their brethren, who have done them no hurt. By the desire of the French and Indians, our brothers, we have come to their assistance, with an intent to drive out the King's soldiers; when driven off, we will return to our own country and leave this to the peaceable enjoyment of its proper inhabitants.

Now if the Indians, our brethren, will join us, we will be very much obliged to them and will give them one Portuguese per month, two dollars bounty, and find them their provisions and the liberty to choose their own officers." [5]

Arnold was able to persuade Chief Natanis and his brother Sabatis to sign an agreement and lead fifty warriors in the expedition. Upon meeting Arnold, Natanis caught a sense about him and dubbed him, "The Dark Eagle," a name that prophesized his very future. "The Dark Eagle comes to claim the wilderness. The Wilderness will yield to the Dark Eagle, but the Rock will defy him. The Dark Eagle will soar aloft to the sun. Nations will behold him and sound his praises. Yet when he soars highest his fall is most certain. When his wings brush the sky then the arrow will pierce his heart." [54] On the 8th day, Arnold reached Point Levi, where he could look across the St. Lawrence River and see Quebec. In a letter to Washington, he laid out his preliminary plan of attack on Quebec, which anticipated his meeting up with Brigadier General Richard Montgomery. Following his education at St. Andrews and Trinity College in Dublin, Ireland, Montgomery served in Canada during the French and Indian War. Finding a passion for farming, this tall, brave, able, humane, and generous son of a wealthy member of Parliament immigrated to America, married the daughter of Robert R. Livingston, and became a delegate to the first Provincial Congress in New York before accepting his commission as a brigadier general. Although his command was short-lived, he proved to be one of our greatest military leaders, being aggressive, decisive, and inductive with the moral and physical courage necessary to endure physical hardships.

To His Excellency General Washington

Point Levi, 8th Nov. 1775

May it please your Excellency

> *My last letter was of the 27th ultimo, from Chaudiere Pond, advising your Excellency that as the detachment was short of provisions by reason of losing many of our bateaus, I had ordered Col. Enos to send back the sick and feeble, and those of his division who could not be supplied with fifteen days provisions, and that I intended proceeding the next day with 15 men to Sartigan to send back provisions to the detachment. I accordingly set out the 28th early in the morning & descended the river, amazingly rapid & rocky for about twenty miles where we had the misfortune to sink three of our bateaus and lose their provisions etc. but happily no lives – I then divided the little provisions left and proceeded on with the two remaining bateaus & six men and very fortunately reached the French inhabitants the 30th at night, who received us in the most hospitable manner & sent off early the next morning a supply of fresh provisions, flour, etc. to the detachment, who are all happily arrived (except one man drowned, one or two sick, & Col. Enos' division who I am surprised to hear are all gone back) and are here & within two or three days march. I have this minute received a letter from*

Brigadier General Montgomery, advising of the reduction of Chambly etc.

I have had about 40 savages joined me & intend as soon as possible crossing the St. Lawrence. I am just informed by a friend from Quebec, that a frigate of 26 guns & two transports with 150 recruits arrived there last Sunday, which with another small frigate & four or five small armed vessels up the river, is all the force they have, except the inhabitants, very few of whom have taken up arms, & those by compulsion, who declare (except a few English) that they will lay them down whenever attacked – the town is very short of provisions but well fortified. I shall endeavor to cut off their communication with the country & which I hope to be able to effect & bring them to terms, or at least keep them in close quarters until the arrival of General Montgomery, which I wait with impatience. I hope at any rate to be able to effect a junction with him at Montreal.

I am, with the greatest respect,
your Excellency's most obedient humble servant,
Benedict Arnold [57]

After British intelligence had discovered the American's plan to cross the St. Lawrence and attack Quebec, they anchored two warships in the river on the **13th** to thwart the attempt. On the **14th**, Arnold informed Washington that he was stuck in a hold mode due to inclement weather, but was going to take a shot at crossing later that night.

To His Excellency General Washington

Point Levi, 14th Nov. 1775

My it please your Excellency

The foregoing is a copy of my last of the 8th instant, by an express sent to me by General Montgomery, who, I am this moment informed, was taken fifteen leagues above this on his return – I have waited three days for the rear to come up, and in preparing scaling ladders etc.

The wind has been so high these three nights that I have not been able to cross the river, but is now moderated and intend crossing this evening with about 40 canoes; to prevent which the Hunter Sloop & Lizard Frigate lie opposite – however expect to be able to evade them. I have received the agreeable intelligence that St. John's is in our hands and Montreal invested. The merchant ships in the harbor (about fifteen) are loading day & night, & four already sailed.

I am, very respectfully,

your Excellency's most obedient and very humble servant,
Benedict Arnold [57]

Working their way around the warships in the dark of night, Arnold ferried 400 men to Wolfe's Cove, three miles above Quebec. To make use of what little diplomatic talents that he had within him, Arnold then called on the Lieutenant Governor of Quebec, instructing him to hand over the city peacefully and nobody would get hurt.

To Hon. Hect. T. Cramahe, Lt. Gov. of Quebec
Camp before Quebec, 14 Nov., 1775
Sir
The unjust, cruel, and tyrannical acts of a venal British Parliament, tending to enslave the American Colonies, have obliged them to appeal to God and the sword for redress. That Being, in whose hands are all human events, has hitherto smiled on their virtuous efforts. And as every artifice has been used to make the innocent Canadians instruments of their cruelty by instigating them against colonies, and opposing them on their refusing to enforce every oppressive mandate, the American Congress, induced by motives of humanity, have at their request sent Genl Schuyler into Canada for their relief. To cooperate with him, I am ordered by his Excellency Genl Washington to take possession of the town of Quebec. I do, therefore, in the name of the United Colonies, demand surrender of the town, fortifications, etc., of Quebec to the forces of the United Colonies under my command; forbidding you to injure any of the inhabitants of the town in their person or property, as you will answer the same at your peril. On surrendering the town the property of every individual shall be secured to him; but if I am obliged to carry the town by storm, you may expect every severity practiced on such occasions; and the merchants who may now save their property, will probably be involved in the general ruin.
I am, Sir, your most obedient humble servant,
B. Arnold [57]

The message failed to get delivered initially, for when the courier approached the fort, he was chased away by gunfire. Arnold wrote another letter on the **15th**, urging the Governor to show some respect.

To the Hon. H. T. Cramahe

Camp Before Quebec, 15th Nov. 1775

88

Sir

I yesterday sent the enclosed with a flag and officer, who approaching near the walls of the town, was, contrary to humanity and the laws of nations fired on, and narrowly escaped being killed. This I imputed to the ignorance of your guards, and ordered him to return this morning, and to my great surprise he was received in the same manner as yesterday. This is an insult I could not have expected from a private soldier; much more from an officer of your rank; and through me, offered to the United Colonies, will be deeply resented; but at any rate cannot be redound to your honor or valor. I am informed you have put a prisoner taken from me into irons. I desire to know the truth of this and the manner in which he is treated. As I have several prisoners taken from you, who now feed at my own table, you may expect that they will be treated in the same manner in future as you treat mine.

I am, Sir, your obedient servant,

B. Arnold [57]

On the **20**[th] Arnold notified Washington of his advance attack and delayed discovery.

To His Excellency General Washington

Point Aux Trembles, Nov. 20, 1775

May it please your Excellency

My last of the 14th instant from Point Levi – the same evening I passed the St. Lawrence without obstruction, except from a barge, on which we fired & killed three men, but as the enemy were apprised of our coming, and the garrison augmented to near seven hundred men, besides the inhabitants, it was thought not proper to attempt carrying the town by storm, but cut off their communication with the country till the arrival of General Montgomery – We marched up several times near the walls, in hopes of drawing them out, but to no effect, though they kept a constant cannonading & killed us one man.

On the 18th having intelligence that Capt. Napier in an armed snow with near 200 men, having made his escape from Montreal, was very near, & that the garrison, furnished with a number of good field pieces intended attacking us the next day, I ordered a strict examination to be made into our arms & ammunition, when to my great surprise I found many of our cartridges unfit for use (which to appearance were good) and that we had no more than five rounds to each man, it was judged prudent in our situation not to hazard a battle but retire to this place, eight leagues from Quebec, which we did yesterday, & are waiting here with impatience the arrival of Genl Montgomery, which we expect in a few days. I have been obliged to send to Montreal for clothing for my people about 650 in the whole, who are almost naked & in want of every necessary – I have been as careful of cash, as possible, but shall soon have occasion for hard money, as the French have been such sufferers from paper heretofore, & mine so large, I thought it not prudent to offer it them at present – I have wrote General Montgomery my situation & wants, which I expect will be supplied by him. Had I been ten days sooner, Quebec must inevitably have fallen into our hands, as there was not a man there to oppose us – however I make no doubt Genl Montgomery will reduce it this winter if properly supported with men which in my opinion, cannot in the whole be less than two thousand, five hundred, though it my possibly be effected with a less number – The fatigue will be very severe at this season, and in this inclement climate.

I have the honor to be with the greatest esteem & respect, your Excellency's most obedient and very humble servant,

Benedict Arnold [57]

Of the original 1,100 men who started out with him, 55 expired while 370 suffering from death, illness, or fear abandoned the task, leaving only 675 survivors. In a letter to Schuyler on the **27th**, Arnold described the difficulties behind them, the relief about them, and the hope before them.

To M General Schuyler

Pointe Aux Trembles, Nov. 27, 1775

Dear Sir

An incessant hurry of business since my arrival in Canada has deprived me of the pleasure of writing you before this, to give you a short sketch of our tour, the fatigue and hazard of which are beyond description...

Thus in about eight weeks we completed a march of near six hundred miles, not to be paralleled in history. The men having with them their greatest fortitude and perseverance hauled their boats up rapid streams, being obliged to wade almost the whole way, near 180 miles, carried them on their shoulders near forty miles, over hills, swamps, and bogs almost impenetrable and to their knees in mire. Being often obliged to cross three or four times with their baggage. Short of provisions, part of the detachment disheartened and gone back; famine staring us in the face; an enemy's country and uncertainty ahead. Notwithstanding all these obstacles, the officers

90

and men, inspired and fired with the love of liberty and their country, pushed on with a fortitude superior to every obstacle, and most of them had not one day's provision for a week.

I have thus given you a short but imperfect sketch of our march. The night we crossed the St. Lawrence, found it impossible to get our ladders over, and the enemy being apprised of our coming, we found it impracticable to attack them without too great a risk. We therefore invested the town and cut off their communication with the country. We continued in this situation until the 20th, having often attempted to draw out the garrison in vain. On a strict scrutiny into our ammunition, found many of our cartridges unserviceable and not ten rounds each for the men, who were almost naked, bare footed and much fatigued. As the garrison was daily increasing and nearly double our numbers, we thought it prudent to retire to this place and wait the arrival of Genl Montgomery, with artillery, clothing, etc., who to our great joy has this morning joined us with about 300 men. We propose immediately investing the town and make no doubt in a few days to bring Gov. Carleton to terms. You will excuse the incorrectness of my letter and believe me with the greatest esteem.

Dear Sir, your friend and very humble servant,
B. Arnold [57]

In a letter to Washington on **December 5ᵗʰ**, Arnold shares the welcome news of Montgomery's arrival.

To His Excellency General Washington

Before Quebec, Dec. 5, 1775

May it please your Excellency

My last of the 20th ultimo from Point aux Trembles, advising of my retiring from before Quebec, make no doubt your Excellency has received. I continued at Point aux Trembles until the 3rd instant, when to my great joy General Montgomery joined us with artillery and about 300 men. Yesterday we arrived here and are making all possible preparation to attack the city, which has a wretched motley garrison of disaffected seamen, marines, and inhabitants, the walls in a ruinous situation, & cannot hold out long. I hope there will soon be provision made for paying the soldiers arrearages, as many of them have families, who are in want. A continual hurry has prevented my sending a continuation of my journal.

I am with very great respect,
your Excellency's most obedient humble servant,
Benedict Arnold [57]

On the same day Washington wrote to him with praise and approval for his accomplishments despite the retreat of Enos, who was arrested for insubordination, but was later acquitted because the majority of his witnesses were in Canada.

To Colonel Arnold

Cambridge, 5 Dec. 1775

Dear Sir

Your letter of the 8 ultimo with a postscript of the 14 from Point Levi, I have had the pleasure to receive – It is not in the power of any man to command success, but you have done more – you have deserved it, & before this I hope, have met with the laurels which are due to your toils, in the possession of Quebec – My thanks are due & sincerely offered to you, for your enterprising & persevering spirit – To your brave followers I likewise present them.

I was not mindful of you or them in the establishment of a new Army – One out of 26 regiments, (likely Genl Putnam) you are appointed to the command of, and I have ordered all the officers with you, to the one or the other of these regiments, in the rank they now bear, that in case they choose to continue in service, & no appointment take place, where they now are, no disappointment may follow – Nothing very material has happened in this camp since you left it – Finding we were not likely to do much in the land way, I fitted out several privateers or rather armed vessels in behalf of the continent, with which we have taken several prizes, to the amount it is supposed of 15,000 pounds sterling – One of them a valuable store ship (but no powder in it) containing a fine brass mortar 1 inch – 2000 stand of arms – shot &c...

I have no doubt but a juncture of your detachment with the Army under Genl Montgomery, is effected before this: If so you will put yourself under his command and will I am persuaded give him all the assistance in your power, to finish the glorious works you begun –

That the Almighty may preserve & prosper you in it, is the sincere & fervent prayer of, Dear Sir, &c.,

G. Washington

P.S. You could not be more surprised than I was, at Enos return with the division under his command. I immediately put him under arrest & had him tried for quitting the detachment without your orders – He is acquitted on the score of provision. [24]

92

In a letter to Schuyler on that same day, Washington praised Arnold's accomplishment and asks him to absorb some inspiration from his example.

To M General Schuyler

Cambridge, December 5, 1775

Dear Sir

Your much esteemed favor of the 22nd ultimate, covering Colonel Arnold's letter, with a copy of one to General Montgomery and his to you, I received yesterday morning. It gives me the highest satisfaction to hear of Colonel Arnold's being at Point Levi, with his men in great spirits, after their long and fatiguing march, attended with the most insuperable difficulties, and the discouraging circumstances of being left by near one third of the troops that went on the expedition. The merit of that officer is certainly great and I heartily wish that fortune may distinguish him as one of her favorites. He will do everything which prudence and valor can suggest, to add to the success of our arms, and for reducing Quebec to our possession. Should he not be able to accomplish so desirable a work with the forces he has, I flatter myself that it will be effected, when General Montgomery joins him and our conquest of Canada be complete.

I am exceedingly sorry to find you so much plagued and embarrassed by the disregard of discipline, confusion, and want of order among the troops, as to have occasioned you to mention to Congress, an inclination to retire. I know that your complaints are too well founded; but I would willingly hope that nothing will induce you to quit the service, and that in time, order and subordination will take the place of confusion and command be rendered more agreeable. I have met with difficulties of the same sort and such as I never expected; but they must be borne with. The Cause we are engaged in is so just and righteous, that we must try to rise superior to every obstacle in it's support; and, therefore, I beg that you will not think of resigning, unless you have carried your application to Congress too far. [24]

I am, Dear Sir, with great esteem & regard, yours, &c.,

G. Washington

Although doubtful about the operation, Montgomery also wrote to Schuyler to acknowledge Arnold's leadership and the effect that it had on his men. In addition he made mention of his brother-in-law, Colonel James Livingston, who had raised and commanded a regiment of Canadian refugees.

To M General Schuyler
Holland House, near the Heights of Abraham, Dec. 5, 1775
My Dear General,
I have been this evening favored with yours of the 19th ultimate and return to you many thanks for your warm congratulations. Nothing shall be wanting on my part to reap the advantage of our good fortune. The season has proved so favorable as to enable me to join Colonel Arnold at Point-aux-Trembles, where I arrived with the vessels Mr. Prescott made us a present of. They carried the few troops, about three hundred, which were equipped for a winter campaign, with the artillery, &c. Col. Livingston is on his way, with some part of his regiment of the Canadians...

I find Colonel Arnold's corps an exceedingly fine one. Immune to fatigue and well accustomed to cannon shot, there is a style of discipline among them much superior to what I have been used to see in this campaign. He himself is active, intelligent, and enterprising. Fortune often baffles the spirited expectations of poor mortals. I am not intoxicated with the favors I have received at her hands, but I do not think there is a fair prospect of success. The Governor has been so kind as to send out of town many of our friends, who refused to do military duty; among them several intelligent men, capable of doing me considerable service – one of them, a Mr. Antill, I have appointed chief engineer... [42]

I am, &c.,
Richard Montgomery

On **December 13th**, Arnold evaded a British frigate and a sloop and crossed the St. Lawrence with 500 men and landed at Wolfe's Cove. Arnold sent another messenger into the city to demand their surrender, but again the messenger was shot at. Montgomery then sent a non-combatant woman to the British Governor of Quebec, Sir Guy Carleton to ask for his surrender, but Carleton's only response was to have the woman arrested. Being outgunned and outside the fort, the Americans commenced a siege on the city, but it could not be prolonged, for many of the men's enlistments were due to expire on the first of the year, and a spring thaw would only bring about British reinforcements. Arnold himself attempted to deliver a request for the British surrender, which was put to the flames and he was turned away with insults.

In the early morning hours of the **31ˢᵗ**, both sides now having about 1,200 men to engage, the American commanders decided on a four-prong assault against the British defenders. Under the cover of a blizzard, Arnold attacked from the northeastern side while Montgomery attacked from the west and south. At precisely four o'clock in the morning, three rockets from the American batteries marked the launch of the attack, although within a few hours, two blasts from British guns would mark the end of it. Montgomery, at the head of his troops, made his advance towards a blockhouse, where a small contingent of soldiers stood brandishing muskets and smoldering wicksticks alongside cannons. He then shouted, "Men of New York, you will not fear to follow where your General leads. March on!" [41] The men charged and the blockhouse erupted with cannon fire, killing Montgomery along with a dozen others. Unfortunately the shock was stronger than the speech, and the column broke and fled.

On the other side of town, Arnold led twenty-five men towards the sound of bells ringing, drums beating, and muzzles blasting. As he charged towards a barrier at the Sault au Matelot, he was struck in his left leg below the knee by a musket ball and crashed to the ground. Refusing to be carried off the field, he struggled up on to his good leg and forged ahead, dragging his bloody limb along. When the main body of the force came up, Arnold resolved to make his way to the hospital one mile away and all the while rallying his men to press on. And press on they did, until they were forced to fight by the bayonet due to a shortage of lead and their powder having to succumb to the weather. After Arnold was treated, Senter recalled the events from the hospital.

Sunday, 31ˢᵗ. – Headquarters was at St. Foy's. Here General Montgomery kept Colonel Arnold with several more of the field officers. The arrangements of the Army was as follows, viz., General Montgomery on the right wing with the majority of the troops from Montreal, &c. Colonel Arnold on the left with his division of "Famine proof Veterans." Colonel Livingston's Canadian Regiment, to assault the walls at St. John's gate, with combustibles for firing the gate, and thereby draw the attention of the enemy that way, and at the same time attempts the walls a little distance with scaling ladders, &c. the place where the General was to assault was on the bank of the St. Lawrence, at the termination of the city walls and where large pickets were substituted. For this purpose instruments were carried to make the breach. Arnold was to attack at the other extremity of the town, where he first expected to be opposed by some small batteries before he arrived in the lower town, where the two extremes were to form a junction. To discriminate our troops from the enemy in action, they were ordered each officer and soldier to make fast a piece of white paper across their caps from the front to the peak of them. Thus matters being arranged in the evening, upon their arms they lay at 4 o'clock in the morn, during which time the General was noticed to be extremely anxious, as if anticipating the fatal catastrophe.

Ruminating in this despondency, back and forth he traversed his room 'till the limited time bade him go forth!

> *"The dawn is overcast, the morning lowers*
> *And Heavenly in clouds brings on the day,*
> *The great, the important day big with the fate*
> *Of Montgomery and his host."*

The decree being fixed, and the assailants determined, though gloomy the prospect in this tremendous storm – snow not less than six feet deep, while yet a heavy darkness pervaded the earth almost to be felt. Thus they went on.

> *"Through winds and storms and mountains of snow,*
> *Impatient for the battle. But alas!*
> *Think what anxious moments pass between*
> *The birth of enterprises and their last fatal periods,*
> *Oh! 'tis a dreadful interval of time,*
> *Filled up with honor all and big with death."*

No sooner had they crossed that bloody plain, American Pharsalia, than the fiery signal was given for the attack. Montgomery at the front of his division forced his way through the strong pickets upon the precipice of the riverbank.

> *"Greatly unfortunate, he fought the cause,*
> *Of honor, virtue, liberty, and his country."*

But a little way had they entered before a dire display from the whole extent of their lines illuminated the air and shock the environs of the city by the tremendous explosion. The discharge was kept up from the whole extent of the city walls incessantly. While fireballs were kept out beyond where they supposed our troops were, thereby to discover them between the walls and their ball, which burnt notwithstanding the depth of snow with amazing advantage to the enemy. not more than an hour had the action continued before the wounded came tumbling in, that the grand ward was directly filled. They continued coming until the enemy rushed out at St. John's Gate and St. Roque's suburbs, and captured the horses and carriages, (the men escaping) which were employed in that service. few of the wounded escaping from their hands, after the capture of the horses, &c., except those wounded slightly.

Daylight had scarce made its appearance when Colonel Arnold was brought in, supported by two soldiers, wounded in the leg, with a piece of a musket ball. The ball had probably come in contact with a cannon, rock, stone, or the like, when it entered the leg which had cleft off about a third. The other two-thirds entered the outer side of the leg, about midway, and in an oblique course passed between the tibia and fibula, lodged in the gastrocnemia muscle at the rise of the tendon Achilles. Where upon examination I easily discovered and extracted it.

Before the Colonel was done with, Major Ogden came in wounded through the left shoulder, which proved only a flesh wound. The Major gave it as his opinion that we should not be successful. The fire and re-fire continued incessant. No news from the General and his party yet, which gave us doubtful apprehensions of their success. Not long had we remained in an anxious suspense before an express came down from the plain informing of the fatal news of his death, and that the remainder of his division had retreated precipitately back to headquarters. We were also immediately advised of the fall of Captain Cheeseman and Mr. McPherson, two gallant young officers, the former commanding one of the New York companies, the latter his aid-de-camp. To this melancholy news was immediately added the capture of Captain Darby and company by a sortie of the enemy from St. Roque's Gate and that the enemy were still without the walls advancing towards the hospital. We soon perceived this to be true, in consequence of which all the invalids, stragglers, and some few of the artillery that were left behind were ordered to march immediately into St. Roque Street with a couple of field pieces under command of Lieut. Captain Wool, who much distinguished himself on this occasion. He took the advantage of a turn in the street and gave the enemy so well directed a fire, as put them to flight immediately. Notwithstanding this, we were momentarily expecting them out upon us, as we concluded Arnold's division, then under the command of Lieut. Col. Green, were all killed.

Under these circumstances we entreated Colonel Arnold for his own safety to be carried back into the country, where the enemy could not readily find him, but to no purpose. He would neither be removed, nor suffer a man from the hospital to retreat. He ordered pistols loaded, with a sword on his bed adding that he was determined to kill as many as possible if they came into the room. We were all now soldiers; even to the wounded in their beds were ordered a gun by their side, that, if they did attack the hospital, to make the most vigorous defense possible.

Orders were also sent out into the villages around the city, to the captains of the militia, to immediately assemble to our assistance. The peasants, however friendly disposed, thought it too precarious a juncture to show themselves in that capacity, and those nigh rather retreated back into the country, than give any assistance. The storm still continued tremendously. Colonel Livingston's Regiment who were employed in firing St. John's Gate made the best of their way off soon after the heavy fire began. Orders were dispatched up to St. Foy's for assistance from the party who were retreated, who assisted but little. An express was sent off to Congress informing of our situation and requesting immediate assistance. No news from Greene's division to be depended on. The prospect was gloomy on every side. The loss of the bravest of Generals, with other amiable officers smote the breasts of all around with inexpressible grief. "Oh, Liberty! Oh, virtue! Oh, my country!" seemed the language of all. [62]

Isaac Senter

While convalescing in his bed, Arnold was asked when they should make their return home, to which he responded, "I have no thoughts of leaving this proud town until I first enter it in triumph. My wound has been exceedingly painful, but is now easy and the Providence, which has carried me through so many dangers, is still my protection. I am in the way of my duty and know no fear." [5] Arnold then sent a battle report to Wooster.

To General Wooster, Montreal

General Hospital, December 31, 1775

Dear Sir

I make no doubt but General Montgomery acquainted you with his intentions of storming Quebec as soon as a good opportunity offered. As we had several men deserted from us a few days past, the General was induced to alter his plan, (which was to have attacked the upper and lower town at the same time,) thought it most prudent to make two different attacks upon the lower town; the one at Cape Diamond, the other through St. Roque's. for the last attack I was ordered, with my own detachment and Captain Lamb's company of artillery. At five o'clock, the hour appointed for the attack, a false attack was made upon the upper town. We, accordingly, made our march. I passed through St. Roque's and approached near a two-gun battery, picketed in without being discovered, which we attacked; it was bravely defended for about an hour, but, with the loss of two hundred men, we carried it. in the attack, I was shot through the leg and was obliged to be carried to the hospital, where I soon heard the disagreeable news that the General was defeated at Cape Diamond, himself, Captain Macpherson, his aide-de-camp, and Captain Cheeseman, killed on the spot with a number of others not known.

After gaining the battery, my detachment pushed on to a second barrier, which they took possession of; at the same time the enemy sallied out from Palace Gate and attacked them in the rear. A field piece, which the roughness of the road would not permit our carrying on, fell into the enemy's hands, with a number of prisoners. The last accounts from my detachment, about ten minutes since, they were pushing from the lower town. Their communication with me was cut off. I am exceedingly apprehensive what the event will be; they will either carry the lower town, be made prisoners, or cut to pieces. I thought proper to send an express to let you know the critical situation we are in, and make no doubt you will give us all the assistance in your power. As I am not able to act, I shall give up the command to Colonel Campbell. I beg you will immediately send an express to the honorable Continental Congress and his Excellency General Washington. The loss of my detachment, before I left it, was about two hundred men, killed and wounded. Among the latter is Major Ogden, who, with Captain Oswald, Captain Burr, and the other volunteers, behaved extremely well.

I have only to add that I am, with the greatest esteem, your most obedient and very humble servant,

B. Arnold

P. S. It is impossible to say what our future operations will be until we know the fate of my detachment. [57]

In his journal, Henry wrote of the agony of defeat suffered on **January 1ˢᵗ 1776**.

It was not until the night of the thirty-first of December, 1775 that such kind of weather ensued as was considered favorable for the assault. The forepart of the night was admirably enlightened by a luminous moon. Many of us, officers as well as privates, had dispersed in various directions among the farm and tippling houses of the vicinity. We well knew the signal for rallying. This was no other than a snowstorm. About twelve o'clock P. M., the Heaven was overcast. We repaired to quarters. By two o'clock we were equipped and began our march. The storm was outrageous, and the cold wind extremely biting. In this northern country the snow is blown horizontally into the faces of travelers on most occasions – this was our case.

January 1st. When we came to Craig's house, near Palace Gate, a horrible roar of cannon took place, and a ringing of the bells of city, which are very numerous and of all sizes. Arnold, heading the forlorn hope, advanced perhaps one hundred yards before the main body. After these followed Lamb's artillerists. Morgan's company led in the secondary part of the column of infantry. Captain Smith followed, headed by Steele, the Captain, from particular causes, being absent. Hendricks' company succeeded, and the eastern men, so far as known to me, followed in due order. The snow was deeper than in the fields, because of the nature of the ground. The path made by Arnold, Lamb, and Morgan was almost imperceptible because of the falling snow; covering the locks of our guns with the lappets of our coats, holding down our heads, (for it was impossible to bear up our faces against the imperious storm of wind and snow), we ran along the foot of the hill in single file. Along the first of our run, from Palace Gate, for several hundred paces, there stood a range of insulated buildings, which seemed to be storehouses; we passed these quickly in single file, pretty wide apart. The intervening spaces were from thirty to fifty yards. In these intervals we received a tremendous fire of musketry from the ramparts above us. Here we lost some brave men, when powerless to return the salutes we received, as the enemy was covered by his impregnable defenses. They were even sightless to us; we could see nothing but the blaze from the muzzles of their muskets.

A number of vessels of various sizes lay along the beach, moored by their hawsers or cables to the houses. Pacing after my leader, Lieutenant Steele, at a great rate, one of these ropes took me under the chin and cast me headlong down a declivity of at least fifteen feet. The place appeared to be either a drydock or a sawpit. My descent was terrible; gun and all was involved in a great depth of snow. Most unluckily, however, one of my knees received a violent contusion on a piece of scraggly ice, which was covered by the snow. On like occasions we can scarce expect, in the hurry of attack, that our intimates should attend to any other than their own concerns. Mine went from me, regardless of my fate. Scrambling out of the cavity, without assistance, divesting my person and gun of the snow, and limping into the line, it was attempted to assume a station and preserve it. these were none of my friends – they knew me not. We had not gone twenty yards in my hobbling gait before I was thrown out and compelled to wait the arrival of a chasm in the line, where a new place might be obtained. Men in affairs such as this seem in the main to lose the compassionate feeling and are averse from being dislodged from their original stations.

We proceeded rapidly, exposed to a long line of fire from the garrison, for now we were unprotected by any buildings. The fire had slackened in a small degree. The enemy had been partly called off to resist the General and strengthen the party opposed to Arnold in our front.

Now we saw Colonel Arnold returning, wounded in the leg and supported by two gentlemen... Arnold called to the troops in a cheering voice as we passed, urging us forward, yet it was observable among the soldiery, with whom it was my misfortune to be now placed, that the Colonel's retiring damped their spirits. A cant term, "We are sold," was repeatedly heard in many parts throughout the line.

Thus proceeding enfiladed by an animated but lessened fire, we came to the first barrier, where Arnold had been wounded in the onset. This contest had lasted but a few minutes and was somewhat severe, but the energy of our men prevailed. The embrasures were entered when the enemy were discharging their guns. The guard, consisting of thirty persons, were either taken or fled, leaving their arms behind them.

At this time it was discovered that our guns were useless, because of the dampness. The snow, which lodged in our fleece coats, was melted by the warmth of our bodies. Thence came that disaster. Many of the party, knowing the circumstance, threw aside their own and seized the British arms. These were not only elegant, but were such as befitted the hand of a real soldier. It was said that ten thousand stand of arms had been received from England in the previous summer for arming the Canadian militia. Those people were loathe to bear them in opposition to our rights.

From the first barrier to the second, there was a circular course along the sides of houses, and partly through a street, probably of three hundred yards or more. This second barrier was erected across and near the mouth of a narrow street, adjacent to the foot of the hill, which opened into a larger, leading soon into the main body of the lower town. Here it was that the most serious contention took place; this became the bone of strife.

The admirable Montgomery by this time (though it was unknown to us) was no more; yet we expected momentarily to join

101

him. The firing on that side of the fortress ceased, his division fell under the command of a Colonel Campbell of the New York line, a worthless chief who retreated without making an effort in pursuance of the General's original plans. The inevitable consequence was that the whole of the forces on that side of the city, and those who were opposed to the dastardly persons employed to make the false attacks, embodied and came down to oppose our division.

Here was sharp shooting. We were on the disadvantageous side of the barrier for such a purpose. Confined in a narrow street hardly more than twenty feet wide, and on the lower ground, scarcely a ball, well-aimed or otherwise, but must take effect upon us. Morgan, Hendricks, Steele, Humphreys, and a crowd of every class of the Army had gathered into the narrow pass, attempting to surmount the barrier, which was about twelve or more feet high and so strongly constructed that nothing but artillery could effectuate its destruction.

There was a construction fifteen or twenty yards within the barrier, upon a rising ground, the cannon of which much overtopped the height of the barrier; hence we were assailed by grapeshot in abundance. This erection we called the platform. Again, within the barrier, and close in to it, were two ranges of musketeers, armed with musket and bayonet, ready to receive those who might venture the dangerous leap. Add to all this that the enemy occupied the upper chambers of the houses, in the interior of the barrier, on both sides of the street, from the windows of which we became fair marks. The enemy having the advantage of the ground in front, a vast superiority of numbers and dry and better arms gave them an irresistible power in so narrow a space.

Humphreys, upon a mound which was speedily erected, attended by many brave men, attempted to scale the barrier, but was compelled to retreat by the formidable phalanx of bayonets within and the weight of fire from the platform and the buildings. Morgan, brave to audacity, stormed and raged; Hendricks, Steele, Nichols, Humphreys, equally brave, were sedate, though under a tremendous fire. The platform, which was within our view, was evacuated by the accuracy of our fire, and few persons dared venture there again.

Now it was that the necessity of the occupancy of the houses, on our side of the barrier, became apparent. Orders were given by Morgan to that effect. We entered – this was near daylight. The houses were a shelter from which we could fire with much accuracy. Yet even here some valuable lives were lost. Hendricks, when aiming his rifle at some prominent person, died by a straggling ball though his heart. He staggered a few feet backwards and fell upon a bed, where he instantly expired. He was an ornament of our little society. The amiable Humphreys died by a like kind of wound, but it was in the street, before we entered the buildings. Many other brave men fell at this place; among these were Lieutenant Cooper, of Connecticut, and perhaps fifty or sixty non-commissioned officers and privates. The wounded were numerous and many of them dangerously so. Captain Lamb, of the York artillerists, had nearly one half of his face carried away by a grape or canister shot. My friend Steele lost three of his fingers as he was presenting his gun to fire; Captain Hubbard and Lieutenant Fisdle were also among the wounded. When we reflect upon the whole of the dangers at this barricade, and the formidable force that came to annoy us, it is a matter of surprise that so many should escape death and wounding as did.

All hope of success having vanished, a retreat was contemplated, but hesitation, uncertainty, and a lassitude of mind, which generally takes place in the affairs of men when we fail in a project upon which we have attached much expectation, now followed. That moment was foolishly lost when such a movement might have been made with tolerable success. Captain Laws, at the head of two hundred men, issuing from Palace Gate, most fairly and handsomely cooped us up. Many of the men, aware of the consequences, and all our Indians and Canadians (except Natanis and another) escaped across the ice which covered the bay of St. Charles, before the arrival of Captain Laws, this was a dangerous and desperate adventure, but worthwhile the undertaking, in avoidance of our subsequent sufferings. Its desperateness consisted in running two miles across shoal ice, thrown up by the high tides of this latitude – and its danger in the meeting with air holes, deceptively covered by the bed of snow.

...About nine o'clock, A. M., it was apparent to all of us that we must surrender. It was done. [57]

John Joseph Henry

Arnold wrote to Wooster again on the **2nd** after receiving a report on his logistics.

To General Wooster

General Hospital, January 2, 1776

Dear Sir

I wrote you, three days since, of our defeat and the death of General Montgomery and others, with all the information I then had of the matter. We have been in suspense, with regard to my detachment, until this afternoon when Major Meigs was sent out with a flag for the officers baggage, who, he says, are all taken prisoners, except Captain Hendricks, Lieutenant Humphreys of the riflemen, and Lieutenant Cooper, who were killed in the action. General Carleton says our loss, in killed and wounded, is a hundred. Major Meigs thinks it does not exceed sixty, and about three hundred taken prisoners, who are treated very humanely. These brave men sustained the force of the whole garrison for three hours, but were finally obliged to yield to numbers and the advantageous situation the garrison had over them. Several other officers, I am told, are slightly wounded. We had the misfortune of losing one brass six-pounder in the engagement and all our mortars were taken from St. Roque's the evening after the engagement. This was the fault of some of the officers who commanded, as they might very easily have been brought away, agreeable to my positive orders for that purpose.

Our force at this time does not exceed eight hundred men including Colonel Livingston's regiment of two hundred Canadians and some scattered Canadian forces amounting to 200 more, many of the troops are dejected and anxious to get home and some have actually set off. I shall endeavor to continue the blockade while there are any hopes of success – for God's sake order as many men down as you can possibly spare, consistent with the safety of Montreal, and all the mortars, howitzers, and shells that you can possibly bring. I hope you can stop every rascal who has deserted from us and bring him back again.

Every possible mark of distinction was shown to the corpse of General Montgomery, who was to be interred in Quebec this day. Had he been properly supported by his troops, I make no doubt of our success. We are short of cash – not more than four or five hundred pounds and only twenty barrels of salt pork. If any can be spared from Montreal, I think best to bring it down and all the butter.

I beg you will transmit a copy of this letter to the honorable Continental Congress and another to his Excellency General Washington. I think it will be highly necessary, with the reinforcement which, I make no doubt, Congress will send, that they should order all the large mortars and howitzers at Crown Point, Ticonderoga, and Fort George on to this place. Monsieur Pelissier, who has a furnace at three rivers, assures me that he can cast any size and number of shells between this and the beginning of April. I hope the honorable Continental Congress will not think of sending less than eight or ten thousand men to secure and form a lasting connection with this country.

I am in excessive pain from my wound,
(as the bones of my leg are affected,)
I can only add that I am, with the greatest esteem, Dear Sir,
your most obedient and very humble servant,
B. Arnold, Colonel, &c.
N. B. Many officers here appear dispirited; your presence will
be absolutely necessary. I don't expect to be in a capacity to act this
two months.

B. Arnold [57]

On the **6ᵗʰ**, Arnold wrote a note to his family to let them know that he was not one of the fallen.

To Hannah Arnold

Camp before Quebec, January 6, 1776

My Dear Sister

Before this reaches you I make no doubt you will have heard of our misfortune of the 31ˢᵗ ultimo and will be anxious for my safety. I should have wrote you before, but a continual hurry of business has prevented me. The command of the Army, by the death of General Montgomery, devolved on me; a task, I find, too heavy under my present circumstances. I received a wound by a ball through the leg, at the time I had gained the first battery at the lower ton, which, by the loss of blood, rendered me very weak. As soon as the main body came up, with some assistance I returned to the hospital, near a mile, on foot, being obliged to draw one leg after me and a great part of the way under the continual fire of the enemy from the walls at no greater distance than fifty yards. I providentially escaped, though several were shot down at my side. I soon learned the death of our General, who attacked the town at the side opposite to me; he behaved heroically; marched up in the face of their cannon, and when he had nearly gained the pass, received the fatal shot, or the town would have been ours. This occasioned the disaster that afterwards happened to my detachment, which, after the General's defeat, had the whole garrison to encounter, under every disadvantage of ground, &c. &c. To return was impossible, as the route was within fifty yards and exposed to the fire of the whole garrison, who had brought several pieces out of one of the gates, which our people would have been obliged to pass. In this situation, they maintained their ground near three hours; but being overpowered with numbers, were obliged to lay down their arms; about three hundred, including Captain Lamb of New York and part of the train were taken prisoners, and as near as I can judge, about sixty killed and wounded. Captain Oswald is among the prisoners; he was with me in a selected party of about twenty-five, who attacked the first battery; behaved gallantly and gained much honor; the prisoners are treated politely, and supplied with everything the garrison affords. Governor Carleton sent to let me know that the soldiers' baggage, if I pleased, might be sent to them, which I shall immediately send. Though the enemy are now double our number, they have made no attempt to come out. We are as well prepared to receive them as can possibly be in our present situation, divided at a distance of two miles. I expect General Wooster from Montreal in a few days with a reinforcement. I hope we shall be properly supported with the troops by the Congress. I have no thoughts of leaving this proud town until I enter it first in triumph. My wound has been exceeding painful, but is now easy, and the surgeons assure me will be well in eight weeks. I know you will be anxious for me in eight weeks. The Providence, which has carried me through so many dangers, is still my protection. I am in the way of my duty and know no fear. [57]

Benedict

Although there is strength in nobility, there is a greater strength in numbers. Had half of that strength not turned back two months prior, the outcome might have been different, but it was not be, for nearly half of what forged on into the fight were either killed or captured. Arnold may have lost the battle, but gained a position for his gallantry when he was promoted to Brigadier General on the **10**th.

Wednesday, January 10, 1776
...Agreeable to the order of the day, the Congress proceeded to the election of two Brigadiers General, and the ballots being taken and examined, Joseph Fry, Esq. was elected Brigadier General for the Army in Massachusetts Bay, Benedict Arnold, Esq., Brigadier General for the Army in the northern department... [26]

In a letter of the **11**th, Arnold gave Congress a report of the Army's present status and laid out his plan to keep up the fight.

To the Honorable Continental Congress
Camp before Quebec, January 11, 1776
Gentlemen
I take the liberty, most heartily, to condole you with the loss of the great, amiable, and brave General Montgomery and those brave

106

men who fell with him. By his death, the command of the Army devolves on me; of course, I have carefully examined his instructions from the honorable Continental Congress and their resolutions respecting this country. I find it strongly recommended to him to conciliate the affections of the Canadians and cherish every dawning of liberty which appears among them; and to assure them of the friendship and protection of the Congress; and to endeavor to form, on a lasting basis, a firm union between them and the colonies by forming a Provincial Congress, and, from that body, giving them a full representation in the Grand Continental Congress. This I am confident, the General labored for with the greatest attention, and with as great a degree of success as could be expected, under the present state of affairs.

The disposition of the Canadians is very favorable to your wishes; (the only bar, of consequence, is Quebec; as this is the key, so, in a great measure, it governs the whole country;) who, having been so long habituated to slavery and having, as yet, but a faint sense of the value of liberty, are naturally timid and distrustful and want every possible encouragement to take an active part. This bar removed, I humbly conceive every other obstacle to a firm and lasting union with Canada, will, of course be removed. So long as Quebec remains in the hands of the enemy, it will not be in our power to assist and protect them; of course, we cannot expect their hearty exertions in our favor. Quebec appears to me an object of the highest importance to the Colonies, and, if proper methods are adopted, must inevitably fall into their hands before the garrison can be relieved. The whole garrison of Quebec, including men, women, and children, is supposed, by gentlemen who left town the beginning of December, to be four thousand.

A gentlemen of veracity assures me that Mr. Alsop, the King's Commissary, told him in confidence that there was not one thousand barrels of flour in the town; and, it was notorious among the merchants, there was not eight thousand bushels of wheat an no convenience for flouring it. provisions of meat were known to be much less that those of bread, though they had some quantity of fish. It is generally agreed, they had short of four months' provisions the 1ˢᵗ December. This cannot be exactly ascertained, as the Governor denied the inhabitants liberty of viewing the stores or giving them any satisfaction in regard to quantity. It appears a blockhead must answer our purpose; it is possible it may not. Will it be prudent to trust an object of such vast importance to the event? With submission, I think it will not. What is to be done? A sufficient force employed to reduce it by a regular siege or assault? If the first is attempted, an addition of three thousand men to our present force will, I make no doubt, be thought necessary; if the latter, at least five thousand. The former, with a vast expense and great waste of ammunition, may prove unsuccessful; the latter, from the extensiveness of the works, I think cannot; and five thousand men will hardly be a sufficient garrison, if the place is taken. I beg leave to recommend the sending a body of at least five thousand men, with an experienced General into Canada, as early as possible; and, in the mean time, that every possible preparation of mortars, howitzers, and some heavy cannon should be made as the season will permit our raising batteries by the middle of March, which may, very possibly, be attended with success, as we can place our mortars under cover, within two hundred yards of the walls and within one thousand of the center of town; and, if supplied with shells, carcasses, &c., can set fire to it whenever we please, which I make no doubt, would reduce the garrison to terms.

I am well assured more than half of the inhabitants of Quebec would gladly open the gates to us, but are prevented by the strict discipline and watch kept over them, the command of the guards being constantly given to officers of the Crown, known to be firm in their interest. The garrison consists of about fifteen hundred men, a great part of whom Governor Carleton can place no confidence in or he would suffer a blockade and every distress of a siege, by seven hundred men, our force consisting of no more at present, including Colonel Livingston's regiment of two hundred Canadians. I have arranged my men in such order as early as possible, if attacked. The men are obliged to lay on their arms constantly and to mount guard every other night. Their duty is exceedingly hard; however, the men appear alert and cheerful, though wanting many necessaries, which cannot be procured here.

I expect General Wooster from Montreal with a reinforcement every minute. I have withdrawn our cannon from the battery and placed them around the magazine, which contains a considerable quantity of powder and ordnance stores, which I am fearful of removing, lest it should make unfavorable impressions on the Canadians and induce them to withdraw their assistance, and Governor Carleton, presuming on our panic, to sally out. I thought it most prudent to put the best face on matters and betray no marks of fear. We are in great want of cash; our finances have never afforded any of consequence to the troops, who make heavy complaints, not without reason. We have often been reduced to a few johannes and never able to procure more than ten days' sustenance beforehand.

108

Our whole dependence has been on Mr. Price, who has done everything in his power and is the only resource we have at present. I have received two petards from Monsieur Pelissier at Three Rivers, who assures me he can supply us with shells by the 1ˢᵗ of April.

Enclosed is a list of officers killed and wounded in the unfortunate attack on Quebec. The prisoners and missing amount to about four hundred. Governor Carleton has permitted the baggage of both officers and men to be sent in, and (strange to tell) treats them with humanity. I think myself, in justice, bound to acknowledge the good conduct and intrepidity of both officers and men of my detachment, who undauntedly marched up in the face of the enemy's cannon; in particular, the volunteers of Captain Oswald, who signalized himself in the attack on their battery and is now a prisoner.

I hope, gentlemen, my being confined to my bed with my wound and a severe fit of the gout, will apologize for the incoherency and inaccurateness of my scrawl;

and that you will believe me,
with respect and esteem, gentlemen,
your most obedient and very humble servant,
B. Arnold [57]

On the **12ᵗʰ**, Arnold gave Congress an updated logistics report along with his intentions on resigning his command due to his injury.

To the Honorable Continental Congress
Camp before Quebec, January 12, 1776
Gentlemen
Since writing the enclosed, General Wooster has acquainted me he cannot leave Montreal, but has sent down Colonel Clinton, to whom I shall resign the command until my would will permit my doing duty, which my surgeon thinks will be four or six weeks. Colonel Clinton acquaints me, we cannot expect more than two hundred men from Montreal. I have put on foot the raising of a regiment of three hundred Canadians, which I make no doubt of effecting. They are to have the same pay and be under the same regulations as the Continental forces. I make no doubt the exigency of our affairs will justify the step I have taken, (though without authority for so doing,) and that it will be approved of by the honorable Continental Congress.

I am, most respectfully, gentlemen,
your most obedient, humble servant,
B. Arnold

P. S. the forts of Niagara and Detroit are an object, which, I make no doubt, the Honorable Congress have in view. Mr. Antill, now on his way down, can inform you in regard to their strength, stores, &c.

B. A. [57]

On the same day, in expectation of a victory and prior to his receiving notice on his promotion, Washington let Arnold know about the consideration of Congress to maintain an American military in Canada.

To Colonel B. Arnold

Cambridge, January 12, 1776

Dear Sir

Your favor of the 5th ultimo from before Quebec enclosing the returns of your detachment – is come to hand. From the account you give of the garrison and state of the walls, I expect soon to hear from you within them, which will give me vast pleasure.

I am informed that there are large quantities of arms – blankets, clothing, & other military stores in that city – these are articles, which we are in great want of here. I have therefore wrote to Genl Montgomery or whoever is commanding officer in that quarter to send me as much as can be spared from thence. If you can assist in expediting their dispatch, you will much oblige me.

I understand that the Congress have it under consideration to raise an Army for the defense of Canada on a new establishment. When I received this information I applied to Congress to know whether it was their intention that you & the officers in your detachment were appointed in this Army as newly arranged, to which I have not received their answer.

The want of so many good officers is felt here, especially in the recruiting service which not go on so brisk as I could wish. I think it will be best for you to settle the arrearages due to your men since October last with the paymaster of the Army at your place – I don't know any better way for you or them to receive it. [24]

I am, Sir, yours &c.,

G. Washington

On the **14th** Arnold wrote his after-action report to Washington.

To His Excellency General Washington

110

Camp before Quebec, January 14, 1776

Dear Sir

I make no doubt you will soon hear of our misfortune on the 31 ultimo and be very anxious to know our present situation. Our loss and repulse struck an amazing panic into both officers and men, and had the enemy improved their advantage, our affairs here must have been entirely ruined. It was not in my power to prevail on the officers to attempt saving our mortars, which had been placed in St. Roque's, of course they fell into the hands of the enemy – Upwards of one hundred officers and soldiers instantly set for Montreal and it was with the greatest difficulty I could persuade the rest to make a stand. The panic soon subsided, I arranged the men in such order as effectually to blockade the city and enable them to assist each other if attacked. It was urged by the officers to move our ammunition and artillery stores of which we had a large quantity and though the risk was great, I could not approve the measure, as it would undoubtedly, have made unfavorable impressions on the minds of the Canadians and induced them to withdraw their assistance, which must have ended in our utter ruin, I therefore put the best face on matters and betrayed no marks of fear. I have withdrawn the cannon from our battery and placed them around the magazine, our present force is only seven hundred, I am in daily expectation of a reinforcement from Montreal of two or three hundred men, I expected Genl Wooster, but find he cannot leave Montreal, Col. Clinton is just arrived, I have put on foot the raising a regt. Of 2 or 3 hundred Canadians, which I make no doubt of affecting, our finances are very low, however I hope we shall be able to rub along, Mr. Price is our only resource and has exerted himself, I wait with great anxiety the arrival of a reinforcement from below, I have wrote the Honorable Congress, my opinion that five thousand men will be necessary to insure us Quebec, though it may possibly be reduced with a less number, it appears a blockade may answer the purpose, I think Quebec an object of too much consequence, to trust it to the event, if reduced five thousand men will be necessary for a garrison.

Your favor of the 5 ultimo is just come to hand. It gives me a most sensible pleasure to have your approbation of my conduct, I beg you'd accept my thanks for the notice you have been pleased to take me and my officers in your establishment. Most of them are provided for in an unexpected manner not very pleasing to me. Enclosed is a list of the killed and wounded, both officers and men behaved with the greatest intrepidity and had not the General been basely deserted by his troops we should doubtless have carried the town, my detachment had carried the first battery, (my being wounded) & the loss of their guides retarded them much, after the death of the General, they sustained the force of the whole garrison for a considerable time, who fired from under cover and had every advantage of situation, their retreat was cut off by the enemy's gaining a narrow defile through which they were obliged to pass, they were overpowered by numbers and obliged to resign though deserving a better fate. Govr Carleton treats them with humanity & has given leave for their baggage to be sent in to them. I heartily congratulate you on the success of your privateers. I think the balance of the last years account is still in our favor, though we have met a sever check here, I hope soon to have the pleasure of seeing Genl Lee or some experienced officer here.

I heartily wish you the protection and blessing of the Almighty & am with very great respect & esteem, Dear Sir,

your obedient humble servant,

B. Arnold [57]

On the **24**th, Arnold gave a detailed report of the British arms supply to Congress.

To the Honorable Continental Congress

Camp before Quebec, January 24, 1776

Gentlemen

I wrote the 14th instant, advising you of our present situation and that of the enemy and took the liberty of presenting you my sentiments on a future plan of operations, for which my zeal for the public service, I hope, will apologize; since which; I have made an estimate (which I now enclose) of such artillery, stores, ammunition, &c., which, I imagine, will be necessary if it is thought proper to carry on a siege in form. Of this I can be no judge, as I know not if powder can be spared from below, or shot, shells, &c., sent up in season. The artillery, except a twelve-inch mortar, (at Crown Point,) is all in this country. I have also enclosed a list of such ammunition, stores, &c., as we have on hand. A list of such articles as can be procured at Montreal, St. John's, and Chambly will be taken and sent you by General Wooster.

I had encouragement from Monsieur Pelissier at Three Rivers, of being furnished with shot, shells, &c., by the 1st of April, of which the bearer, Major Ogden, will inform; this measure, I hope, will meet your approbation, as the expense of bringing shells from below will be great, and, if not wanted here, the cost will be trifling.

112

It is very probable the city would surrender before half or perhaps one quarter of the shot, shells, &c., in my memorandum were expended; but if they should make an obstinate resistance, perhaps the whole will be necessary.

A gentleman, now present, assures me that the King's magazines, containing upwards of three thousand barrels of powder are full, and that three hundred barrels, his private property, taken from him by the government, was obliged to be stored in a private vault; add to this ten thousand stand of arms, seven thousand of which are new, and arrived last summer, also seven thousand complete suits of new clothing with a large artillery stores; two frigates with a number of other vessels in the harbor, &c, &c., &c. the above mentioned articles, exclusive of securing an extensive country in our interest, and liberating three or four hundred of our brave men, appears an object of the greatest importance to us under our present circumstances. I make no doubt every necessary measure will be adopted for reducing the city.

Yesterday arrived here, a reinforcement of one hundred men from Montreal; sixty men are soon expected. We are still very weak handed. Of course the duty is severe; however, the enemy have not dared to come out, though they are double our number. Desertions from the garrison are frequent. They are in want of fuel and have attempted to supply themselves by cutting down the houses in St. Roque's suburbs, (under their guns,) to prevent which, I have burnt most of them, with several vessels they had broke up; every artifice is used by Governor Carleton to procure provisions and induce the Canadians to take up arms against us, to no effect, though seconded by the clergy, our bitter enemies. I make no doubt of continuing the blockade until a proper reinforcement arrives to make use of more coercive measures.

Major Ogden, the bearer of this to Montreal, who came out with me a volunteer, proposes going down to Philadelphia. I beg leave to recommend him as a gentleman who has acted with great spirit and activity through our fatiguing march and at the attack of Quebec in which he was wounded.

General Montgomery, on his arrival in this country, was pleased to appoint Mr. John Halstead as Commissary; he is a gentleman who has been very active and zealous in our cause; and is a merchant, capable in his department, in which I beg leave to recommend his being continued.

Our finances are low; we have been obliged to beg, borrow, and squeeze to get money for our subsistence; and, but for Mr. Price, *who has been our greatest resource, we must have suffered. I have agreeable intelligence that the paymaster is at hand.*

I am, with great esteem, gentlemen,
your most obedient and very humble servant,
Benedict Arnold [57]

On the same day, Schuyler pleaded for supplies from Hancock and requested that Captain Jacobus Wynkoop be appointed under Commodore William Douglass.

To the Honorable John Hancock, esq.

January 24, 1776
Dear Sir

I have just now received a letter from the Committee of Safety at New York enclosing copies of the resolutions of Congress of the 8th of January. They observe "that several things are left indeterminate" in that resolve which orders a large quantity of provisions and stores to be sent to Fort George. In answer I wrote them that "I cannot believe Congress intended anything more by sending the resolution to them than that they should supply me with what I might want. The almost impossibility of sending a large quantity from New York to Fort George at this season wound countenance this construction."

They have also wrote me on the subject of the shipwrights. I have given them an extract of what I have above said to Congress on the occasion and requested that they would not send any until I applied for them.

They also seem to think that they were to procure bateau men and ask what wages are to be allowed them – I have promised to write to Congress on that head. I believe that they would be best got in the vicinity of this place. If Congress thinks so I wish to know what pay to allow to the officers and men.

Congress will please to attend to the Naval Department in this quarter – perhaps Commodore Douglass will remain – I could wish a Capt. Wynkoop to be employed under him. He is active and brave.

I am, &c.,
Ph. Schuyler [18]

On the 17th, Washington had received the grim report and sent his regrets to Arnold on the 27th, still without notice of his promotion.

To Colonel B. Arnold

Cambridge, January 27, 1776

114

Dear Sir

On the 17th instant I received the melancholy account of the unfortunate attack on the city of Quebec, attended with the fall of General Montgomery and other brave officers & men, & your being wounded – This unhappy affair affects me in a very sensible manner & I sincerely condole with you upon the occasion. But in the midst of distress, I am happy to find that suitable honors were paid to the remains of Mr. Montgomery & our officers & soldiers who have fallen into their hands, treated with kindness and humanity.

Having received no intelligence later than the copy of your letter of the 2nd to Genl Wooster, I would fain hope that you are not in a worse situation than you were then, though I confess I have greatly feared that that those misfortunes would be succeeded by others, on account of your unhappy condition & the dispirited state of the officers & men. If they have not, I trust when you are joined by three regiments now raising in this and & the governments of Connecticut & New Hampshire – & two others ordered by the Congress from Pennsylvania & the Jerseys with the men already sent by Col. Warner, that these misfortunes will be done away and things resume a more favorable & promising appearance than ever.

I need not mention to you the great importance of this place & the consequent possession of all Canada in the scale of American affairs – you are well apprised of it – to whomever it belongs, in their favor probably, will the balance turn – if it is ours, success I think will most certainly crown our virtuous struggles – If it is in theirs, the contest at best will be doubtful, hazardous, and bloody. The glorious work must be accomplished in the course of this winter, otherwise it will become difficult, most probably, impracticable – for administration knowing that it will be impossible to reduce us to state of slavery & arbitrary rule without it will certainly send a large reinforcement there in the spring – I am fully convinced that your exertions will be invariably directed to this grand object & I already view the approaching day when you and your brave followers will enter this important fortress with every honor & triumph attendant on victory and conquest, then you will have added the only link wanting in the great chain of Continental union & render the freedom of your country secure.

Wishing you a speedy recovery & the possession of those laurels, which your bravery & perseverance justly merit,

I am, Dear Sir, &c.,

G. Washington [24]

On **February 1ˢᵗ**, one month after the fighting had gone from start to finish, *The New York Packet* furnished its own battle report.

New York Packet, February 1, 1776

Canada   The Americans have made an unsuccessful attack upon the town of Quebec. General Montgomery finding his cannon too light to effect a breach, and that the enemy would not hearken to terms of capitulation, formed a design of carrying the town by escalade. In this he was encouraged by the extensiveness of the works, and the weakness of the garrison. When everything was prepared, while he was awaiting the opportunity of a snowstorm to carry his design into execution, several of his men deserted to the enemy. His plan, at first, was to have attacked the upper and lower town at the same time, depending principally for success upon the upper town. But discovering, from the motions of the enemy, that they were apprised of his design, he altered his plan, and, having divided his small Army into four detachments, ordered two feints to be made against the upper town, one by Colonel Livingston at the head of the Canadians, against St. John's gate, the other by Captain Brown, at the head of a small detachment, against Cape Diamond, reserving to himself and Colonel Arnold, the two principal attacks against the lower town.

At five o'clock this morning, the hour appointed for the attack, the General, at the head of the New York troops, advanced against the lower town. Being obliged to take a circuit, the signal for the attack was given and the garrison alarmed before he reached the place. However, pressing on, he passed the first barrier, and was just opening the attempt on the second, when, by the first fire from the enemy, he was unfortunately killed, together with his aide-de-camp, Captain J. McPherson, Captain Cheeseman, and two or three more. This so dispirited the men, that Colonel Campbell, on whom the command devolved, found himself under the disagreeable necessity of drawing them off.

In the meanwhile Colonel Arnold, at the head of about three hundred and fifty of those brave troops, (who with unparalleled fatigue penetrated Canada under his command,) and Captain Lamb's company of artillery, had passed through St. Roque's' gate, and approached near a two gun battery, picketed in, without being discovered. This he attacked, and though it was well defended for about an hour, carried it, with the loss of a number of men. In this attack, Colonel Arnold had the misfortune to have his leg splintered by a shot and was obliged to be carried to the hospital. After gaining the battery, his detachment passed on to a second barrier, which they took possession of. By this time the enemy, relieved from the other attack, by our troops being drawn off, directed their whole force against his detachment, and a party sallying out from Palace gate attacked them in the rear. These brave men sustained the whole force of the garrison for three hours, but finding themselves hemmed in, and no hopes of relief, they were obliged to yield to numbers, and the advantageous situation the garrison had over them.

After this unfortunate repulse, the remainder of the Army retired about eight miles from the city, where they have posted themselves advantageously, and are continuing the blockade, waiting for the reinforcements which are now on their march to join them. [50]

On the same day, Arnold reported the first enemy movements since the battle to John Hancock, President of the Continental Congress, as well as a matter regarding the promotion of one Major John Brown. Raised by a rich uncle in Boston, Hancock attended the Latin School and Harvard University before inheriting his uncle's business and becoming one the wealthiest men in Massachusetts. His political career started as a member of the General Court followed by heading a town committee to investigate the "Boston Massacre." He was elected President of the Massachusetts Provincial Congress, served as Chairman of the Massachusetts Committee of Safety and as a member of the First Continental Congress before being elected President of the Second Continental Congress.

To the Honorable John Hancock, Esq.
Camp before Quebec, February 1, 1776
Dear Sir
I have the pleasure of acquainting you we still hold our ground before Quebec and keep the enemy closely blockaded, though we have received but a small reinforcement of one hundred and fifty men from Montreal. The enemy have, within this ten day, sallied out twice at Palace Gate with about four or five hundred men, with a view of seizing two field pieces we have on that side; our men advanced briskly to attack them when they made a precipitate retreat under cover of their guns. I make no doubt of holding our ground as we expect a reinforcement daily, which we are anxiously awaiting for, as the duty is very severe.

117

I have taken the liberty, in former letters to the Honorable Continental Congress, to give my opinion in regard to men and measures necessary for the reduction of Quebec. The necessary ways and means for supporting those men I have omitted, as General Montgomery, in his lifetime, transmitted you his sentiments on the matter, as well as on the necessary measures for forming a lasting union between this country and the colonies. I have only to observe, if the capital is taken I believe paper money will soon have a currency.

Major John Brown, who came down with General Montgomery, with about one hundred and sixty men collected from different regiments, now assumes and insists on the title of Colonel, which he says, the General promised him at Montreal. That the General promised him promotion, he told me sometime before his death. When Major Brown wrote to remind him of his promise, the General handed me his letter and told me at the same time, as Colonel Easton and Major Brown were publicly impeached with plundering the officers' baggage taken at Sorrel, contrary to articles of capitulation and to the great scandal of the American Army, he could not, in conscience or honor promote him until those matters were cleared up. He then sent for Major Brown and told him his sentiments on the matter very freely; after which I heard of no further application for promotion. This transaction Colonel Campbell, Major Dubois, and several gentlemen, were knowing to. As Colonel Easton and Major Brown have, doubtless, a sufficient share of modest merit to apply to the Honorable Continental Congress for promotion, I think it my duty to say the charge before mentioned is the public topic of conversation at Montreal and among the officers of the Army in general; and, as such conduct is unbecoming the character of gentlemen or soldiers, I believe it would give great disgust to the Army in general if those gentlemen were promoted before those matters were cleared up.

This will be delivered to you by Mr. David Hopkins, a gentleman who came out a volunteer with me; his spirited conduct, both on march and since our arrival in this country, merit my recommendation to your notice, of which I think him worthy.

I am with the greatest respect and esteem, Dear Sir,
your most obedient and humble servant,
Benedict Arnold

P. S. The contents of the enclosed letter I do not wish to be kept from the gentlemen mentioned therein; the public interest is my chief motive for writing. I should despise myself were I capable of *asserting a thing in prejudice of any gentlemen without sufficient reasons to make it public.*

B. A. [57]

On the **5ᵗʰ**, Congress conceded with Schuyler's needs and desires in regards to supplies, shipwrights, and the appointment of Wynkoop.

Monday, February 5, 1776

The committee to whom General Schuyler's letters were referred, brought in their report, which being taken into consideration: thereupon

Resolved, That the resolution of Congress of the 8ᵗʰ day of last month, for sending shipwrights from the cities of New York and Philadelphia, to build bateaus at Ticonderoga, be superseded; and that General Schuyler be desired to employ any artificers, as he shall think proper, in that business.

That General Schuyler be desired to procure skillful persons to assist General Wooster in exploring the river St. Lawrence and to construct armed boats to be kept there according to a former resolution of Congress.

That General Schuyler be desired to employ any such bateau men as are in and near Albany, instead of those it was recommended to the Convention of New York to procure, upon the best terms he can and to acquaint Congress for what wages they will serve.

That Captain Wynkoop be employed under Commodore Douglass in the naval department. [26]

On the **12ᵗʰ**, Arnold requests a paymaster from Hancock to account for expenses.

To Hon. John Hancock

Camp before Quebec, February 12, 1776

Dear Sir

My last was of the 1ˢᵗ of February since which nothing has occurred worth notice, except several desertions from the garrison, who are much distressed for fuel, and must burn their houses and shipping; they are at short allowance of provisions, and obliged to mount guard every other night, which has made great uneasiness among the seamen, who are the principal part of the garrison.

I have just received the resolves of the Honorable Continental Congress, as late as 10ᵗʰ of Janry and beg leave to present them my

119

respectful compliments and sincere thanks for the honorable mark of esteem they have been pleased to confer on me, which I shall study to deserve.

The multiplicity of accounts which daily arise here, and many which originated in the life of Genl Montgomery, together with those of the commissaries & quartermasters, (which in my opinion ought often to be adjusted) as well as those of Col. Livingston's regiment and many others, (which are intricate) and do not immediately fall under any particular department, renders it impossible for a commanding officer to pay that attention to them which they deserve and at the same time do his duty as a soldier, I have therefore to request that the Honorable Continental Congress, would take into their consideration, the directing the paymaster to adjust those accounts, or appointing a committee for that purpose, who, I make no doubt, would find full employment, prevent many frauds, and greatly accelerate the public business.

We have been reinforced with only one hundred & seventy five men, our whole force is about eight hundred effective men, we have about two hundred, sick & unfit for duty, near fifty of them with the small pox, the Canadians, in most of the parishes, inoculate for their own safety.

I am with great esteem, Dear Sir,
your most obedient and humble servant,
Benedict Arnold [57]

Arnold followed up with a status report to Washington on the 27th.

To His Excellency General Washington
Camp before Quebec, February 27, 1776
Dear General
I wrote you the 14th ultimo of our situation and prospects, since which nothing of consequence has occurred here. The enemy to the number of about five hundred have twice sailed out at Palace Gate with design of seizing our field pieces, (near the Nunnery) but on our troops, advancing to attack them, they made precipitate retreat under cover of their guns – desertions from the garrison are frequent by which we learn they are much distressed for fuel & must soon burn their houses & ships – Two officers taken at St John's were lately sent with a flag to the walls with a view of getting their families at liberty, but were refused admittance, which I am told by several deserters incensed by the inhabitants very much and caused a great uneasiness

in the garrison, who I believe begin to grow heartily tired of salt provisions and confinement. We have received a reinforcement of four hundred men, many are daily coming in, I hope in the course of this month we shall have four or five thousand men – I am fearful we shall not be supplied with shot, shells, and mortars etc. I am therefore preparing ladders for an assault if necessary – the extensiveness of the works I think will render their defiance impracticable.

I have this minute the pleasure of your favor of the 27th ultimo, I am greatly obliged to you for your good wishes and the concern you express for me. Sensible of the vast importance of this country, you may be assured my utmost exertions will not be wanting to effect your wishes in adding it to the United Colonies, I am fully of your opinion that the balance will turn in whose favor it belongs. The repeated successes of our raw, undisciplined troops over the flower of the British Army, the many unexpected and remarkable occurrences in our favor are plain proofs of the overruling hand of Providence and justly demands our warmest gratitude to Heaven which I make no doubt will crown our virtuous efforts with success. No doubt administration will exert themselves in sending a large force this way in the spring, but if we are fortunate enough to reduce the city before they arrive, I make no doubt of keeping it, as we shall have the interest of the country in general to which the raising two regiments of Canadians (which Congress have ordered) will not a little conduce.

I am sorry to inform you notwithstanding every precaution that could be used , the small pox has crept in among the troops, we have near one hundred men in the hospital, in general it is favorable, very few have died, I have moved the inhabitants of the vicinity of Quebec into the country and hope to prevent its spreading any further.

The severity of the climate, the troops very ill clad and worse paid, the trouble of reconciling matters among the inhabitants, and lately, an uneasiness among some of the New York and & other officers, who think themselves neglected in the new arrangement, while, those who deserted the cause and went home last fall have been promoted. In short, the choice of difficulties I have had to encounter has rendered it so very perplexing that I have often been at a loss, how to conduct matters.

As General Schuyler's ill state of health will not permit his coming this way, I was in hopes Genl Lee or some experienced officer would have been sent to take the command here. The services requires a person of greater abilities and experience than I can pretend to. Genl Wooster writes me his intentions of coming down here, I am afraid he will not be able to leave Montreal.

I have the pleasure to inform you my wound is entirely healed and I am able to hobble about my room, though my leg is a little contracted and weak. I hope soon to be fit for action. We are waiting impatiently, expecting to hear some of the capital blow being struck with you.

I beg my compliments to the gentlemen of your family and am with great respect & esteem, Dear General, your obedient and very humble servant,

B. Arnold [57]

IV
Valcour Island

On **March 8th**, having received the approval of Congress for Wynkoop's appointment, Schuyler summoned him through Nathaniel Woodhull. Born in the town of Mastic, New York on Long Island in 1722, Woodhull had fought in the French and Indian War and served in the Assembly and held a current commission as a brigadier general of militia along with a position as President of the New York Provincial Congress.

To Nathaniel Woodhull, Esq.

Albany, March 8, 1776

Sir

I am honored with yours of the 4th instant. The Continental Congress has resolved that Captain Wynkoop should be employed upon the Lakes under Commodore Douglass. Whether the latter gentleman means to engage in that service I do not know; of this, Congress can very speedily inform itself, as he resides near New York. Should he not engage, there is no person I would more willingly have to command the vessels than Captain Wynkoop. At any rate, I wish you to send him up the soonest possible, with a sufficient number of sailors for the two schooners and sloop.

I am, Sir, your most obedient and very humble servant,

Ph. Schuyler[25]

To give Arnold some backing, Congress on the **20th** ordered Benjamin Franklin, Samuel Chase, and Charles Carroll to Canada to let them know exactly what Congress had in mind regarding their well being during the American rebellion against Great Britain. Born in 1706, Franklin was born and raised in Boston where he spent his free time and work earnings to buy books and devour knowledge from them. After learning a trade as a pressman in his brother's print shop, he moved to Philadelphia where he became a noted writer, editor, inventor, entrepreneur, and scientist while owning and operating *The Pennsylvania Gazette* newspaper. His experiments and observations on electricity awarded him Master's degrees from Harvard, Yale, and William and Mary. As a prominent citizen in the "city of brotherly love," he is credited with establishing a circulating library, fire company, academy, philosophical society, and militia infantry. His political career began as a clerk of the Assembly before becoming an ambassador in England and member of the Second Continental

Congress. After studying law in Annapolis, Chase became a prominent lawyer and rallied for independence as a member of the Maryland Assembly, Committee of Safety, the 1st Maryland Convention, Committee of Correspondence, and the Continental Congress. Carroll was born in Annapolis, attained his formal education throughout Europe, and studied law at the Middle Temple in London. Upon returning the America, he sought the hand of a woman with more than just good looks; he wanted someone of wealth, someone with a heritage, someone that he could relate to, so he married his cousin. Following his authorship on several articles protesting Britain's taxation on the colonies, he was appointed as a member of the Committee of Correspondence, the Maryland Convention, Council of Safety, and the Continental Congress.

In Congress, March 20, 1776
Instructions to Benjamin Franklin, Samuel Chase, and
Charles Carroll, Esquires
Gentlemen
You are, with all convenient dispatch, to repair to Canada and make known to the people of that country the wishes and intentions of Congress with respect to them.

Represent to them that the arms of the United Colonies having been carried into that province for the purpose of frustrating the designs of the British Court against our common liberties, we expect not only to defeat the hostile machinations of Governor Carleton against us, but that we shall put it in the power of our Canadian brethren to pursue such measures for securing their own freedom and happiness as a generous love of liberty and sound policy shall dictate to them...

By order of Congress
John Hancock, President [25]

On the **23rd**, the New York Committee of Safety endorsed Wynkoop to serve on the lakes following the endorsement of Douglass, who was unavailable to do so, as recorded in the minutes.

Die Sabatti, A.M. March 23, 1776
A letter from Major Douglass, as to the service on the lakes, and which was received yesterday, was read and filed.
He says he will proceed to the lakes when he receives the command of Continental Congress or the General if his health will

permit and in the meantime will serve his country and desires the committee would assist and forward Mr. Wynkoop.

A draft of a letter to the delegates of this Colony, relative to the command on the lakes and recommending Captain Wynkoop was read and approved, and is in the words following, to wit:

To the New York Delegates in Continental Congress

$$\text{In Committee of Safety}$$
$$\text{New York, March 23, 1776}$$

Gentlemen

On the 16ᵗʰ instant, the Provincial Congress, then about to adjourn, received a letter from Major General Schuyler (dated the 8ᵗʰ) respecting Major Douglass and Captain Wynkoop, of which we enclose a copy, No. 1.

The Provincial Congress immediately sent for Capt. Wynkoop, read the General's letter to him, delivered him a copy, desired him to call on Major Douglass with it, an return an answer the speediest possible.

On the 18ᵗʰ, Capt. Wynkoop informed the Committee of Safety that he had called on Major Douglass, (who is in Col. Ward's regiment in King's County), and delivered him a copy of the General's letter. That Mr. Douglass had intimated that he was now in service, that it would be at least two months before he could attend at the lakes if his health would then permit. The Committee therefore wrote to Major Douglass and on the 21ˢᵗ received his answer of which we enclose you copies No. 2 and 3.

The season is so far advanced that the service must suffer if the vessels on the lakes are not immediately employed. We have prevailed on Capt. Wynkoop by this reason only, to engage seamen and proceed to the General with all possible dispatch. We beg leave through you to inform Congress that Capt. Wynkoop was bred a mariner, has frequently been master of mercantile vessels, served with reputation last war, both in the land and marine departments; we think him an officer of merit and we have heard his conduct in the last campaign highly applauded. We have promised to recommend Mr. Wynkoop to Congress for the command of the vessels on the lake. This we do with the greatest cheerfulness, as we think him equal to the command and worthy of the trust; and from General Schuyler's letter, we are induced to believe it would not be disagreeable to him. We do not wish to impose Capt. Wynkoop's services on Congress in this command if it is not perfectly agreeable to them; and should the Congress think proper to order Major Douglass or any other gentleman to go up to take the command, we pray their determination may be speedy, that the service may not suffer, as Capt. Wynkoop will not continue in that service under Major Douglass.

We are, gentlemen, &c., [18]

(Signed by the Members of the Committee of Safety in New York)

On **April 3rd** Washington notified Arnold that relief was on the way via Major General John Thomas. He also made a reference to an artillery appointment that would later dismantle the success of his treason. Born in 1725, Thomas studied and practiced medicine in his native town of Marshfield, Massachusetts before moving to Kingston and serving in eight campaigns during the French and Indian War. Between the wars he returned to his practice and became a justice of the peace. With the rise of the Revolution, he accepted a commission as a brigadier general of militia and took possession of Dorchester Heights before taking possession of a Continental command of troops retreating from Canada.

To B General Arnold

Cambridge, April 3, 1776

Sir

Your favor of the 27th February is come to hand. I much fear you will be much disappointed in that month as the lakes were impassible.

Major General Thomas will long before you receive this have informed you the success of our operations here. We have no certain accounts of their destination, it is generally believed they are gone to Halifax. (If true) it is probable they will attempt to penetrate Canada on the opening of the St. Lawrence, I hope before that happens, you will be in full possession of Quebec & have its avenues well secured, upon which depends the fate of this campaign in these parts.

I dispatched two company's of Colonel Knox's regiment of artillery to you from hence two mortars, etc, as you will see at foot hereof if anything else is wanting that cannot be had in Canada & in my power to send, they shall be forwarded with all possible expedition upon my being informed thereof – the chief part of the troops are marched from hence towards New York. I will set off tomorrow if the enemy will not find us full employment & it is necessary you may expect a detachment from thence to your assistance – I am very sorry that the gentlemen of New York & other officers should think themselves neglected in the new arrangement – it is true that I reserved places in the Army for those officers who went from hence under your command – the Congress have since informed

126

me that they would be provided for in the Army raised for Canada. I was not acquainted with the gentlemen who complain nor with their circumstances, there is little doubt but their merits will be rewarded in due time – I am very sensible of the many difficulties you have had to encounter. Your conduct under them does you great honor – as General Thomas will take the burden off your shoulders, I hope you will gather strength sufficient to assist in finishing the important work you have with so much glory to yourself & service to your country hitherto conducted – as I am informed that there is a furnace somewhere near you, where shells & shot of any size can be cast, I would recommend to General Thomas to have what quantity of each that may be wanting immediately prepared, the roads are so very bad that it is impossible to send you any great number of these necessary articles from hence, I have appointed Capt. Lamb who is prisoner in Quebec to be second major in the regiment of artillery commanded by Col. Henry Knox. The gentlemen of this family return you their compliments and my best wishes attend General Thomas.

I remain, Sir, yours &c.,

G. Washington [24]

Along with the arrival of spring, came a new strategy to defend the Lake Champlain region from a British invasion. In April from his headquarters in Montreal, Arnold made a proposal to construct an American Navy made up of shallow water vessels that were capable of sailing where the larger British ships couldn't. Benjamin Franklin, serving as Chairman of the Pennsylvania Committee of Safety, approved the plan and commissioned the construction of the first two galley ships with more to follow. Galley ships measured seventy to eighty feet in length, bearing two short masts, triangular pivoting sails, oars, and rounded hulls. Their design allowed for exceptional maneuverability, making them to be the perfect battleship for the shoal depths and changing winds of Lake Champlain. While Arnold was chosen to oversee construction, based on his familiarity of vessels as a former merchant mariner, the Committee of Safety in New York ordered Wynkoop to take command of the lakes on the 13th.

In Committee of Safety, New York, April 13, 1776
Ordered, That Captain Jacobus Wynkoop do enlist the number of mariners desired by Major General Schuyler for the service of the lakes, with all possible dispatch. That Captain Wynkoop proceed to Albany with said mariners to General Schuyler, and take his

127

directions as to the vessels on the lakes, until the Honorable Continental Congress shall have appointed him to that command or some other gentleman shall arrive at the lakes authorized to take the command.

Extract from the minutes:

John McKesson, Secretary [25]

Feeling useless under Wooster, Arnold transferred to Montreal where he notified Schuyler on the **20**[th] that the Army hadn't seen much improvement compared to his report to Washington almost two months ago. He also mentioned that he had ordered Colonel Moses Hazen to take command of Chambly, to oversee the construction of four gondolas, and St. John's. Hazen was a wealthy veteran of the French and Indian War who had maintained a farm, forge, sawmill, and glass-making house in Montreal prior to the Revolution. When the present war broke out, he served as a courier to Carleton in an effort to protect his properties. In a proverbial game of tug-o-war, he was arrested by the Americans, rescued by the British, arrested by the British, and forced to flee to Quebec where he sided with the Americans in which he served under Montgomery during the fateful attack.

To General Schuyler

Montreal, April 20, 1776

Dear General

I hope you will pardon my neglect in not writing you for so long a time, when I acquaint you that I have, from time to time, communicated every material intelligence to General Wooster, who, I make no doubt, has transmitted the same to you. The 1st *instant he arrived at camp before Quebec. On the 2*[nd]*, I had, on an alarm, occasion to mount my horse, who unluckily fell on me and violently bruised my lame leg and ankle, which confined me until the 12*[th]*, at which time I left the camp and arrived here yesterday. Had I been able to take an active part, I should by no means have left the camp; but as General Wooster did not think proper to consult me in any of his matters, I was convinced I should be of more service here than in the camp and he very readily granted me leave of absence until covered from my lameness.*

Enclosed is a list of our force before Quebec; which I am sorry to say is very inconsiderable and illy supplied with every requisite to carry on a siege that I am very dubious of their success. The 2nd *instant we opened a battery of three guns and one howitzer on*

128

Point Levi; another battery of six guns, two howitzers, and two small mortars on the Heights of Abraham, and one of two guns at the traverse were nearly completed when in came away. To supply the whole, there are only three or four tons of powder and ten or twelve of shot, no engineer, and few artillerymen. Two fire ships – one at Orleans and on at Point aux Trembles – were nearly completed to attempt burning their ships as soon as the ice will admit of it. We have few seamen (and not one good commander) to man those vessels or I should conceive great hopes of their success.

Our Army are supplied with provisions to the 10th of May, after which their only resource for meat is from below. This country (which is not plentiful at best) is nearly exhausted of beef. We can procure a supply of flour if furnished with cash. I am now stretching our credit for that purpose which is at a low ebb.

I cannot help lamenting that more effectual measures have not been adopted to secure this country in our interest, an object which appears to me of the highest importance to the colonies. Colonel Hazen, who is a sensible judicious officer, and well acquainted with this country, has shown me his letter to you of the 1st instant. I am sorry to say I think most of his remarks but too true; and that if we are not immediately supported with eight or ten thousand men, a good train of artillery, and a military chest well furnished, the Ministerial troops, if they attempt it, will regain this country and we shall be obliged to quit it. The fatal consequences of which are too obvious...

I am, with great respect and esteem, Dear General,
your obedient and humble servant,
Benedict Arnold [25]

The race to build an American fleet was on as more and more British warships arrived in Quebec on **May 6th**, laden with food, supplies, ammunition, and 8,000 men under Major General John Burgoyne. Appointed as Carleton's second in command, Burgoyne had previously made his mark by gallantly establishing the first light horse units in the British Army, which were proven effective during assignments in Portugal and Spain during the Seven Years' War. He acquired the name of "Gentleman Johnny" as a tribute of his humanity towards his men, rather than the harsh discipline that was the norm for training new recruits, by combining the best of the French and Prussian disciplines. His style of leadership rather than dictatorship was similar to that of Arnold's, that along with his ambitious, pretentious, and vain personality proved him to be a most worthy adversary. Also arriving with Burgoyne were Major General

Wilhelm, Baron von Riedesel and the wise and daring Lieutenant Colonel Simon Fraser. Both were proven veterans of the previous war against the French, Riedesel fighting in Europe and Fraser in America. The supplies that Burgoyne had brought over from the British Empire were the very things that were diminishing throughout the American Army. The only thing that was growing for them was the spread of smallpox. Given these factors, the decision to evacuate Canada was made by Thomas. On the 7th, Schuyler, under his own authority, ordered Wynkoop to Lake Champlain.

To Captain Wynkoop

Fort George, May 7, 1776

Sir

You are immediately to repair to Ticonderoga and take command of all the vessels on Lake Champlain, which you will with the greatest expedition put in the best condition possible for immediate service.

I am, Sir, your humble servant,
Ph. Schuyler [25]

From Montreal on the 8th, Arnold wrote to Washington, pleading for the expected help to arrive.

To His Excellency General Washington

Montreal, May 8th 1776

Dear General

Your favor of the 3rd April I received a few days since & should have answered by the last post, but was obliged to go to Chambly to give directions about some gondolas building there. I heartily congratulate you on the success of your arms against Boston & am sorry it is not in my power to give you a more pleasing account of our affairs in this country, where wear no favorable aspect at present. Genl Thomas arrived here about ( ) days since & has joined the Army before Quebec. General Wooster is disgusted and expected here daily. Our Army consists of few more than two thousand effective men & twelve hundred sick & unfit for duty chiefly with the small pox, which is universal in the country. We have very little provisions, no cash, & less credit & until the arrival of the heavy cannon & two mortars from Cambridge, our artillery has been trifling; the mortars I expect will reach camp tomorrow & shells can be supplied from the three rivers. I hope they will have the desired effect. The want of cash has greatly retarded our operations in this country. We are fortifying two very important posts which command the river at Richelieu, fifteen leagues above Quebec and at Jacques Cartier which commands a pass between two mountains eleven leagues above Quebec: If succors should arrive before we can posses ourselves of Quebec, I hope we shall be able to maintain these two posts until a reinforcement arrives to our assistance, which we are told are on their way here. These are the only posts that secure the river, until you approach near Montreal and of so much consequence, that nothing but superior numbers will oblige us to abandon them.

I have mounted three 24 pounders on a gondola & armed several bateaus, which go down the river tomorrow. These with a schooner mounting ten guns & a gondola mounting one twelve pounder are all the force we have in the river. Four other gondolas are building at Chambly calculated to mount three heavy pieces of cannon, but will not be completed these two weeks. Tomorrow I set off for the Army with no very agreeable prospects before me. Should the enemy receive any considerable reinforcement soon, I make no doubt we shall have our hands full. At any rate, we will do all that can be expected from raw troops, badly clothed and fed, & worse paid, & without discipline, & trust the event to Providence. We have received advice that the 8th Regt of about 400 men with a number of savages are coming down from the upper countries. I have posted 500 men at the Cedars, a narrow pass 15 leagues above this place. They have two pieces cannon & well entrenched by which the enemy must pass. I have only time to beg you will accept my best wishes & respectful compliments & make the same to the gentlemen of your family.

I am most respectfully, Dear General,
your most obedient & very humble servant,
Benedict Arnold [25]

On the **11th**, although the outcome didn't look good for the Americans, Arnold made a pledge to Schuyler that he would do all that he could to keep the up fight in Canada for the sake of his men, the duty to his Country, and the honor for himself.

To General Schuyler

Montreal, May 11, 1776

Dear General

By the bearer you will receive letters from the honorable Commissioners, advising you of our situation and prospects in respect to provisions, &c. You will also have enclosed a copy of a letter from General Thomas to me, dated at Deschambault, by which you will see the distressed and critical situation of our Army, which I can hardly flatter myself will be better, at least for some time. Indeed we have everything to fear if the enemy's reinforcements are as considerable as we have reason to think and they improve their advantage. I tremble for the sake of our scattered, sick, starved, and distressed Army, as well as for our friends in this country, many of whom will lose their all if we are obliged to evacuate it. Salted provisions are not in this country, very little fresh, and that miserably poor; our whole dependence is on you. More troops will add to our distress, unless they are supplied with provisions, which must be forwarded on to us immediately, or we shall not be able to continue in the country or return home. I shall set out for the Army in two hours and proceed from the Sorrel with the gondola and heavy cannon, if there should be any prospect of our maintaining our post at Deschambault, of which I expect to be able to judge better when I arrive at the Sorrel. You may depend that everything in my power will be done to keep possession of this Country, which has cost us so much blood and expense.

I am with my best wishes, very respectfully, Dear General, your most obedient, humble servant,

B. Arnold

P. S. Flour can be procured in this Country, provided we keep possession of this part of it. A magazine will be immediately established at St. John's to secure our retreat.

B. A. [25]

On the **18**[th], Arnold made a surprise attack at St. John's and captured a 70 ton sloop bearing a pair of 6-pounders, which the Americans later renamed the *Enterprise*. On the **25**[th], Arnold notified the Commissioners of Canada that he would be attempting a rescue mission for 474 soldiers and officers who had recently been taken prisoner after a battle at the Cedars.

To the Honorable Commissioners

La Chine, May 25, 1776

Gentlemen

One of our men this moment came in who was taken at the Cedars; he made his escape this morning and says we have lost only ten privates killed, the rest are prisoners at St. Anne's and the Cedars; the enemy lost double that number. They were last night within three miles of us, with three hundred savages, fifty regulars, and two hundred and fifty Canadians, with our two pieces of cannon. But on hearing that we had a large body of men here, they made a precipitous retreat. He left them above Point Claire; they have only twenty-one canoes, which will carry eight or nine men on an average. I intend to send off four hundred men in bateaus immediately, to proceed to the Isle Perot, and endeavor to cut off the enemy's retreat. I expect they will make some stay at Fort St. Anne's by which it may possibly be effected. Pray hurry on the men as fast as possible. I shall push them on from this immediately. We have so much water craft that we can always keep up a communication between those on land and those on water, and be able to act in concert.

I am, gentlemen, your obedient, humble servant,

Benedict Arnold [25]

After a heated debate between himself and Hazen, Arnold led the assault on La Chine on the **26**[th] and although he failed to rescue the prisoners, he succeeded in negotiating their release, but not without another shouting match. On the **27**[th], he placed his report to the Commissioners.

To the Honorable Commissioners

St. Anne's, May 27, 1776

Gentlemen

I wrote you from La Chine yesterday morning that the Army marched at six o'clock from this place. We arrived here with the main body at six o'clock P. M., when we discovered several of the enemy's bateaus taking our unhappy prisoners off an island at one league distance from us. Words cannot express our anxiety, as it was not in our power to relieve them; our bateaus were a league behind, coming up the rapids very slowly. I sent several expresses to hurry them; however, it was sunset before they arrived and I could embark all my people; previous to which arrived some Caughnawaga Indians, whom I had sent early in the morning to the savages, demanding a surrender of our prisoners; and, in case of refusal and that any of them were murdered, I would sacrifice every Indian who fell into my hands, and would follow them to their towns, and destroy them by fire and sword. The answer I received was that they had five hundred of our prisoners collected together and that if we offered to land and attack them at Quinze Chiens, where they were posted, they would immediately kill every prisoner, and give no quarter to any who should fall into their hands hereafter. Words cannot express my feelings at the delivery of this message: torn by the conflicting passions of revenge and humanity, a sufficient force to take ample revenge, raging for action, urged me on one hand; and humanity for five hundred unhappy wretches, who were on the point of being sacrificed if our vengeance was not delayed, plead equally strong on the other. In this situation I ordered the boats to row immediately for the Island, where our prisoners had been confined; where we found five unhappy wretches, naked and almost starved; the rest, they informed me, were all taken off by the savages just before, except one or two, who, being unwell, were inhumanely butchered. I immediately ordered the boats to row for Quinze Chiens, about four miles from the Island, on the main land; there the enemy had two brass six-pounders, were entrenched round the church, and well fortified. They began firing upon us when we approached within three-quarters of a mile from the shore, with their cannon and small arms. We rowed in shore without returning a shot; by this time it was so dark we could not distinguish a man on shore, and as we were unacquainted with the ground, and our people much fatigued, I judged it most prudent to return to St. Anne's. on our arrival I called a council of war, who were unanimous in attacking the enemy early in the morning. At two o'clock in the morning, Lieutenant Parke was sent to me with a flag, and articles for exchange of prisoners, entered into by Major Sherburne and Captain Forster; one article was, that there should be an exchange of prisoners of equal rank, and that our troops should be under an obligation not to take up arms again; but the King's troops were to be at full liberty. This article I rejected and dispatched Lieutenant Parke to acquaint Captain Forster that I would enter into articles for an exchange of prisoners on equal terms; which, if he refused, my determination was to attack him immediately; and if our prisoners were murdered, to sacrifice every soul that fell into our hands. Captain Forster agreed to these terms and sent them back signed. As they were not so explicit as I judged necessary, with some alterations and explanations I returned them. Enclosed you receive a copy as finally agreed to. This matter was finished at six o'clock this evening and tomorrow morning part of the prisoners are to be sent to Caughnawaga. You may be surprised that six days were allowed for the delivery of the prisoners and the hostilities should in the meantime cease; this does not include the savages. Captain Forster pretended it was not in his power to fix on any particular time for that purpose, but would engage on his honor to deliver them as soon as possible, and proposed if it could be done in less time, hostilities should then commence; of which Captain Forster is to determine and acquaint me this evening.

The base hypocritical conduct of the King's officers, their employing savages to screen them in their butcheries, their suffering the prisoners to be killed in cool blood, I will leave with you to comment on. I observed to Captain Forster that it appeared very extraordinary to me that he could influence the savages to deliver up the prisoners, and could not keep them from being murdered in cool blood or prevent their being stripped naked, contrary to the agreement made with the garrison at the Cedars.

I intend being with you this evening to consult on some effectual measures to take with these savages and still more savage British troops, who are still at Quinze Chiens. As soon as our prisoners are released, I hope it will be in our power to take ample vengeance or we will nobly fall in the attempt.

I am, with great respect and esteem, gentlemen,
your obedient, humble servant,
Benedict Arnold [25]

On the **31**[st], Schuyler notified Washington that the first artisans for the Champlain fleet had been dispatched to the shipyards at Skenesborough (Whitehall).

To His Excellency General Washington
Fort George, May 31st, 1776
Dear Sir
Your Excellency's letter of the 22nd instant was delivered me last evening. I learn with particular satisfaction that Congress has requested your attendance to advise with them on the measures necessary to be adopted for the present campaign. I foresee many salutary consequences from this step.

This morning thirty carpenters left this to repair to Skenesborough, by way of Ticonderoga in order to construct gondolas, although nothing is prepared for building them – I hope nevertheless to finish one in a short time, at least, I will do everything in my power to complete it the soonest possible, and for that purpose; I shall leave this tomorrow to put all in train. Since General Sullivan's departure, I have finished sixty bateaus, nor shall I cease until I am advised by your Excellency that no more troops are coming this way...

I wish a person that understood the construction of the best gondolas was sent up to express to me, for – although they should not be able to get down the Falls of Chambly, yet they will be of service on Lake Champlain should our Army be obliged to retreat. The vessels we have there (except the Royal Savage) are of very little force...

I am, Dear Sir, ever most sincerely,
your Excellency's most obedient, humble servant,
Ph. Schuyler [84]

On **June 2nd**, Arnold gave an account of the situation to Congress based on an analysis given by Colonel John De Haas, a veteran of the French and Indian War from Pennsylvania, whose unit would later save Arnold from being captured by driving off an enemy column.

To the Honorable Commissioners of Congress
Montreal, June 2, 1776
Gentlemen
On my return to this place, I received intelligence from Colonel De Haas that the enemy had abandoned their post at Quinze Chiens, the 30th ultimo, and were seen next morning three miles above the Cedars. On their way up they made a precipitate retreat, and left behind them a quantity of flour. I repeated my order to Colonel De Haas to burn and destroy the town and inhabitants of Canassadaga and afterwards to destroy the fort at St. Anne's and retire to La Chine. Last evening an express arrived from him, who advises that on the 31st they received intelligence by some Frenchmen that seven hundred Indians were arrived at Canassadaga from the upper countries and were on the point of attacking St. Anne's, on which Colonel De Haas called a council of war, which concluded it best retire from the fort. The express came away at three o'clock P. M. and the troops were to leave it immediately after. The advice Colonel De Haas received from the Frenchmen appears to me very vague and uncertain; neither do I believe a single Indian has arrived from above. The orders I sent Colonel De Haas were very positive; and how he should think of calling a council to determine if he should obey them, appears to me very extraordinary. A fatality seems to attend every of our enterprises. Enclosed are sundry depositions respecting the affair at the Cedars. Our prisoners are most of them delivered up. I have sent all the sick from this to Isle-aux-Noix. Nothing new from below since you left us. Our future conduct must be governed by advice from that quarter. I am making every possible preparation to secure our retreat. I have secured six tons of lead, ball, and shot. Merchandise or the inhabitants I have not as yet taken hold of; I intend it tomorrow. It is impossible to know one hour beforehand the necessary steps to be taken. Everything is in the greatest confusion; not one contractor, commissary, or quartermaster; I am

obliged to do the duty of all. I wish with all my heart we were out of the country. We had much better begin anew and set out right and methodically.

Enclosed is the list of the prisoners who came into Caughnawaga, attested by Captain Osgood, who was appointed on my part to receive them. They were fired at on their leaving Quinze Chiens and narrowly escaped. Major Sherburne will deliver you this, to whom I beg leave to refer you for particulars.

I am with great esteem and affection, gentlemen,

your obedient, humble servant,

B. Arnold [25]

Although he had received permission from Congress to take what he needed from the inhabitants of Montreal, Arnold knew it could not sustain them to victory when he learned that the British were planning to envelope the Army. In a letter of the 10th to Brigadier General John Sullivan, he let known his intentions to abandon Canada, but would only do so as the last man standing. He also made it known that Hazen posed to be a threat to Canadian diplomacy by failing to secure supplies of the local inhabitants. Sullivan had been born in Somersworth, New Hampshire across the Salmon Falls River from Berwick, Maine and studied law at Portsmouth before receiving a commission as major in the New Hampshire Militia. After his appointments to the Provincial Congress and 1st Continental Congress, he was commissioned as one of eight brigadier generals when the fighting began and took part in the siege at Boston. Like Arnold, he was a bold and brave showman whose overt sensitivity to his mistakes led to a rage beyond control of which he displayed following his recent loss at Three Rivers.

To General Sullivan

Chambly, June 10, 1776

Dear General

I went to St. John's yesterday, where I found everything in the greatest confusion – not one stroke done to fortify the camp – the engineer a perfect sot – at that and this near three thousand sick. I have given orders that the sick draw only half rations in future. I have ordered Colonel Antill to St. John's, and an abattis and lines to be immediately begun, to enclose the two old forts and an encampment, sufficient to hold six thousand men. I am fully of opinion not one minute out to be lost in securing our retreat, and saving our heavy cannon, baggage, and provisions. The enemy will never attack you at

Sorrel. Their force is doubtless much superior to ours and we have no advice of any reinforcements. Shall we sacrifice the few men we have by endeavoring to keep possession of a small part of the country, which can be of little or no service to us? The junction of the Canadians with the Colonies – an object, which brought us into this country – is at an end. Let us quit then and secure our own country before it is too late. There will be more honor in making a safe retreat than hazarding a battle against such superiority which will doubtless be attended with the loss of our men and artillery and the only pass to our country. These arguments are not urged by fear for my personal safety. I am content to be the last man who quits the country and fall, so that my country may rise. But let us not all fall together.

The goods I seized at Montreal and sent to Chambly, under the care of Major Scott, have been broken open, plundered, and huddled together in the greatest confusion. They were taken in such a hurry it was impossible to take a particular account of them. Each man's name was marked on his packages. When Major Scott arrived at Chambly, he received your positive orders to repair to Sorrel. The guard was ordered to return and the goods to be delivered by Colonel Hazen to be stored. He refused receiving or taking any care of them, by which means, and Major Scott's being ordered away, the goods have been opened and plundered, I believe to a large amount. It is impossible for me to distinguish each man's goods or ever settle with the proprietors. The goods are delivered to Mr. McCarthy. This is not the first or last order Colonel Hazen has disobeyed. I think him a man of too much consequence for the post he is in. I am giving him orders to send directly to St. John's all the heavy cannon, shot, powder, bateaus, valuable stores, and the sick. I go to Montreal immediately and beg to have your orders as soon as possible, for my future conduct.

I am with respect and esteem, Dear General,
your obedient humble servant,
B. Arnold
P. S. If you should think proper to retire to St. John's, will it not be best to order a number of carts to be ready here from all the neighboring parishes and enforce your order by sending a number of armed men to secure them?

B. A. [25]

On the **12**[th], Schuyler begged Washington to send men and supplies to build the fleet, because Arnold had detected that the British were gathering supplies to build their own.

To His Excellency General Washington
                    Albany, June 12ᵗʰ, 1776, 4 o'clock P. M.
Dear Sir
    The letter, which I had the honor to write to you yesterday, I delivered to General Wooster who sailed this day.
    I have within this half hour received a letter from General Arnold of which the enclosed is a copy. I fear the next will announce the evacuation of Canada by our troops, probably with loss, as I fear that not a sufficient attention has been paid to a recommendation of mine to bring all the bateaus that could possibly be spared from Sorrel to St. John's.
    I shall immediately dispatch an express to Fort George to send bateaus to St. John's, but after all the number will be very small for want of men to navigate them, I suppose one hundred and twenty at least are at Lake George.
    I am not under the least apprehension that the enemy will be able to cross Lake Champlain, provided that our Army is able to retreat into that lake, that ammunition is speedily sent up, and further supply of pork forwarded without delay to this place.
    Your Excellency will perceive that Genl Arnold informs me that the enemy have the frames &c for gondolas on board. we should therefore build a number of these vessels with all possible dispatch. One is now on the stocks, but we want people that understand the construction of them. I have some time ago begged Congress to send one express, let me entreat that some more capable persons may be sent up & twenty shipwrights with them.
    As I fear the sawmills will not be able to saw a sufficient number of plank, I wish to have a dozen of whipsaws & files sent up with all possible dispatch.
    I shall order all the bateaus that do not go to St. John's out of Lake George to Ticonderoga that they may be ready at that place to be sent to Skenesborough to convey the Militia should they be sent up.
[18]
                    I am with every respectful sentiment,
            your Excellency's most obedient, humble servant,
                                    Ph. Schuyler

On the **13ᵗʰ**, Arnold gave Schuyler a last minute logistical report before he made a run for the border.

You may expect soon to hear of our evacuating Canada or being prisoners. [25]

At the rear of 8,000 men, Arnold pushed the retreat south while taking what he could and burning the rest, with the British just one hour behind him in pursuit. On the 13th, true to his word at the time, Arnold was the last man to leave the unconquered area of Canada. As an advance guard of British grenadiers galloped towards him, withdrew his pistol, aimed, and fired, killing his own horse before escaping into a boat bound down river towards Albany. On the 16th, Arnold notified Sullivan that he made his great escape and was determined not to be pursued.

To Honorable B Genl Sullivan, Chambly
La Prairie, June 16, 1776 – 11 o'clock A. M.
Dear General
I have received your letter from Sorrel of the 14th instant, at three o'clock, previous to which I had destroyed all the knees, &c. In the morning, I sent Captain Wilkinson express to you; at three o'clock he met the enemy at Varenne and narrowly escaped being taken; at five he arrived at Montreal; at seven P. M. I embarked the whole garrison in eleven bateaus and got safe over. The rain made it seven o'clock before carts could be procured at Longueil and La Prairie to carry the sick and baggage. The whole are safe here, with some rum, molasses, wine, &c., seized at Montreal. The salt could not be got over. We have destroyed all the bateaus and will break down all the bridges in our rear. I expect to be at St. John's at five o'clock this evening. We have thirty carts, which I will send to Chambly as soon as they are discharged of their loading. Four or five of the enemy's vessels are as high as Vercheres or Varenne. Our people saw their troops at the latter place and a Frenchman from Montreal says they mounted guard there last. The number of the enemy is very considerable. No particular account has been received of their movements.
I am very respectfully, Dear Sir, your obedient and humble servant,
B. Arnold [25]

On the 17th, Congress gave the Canadian command to Major General Horatio Gates, gave Schuyler the green light to complete the fleet, and read over Arnold's prisoner report. After rising through the British ranks during the French and Indian War, Gates had immigrated to America and settled in Virginia with the help of his

140

friend at the time, George Washington. Upon Washington's appointment as Commander-in-Chief, Gates was assigned as his first adjutant general. Working under the Commander-in-Chief as his administrator, he proved to be an accomplished, tireless, and faithful servant, but like Arnold, Gates had an abrasive personality towards those who got in his way. This along with his older than actual appearance of thinning gray hair and spectacles on a beefy body with stooped shoulders had garnered him to be known as "Granny Gates" among his men and "the old midwife" by his British counterpart, Burgoyne.

Monday, June 17, 1776
...Resolved, That General Washington be directed to send Major General Gates into Canada, to take command of the forces in that province...

That General Schuyler be directed to make a good wagon road from Fort Edward to Cheshire's; to clear Wood Creek and to construct a lock at Skenesborough, so as to have a continued navigation for bateaus from Cheshire's into Lake Champlain; to erect a grand magazine at Cheshire's and to secure it by a stockaded fort; to erect a sawmill on Schoon Creek; to order skillful persons to survey and take the level of the waters falling into Hudson's River near Fort Edward, and those which fall into Wood Creek at Cheshire's.

That he be directed to have a greater number of boats and hands kept on Hudson's River at different stations between Albany and Fort Edward in order to save the expense of waggonage.

That he be empowered to appoint proper officers to superintend the carriage by land and transportation by water of provisions, military stores, and other things into Canada, that neither waste nor delay may arise therein.

That he build with all expedition, as many galleys and armed vessels as, in the opinion of himself and the General Officer to be sent into Canada, shall be sufficient to make us indisputably masters of the Lakes Champlain and George; and that, for this purpose, there will be sent to him a master carpenter acquainted with the construction of the galleys use on the Delaware, who shall take with him other carpenters and models also if requisite.

And that it be submitted to General Schuyler, whether a temporary fortification or entrenched camp, either at Crown Point or opposite Ticonderoga, may be necessary...

The committee, to whom was referred, the cartel between Brigadier General Arnold and Captain Forster, for the exchange of prisoners, and several papers relating thereto, brought in their report, which was read:... [26]

That same day, in considering a new commander for Canada, Washington realized even at this early point in Arnold's military career that his strong points were equal to that of his weak points as revealed in a letter to Congress.

To the President of Congress

New York, June 17, 1776

Sir

The enclosed came to my hands, as a private letter from General Sullivan. As a private letter, I lay it before Congress. The tendency (for it requires no explanation) will account for the contrast between it and the letter of Genl. Arnold.

That the former is aiming at the command of Canada, is obvious. Whether he merits it or not, is a matter to be considered; and that it may be considered with propriety I think it my duty to observe, as of my own knowledge, that he is active, spirited, and zealously attached to the cause; that he does not want abilities, many members of Congress, as well as myself, can testify. But he has his wants and he has his foibles. The latter are manifested in a little tincture of vanity and in an over-desire of being popular, which now and then leads him into some embarrassments. His wants are common to us all; the want of experience to move upon a large scale; for the limited and contracted knowledge which any of us have in military matters stands in very little stead; and is greatly over balanced by sound judgement, and some knowledge of men and books; especially when accompanied by an enterprising genius, which I must do Genl. Sullivan the justice to say, I think he possesses; but as the security of Canada is of the last importance to the well being of these Colonies, I should like to know the sentiments of Congress, respecting the nomination of any officer to that command. The character I have drawn of Genl. Sullivan is just, according to my ideas of him. Congress will be pleased therefore to determine upon the propriety of continuing him in Canada or sending another, as they shall see fit. Whether Genl. Sullivan knew of the promotion of Genl. Gates (at the time of his writing) and that he had quitted the department he left him in when he marched his brigade from hence to Canada I cannot

142

undertake to say, nor can I determine whether his wish to be recalled
would be changed by it if he did.
I shall add no more than my respectful compliments to Congress
and that I have the honor to be &c.,
G. Washington [24]

On the **24th**, Schuyler claimed his first victory in building the fleet with the completion of the first vessel.

To His Excellency General Washington

Albany, June 24th, 1776

Dear Sir

...One gondola is finished at Skenesborough and a second is already planking, and I hope if my health permit me, when I return from the westward to build one every six days. [18]

I am, Dear Sir, with the greatest respect,
your Excellency's most obedient, humble servant,
Ph. Schuyler

On the **25th**, Arnold laid out his plan to build the Nation's first Navy. In his letter to Washington, he makes mention of Brigadier General William Thompson, who was captured after the debacle at Three Rivers. Thompson was an Irish immigrant from Pennsylvania who became a surveyor and justice of the peace before serving in the French and Indian War. After the British crashed the "Boston Tea Party" by closing the port of Boston, he was elected as a member of the Committee of Correspondence and the Committee of Safety. Following the contest at Concord, he was placed in command of a rifle battalion that successfully repelled enemy attacks at Boston.

To His Excellency General Washington

Albany, June 25th 1776

Dear General

By this express, you will receive advice from General Schuyler of our evacuating Canada, an event which I make no doubt (from our distressed situation) you have some time expected, the particulars of General Thompson's repulse & captivity, as nearly as could be ascertained, have been transmitted to you. On advice of which, very direct intelligence that the enemy were greatly superior to us in numbers, I advised General Sullivan to secure his retreat by retiring to St. John's. He was determined to keep his post at Sorrel, if possible & did not retire until the 14th instant at which time the enemy were as *high up with their ships as the Sorrel – The 15ᵗʰ at night when the enemy were at twelve miles distance from me I quitted Montreal, with my little garrison of three hundred men. The whole Army with their baggage & cannon, (except three heavy pieces left at Chambly), arrived at St. John's the 17ᵗʰ & at the Isle Aux Noix the 18ᵗʰ previous to which it was determined by a council of war at St. John's that in our distressed situation, (one half of the Army sick & almost the whole, destitute of clothing & every necessary of life except salt pork & flour). It was not only imprudent but practicable to keep possession of St. John's.*

Crown Point was judged the only place of health & safety to which the Army could retire and oppose the enemy, it was found necessary to remain at the Isle aux Noix for some few days until the sick heavy cannon etc. could be removed, General Sullivan did not choose to leave the Isle aux Noix until he received positive orders for that purpose & thought it necessary for me to repair to this place & wait on General Schuyler. I arrived here last night & am happy to find him of our sentiments. In quitting the Isle aux Noix, which from its low situation, is rendered very unhealthy & from the narrow channel leading to it from the south part of Lake Champlain of six miles in length & from three to eight hundred yards in breadth is rendered very insecure, as the enemy by light pieces of cannon and small arms, might render all access to it dangerous if not impracticable. It now appears to me of the utmost importance that the lake be immediately secured by a large number of (at least twenty or thirty) gondolas, row galleys, & floating batteries. The enemy from undoubted intelligence have brought over a large number (it is said one hundred) frames for flat bottomed boats designed to be made use on Lake Champlain and from their industry & strength will doubtless become masters of the lake unless nerve on our part is strained to exceed them in a naval armament. I think it absolutely necessary that at least three hundred carpenters be immediately employed, fifty sent from Philadelphia, who are acquainted with building those kind of craft would greatly facilitate the matter. A particular return of the Army could not be obtained, in our hurry and confusion it will be transmitted to you in a few days, I believe the whole about seven thousand & at least one half of them sick & unfit for duty, but daily recovering upwards of one thousand more are yet to have the small pox. The enemy, from the best intelligence that can be obtained, are near ten thousand, exclusive of Canadians & savages, few of the latter have joined them as yet.

144

I make no doubt it will be thought necessary to repair Crown Point or build a new fort near that place, the former from the advantage of its situation & the fine barracks nearly completed will I believe be thought most proper, I make no doubt but General Gates, whom I am happy to hear, is on his way here, will pay immediate attention to it.

I flatter myself our arms under your immediate direction will meet with more success than they have done in this quarter; I make not the least doubt our struggles will be crowned with success.

I am with every friendly wish, most respectfully, Dear General, your affectionate & obedient humble servant,

B. Arnold [18]

Following his arrival in Albany on the **30**[th], Gates held a meeting with Schuyler to establish a common understanding of their commands. Schuyler felt that Gates no longer had a command because the Army was no longer in Canada, while Gates felt that he maintained command of the Army regardless of its position. The two then agreed to let Washington and Congress decide, prompting Schuyler to write to Washington for clarification on **July 1**[st].

To His Excellency General Washington

Albany, July 1, 1776

Dear General

...I did not know that he then claimed a right to control my orders with respect to the Army, even if it should be at Crown Point, nor could I imagine he thought so, as your Excellency's instructions to him gave, as I conceive, not the least color for it. Your last letter to me holds up a contrary idea and so does every resolution of Congress hitherto transmitted to me; but that General Gates conceived, and still does, that the Army is immediately under his command, I had a very few hours after the most convincing proof of, as your Excellency will observe from the enclosed paper, which I hastily drew up immediately after the discourse, and which I desired General Gates to read, that no misunderstanding might arise for want of recollecting what had been said and which he acknowledges contains the substance of what passed between us...

If Congress intended that General Gates should command the Northern Army, wherever it may be, as he assures me they did, it ought to have been signified to me and I should then have immediately resigned the command to him; but until such intention is properly conveyed to me I never can. I must, therefore, entreat your

145

Excellency to lay this letter before Congress, that they may clearly and explicitly signify their intentions, to avert the dangers and evils that may arise from a disputed command; for after what General Gates has said, the line must be clearly drawn, as I shall until then stand upon accordingly with General Gates that I would otherwise with pleasure waive; but that the service may not be retarded, nor suffer the least from a difference of opinion between General Gates and me, I have determined to remain here, although I had, before this affair came to light, mentioned to him my intentions of going up with him.

As both General Gates and myself mean to be candid and wish to have the matter settled without any of that deception which would disgrace us as officers and men, we have agreed to speak plain and to show each other what we have written to you upon the occasion, and as he has accordingly read the whole of what I have above said.

Since writing the above, General Gates has shown me the resolutions of Congress of the 17th instant, which confirm me in the opinion I have entertained, that he was only to command the Army in Canada and that I had no control upon him when there...

I am, Dear General, most respectfully, your obedient humble servant,

Ph. Schuyler [25]

As fifty-six members of the Continental Congress approved the Declaration of Independence on the 4th, His Majesty's military was sailing into New York Harbor with 34,000 troops aboard 479 warships in order to protest the document and form a naval blockade. Their plan was to sail up the North (Hudson) River to Albany where Sir William Howe would rendezvous with Sir Guy Carleton's northern fleet to gain control of the river and separate New England from the rest of the Country. Born in 1729, Howe was an aristocrat who attended school at Eton, fought with valor in the French and Indian War, and was an illegitimate uncle of King George III. While serving in Parliament, he condemned his government's coercive policy towards the American colonies and crossed the Atlantic to end hostilities and restore the peace. Shortly after his arrival in Boston, he not only formulated the attack on Breed's Hill, but he led the charge as well, demonstrating undaunted courage under fire. His primary mistake was in forming lines as he had done on the plains instead of columns as should be done on a hill. After three assaults, he had gained the ground, but at a cost of fifty percent casualties. Seeing the carnage before him, he vowed never to take such an aggressive approach again. This attitude along with his interest in conquering

146

acres instead of armies would eventually lead to their inevitable surrender at Yorktown. As a leader, his men described him as a tall figure, well proportioned, graceful, generous, and approachable, but as a strategist, he was sedentary, timid, and inconsistent. The British plan to meet at Albany looked good on paper, but there was just one problem; it lacked depth. The waters of the Richelieu River connecting the St. Lawrence and Champlain were only shallow enough to allow a man to wade across them, not a ship. On the 7th, Captain Charles Douglas, who had served on the St. Lawrence during the Seven Years' War, ordered Lieutenant John Starke to have the fleet dismantled, carried twelve miles overland to St. John's, and reconstructed under the guidance of Captain Thomas Pringle.

To Mr. John Starke, Commanding as Lieutenant
His Majesty's Armed Schooner Maria
                    By Charles Douglas of his Majesty's Ship Isis
                    & Senior Officer in the River St. Lawrence
        Whereas His Majesty's Service requires that a sufficient naval force be with all speed got ready on the Lake Champlain; And whereas it is hoped & thought through the indefatigable zeal of his servants of the Army & Navy in their Country's cause hitherto so manifest the hull of His Majesty's schooner which you command may be transported by land beyond these rapids.
        You are hereby required & directed to exert yourself accordingly to the utmost of your power under the direction of Captain Pringle of His Majesty's armed ship the Lord Howe cooperating therein with the General Officers, engineers & other officers of His Majesty's Army respectively. And should the success of this important enterprise demand the taking down of the said schooner near to the water's edge as she now floats, leaving nothing but the timbers standing; you are hereby authorized to acquiesce in her being taken down to within two streaks of her present line of flotation accordingly; and moreover directed to be yourself aiding & assisting therein as occasion may require.
        For all which this shall be your order.
        Given under my hand on board His Majesty's Schooner Maria at the foot of the rapids of Chambly in Canada the 7th July 1776
                                    Chs Douglas [18]

In a council of war at Crown Point on that same day, Arnold proposed the construction of the first American Navy on Lake Champlain to intercept the British attempt to sever the Colonies. One of the officers present was Baron de Woedtke who was born in Prussia and sent to America with an endorsement from Benjamin Franklin after having served under Frederick the Great.

At a Council of War held at Crown Point
July 7th 1776
The Honorable Major General Schuyler – President
Members:
Honorable Major General Gates
Brig. Genl Sullivan
Brig. Gen Arnold
Brig. Genl De Woedtke

Resolved, that under our present circumstances, the post of Crown Point is not tenable & that with our present force, or one greatly superior to what we may reasonably expect, it is not capable of being made so this summer.

Resolved therefore, that it is imprudent to retire immediately to the strong ground on the east side of the lake opposite to Ticonderoga, with all the healthy and uninfected troops, & that the sick and infected with the small pox be removed to Fort George. It appearing clearly to the council, that the post opposite to Ticonderoga, will the most effectually secure the Country & removing the infected with the small pox, anticipate every objection that may at present retard the Militia (ordered from Congress) from joining the Army.

That the most effectual measures to be taken to secure our superiority on Lake Champlain, by a Naval Armament of gondolas, row galleys, & armed bateaus.

That one or more surveyors be immediately employed to trace out a road between the high ground opposite to Ticonderoga, & the road leading to Skenesborough to the northern settlements. –
P. Schuyler, B. Arnold, H. Gates, B. D. Woedtke, J. Sullivan [18]

At the meeting, Arnold requested that 1,000 men be assembled to construct, sail, and engage the enemy with one man-o-war, eight row galleys, and eight gondolas. The council agreed to the construction of all ships except the man-o-war, which would cost too much time, material, and manpower. Arnold was also given the position of Commander of the Lakes, with Major General Horatio Gates above him in command of Ticonderoga. On the 8th, Hancock directed Gates to put personal grievances aside in order to keep his eye on the mission and not on Schuyler's position. This was done with no further argument from Gates, who took command of Ticonderoga, while Schuyler returned to Albany.

To M General Gates

Philadelphia, July 8ᵗʰ, 1776

Sir

The Congress being informed by letter from General Schuyler to General Washington, which was laid before them at the request of the former, and by your own consent, that a difference of opinion has arisen between General Schuyler & yourself, with regard to the command of the Army in the Northern Department, they immediately took the matter into consideration and have this day come to the enclosed resolution, which I do myself the honor of transmitting in obedience to their commands.

You will there perceive that Congress is of opinion, your command was totally independent of Genl Schuyler, while the Army was in Canada, but no longer, and indeed, the terms in which the Resolve, relative to your appointment, is conceived, seem to show that this was their intention. You were expressly, by that resolve, to take the command of the troops in Canada, words, which strongly imply that they had no design to divest Genl Schuyler of the command while the troops were on this side of Canada. I am however to inform you, that Congress highly approves your resolution and magnanimity that the public service should receive no detriment from any difference of opinion on the occasion. It is their most earnest desire, you will go on to act in the same manner, and cultivate harmony in all your military operations. A good understanding and mutual confidence are so essentially necessary in order to give success to our measures, that I am convinced, they will take place on all occasions between you.

He deserves most of his Country and will undoubtedly meet with the greatest applause, in whatever rank or station he may be, who renders her the most useful and signal services.

I have the honor to be, Sir, with great respect & esteem, your most obedient & very humble servant,

John Hancock
President [67]

That same day, in a letter to Schuyler, he gave the same explanation for the assignments, but expressed his thanks for not putting politics before protocol.

...The Congress highly approves of your patriotism and magnanimity in not suffering any difference of opinion to hurt the public service... [67]

On the **10**th, Lieutenant Colonel Thomas Hartley, a lawyer from Pennsylvania who had served as a member of the Committee of Observation and deputy to the provincial conferences, reported to Arnold that the British were in fact building a fleet of their own at the north end of Lake Champlain.

To Brigadier General Arnold

Crown Point, 10 July 1776

Sir

In pursuance of General Sullivan's orders, I set off from hence on the 5th instant in the afternoon. We had a very great storm that evening which had nearly destroyed several of our boats, and much injured our arms and ammunition. Against a very strong north wind we arrived the second evening at Cumberland Head, proper dispositions were made to provide against a surprise or oppose an enemy if any should appear...

At Hays' we found Hays, Cross, and two other men and by some address we collected the following intelligence – that Cross' father in law had been there within a few days, that he had informed that Generals Carleton and Frazer were at St. John's with a considerable body of Hanoverian and other troops, that they were repairing the works at St. John's, and that seamen were daily employed in cutting wood between that place and the Isle aux Noix, that they were building 3 sloops and 2 schooners at St. John's, which they expected would be soon finished and that they intended immediately to proceed to Crown Point & that the enemy did not mean to injure any of the common people in those settlements...[18]

I am, Sir, your most humble servant,
Thomas Hartley, Lt. Col.
4th Battalion of Pennsylvania

From Crown Point, Arnold issued his initial shipbuilding report to Gates and requested intelligence on Howe's progress from New York.

To Major General Gates

Crown Point, July 10, 1776

Dear General

150

Colonel Hartley arrived from a tour down the lake last night. Enclosed is a copy of his journal. I make no doubt the enemy have a number of vessels in forwardness and will exert themselves in building to command the lake.

I have made a draft of the artisans and have sent you a number of each, as per the enclosed memorandum. I have ordered the oar makers to go between this and Skenesborough. If timber cannot be procured there, they must return here, where it is plenty. I believe the armorers will be wanted at Ticonderoga and some few of the blacksmiths. The others will have employ at Skenesborough. All the house carpenters you doubtless want. The ship carpenters are divided into gangs of fifteen each and will most or all of them be wanted at Skenesborough. I have employed officers to command the artisans, which I believe will expedite the works. I have ordered to Ticonderoga some boards, plank, etc. All that can be procured will be forwarded to you immediately.

I am anxious to hear from New York. You will be kind enough to transmit to General Schuyler a copy of Colonel Hartley's journal.

I am with esteem and affection, Dear General, yours, &c., &c,
B. Arnold

N. B. I sent you about four tons lead yesterday in sheets & ball, & have three tons remaining on hand. None can be found in this fort.

B. A. [18]

Impatient to get the gondolas completed, Gates summoned Arnold to Ticonderoga on the **13**[th] to get the contractors to move with a purpose.

To Brigadier General Arnold
Headquarters Ticonderoga, July 13, 1776
Dear Sir
I am anxious to have you here as soon as possible, as maintaining our naval superiority is of the last importance. I labor continually to get the Commodore to Crown Point with the vessels, but am baffled by the laziness of the artificers or the neglect of those whose duty it is to see them diligent at their work. I hourly expect one or two more gondolas from Skenesborough and shall labor all in my power to get them rigged and armed. I am certain you will not lose a moment in forwarding the troops and stores from the point. We shall be happy or miserable, as we are or are not prepared to receive the enemy.

I am your affectionate humble servant,
Horatio Gates [18]

On the **15ᵗʰ**, Arnold responded that he was relieved to hear the New York report and claimed his commitment to America's first fleet. The news of New York was delivered by his second in command, Brigadier General David Waterbury, a true asset to Arnold on more than one account. The first benefit was his having extensive maritime experience; his second was his extensive military experience as a veteran who had fought in the battles of Lake George and Ticonderoga during the French and Indian War and served under Montgomery during the attack on Quebec.

To Major General Gates

Crown Point, July 15, 1776
Dear General
I received your favors of the 13ᵗʰ and 14ᵗʰ last evening, also a letter this minute respecting the cattle. I am heartily rejoiced at the good news from New York by General Waterbury. I make no doubt the enemy will be baffled in all their efforts. The paymaster is gone this minute for Ticonderoga. Two companies of the train went off early this morning. six regiments were ordered off; so many artillery stores, &c., were remaining, that only four could be supplied with the bateaus. If bateaus arrive this evening, the whole will go off tomorrow morning. tomorrow I expect to have the pleasure of seeing you. We want oars for nearly thirty bateaus lying here, which are at present useless, as none can be procured. We have few cattle on hand; eight or ten yoke may be procured, which the commissary will send to Ticonderoga. Tomorrow Colonel Bedel and Major Butterfield are ordered up and go off immediately. You may depend on my utmost exertion in forwarding our naval armament, on which I think much depends.

I shall detain the inhabitants brought up from below for the present and shall be obliged to leave a small party here. I am at a loss whether I shall remove the families on the Point or not; most of them are unfriendly. I will forward on the troops as fast as possible. All that are able will be sent off by land.

I am with great esteem and affection, Dear General,
your obedient humble servant,
B. Arnold
P. S. If oars can be spared, pray send us one hundred and fifty. [25]

152

Gates followed this up with another letter to Arnold on the 17th, stating that he was unimpressed with Wynkoop and needed to have the best man for the job to lead the fleet.

To Major General Arnold

Ticonderoga, 17th July 1776

Sir

    As I am entirely unacquainted with the Lake below Crown Point, I send the Commodore with the largest & best schooner, to receive his instructions from you in regard to this cruise he ought to make; I think until the rest of the vessels are fitted, it will not be advisable to send this schooner into the narrow part of the lake below. I wish you were here to give directions to putting our whole squadron afloat. It seems to me they are very tardy about it, but am entirely uninformed as to Marine affairs. I like Capt. Mayhew whom you sent here, but I think the Commodore seems slow & wish he retain all that prowess for which he says he was s famous last war. It is of the greatest consequence to our affairs to have the armed vessels commanded by men of firmness & approved courage.

I am, Sir, &c.,

Horatio Gates [18]

    On the 23rd, Arnold arrived at Skenesboro and sent a progress report to Gates the following day.

To Hon. Major General Gates

Skenesborough, July 24, 1776

Dear General

    I arrived here last evening and found three gondolas on the stocks; two will be completed in five or six days, the row galley in eight or ten days. Three other gondolas will be set up immediately and may be completed in ten days. A company of twenty-seven carpenters from Middletown are cutting timber for a row galley on the Spanish construction to mount six heavy pieces of cannon. One hundred carpenters from Pennsylvania and Massachusetts will be here this evening. I shall employ them on another row galley. In two or three weeks, I think we shall have a very formidable fleet. No canvass or cordage is yet arrived, though much wanted. Not one syllable of news from below. There are only one hundred barrels of pork and two hundred of flour here. I have desired Mr. Schuyler to purchase beef for the troops and workmen here. A commissary of provisions is much wanted here and will be more so when the militia arrive, who are daily expected. If Mr. Taylor can be spared, he will be a proper person to send and may purchase a considerable quantity of beef in this neighborhood. I hope the vessels and gondolas will not be retarded for want of seamen or Marines. Those seamen who were sent from Crown Point with Captain Mayhew and afterwards joined their regiments, I would wish were ordered on board the vessels and gondolas. We shall not be able to procure a sufficient number without them.

The mills at Cheshire's are sawing and will produce about four thousand feet of boards each day. All that can be sawed in two weeks will be wanted here. I have ordered the next gondolas that go down to be loaded with boards. I think it will be best to send to Onion River for the boards there and for a parcel lying between Ticonderoga and Crown Point. Mr. Hay can inform where they lie. As soon as I can give the carpenters proper instructions and set them at work, I will return to Ticonderoga.

I am very respectfully, Dear General,
your obedient and humble servant,
B. Arnold [25]

While the tradesmen were busy with their building, Arnold did some reconnaissance around the lake, taking soundings to measure depths and scout out potential ambush sites. He also went to the local lumber mills and selected over 20,000 feet of timber himself that would be used to sail him into history. With the battle destined before him, Arnold wrote out his last will and testament and sent it to his sister Hannah in New Haven. As Arnold scrambled to gather men and materials in the great race to command Champlain, he was summoned to appear in front of a court martial on the **26**[th] at Ticonderoga to answer thirteen charges filed against him by Lieutenant Colonel John Brown. The charges included: slandering Brown, depriving him of a promotion, labeling him a liar, defamation of character, promoting smallpox inoculation, starving his men at Quebec, plundering Montreal, plundering the personal belongings of British prisoners in Canada, cruelly destroying whole villages, exchanging prisoners illegally, and great misconduct. Congress had set up a committee of officers that were all junior to Arnold in rank, to investigate the charges. As he began to fortify his defense against Brown, Arnold also began his offensive campaign against Hazen by filing a formal court martial. On the **28**[th], a formal ceremony and public reading of the Declaration of Independence was made followed by enthusiastic cheers under the roar of a thirteen-gun salute. After careful consideration of the issues at hand, Gates sent a praising report of Arnold's character to Congress, endorsing him to command the country's new Navy.

To Hon. John Hancock, Esquire

Ticonderoga, July 29, 1776

Sir

I am but just now honored with the receipt of your letter of the 8th instant with the resolves of Congress enclosed. As their resolves will ever be held sacred by me, they may be assured of my implicit obedience to them... Affairs here begin to wear a less gloomy aspect. The carpenters are all got to Skenesborough from the different colonies and our fleet is increasing rapidly as it ought. General Arnold, ever active and anxious to serve his country, is just returned from Skenesborough, where he has been to give life and spirit to our dockyard.

Two schooners and a sloop will be at Crown Point this evening, well manned and armed; four gondolas will follow in a day or two. When what we have finished get to Crown Point, we shall have as many armed vessels there as will carry fifty-two pieces of cannon, with all the swivels we have to mount. More swivels are written for to New York and we shall collect all the heavy cannon we can from Albany and the posts upon the communication thither. I wish they may be sufficient. More should be sent could they be procured. The militia begin to come to Skenesboro from when I do not propose to remove them until all the danger of the small pox is far removed from us...

General Arnold, who is perfectly skilled in naval affairs, has most nobly undertaken to command our fleet on the lake. With infinite satisfaction I have committed the whole of that department to his care, convinced that he will thereby add to the brilliant reputation he has so deservedly acquired...

In the meantime, I have appointed the three eldest colonels to command brigades – Colonel Stark, Colonel Reed, and Colonel St. Clair. Should the conduct of gentlemen be such as to merit approbation, (of which I have not the least doubt) I am confident the Congress will show them some honorable mark of esteem... [25]

I am your affectionate humble servant,

Horatio Gates

After one week of attacks to his character by lower ranked officers, Arnold, who was unable to produce proof for his defense, couldn't take any more and told each of his accusers to put their muzzles where their mouths were in a letter on **August 1st**.

To the Court Martial

Ticonderoga, August 1, 1776

Gentlemen

The very extraordinary vote of the court and directions given to the President and his still more extraordinary demand are in my opinion ungenteel and indecent reflections on a superior officer, which the nature and words of my protest will by no means justify; nor was it designed as you have construed it. I am not very conversant with courts martial, but this I may venture to say, they are composed of men not infallible. Even you may have erred. Congress will judge between us; to whom I will desire the General to transmit the proceedings of this court. This I can assure you, I shall ever, in public or in private, be ready to support the character of a man of honor. As your very nice and delicate honor, in your apprehension, is injured, you may depend, as soon as this disagreeable hearing is at an end, (which God grant may soon be the case,) I will by no means withhold from any gentlemen of the court the satisfaction his nice honor may require.

Your demand I shall not comply with.

B. Arnold [25]

In a letter to Gates on the **6th**, the President of the Court-Martial, Colonel Enoch Poor, reflected his disapproval of Arnold's behavior during the proceedings against Hazen. Born in Andover, Massachusetts, Poor was raised on the family farm and became apprenticed to a cabinetmaker before he served in the French and Indian War. After moving to Exeter, New Hampshire, he became a trader, ship builder, and member of the Provincial Congress. Upon the birth of the American rebellion, he commanded one of three regiments that were raised after the battle of Lexington and led them into Boston and Canada.

To the Hon. Major General Gates

Ticonderoga, August 6, 1776

Sir

We do not make a doubt of your having heard that this court has taken umbrage at some part of General Arnold's behavior in the course of his prosecution of Colonel Hazen.

We are sensible men of rank and should be treated with delicacy. We are also sensible that it is our duty to maintain the dignity and authority of the court martial; and that an attempt to lessen the one, or render the other contemptible, is proportionally a greater offence as the person who makes the attempt is in station more elevated, and that passing over such attempts must have the worst effects on the discipline of the Army.

We know we have power to compel parties before us to decent behavior and to punish insults offered to us. It is a power incident to courts and without which they would be ridiculous and nugatory. It is a power, however, we wish not to exercise in the case of General Arnold especially; a power, however, we must use in his case, unless he gives the court the satisfaction they have demanded. Justice to the Army and to our country require it of us. The case is shortly this:

A witness was offered to the court to support the charge brought by General Arnold against Colonel Hazen, to whom exception was taken that he was interested in the event of the trial and therefore not admissible. The court, after hearing the allegations of both parties, adjudged that he was interested and rejected him. Other witnesses were called and the trial went on; after some time, General Arnold again pressed for the admission of the above witness, at the same time observing to the court, that he would enter a protest on their minutes, unless his request should be granted. He was refused. He then offered his protest again against our proceedings, couched, as we think, in indecent terms, and directly impeaching the justice of the court. If he thought by his protest to stop the proceedings, he certainly has not considered how far the practice would lead. If either party has a right to stop the proceedings by protest, both parties must have the right, and there then needs nothing more to secure every offender from punishment. And on the other hand, it would expose a person who might have the misfortune to be obnoxious to his superior officer to perpetual persecution. However conscious of his innocence, in vain would he expect redress from a General Court Martial, for in the very moment of a well-founded expectation of an honorable acquittal, a protest appears and blasts it all, and sends him back to his room a melancholy prisoner. But on the contrary, if his design was no more than by an entry of his protest upon the minutes, to operate against the justice and equity of our proceedings, we must and do consider ourselves as an improper conveyance to our superiors of that protest, which was so replete with crimination and abuse. We could add that the illiberal sentiments of the protest were not the only injury offered us. The whole of the General's conduct during the course of the trial was marked with contempt and disrespect towards the court; and by his extraordinary answer, has added insult to injury.

We mention these things that you may know what were our motives in this matter. And our principal design is this, that through you General Arnold may know the light in which we have seen this matter, which we flatter ourselves you will readily see the propriety of. And from the regard you have for the honor, the discipline, and subordination of the Army, you will not by a sudden dissolution, put it out of our power to obtain that satisfaction we are entitled to.

By order of the Court Martial:
Enoch Poor, President [25]

Putting his focus back on the fleet, Arnold gave Gates an update on the 7th.

To Hon. General Gates

Skenesborough, August 7, 1776
Dear General

I found on my arrival here last evening the galleys much more forward than I expected. Three will be launched in two weeks if not sooner, and timber is cut for three or four others. The carpenters are very industrious and spirited. Nothing will retard the building but want of plank and iron. I have written Captain Varick to hurry on the latter and have ordered the carpenters to omit building more gondolas than those on the stocks; as they take a large quantity of plank and retard the building of the galleys, which are of more consequence. One gondola will be launched tomorrow and the eighth and last in a few days. The seamen will be drafted this afternoon and tomorrow I hope to have the pleasure of seeing you at Ticonderoga.

I am with sentiments of esteem and respect, Dear General,
your obedient humble servant,
B. Arnold

P.S. Militia come in fast. Nothing new at Albany the 4th instant.

B. A. [25]

A List of the Navy of the United States of America on Lake Champlain
Aug. 7th, 1776

Vessel	*Name*	*Car. Guns*	*Swivels*	*Men*
Row Galley	*Congress*	*6*	*16*	*80*
	Washington	*6*	*16*	*80*
	Schuyler	*6*	*16*	*80*
	Lee	*6*	*10*	*65*
Schooner	*Royal Savage*	*12*	*10*	*60*
		Gar. Guns	*Swivels*	*Men*
Sloop	*Enterprise*	*10*	*10*	*60*
Schooner	*Revenge*	*8*	*10*	*40*
	Liberty	*8*	*8*	*35*
Gondola	*New Haven*	*3*	*8*	*45*
	Providence	*3*	*8*	*45*
	Boston	*3*	*8*	*45*
	Spitfire	*3*	*8*	*45*
	Philadelphia	*3*	*8*	*45*
	Connecticut	*3*	*8*	*45*
	New Jersey	*3*	*8*	*45*
	New York	*3*	*8*	*45*

N. B. Each galley mounts two 24-pounders, two 12-pounders, & two 6-pounders. Each gondola mounts one 12 & two 9-pounders.
The sloop & schooner carry three 4 & 6-pounders.
6 gondolas end complete – one galley launched.
The sloop and schooners completed – the whole will be ready completed in the course of this month & four other galleys will be completed by the middle of September. [18]

That same day, Hazen was acquitted on all accounts.

Headquarters, August 7, 1776

Colonel Moses Hazen, tried at a general court martial, of which Colonel Poor is President, and charged with neglect of duty in general and in particular for refusing to receive into the store the goods General Arnold sent to Chambly by Major Scott and not placing proper guards and suffering them to be plundered. The court having deliberately weighed and considered the charge against Colonel Hazen are clearly of opinion it is without foundation; they do therefore adjudge him not guilty and unanimously acquit him with honor. The General confirms the sentence of the court martial and orders Colonel Hazen to be released from his arrest. [25]

With the court martial concluded, Gates issued his official orders for Arnold to take the lake.

Orders and instructions for the Hon. Benedict Arnold, Esq., Brigadier General in the Army of the United States of America.

Upon your arrival at Crown Point, you will proceed with the fleet of the United States under your command down Lake Champlain to the narrow pass of the lake made by the Split Rock or to the other narrow approach down the lake made by Isle-aux-Tetes and the opposite shore. You will station the fleet in the best manner to maintain the possession of those passes according as your judgement shall determine, cautiously avoiding to place the vessels in a manner which might unnecessarily expose them to the enemy's heavy artillery from the shore. You will most religiously observe that it is my positive order that you do not command the fleet to sail blow the pass of the Isle-aux-Tetes, above mentioned, incessantly reflecting, that the preventing the enemy's invasion of our country is the ultimate end of the important command with which you are now intrusted. It is a defensive war we are carrying on, therefore no wanton risk or unnecessary display of the power of the fleet is at any time to influence your conduct. Should the enemy come up the lake and attempt to force their way through the pass you are stationed to defend, in that case you will act with such cool, determined valor, as will give them reason to repent their temerity. But if, contrary to my hope and expectation, their fleet should have so increased as to force an entrance into the upper part of the lake, then, after you shall have discovered the insufficiency of every effort to retard their progress, you will, in the best manner you can, retire with your squadron to Ticonderoga. Every vessel in the fleet being furnished with a bateau, you will have it in your power to keep out scout boats at night and occasionally to annoy the enemy's small craft. In the daytime your boats can act, when opportunity offers, under cover of the cannon of your fleet.

As the most Honorable Congress of the United States rest a great dependence on your wise and prudent conduct in the management of this fleet, you will on no account detach yourself from it, upon the lesser services above mentioned. A resolute but judicious defense of the northern entrance into this side of the continent is the momentous part, which is committed to your courage and abilities. I doubt not you will secure it from further invasion.

As I am entirely unacquainted with Marine affairs, I shall not presume to give any directions respecting the duty and discipline of the seamen and Marines on board the fleet.

I have traced the great outline of that service which your country expects from the rank and character you have acquired. I have, as is my duty, fixed the limits beyond which you are not to go. But you must communicate that restriction to nobody. I wish, on the contrary, that words occasionally dropped from you, with that prudence which excludes every sort of affection, and which I believe, you possess, may, together with all your motions, induce our own people to conclude it is our real intention to invade the enemy, which, after all, may happen. It will keep up their spirits without affecting your reputation, whatever may be the event.

It only remains for me to recommend you to the protection of that power upon whose mercy we place our hopes of freedom here, and of happiness hereafter. You will frequently report the state and situation of your fleet and of every interesting occurrence.

Given at Ticonderoga, this 7ᵗʰ day of August, 1776
Horatio Gates, Major General [25]

As Arnold was gaining more experience and responsibility, Washington wrote to Congress to promote more officers to the General staff, with consideration of their experience and ability to accept responsibility.

To the Hon. John Hancock, &c.

New York, August 7, 1776
Sir

In my letter of the 5ᵗʰ, which I had the honor of addressing you, I begged leave to recall the attention of Congress to the absolute necessity there is for appointing more General Officers, promising, at the same time, by the first opportunity, to give my sentiments more at large upon the subject.

Confident I am that the postponing this measure has not proceeded from motives of frugality, otherwise I should take the liberty of attempting to prove that we put too much to the hazard by such a saving. I am but too well appraised of the difficulties that occur in the choice. They are, I acknowledge, great; but at the same time it must be allowed that they are of such a nature as to present themselves whenever the subject is thought of. Time, on the one hand, does not remove them; on the other, delays may be productive of fatal consequences.

This Army, though far short as yet of the numbers intended by Congress, is by much too unwieldy for the command of any one man, without several Major Generals to assist. For it is to be observed, that a Brigadier General at the head of his brigade is no more than a Colonel at the head of a regiment, except that he acts upon a larger scale. Officers of more general command are at all times wanted for the good order and government of an Army, especially when the Army is composed chiefly of raw troops; but in an action, they are indispensably necessary. At present there is but one Major General for this whole department and the flying camp; whereas, at this place alone, less than three cannot discharge the duties with that regularity there ought to be.

If these Major Generals are appointed, as undoubtedly they will, out of the present Brigadiers, you will want for this place three Brigadiers at least. The Northern Department will require one, if not two, (as General Thompson is a prisoner and the Baron de Woedtke reported to be dead or in a state not much better,) there being at present only one Brigadier (Arnold) in all that department. For the Eastern Governments there ought to be one, or a Major General, to superintend the regiments there and to prevent impositions that might otherwise be practiced. These make the number to be wanted six or seven; and who are to be appointed, Congress can best judge. To make Brigadiers of the oldest Colonels would be the most exceptionable way; but it is much to be questioned whether by that mode the ablest men would be appointed to office. And I would observe, though the rank of Colonels of the Eastern Governments was settled at Cambridge last year, it only respected themselves, and is still open as to officers of other governments. To pick a Colonel here and there through the Army, according to the opinion entertained of their abilities, would no doubt be the means of making a better choice, and nominating the fittest persons; but then their senior officers would get disgusted, and more than probable, with their connections, quit the service. That might prove fatal at this time.

To appoint gentlemen as brigadiers, that had not served in the Army, (in this part of it at least,) would not would any one in particular, but hurt the whole equally and must be considered in a very discouraging light to every officer of merit. View the matter, therefore, in any point of light, you will see there are inconveniences on the one hand and difficulties on the other, which ought to be avoided. Would they be remedied by appointing the oldest Colonels from each state? If this mode should be thought expedient, the enclosed list gives the names of the Colonels from New Hampshire to

Pennsylvania inclusive, specifying those who rank first, as I am told, in the several colony lists...

The paymaster informs me he received a supply of money yesterday. It came very seasonably, for the application and clamors of the troops had become incessant and distressing beyond measure. There is now two months pay due them.

I have the honor to be, with great esteem, your most obedient servant,

G. Washington [25]

Arnold arrived to take command of the fleet at Crown Point on the **16**[th], but on the **17**[th], he came upon another command conflict similar to the one with Ethan Allen during his assault on Quebec. When word arrived that British advance parties were planning an assault on an expedition of men, who were out gathering more timber at Crown Point. In an instant, Arnold dispatched 100 troops to escort the lumberjacks back to the fort. Arnold then issued an order to Captain Isaac Seamon of the schooner *Revenge* and Captain Premiere of the schooner *Liberty* to head south.

To Captain Seamon

Crown Point, August 17, 1776

Sir

You will immediately get your vessels under sail and proceed down the lake seven or eight miles. If you make any discovery of the enemy you will immediately give me notice; if none, return as soon as possible.

B. Arnold, Brigadier General [25]

The schooners did as ordered, but Captain Jacobus Wynkoop, who was appointed Commodore of the Lake by Schuyler, had halted the schooners by firing a shot across their bows. After reading Arnold's orders to the schooner, Wynkoop challenged his authority.

To Brigadier General Arnold

On board the Royal Savage, August 17th*, 1776*

Sir

I find by an order you have given out that the schooners are to go down the lake. I know no orders but what shall be given out by me. If an enemy is approaching I am to be acquainted with it and know how to act in my station.

I am, Sir, yours,

Jacobus Wynkoop

Arnold then demonstrated his authority by putting Wynkoop in his place.

To Captain Wynkoop

Headquarters at Ticonderoga, August 17ᵗʰ, 1776

Sir

I am surprised you should pretend to contradict my orders. I acquainted you some time since that the Commander-in-Chief had appointed me to take command of the Navy on the Lakes, had I not received this appointment from my rank in the Army and as Commander-in-Chief of this post. It is your duty to obey my orders, which you have received and executed for some time past. You surely must be out of your senses to say no orders shall be obeyed but yours. Do you imagine that Congress has given you a superior command over the Commander-in-Chief, or that you are not to be under his direction? If you do not suffer his orders to be immediately complied with, I shall be under the disagreeable necessity of convincing you of your error by immediately arresting you.

B. Arnold,
B Genl & Commr-in-Chief
of the Fleet on Lake Champlain [25]

In explaining the situation to Gates, Arnold confirmed his appointment by him while Wynkoop claimed that Schuyler had given him command of the lake and he wasn't going to be second to anyone except Washington.

To Major General Gates

Crown Point, August 17ᵗʰ 1776, Saturday Night, 8 o'clock

Dear General

About two o'clock this afternoon Colonel Hartley acquainted me, that a party of his men who were posted seven miles down the lake, as a covering party to the oar makers, had made a large fire as a signal that the enemy were approaching. I sent Colonel Hartley with one hundred men to secure the retreat of the party if attacked and ordered the two light schooners down the lake to cover them. They were no sooner under way than Commander Wynkoop fired a shot & brought them to, and soon after sent me a note (copy of which I enclose with my order to the Captains of the schooners and answer to the Commodore's note). I waited some time expecting the vessels to sail, but finding they did not, I went on board the Commodore when he ordered them under sail, he refuses to be commanded by anyone and imagines his appointment, (which is by General Schuyler) cannot be superceded. I have shown him such parts of your instructions as I thought necessary, which has brought him so far to reason. He says if you think proper, he will quit the vessel. I have given him to understand that I shall at all events pursue your orders & that if he did not incline to remain in the service, he would not be compelled to it. Colonel Hartley is not yet returned.

I am with sentiments of respect and esteem &c.,

B. Arnold [18]

To Major General Gates

Crown Point, August 17, 1776

Sir

I have understood that General Arnold is to have the command of the Navy; and if that be so, he ought o have shown me his power to it; but instead of that, he sent an order for two of the schooners to get under way and go down the lake, upon some information he had of the approach of the enemy. was it not his duty to have communicated it to me, and my orders to have been given to the vessels? I have contradicted them, till he acquainted me with some accounts of the enemy and then I immediately issued out my orders for them to go down. Sir, if that be the case, I would be glad of my dismission from the service, for I accepted of this command upon these conditions. Major General Schuyler has a letter which I brought up to him from Congress, that no man was to take the command from me; and when he read the letter, he told me I need not to fear, that no one should have it but me; and the Congress of New York promised me that if any one should arrive here authorized to take the command by the honorable Continental Congress, I wish to be dismissed from the service, and have the command of one of the frigates building up the North River, for I am resolved to go under command of no man. I will receive general orders to sail and how far, and will obey the Commander-in-Chief's orders; but if I have the command, I expect to give orders to the captains of the fleet when I receive them from the Commander-in-Chief. I refer your honor to a copy of my warrant, a copy of Major General Schuyler's letter, and his orders, here enclosed.

Sir, if you find my grievance well founded, I hope your Honor will be pleased to redress it.

I am, Sir, with all due respect,

your Honor's most obedient and very humble servant,
Jacobus Wynkoop, Commander [18]

Arnold sent a report of the communication to Gates that night, whose response of the **18th** stated that Wynkoop was to be apprehended and brought before him.

To General Arnold

Ticonderoga, 18th August 1776

Sir

I have this moment received your letter from Crown Point of yesterday evening. It is my orders you instantly put Commodore Wynkoop in arrest and send him prisoner to headquarters at Ticonderoga. You will at the same time acquaint the officers of the fleet that such of them as do not pay an implicit obedience to your commands are instantly to be confined & sent to me for trial.

I am, Sir, &c.
H. G. [18]

Gates then notified Schuyler of the finality of his decision regardless of command.

To General Schuyler

Ticonderoga, 18th August 1776

Dear General

Thursday, General Arnold went to Crown Point to take the command of the fleet, collected there, enclosed is a copy of my orders to him, which he read and much approved before his departure from hence. Late last night, I received the within letter from the General with an extract of what passed between him and Mr. Wynkoop, which you will also find in the packet together with my letter at daylight this morning, in consequence of General Arnold's letter to me. I shall send Mr. Wynkoop to Albany immediately on his arrival here and I dare say you will without scruple forthwith dismiss him the service. He ought, upon no account, to be again employed. Many officers of rank in this department say he is totally unfit to command a single vessel at this important hour of business. I would not submit this affair to a general court martial here, least they should have doubts how to decide upon it, as the Continental Articles of War make no provision for so extraordinary a circumstance. The times will not admit of trifling. Decision alone must govern these occasions.

I expect Genl Waterbury by Saturday night with the row galleys. As he is an able seaman and a brave officer, I intend he shall join Genl Arnold with the rest of the squadron the instant they can be armed and equipped. As Genl Arnold and he are upon the best terms, I am satisfied no dispute about command or want of confidence in each other will retard the public service.

I am, Dear General, &c.

Horatio Gates [18]

Upon receiving his response from Gates, Arnold notified Wynkoop that he was to be placed into custody at his earliest convenience.

To Jacobus Wynkoop, Commander

Crown Point, August 18, 1776

Sir

The following is a paragraph of a letter and orders I have just received from the Honorable Major General Gates, viz:

'It is my order you immediately put Commodore Wynkoop in arrest and send him prisoner to headquarters at Ticonderoga.

Horatio Gates'

In consequence of the above order, I do hereby put you in arrest, of which you will take notice and govern yourself accordingly. A boat and hands shall be ordered this evening or tomorrow morning to attend you to Ticonderoga. Please to let me know what time will be most agreeable.

I am your humble servant,

B. Arnold, Brigadier General [25]

Getting back to the business at hand, in order to assemble some capable navigators for the battle with the Brits, Arnold went so far as to try to pull people out of their sick beds.

To Dr. Thomas (Jonathan) Potts at Fort George

Crown Point, August 18, 1776

Dear Sir

You have one Robert Aitkins in your hospital, who is an exceeding good pilot for this lake. If his health will possibly admit of his coming here, I beg you will let him have such necessaries as he may want & dispatch him as soon as possible. He belongs to Major Bigelow of the train.

I am, Dear Sir, &c.

P. S. I hope no time will be lost in sending a surgeon, the fleet will be detained until one arrives. – B. A. [18]

Although the letter is addressed to his brother Thomas Potts, it is believed that Arnold had intended the letter for Jonathan Potts, who had been recently appointed by Congress as Surgeon for the Troops on the Canadian Expedition. Potts had been born to an influential family in Popodickon, Pennsylvania, where he received a classical education before delivering the valedictory address to his fellow graduates from the College of Philadelphia (now University of Pennsylvania) with one of the first medical degrees ever to be received in America. With striving ambition, he started a practice and apothecary shop in Reading, Pennsylvania and became a member of the Committee of Safety and Provincial Congress. Meanwhile, Wynkoop, not being notified of Arnold's command beforehand, soon realized his mistake and apologized for it, an apology, which Arnold accepted and transmitted to Gates.

To Major General Gates

Crown Point, August 19, 1776
Dear General
    I received yours of yesterday and have ordered Commodore Wynkoop to headquarters. No other person in the fleet has disrespected my orders. I believe the commodore was really of opinion that neither of us had authority to command him. He now seems convinced to the contrary and is sorry for his disobedience of orders. If it can be done with propriety, I wish he may be permitted to return home without being cashiered.
    I am very respectfully, Dear General, your obedient humble servant,
B. Arnold [25]

On the **23rd**, in addition to two more vessels and men to command them, Arnold finally got his physician along with a New York minute of news from Gates.

To General Arnold

Ticonderoga, 23rd August 1776
Dear General
    This will be delivered to you by Doctor McCrea, whom at the recommendation of Doctor Potts, I have appointed first surgeon to the fleet under your command. He has instruments & medicines, two

things much in request with you. Mr. Francis Hagan accompanies Mr. McCrea as his assistant surgeon. I cannot procure any instruments for him here, but wish you could hire Doctor Speram's for the voyage. You are, I am told, acquainted with Doctor McCrea. I am assured his abilities are their own recommendation. Another gondola sails from hence this morning & the row galley will sail tomorrow. Yesterday, Mr. Titcomb, master carpenter from Skenesborough, returned tither from hence, he got a good recruit of ship carpenters, twelve of his gang being now sick. He is a fine looking fellow and seems desirous to command the row galley he has just finished, he possesses himself a seaman, from the sense and manly appearance of Mr. Titcomb, I think you would do well to appoint him, but I shall not interfere further than to recommend him. I wrote yesterday to General Waterbury, to spur him up to reinforce you with all speed with the row galleys. I am confident he will exert himself to join you as expeditiously as possible. The rumor we heard of an action at New York proves premature. The enemy had embarked from Staten Island, but not landed again when the last accounts came from thence. It is positively asserted that the Hessian General had sent to Genl Washington, to know what treatment the prisoners of that principality were to expect & was answered that they must expect to be treated as hirelings. May health honor & success attend you.

I am, Dear General, &c.

Horatio Gates

Capt. Thatcher of Col. Swift's regiment is just come from Govr Trumbull's where I sent him express. He says you had consented to his commanding a row galley. He seems very fit to do it. [18]

Arnold agreed to Gates' endorsements and on the **24**[th], he activated ten ships that were worthy of sea and strife to head north onto the aquatic battlefield of Lake Champlain. At the front of the column was Arnold aboard the 200-ton, twelve-gun sloop *Royal Savage*, commanded by Captain David Hawley, followed by the ten-gun sloop *Enterprise*, the eight-gun schooners *Revenge* and *Liberty*, and six gondolas *Boston, Connecticut, New Haven, New York, Philadelphia, and Providence*.

On the **29**[th], Schuyler explained the circumstances regarding Wynkoop to Gates.

To the Hon. General Gates

Albany, August 29, 1776

169

Dear General

...Captain Wynkoop has presented me a memorial to Congress, with a request to have it forwarded to them, copy of which I enclose. When I recommended him to the command of the vessels on Lake Champlain, they were few and the Army in Canada; and although I believe him brave, yet I do not think him equal to the command of such a fleet as we now have there. His appointment by the New York Congress you will perceive is only temporary, until another should be appointed; he could, therefore, have no reason to complain, even if an officer of inferior rank to General Arnold had been ordered to take the command...

I am, Dear General, with every friendly wish,
your most obedient, humble servant,
Ph. Schuyler [25]

Meanwhile back in court, the officers had called for Arnold to be put under arrest for challenging them to a duel, but Gates went to bat for him on **September 2nd** in a letter to the president.

To Hon. John Hancock, Esq.

Ticonderoga, September 2, 1776

Sir

...By this conveyance your Excellency will receive a large packet, containing the proceedings of a general court martial held by my order, upon Colonel Hazen, on a complaint exhibited by Brig. General Arnold. The warmth of General Arnold's temper might possibly lead him a little farther than is marked by the precise line of decorum to be observed before and towards a court martial. Seeing and knowing all circumstances, I am convinced there was a fault on one side, the was too much controversy on the other. here again I was obliged to act dictatorially and dissolve the court martial the instant they demanded General Arnold to be put in arrest. The United States must not be deprived of that excellent officer's service at this important moment. I wish your Excellency would represent this affair in the most favorable light to Congress. Upon such occasions there is a way to satisfy complainants without publicly disgracing those complained of, especially when a General officer of acknowledged merit is a party concerned...

With every sentiment of esteem and respect,
I am, Sir, your most obedient and most humble servant,
Horatio Gates [25]

In a letter to Gates on the 7th, Arnold reported one skirmish that his men had encountered on the lake and another that his reputation had encountered in Philadelphia according to a letter from Samuel Chase.

To Major General Gates

Windmill Point, September 7th 1776

Dear General

I wrote you from the 2nd instant from Willsborough by Lieut. Calderwood, the same evening anchored at Schuyler's Island, & on the 3rd instant arrived safe at this place, which is 4 or 5 miles from the Isle aux Tete's occupied by the enemy, and several hundred men encamped, between that & us, who the evening of our arrival made a precipitous retreat.

I have posted my guard boats at a point running into the lake about one mile below us, the enemy's boats have several times appeared on the lake with a view of decoying our boats but I have never suffered them to be pursued. Lieutenant Whitcomb arrived here the 5th in the evening and went off the same night with three men for St. John's on the west side, I sent off Ensign McCoy early this morning on the east side with three men, they are to send me intelligence from time to time; I expect to hear from them tomorrow. Early yesterday morning the boats were ordered on shore to cut fascines to fix on the bows and the sides of the gondolas to prevent the enemies boarding and to keep off small shot. One of the boats went on shore contrary to orders before the others were ready, they were attacked by a party of savages, who pursued them into the water. They all reached the boat, but before they could row off, three were killed and six wounded. The party was headed by a regular officer, who called to our people to resign themselves, on our firing a few shot among them they immediately dispersed. A party was sent on shore who found a laced beaver hat, the button marked the 47th regiment. The Lee and gondola arrived here yesterday morning, we are moored in a line across the lake in such a manner, it will be impossible for a bateau to pass us.

I hope the galleys are nearly completed, the force of the enemy is uncertain, however they have this advantage that they can man all their bateau with soldiers whenever they think proper to attack us and our vessels are so low that numbers may carry them by boarding, this must be attended with great loss on their side, as I am positive they will not be able to surprise us. If I find the enemy have a considerable naval force I design to retire to Cumberland Head or Schuyler's

171

Island until joined by the three row galleys, which will be superior to all our present force, when the whole are joined, I believe the Isle La Motte will be the best stand as the enemy can bring nothing against us by land nor will they dare to come on the island, as by our guard boats we can prevent any boats going from Missisque Bay. As you have more troops at Ticonderoga than you want, will it not be prudent to send up one thousand or fifteen hundred men, who might encamp on the Isle La Motte and be ready at all times to assist us if attacked; twenty men to a bateau will be sufficient, they might load under cover of the vessels, push out and fire, & retire under cover again, & if the enemies boats should make their principal attack on any particular vessel, these bateau might assist her; each should be fixed for a swivel in each end and if they are armed one should be fixed in them. If you should think it necessary to send a detachment, it will be necessary to bring entrenching tools, that they may cover themselves from small arms.

We have but very indifferent men in general, great part of those who shipped for seamen know very little of the matter. Three or four good gunners are wanted. Enclosed is a list of our sick, who increase fast, I have sent up in three bateau 23 men, who will be of no service for some time, I wish 50 seamen could be procured and sent down. I enclose you a letter from Samuel Chase Esq. you will observe he requests an explanation of your letter to Mr. Adams. He observes my character is much injured by a report prevailing in Philadelphia of my having sequestered the goods seized in Montreal, as you have had an opportunity of hearing that matter canvassed on the trial of Colonel Hazen, I beg you will be kind enough to write your sentiments to him on the matter. I cannot but think it extremely cruel, when I have sacrificed my ease, health, and great part of my private property in the cause of my country, to be culminated as a robber and thief, at a time when I have it not in my power to be heard in my own defense.

The 15th of August when we left Ticonderoga the fleet was supplied for thirty days, which time is elapsed except 6 days, we have on board the fleet six or eight days provision besides twenty barrels of flour, left at Crown Point to be baked, and ten barrels of pork which I have ordered Lieutenant Calderwood to bring down, which will serve the fleet to the 20th, as the lake is often difficult to pass for a number of days we ought to have at least one month's provisions on hand. Major Greer goes up with the sick to whom I must refer you for particulars.

We are very anxious to hear from New York, hope soon to have that pleasure by one of the galleys, which I think must be completed by this time.

Please to make my compliments to the gentlemen of your family and believe me with much respect, esteem, and affection,

Dear General,

I am your most humble servant,

B. Arnold [18]

On the **8th**, Arnold notified Gates that he had launched the fleet to its first defensive position at the Isle La Motte at the northern end of the lake.

To Major General Gates

Isle La Motte, September 8th 1776

Dear General

When I wrote the foregoing letter I designed sending off the bateau last evening but was prevented by the stormy weather. Last night the enemy was heard by the guard boats and the people on board the vessels near inshore on both sides of us, several trees were felled and lights discovered. I believe the enemy were erecting batteries, which might have injured us as the lake is only one and a quarter miles over and their design was doubtless to have attacked us both by land and water at the same time. I make no doubt we should have been more than a match for them, but did not think it prudent to run any risk, as it would answer no good purpose. I therefore ordered the fleet underway this morning, and at 2 o'clock P. M. anchored at this place. Here the lake is about two miles over and safe anchorage. We effectually secure any boats passing us – just as we came to anchor, Lieutenant Brooks came on board, sent down by Colonel Hartley in consequence of hearing our cannon fired at the Indians on Sunday morning. I have thought it necessary to dispatch him back again that you may be out of suspense with regard to us. Four guard boats are constantly out, the rounds go every two hours at night, and every precaution is taken to prevent being surprised.

Our men are extremely bare of clothing and the season is coming on severe & more so on the water than land. If a watchcoat or blanket & one shirt could be sent for each man, it will be of great service for them. Rum is another necessary article. When the Howitz arrive, I beg three or four of six inches may be sent us mounted, on field carriages, with shells &c. &c. 50 swivels are much wanted, the last vessels have none. [18]

I am with much respect, esteem, and affection, Dear General,
your humble servant,
B. Arnold

On the **15ᵗʰ**, Arnold revealed a great little ambush site behind Valcour Island, just south of Plattsburgh.

To Hon. Major General Gates

Isle La Motte, September 15ᵗʰ 1776

Dear General

Your favor of the 12ᵗʰ instant was delivered me last night by Ensign Botsford, who narrowly escaped being lost in his passage down and was obliged to throw overboard three barrels of provision to lighten the bateau. I am happy to find, you approve of my returning from the Isle aux Tetes (Rouse's Point), *our present situation is five miles to the southward of Point aux Fire and two miles to the southward of the north end of Isle La Motte, at a part of the island where the lake is one and a half to two miles over, to the southward of us there is no part of the lake less than two miles over and entirely out of the reach of any batteries that can possibly be erected by the enemy of whose naval force I have been able to procure no other intelligence, than from a deserter one Thomas Day whom I have sent you by Ensign Botsford with his examination; which is enclosed. I have heard nothing from Lieutenant Whitcomb or Ensign McCoy since they left the Isle aux Noix, from which a man returned from each party, who agree that there is about one thousand men encamped there, they saw no watercraft except bateau.*

I have dispatched a Frenchman to St. John's for intelligence, whom I found in the Bay of Missisque, he has promised to return in four days with intelligence. If I hear nothing from St. John's soon, I design making a remove to the Island Valcour until joined by three galleys. There is a good harbor and if the enemy venture up the lake it will be impossible for them to take advantage of our situation, if we should succeed on our attack on them it will be impossible for any of them to escape, if we are worsted our retreat is open and free, in case of wind which generally blows fresh at this season our craft will make good weather, when their bateaus cannot keep the lake.

I am glad to hear General Waterbury has taken charge of the galleys, I make no doubt they will soon be completed, my best pilot I sent up by Major Greer.

I requested General Schuyler to send for four captains for the galleys, since which I have appointed only two, at that time three galleys were nearly finished and four others ordered to be put on the stocks, which still left a vacancy for one captain. Captain Warner is one of the four which was requested: one of the others I wish sent for the Royal Savage, the third for the galley on the stocks and the fourth for one of the others ordered to be built, which ought to be put on the stocks long before this. The greatest part of the timber was cut for the four last galleys before I left Skenesborough, and as the carpenters and materials are procured, will it not be prudence and economy to have them completed.

In my last I wrote you were provided to the 20th instant. For that calculation I computed ten barrels of pork and twenty of flour left at Crown Point, which I ordered to be sent down in the last gondola, the order was neglected and the provisions left behind so that the supply sent now will provide us no longer than the 26th instant unless supplied by the inhabitants on the lake of which there is little prospect. Cannot a Frenchman or two, who is acquainted in Canada and can be depended upon, be sent me with the tobacco. I keep the two small schooners continually cruising above and below us. The countersign is never given until four o'clock, two guard boats are posted every night two miles below us, at a proper distance to discover the approach of the enemy, another boat goes the rounds every two hours all night, every ship keeps half her men constantly on deck under arms, and matches lighted, it will be impossible for the enemy to surprise us.

I am greatly obliged to you for the friendly notice you have taken of me in your public letter, which I make no doubt will have the desired effect.

I am surprised you have received no particular accounts of the Battle on Long Island, the severe check of the enemy have met with will doubtless dispirit them greatly and will I hope prove a happy prelude to our future success, I hope you will soon have the particulars of the affair. The act of independence, I will send, agreeable to your direction.

I am with sentiments of respect and esteem, Sir,
your most obedient and most humble servant,
B. Arnold [18]

On the **18th**, Arnold gives Gates an update on the progress and possible intentions of the British fleet. Based on a long awaited report given to him by Lieutenant Benjamin Whitcomb, Arnold knew that if they build it, they will come.

175

To Hon. Major General Gates

Isle La Motte, September 18*th* 1776

Dear General

My last was the 16*th* instant by Ensign Botsford; the next morning, Lieutenant Whitcomb and his party returned from St. John's with two prisoners, Ensign Sanders and a corporal of the 29*th* regiment, who were taken between St. John's and La Prairie. The ensign says there is a ship on the stocks at St. John's, designed to mount twenty guns, nine and twelve pounders, several schooners, and small craft; but seems ignorant as to their size and numbers. He says there was talk of crossing the lake soon; but in general it was thought they would not cross this fall. Both him and the corporal seem cautious of giving any information...

I am inclined to think, on comparing all accounts, that the enemy will soon have a considerable naval force. The ship, the ensign says, will be completed in two weeks and is to be manned from the Navy in the river.

I make no doubt of their soon paying us a visit, and intend first fair wind to come up as high as Isle Valcour, where 'tis a good harbor, and where we shall have the advantage over the enemy; and if they are too many for us, we can retire. I believe their Army crossing the lake, depends entirely on the advice they may receive from New York.

I beg that at least one hundred good seamen may be sent me as soon as possible. We have a wretched motley crew, in the fleet; the Marines, the refuse of every regiment, and the seamen, few of them, ever wet with salt water. We are upwards of one hundred men short of our compliment.

Ensign Bush arrived here last night and brought four beeves, which is all the fresh provisions we have received. By him I send up Lieutenant Whitcomb and his prisoners. I could wish to have a six or eight inch howitz mounted in two or three of the galleys. If they are arrived, they will be of infinitely more service than guns especially to attack a large vessel. If the grape and chain shot is arrived, I beg it may be sent with some good slow match and three cables and anchors. We have not a spare one in the fleet and the blowing season is now coming on. There is a small brass royal at Ty, which, with a hundred shells and a gunner, may be very useful to us. I am anxiously waiting to hear the particulars of the affair at New York; we are told our troops have evacuated Long Island. This I cannot credit.

I am with sentiments of respect and esteem, Sir,

your most obedient and most humble servant,

B. Arnold [25]

On the same day, a British logistics report showed Arnold's concerns to be true, for they had indeed produced a considerable naval force.

"Force on the Lake Tolerably Exact, on Sept. 18th 1776"

Inflexible   will be ready in 8 days   16. . 12 lbs. & 2. .9 lbs.
Commanded by Lieut. John Schanck of his Majesty's armed ship *Canceaux*

Maria   quite ready   14. . 6 lbs.
Commanded by Lieut. John Starke

Carleton   ditto   12. . 6 lbs.
Commanded by Lieut. James Richard Dacres of the *Blonde*

Radeau   ditto   6. . 24 lbs. – lower deck
(*Thunderer*)   6. . 12 lbs. – quarter deck
                                               2. . 12 lbs. – forecastle
                                               2 howitzers – most use
Commanded by Lieut. John Stone of the *Lizard*

Retaken gondola   (*Loyal Convert*)   6. . 6 lbs. & 2. . lbs.
Commanded by Lt. Edward Longcroft of the *Brunswick*

6 gunboats   each   1. . 9 lbs.
8 gunboats   each   1. . 6 lbs.
14 gunboats   Army guns of different caliber howitzers
Each of the above commanded by a Petty Officer

4 long boats   each   1. . 3 lbs.

26 other transport long boats to convey provisions and about 450 bateaus for the conveyance of troops. [18]

In a letter to Gates on the **21**[st], Arnold reported another skirmish at Vermont's Isle La Motte and confirmed the strategic benefits of the bay between the New York shore and Grand Isle in the middle of the lake known as Valcour.

To Hon. Major General Gates

Bay St. Amand, September 21, 1776

Dear General

My last was the 18*th* instant, by Lieutenant Whitcomb. The next day at noon weighted anchor with the whole fleet, which arrived here the same evening. This is a fine bay and good anchorage, two leagues to the northward of Cumberland Head, on the west shore. The Liberty was ordered to cruise off the Isle-la-Motte until two o'clock and then join the fleet. On her return, opposite the Isle-la-Motte, a Frenchman came down and desired to be taken on board; the captain suspected him and went near the shore with his boat, stern in, swivels pointed, and match tiled; the Frenchman waded near a rod from the shore, but when he found he could decoy the boat no farther, he made a signal to the enemy, when three or four hundred Indians, Canadians, and regulars rose up and fired on the boat; they wounded three men. The boat returned the fire with their swivels and small arms, and the schooner fired several broadsides of grape before they dispersed, though several were seen to fall. On their way down, they discovered a large party of savages on the western shore; they imagined two or three hundred. They have a large number of white birch canoes, with which they can pass us in the night and in the daytime secure them in the bushes. It will be dangerous sending down single boats. I have sent up the Liberty to guard the return boats and bring down the medicines &c. The surgeons can be of no use to us without. Captain Hawley is appointed to the Royal Savage.

I must renew my request for more seamen and gunners; there is plenty of the former in the Army, provided they have liberty of enlisting. Though it is a bad precedent, this emergency will justify the measure. I am greatly at a loss what could have retarded the galleys so long. I verily believe if we are attacked this fall by the enemy, it will be in the course of a week or ten days; the want of those galleys may decide the contest against us.

I am surprised our intelligence from New York is so imperfect. I hope we shall soon have the particulars. The tobacco papers were delivered me. I will endeavor to send them soon. The articles I wrote for in my last, I hope will be sent if possible. I have sent up Mr. Dunn to collect the shot and other articles I want and bring them down.

We had an exceeding gale here the 20*th* and a prodigious sea. The galleys rode it out beyond my expectation.

I have sent two boats to sound round the Island Valcour, who report that it is an exceeding fine and secure harbor. I am determined *to go there the first fair wind, as the fleet will be secure and we can discover the enemy if they attempt to pass us up the east bay on the back of Grand Isle. I make no doubt you will approve of this measure; if not, I will return to any of my former stations. We are as well prepared for the enemy as our circumstances will allow: they will never have it in their power to surprise us. The men are daily trained to the exercise of their guns, and if powder was plenty, I would wish to have them fire at a mark with their great guns often. At present we cannot afford it.*

I wish the workmen could all be employed on one galley and finish her first, that something might be added to the fleet. I cannot help thinking that they are hindering each other; there was all the material sufficient for one when I came away. I hope they will not mount twelve-ponders, if eighteens or twenty-fours can be procured.

I am with great respect and esteem, Dear General, your affectionate obedient humble servant,
B. Arnold
P. S. The drafts from the regiments at Ticonderoga are a miserable set; indeed the men on board the fleet in general are not equal to half their numbers of good men.

B. A. [18]

On the **26**[th], Gates gave Arnold a logistics report, making the point that he could not send what he did not have. In closing, he sent a report of a skirmish involving Colonel John Trumbull, the Governor's son and his regards to Arnold's third in command, Colonel Edward Wigglesworth, a third generation Harvard graduate. Born in 1756, young Trumbull had also graduated from Harvard and applied his craft of drawing in order to reveal the layout of enemy entrenchments at Boston, which granted him an appointment as one of Washington's aides and presently as deputy adjutant general to Gates.

To Brigadier General Arnold
26th *September 1776*
Dear General
Yesterday I received your letter of the 21st *instant. I hope your little schooner had ample satisfaction for the injury her people suffered in the bateau.*
This will be delivered to you by Captain Warner of the Trumbull Row Galley. She carries you a fine reinforcement of seamen & besides is herself a considerable addition to your squadron. The schooner & the two other galleys will follow Sunday or Monday at

farthest; but the cordage is not yet arrived and General Waterbury assures me that if your estimate was as large as you mention it to have been, not more than a third of it can have been sent; as more than twenty coils of rigging are now wanted for the galleys already built. The powder wrote for so long ago is not even in part received at Ticonderoga; economy is the word. You cannot be more anxious to have all the galleys with you than we are to send them. Be satisfied; more cannot be done than is done to dispatch them.

  Col. Trumbull writes you an account, or rather, rumor of action that happened last Sunday near Turtle Bay. When any thing to be depended upon arrives, I will send it to you without delay. Enclosed is Dr. Potts' letter to me, which I received last night. My affectionate compliments to Col. Wigglesworth.

I am, &c.,
Horatio Gates [18]

  On the **28**[th], Arnold wrote to Gates from his new concealed position behind Valcour Island.

To Hon. Major General Gates

Isle Valcour, Sept 28th *1776*

Dear General

  My last was from the Bay St, Amont the 22nd *instant by Capt Dunn, which make no doubt you have received. The next day the fleet arrived safe at this place, (which is an excellent harbor) we are moored in a small bay on the west side of the island as near together as possible & in such form that few vessels can attack us at the same time & then will be exposed to the fire of the whole fleet.*

  The 25th *I dispatched into Canada a German who was mate of the Revenge & a New England man, who speaks French well, both are sensible fellows & may be depended on, they are extremely well acquainted with the country, go in character of deserters, & have proper instructions & credentials. (Sixteen of each sort) sewed up between the sols of their shoes. As they run a great risk, I have promised them (in case they succeed) five hundred dollars between them; as soon as they know the success of their embassy, they are to return. One of them was a Ranger with Major Rogers all last war, has since lived in Canada & knows the woods perfectly. Two men are stationed on the Isle La Motte to watch the motions of the enemy.*

  Early yesterday morning Sergeant Strictland with twelve men in a provision bateau passed this place & went as far as Point Au Fere, but not finding the fleet returned. The Revenge (on a cruise) picked them up at 6 o'clock last night, the sergeant took the schooner for an enemy & stupidly destroyed all his letters & papers when she was at a distance from him, which was very mortifying to me as I am deprived the pleasure of your letter & have a long time anxiously waited for the particulars of the affair at New York. This fellow can give me no manner of intelligence respecting the galleys or anything else. I expect them every minute, as the time is elapsed in which you wrote they would be ready.

Colonel Hartley writes me that one galley was expected at Crown Point the 26th & that the others would be there the 27th, there is a fine wind for the enemy to come down. If they appear too strong for us, I will retire until I meet the galleys.

I am with great respect and esteem, Dear General, your affectionate obedient humble servant, B. Arnold [18]

With only half of his fleet completed, Arnold had to change his battle plan to one of a defensive ambush than the offensive attack that he was hoping to conduct, as revealed in a letter to Gates on **October 1st**.

To Hon. Major General Gates

Valcour, October 1, 1776

Dear General

Last night the Trumbull galley arrived here, and Captain Warner delivered me your letter of the 26th ultimo. I was rejoiced to hear she brought a reinforcement of seamen. I expected at least one hundred, but, was much surprised when Captain Warner informed he had not one save his own ship's company. I hope to be excused (after the requisitions so often made) if with five hundred men, half naked, I should not be able to beat the enemy with seven thousand men, well clothed, and a naval force, by our best accounts, near equal to ours. The Trumbull is a considerable addition to our fleet, but not half finished or rigged; her cannon are much too small.

I wrote in July for cordage sufficient for eight galleys; I then supposed that number would be built. I am surprised at their strange economy or infatuation below. Saving and negligence, I am afraid, will ruin us at last.

Colonel Trumbull writes me a very imperfect account of the affairs at New York. I am all impatience to hear the particulars and know the event.

Enclosed is a list of sundry articles which I have sent Lieutenant Calderwood to bring down, if to be had. Great part of my seamen and Marines are almost naked. The weather has been very severe for some time. I don't expect to be able to keep my station above fourteen days longer. We have continual gales of wind and the duty very severe.

I ordered the captain of the Liberty to stay no longer than to overhaul his vessel, which might have been done in forty-eight hours. I beg you will be kind enough to order him back immediately. If he brings materials, his vessel may be here in one day.

This minute Sergeant Stiles is returned from a scout to the Isle-aux-Noix, where he was sent this day week. Enclosed is his examination, by which it appears the enemy are exerting every nerve to augment their Navy, doubtless with a design to cross the lake this fall or be an overmatch for us next spring.

Colonel Wigglesworth joins me in respectful compliments.

I am, Dear General, your affectionate and obedient humble servant,

B. Arnold [25]

On the **10th**, Arnold expressed his relief to Gates when the much-needed clothing had finally arrived and assured him that he would not jump the gun if the enemy appears.

To Major General Gates

Valcour, Oct. 10th, 1776

Dear General

Your favor of the 3rd instant was delivered to me on the 7th by Captain Premiere. I am much surprised so little attention is paid to us by the good people below, I should have imagined, two hundred seamen could have been sent us in three or four months after they were so pleasingly wrote for. I make not the least doubt there has been the greatest industry used at Ticonderoga in fitting out the fleet, I am glad to hear the other galley is so forward, I expect to see her the first fair wind.

The clothing which is arrived is a sufficient supply of the kind we much want; one hundred pair shoes & hose, one hundred watch coats, fifty pair breeches, & twenty blankets & hats or caps. We are provisioned for about ten days.

You may depend I shall do nothing of consequence without consulting Genl Waterbury & Colonel Wigglesworth, both of whom I esteem judicious, honest men & good soldiers. We cannot at present determine how long it will be requisite to remain here. One minute sooner than is prudent & necessary.

I have received no late intelligence from the northward, the loss of the small canoes (all we had) has prevented my sending out small parties. I have wrote Colonel Trumbull to send me three or four which may be procured at Crown Point.

I am of opinion with you respecting the battery building at river a cote, that the enemy are acting on the defensive, they are at the same time exerting themselves to augment their Navy & if they hear (in time) that Lord Howe is in possession of New York, they will doubtless attempt a junction with him. If they think it practicable, their fleet, I make no doubt in the course of this month will be very formidable, if not equal to ours.

I have taken two 4-pounders from the Liberty for the Trumbull & three of her small guns, there are others at Crown Point suitable for her & Colonel Hartley may be supplied with large ones for his castle from Ticonderoga. The schooner goes up for provisions. I wish she may be immediately dispatched back – the guns may be ready when she returns, at present, she does not want them.

I am extremely glad you have represented to Congress & Genl Schuyler the absolute necessity of augmenting our Navy on the Lake. It appears to me an object of the utmost importance, I hope measures will be immediately taken for that purpose. There is water between Crown Point & Point aux Feu for vessels of the largest size. I am of opinion that row galleys are of the best construction & cheapest for this lake, perhaps it may be well to have one frigate of thirty six guns, she may carry eighteen pounders on the lake & will be superior to any vessel that can be built at & floated from St. John's. Carpenters ought to be immediately employed to cut timber & plank & three hundred set at work at Skenesborough the 1st of February. Of these matters I hope we shall have time to confer hereafter.

General Waterbury and Colonel Wigglesworth join me in affectionate compliments.

I am with great esteem and regard, Dear General, your obedient and humble servant,
B. Arnold

P. S. If you have read Price's pamphlet, sent to you by Mr. Franklin, I will take the loan of it a favor.

B. A. [25]

That same day, the ten-gun row galleys: *Congress*, *Trumbull*, and *Washington* joined the fleet in a crescent shaped battle line.

183

Strategically anchored stem to stern just one half-mile north of the southern tip of the island, the guns of the ships providing deadly coverage from both the north and south approaches. Arnold was playing hide to the British Navy's seek, which had been searching for him behind coastal islands and inside shore-line coves to the north. On the morning of the 11th, Arnold transferred his flag from the *Royal Savage* to the *Congress* in the center of the line with Waterbury in the *Washington* on the right flank and Wigglesworth in the *Trumbull* on the left. At about 10 o'clock the *Revenge* returned from its patrol to report the approach of the British fleet. Carleton and Pringle sailed aboard the flagship schooner *Maria*, which was named in honor of Carleton's wife, placed under the command of Lieutenant John Starke, and armed with 14 six-pounders. The schooner *Carleton*, commanded by Lieutenant James Richard Dacres, carried 12 six-pounders. The captured American gondola, *Loyal Convert* hailed 7 nine-pounders under the command of Lieutenant Edward Longcroft. The radeau *Thunderer* supported 6 twenty-four pounders, 6 twelve-pounders, and 2 howitzers under Lieutenant John Stone and measured ninety-one feet in length. The 180-ton *Inflexible*, commanded by the mechanically gifted Lieutenant John Schanck, a man from Fifeshire, Scotland with nineteen years at sea, bore 16 twelve-pounders and a pair of nines under three masts.

Upon hearing this, Arnold dispatched Wigglesworth to observe their motions, which he later reported back that they had rounded the island. Arnold ordered the *Royal Savage* and the three galleys under way to act as decoys and draw the enemy in. Not wanting to become enveloped by the enemy, Waterbury suggested that all ships engage the enemy on the lake while the wind was in their favor, but Arnold held firm to his strategy to fight them on his terms. One of the decoys caught the attention of Dr. Robert Knox, the physician to the British fleet, who spied the vessel just as it disappeared behind Valcour. Upon sighting it, he alerted Pringle aboard the *Maria*, who dispatched a tender to investigate. The tender approached the island cautiously, muskets at the ready. Peering around the opposite side, the crew discovered Arnold's floating fortress in a firing squad formation, their guns pointing straight at them. Having just been served an eyeful of how the Americans spent their summer vacation, the tender dashed back out towards the center of the lake. With a single shot from a signal gun, the tender passed the word, "it's on." As the drummers beat to quarters, men on all decks race to their assigned positions. Pre-battle butterflies fill the stomachs of all, but the look in every man's eyes mirrors the man next to him, a look confirming the bond between them, the look of courage, King, and country.

The British tacked to approach, but were struggling against a south wind, just as Arnold had hoped for. Unfortunately on its way back to the formation, the same wind caught the *Royal Savage* leaving it exposed and vulnerable. When the *Inflexible* got within firing range of her, the British launched a barrage of chain shot, which shredded sails, lines, rigging, and the ability to maneuver. This was followed by a wind shear that pushed the *Savage* towards the island's southwest shore, where it became suspended on a shallow ledge. Coming in for the kill, the *Inflexible* fired a lethal dose of shells through her stern railing severing life and limb before she ran aground and pitched halfway on her side like a beached whale. A longboat was lowered by Hawley from the *Savage* for men to fill while others leaped into the water and swam for the island. There they fended against Indians that had landed on both shores to fire on the Americans. When the British witnessed Hawley trying to tow the *Savage* off from the shallows, they opened up and sank him. From the *Loyal Convert*, Longcroft ordered a boarding party onto the *Savage*, which captured twenty prisoners before turning the ship's guns on the American fleet.

On board the *Congress*, the men were led by Arnold's example up close and personal. With his own bare hands, he aimed a bow gun at the *Maria* that sent a shot sailing between Governor Guy Carleton and his brother Thomas, the quartermaster general, which exploded behind them and sent them both to the deck. The explosion brought Pringle to order the *Maria* out of the bay and the gunboats to move in, but they were soon sunk by American cannon blasts as they tried to gain the advantage in the shallow waters. One precision shot from another American ship ignited the magazine in a Hessian gunboat, causing a massive explosion that launched men into the water. Other bateaus came to their rescue, but were nearly swamped by the overcrowding. While the *Inflexible* was harpooning the *Savage*, the *Carleton* pursued the *Enterprise* into the bay before Dacres realized that it was a trap. Like a man against a firing squad, the American fleet unleashed a murderous volley of cannon fire against the lone Brit ship. As she turned to port to fire her cannons, she received another violent barrage. The anchor line was dropped, but was severed by a shot that could not have been more accurate, which set her adrift with her bow into the wind and into the blazing guns before her, raking her hull and taking virtually every life on deck. As Dacres was knocked unconscious and a Midshipman Brown officer suffered the loss of an arm, nineteen-year-old, Midshipman Edward Pellew from Dover, England summed up the courage to free the ship from its snare. With hot metal flying all around him, he climbed out onto the bowsprit and struggled to swing the jib sail to windward. Although unsuccessful in his efforts, his gallantry inspired the crew to keep up the fight until two longboats under John Curling and Patrick Carnegy maneuvered close enough to catch a towrope from him and haul her out of harm's way. Once it had cleared, the *Inflexible* took its place, but withdrew shortly afterwards as well. The *Thunderer* then moved in to serve as relief for the *Inflexible*, but the onset of dusk prevented her from inflicting any significant retaliation. According to a diary entry made by a British sailor named, Joshua Pell, Jr., the wind served as an ally to the Americans.

10th Oct'r – Our little squadron sailed from Point au Fer toward the upper or great lake; about 12 o'clock on the 11th, one of our armed boats spied their fleet at anchor in the Bay of Valcour. Our armed boats immediately rushed in amongst them and engaged them without waiting for orders; the Carleton went to their assistance and kept a continual firing until dark, during which time we destroyed a schooner called the Royal Savage and greatly damaged another. Unluckily for us, the wind changed and hindered the other part of our squadron from giving the Carleton any assistance. Had it not happened, in all probability, the Rebels whole fleet would have been destroyed. Our loss consist in two armed boats been sunk; about ten men killed and sixteen wounded. The loss of the Rebels is not positively known.

I do justice to Capt'n Dacres, he behaved like a true British Tar; he was engaged by five of them together and when ordered to join his squadron, he would not till the General's own boat came on board with positive orders to desist.

The Rebel's fleet consisted of sixteen sail of schooners, sloops, and row galleys. The Rebels anchored close under the land and our Indians did them considerable damage with their small arms from the shore. [18]

As the sun fell below the horizon, so did the sound of the guns. While the British were busy raiding and torching the abandoned *Royal Savage*, Arnold held a battle assessment briefing in his cabin. The casualties totaled about sixty including every officer on the *Lee* and half of the officers on the *Washington*. Several ships had also sustained heavy damage and were leaking. The *Congress* had been drilled a dozen and a half times; the *Philadelphia,* commanded by Captain Benjamin Rue, had taken a twenty-four pound shot from the *Thunderer* and was sinking beyond repair; the *Royal Savage* had been set afire and was burning beyond recognition; the mainmast of the *Providence* looked as though it had taken a shark bite from a great white; and the foremast of the *Washington* was completely shot through. With three-quarters of their powder spent, Arnold knew that they would not be able to sustain another full day of fighting, but if they were still afloat, then they could still flee. He decided to make a run for it, thirty-five miles south to Crown Point. In order to maintain noise discipline, he had the wounded transferred to the galley cabins so that the enemy could not hear their groans and had all of the oars muffled with sheepskins so as to prevent detection of their movement. As the flames from the *Royal Savage* delivered the perfect distraction, the evening mist rising off the lake on a moonless night served as the ultimate mask, now making the American fleet virtually invisible. At 7 o'clock that evening, Arnold had the formation wheel to the south, form a single line, and attach a shrouded lantern to each bow. With a galley in the lead and Arnold providing rear security, the flotilla filed out in stealth right under the enemy's nose, thus giving a new meaning to the term, "the fog of battle."

When the sun and mist of the fog rose on the next morning of the 12th so did the eyebrows of the British, who were shocked to see that Arnold and his fleet had slipped by unnoticed. Carleton was furious and immediately ordered patrol boats to the north, thinking that Arnold would take this opportunity to attack the now unguarded British post at Windmill Point. At about noontime, a boat did discover their true bearing to the south and alerted the fleet, which continued its deadly pursuit. During a repair stop at Schuyler's Island, just six miles south of the offensive, Arnold sent a report of the engagement to Gates.

To Hon. Major-General Gates
                                      Schuyler's Island, Oct. 12, 1776
Dear General
        Yesterday morning at eight o'clock, the enemy's fleet, consisting of one ship mounting sixteen guns, one snow mounting the same number, one schooner of fourteen guns, two of twelve, two sloops, a bomb-ketch and a large vessel, fifteen or twenty flat-

bottomed boats or gondolas carrying one twelve or eighteen-pounder in their bows appeared off Cumberland Head. We immediately prepared to receive them. The galleys and Royal Savage were ordered under way; the rest of our fleet lay at anchor. At eleven o'clock they ran into the wind of Valcour and began the attack. The schooner, by some bad management, fell against the wind and was first attacked; one of her masts was wounded, and her rigging shot away. The Captain thought prudent to run her on the point of Valcour, where all the men were saved. They boarded her, and at night set fire to her. At half past twelve the engagement became general and very warm. Some of the enemy's ships and all her gondolas beat and rowed up within musket-shot of us. They continued a very hot fire with round and grapeshot until five o'clock, when they thought proper to retire to about six or seven hundred yards distance and continued the fire until dark.

The Congress and Washington have suffered greatly; the latter lost her first lieutenant killed, captain and master wounded. The New York lost all her officers except her captain. The Philadelphia was hulled in so many places that she sunk in about one hour after the engagement was over. The whole killed and wounded amounts to about sixty. The enemy landed a large number of Indians on the island and each shore, who kept an incessant fire on us, but did little damage. The enemy had, to appearance upwards of one thousand men in boats, prepared for boarding. We suffered much for want of seamen and gunners. I was obliged myself to point most of the guns on board the Congress, which I believe did good execution. The Congress received seven shots between wind and water, was hulled a dozen times, had her mainmast wounded in two places and her yard in one. The Washington was hulled a number of times, her mainmast shot through, and must have a new one. Both vessels are very leaky and want repairing.

On consulting with General Waterbury and Colonel Wigglesworth, it was thought prudent to return to Crown Point, every vessel's ammunition being nearly three-fourths spent. At seven o'clock, Colonel Wigglesworth, in the Trumbull, got under way, the gondolas and small vessels followed, and the Congress and Washington brought up the rear. The enemy did not attempt to molest us. Most of the fleet is this minute come to anchor. The wind is small to the southward. The enemy's fleet is under way to leeward and beating up. As soon as our leaks are stopped, the whole fleet will make the utmost dispatch to Crown Point, where I beg you will send ammunition and your further orders for us. On the whole, I think we have had a very fortunate escape and have great reason to return our humble and hearty thanks to Almighty God for preserving and delivering so many of us from our more than savage enemies.

I am, Dear General, your affectionate, humble servant,

B. Arnold

P. S. I had not moved on board the Congress when the enemy appeared and lost all my papers and most of my clothes on board the schooner. I wish a dozen bateaus, well manned, could be sent immediately to tow up the vessels in case of a southerly wind.

I cannot, in justice to the officers in the fleet, omit mentioning their spirited conduct during the action.

B. A. [19]

Upon disembarking from the repair and assessment at Schuyler's Island, Arnold decided to have the ordnance from the *New York* and *Providence* transferred so that they could be taken out back and shot, or rather, taken out into deeper water and sunk. The *Jersey* was deemed so waterlogged that it wouldn't even take a flame, so rather than trying to drag it out to deep water, he just left it there. The fleet launched again for Crown Point when the enemy reappeared in the early afternoon, but fortune favored the bold Americans with another southerly wind that kept the British at bay. As they attempted to catch up, Arnold's oarsmen continued their southward evasion against the wind and the driving rain all day long and into the night.

On the morning of the 13th, it was discovered that the fleet had only reached Willsborough, a mere seven miles from Schuyler's Island and a full twenty-eight miles from their objective of Crown Point. The British fleet was still far behind for the moment, but they soon caught the wind at their back and gained on the Americans in no time. Waterbury, aboard the *Washington*, requested permission from Arnold to run aground and fire the ship, but Arnold refused, pressing him to press on to the narrows known as Split Rock, halfway between Schuyler's Island and Crown Point. At about noontime the *Inflexible* and the *Maria* rushed upon the waterlogged *Washington* just short of Split Rock. Before Waterbury was able to fire his first shot, the *Inflexible* fired five. Wanting to save his crew of one hundred rather than sacrifice them, Waterbury ordered the colors down. Arnold on the other hand kept up the fight for another five hours. Although gallantry abounded him, by late afternoon the *Congress* took its final toll when the *Carleton, Inflexible, and Maria* surrounded it and unleashed a merciless bombardment. When the ammunition ran dry for the Americans, Arnold pressed on into the shallows of Ferris Bay (Button Bay) to make his last stand where the enemy could not pursue him. Once there he cleared the survivors before setting fire to the *Congress* and the gondolas with flags flying and led his men on foot along the Vermont shore to Chimney Point. After ferrying across to Crown Point for a brief recuperation, he then put the fort to the torch before making for Ticonderoga with the remaining vessels in his fleet: the *Trumbull, Enterprise, Revenge,* and one unidentified gondola. In his journal, Captain George Pausch of the Royal Navy recorded his side of the battle.

Windmill Point, Lake Champlain
11ᵗʰ October – We raised our anchor, and, with a favorable wind, got very early under sail. At 5 o'clock in the morning, we received orders to get in readiness for an engagement. About half after ten, we heard the sound of artillery; and soon after, under a splendid and suspicious and auspicious wind, the bateau met the enemy's ships in a bay behind an island. The first sight, encountered by our advanced guard, was a frigate of the enemy stuck fast on a stone cliff or island and abandoned; and soon after we saw two other frigates sending forth a lively fire. Besides this they had several armed gondolas, which, one after another, emerged from a small bay of the island firing rapidly and effectively. Every once in a while they would vanish in order to get breath and again suddenly reappear.

Our attack with about 27 bateau armed with 24, 12, and 6 pound cannon and a few howitzers became very fierce; and, after getting to close quarters, very animated. But now our frigates approached. One of them, the 'Maria', having his Excellency, Von Carleton on board, advanced and opened a lively cannonade. This one was replaced by the frigate, 'Carleton'; and as she in turn retreated, the 'Inflexible' took her place only to retreat as the others had done. One of the enemy's frigates, two of which were at echelier, or rather at echelon, one behind the other, began to careen over on one side, but in spite of this continued her fire. The cannon of the rebels were well served; for, as I saw afterwards, our ships were pretty well mended and patched up with boards and stoppers.

Close to one o'clock in the afternoon, this naval battle began to get very serious. Lieutenant Dufais came very near perishing with all his men; for a cannonball from the enemy's guns going through his powder magazine, it blew up. He kept at a long distance to the right. The sergeant, who served the cannon on my bateau, was the first one who saw the explosion, and called my attention to it as I was taking aim with my cannon. At first, I could not tell what men were on board; but directly, a chest went up into the air, and after the smoke had cleared away, I recognized the men by the cords around their hats. Dufais' bateau came back burning; and I hurried toward it to save, if possible, the Lieutenant and his men, for, as an additional misfortune, the bateau was full of water. All who could, jumped on board my bateau, which being thus overloaded, came near sinking. At this moment, a Lieutenant of artillery by the name of Smith, came with his bateau to the rescue, and took on board the Lieutenant, Bombardier Engell, and one cannoneer. The remainder of Dufais' men, viz: nine cannoneers and nine sailors remained with me; and these, added to my own force of 10 cannoneers, 1 drummer, 1 Sergeant, 1 boy and 10 sailors – in all 48 persons – came near upsetting my little boat, which was so over-laden that it could hardly move. In what a predicament was I? Every moment I was in danger of drowning with all on board, and in the company, too, of those I had just rescued and who had been already half lost! It being, by this time, nearly evening, the bateau retired. The radeau arrived at dusk, because although we had a favorable wind, it was light, and it made, in consequence, but little headway. Anyway, the 4-pounders did their best in firing at the frigates of the enemy. The distance, however, was too great, so that no ball was effective and the approach of night prevented our advancing nearer. This night, a chain was formed of all the bateaus; and every one had to be wide awake and on the alert. The Captain's frigate, which had run aground, was set on fire at dusk by the orders of his Excellency; and her ammunition, blowing up, caused a fine fire lasting all night. Up to this time, nothing more occurred; for the enemy's frigates remained in the same place where they had acted on the defensive.

12th October – Toward morning, however, it was clear that they had escaped. A pursuit was begun and some vessels were captured. Five large and small vessels, which had entered a bay on the left shore were set on fire and abandoned by the enemy.

13th October – The following night, my bateau, together with some other armed English bateau, lost sight of the fleet on the lake; and we were thus forced to continue rowing by guesswork the entire night that we might not be left behind. The next morning at daybreak, we were lucky enough to meet a few English vessels, which had met with the same experience as I had. Others followed in my rear, so that I *arrived in time (ahead of some and behind others) at 9 o'clock A. M. at Crown Point...*[18]

Lieutenant James Hadden of the Royal Artillery had this to say:

About the 5ᵗʰ of October everything being ready, a fleet consisting of one ship, two schooners, one radeau, one gondola, and 22 gunboats proceeded from St. John's up the Sorrel River to the entrance of Lake Champlain at the Isle aux Noix, 15 miles from St. John's...

The 10ᵗʰ October the fleet proceeded to the south end of Isle la Motte on the eastern side of Lake Champlain, which afterwards widens very considerably, to about 12 or 15 miles in many places.

The 11ᵗʰ October the Army arrived at Point au Fer under Gen. Burgoyne and early in the morning the fleet proceeded under Gen. Carleton and Captain Pringle of the Navy. A large detachment of savages under Major Carlton also moved with the fleet in their canoes, which were very regularly ranged. These canoes are made of birch bark and some of them brought 1500 miles down the country, several of which would contain 30 people. The savages paddle them across the lakes and down the rivers with great dexterity, and being very light, they are carried across any breaks in the water communication; they land every night, most of which they dance and sing. In wet weather they prop up one side and lay under the canoe.

About 11 o'clock in the morning one of the enemies vessels was discovered and immediately pursued into a bay on the eastern shore of the lake, where the rest of the fleet was found at an anchor in a form of a crescent between Valcour Island and the continent. Their fleet consisted of 3 row galleys, 2 schooners, 2 sloops, and 8 gondolas, carrying in all 90 guns. That of the British carried only 87 pieces of ordnance including 8 howitzers. The pursuit of this vessel was without order of regularity; the wind being fair to go down the lake enabled us to overtake the vessel before she could (by tacks) get in to the rest of their fleet, but lost to us the opportunity of going in at the upper end of the island and attacking the whole at once. The vessel, which proved to be the Royal Savage taken by them from St. John's last year, carrying 14 guns, was run on shore and most of the men escaped onto Valcour Island, in effecting which they were fired upon by the gun boats. This firing at one object drew us in a cluster and four of the enemies vessels getting under weigh to support the Royal Savage fired upon the boats with success. An order was therefore given by the commanding officer for the boats to form across the bay: this was soon effected though under the enemy's whole fire and unsupported, all the King's vessels having dropped too far to leeward. This unequal combat was maintained for two hours without any aid, when the Carleton schooner of 14 guns and 6 pairs got into the bay and immediately received the enemies whole fire which was continued without intermission for about an hour, when the boats of the fleet towed her off and left the gun ammunition to maintain the conflict. This was done till the boats had expended their ammunition, when they were withdrawn...

The boats were now formed between the vessels of the British fleet, just without the enemy's shot, being withdrawn a little before sunset and the Royal Savage blown up: this last was an unnecessary measure as she might at a more leisure moment have been got off, or at all events her stores saved, and in her present position no use could be made of her by the enemy, night coming on and a determination to make a general attack early next morning.

The Rebels having no land force, the savages took post on the main and Valcour Island; thus being upon both flanks they were able to annoy them in the working of their guns; this had the effect of now and then obliging Rebels to turn a gun that way, which danger the savages avoided by getting behind trees. The boats having received a small supply of ammunition were unaccountably ordered to anchor under cover of a small island without the opening of the bay.

The enemy, finding their force diminished and the rest so severely handled by little more than 1/3 the British fleet, determined to withdraw towards Crown Point, and passing through our fleet about 10 o'clock at night effected it undiscovered; this the former position of the gun boats would probably have prevented. All the enemy vessels used oars and on this occasion they were muffled. This retreat did great honor to Gen. Arnold, who acted as Admiral to the Rebel fleet on this occasion. The wind changing prevented the success of his attempt and, making but little way in the night, they were scarcely out of sight when their retreat was discovered at daybreak. The British fleet stood after them and gained ground considerably till the violence of the wind and a great swell obliged both fleets to anchor. towards evening, the weather was more moderate and the fleet proceeded, the boats using their oars to make head against the wind. The Rebel vessels, gaining little way when under sail from the violence of a contrary wind and thinking we were at an anchor, remained so all night, and though the British fleet gained but little by a contrary conduct, that little enabled them to overtake the enemy next day when the wind proved fair. Our ship and schooners being better sailors first came up with the Rebel fleet and retarding their movements till the whole were in sight. Three of the stern-most vessels struck their colors, in one of which was Brig. Gen. Waterbury, their second in command. Arnold ran his own vessel and 5 others on shore and set fire to them. The three foremost only escaped to Ticonderoga; as did Gen. Arnold with most of the crew's of the burnt vessels... [20]

Carleton sent a brief message of what he called a British victory to Douglas and Lord George Germain on the **14th**. Born in 1716, Germain was a graduate of Trinity College in Dublin, Ireland who served as a member to Parliament and as a promising veteran of the Seven Years' War until his last campaign in which he refused to obey an order to attack and allowed the enemy to escape. He was a tall, robust, and active man who appeared to be a distant snob in public, while being rather agreeable in private. On the **15th**, Arnold safely delivered his men to Ticonderoga, where he sent a report of the engagement to Schuyler.

To Hon. Major General Schuyler

Ticonderoga, Oct. 15, 1776

Dear General

I make no doubt that before this you have received a copy of my letter to General Gates, of the 12th instant, dated at Schuyler's Island, advising of an action between our fleet and the enemy the preceding day, in which, we lost a schooner and a gondola. We remained no longer at Schuyler's Island than to stop our leaks and mend the sails of the Washington. At two o'clock P.M. on the 12th, we weighed anchor with a fresh breeze to the southward. The enemy's fleet at the same time got underway; our gondola made very little way ahead. In the evening the wind moderated and we made such progress that at six o'clock the next morning we were off Willsborough, twenty-eight miles from Crown Point and the enemy's fleet were very little way above Schuyler's Island. The wind then breezed up to the southward so that we gained very little by beating or rowing; at the same time the enemy took a fresh breeze from the northeast and by the time we had reached Split Rock, they were alongside of us. The Washington and Congress were in the rear, the rest of our fleet was ahead, except two gondolas sunk at Schuyler's Island. The Washington galley was in such a shattered condition and had so many men killed and wounded, she struck to the enemy after receiving a few broadsides. We were then attacked in the Congress galley by a ship

194

mounting twelve eighteen-pounders, a schooner of fourteen sixes, and one of twelve sixes, two under our stern and one on our broadside within musket shot.

They kept an incessant fire on us for about five glasses (2½ hours) with round and grapeshot, which we returned as briskly. The sails, rigging, and hull of the Congress were shattered and torn in pieces and the first lieutenant and three men were killed. To prevent her falling into the enemy's hands, who had seven sail around me, I ran her ashore in a small creek ten miles from Crown Point on the east side and after saving our small arms, I set her on fire with four gondolas. With those crews, I reached Crown Point through the woods that evening and very luckily escaped the savages, who waylay the road in two hours after we passed. At four o'clock yesterday morning I reached this place, exceedingly fatigued and unwell, having been without sleep or refreshment for near three days. Of our whole fleet, we have saved only two galleys, two small schooners, one gondola, and one sloop. General Waterbury, with one hundred and ten prisoners, was returned by Carleton last night. On board the Congress, we had twenty-odd men killed and wounded with our whole loss amounting to eighty odd. The enemy's fleet was last night three miles below Crown Point; their Army is doubtless at their heels. We are busily employed in completing our lines and redoubts, which, I am sorry to say, are not so forward as I could wish. We have very few cannon, but are mounting every piece we have. It is the opinion of General Gates and St. Clair that eight or ten thousand militia should be immediately sent to our assistance if they can be spared from below. I am of the opinion that the enemy will attack us with their fleet and Army at the same time. The former is very formidable, a list of which I am favored with General Waterbury, and have enclosed.

The season is so far advanced and our people are daily growing healthier. We have about nine thousand effectives and if properly supported, make no doubt of stopping the career of the enemy. all your letters to me of late have miscarried. I am extremely sorry to hear by General Gates that you are unwell. I have sent you by General Waterbury a small box containing all of my public and private papers and accounts, with a considerable sum of hard and paper money, which I beg the favor of your taking care of.

I am, Dear General, your most affectionate humble servant,

B. Arnold [18]

On the same day, Carleton completed his report to Burgoyne, which he had started on the 12th.

195

To General Burgoyne

On board the Maria off Isle Valcour, October

Sir

We found the Rebel fleet yesterday morning behind the Island of Valcour apparently, and as we hear since from prisoners, unapprised either of our force or motions. One of their vessels perceived us only a little before we came abreast of the island and our van got to the southward of it time enough to stop them just as they were making off. They then worked back into the narrow part of the passage between the island and the main, where they anchored in a line. Their principal vessel, the Royal Savage, one of the first endeavoring to get out, in her confusion, upon finding our ships before her, ran upon the south end of the island and our gunboats got possession of her. Upon finding she could not get off, she was afterwards set fire to and she blew up. Her crew except twenty, who were made prisoners, got on shore.

After we had, n this manner, got beyond the enemy and cut them off, the wind which had been favorable to bring us there, however entirely prevented our being able to bring our whole force to engage them, as we had a narrow passage to work up, ship by ship, exposed to the fire of their whole line. The gunboats and Carleton only got up, and they sustained a very unequal cannonade of several hours, and were obliged to be ordered to fall back, upon our finding that the rest of the fleet could not be brought up to support them. We then anchored in a line opposite the Rebels within the distance of cannon shot, expecting in the morning to be able to engage them with our whole fleet, but to our great mortification we perceived at daybreak that they had found means to escape us unobserved by any of our guard boats or cruisers, thus an opportunity of destroying the whole Rebel naval force at one stroke was lost, first by an impossibility of bringing all our vessels into action, and afterwards by the great diligence used by the enemy in getting away from us.

We have been attempting to get up with part of them, which is still in our sight this morning, but the wind blowing very strong from the southward we have been obliged to give over the chase for the present: the enemy however is retarded as well as us. We have had one gunboat, which was served by the Hessian Artillery, sunk; and about thirty men, sailors and artillery, have been killed and wounded.

14th Oct. – Just as I had finished the above and I could not but be very dissatisfied, the wind sprung up fair and enabled us, after a long chase yesterday, to get up to the Rebels, and in our second *action, we have been much more successful; only three of their vessels, as you will see by the list enclosed having escaped. Their second in command Mr. Waterbury struck to us in the Washington galley, but Arnold run that he was on board of on shore and set fire to her and several others of his vessels.*

This success cannot be deemed less than a complete victory; but considering it was obtained over the King's subjects, that, which in other circumstances ought to be a proper cause of public rejoicing, is, in these, matter only of great concern, and therefore though it may be right to communicate it to the troops, yet I dare say they think with me, that we should suppress all signs of triumph on the occasion.

The Rebels upon the approach of the shattered little remains of their fleet, set fire to all the buildings in and about Crown Point, abandoning the place and retired precipitately to Ticonderoga.

The sooner Fraser's Brigade with all the matter I wrote about yesterday arrive the better; I shall then be able to see what is to be done.

I am, &c.

Guy Carleton [18]

Pringle also made his report of the same to the Secretary of the Admiralty, Philip Stephens who had been born in Essex, England in 1725, entered the Royal Navy at an early age, and later served in the House of Commons.

To Philip Stephens
                        On board the Maria off Crown Point, 15th October 1776
Sir

It is the greatest pleasure that I embrace this opportunity of congratulating their Lordships upon the victory completed on the 13th of this month by His Majesty's fleet under my command upon Lake Champlain. Upon the 11th I came up with the Rebel fleet commanded by Benedict Arnold: they were at anchor under the Island Valcour to the west side of the continent. The wind was so unfavorable, that for a considerable time nothing could be brought into action with them; but the gunboats, the Carleton schooner, commanded by Mr. Dacres, (who brings their Lordships this) by much perseverance at last got up to their assistance; but as none of the other vessels of the fleet could then get up, I did not think it by any means advisable to continue so partial and unequal a combat; consequently. With the approbation of his Excellency General Carleton, who did me the honor of being on board the Maria, I called off the Carleton and gunboats, and brought the whole fleet to anchor in a line as near as possible to the rebels, that their retreat might be cut off; which purpose was however frustrated by the extreme obscurity of the night; and in the morning the Rebels had got a considerable distance from us up the lake.

Upon the 13th I again saw eleven sail of their fleet making off to Crown Point, who, after a chase of seven hours, I came up with in the Maria, having the Carleton and Inflexible a small distance astern; the rest of the fleet almost out of sight. The action began at twelve o'clock and lasted two hours; at which time Arnold, in the Congress galley, and five gondolas, ran on shore and were directly abandoned and blown up by the enemy, a circumstance they were greatly favored in, by the wind being off shore and the narrowness of the lake. The Washington galley struck during the action and the rest made their escape to Ticonderoga.

The killed and wounded in His Majesty's fleet, including the artillery in the gunboats, do not amount to forty, but from every information I have yet got, the loss of the enemy must indeed be very considerable.

Many particulars which their Lordships may wish to know I must at present take the liberty of referring you to Mr. Dacres for; but I am well convinced his modesty will not permit him to say how great a share he had in this victory, give me leave to assure you, that during both actions, nothing could be more pointedly good than his conduct. I must also do the justice the officers and seamen of this fleet merit; by saying that every person under my command exerted themselves to act up to the character of British Seamen. [18]

I am, &c.

Thomas Pringle

On the **21st**, an account of the battle was printed in a New Jersey newspaper.

Newark, in East Jersey, October 21, 1776

On the 11th instant, a hot engagement commenced on Lake Champlain, between the fleet under the command of General Arnold and that commanded by General Sir Guy Carleton, which continued almost the whole day, and, for the most part, was greatly in favor of General Arnold, but terminated to the advantage of General Carleton.

William Briggs, a seaman belonging to the Washington galley on the lake, arrived here last Thursday. He says that the English fleet consists of thirty-six sail, from a twenty-gun ship to a gunboat, the whole commanded by General Sir Guy Carleton, General Burgoyne being indisposed; that two gondolas belonging to the English were sunk, and their crews perished; and that eleven of our vessels out of sixteen were taken, or run ashore and destroyed; that the vessel commanded by General Arnold was run ashore and blown up. The Washington galley, under the command of General Waterbury, and the crew, amounting to one hundred and four, were treated with much politeness, the wounded part taken great care of, all discharged upon their parole, and guarded through the woods by some soldiers, lest they fall in with the Indians, who were there in great numbers; that the land forces did not come out with the fleet, but were to follow in a day or two, and, it was said, would invest Ticonderoga last Sunday. Our troops at that post consisted of ten thousand effective men, well supplied and in high spirits. A bomb ketch did damage to our vessels, many of the shells being thrown on board with great exactness. Our loss in the engagement not known; there were four killed and some wounded on board the Washington galley.

Colonel Dayton's battalion is ordered from Fort Stanwix to Ticonderoga and is to be replaced by Colonel Nicoll's from the German Flats. The Militia of the Counties of Albany, Tryon, &c., were all in motion. [25]

The *Pennsylvania Gazette* followed with their own story of the shootout on the **23rd**.

Pennsylvania Gazette
Wednesday, October 23, 1776
Philadelphia, October 23.
Intelligence received in Congress, October 21st, from the Middle and Northern Departments.
That on the 11th instant, at 8 o'clock in the morning, the enemy's fleet on Lake Champlain, consisting of one ship mounting 16 guns, one snow mounting the same number, one schooner of 14 guns, two of twelve, two sloops, a bomb ketch, and a large vessel, (her force unknown) with fifteen or twenty flat bottomed boats or gondolas, carrying one 12 or 18 pounder in their bows, appeared off Cumberland Head: General Arnold with his forces immediately prepared to receive them. At 11 o'clock the attack began, at half past 12 the engagement became general and very warm; some of the enemy's ships and all their gondolas beat up and rowed within

musket shot of our fleet. They continued a very hot fire with round and grapeshot till 5 o'clock when they thought proper to retire about six or seven hundred yards distance and continued there until dark. Gen. Arnold and his troops conducted themselves during this action with great firmness and intrepidity, and made a better resistance than could have been expected against a force so greatly superior – the whole of our killed and wounded amounted to about 60. The *Philadelphia* gondola and a schooner were lost in the engagement, but all the men were saved. The enemy landed a large number of Indians on Schuyler's Island and on each shore, who kept up an incessant fire, but did little damage. The enemy had to appearance upwards of 1000 men in bateaus prepared for boarding.

The enemy's force being so greatly superior, it was determined in Council to remove to Crown Point in order to refit and collect our force. At 2 o'clock P.M. the 12th, our fleet weighed anchor with a fresh breeze to the southward: the enemy's fleet at the same time got underway: our gondolas made very little headway. In the evening the wind moderated and we made such progress that at six o'clock next morning we were about 28 miles from Crown Point. The enemy's fleet was very little above Schuyler's Island, the wind breezed up to the southward, so that we gained very little by beating or rowing; at the same time the enemy took a fresh breeze from the N. E. and, by the time we had reached Split Rock, were along side of us. The *Washington* and the *Congress* were in the rear, the rest of our fleet were ahead, except two gondolas sunk at Schuyler's Island. The *Washington* galley was in such a shattered condition, and had so many men killed and wounded, that she struck to the enemy after receiving a few broadsides. The *Congress* was then attacked by a ship mounting 12 eighteen pounders, a schooner of 14 sixes, and one of 12 sixes; two under her stern and one on her broadside, within musket shot. The enemy kept up an incessant fire about five glasses with round and grapeshot, which was returned as briskly. The sails, rigging, and hull of the *Congress* were shattered and torn in pieces; when, to prevent her falling into the enemy's hands, Gen. Arnold, who was on board, ran her ashore in a small creek ten miles from Crown Point, where after taking out her small arms, she was set on fire with 4 other gondolas; with whose crews the General reached Crown Point that evening, luckily escaping the savages, who waylaid the road in two hours after he had passed it. Of our whole fleet we have saved two galleys, two schooners, one gondola, and one sloop.

Gen. Arnold behaved with such intrepidity, that he covered the retreat of the few vessels we saved at the expense of one third of his crew. Our commanders and men behaved most gallantly; some vessels having lost all their officers, fought notwithstanding and refused to yield, but with their lives. The enemy acknowledge our bravery and confess their loss of men equal to ours.

Our troops are now busily employed in completing the lines, redoubts, &c. at Crown Point, expecting the enemy to attack them with their fleet and Army. But as the season is now far advanced and our men are daily growing in health, they have the most flattering expectations of maintaining their post against any force the enemy can bring.

N.B. Two of the enemy's gondolas were sunk the first day by our fleet, and one blown up with 60 men... [18]

On the **24th**, Waterbury wrote his account of the battle with an explanation of his capture to Hancock.

To the Hon. John Hancock, Esq.,
President to the Continental Congress

Stamford, October 24, 1776

Honored Sir

I have now returned home on parole. Your Honor has undoubtedly heard of my misfortune of being taken prisoner on the 13th instant on Lake Champlain. I shall give your Honor a short sketch of our engagement, which is as follows:

On Friday morning of the 11th instant, our alarm guns were fired that the enemy was off Cumberland Head. I immediately went on board of General Arnold and told him that I give it as my opinion that the fleet ought immediately come to sail and fight them on a retreat in main lake, as they were so much superior to us in number and strength, and we being in such a disadvantageous harbor to fight a number so much superior, and the enemy being able with their small boats to surround us on every side, as I knew they could, we lying between an island and the main. But General Arnold was of the opinion that it was best to draw the fleet in a line where we lay in the Bay of Valcour. The fleet very soon came up with us and surrounded us, when a very hot engagement ensued ten o'clock in the morning till towards sunset, when the enemy withdrew. We immediately held council to secure a retreat through the fleet to get to Crown Point,

201

which was done with so much secrecy, that we went through them entirely undiscovered. The enemy, finding next morning that we had retreated, immediately pursued us. The wind being against us and my vessel so torn to pieces that it was almost impossible to keep her above water; my sails were so shot that carrying sail split them from foot to head and I was obliged to come to anchor at twelve o'clock to mend my sails. When we had completed that, we made sail just at evening. The enemy still pursued all night. I found next morning that they gained upon us very fast and that they would soon overtake me. The rest of the fleet all being much ahead of me, I sent my boat on board of General Arnold to get liberty to put my wounded in the boat and send them forward, and run my vessel on shore and blow her up. I received for answer, by no means to run her ashore, but to push forward to Split Rock, where he would draw the fleet in a line and engage them again; but when I came to Split Rock, the whole fleet was making their escape as fast as they could and left me in the rear to fall into the enemy's hands. But before I struck to them, the ship of eighteen twelve-pounders and a schooner of fourteen six-pounders had surrounded me, which obliged me to strike, and I thought it prudent to surrender myself prisoner of war. As soon as I was taken, General Arnold, with four gondolas, ran ashore and blew up the vessels ahead of me. One thing I have omitted in the former part of my letter, that is, the Royal Savage ran ashore on the point of Valcour, in the first engagement and was lost.

I will give the strength of the British fleet upon the lake: One ship carrying six twenty-four-pounders, brass; four eight-inch howitzer; one ship, eighteen twelve-pounders; one schooner, fourteen six-pounders; one schooner, twelve six-pounders; two gondolas, one carrying six, the other four carriage guns; twenty-eight rowboats, carrying one gun each; from eighteen to twelve-pounders, and some of them carrying howitzers. This is the truest account that I am able to give.

Sir, I would have waited on the Congress in person, had it not been that my parole confined me to Connecticut. But I hope that I shall not be neglected in being exchanged, if any opportunity there be.

I remain, Sir, with the greatest esteem,
your Honor's most obedient and very humble servant,
David Waterbury, Junior [25]

As snow had capped the mountains just west of Valcour, signaling the approach of winter, the threat of having the Royal Fleet iced in for the season literally froze their schedule and forced them to cancel any further plans to penetrate into the Colonies until spring. A **November 2nd** journal entry by Lieutenant William Digby of the Royal Navy revealed one last act of decency by the British before returning to Canada for the winter; committing our fallen comrades to the Earth.

November 2 – We embarked in our bateaus and long boats for Canada & proceeded about 17 miles where our small fleet was obliged to put into a creek, the wind blowing very fresh, though fair for us, but causing a deep swell which was not safe for the bateaus, as to the long boats there was but little danger. Our soldiers called this place Destruction Bay, and not ineptly, as there we saw the great execution the enemy suffered from the fire of our fleet in the engagement on the 11th and 13 October. Some of their dead were then floating on the brink of the water, just as the surf threw them, these were ordered to be directly buried. During the night it blew fresh & was attended with a fall of snow, which was the first we had experienced. [18]

Later on the 26th of February the following year, after getting a bad rap for being captured, Waterbury pleaded his case to Gates, criticizing Arnold and operations as his reasons to surrender.

To Major General Gates
                                    Stamford, February 26th AD 1777
Dear General
*   After suitable regards to your honor, I would acquaint you I have lately heard there was many things said to my disadvantage at Ticonderoga after I left there last fall. I think it was taking a great advantage of a man's character, biting behind his back. I think it would have been no more than using me well if any man had anything against my conduct to have talked that over while I was present, and in particular, General Arnold, as I told him in your house at Ticonderoga that I was taken in consequence of the orders I received from him by the Captain of the Marines. I believe your Honor is never had the particulars of that affair and proceedings in the lake and on that account I will give you the whole as near as can be spoke:*
*   When I left Ticonderoga I took your orders and meant to follow them as nigh as possible: my orders were to put myself under Genl Arnold & to follow his directions, & I think I did. Had I not, I should went ashore as he did: as here I will give you an account of the whole. When the fleet first appeared off of Cumberland Head, I*

203

went on board of the Genl and told him I gave it as my opinion that our fleet ought to come to sail and not lie where we should be surrounded: and I think it was in your orders not to be surrounded if it could be avoided, but Genl Arnold said he would fight them in the Bay of Valcour & on that account we formed up in a line and fought them seven hours and then Genl Arnold thought it best to retreat: and I thought it best likewise as I thought it best when the enemy were off Cumberland Head & so formed at Split Rock where the enemy could not get round us as they did at Valcour. It was agreed that Col. Wigglesworth to lead the front and for Genl Arnold to go in the rear and myself with him and so we set off and we came down to Schuyler's Island. The wind came right ahead and so I went to turning to windward all night and I did not gain any for my vessel was very dull and the next morning about ten or eleven, the bolt broke off my sails being shot away. My foresail split from foot to head and I came to by Schuyler's Island and made it and a little before sunset, I made sail again and rowed and carried all night. Next morning I was about half way between the Brothers and Split Rock and the enemy to the south of the Brothers and General Arnold about two miles ahead of me and the rest of the fleet scattered about seven miles in length. I found it began to grow calm, and I knew the next wind would be north and the enemy could spread so much sail and our vessel so much torn and dull I thought it best to put my wounded men into the boats and send them to Ticonderoga and so rowed my galley ashore and blew her up while it was calm, but I thought it not best to do this without consulting the commander and so I sent my boat forward to take General Arnold's opinions on the matter and I received for answer by no means to run ashore but to get forward as fast as possible and he would stop the fleet at Split Rock and there make a stand – and with that I encouraged my men and the wind calm at north and I got up two gondola's sails I had aboard for topsails, but all would not do for she was much damaged and a great deal of water in her & was a dull sailer: but I made it out to get five miles below Split Rock before I was taken and I found my vessel to make any stop for me but all made the best of their way for Crown Point and General Arnold being next ahead and found he should be run ashore.

Although I was kept from that privilege by his orders: I have heard there has been something said about there being no firing on board of my vessel while on said retreat. As to that, General Arnold kept close under the east shore and so did I and the enemy came down under the west shore. If I had bore away to have my stern chasers bear on them, I should have been ashore a mile or two before I was *taken. General Arnold fired two or three guns before he went ashore, but I am sure they went fifty yards to the east of the enemy. As to my part I always thought it best to fire something near an enemy or not fire at all: but as to my vessel, she was so shattered she was not able to bare firing. As to my part I thought we were all friends while we were at Ticonderoga. As to my part it is above thirty years since I first went in the service and I believe I have been in as many battles as any man in Connecticut and I never heard any such thing about my self before. I am a man that strictly observes my orders from my superior and should if I was taken ten times. As to my part I do not think the retreat was conducted all to gather well for to be scattered for seven miles in length it was too much. We had no written orders for signals as there ought to have been or General Arnold ought to have been in the rear on a retreat for what could I do, he being ahead and I could not overtake him: and had no signal to go by: and had orders to run ashore: and the enemy a going three feet to our one. If any gentleman had been on board of me and have kept me clear from being taken I should have been glad and keep to my orders.*

I would give your Honor to understand that I am very uneasy in my situation and much long for the time when I shall be exchanged: but I do not doubt of your Honor's goodness in doing me what service you can on the account.

And am with sincere regard &c.
David Waterbury Jr. [18]

Although Arnold had lost the Battle of Valcour Island, he won a delaying action that cancelled Carleton's plans to sail south and meet up with General Howe's forces sailing north. With the approach of winter, the threat of having the Royal fleet iced in for the season literally froze their schedule. Howe and Burgoyne would try again next year, and Arnold would once again succeed in defeating their course of action.

V
Providence

Two months following Arnold's first bout with British warships, Washington dispatched him to New England to repel them again on the **14th of December 1776**, this time in New England.

To B General Arnold
Headquarters Bucks County, State of Pennsylvania, 14 December
1776
Dear Sir
Having received advice from Govr Trumbull of the 6th instant that a large fleet of the enemy's men of war and transports had appeared off New London, without doubt with an intent to make a descent either there or some part of the coast of New England and he desiring some General officers might be sent to take the command of the militia who were assembling. I must desire that you would immediately repair to the states of New England and in whichever of them you find the enemy landed or likely to land, that you will in conjunction with Major Genl Spencer, who I have ordered upon the same service, take such measures as in your opinion will be most likely to give opposition to and frustrate the intents of the enemy.
I shall be glad to hear from you upon your arrival in New England with a state of matters as you find them and have full confidence in your exerting yourself in this as upon former occasions.
I am, Dear Sir, with great esteem & regard,
your most obedient servant,
G. Washington [24]

Arnold did as ordered and reported back to Washington on **January 13, 1777** that the British Army under General Henry Clinton was leaving the region (thanks again to the arrival of unseasonable weather for fighting) and was heading back to New York. Born into aristocracy, Clinton was the widower of a woman more than half his age, a veteran of the Seven Years' War, and the older brother of George Clinton, the second generation Governor of New York. Although urgency and audacity were not among his strong points, he was aggressive in the planning and conduct of a battle, and his gallant implementation against orders won him the Battle of Bunker Hill. He displayed more of his bold strategic talents with his envelopment maneuver at the battle of Long Island and in the capture of Newport, Rhode Island.

To His Excellency General Washington

Providence, January 13th 1777

Dear General

Yesterday I arrived here, having previously done all in my power to forward on the militia, from Massachusetts Bay and Connecticut upwards of six thousand of which I hope are in the Jerseys before this time.

There is at this place & in the vicinity about two thousand men, part of six thousand ordered from the New England states, the others are on their march & expected in a few days. The enemy's force on Rhode Island by the best intelligence is five or six thousand, one half foreigners & some few invalids. We are informed by several persons who left Newport within a few days that Genl Clinton is going home in the Asia & has sent his baggage on board & that the troops have orders to hold themselves in readiness to embark at a minutes notice (perhaps for New York), I believe they have no intention of penetrating the country at present. I beg leave (though late) to congratulate your Excellency on your success at Trenton. It was a most happy stroke and has greatly raised the sinking spirits of the country.

We this minute have advice by a letter from Governor Trumbull of your further success near Princeton & a report says Generals Putnam & Mifflin have killed & taken two regiments near Bristol. We believe this true as intelligence comes from Newport. People in general are in high spirits, this seems a most favorable crisis to dislodge the enemy from the country, Heaven grant your Excellency may be able to effect it & may peace & laurels crown your successes.

About twelve or fifteen hundred of the enemy are dispersed in all the farm houses on Rhode Island, as soon as the militia arrives I hope we shall be able to give a good account of some of them.

I beg leave to recommend to your Excellency, Capt. Samuel Mansfield to command a company of artillery. He was a lieutenant of artillery last summer in the northern department and afterwards, captain of a galley. In two actions, behaved with great prudence and bravery, being anxious to continue in the service & much wanted here, I have desired him to engage a number of men. If your Excellency should think proper to appoint him, his company will soon be filled up & I dare to be responsible for his good conduct.

A quartermaster is much wanted here, one is appointed by the state for their own troops, but they are not able to furnish him with cash.

I beg the favor of your respect to Capt. Mansfield & am always of perfect respect & esteem, Dear General, your most obedient humble servant, B. Arnold [84]

On the **22**[nd], Washington made a manpower plea to Congress, asking them to send more generals by means of promotions, naming John Cadwalader and Benjamin Lincoln as his recommendations, but failing to include Arnold. Educated at the College and Academy of Philadelphia (now University of Pennsylvania), Cadwalader was a wealthy merchant with polished manners who served as a member of the Philadelphia Committee of Safety prior to the Revolution. While the ignition of hostilities brought about his position as a colonel of a Philadelphia battalion, his performance as a good disciplinarian in planning Washington's attack on Trenton yielded his commission as a militia brigadier.

Although Lincoln only held a common school education, his being raised on the family farm and brewery in Hingham, Massachusetts provided a foundation for him to become an able and industrious young man, who at age sixteen had enlisted in the militia during the French and Indian War. His efforts granted him a wealth of public positions including: town clerk, justice of the peace, deacon of the Unitarian Church, a member of the legislature, Provincial Congress, secretary, a member of the Committee on Supplies, and a short term as President. During the opening phase of the war he was promoted to the rank of lieutenant colonel of militia and advanced quickly through the ranks. Being ethical, reliable, smart, and discreet along with having patience and a good sense of humor, he was a popular figure amongst his peers, yet having the leadership ability to direct a bombardment to disperse the British fleet south of Boston made him popular with Washington. Unfortunately this victory was followed by a devastating defeat at the battle of White Plains, where many of his men were killed, wounded, captured, or chased home by the Hell that is war. Washington's recommendation apparently comes from viewing Lincoln's most recent leadership abilities displayed at Fort Independence in New York, where he took over command of Major General William Heath's mismanaged troops.

To the President of Congress

Morristown, January 22, 1777

Sir

My last to you was on the 20th instant...

I shall be glad to know what stock of small arms you at present have and what are your expectations shortly. The necessity that we have been, and are now under, of calling in and arming the Militia, scatters our armory all over the world in a manner, their officers are so irregular that they generally suffer their men to carry home everything that is put into their hands, which are forever lost to the public. The new raised regiments will call for a great number of arms and I do not at present see how they are to be supplied. The increase of our Army will occasion an increase of Brigadier Generals, thirty at least will be necessary for the ensuing campaign for supposing the regiments to be full, three will be sufficient to a brigade. These promotions had better be thought of and made in time, that I may be able to arrange the Army properly, as fast as it is raised. Three brigades will form a proper division of the Army for a Major General's command, consequently there is need of promotions in that line also.

As our Army will be more divided in the ensuing campaign than it has been, there appears to me a necessity of introducing the rank of Lieutenant General into the Army.

I would again beg leave to recall the attention of Congress to the appointment of Genl officers. I will not suppose the nomination of them is postponed upon a saving principle; because the advantage in having proper officers to examine the payrolls of their several regiments and compare them with the returns of their brigades, to see that the regiments are provided with what is proper, and that no more than a sufficiency is allowed to keep officers to their duty and not while the spirited officer is encountering all the fatigue and hardship of a vigorous campaign; suffer a number of others, under various frivolous pretenses and imaginary sicknesses to enjoy themselves at the public expense in ease and comfort by their own firesides. I say, if the appointments are withheld upon covetous principles, the Congress are mistaken, for I am convinced that by the correction of many abuses which it is impossible for me to attend to, the public will be benefited in a great degree in the article of expense. But this is not all. We have a very little time to do a very great work in the arranging, providing for, and disciplining one hundred and odd battalions, not to be accomplished in a day; nor is it to be done at all with any degree of propriety, when we have once entered upon the active part of the campaign; these duties must be branched out or they will be neglected and the public injured. Besides, were the Brigadiers appointed, they might be facilitating the recruiting service, they would have time to get a little acquainted with their brigades, the wants of them, and ease me of the great weight and burden which I at present feel.

On whom the choice will, or ought to light, I can not undertake to say; in a former letter, I took the liberty of submitting to the consideration of Congress, the propriety of appointing out of each state, Brigadiers to command the troops of that state, thinking as a distinction is now fixed, a spirit of emulation might arise by this means; at any rate, I shall take the liberty of recommending Genl Cadwalader as one of the first for the new appointments, I have found him a man of ability, a good disciplinarian, attentive to service, firm in his principles, and of intrepid bravery. I shall also beg to recommend Col. Read to the command of the horse, as a person in my opinion every way qualified; for he is extremely active and enterprising, many signal proofs of which he has given this campaign. For the rest, the Members of Congress can judge better than I can; I can only say, that as the Army will probably be divided in the course of the next campaign, there ought, in my opinion, to be three Lt. Generals, nine Major Generals, and 27 Brigadiers; new Brigadiers will then be to nominate...

P. S. I did not recollect Major General Lincoln in the provincial service of Massachusetts; he is an excellent officer and worthy of your notice in the Continental line. [24]

Following his initial reconnaissance, Arnold wrote back to Washington with a plan of attack on the **31ˢᵗ**.

To His Excellency General Washington

Providence, January 31, 1777

Dear General

By the best intelligence we have been able to procure of the enemy's force on Rhode Island, they consisted of about six thousand men, eleven regiments of British and four of Hessians. Two thousand embarked the 21st instant in twenty four transports & sailed from Newport three days since supposed for New York, as they were seen of New London, part of the remainder, believed about fifteen hundred are dispersed over the island. In seeming great security, they have a small fort opposite Bristol Ferry & are raising a work opposite Foggland Ferry. One of their frigates was lately drove from thence & was yesterday replaced by a fifty gun ship & two tenders, which we *are preparing to attack by guns on shore & our galleys, which are ordered down.*

At a council of General officers held a few days since it was advised, to land a body of eight thousand men (if they can be procured) on Rhode Island and attack the enemy in the following manner; five thousand men with proper artillery to embark at Howlands Ferry & land nearly opposite Foggland Ferry and take post on high ground under cover of a thick wood on the middle of the island, six miles this side of Newport. Three thousand men to embark at Bristol and Howlands Ferry and attack the enemy in the different posts, a diversion to be made by a party from Seconnet who are to land three miles this side of Newport. At the same time two fireships are to be sent into Newport among the transports – two frigates & two galleys are to be placed between Bristol & Howlands Ferry, which with the batteries will effectively secure our retreat.

We are making every necessary preparation of boats, artillery, etc., which will be complete in two or three weeks. Nothing will be wanting but men, we have at present only four thousand, not more than one thousand more (of the six ordered) can be expected, with this number, as they are chiefly raw militia, I believe your Excellency will not think it prudent for us to make a general attack. The deficiency, I know of no way of making up but by calling in four or five Continental Regts from the states of Massachusetts Bay & New Hampshire, if this number can be procured, we have a good prospect of dislodging the enemy from Newport, if not, we must be content to harass them with small parties. I suppose Major General Spencer has wrote your Excellency very particularly on the subject & will wait for your directions in the matter.

This will be delivered to your Excellency by Capt. Mansfield, whom I recommended in my last as a proper person to command a company of artillery, if your Excellency should think proper to appoint him, I beg the favor that he may be allowed to return here immediately.

I am with sentiments of great respect & esteem, Dear General,
your affectionate & most obedient humble servant,
B. Arnold [84]

On **February 6**[th] from his headquarters at the Ford Mansion in Morristown, New Jersey, Washington responded to Arnold's war plan telling him to proceed with caution. The mansion is still in operation today as a historical visitor's center.

To B General Arnold

Headquarters Morristown, February 6, 1777

Dear Sir

I was this evening favored with your letter of the 30th ultimo and am sorry to find the forces now assembled in Rhode Island are not competent to the projects you have in view. The propriety of the attack or of the plan, I cannot determine. The map you sent and for which I return you my thanks, gives me an idea of the situation of the island but not so accurately as to pronounce upon the matter with precision. If the attack can be made with a strong probability, almost amounting to a certainty of success, it is much to be desired, otherwise I would not advise it – for as a favorable issue would be productive of the most valuable & important consequences, so on the other, a miscarriage would lead to those of the most melancholy nature. I have wrote Genl Spencer on the subject wishing everything respecting the measure to be duly weighed previous to an attempt and consented that if after mature deliberation had of all circumstances the officers esteem advisable, that four or five Continental regiments may be called in aid. I suggested to him the difficulty of passing a river to attack an enemy & of making a good retreat in case of a repulse. This is obvious & I am satisfied will not escape your attention. Whatever may be determined on, I trust will be founded in prudence and I hope crowned with success.

Nothing of consequence has occurred of late in the military line in this quarter. The enemy still remain in Brunswick – Our force is at the neighboring posts to prevent as much as possible their obtaining forage and supplies of provision.

I am, Dear Sir, yours &c.,

G. Washington [24]

On the 7th, Arnold alerted Washington of potential security leaks and made a plea to strengthen the American naval forces.

To His Excellency General Washington

Providence, February 7, 1777

Dear General

Your favor of the 26th ultimo I had not the pleasure of receiving until the 3rd instant – am sorry to hear the militia have not yet suffered enough to expect them to size in their own defense and expel these inhuman enemies from the Country. I am not however, *without hopes your Excellency will be able to finish this campaign with great honor & advantage to our Country.*

My letter of the 1ˢᵗ instant by Capt. Mansfield, I hope your Excellency has received before this. General Spencer is at Boston endeavoring to procure a body of men & number of bateaus. Our numbers are very little augmented since my last at this place and the environs, (which are extinctive posts) we have near five thousand men, a great part of whom are the militia of this state, ordered out monthly, on whom little or no dependence can be placed.

Three days since a flag of truce arrived from Newport, with four prisoners only, I believe with no other intent but to procure intelligence. Yesterday a flag was sent was sent from this state with fifty prisoners, among whom are, nine officers, one of which (a very intelligent person), has had free access to all our works in this town & the neighborhood & is well acquainted with all our preparations. I have remonstrated to the Governor & council of sending these officers at this juncture & have endeavored to prevail on Genl Spencer to prevent it, but to no purpose – I am fully convinced that by means of these flags the enemy will be acquainted with our most secret movements.

The prisoners sent to Newport by this state will leave a balance of near thirty men due them, to which may be added fifty I sent to Lord Percy yesterday – who came from New Hampshire & one hundred go tomorrow or next day – who were sent from Massachusetts Bay – amounting in the whole to one hundred & eighty. As the enemy had no prisoners at Newport when the flag came away, I have wrote Lord Percy, requesting him, to advise Lord Howe by first opportunity of the receipt, of these prisoners, that the exchange may take place in New York. As soon as the flag returns, I will forward the receipts for the prisoners to your Excellency by express.

The Continental ships at this place & Boston have little more than half their compliment of men, who are allowed by the states to enlist into the standing regts by which means & the passivity of some of the officers, the ships will soon be deserted I cannot help thinking that bad policy at this juncture, when those ships being clean and new might keep the seas & greatly distress the enemy by taking their transports and Provision ships & being perfectly well acquainted with the coast, might at any time make a harbor if some more effective measures are not adopted with respect to our Navy, we had much better be without it. The men now in the ships might be of great service in the Army & a great saving made thereby – there is nothing to detain the ships at this place but want of hands or heads, I am not sure which.

I am with great respect & esteem, Dear General,
your most obedient humble servant,
B. Arnold [84]

On the **20th** Washington responded in agreement with Arnold's concerns and explained that seapower was based on supply and demand.

To B General Arnold

Headquarters Morristown, February 20, 1777
Dear Sir

I was yesterday favored with yours of the 7th instant. It has somehow or other generally happened that we have been obliged to send in our prisoners at the most inconvenient times, but when they are brought down for the purpose of exchange, it seems hard to send them back, especially as they did not fix upon the time themselves. I am so well convinced that the officers are enabled to do us harm by staying in the country and making themselves acquainted with our situation, that I have ordered Govr Trumbull to send in eleven that were taken at Princeton if they can be conveyed to any of your posts and sent in by a way in which they will see little of your disposition; it will be better than sending them by land to Kingsbridge. Whenever any officers go in from your quarter only send me the return and I will take care to ask for such in exchange as have a right to preference from length of captivity.

If the accounts we have lately received of the reinforcement of the enemy at Brunswick be true, few can be left at Rhode Island; it is said Lord Percy has arrived at Amboy within a few days.

The eastern states have in so many instances departed from the line of conduct agreed to in Congress for the enlistment of the new Army that I do not wonder at their stripping the ships to fill the regiments, but they will find that as soon as the seamen have spent the bounty they will run back and get on board the ships again.

If the enemy will give us time to collect an Army levied for the war, I hope we shall set all our former errors to rights.

I am, yours &c.,
G. Washington [24]

After spending a few weeks debating Washington's request to expand the officer corps, Congress at long last chose to promote five of them to the rank of Major General on **February 19th**, based on their numbers.

Wednesday, February 19, 1777
...Resolved, That in voting for general officers, a due regard shall be had to the line of succession, the merit of the persons proposed, and the quota of troops raised and to be raised by each State. [26]

Among those promoted were: William Alexander (Lord Stirling) of New Jersey, Thomas Mifflin and Arthur St. Clair of Pennsylvania, Adam Stephen of Virginia, and Washington's recommendation, Benjamin Lincoln. Born in New York City in 1726, Alexander was a well-educated local merchant in New York before serving in the French and Indian War. He acquired his Lordship while on a trip to England in which he invested a considerable amount of time and money in order to prove his relationship to royalty, the first earl of Stirling. Upon his return to America, his Lordship married the sister of Governor William Livingston, became surveyor-general, a member of the New Jersey Provincial Council, and a founder and early governor of King's College (now Columbia University). Following the commencement of the Revolution, he was appointed colonel of the 1st New Jersey regiment and directed the construction of Forts Lee and Washington along with Fort Stirling on Brooklyn Heights before serving in the battles on Long Island and at Trenton.

Mifflin was born into a wealthy Quaker merchant family in Philadelphia and graduated from the College of Pennsylvania to become a merchant himself. Entering into politics as a moderate Whig, his views to that of a radical from the time he served as a member of the Provincial Assembly until he was elected as Philadelphia's representative in the First Continental Congress. His impressive ability to recruit and train troops in the early stages of the war attracted the attention of Washington, who appointed him aide-de-camp and later as quartermaster general. Born in Thurso, Scotland, St. Clair had been educated at the University of Edinburgh and studied medicine before coming to America to serve in the French and Indian War. After settling for a short time in Boston, he purchased 4,000 acres in Ligonier Valley, Pennsylvania where he was appointed to several civic positions and was commissioned a colonel in the militia, later serving at Three Rivers, Trenton, and Princeton as a Continental officer. Born in Aberdeenshire, Scotland in 1721, Stephen

216

graduated from the University of Aberdeen and the University of Edinburg before serving in the Royal Navy as a surgeon. After immigrating to America, he settled in the northern Shenandoah Valley of Virginia where he became a wealthy landowner and fought alongside Washington during the French and Indian War. Between the wars he served as a practitioner, sheriff, justice of the peace, and fought against Washington in a bitter run for burgess of Fredericksburg. During the Revolution he served as a member of the Committee of Safety, delegate to the Virginia Convention, held an appointment by the House of Burgesses, and was commissioned colonel in the 4th Virginia Regiment. In the field, he displayed bold and negligent spontaneity due to his drinking which almost compromised Washington's advance on Trenton when he prematurely sent his men dangerously close to the town and exchanged fire with a few Hessians.

Washington did not learn of this from an official report, but rather had read it in the newspaper and saw one common denominator; all of them were junior to Arnold in service and ability. Thinking that there must have been some mistake and fearing that Arnold's temperament would force him to resign, Washington wrote back to him on **March 3rd**, urging him not to panic, nor to submit his resignation out of anger.

To Brigadier General Benedict Arnold
Morristown, March 3, 1777
Dear Sir
I am to acknowledge the receipt of your favor of the 10th of last month with the enclosed papers.
I must recall your attention to what I have before said on the subject of your intended attack. You must be sensible that the most serious ill consequences may and would probably result from it in case of failure, and prudence dictates that it should be cautiously examined in all its lights. Before it is attempted. Unless your strength and circumstances be such that you can reasonably promise yourself a moral certainty of succeeding, I would have you by all means to relinquish the undertaking and confine yourself in the main to a defensive opposition.
We have lately had several promotions to the rank of major general and I am at a loss whether you had a preceding appointment, as the newspapers would announce, or whether you have been omitted through some mistake. Should the latter be the case, I beg you

will not to take any hasty steps in consequence of it; but will allow time for recollection, which, I flatter myself, will remedy any error that may have been made. My endeavors to that end will not be wanting.

As I am with great respect, Dear Sir,
your most obedient servant,
G. Washington [24]

During one stop in Boston, Arnold had met and fallen for sixteen-year-young lady by the name of Betsy DeBlois, whom he attempted to woo with a trip to the mall (or the period equivalent) as revealed in a letter to the wife of Brigadier General Henry Knox on the **4th**. Knox was a robust and enterprising boy from Boston, who found work as a clerk in a bookstore when he was just nine. His discoveries of military history inspired him to enlist in a local militia company when he was eighteen and on his twenty-first birthday, he opened his own bookstore. With the commencement of the war, this tall and beefy young man of Scotch-Irish decent was appointed to take charge of the artillery, which he did thanks to the efforts of Arnold and Allen capturing Ticonderoga. His noble train of artillery traveled more than 300 miles in less than six weeks over the snow and through the woods to the top of Dorchester Heights, thus forcing the British to evacuate and eradicate their siege of Boston. This feat strengthened his reputation for daring and resourcefulness, which enabled him to become one of Washington's closest friends and advisor's throughout the war. His enduring optimism in the toughest branch of the Army helped to maintain the fortitude of his men whose spirits had been buried by an avalanche of hardships. Although he and his men had suffered the agony of defeat at the battle of Long Island, their precision and mobility allowed them to share in the thrill of victory at Trenton and Princeton.

Mrs. Knox, Boston

Watertown, 4th March, 1777

Dear Madam

I have taken the liberty of enclosing a letter to the heavenly Miss Deblois, which I beg the favor of your delivering with the trunk of gowns, &c., which Mrs. Colburn promised me to send to you. I hope she will make no objection to receiving them. I make no doubt you will soon have the pleasure to see the charming Mrs. Emery and have it in your power to give me the favorable intelligence. I shall remain under the most anxious suspense until I have the favor of a

line from you, who if I may judge, will from your own experience consider the fond anxiety, the glowing hopes, and chilling fears that alternately possess the heart of Dear Madam,
your most obedient and humble servant,
Benedict Arnold [5]

After asking Arnold to put his emotions on hold, Washington wrote a letter of inquiry regarding the recent promotions to Congressman Richard Henry Lee on **March 6th**. After receiving his elementary education from private tutors, Lee had attended higher education in Yorkshire, England to study law, which allowed him to become a justice of the peace in his home state of Virginia. His status as an aristocrat enabled him to follow in the footsteps of his ancestors and enter into the House of Burgesses in which he sought out progressive plans for the colonies and opposed the Parliamentary plan to tax them. As a member of the newly developed Congress, Lee endorsed the idea that each colony should adopt its own government and that Independence should be established in a form of separation from the King, not the country. He later put that endorsement in writing by signing his name on the Declaration.

To Hon. Richard Henry Lee
Morristown, March 6, 1777
Dear Sir
I am anxious to know whether General Arnold's non-promotion was owing to accident or design; and the cause of it. Surely a more active, a more spirited, and sensible officer fills no department in your Army. Not seeing him then on the list of major generals, and no mention made of him, has given me uneasiness, as it is not to be presumed (being the oldest brigadier) that he will continue in the service under such a slight. I imagine you will lose two or three other very good officers by promoting yours or adequate ones over them. My public letters will give you the state of matters in this quarter and my anxiety to be informed of the reason for Arnold's non-promotion gives you the trouble of this letter.
Being very sincerely, Dear Sir, your most obedient and affectionate,
G. Washington [24]

Arnold replied to Washington on the **11th**, promising not to be a loose cannon towards Congress, yet, with all due respect, he let it be

219

known that he was disappointed and asked for an investigation to prove his worthiness of the promotion.

To His Excellency General Washington
                              Providence, Rhode Island, March 11*th*, 1777
Dear General

    I am now to acknowledge your Excellency's favors of the 6*th* & 20*th* ultimo & 3*rd* instant. On receipt of the former, I was ordered to Boston with a view of collecting four or five Continental battalions for our intended attack. On my return Genl Spencer thought it necessary for me to go to Pt. Judah from whence I returned last night & was then presented with your Excellency's favors of the last date – prior of the receipt of which we have laid aside all thoughts of making a general attack on Rhode Island. The new levies of the Massachusetts Bay being all ordered to Ticonderoga & those of Connecticut inoculated for the small pox deprives us of the aid of Continental troops, on whom we had placed our chief dependence.

    When the attack was first proposed, we had reason to think your Excellency had a force superior to the enemy in the Jersey's, I am sorry to say we now have reason to think the case is altered. After duly weighing the matter, considering the difficulties, making good a retreat, and the fatal consequences attending a failure of success, I was dubious of the propriety of the attack. As the enemy now rests secure & easy in their quarters, I am fully of opinion it will be imprudent to force them to action until our new levies are in a manner complete. From our strength & numbers who do not exceed four thousand raw militia, we have no reasonable prospect of succeeding against four thousand well-disciplined troops. Notwithstanding the Assembly of this State have lately requested General Spencer to make an attack on the enemy at Rhode Island, which he seems inclined to do & the militia are collecting for the purpose. It is proposed to attack the north end of the island with three thousand men, I am much averse to this plan as I am fearful it will bring on a general action & end in our disgrace or cause the troops in Newport to embark, both of which I wish to avoid at this critical juncture. From some of our own people & several deserters from the enemy, we are informed they are near four thousand strong, it is said two thousand have lately arrived at Newport from New York. I am rather inclined to think that a body of men lately sent to Martha's Vineyard for stock. Ten transports passed Pt Judah this day week to the westward & appeared full of troops, twenty odd sail are gone to England & fifty sail remain at New York.

I am greatly obliged to your Excellency for interesting yourself so much in my behalf in respect to my appointment, which I have had no advice of, and know not by what means it was announced in the papers. I believe none but the printer has a mistake to rectify. Congress, undoubtedly, have a right of promoting those whom, from their abilities, and their long and arduous services, they esteem most deserving. Their promoting junior officers to the rank of major general, I view it as a very civil way of requesting my resignation, as unqualified for the office I hold. My commission was conferred unsolicited and received with pleasure only as a means of serving my country. With equal pleasure I resign it, when I can no longer serve my country with honor. The person who, void of the nice feelings of honor, will tamely condescend to give up his right, and retain a commission at the expense of his reputation, I hold as a disgrace to the Army and unworthy of the glorious cause in which we are engaged. When I entered the service of my country my character was not impeached. I have sacrificed my interest, ease, and happiness in her cause. It is rather a misfortune than a fault that my exertions have not been crowned with success. I am conscious of the rectitude of my intentions. In justice, therefore, to my own character and for the satisfaction of my friends, I must request a court of inquiry into my conduct. And though I sensibly feel the ingratitude of my countrymen, every personal injury shall be buried in my zeal for the safety and happiness of my country, in whose cause I have repeatedly fought and bled, and am ready at all times to risk my life. I shall avoid any hasty step that may tend to injure my country.

Particular attention shall be paid to your Excellency's commands respecting the prisoners.

I have the honor to be with very great respect & esteem, your Excellency's most obedient & very humble servant,

B. Arnold [84]

On the **26**[th], Arnold followed up his previous letter to Washington with information on his current status as well as the enemy's status under Captain Sir Peter Parker. Born in 1721, Parker served in European campaigns and in the Seven Years' War before coming to fight the American Rebellion in Charleston, South Carolina and Long Island.

To His Excellency General Washington

Providence, March 26th *1777*

Dear General

I was made unhappy a few days since by hearing your Excellency was exceeding ill with fever, soon after had the pleasure hearing by Mr. Learned you were so far recovered as to be able to ride out. My fears have not entirely subsided, I am still anxious for your safety and apprehensive your zeal for the public service will induce you to exert yourself before you are perfectly recovered.

I wrote your Excellency the 11th instant, since which our intended expedition against Rhode Island is laid aside, we now confine ourselves to a defensive opposition only. Desertions from the island are frequent, the most intelligent persons agree the enemy have six battalions of Hessians and four of British troops, the whole about four thousand men. Several inhabitants who came from Newport the evening of the 23rd & 25th instant say that all the enemies transport ships are hauled of from the wharves, their water in, sails bent & ready for sailing. Sir Peter Parker has sent his baggage on board & was to embark soon. It is said by their seamen, they are bound to New York & probably join General Howe.

In my last, I intimidated to your Excellency, the impossibility in my remaining in a disgraceful situation in the Army; my being superceded must be viewed as an implicit impeachment of my character. I therefore requested a court of inquiry into my conduct, I believe the time is near at hand when I can leave this department without any damage to the public interest. When that is the case, I will wait on your Excellency, not doubting my request will be granted and that I shall be able to acquit myself of every charge, malice, or envy can bring against me.

General Spencer writes your Excellency very particularly by this opportunity.

I have only to add my sincere wishes for your restoration to perfect health and preservation in every danger and am very respectfully, Dear General, your affectionate & most obedient humble servant,

B. Arnold [70]

In his report to Washington, Major General Nathanael Greene stated that the promotions made by Congress were based upon the fact that Connecticut already held two major generals at the time and did not justify a third appointment. These officers were Israel Putnam from Pomfret and Joseph Spencer from Haddam, the latter of whom was the sixty-six year old veteran of the French and Indian War whom Arnold was serving with at that very moment. As a bright and energetic young man before the war, Greene had served as a deputy to the General Assembly in Rhode Island and as a brigadier of militia. At 33, as an independent student of military science, he was appointed as the youngest brigadier in the Continental Army at the commencement of the war and placed in command of troops that reoccupied Boston. Although he lost Fort Washington along with 5,000 men to the British, he later proved himself a capable officer by repelling enemy troops during Washington's retreat to Hackensack and attacking them in Trenton.

Putnam, born in 1718, was one of eleven children in his wealthy family from Salem, Massachusetts, who later married and moved to Pomfret, Connecticut. Bearing a medium height on a powerful frame, he acquired a large farm as a young man before he served in the French and Indian War as one of Rogers' Rangers. The Rangers were an elite special-forces group made up of Colonial warriors under the brave, rugged, and renegade wilderness leader, Major Robert Rogers from Dunbarton, New Hampshire. Back in the day, Rangers led the way. Thank God some things never change. Hooah! After settling back down on the farm, Putnam became an active member of the "Sons of Liberty," the General Assembly, and held a position as a selectman. Two years after he was widowed himself, he married a wealthy widow and opened a tavern named, "The General Wolfe" that served as a gathering place for former soldiers and patriots. After being elected Chairman of the Committee of Correspondence, he was commissioned as a lieutenant colonel in the militia. While plowing his field, he received word about the conflict at Concord, jumped on his horse, ordered the militia to Cambridge, and rode the 100 miles in 18 hours. At the siege of Boston, he was appointed major general by Washington to lead the centerline of the Army and was dispatched to New York to command the works at Brooklyn Heights. Although his self-confidence seemed overwhelmed by his sparse education, the activity and bravery of "Old Put" was a leading spirit at Bunker Hill and in the battles that followed at Long Island and Harlem Heights.

This decision by Congress to promote general officers by state was not what Washington had intended in his earlier letter to Hancock, a detail which he did not reveal to Arnold on **April 3rd**.

To B General Arnold

Headquarters Morristown, April 3, 1777

Dear Sir

It is needless for me to say much upon a subject, which must undoubtedly give you a good deal of uneasiness. I confess I was surprised when I did not see your name in the list of Major Generals, and was so fully of opinion that there was some mistake in the matter. As you may recollect, I desired you not to take any hasty step before the intention of Congress was fully known. The point does not now admit of a doubt, and is of so delicate a nature that I will not even undertake to advise. Your own feelings must be your guide. As no particular charge is alleged against you, I do not see upon what ground you can demand a court of inquiry. Besides, public bodies are not amenable for their actions. They place and displace at pleasure; and all the satisfaction that an individual can obtain when he is overlooked is, if innocent, a consciousness that he has not deserved such treatment for his honest exertions. Your determination not to quit your present command while any danger to the public might ensue from your leaving it, deserves my thanks, and justly entitles you to the thanks of your country.

General Greene who has lately been at Philadelphia, took occasion to inquire upon what principle the Congress proceeded in their late promotion of General officers. He was informed that the members from each state seemed to insist upon having a proportion of general officers adequate to the number of men, which they furnish, and that, as Connecticut had already two major generals, it was their full share. I confess this is a strange mode of reasoning, but it may serve to show you that the promotion, which was due to your seniority, was not overlooked for want of merit in you.

I am, Dear Sir, your most obedient servant,
G. Washington [24]

After John Brown had gotten the runaround from Congress and Gates, he took matters into his own hands in which he published and distributed a pamphlet in his hometown of Pittsfield, Massachusetts maligning Arnold's character. Brown had made the prophetic claim against him when he stated on the 12th that, "Money is this man's God, and to get enough of it he would sacrifice his country." [79] Upon hearing of the article, Arnold requested to debate the issue.

My character is much injured by a report prevailing in Philadelphia of my having sequestered the goods received in Montreal. I cannot but think it extremely cruel, when I have sacrificed my ease, health, and a great part of my private property in the cause

224

of my country, to be calumniated as a robber and a thief; at a time, too, when I have it not in my power to be heard in my own behalf. [79]

I am, &c.,

B. Arnold, M. Genl

VI
Ridgefield

On Friday the 25th, twenty-six British ships appeared off Norwalk, Connecticut and were standing in for Cedar Point. The opportunity to brighten his reputation came in the early hours of the 26th, when Arnold awoke to the sound of someone pounding on his door to deliver the news. A courier announced that the British had just invaded Connecticut from the shore of Compo Beach and were headed to the American ammunition stores at Danbury. Arnold darted towards Danbury at the head of one hundred New Hampshire Militia, but was too late to stop the fiery destruction of the supply depots.

On the 27th, British troops under Governor William Tryon marched through the rain into Ridgefield and torched the homes of patriots and the Presbyterian Church, which served as a military warehouse. Born in Northamptonshire, England in 1725, Tryon had served in the Army before marrying a woman of significant wealth, whose influence granted him the appointment of lieutenant governor of North Carolina and then governor. He led the colony as a firm, able, and vigorous administrator before making the move to New York where he established a brilliant militia force. In a visit to the Indian country, he purchased a large tract of land and thus established Tryon County west of Albany. When Arnold learned of the redcoats next rendezvous, he made a forced march leading 500 Connecticut militia to Ridgefield arriving at 11 o'clock in the morning. Against a force of 2,000 British regulars, he ordered the militia to form a barricade of carts, logs, stones, and earth in an attempt to cut them off from their return to their ships. The militia repelled three charges before retreating from a flanking bayonet attack. While charging into the attack, Arnold's horse was shot out from under him causing him to get trapped under the horse. A "tory" (a.k.a. a loyalist, one who is loyal to England) named Coon from New Fairfield ran up to him leading with his bayonet and shouted, "Surrender, you are my prisoner!" [41] Arnold yanked his foot free and replied, "Not yet!" before he leaped to his feet, drew his pistol, and fired a direct hit just before the soldier reached him. [41] He then vaulted a fence and escaped through a swamp under a hail of musket fire, only to be missed again, as his horse was later discovered to have been struck nine times. His being missed was nothing short of a miracle. In an attempt to cut the British off at the Hudson River, Arnold sent a report to Brigadier General Alexander McDougall, reporting his actions along with Wooster, who had advanced to major general, and Brigadier General Gold Sellick Silliman. A native of nearby Fairfield, Connecticut, Silliman was a Yale graduate who served as judge of the Connecticut superior court and had fought at Long Island and White Plains.

To Honorable General McDougall
                                    W. Redding, April 27th 1777, 10 o'clock a. m.
Sir

On Friday evening last, the enemy landed about 2,000 men at Compo 8 miles west of Fairfield and on Saturday at 2 o'clock p. m. reached Danbury, which was abandoned by a handful of our men. The enemy immediately began burning and destroying our magazines of provision, &c. Last night at half past eleven, General Wooster, General Silliman, and myself with six hundred militia arrived at Bethel, 8 miles from Danbury. The excessive heavy rains rendered our arms useless and many of the troops were much fatigued, having marched 30 miles in the course of the day without refreshment. At 6 this morning we divided the troops into two divisions, being uncertain if they would return via Fairfield or Norwalk. One division was stationed on each road, on a crossroad where they could support each other. we have this minute information that at 9 this morning the enemy set fire to the meetinghouse and most of the buildings in town and had taken the route to Newbury (Ridgebury) *leading either to Peekskill or Tarrytown. We imagine they are destined for the latter as we hear they landed eight hundred men there yesterday morning. we propose following them immediately in hopes of coming up with their rear and hope you will be able to take them in front. Our loss at Danbury is great, but I hope not irreparable.*

I am with esteem, Sir, your most obedient, humble servant,
                                                        B. Arnold {79}

After a night's rest, the British resumed their march toward Norwalk and Compo on the morning of the 28th. Seizing the moment, five hundred men under Colonel Huntingdon and a battalion of New York Artillery under Colonel John Lamb formed a line on the western side of the Saugatuck Bridge (Westport) to cut them off. Lamb was a successful wine merchant from New York, who qualified as an artilleryman by his mathematical experience and independent studies in gunnery. Montgomery, whom he served under in capturing Montreal, thought of Lamb as a "restless genius" with "a bad temper;" a brave, intelligent, and active officer, but "very turbulent and troublesome." [86] Following Montgomery's death and Arnold's injury during the attack on Quebec, Lamb assumed command, but was also wounded shortly thereafter, an injury that cost him the loss of his left eye. The inevitable loss of the battle made him a prisoner for the next several months. Upon receiving intelligence of the American's blockade, the British outflanked them and crossed the creek above the bridge, but were pursued and fired upon by Arnold's militia. When the British reached Compo, the Royal Marines counterattacked and drove off the militia long enough to secure the boarding of the main Army. During this engagement Arnold lost another horse from under him before the fleet weighed anchor at sunset. A souvenir from the battle in the form of a cannonball can be found lodged in the wall of the Keeler Tavern at the south end of the village. Arnold wrote again to McDougall to report their escape.

To Honorable General McDougall
 Saugatuck, 3 miles East Norwalk, 28th April 1777, 6 o'clock p. m.
Sir
 Soon after I wrote you yesterday I found the enemy were on their march for Ridgefield. At 11 0'clock we arrived there about one hour before them with 500 men. We had little time to make a disposition of our troops, when a smart action began which lasted about one hour. Our troops were obliged to give way to superior numbers; I found it impossible to rally them and ordered a stand to be made at this place. At 11 o'clock this morning we met the enemy with 500 militia about two miles from this place, when a skirmishing began between the flanks and soon became general, which continued until five o'clock, when the enemy gained a height under cover of their ships and embarked before night. At the beginning of the action Col. Huntington joined me with 500 men and before it was over a small number of General Wadsworth's Brigade. General Wooster, whose conduct does him great honor, was mortally wounded yesterday. Lieut. Col. Gold killed and Col. Lamb wounded. Our loss otherwise is not great, about twenty killed and wounded. Many of the officers and men behaved well. The militia as usual I wish never to see another of them in action. The enemy's loss is uncertain, as they carried off most of their killed and wounded. Several prisoners have fallen into our hands. As soon as the troops were embarked, the fleet got under way and stood to the eastward. Extreme hurry and fatigue obliges me to request your advising his Excellency General Washington of the above matters.
 I am very respectfully, Sir, your most humble and obedient servant,

In a letter to a friend, a British officer also gave his account of the raid during that week.

21 April   Embarked on the North River 1600 Regulars & 500 Provincials – commanded by Major Genl Tryon - & Brig Genls Agnew – Sir Wm Erskine & Govr Browne. Two frigates proceeded immediately after up the North River where the public concluded the expedition was intended; but early the next morning the 22nd a westerly breeze favored our passage through Hell Gate to Whitestone 16 miles down the sound. Here we were met by the Senegal & Swan sloops & detained by a contrary wind.

The 24 a westerly breeze released us & carried us the 25 to a spacious bay called Capone Bay 5 short miles from Norwalk Harbor. The troops were immediately landed without any opposition & everything necessary disembarked.

We encamped or rather lay on our arms & early on the 26 marched forward with 6 pieces of artillery. About 7 miles from sea we were attacked by a small ambush from a marsh, but we soon dislodged them, killed 5, & took a few prisoners - & proceeded with very little opposition to Danbury, where we found the greatest magazine the Rebels had ever collected: & full leisure to destroy it – viz. About 4000 bbls of beef & pork; 5000 bbls of flour; 100 puncheons of rum; a vast quantity of rice, coffee, salt, sugar, medicines, tents, clothing, shoes, wagons – harness – made up ammunition &c – the exact quantities unascertained. We sent several detachments to destroy what we learned were concealed by the Rebels in Copse's at a mile & two miles distance, & then left the town in flames & proceeded Ridgefield, where, as at Danbury, we found the meeting house full of stores, which we also set fire to & to several houses.

We marched all night unmolested, but the militia began to harass us early on the 27 & increased & increased every mile, galling us from their houses and fences – several instances of astonishing audacity marked the Rebels in this route. Four men from one house fired on the Army & persisted in defending it till they perished in its flames. One man on horseback rode up within 15 yards of our advanced guard, fired his piece, & had the good fortune to escape unhurt. Within about 5 miles of the sea we found Arnold had taken post very advantageously with a body of 500 men; most of them he had marched from Peekskill 32 miles distance; which obliged us to form

230

& lose no time in charging the Rebels who were active in throwing up breastworks & constructing a battery for three 6 pounders.

Arnold & Wooster opposed us with more persistency than skill – the first narrowly escaped; leaving his horse dead & his pistols dropped a few yards off; the other was mortally wounded in the belly & left to die on the field by his son, who behaved remarkably well, refusing quarter & died by the bayonet.

Major Stuart, a volunteer on this expedition, has gained immortal honor; he perceived first, the battery which the enemy had nearly completed & rushing on with 10 or 12 spirited men by his example drove them out of it in the face of three 6 pounders, which were well served, but ineffectual – the line followed & the Rebels presently retreated on all sides, leaving us a complete victory – their cannon &c &c. and with less loss than we could have expected; for the enemy opposed us with great bravery – many opening their breasts to the bayonets with great fury & our ammunition began to be very scarce. We have not lost above 70 killed & not one officer & we have about half as many prisoners: they are better clothed than last year. among our wounded are Genl Agnew in the breast near the shoulder – Majors Hope & Thorn; Capt Hastings slightly & Capt Lyman of Brown's corps dangerously. The Genl gave public thanks to this corps on the beach for their very distinguished behavior.

We re-embarked the 28 in good order though exceedingly fatigued, having marched at least 35 miles the way we went & not slept from Friday evening to this day six o'clock in the evening, which affords me this hasty moment to write you. I shall think of many particulars hereafter, such as that the Rebels murdered 13 tories, as they called them for opening their houses to us on our March to Danbury &c. After so long a letter, I shall not venture to add any intelligence of the general state of things in the Jerseys – only that the Rebel enlistments to the southward are not yet completed & those to the northward may probably nearly fail: & this coup by Gov Tryon may go nigh to carry the defection of Connecticut & Rhode Island provinces from the Rebel cause. Three of their papers, which I enclose, show that it is supported on crutches. [18]

On the **30th**, a report of the battle was printed in the local paper.

Connecticut Journal, Wednesday, April 30, 1777
New Haven, April 30

On Friday the 25th instant, twenty-six sail of the enemy's ships appeared off Norwalk Islands, standing in for Cedar Point, where they anchored at 4 o'clock P. M. and soon began landing troops; by 10 o'clock they had landed two brigades, consisting of upwards of two thousand men, and marched immediately for Danbury, where they arrived the next day at 2 o'clock P. M. The handful of Continental troops there were obliged to evacuate the town, having previously secured a part of the stores, provisions, &c. The enemy on their arrival began burning and destroying the stores, houses, provisions, &c. On the appearance of the enemy, the country was alarmed.

Early the next morning Brigadier General Silliman with about five hundred militia, (all that were collected) pursued the enemy; at reading he was joined by Major General Wooster and Brigadier General Arnold. The heavy rain all the afternoon, retarded the march of our troops so much that they did not reach Bethel (a village two miles from Danbury) till 11 o'clock at night, much fatigued, and their arms rendered useless by being wet. It was thought prudent to refresh the men and attack the enemy on their return. Early the next morning, (which proved rainy) the whole were in motion, two hundred men remained with General Wooster, and about four hundred were detached under General Arnold, and General Silliman, on the road leading to Norwalk.

At 9 o'clock A. M. intelligence was received that the enemy had taken the road leading to Norwalk, of which Gen. Wooster was advised and pursued them, with whom he came up about 11 o'clock, when a smart skirmishing ensued in which Gen. Wooster, who behaved with great intrepidity, unfortunately received a wound from a musket ball through the groin, which it is feared will prove mortal. Gen. Arnold, by a forced march across the country, reached Ridgefield at 11 o'clock, and having posted his small party (being joined by about 100 men) of 500 men, waited the approach of the enemy, who were soon discovered advancing in a column with three field pieces in front, and three in rear, and large flank guards of near two hundred men in each.

At noon they began discharging their artillery, and were soon within musket shot when a smart action ensued between the whole, which continued about an hour, in which our men behaved with great spirit, but being overpowered by numbers, were obliged to give way, though not until the enemy was raising a small breastwork, thrown across the way, at which Gen. Arnold had taken post with about two hundred men (the rest of our small body were posted on the flanks) who acted with great spirit. The General had his horse shot under him when the enemy were within about ten yards of him, but luckily received no hurt, recovering himself he drew his pistols and shot the soldier who was advancing with his fixed bayonet. He then ordered his troops to retreat through a shower of small and grapeshot. In this action the enemy suffered very considerably, leaving about thirty dead and wounded on the ground and besides a number unknown buried. He had the misfortune of losing Lieut. Col. Gold, one subaltern, and several privates killed and wounded.

At 9 o'clock A. M. the 28th, about 500 men were collected at Sagatuck bridge, including part of two companies of Col. Lamb's battalion of Artillery, with three field pieces under command of Lieut. Col. Oswald, 1 field piece with part of the artillery company from Fairfield, sixty Continental troops, and three companies of volunteers from New Haven, with whom Generals Arnold and Silliman took post about two miles above the bridge. Soon after the enemy appeared in sight, their rear was attacked by Col. Huntington, (commanding a party of about 500 men) who sent to Gen. Arnold for instructions and for some officer to assist him. General Silliman was ordered to his assistance; the enemy finding our troops advantageously posted, made a halt, and after some little time, wheeled off to the left and forded Sagatuck river, three miles above the bridge. Gen. Arnold observing this motion, ordered the whole to march directly for the bridge in order to attack the enemy flank. Gen. Silliman, at the same time to attack their rear; the enemy by running full speed had past the bridge on Fairfield side with their main body before our troops could cross it. Gen. Silliman finding it impossible to overtake the enemy in their rear proceeded to the bridge; when the whole were formed, they marched in two columns, with two field pieces on the right, the other on the left of the enemy, when a smart skirmishing and firing of field pieces ensued, which continued about three hours. The enemy having gained the high hill of Compo, several attempts were made to dislodge them, but without effect. The enemy landed a number of fresh troops to cover their embarkation, which they effected a little before sunset, weighed anchor immediately, and stood across the sound for Huntington, on Long Island.

Our loss cannot be exactly ascertained, no return being made. It is judged to be about sixty killed and wounded. Among the killed are: 1 Lieut. Col., 1 Capt., 4 subalterns, and

233

Dr. David Atwater of this town, whose death is greatly lamented by his acquaintance. Among the number wounded are Col. John Lamb; Anar Bradley and Timothy Gorham, volunteers from New Haven, though not mortally.

The enemy's loss is judged to be more than double our number and about 20 prisoners. The enemy on this occasion behaved with their usual barbarity, wantonly and cruelly murdering the wounded prisoners who fell into their hands, and plundering the inhabitants, burning and destroying everything in their way.

The enemy the day before they left Fairfield were joined by 10 sail, chiefly small vessels.

Since the enemy went off, a number of disaffected persons, who it is supposed intended to join them, have been taken into custody. [18]

On **May 2nd**, Congress motioned to award Arnold with the promotion he so deserved, which would have been totally acceptable to him, but the members failed to restore his placement above the five officers who were promoted earlier.

In CONGRESS

The DELEGATES of the UNITED STATES of New Hampshire, Massachusetts Bay, Rhode Island, Connecticut, New York, New Jersey, Pennsylvania, Delaware, Maryland, Virginia, North Carolina, South Carolina, and Georgia, TO

Benedict Arnold, Esquire

We reporting special Trust and Confidence in your Patriotism, Valor, Conduct, and Fidelity, DO by these presence, constitute and appoint you to be

Major General

in the Army of the United States, raised for the defense of American Liberty, and for repelling every hostile invasion thereof. You are therefore carefully and diligently to discharge the duty of *Major General* by doing and performing all manner of things thereunto belonging. And we do strictly charge and require all officers and soldiers under your command, to be obedient to your orders as *Major General*, and you are to observe and follow such orders and directions from time to time, as you shall receive from this or a future Congress of the United States, or Committee of Congress, for that purpose appointed, or Commander-in-Chief for the time being of the Army of the United States, or any other of your superior officers, according to the Rules and Disciplines of War, in pursuance of the trust reposed in you. This Commission to continue in force until revoked by this or a future Congress.

Dated at *Philadelphia, May 2nd 1777.*

By order of the Congress:

John Hancock   President [87]

VII
Peekskill

On **May 8th**, Washington appointed Arnold to a command in the Hudson Highlands.

To M General Arnold
                          Headquarters, Morristown, May 8th, 1777
Dear Sir
          I am happy to find that a late resolve of Congress, of the 2nd instant, has restored you to the Continental Army. The importance of the post at Peekskill, and its appendages, has become so great, that it is now necessary to have a major general appointed to the command of it. You will therefore immediately repair to that post, and take charge of it, 'till a general arrangement of the Army can be affected, and the proper province of every officer assigned.
                          I am, Sir, your most obedient servant,
                          G. Washington [24]

On the **12th**, Arnold visited Washington and requested to speak to Congress in person to square his debts and request an adjustment to his seniority. Washington accepted his request and sent him along with a letter of endorsement. Although Arnold did receive his advancement in rank, it was only a partial gain, for Congress did not restore the date of his rank to be equal to those who were promoted over him until later.

To the President of Congress
                          Headquarters Morristown, May 12, 1777
Sir
          This will be delivered to you by General Arnold, who arrived here today on his way to Philadelphia. He seems to be anxious to settle his public accounts and waits on Congress, hoping they will appoint a committee of their body, or of such gentlemen as they shall judge proper, to take the matter into consideration. This he considers the more necessary, as he has heard, some reports have been propagated injurious to his character as a man of integrity. If any such aspirations lie against him, it is but reasonable, that he should have an opportunity of vindicating himself and evincing his innocence.
          I find, he does not consider the promotion, Congress have been pleased to confer upon him, sufficient to obliterate the neglect

arising from their having omitted him in their late appointments of Major Generals. He observes, it does not give him the rank he had a claim to from seniority in the line of Brigadiers; and that he is subject to be commanded by those, who had been inferior to him. He further adds that Congress in their last resolve respecting him, have acknowledged him competent to the station of Major General and therefore have done away every objection implied by their former omission. It is needless to say anything of this gentleman's military character. It is universally known, that he has always distinguished himself as a judicious, brave officer, of great activity, enterprise, and perseverance.

I have the honor to be &c.,

G. Washington [24]

When the matter remained as an issue months later, Arnold challenged Congress to conduct an investigation on the **20ᵗʰ**.

To the Hon. Continental Congress

May 20, 1777

Gentlemen

I am exceedingly unhappy to find that, having made every sacrifice of fortune, ease, and domestic happiness to my country, I am publicly impeached of a catalog of crimes which, if true, ought to subject me to disgrace, infamy, and the just resentment of my countrymen. Conscious of the rectitude of my intentions, however I have erred in judgement, I must request the favor of Congress to point out some mode by which my conduct, and that of my accusers, may be inquired into, and justice done to the innocent and injured. [5]

I have the honor to be, &c.,

B. Arnold, Major General

On the evening of the **21ˢᵗ**, Arnold presented several letters that he had salvaged from the Canadian campaign in order to gain restitution for $55,000 that he could not well account for with receipts. In presenting his case, he pointed out that although he had requisitioned Congress for a paymaster, Congress had failed to appoint one to him. He added that the funds that he had divided with his divisional commanders were captured along with their records on the march to Quebec, as well as records from the French Canadians that were lost on board the *Royal Savage* when it was burned. Many members of Congress had some difficulty with a number of his accounts, because he was calling for a series of extravagant charges in his own favor, dubious in character, and unreasonable in value. In addition, they claimed that he owed them close to $9,000 for advances made to him prior to the Quebec campaign. Although John Adams had agreed with Arnold on the John Brown issue, as he mentioned in a letter to his wife on the 22nd, he was also fed up with him being on a power trip. John Adams, like his second cousin Samuel, was also born in Braintree, Massachusetts; a vain, verbal, and vivacious Harvard graduate who opposed the acts of England to tax the colonies without representation. Although unlike Sam, John fully pursued the study of law, was admitted to the bar, started his own practice, and published his opinions on a strictly legal basis, not a violent one. Becoming the principal legal council to the patriot party, he opposed mob violence, although he supported his cousin's actions at the "Boston Tea Party." As a member of the 1st Continental Congress he assisted in drafting the Declaration, acted as a signer, served on the Board of War, and secured a committee to establish a military academy for the Army.

I spent last evening at the war office with General Arnold... He has been basely slandered and libeled. The Regulars say, "He fought like Julius Caesar." I am wearied to death with the wrangles between military officers high and low. They quarrel like cats and dogs and they worry one another like mastiffs, scrambling for rank and pay like apes for nuts. [1]

On the 30th, seeing that Arnold had lost a mare or two in a job-related accident, Congress agreed to rustle up some fresh transportation for him.

Resolved, that the quartermaster general be directed to procure a horse and present the same, properly comparisoned, to Major General Arnold, in the name of this Congress, as a token of their approbation of his gallant conduct in the action against the enemy in the late enterprise to Danbury, in which General Arnold had one horse killed under him and another wounded. [26]

Washington writes to Arnold on **June 7th** requesting intelligence on the enemy's fleet, and asks that he communicate between his field commanders by means of stealth.

To M General Arnold

Headquarters Middlebrook, June 7, 1777

Dear Sir

I imagine that since Genl Schuyler's departure from Philadelphia you command there. I therefore enclose you the evidence of a person very lately from New York, from which as well as from other information it appears that a fleet is upon the point of sailing from New York. If Philadelphia should be the place of destination they will make their appearance in Delaware Bay soon after they leave the hook. I therefore desire that you will as soon as you are certain that the fleet is in the bay, give me the earliest notice by the expresses that are posted on the road between this and Philadelphia. Before you send notice to me, be sure that you are not deceived by the signal guns, which I am told have been fired several times without any grounds for so doing. A move of this Army upon a false alarm might prove fatal.

Could not you and Genl Sullivan contrive to give each other notice by signals. We can do it by making lights upon the heights near Princetown and at this place, but I am afraid it will be difficult between Princetown and Philadelphia because the ground is low.

I am, &c., [24]
G. Washington

On the **16th** Arnold wrote to Washington with his predictions for the British to march on Philadelphia.

To His Excellency General Washington
Coryells Ferry, June 16th 1777 8 o'clock P.M.
My Dear General

I wrote your Excellency yesterday that the boats, scows, etc. were sent up the river eleven miles to a place called Tohegan (Tohickon), *except such as were necessary here, which would be secured from the enemy in case of their approach, since which I have had no direct and but very imperfect intelligence from your Excellency. I am at a loss if any part of your Army has removed from Middlebrook and more so of your Excellency's intentions. The enemy I am informed are at Somerset Heights, entrenching General Sullivan is at Flemington with sixteen hundred Continental troops, the Jersey militia & one thousand men; I have sent him from this place half Continental, the others militia. I expect Colonel Bull here tomorrow with five hundred-state troops part of two battalions engaged for the war. General Mifflin writes me yesterday, the city militia will move this morning, I am informed there is about two thousand of them. They bring ten pieces cannon four, sixes, twelve pairs & one royal howitzer, two hundred tents, one thousand felling axes, one thousand*

240

spades & shovels. One quarter part of the militia of this state are ordered out immediately except two of the western counties, the whole, including the city militia, I am informed will make ten thousand men. Three thousand of the southern Continental troops are on their march & will be in Philadelphia in the course of a week. Six heavy pieces cannon, four galleys & ten armed boats are arrived at Bristol & Trenton Ferries. The enemy must be desperate indeed if they attempt to push for Philadelphia. as the militia can be but ill spared at this busy season, I wish to know as early as possible your Excellency's orders respecting them if you wish to have them in the Jerseys or on this side the Delaware. If the latter for the defense of the passes on the river, one half will effectually answer the purpose. I have examined & enclosed your Excellency a sketch of the passes between this and Trenton Ferry. Four or five thousand men with a few pieces cannon will effectually guard the whole as far down as Philadelphia with the assistance of the galleys & armed boats against twenty thousand men. Above Corryells Ferry I am convinced the enemy will never attempt to pass. I hope the troops will be ordered for a different purpose that of securing the enemy where they are in the Jerseys. If they are detained here I shall employ them in fortifying the banks of the river against the passes.

I have sent of this evening via Flemington four wagons, musket cartridges quantity six thousand, under an escort of seventy-five men.

> *I have only to add with great respect & esteem,*
> *I am your Excellency's most obedient humble servant,*
> *B. Arnold* [84]

On the **17th**, Washington made his own speculations regarding the enemy's intentions.

To M General Arnold
> *Headquarters Camp Middlebrook, June 17th, 1777*

Dear Sir
I have received your favor of the 16th instant. You mention a want of intelligence respecting my situation and that of the enemy. As to mine, the main body of our Army is encamped at Middlebrook and a considerable force under Genl Sullivan lies at Sourland Hills. Our position is strong and with a little labor will be rendered much more so. The passes in the mountains are most of them extremely difficult of access and cannot be attempted without the most eminent hazard. Our right is our only weak part, but two or three redoubts will pretty

241

effectually remedy its defects. As to the enemy they are very strongly posted, their right at Brunswick and their left at Somerset. They are well fortified on the right and have the Raritan in front and millstone on the left.

In this situation an attack upon them would not be warranted by a sufficient prospect of success and might be attended with the most ruinous consequences. My design is to collect all the force that can possibly be drawn from other quarters to this post, so as to reduce the security of this Army to the greatest certainty possible and to be in a condition of embracing any fair opportunity that may offer to make an attack on advantageous terms. In the meantime I intend by light bodies of militia, seconded and encouraged by a few Continental troops, to harass and diminish their numbers by continual skirmishes.

I have ordered all the Continental troops at Peekskill, except the number requisite for the security of the post, to hasten on to this Army, and shall call a part of Genl Sullivan's troops to reinforce our right; leaving the rest at and about Sourland Hills to gall the flank and rear of the enemy. in case of any movement towards us he is to give them all the annoyance he can on the rear and flank according to circumstances.

The views of the enemy must be to give a severe blow to this Army and to get possession of Philadelphia. Both are objects of importance; but the former of far the greatest. While we have a respectable force in the field, every acquisition of territory they may make will be precarious and perhaps burdensome – but were this not the case – I am clearly of opinion that they will not move towards Philadelphia without first endeavoring to disable us and prevent our following them. The risk would be too great to attempt to cross a river, where they must expect to meet a formidable opposition in front and would have such a force as our hovering on their rear. They might possibly succeed, but the probability would be infinitely against them. Should they however be imprudent enough to make the attempt, I shall keep close upon their heels and do everything in my power to make the project fatal to them.

But besides the argument for their intending in the first place a stroke at this Army drawn from the policy of the measure – every appearance coincides to confirm the opinion – had their design been in the first instance to cross the Delaware, they would probably have made a secret rapid march towards it and not halted as they have done to awaken our attention and give us time to make every preparation for obstructing them. Instead of that they have only advanced to a position convenient for an attack upon our right, which as I before observed is the part they have the greatest likelihood of injuring us in and added to this consideration, they have come out as light as they could, leaving all their baggage, provisions, except enough to subsist them two or three days at a time, boats and bridges at Brunswick which forcibly contradicts the idea of an immediate expedition towards the Delaware.

It is a happy circumstance that so great an animation prevails among the people. I wish to let it operate and bring as many as possible together, which will be a great discouragement to the enemy by showing that the spirit of opposition runs so high; and at the same time will inspire the people with confidence in themselves by discovering to every individual the zeal and attachment of others – but after they are collected together a few days – I would have the greater part of them in a good humor and make them willing to turn out again in any emergency. It will be proper to concert signals with them for a month or as much more as they can be induced to consent to – if this can be done, they may be made to render very essential service.

Forward all the Continental troops by a safe route as fast as they arrive – but send over no more militia 'till further orders. I approve of your fortifying such places as you judge most likely to frustrate any attempt of the enemy to pass the river.

I am with regard, Dear Sir, your most obedient servant,
G. Washington [24]

With the arrival of Brigadier General James Potter, Arnold wrote back to Washington on the **20**[th] wanting to return to Philadelphia and collect his pay. Born in Ireland back in '29, Potter came to America as a boy and settled in Cumberland County, Pennsylvania, where his father became the first sheriff. During the French and Indian War, he rose through the ranks in the border militia and in the present war he was commissioned as a colonel and elected as a member of the Provincial Convention.

To His Excellency General Washington
Coryells Ferry, June 20th *1777*
Dear General
Your favor of the 17th *instant I received the next morning & immediately communicated the contents to Congress, at the same time recommended the posting two thousand men on the Delaware from this place to Bristol & fifteen hundred at the posts below Philadelphia to complete the works already began & raise such new ones, as are*

*necessary. The state regiment formerly commanded by Colonel Bull,
now by Colo. Stewart, is on its march to join your Excellency, this
will be delivered by Capt. Patrick Anderson, who has the advance
guard & is charged with a letter and fourteen half johannes & three
guineas for Lieut. Colonel Thos. Bull a prisoner in New York, which
beg the favor of your Excellency to forward.*

*I went yesterday from this to Trenton by the rivers bank &
carefully examined all the passes, I am fully of opinion two thousand
men will effectually guard them with some few works, which will be
immediately moved up. Brigr Genl Potter is posted here, I am just
setting off for Trenton, where I shall continue until further orders.
Genl Mifflin I am told will be here this evening on his way to join
your Excellency. Last evening I received a line from Genl Sullivan
who writes me the enemy had abandoned their posts at Somerset &
were retiring to Brunswick.*

*I am ordered by Congress to remain at this post or Trenton
until I received further orders from your Excellency as there are no
troops posted here except militia, who have a sufficient number of
officers. I can be of little service here if I am not wanted with the
Army, I should be glad to return to Philadelphia as my accounts with
the public have not yet been settled owing to Mr. Milligan, one of the
commissioners being out of town.*

I am very respectfully, Dear General, your obedient humble servant,

B. Arnold [84]

244

VIII
Stanwix

On the morning of **July 5th**, Major General Arthur St. Clair was startled to discover that a British flag was flying high atop Sugar Loaf, a higher elevation just to the southwest of Fort Ticonderoga. While the Americans were short of men to man the position, the British were not. The position was taken as a directive from Burgoyne's second in command and first in the artillery, Major General William Phillips, whose proven initiative advanced him rapidly through the ranks during the Seven Years' War. Setting his sights on conquering the heights, he declared, "Where a goat can go a man can go and where a man can go he can drag a gun." [53] With this order in hand, his troops scaled up the mountain and carved a road in just two days time to mount cannon near the top aimed down at the fort. With the possibility of precipitation in the forecast, in the form of cannonballs, the Americans held a council of war and concluded that their only response was to retreat south in order to live to fight another day. During their stealthy escape, they were discovered by the enemy and engaged in hot pursuit. Although the Americans got away, much of their arms, baggage, and stores did not, much to the Brits delight. Schuyler then led the Americans on a one hundred-mile southward retreat to Stillwater on the west bank of the Hudson, east of Saratoga Lake. With Ticonderoga secured, Burgoyne headed directly for Fort Edward from Skenesboro, a task in which he was to discover that although the shortest distance between two points is a straight line, it is not always the quickest. In the predawn hours of the **7th**, American troops were ambushed and brought to battle again when British forces under St. Clair caught up with them at Hubbardton, Vermont. Given the volume of activity in the north, Washington requested Arnold's presence back in the field on the **10th**.

To Hon. John Hancock, Esq.

Morristown, July 10th, 1777

Dear Sir

If the event mentioned by General Schuyler should not have happened, we cannot doubt, but General Burgoyne has come up the lake, determined, if possible, to carry his point, I mean, to possess himself of our posts in that quarter, and to push his arms further. Supposing this not to have happened, as our continental levies so deficient in their number, our security and safety will require, that aids from the militia should be called forth, in case of emergency. If it has, there is now an absolute necessity for their turning out to check General Burgoyne's progress, or the most disagreeable consequences may be apprehended. Upon this occasion, I would take the liberty to suggest to Congress, the propriety of sending an active, spirited, officer to conduct and lead them on. If General Arnold has settled his affairs, and can be spared from Philadelphia, I would recommend him for the business, and that he should immediately set out for the northern department. He is active, judicious, and brave, and an officer in whom the militia will repose great confidence. Besides this, he is well-acquainted with that country, and with the roads and most important passes and gorges in it. I do not think he can render more signal services, or be more usefully employed at this time, than in this way. I am persuaded his presence and activity will animate the militia greatly, and spur them on to a becoming conduct. I could wish him to be engaged in a more agreeable service, to be with better troops; but circumstances call for his exertions in this way. And I have no doubt of his adding much to the honor he has already acquired. [24]

I am your most faithful and most humble servant,
G. Washington.

Although a committee was formed to investigate Arnold's reimbursements, the matter was not pursued with haste, to which Arnold wrote to Congress complaining of the delay and tendered a resignation of his commission on the **11th**. He declared that he was driven to this step only by a sense of the injustice that he had suffered and professing an ardent love of his country, and his readiness to risk his life in its cause, claiming that "honor is a sacrifice no man ought to make; as I received, so I wish to transmit it inviolate to posterity." [69] After receiving Washington's endorsement for his leadership, Hancock sent Arnold to deal with Burgoyne, who was headed for Albany.

To Major General Benedict Arnold

Philadelphia, July 12ᵗʰ, 1777
Sir

I have the honor to enclose you an extract of a letter from Genl Washington from which you will perceive the General is of opinion "a brave, active, and judicious officer" should be immediately employed in collecting the Militia to check the progress of Genl Burgoyne, as very disagreeable consequences may be apprehended if the most vigorous measures are not taken to oppose him.

246

The Congress therefore concurring in opinion with General Washington, who has strongly recommended you for this purpose, have directed you to repair immediately to headquarters to follow such orders as you may receive from him on the subject.
I have the honor to be, with respect, Sir, your most obedient servant,
J. H. President [67]

Not being able to resist the call to battle, he asked for the suspension of his resignation and accepted the order. Placing his trust in the justice of his claims for future reparation, he made his way north to Fort Edward and arrived on the **21**[st]. On the **23**[rd], two weeks after the charges were made; Congress cleared Arnold of all complaints made against him by John Brown. On the **24**[th], Washington advised Schuyler to send Arnold to secure Fort Schuyler and for Lincoln to secure the area. Originally named Fort Stanwix during the French and Indian War, the garrison retains this name today and is open to the public just west of the Mohawk River in the present town of Rome, New York, eighty miles west of Albany.

To M General Schuyler
　　　　　　　　　Headquarters Ramapo, 24 July 1777
Dear Sir
　　　Your two favors of the 21st *and 22*[nd] *with their enclosures are come to hand...*
　　　You intimate the propriety of having a body of men stationed somewhere above the Grants. The expediency of such a measure appears to me evident; for it would certainly make General Burgoyne very circumspect in his advances, if it did not totally prevent them. It would keep him in continual anxiety for his rear, and oblige him to leave the posts behind him much stronger than he would otherwise do, and would answer many other valuable purposes. General Lincoln could not be more serviceable, than in command of this body, and no person could be more proper for it.
　　　From the view I have of the matter, I should also think it necessary to send General Arnold or some other sensible, spirited officer to Fort Schuyler, to take care of that post, keep up the spirits of the inhabitants, and cultivate and improve the favorable disposition of the Indians. This is recommended on the supposition that anything formidable should appear in that quarter.
　　　　　　　　　　　　　　I am, Dear Sir, &c. [68]
　　　　　　　　　　　　　　　　G. Washington

Following his arrival at Fort Edward, Arnold wrote to Washington on the 27th and described the savagery that his men had been subjected to. One of the officers present with Arnold was Brigadier General Abraham Ten Broeck, a prudent and practical-minded merchant from Albany, a member of the Colonial Assembly and Provincial Congress, husband to Elizabeth Van Rensselaer, and brother-in-law to Philip Livingston, signer of the Declaration.

To His Excellency General Washington

Snook Kill (N.Y.) 27 July 1777

Dear General

    I arrived at Camp Fort Edward the 21st instant and should have done myself the honor of writing your Excellency immediately on my arrival, but was informed by Genl Schuyler that he had communicated every intelligence in his power by an express sent off the day before my arrival. The day after coming here the Army was divided into two divisions & headquarters moved to Moses Creek three miles below this place. I am stationed at this place with Nixon's & Learned's brigades of Continental troops, Genl Ten Broeck's brigade & Col. Ashley's battalion of Militia, the former consisting of 1,779 including officers, the latter about thirteen hundred, badly clad & armed.

    The want of salted provisions of which we have not one day's allowance has prevented our sending out any considerable parties of men on scouts, by which reason we have been deprived of intelligence from the enemy, except such as is very vague and uncertain, the woods being so full of Indians, Canadians & regulars that it is almost impossible for small parties to escape them. We are daily insulted by the Indians, who on the 22nd instant, attacked our picket guard, killed & scalped five men, wounded nine & took one prisoner. On the 24th they killed & scalped two officers between Fort Edward & our lines. Yesterday morning our picket at Fort Edward, where we have one hundred men advanced, was attacked by a large party of Indians & regulars, some of my officers were of opinion there was one near one thousand men of the enemy.

    The advanced guard retired to the main body with the loss of one lieut. & five privates, killed & scalped four wounded, the Indians took two women prisoners from a house near the fort, carried them to the regular troops, who were paraded near the fort where they were shot, scalped, stripped, & butchered in the most shocking manner, one of them, a young lady of family, who has a brother, an officer in the regular service. I immediately detached a thousand men, one half

248

to take them in rear, the other in front, who would have accomplished their purpose, but for a heavy shower of rain which wet their arms and ammunition & gave the enemy time to retire, several of our small scouting parties are missing & have probably fell into the hands of the enemy.

I have five or six now out but expect little from them. The regular troops are prevented from deserting by the Indians between us so that every source of information is in a manner cut off. Colonel Warner is at Bennington with seven hundred militia, a considerable number are expected to join him soon, I am this minute informed General Glover's brigade is arrived at Albany. I wish Colo. Morgan's regt would be spared to this department, I think we should then be in a condition to see Genl Burgoyne with all his infernals on any ground they might choose if we could be supplied with salt provisions, we might beat up his quarters at Skenesborough.

We are very anxious to know the destination of General Howe, I believe we shall be able to manage Genl Burgoyne when reinforced by General Glover. General Schuyler writes your Excellency very full. I have not had the pleasure of seeing him these two days.

I have the honor to be with great respect & esteem, your Excellency's most obedient humble servant,

B. Arnold

P.S. Justice obliges me to observe I believe Genl Schuyler has done everything a man can do in his situation, I am sorry to hear his character has been so unjustly aspersed & slandered.

B. A. [84]

Another savage act had also occurred on that day, the murder of a beautiful young woman named Jane McCrea, a tory sympathizer and daughter of a Presbyterian minister from New Jersey. McCrea had been travelling from Fort Edward to Fort Anne to see her fiancé, Lieutenant David Jones of Burgoyne's Army, along with Sarah McNeil, a cousin of Simon Fraser, who was recently promoted to brigadier general after his success at Three Rivers. While enroute to Fort Anne, a skirmish broke out between Indians and Americans forcing the two women to hide in a nearby house, but she was captured and scalped by an Indian named Wyandot Panther, also under Burgoyne. Word of the atrocity spread quickly among the inhabitants, as did the dramatic intensity of the story, for if Burgoyne's native warriors were willing to kill an innocent woman who was attached to one of his own men, then surely they would show no mercy to those against him. This upheaval of resentment caused a surge of new patriots taking up arms for the cause of liberty.

Having trampled through a trackless wilderness of thick woods laden with marshes, ravines, and streams, oh my, it took Burgoyne and his Army all of twenty days to travel twenty-two miles, eating up much of his provisions along the way to finally arrive at Fort Edward on the **30th**. To make the trip more interesting, Schuyler had dispatched a thousand axemen to strategically drop large trees along the route for Burgoyne's men to climb over, under, and around. Utilizing more of Mother Nature's palette, Schuyler's men also dug ditches to expand the wetlands along the way (a no-no under today's environmental laws). On **August 1st**, Congress ordered Schuyler and St. Clair to Washington's headquarters for a court of inquiry regarding the loss of Ticonderoga to the enemy. In a letter to Washington on the **2nd**, New England delegates politically endorsed Gates to serve as the new commander of the Northern Department. Washington, who couldn't agree at all with their selection, asked to be excused from the assignment, but Congress followed up their endorsement with orders and with that, Gates headed north.

That same day, over a thousand British forces under Lieutenant Colonel Barry St. Leger then marched from Oswego into the Mohawk Valley (Rome), demanded the surrender of Fort Stanwix under twenty-eight year old Colonel Peter Gansevoort whose refusal brought about an armed standoff. St. Leger had served as a good leader in frontier warfare in the French and Indian War. Gansevoort was an energetic, resolute, and competent soldier from nearby Albany who had been commissioned as a major in the 2nd New York regiment when he served under Montgomery in Montreal and Quebec before being put in command of Fort George from March through November of last year. Serving alongside Gansevoort was Lieutenant Colonel Marinus Willett from New York, a graduate of Kings College (now Columbia University) who became a wealthy merchant and property owner before serving in the French and Indian War. He took action against the British in New York City at the start of the Revolution and served under Montgomery during the Canadian invasion before attacking enemy troops that had disembarked at Peekskill, New York to destroy magazines and storehouses. On the **5th**, Arnold alluded to Brown's handbill in his letter to Gates, declaring that nothing would deter him from doing his duty in honor of his country.

To General Gates

August 5, 1777

Dear Sir

   A few days since I was informed that Congress had accepted my resignation. I have had no advice of it from the President. No public or private injury or insult shall prevail on me to forsake the cause of my injured and oppressed country until I see peace and liberty restored to her, or nobly die in the attempt. [61]

I am, &c.,

B. Arnold

   On the 6th, American militia under Brigadier General Nicholas Herkimer had been ambushed by a detachment of Burgoyne's troops and Mohawk Indians under Joseph Brant near the Oriskany Indian village while enroute to support Gansevoort. Brant, known among the Iroquois as the warrior leader, Thayendanegea, was the son of a Mohawk warrior who adopted his name after his Indian mother remarried following his father's death. After fighting in the Lake George Campaign of the French and Indian War, he studied English in Lebanon, Connecticut before leading Iroquois warriors in Pontiac's Rebellion. While serving as Sir Guy Johnson's secretary he was presented at court in London, where a portrait was made of him before returning to America to fight in the Cedars. The ambush quickly turned into a six-hour battle and although he died from his wounds ten days later, Herkimer is remembered as a true leader, a man with a cool head and a devout faith. He was born in 1728 near what is now Herkimer, New York and later became Chairman of the Committee of Safety before accepting an appointment as head of the militia. After the initial relief forced was cut off from reaching Stanwix, Arnold attended a council of war on the 12th held by Schuyler, who proposed to save the besieged troops inside the fort, but the council did not want to risk another ambush nor did they think that the Army was strong enough to go up against St. Leger if they did make it that far. In wanting to make up for his evacuation of Ticonderoga, he exclaimed, "Gentleman, I am willing to take responsibility upon myself; where is the Brigadier who will take command of the relief? I shall beat up for volunteers tomorrow." Arnold was the first to volunteer and by noon on the 13th, eight hundred men from Brigadier General Ebenezer Learned's Brigade had assembled for the rescue mission. Learned, who was fifty at the time, hailed from Oxford, Massachusetts where he grew up to serve in the French and Indian War before serving as a delegate to the

Provincial Congress. Upon hearing the shot heard 'round the world, this solid principled patriot led his minutemen on a march to Cambridge, where he was assigned to the left wing of the Army. After mediating the evacuation of British forces from Boston, he personally unbarred the gates on St. Patrick's Day to admit patriot troops back into the city. Following his efforts to help organize militia around Forts Edward and Anne, he then coordinated the extraction of stores at Ticonderoga prior to the American's evacuation. For Arnold's prime example of followership in the Stanwix situation, Schuyler expressed his appreciation for the record.

To General Arnold

August 13, 1777

Dear Sir

It gives me great satisfaction that you have offered to go and conduct the military operations in Tryon County. [42]

I am, &c.,

Philip Schuyler

While Arnold was enroute to Stanwix, Burgoyne, in search of food and supplies, ordered his troops to raid American stores at Bennington, Vermont. A battle ensued on the 16th when they clashed with Brigadier General John Stark's troops and Green Mountain Boys under Seth Warner, who inflicted hundreds of casualties, captured an equal amount of prisoners, and caused just as many of Burgoyne's Indians to flee. These losses had reduced the strength of the Royal Army by as much as fifteen percent, while offering a significant gain for the American arms supply. The effect of the loss for the British was doubled by the fact that the raiding party failed to obtain the store of supplies that they had set out for, which was getting desperately low in camp. Born and raised in the wilderness region of Londonderry, New Hampshire in 1728, Stark acquired incredible talents in hunting and athletic endeavors that served him well as a member of Rogers' Rangers during the French and Indian War. When the Revolution kicked off at Lexington and Concord, he led several hundred of his neighbors to Cambridge where he was appointed as a colonel and assumed command at Bunker Hill. He later served in Canada and fought at Trenton and Princeton. Arnold reached Fort Dayton on the 20th and wrote to Gates from the German Flats (now Herkimer) on the 21st declaring that he was willing to give all or die trying to aid in the fort's defense.

To General Gates
                                    German Flats, August 21, 1777
Dear General
   *Your favor of the 19th instant was delivered to me last evening
and happy to hear you are well and have joined the Army...*
   *I leave this place this morning with twelve hundred
Continental troops and a handful of militia, for Fort Schuyler, still
besieged by a number equal to ours, nothing shall be omitted that can
be done to raise. You will hear of my being victorious or no more and
as soon as the safety of this part of the country will permit I will fly to
your assistance.* [61]
                    *Adieu, Dear General, & believe me with great sincerity,
                              your friend & obedient, humble servant,
                                                        B. Arnold*

   With stealth and silence, Willett made his way through St.
Leger's lines and informed Arnold that Gansevoort was putting up
one hell of a fight at the fort, but with the Indians supporting the
British, their combined forces numbered twice as many as those under
Arnold. Given these stats, Arnold called on Gates for additional
reinforcements, only to learn later that none were available.

To Honorable General Gates
                                    German Flats, August 21, 1777
Dear General
   *Since I wrote the enclosed, a number of the Oneidas have
arrived, several of whom have been at Fort Schuyler within these few
days & say the enemies force is greatly superior to ours, this
intelligence is confirmed by several prisoners and as Colonel Willett,
the bearer, is fully of opinion there is no danger of the Fort's
surrendering for some time, a council of war are fully of opinion that
we ought not to hazard our little Army until reinforced or a
miscarriage would probably be attended with the most fatal
consequences. Enclosed you have the resolutions of the council, I
must beg you will send me such a reinforcement as will in all
probability secure to our success, which I make no doubt you will be
able to spare, one thousand light troops I believe will be sufficient. I
beg they may have no baggage except one shift of clothes if sent of by
companies or small detachments, in which case their tents may be
sent on in wagons. If it is not in your favor to spare us a
reinforcement, you will please to give your relative orders, which
shall be obeyed at all succumb...*

Adieu, Dear General, and believe me with great sincerity,
your friend and obedient humble servant,
Benedict Arnold [84]

If Gates was unable to provide the necessary troops, Arnold would need a backup plan to break the British hold on the fort, something that would rattle their teacups. The opportunity came when a Mohawk Dutchman named Hon Yost Schuyler had been arrested and sentenced to hang for rallying men for the British cause. Upon hearing of his arrest and sentence, his mother and brother they hurried to Fort Dayton and beseeched mercy from Arnold. Even though the convict was a distant cousin of General Philip Schuyler, Arnold refused to entertain their plea. His fate seemed to be sealed until Arnold got an idea from Lieutenant Colonel John Brooks. Following a seven-year apprenticeship to a physician, Brooks became a doctor and had served at the battles of Concord, Bunker Hill, White Plains, and Long Island.

If Yost was known for his political status as well as being a wild and crazy guy, Arnold could use these traits to his advantage. Knowing that the Indians treated people with Hon Yost's mental condition with fear and respect, believing that the great spirits were speaking through them, he would grant his release on one condition. Hon Yost would have to deliver an alarming report to the British at Stanwix that Arnold was approaching with a massive force. With an Oneida Indian as his guide and his proctor, and his brother as an insurance policy left behind, Hon Yost arrived with at the British camp wearing a coat riddled with bullet holes and revealed in exhaustion that Arnold was marching forth with a considerable number of men. Arnold's name certainly got the attention of the British for he had well earned his reputation as an aggressor from his initial attack and last stand on Lake Champlain. Yost got the attention of the Indians as well, for they just happened to be holding a council of war to decide to remain after the losses they recently suffered at the Battle of Oriskany. When the Indians asked how many men was Arnold leading, Yost looked up at a nearby tree and jabbed his finger at it repeatedly as if counting the leaves. Hon Yost was brought before St. Leger and explained that the bullet holes in his coat were fired at him after he escaped from his march to the gallows for his rallying speeches. Just then the Oneida Indian arrived to confirm Hon Yost's story.

That was it for the Indians, when the Great Spirit sends one who is speaking in tongues about a retaliation storm approaching and a brother native claims the same, it's time to leave. Considering the numbers that were lost at the recent Battle of Oriskany, they scolded St. Leger, declaring, "You mean to sacrifice us. When you marched down you said there would be no fighting for us Indians; we might go down and smoke our pipes; whereas numbers of our warriors have been killed and you mean to sacrifice us also." [42] They then fled in a panic, yet before they departed, they murdered some officers and plundered their liquor and clothing, and "became more formidable than the enemy they had to expect," according to St. Leger. [42] Without the support of the natives who made up half of their force, the British joined in the mad rush to get out alive, leaving behind a sizable amount of baggage, tents, arms and most of all, Fort Stanwix, giving Arnold a decisive victory without him firing a single shot. For the American's who lost so much in the flight from Ticonderoga, this payback was sweet. In his journal, Dr. James Thacher wrote of the ruse. Born in 1754, Thacher was apprenticed to a local physician before starting his own practice in his hometown of in Barnstable, Massachusetts. Following the carnage at Concord he served in the hospital at Cambridge and at Ticonderoga before Burgoyne had recently forced him out with the rest of the troops in which he transferred his wounded to the hospital at Albany.

August, 1777 – An object, which cannot be accomplished by force, is often obtained by means of stratagem. Lieutenant Colonel John Brooks, an intelligent officer from Massachusetts, (being in advance of Arnold's party marching to relieve Fort Schuyler), with a small detachment, fortunately found one Major Butler, a noted officer among the Indians, endeavoring to influence the inhabitants in their favor, and he was immediately secured. A man also by the name of Schuyler, who was a proprietor of a handsome estate in the vicinity, was taken up as a spy.

Colonel Brooks proposed that he should be employed as a deceptive messenger to spread the alarm and induce the enemy to retreat. General Arnold soon after arrived and approved the scheme of Colonel Brooks; it was accordingly agreed that Schuyler should be liberated and his estate secured to him on the condition that he would return to the enemy and make such exaggerated report of General Arnold's force as to alarm and put them to flight. Several friendly Indians being present, one of their head men advised that Schuyler's coat should be shot through in two or three places to add credibility to his story.

Matters being thus adjusted, the imposter proceeded directly to the Indian camp, where he was well known, and informed their warriors that Major Butler was taken, and that himself narrowly escaped, several shots having passed through his coat, and that General Arnold with a vast force was advancing rapidly towards them. In aid of the project, a friendly Indian followed and arrived about an hour after with a confirmation of Schuyler's report.

This stratagem was successful: the Indians instantly determined to quit their ground and make their escape, nor was it in the power of St. Leger and Sir John Johnson with all their art of persuasion to prevent it. when St. Leger remonstrated with them, the reply of the chiefs was, "When we marched down, you told us there would be no fighting for us Indians; we might go down and smoke our pipes; but now a number of our warriors have been killed and you mean to sacrifice us." The consequence was that St. Leger, finding himself deserted by the Indians, to the number of seven or eight hundred, deemed his situation so hazardous that he decamped in the greatest hurry and confusion, leaving his tents with most of his artillery and stores in the field. General Arnold with his detachment was now at liberty to return to the main Army at Stillwater; and thus have we clipped the right wing of General Burgoyne.

In the evening, while on their retreat, St. Leger and Sir John got into a warm altercation, criminating each other for the ill success of their expedition. Two Sachems, observing this, resolved to have a laugh at their expense. In their front was a bog of clay and mud; they directed a young warrior to loiter in the rear, and then on a sudden run as if alarmed, calling out, "They are coming, they are coming!" on hearing this, the two commanders in a fright took to their heels, rushing into the bog, frequently falling and sticking in the mud, and the men threw away their packs and hurried off. This and other jokes were several times repeated during the night for many miles. [76]

James Thacher

On the **22nd**, Gansevoort sent his thanks to Arnold.

To the Hon General Arnold

Fort Schuyler, 22 Aug 1777
Dear Sir

This morning at 11 o'clock I began a heavy cannonade upon our enemies works – which was immediately returned by a number of

256

shells & cannon. About three o'clock several deserters came in who informed me that General St Leger with his Army was retreating with the utmost precipitation. Soon after which I sent out a party of about sixty men to enter their camp, who soon returned & confirmed the above account.

About seven o'clock this evening Hon Yost Schuyler arrived here and informed me that General Arnold with two thousand men were on their march for this place in consequence I send you this information.

I am, Dear Sir, yours,
Peter Gansevoort, Colo. [15]

IX
Saratoga

In a meeting at Gates' headquarters on Van Schaick's Island on **September 1st**, Arnold concurred with Gates that Burgoyne's next move would be to head for Albany. Gates then dispatched Arnold to London's Ferry to take command of the Brigades led by Generals Poor and Learned, along with Morgan's battalion. On the **9th**, Arnold also acquired the New York and Connecticut Militia brigades when the American troops reached Stillwater, where the Hudson meets the Mohawk River, and made plans to make their defensive stand here. Arnold on the other hand yearned for a more advantageous playing field and set out to scout the region with the Army's chief engineer, Thaddeus Kosciuszko. Together they found it; an area about four miles to the north called Bemis Heights, named for Jotham Bemis, a local farmer and tavern owner. Gates dispatched Colonels James Wilkinson and Udny Hay to scout the proposed site, when they returned and confirmed, gates investigated it himself and verified their observations. The bluff was surrounded by river, ravines, and ridges, all bordered by forests and totally out of the Briton's element of fighting in an open field. Running below the bluff was the only road to Albany on this side of the river that Burgoyne would have to take in order to reach his objective, the perfect place to lure him into a funnel. A commanding position to say the least, but not a conquering one, at least not until seven thousand men under the direction of Kosciuszko, erected redoubts, earthworks, bivouacs, and abatis (forts, foxholes, campsites, and trenches with felled trees in them as barricades). Meanwhile, men under Colonel Jeduthan Baldwin constructed a raft-bridge across the Hudson measuring over nine hundred feet in length to get supplies and artillery from across the river. As a boy in his native Poland, Kosciuszko studied drawing, mathematics, and French. After graduating from the Royal Military School in Warsaw with the rank of First King's Cadet, he was commissioned as an instructor and went on to further studies at the Ecole Militaire in Paris, before finishing his studies in engineering and artillery at Mezieres. With borrowed money, he set out across the ocean to America as a modest lover of liberty, arriving in Philadelphia, where he developed fortification plans for the Delaware River and was awarded a commission as a Colonel of Engineers. He was later awarded the top slot of chief engineer for his development of the fortification plans for Fort Mercer along the Jersey shore. In viewing the impressive American defenses on the **10th**, Gates wrote to

John Hancock and declared, 'A few days, perhaps hours, will determine whether General Burgoyne will risk a battle or retire to Ti...' [53]

It was at this time that dissention in the ranks set in when three officers who had served under Schuyler, Gates' political nemesis, had joined Arnold's staff. Twenty-four-year-old Lieutenant Colonel Richard Varick was born in Hackensack, New Jersey and had studied and practiced law in New York City upon the birth of our Nation. Upon which he received a commission as a captain under McDougall, an appointment as secretary to Schuyler, and his present position as deputy commissioner general of musters. Twenty-one year old Major Matthew Clarkson had previously served as a volunteer in the battle of Long Island and had referred his cousin, Lieutenant Colonel Henry Brockholst Livingston, to serve as Arnold's aide-de-camp. Born and raised in New York City, Clarkson's cousin was the son of New York Governor William Livingston. After graduating from the College of New Jersey (now Princeton University), he received a captain's commission at the outbreak of the war and was promoted to major as Schuyler's aide-de-camp.

Although they were brothers in arms, they rivaled in command and the feeling soon spread among the staff members as well, who got into a few brawls themselves. The riff was the resentment that Gates felt towards Schuyler for beating him out of the command at Ticonderoga. When Gates expressed his feelings to Arnold regarding his new staff officers, Arnold brushed it aside, wanting to tend to the matter at hand, acting like the warrior he *was*. This lack of concern by Arnold then made Gates grow suspicious of him as well, wondering whether Arnold would remain true to him or to Schuyler and his boys. Gates later took the first step in stripping Arnold's power to demonstrate his own when he had Wilkinson, his deputy adjutant general, annex three of Arnold's New York Militia regiments over to Brigadier General John Glover. Wilkinson was born in from Benedict, Maryland and had marched with Arnold on the quest for Canada before serving under Washington at Trenton and Princeton. A former ship-owner and merchant like Arnold, Glover was a short, heavyset redhead who served in the French and Indian War prior to his immense contributions in the Revolution in which he raised, equipped, and trained 1,000 fishermen to attack British supply ships in Massachusetts Bay. He later coordinated the evacuation of Washington's troops from Long Island and after the battle of White

Plains, coordinated Washington's famous crossing of the Delaware to attack Trenton. When Arnold confronted Gates about the reassignment of his troops, Gates brushed it off with the same carefree way that Arnold held for the assignment of his aides, adding that he would remedy the situation, but he didn't. Once again Arnold was outranked and outflanked.

After the Army moved onto the heights on the **12th**, Arnold settled into his headquarters which was the home of a local farmer named John Neilson, while Gates placed his headquarters a safe distance to the south. On the **13th**, seeing that a trek along the east side of the Hudson to Albany would resemble the one from Skenesborough, Burgoyne crossed the Hudson at Saratoga with seven thousand troops. That same day, Arnold led a detachment to reconnoiter their encampment and captured eight prisoners in the process. The American fortifications were completed by the **15th** with a total of nine thousand men who were ready, willing, and able to defend them. Unbeknownst to either Army at the time, Lincoln at Pawlet had dispatched three bodies of 500 men to retake possession of Ticonderoga, presently under the command of British Brigadier General Powell. Those under Colonel Woodbridge would first take Skenesboro before sweeping south to Forts Anne and Edward. Colonel Johnson led a second group to attack Mount Independence, the elevated heights across the river and to the south of Ticonderoga, thus obtaining air superiority. Last but not least, Arnold's own adversary, John Brown, was to attack a landing at the foot of Lake George, release American prisoners that were being held there, and make an assault on the fort. It took a few days, but they did it.

Upon learning that Burgoyne had cleared all artillery out of the posts at Skenesborough, Fort Anne, Fort George, Fort Edward, and one south of Lake George, Gates dispatched a letter to Governors Clinton and Trumbull and the Committees of Safety in Albany, Bennington, Berkshire County in Massachusetts on the **17th** stating that, "it is evident the General's design is to risk all upon one rash stroke," which he did. [53] When the fog lifted on the **19th**, American pickets reconnoitering the area observed British troops forming up to march along the river road near their encampment at Sword's Farm and passed the word onto Gates, who did absolutely nothing. Arnold stood up and urged Gates to attack before the British were able to make the first move. Guided by feelings of resentment and insecurity, Gates refused the idea. Arnold debated that if they took the road, surely they would be covered, but if they advanced onto the unoccupied highground to the west of Bemis Heights, then they could repeat the Ticonderoga takeover. Again Gates rejected his wisdom. Arnold argued that if he could attack them in the woods, the British would not be able to fight as a unit, and if Arnold's men did get into a scrape, they could retreat back into the fortifications. The British buried their fallen comrades in mass graves, separating officers from enlisted, and leaving severed heads and limbs aboveground. Burgoyne, thinking like the true strategist that he was, did just as Arnold had suspected, but on a broader scale. He divided his forces into three separate branches with Riedesel and Phillips approaching from the river road on the left; Fraser taking the north road and maneuvering to the right; and himself with Brigadier General James Hamilton appearing in the center from the Great Ravine. This would allow them to all converge on John Freeman's Farm. This three-pronged attack would hopefully gain him the fighting victory that he yearned for, one that was denied to him when St. Clair chose flight over fight at Ticonderoga.

Gates finally allowed Colonel Daniel Morgan's riflemen to perform a reconnaissance in force with the support of Captain Henry Dearborn's light troops. Dearborn was a large and commanding man of integrity and frank manners from New Hampshire who had practiced medicine and passed his leisure time studying the art of war. This time spent was proven to be put to good use under Colonel John Stark at Bunker Hill and under Arnold during the march and assault on Quebec. Morgan and Dearborn had been dispatched from the left wing of the Army under Arnold. Other units included the New Hampshire Continental regiments of Colonels Cilley, Hale, and Scammell; the New York regiments under Colonels Henry Beekman Livingston and Van Cortlandt; and Connecticut Militia regiments under Colonels Cook and Lattimer. Born in Mendon (now Milford), Massachusetts, Scammell was a Harvard graduate with a good sense of humor who became a teacher before serving as a surveyor and mapmaker in New Hampshire. After studying law, he entered the Revolution serving in Boston, Canada, and on Long Island. Livingston, a New York native born in 1950, was the son of Robert R. and served under Montgomery at Quebec before serving as an aid-de-camp to Schuyler. Born in New York City in 1749, Van Cortlandt had grown up in Croton, New York and was educated at Coldenham Academy and King's College (now Columbia University) before becoming a surveyor. When push came to shove with England, he became a member of the Provincial Convention and Provincial Congress, before accepting an appointment in the 4th battalion in the New York Infantry.

Arnold rode between the two advance units to coordinate their positions, placing Morgan's sharpshooters behind trees, fences, and huts at the inside corner woods area of Freeman's Farm and lining up Dearborn's men at the south end. In the woods, Morgan and major Jacob Morris communicated with their men through a series of whistles and turkey calls. Soon after the sharpshooters positioned themselves behind trees, fences, and huts at the south end of Freeman's Farm, British skirmishers under Major Gordon Forbes emerged from the woods at the north end. Morgan's men took the first shot, dropping several British officers including Captain David Monin of the British Canadians while fighting alongside his eleven-year-old son. A shot from a prone position from one of Morgan's men apparently took out Lieutenant John Don of the 21st Foot Regiment, who was struck in the chest and sprang up as high as a man before falling dead, according to Lieutenant Thomas Anburey. The riflemen then charged after the fleeing redcoats, but were countered with a British artillery blast from three and six pound cannons that were hidden in the woods. After losing nineteen of his twenty-two artillery men, British Lieutenant James Hadden had his hat shot off while trying to spike one of his cannons, lest it be turned against him by the Americans. Captain Charles Green, an aide-de-camp to Phillips, who was riding atop an elaborately laced and embroidered saddle, was struck down while delivering a message to Burgoyne, being mistaken for Burgoyne himself. After receiving the first battle report, Gates allowed Brigadier General Enoch Poor to send in two New Hampshire regiments as reinforcements under Cilley and Scammell. Once on the scene, Arnold led them to repel the enemy at the east end, but was driven back with ferocity. Seeing a gap between Burgoyne's center and his right wing under Fraser, Arnold led in several regiments to divide the two forces. During one of Arnold's many assaults he directed Van Cortlandt's Second New York Regiment to attack Fraser's force on the left. He also called for volunteers among the 8th Massachusetts under William Hull and directed three hundred of them to support Poor's brigade. Back at headquarters, Arnold requested Gates to order a full attack with each charge to finish the fight. Gates denied the request several times before giving in to allow Learned's brigade to be dispatched. A report then reached headquarters noting that no advantage was yet to be seen by either side, which fired up Arnold's spirit all the more to change that report, as revealed in Wilkinson's memoirs. Born in 1754, Lewis was a recent graduate from Princeton, who studied law before joining the Army in the summer of '75 as a captain in the New York Militia serving at Cambridge and New York City. The following year he was promoted and appointed deputy quartermaster general of the Northern Army before becoming chief of staff to Gates.

It is worthy of remark, that not a single General officer was on the field of battle on the nineteenth of September, until the evening, when General Learned was ordered out. About the same time, General Gates and Arnold were in front of the center of the camp, listening to the peal of small arms, when Colonel M. Lewis returned from the field and reported the indecisive progress of the action, at which Arnold exclaimed, 'By God I will soon put an end to it,' and clapping spurs to his horse, galloped off at full speed. Colonel Lewis observed to Gates, "You had better order him back; he may, by some rash act, do mischief.' I was instantly dispatched, overtook, and remanded Arnold to camp. [5]

James Wilkinson

As the blazing sun set below the horizon, so did the sound of the guns cannons and muskets, but all was not quiet on the western front as the air was filled with the sound of brave men groaning in pain from their battle wounds. The British buried their fallen comrades in mass graves, separating officers from enlisted, and leaving severed heads and limbs aboveground. As night fell on Freeman's Farm, the conflict transformed from one of man vs. man to man vs. beast, as wolves came down from the hills following the smell of blood to its source. Inside the overwhelmed, makeshift hospital the British spent the better part of the 20th licking their wounds as they tried to recoup from the worst beating they had ever taken from a bunch of rebels with casualties amounting to more than six hundred killed, injured, or captured. Digby, who went up against Arnold at Valcour Island, wrote of the battle as part of the Shropshire Regiment.

19th. At daybreak, intelligence was received that Colonel Morgan, with the advance party of the enemy consisting of a corps of riflemen, were strong about three miles from us; their main body amounting to great numbers encamped on a very strong post about half a mile in their rear; and about 9 o'clock we began our march, every man prepared with 60 rounds of cartridge and ready for instant action. We moved in three columns, ours to the right on the heights and farthest from the river in thick woods. A little after 12 our advanced pickets came up with Colonel Morgan and engaged, but from the great superiority of fire received from him – his numbers being much greater – they were obliged to fall back, every officer being either killed or wounded except one, when the line came up to their support and obliged Morgan in his turn to retreat without loss.

About half past one, the fire seemed to slacken a little; but it was only to come on with double force, as between 2 and 3 the action became general on their side. From the situation on the ground, and their being perfectly acquainted with it, the whole of our troops could not to be brought to engage together, which was a very material disadvantage, though everything possible was tried to remedy that inconvenience, but to no effect. Such an explosion of fire I never had any idea of before, and the heavy artillery joining in concert like great peals of thunder, assisted by the echoes of the woods, almost deafened us with the noise. To an unconcerned spectator, it must have had the most awful and glorious appearance, the different battalions moving to relieve each other, some being passed and almost broke by their superior numbers. The crash of cannon and musketry never ceased till darkness parted us, when they retired to their camp, leaving us masters of the field; but it was a dear-bought victory if I can give it that name, as we lost many brave men. The 62nd had scarce 10 men a company left, and other regiments suffered much, and no very great advantage, honor excepted, was gained by the day.

On its turning dark we were near firing on a body of our Germans, mistaking their dark clothing for that of the enemy. General Burgoyne was everywhere and did everything that could be expected from a brave officer and Brig. Gen. Fraser gained great honor by exposing himself to every danger. During the night we remained in our ranks and though we heard the groans of our wounded and the dying at a small distance, yet could not assist them till morning, not knowing the position of the enemy, and expecting the action would be renewed at daybreak. Sleep was a stranger to us, but we were all in good spirits and ready to obey with cheerfulness any orders the General might issue before morning dawned. [20]

Another version of the battle was printed in the *Churchill Papers* on that very same day.

Churchill Papers

New York   Yesterday, about noon, the two armies met near Stillwater, and a most obstinate and bloody battle ensued. The advanced parties of the Americans, which were composed of Morgan's riflemen and Dearborn's infantry, received the first fire of the enemy, and a little after two o'clock the action became general. The right wing of the British forces was commanded by Burgoyne in person, the left by Phillips and Reidesel, and the center, covered by Fraser and Breymann, was supported by the savages, Canadians, and renegade provincials and tories. Never was more bravery or determination shown. For upwards of three hours the blaze from the artillery and small arms was incessant, and sounded like the roll of the drum. By turns the British and Americans drove each other, taking and retaking the field pieces, and often mingling in a hand to hand wrestle and fight. Scammell fought like a hero, leading his regiment where the fire was the hottest, and did not leave his post until he was wounded and taken off the field. The British artillery was well served, and worked with sad havoc among our poor fellows, who are the more to be wept, for their gallantry and devotion to their country. The cannon of the British was lost to us only for the want of horses to draw them off. Arnold rushed into the thickest of the fight with his usual recklessness, and at times acted like a madman. I did not see him once, but S. told me this morning that he did not seem inclined to lead alone, but as a prominent object among the enemy, showed itself, he would seize the nearest rifle-gun and take deliberate aim.

During the action a party of our men got up into some trees, and as the clouds of smoke opened, poured in upon the enemy single shot. In this manner several of the officers were killed or wounded. One of Brook's regiment says he silenced two fellows with laced coats, and it is said that Burgoyne had a narrow escape.

At sundown the action was less furious, and a little after dark a greater part of the two armies retired from the field. Some of our men did not come off until near midnight. In the midst of so much destruction, it is a wonder how any of them escaped; "but it is in this cause," as old Emerson used to say about the hens that laid every day in the year but Sunday, "Providence is with 'em." [50]

Although while the contest in the Hudson Highlands closed with a draw, the campaign in Philadelphia ended in a rout when Howe ordered Major General Charles Grey to seize the capital city, thus driving Congress to relocate to York, ninety miles to the west. Born in Howick, England in 1729, Grey had fought in the Seven Years' War and served as an aide-de-camp before doing battle with the Americans across the pond. He acquired the nickname "no flint Grey" when he ordered his men to remove the flints of their muskets, in order to prevent anyone from firing early and losing their element of surprise, and made a successful stealth attack on American forces under Brigadier General Anthony Wayne.

Before the sun rose on the 21st, spirits rose among Burgoyne's camp when he received a most attractive offer from his comrade in New York, Sir Henry Clinton. His letter informed Burgoyne that he would attack the defenses just south of West Point with a significant force in order to help clear the river. All he needed was the arrival of fresh troops on their way from England to assure that New York was not left unattended and the assault on the forts to be overwhelming, for if he were outflanked, he would have to retreat back to New York.

To General Burgoyne
                                            September 12, 1777
Dear Sir:
   You know my good will and are not ignorant of my poverty of troops. If you think 2000 men can assist you effectually, I will make a push at Fort Montgomery (just south of West Point) *in about ten days. But ever jealous of my flanks if they make a move in force on either of them I must return to save this important post. I expect reinforcement every day. Let me know what you wish.*

                                            I am, &c.,
                                            Sir Henry Clinton

Interpreting that Clinton was going to come all the way up the Hudson, Burgoyne eagerly accepted his offer and pleaded with him to hurry for he could only hold out until October 12th before he must withdraw to Ticonderoga for the winter. Unfortunately Burgoyne's letter must have been lost or intercepted along the way for Clinton never got it, nor did he get orders from Howe to leave the New York metropolitan area and sail that far up the Hudson. Confident that help was on the way, Burgoyne changed his tactical plan from offensive to defensive in order to buy time for Clinton to make the 160-mile trip. In order to establish this, the British erected a series of fortifications north of the American position that included two redoubts on Freeman's Farm to the north and east of Barber's Wheat Field that

267

anchored the British right flank and the road to Quaker Springs. Major Alexander Lindsay Balcarres commanded the defense to the east while the northern site was under Lieutenant Colonel Heinrich Breymann. Born in 1752, Balcarres was a tough aristocratic earl who had served under Carleton at Three Rivers and Burgoyne at Ticonderoga and Hubbardton, Vermont, where his life was spared by thirteen bullets that had passed through his coat. Although the hardnosed disciplinarian Breymann got off with only five bullet holes through his coat and a flesh wound in his leg at the battle of Bennington, his reputation suffered more when he failed to reinforce Colonel Friedrich Baum in time, forcing him to surrender.

The Americans were celebrating something of their own when cheers were heard coming from their camp followed by a thirteen-gun salute. The British had no idea what all the fuss was about until one of their own who had been taken prisoner on the 19th, had escaped, raced into the camp, and announced that the American's had retaken Ticonderoga. Burgoyne had just lost his only nearby safe haven and the morning frost was already beginning to reveal the onslaught of winter. Things did not look good for Burgoyne, he had his back to the river, the American Army growing in numbers to the north and south, and he was running low on provisions. Back in the American camp, seeing that Gates had lost the opportunity to take the field in the recent engagement, Arnold offered him a second chance to get it right.

To General Gates
Sir
 I think it my duty (which nothing shall deter me from doing) to acquaint you, the Army is becoming vigorous for action. The militia (who compose a quarter part of the Army) are already threatening to go home. One fortnight's inaction will, I make no doubt, lessen your Army by sickness and desertion, at least four thousand men, in which time the enemy may be reinforced and make good their retreat. I have reasons to think that, had we improved the 20th of September, it might have ruined the enemy. That is past; let me entreat you to improve the present time. [42]

I am, &c.,
B. Arnold

Hearing praise after praise from troops recalling Arnold's showmanship in the battle, yet not hearing any for his part in coordinating it, Gates' feelings towards Arnold grew more incessant. In retaliation for this imagined lack of respect, Gates refused to mention him in the battle report written to Congress. Arnold, who for obvious reasons was insulted by this action, later became infuriated when Gates removed Morgan's corps from under his command on the 22nd. Arnold marched over to Gates' headquarters and burst in on him, which unleashed a heinous shouting match between the two, forged with curses and hatred. Gates claimed that he had no knowledge of Arnold holding the rank of a major general (referring to his threat to resign from the Army when he had been passed over for promotion) nor the command of any troops whatsoever. To conclude his side of the political debate, Gates announced the matter to regardless, for he had ordered Lincoln to return as a division commander and would have no further use for Arnold. In a letter to Schuyler, Varick gave credit where credit was due.

To Major General Schuyler
September 22, 1777
Dear Sir
    Gates seems to be piqued that Arnold's division had the honor of beating the enemy on the 19th. This I am certain of: Arnold has all the credit of the action; and this I further know, that Gates asked where the troops were going when Scammell's battalion marched out, and upon being told, he declared no more troops should go; he would not suffer the camp to be exposed. Had Gates complied with Arnold's repeated desires, he would have obtained a general and complete victory over the enemy. But it is evident to me he never intended to fight Burgoyne until Arnold urged, begged, and entreated him to do it.
[5]
I am, &c.,
Richard Varick

    That evening, Arnold addressed his command issue to Gates in a letter to make it official.

To General Gates
Camp at Stillwater, September 22, 1777
Sir
    When I joined the Army at Vanschaak's Island the 1st instant, you were pleased to order me to London's Ferry to take the command of Generals Poor and Learned's Brigades and Colonel Morgan's battalion of riflemen and light infantry. Your command was

immediately obeyed. I have repeatedly since received your orders respecting those corps as belonging to my division, which has often been mentioned in General Orders, and the gentlemen commanding those corps have understood themselves as in my division. On the 9th instant, you desired me to annex the New York and Connecticut Militia to such brigades as I thought proper in my division, which I accordingly did and ordered the New York Militia to join General Poor's brigade and the Connecticut Militia to General Learned's. The next day, I was surprised to observe in General Orders the New York Militia annexed to General Glover's brigade, which placed me in the ridiculous light of presuming to give orders I had no right to do, and having them publicly contradicted, which I mentioned to you as I thought it a mistake of the Deputy Adjutant General. You then observed the mistake your own and that it should be mentioned as such in the ensuing orders, which has never been done.

On the 19th instant, when advice was received that the enemy was approaching, I took the liberty to give it as my opinion that we ought to march out and attack them. You desired me to send Colonel Morgan and the light infantry and support them. I obeyed your orders and before the action was over I found it necessary to send out the whole of my division to support the attack. No other troops were engaged that day except Colonel Marshall's regiment of General Paterson's brigade.

I have been informed that in the returns transmitted to Congress of the killed and wounded in the action the troops were mentioned as a detachment from the Army and in the orders of this day I observe it is mentioned that Colonel Morgan's corps not being in any brigade or division of this Army are to make returns and reports only to headquarters, from whence they are alone to receive orders. Although it is notorious to the whole Army they have been in and done duty with my division for some time past.

When I mentioned these matters to you this day, you were pleased to say in contradiction to your repeated orders that you did not know that I was a Major General or had any command in the Army. I have ever supposed a major general's command of four thousand men a proper division and no detachment, when composed of whole brigades forming one wing of the Army and that general troops if guilty of misconduct or cowardly behavior in time of action were justly chargeable as a division. If on the other hand, they behave with spirit and firmness in action they were justly initiated to the applause due to a brave division, not detachment, of the Army. Had my division behaved ill, the other divisions of the Army would have thought it extremely hard to have been amenable for their conduct. I mentioned these matters as I wish justice due to the division, as well as particular regiments or persons.

From what reasons I know not, as I am conscious of no offense or neglect of duty, but I have lately observed little attention paid to any proposals I have thought it my duty to make for the public service and when a measure I have proposed has been agreed to it has immediately been contradicted. I have been received with the greatest coolness at headquarters and often treated in such a manner as must mortify a person with less pride than I have and in my station in the Army. You observed that you expected General Lincoln in a day or two when I should have no command of a division, that you thought me of little consequence to the Army and that you would with all your heart give me a pass to leave it whenever I thought proper. As I find your observation very just that I am not or that you wish me of little consequence in the Army and as I have the interest and safety of my country at heart, I wish to be where I can be of the most service to them. I therefore, as General Lincoln has arrived, request your pass to Philadelphia with my aid de camp and three servants, where I propose to join General Washington and may possibly have it in my power to serve my country, though I am thought of no consequence in this department. [20]

I am, &c.,

B. Arnold

Upon receiving Arnold's request to depart the premises, Gates sent him a brief, unsealed note stating that he had written to John Hancock granting him permission to leave the camp if he wished. Arnold protested the open pass from Gates and gave serious consideration to making haste for Philadelphia, which didn't sit well with the troops who admired his leadership abilities. On the **23rd**, Gates issued a sealed letter to Arnold to offer him satisfaction and be done with the matter.

To General Arnold

Headquarters, September 23, 1777

Dear Sir

You wrote me nothing last night but what had been sufficiently altercated between us in the evening. I then gave such answers to all your objections as I think were satisfactory. I know not what you mean by insult or indignity. I made you such replies only as I conceived proper. As to the opened letter I sent you to Mr. Hancock,

it was the most civil method I could devise of acquainting Congress with your leaving the Army and is to all intents and purposes as full a pass as can be desired. I sent it unsealed as being more complacent to you and is what is commonly done upon such occasions. That not being so agreeable to you as a common pass, I send you one enclosed.
[20]

I am, &c.,
H. Gates, Major General

Fearing the loss of Arnold's presence during such a vital campaign, Henry Brockholst Livingston appealed to Schuyler to intervene and prevent his leaving.

To Major General Schuyler
Camp on Bemis Heights, September 23, 1777
Dear Sir
I am this moment honored with your favor of the 21ˢᵗ by Major Franks. General Lincoln arrived here last night and part of his infantry came today; the remainder are expected tomorrow. I wrote you some time since of his having detached two parties to Ticonderoga and Fort Independence. Colonel Varick has given you the particulars of their success. I cannot persuade myself that the mount will be taken.

I am much distressed at Genl Arnold's determination to retire from the Army at this important crisis. His presence was never more necessary. He is the life and soul of the troops. Believe me, Sir, to him and to him alone is due the honor of our late victory. Whatever share his superiors may claim they are entitled to none. He enjoys the confidence and affection of officers and soldiers. They would, to a man, follow him to conquer or death. His absence will dishearten them to such a degree as to render them of but little service.

The difference between him and Mr. Gates has arisen to too great a height to admit of a compromise. I have, for some time past, observed the great coolness and, in many instances, even disrespect with which Genl Arnold has been treated at headquarters. His proposals have been rejected with marks of indignity, his own orders have frequently been contravened, and himself set in a ridiculous light by those of the Commander-in-Chief. His remonstrations, on those occasions, have been termed presumptuous. In short he has pocketed many insults for the sake of his country. Which a man of less pride would have resented.

272

The repeated indignities he received at length roused his spirit and determined him again to remonstrate. He waited on Mr. Gates in person last evening. Matters were altercated in a very high strain. Both were warm, the latter rather passionate and very assuming. Towards the end of the debate Mr. Gates told Arnold, "He did not know of his being a Major General. He had sent his resignation to Congress. He had never given him the command of the Army. Genl Lincoln would be here in a day or two, that then he should have no occasion for him, and would give him a pass to go to Philadelphia, whenever he chose."

Arnold's spirit could not brook this usage. He returned to his quarters, represented what had passed in a letter to Mr. Gates and requested his permission to go to Philadelphia. This morning, in answer to his letter, he received a permit, by way of a letter directed to Mr. Hancock. He sent this back and requested one in a proper form, which was complied with. Tomorrow he will set out for Albany.

The reason of the present disagreement between two old cronies is simply this – Arnold is your friend. I shall attend the General down. Chagrining as it may be for me to leave the Army at a time when an opportunity is offering for every young fellow to distinguish himself, I can no longer submit to the command of a man whom I abhor from my very soul. This conduct is disgusting to everyone but his flatterers and his dependents, among whom are some who profess to be your friends. A cloud is gathering and may before long burst on his head.

B. Livingston [20]

To show their loyalty for Arnold, he was presented with a petition signed by every officer except Gates and Lincoln, beseeching him to stay. Knowing that leadership is a two-way street, Arnold obliged and remained with his men. On the **24th**, Clinton's long awaited troops arrived from England after first embarking on their three month crossing of the Atlantic. That same day, along with some intel on the red Army, Livingston shared the news of Arnold's reconsideration with Schuyler.

To Major General Schuyler

September 24, 1777

Dear Sir

I wrote you last evening and was in hopes to have had the pleasure of seeing you today, but as the enemy are hourly expected, General Arnold cannot think of leaving camp. Three deserters came in this morning and it was rumored in the camp when they came off that we were to be attacked this day. Burgoyne yesterday harangued the soldiers and told them he was determined to leave his bones on the field or force his way to Albany. He has about one month's salt provisions in his camp. Three tories were just now brought in by the Oneidas; they confirm the report of the deserters, and add that the enemy acknowledged publicly to have lost 700 killed and wounded in the late battle, and plume themselves with a confidence that our loss might have been at least double.

General Arnold's intention to quit this department is made public, and has caused great uneasiness among the soldiers. To induce him to stay, General Poor proposed an address from the General officers and Colonels of his division, returning him thanks for his past services, and particularly for his conduct during the late action, and requesting him to stay. The address was framed and consented to by Poor's officers. Those of General Learned refused. They acquiesced in the propriety of the measure, but were afraid of giving umbrage to General Gates – a paltry excuse for officers of rank to allege in excuse for not doing their duty. As this method has failed, I see no other way left to bring about a reconciliation but by the interposition of the General officers. This has been proposed to Lincoln. He is now anxious for Arnold's stay and will push the matter. I hope he may succeed, as I think he is an officer of too much moment to be neglected – though it may be a mortifying situation for any gentleman of spirit to submit to the petulant humors of any man, be his rank ever so high.

> I am with due respect and esteem, Sir, your friend,
> Henry B. Livingston [5]

On the 25th, Schuyler expressed his relief to Varick regarding Arnold's decision to keep the fight.

To Colonel Varick

September 25, 1777

Sir

I am pleased to hear that our gallant friend General Arnold has determined to remain until a battle shall have happened or General Burgoyne retreats. Everybody that I have conversed with on the subject of the dispute between Gates and him thinks Arnold has been extremely ill-treated. He (Gates) will probably be indebted to him for the glory he may acquire by a victory; but perhaps he is so *very sure of success that he does not wish the other to come in for a share of it.* [5]

I am, &c.,

Philip Schuyler

Meanwhile, Gates, refusing to issue a formal order of Arnold's command status and instead choosing to ignore his concerns, had put their debate at a standoff. Having not heard from Clinton as expected, Burgoyne was pleading for him on the **28**th as he wrote, '...an attack or even the menace of an attack upon Fort Montgomery must be of great use, as it will draw away great part of their force and I will follow them close. Do it, my dear friend, directly.' [53] On **October 3**rd, Clinton sailed up the Hudson River from New York armed with 3,000 fresh troops to clear the river as promised and disembarked a part of his force at Tarrytown on the **4**th, which marched north towards Peekskill. Word spread about the eminent attack, causing Israel Putnam to call for an alarm in Peekskill before the British returned to their ship, completing their feint. On the **5**th, Clinton feinted again at Verplank's Point, just below Peekskill, this time with his full strength of three thousand. With the abundant number of enemy troops arriving on the eastern shore, Putnam called for reinforcements from Clinton's true target points, Fort Montgomery and the one adjacent to it Fort Clinton, commanded by Henry's brother, Governor George, leaving a paltry six hundred men to defend them. With a thousand men to secure any crossing of American reinforcements from Verplank's Point, Clinton sailed over to the other side in the early morning fog on the **6**th to disembark at Stony Point. From there, they marched through the woods northward and split up into two assault groups with Lieutenant Colonel Campbell leading the attack on Fort Montgomery and Sir Henry leading the attack on Fort Clinton. When the two opposing advanced guards met and exchanged fire, Governor George left Fort Clinton under the command of his brother James and crossed Popolopen Creek to take command of Fort Montgomery. When the Governor rejected a call from the British to surrender the American forts, the invading Army poured two thousand forces against the river strongholds and drove the six hundred to defeat. Although George and James escaped with their lives, three hundred of their comrades did not. After putting the two river forts to the torch, Sir Henry followed up these attacks on the **7**th with an assault on Fort Constitution, directly across from Fortress West Point. After making his way a dozen miles up the river, Governor George, unaware that a third river fort had just fallen to the enemy, wrote to the Council of New York to announce the loss of two key defenses built to protect the Point.

To the Council of New York

New Windsor, October 7, 1777

Gentlemen

 The extreme fatigue I have undergone this three past days and the want of rest for an equal number of nights renders me unfit to write you matters of so serious consequence to this state as I have to communicate. I am able only briefly to inform you that yesterday about ten o'clock a.m. an advanced party was attacked by the enemy at Doodletown about 2½ miles from Fort Montgomery. They consisted of about 30 men; the enemy, by appearance and accounts after received, of 5000. They received the enemy's fire, returned it and retreated to Fort Clinton.

 Soon after I received intelligence that the enemy were advancing on the west side of the mountain with design to attack us in rear. Upon this I ordered out Lieut. Colo. Brown and McClaghey with upwards of 1900 men towards Doodletown and a brass field piece with a detachment of 60 men to a very advantageous post in the road to the furnace. They were not long out before they were both attacked by the enemy with their whole force. Our people behaved with spirit and must have made great slaughter of the enemy. I strengthened the party in the furnace road to upwards of 100 but they were obliged to give way to so superior a force as the enemy brought against them. They kept their field piece in full play at them till the men who worked it were drove with fix bayonets, then spiked it and retreated with great good order to a 12 pounder which I had ordered to cover them and from thence in the fort. I immediately posted my men in the most advantageous manner for the defense of the post and it was not many minutes before as well our post as Fort Clinton were invaded on all sides and in a most incessant fire kept up till night and even after dusk, when the enemy forced our lines and redoubts at both posts, and the garrisons were obliged to fight their way out – as many as could as were determined not to surrender – and many have escaped.

 I was summoned, sun an hour high, to surrender in five minutes and thereby prevent the effusion of blood. I sent Lieut. Colo. Livingston to receive the flag, who informed them that he had no orders to treat them except to receive their proposals if they meant to surrender themselves as prisoners of war in which case he was empowered to assure them good usage. About 10 minutes after they made a general and desperate attack on both posts which was resisted with great spirit, but we were at length overpowered by numbers and they gained possession of both posts. Officers and men behaved with great spirit, as well Continental troops as militia. Our loss in slain cannot be great considering the length of the action. My brother Genl Clinton is wounded and I believe made prisoner. This is the case with Major Logan. The number of our missing I cannot ascertain. The ships are both burnt and Fort Constitution demolished by our people without my orders but I can't as yet condemn the measure. The officers all say it was right. I am clear it was as to the fort after removing artillery and stores, which has not been done. the ships I hoped might have been saved.

Genl Putnam will retreat to near Capt Haights about 3 miles from Mr. Van Wyck and I mean to rally my broken but brave forces and advance tomorrow on Butter Hill. Genl Putnam is to send Colo. Webb's regiment to join me.

I beg you will give me the substance of this account to Genl Gates in answer to his letter to me. I have only to add that I greatly respect the loss of these posts but I am consoled with the full persuasion that they have bought them dear and that I have done the most in my power to save them. [20]

Meanwhile as the first frost appeared one hundred miles to the north and fearing that his troops would starve before help would arrive, Burgoyne reluctantly resumed his offensive with a reconnaissance in force to see what Gates was up to. Burgoyne was in for a big surprise, because Gates was up to over 10,000 men as scores of militia came pouring in from all over. This was to take an extremely heavy toll on him as his forces had whittled down to 5,000 following the losses from the first engagement and the desertions that followed. Regardless, Burgoyne once again divided his forces three ways and once again he probed the highground to the west. Although neither Army had changed its position since the preceding battle, the view of the surroundings had transformed itself from a sea of emerald green to a vibrant mixture of red, orange, and yellow as the fall foliage spread across the vast expanse of the Highlands. Each tree giving the illusion of a thousand flames dancing in the wind. From the number of deserters in Burgoyne's camp, Gates learned that provisions were running low and it was only a matter of time before he had to succumb to either fight or flight. A mixture of feelings welled inside him to trust but verify these accounts, so he dispatched Wilkinson to get a fix on their activities in order to gain intelligence on their intentions.

From a distance of 300 hundred yards under the cover of the woods, Wilkinson could see enemy troop and artillery movements heading towards Barber's wheat field, which was being prepared by soldiers, thatching the wheat and loading it onto wagons. He also observed three British officers (Burgoyne, Phillips, and Riedesel) climb on top of an abandoned cabin and peer through their spyglasses to view the American formations, but were unable to see anything. After fifteen minutes, he returned to headquarters and reported the news to Gates, who commenced offenses by sending Morgan and Dearborn's men to the left of Freeman's Farm, Learned to the center, and Poor, who was previously under Arnold, to the right. Being the first on the scene, Poor's brigade positioned themselves in the woods as six and twelve-pound British cannon blasts initiated the engagement. Major John Dyke Acland's grenadiers immediately followed up by launching a series of musket salvos before Acland commanded, "Fix bayonets and charge the damned rebels." [53] As the wave of British steel rushed towards them, Cilley ordered Poor's men to do the same who succeeded in gouging the advancing line of grenadiers. Once the gap was sighted, Poor's men advanced, sending the enemy running in the opposite direction without even stopping to pick up their wounded, Acland being among the casualties. Cilley even went as far as jumping on top of a captured twelve-pounder, waving his sword high in the air, and rallying his men to turn it on the enemy, which they did. Wilkinson recalled his actions and observations, but followed the political lead of Gates by omitting any mention of Arnold.

On the afternoon of the 7th of October, the advanced guard of the center beat to arms; the alarm was repeated throughout the line and the troops repaired to their alarm posts. I was at headquarters when this happened, and with the approbation of the General, mounted my horse to inquire the cause; but on reaching the guard where the beat commenced, I could obtain no other satisfaction but that some person had reported the enemy to be advancing against our left. I proceeded over open ground and ascending a gentle slope in front of the guard, I perceived, about half a mile from the line of our encampment, several columns from the enemy, 60 or 70 rods from me, entering a wheat field which had not been cut and was separated from me by a small stream; and without my glass I could distinctly mark their every movement. After entering the field, they displayed, formed the line, and sat down in double ranks with their arms between their legs. Foragers then proceeded to cut the wheat or standing straw, and I soon after observed several officers, mounted on the top of a cabin, from whence with their glasses they were endeavoring to reconnoiter our left, which was concealed from their view by intervening woods.

Having satisfied myself, after fifteen minutes attentive observation, that no attack was mediated, I returned and reported to the General, who asked me what appeared to be the intentions of the enemy.

"They are foraging and endeavoring to reconnoiter your left; and I think, Sir, they offer you battle."

"What is the nature of the ground and what your opinion?"

"Their front is open and their flanks rest on woods, under cover of which they may be attacked; their right is skirted by a lofty height. I would indulge them."

"Well then, order on Morgan to begin the game."

I waited on the Colonel, whose corps was formed in front of our center, and delivered the order; he knew the ground and inquired the position of the enemy: they were formed across a newly cultivated field, bordering on a wood and a small ravine formed by the stream before alluded to; their light infantry on the right, covered by a worm fence at the foot of the hill before mentioned, thickly covered with wood; their center composed of British and German battalions. Colonel Morgan, with his usual sagacity, proposed to make a circuit with his corps by our left, and under cover of the wood to gain the height on the right of the enemy, and from thence commence his attack, so soon as our fire should be opened against their left; the plan was the best which could be devised, and no doubt contributed essentially to the prompt and decisive victory we gained... [20]

James Wilkinson

As Morgan, Dearborn, and Poor kicked off the contest, Lieutenant Colonel John Brooks of Massachusetts recalled the events that followed as one of several officers dining with Gates and Arnold at Headquarters that afternoon.

I was among the company and well remember that one of the dishes was an ox's heart. While at table, we heard a firing from the advanced picket. The armies were about two miles from each other. the firing increasing, we all rose from the table; and General Arnold, addressing General Gates, said, "Shall I go out and see what is the matter?"

279

General Gates made no reply, but upon being pressed, said, "I am afraid to trust you, Arnold." To which Arnold answered, "Pray let me go. I will be careful, and if our advance does not need support, I will promise not to commit you."

Gates then told him he might go and see what the firing meant.

[60]

John Brooks

With Lincoln along for the ride to keep him on a leash, Arnold trotted towards the lines; the sound of the drums and the guns, each beating a war cadence that resonated deep in his heart. In viewing the fight, they saw that once again the British forces were divided three ways and that a sizeable enemy force was aiming towards the Army's left flank, which was open and vulnerable. Within a half-hour of leaving headquarters, the two officers returned and reported their concern to Gates. Lincoln advised him that their lines were in great danger if reinforcements were not sent in right away, to which Gates said that he would order Morgan and Dearborn to make a wide sweep around to the left and outflank them. Arnold protested such a weak response to which Gates dismissed his input. Lincoln emphasized the need for more forces, which Gates accepted, sending regiments from Learned's and Brigadier General John Nixon's brigades, but when Arnold had returned to the field to observe further action with Lincoln, Gates called him back and confined him to quarters.

While there, Arnold learned from a courier that the British had advanced deep into the wheat field. He paced about like a caged animal, listening to the blast of six and twelve pounders beating away like a virtual orchestra of ordnance, cursing every step. He couldn't believe it, he, who yearned for the surge of war and knew how to lead men in battle, was being forbidden from serving his country and maybe even saving it? The hell he wasn't. Having "impatience" as a virtue, Arnold abandoned his quarters and called out to his aids, "No man shall keep me in my tent today. If I am without command, I will fight in the ranks; but the soldiers God bless them, will follow my lead. Come on, victory or death!" [5] He then mounted his mare, brandished his word, and charged into the smoke and sound of the guns. Gates spotted Arnold galloping off and sent Major John Armstrong out to retrieve him, but all he caught was a flurry of dust and a glimpse of the rear of a big brown horse. He continued to pursue him for the next half-hour, but just couldn't keep up, for Arnold was all over the field. Another officer that was leading from

280

the front rather than pushing from the rear was General John Burgoyne, who was sharply dressed in his red regimentals while giving directions atop his horse.

Arnold came upon the rear of Learned's brigade and asked whose group it was. A soldier called out, "Colonel Lattimer's, Sir," to which Arnold replied, "My old Norwich and New London friends, God bless you! I am glad to see you. Now come on, boys; if the day is long enough, we'll have them all in hell before night." [5] The men responded with a great cheer as Arnold spurred his horse to the front of the brigade. With a wave of his sword, he led three regiments of Lattimer's men up the slope to attack a disciplined line of Brunswickers under Brigadier General Johann Friedrich von Specht. Shortly afterwards, units from the Rhetz and Hesse-Hanau regiments reinforced Specht and drove Arnold's men back. To gain more manpower, Arnold sought out Morgan's men, who were engaged in a vicious firefight with Balcarres's light infantry under the present direction of Fraser. Samuel Woodruff, a volunteer under Gates, recollected Arnold's leadership in helping to take out the competition, one Simon Fraser, who had recently been promoted to brigadier general for his success at Three Rivers. For Arnold, a little help from Timothy Murphy's smoothbore up in a tree was all he needed and the deed was done. Murphy was a man of medium height, above average strength and speed, and a dark complexion, who had served well in the Boston siege, at Long Island, and in the New Jersey campaign.

...Soon after the commencement of the action, General Arnold, knowing the military character and efficiency of General Fraser, and observing his motions in leading and conducting the attack, said to Colonel Morgan, "That officer upon a gray horse is of himself a host and must be disposed of – direct the attention of some of the sharp-shooters among your riflemen to him."

Morgan nodded his assent to Arnold, repaired to his riflemen, and made known to them the hint given by Arnold. Immediately upon this, the crupper of the gray horse was cut off by a rifle bullet, and within the next minute another passed through the horse's mane a little back of his ears.

An aid of Fraser, noticing this, observed to him, "Sir, it is evident that you are marked out for particular aim; would it not be prudent for you to retire from this place?"

Fraser replied, "My duty forbids me to fly from danger," and immediately received a bullet through his body. A few grenadiers were detached to carry him to the Smith (Taylor) *House.* [20]

Samuel Woodruff

Burgoyne had also been in the sights of Morgan's snipers, who passed bullets through his hat, his coat, and his horse, but had missed their primary target. With Fraser out of the way, Arnold was able to diminish the British Artillery, which fled into a place called "bloody knoll," named for the damaging effect that it had on the British from Poor's brigade. Morgan and Dearborn had swept away the flanks of the British line, leaving Riedesel's grenadiers and jagers to fight for themselves. Arnold then led a charge towards the Balcarres' Redoubt with the support of Paterson's and Glover's men, but were soon driven back. Looking off to the left, Arnold saw Learned's brigade attempting to penetrate an opening in the abattis between the Balcarres and Breymann Redoubts. He bolted to the head of the brigade and drove them forward, directing Colonel Brooks to assault the redoubt. A fusillade of grapeshot erupted from within as the Americans attacked with muskets and guts. Spurring his horse again, Arnold rode through a gauntlet of gunfire launched from the American line and the enemy position. Once again playing the part of the miracle worker, he came through unscathed, although his horse was bleeding in a couple of places. He then ordered Wesson and Livingston's regiments along with Morgan's riflemen to make a direct assault. As the men's spirits rose, so did their success in gaining ground and guns. Seeing his men and munitions being swept away, Burgoyne sent orders via an aide, Sir Francis Clarke, for the whole detachment to fall back in an attempt to save some of his cannons; unfortunately for Burgoyne, someone shot the messenger. After Balcarres himself was struck down by a fatal shot, his redoubt soon followed.

When Arnold spied some of the Balcarres defenders retreating to Breymann's Redoubt, he saw the open gap between the two forts as a huge welcome mat. He directed Morgan to make a frontal attack on the Breymann Redoubt from the west while he charged forward leading a portion of Brooks' regiment straight up the middle to attack from the east. Inside the fort, Breymann cursed and swung at his own men with his sword to keep them from fleeing before he himself was struck down by friendly fire, or rather friendless fire, for moments after Breymann fell so did the redoubt as his men fled in droves.

Upon entering the sallyport at the rear of the fort, a volley of fire from the last to leave brought down Arnold's horse followed by one fateful musket ball from a wounded German private that struck him in the left leg above the knee. But he was not deterred from this for he called out, "Rush on my brave boys, rush on," which they did victoriously, their sweaty faces blackened with burnt powder. [5] When Private John Redman made a bayonet charge at the Hessian soldier who shot him, Arnold called out, "Don't hurt him, he did but his duty, he is a fine fellow." [5] Officers rushed over to carry Arnold off the battlefield, but he waved them away. Captain Henry Dearborn asked him where he was hit, to which Arnold replied, "In the same leg, I wish it had been my heart." [57] Armstrong finally caught up with him to direct him back to headquarters, but instead, he was placed on a litter and carried to the hospital by members of Asa Bray's Connecticut Militia company as the only American officer to be wounded in the battle. In his journal, Captain Ebenezer Wakefield recalled the energy elicited by Arnold during both engagements.

> *A persistent effort has been made from the day of the battle to rob Arnold of the glory. Being attached to Dearborn's light Infantry, which had a conspicuous part of the battles of the 19th of September and the 7th of October, I had the opportunity of witnessing the principal movements of both, and therefore speak from personal knowledge.*
>
> *I shall never forget the opening scene of the first day's conflict. The riflemen and light infantry were ordered to clear the woods of the Indians. Arnold rode up, and with his sword pointing to the enemy emerging from the woods into an opening partially cleared, covered with stumps and fallen timber, addressing Morgan, he said, "Colonel Morgan, you and I have seen too many redskins to be deceived by that garb of paint and feathers; they are asses in lion's skins, Canadians and tories; let your riflemen cure them of their borrowed plumes."*
>
> *And so they did; for in less than fifteen minutes the "Wagon Boy," with his Virginia riflemen, sent the painted devils with a howl back to the British lines. Morgan was in his glory, catching the inspiration of Arnold, as he thrilled his men; when he hurled them against the enemy, he astonished the English and Germans with the deadly fire of his rifles.*
>
> *Nothing could exceed the bravery of Arnold on this day; he seemed the very genius of war. Infuriated by the conflict and maddened by Gates' refusal to send reinforcements, which he*

*repeatedly called for, and knowing he was meeting the brunt of the
battle, he seemed inspired with the fury of a demon.*

E. Wakefield [20]

In another letter to Schuyler, Ebenezer Mattoon wrote of
Arnold's defiance to Gates and dedication to glory.

*...About one o'clock of this day, two signal guns were fired on
the left of the British Army, which indicated a movement. Our troops
were immediately put under arms and the lines manned. At this
juncture Gens. Lincoln and Arnold rode with great speed towards the
enemy's lines. While they were absent, the picket guards on both sides
were engaged near the river. In about half an hour, Generals Lincoln
and Arnold returned to headquarters, where many of the officers
collected to hear the report, General Gates standing at the door.*

*Genl Lincoln says, "Genl Gates, the firing at the river is
merely a feint; their object is your left. A strong force of 1,500 men
are marching circuitously to plant themselves on yonder height. That
point must be defended or your camp is in danger."*

*Gates replied, "I will send Morgan with his riflemen and
Dearborn's infantry."*

Arnold says, "That is nothing; you must send a strong force."

*Gates replied, "Genl Arnold, I have nothing for you to do; you
have no business here."*

Arnold's reply was reproachful and severe.

*Genl Lincoln says, "You must send a strong force to support
Morgan and Dearborn, at least three regiments."*

*Two regiments from Genl Learned's brigade and one from
Genl Nixon's were then ordered to that station and to defend it at all
hazards. Generals Lincoln and Arnold immediately left the
encampment and proceeded to the enemy lines.*

*In a few minutes, Capt. Furnival's company of artillery, in
which I was lieutenant, was ordered to march towards the fire, which
had now opened upon our picket in front, the picket consisting of
about 300 men. While we were marching, the whole line, up to our
picket or front, was engaged. We advanced to a height of ground,
which brought the enemy in view and opened our fire. But the
enemy's guns, eight in number and much heavier than ours, rendered
our position untenable.*

*We then advanced into the line of infantry. Here Lieutenant
M'Lane joined me. In our front there was a field of corn. In which the
Hessians were secreted. On our advancing towards the cornfield, a*

number of men rose and fired upon us. M'Lane was severely wounded. While I was removing him from the field, the firing still continued without abatement.

During this time, a tremendous firing was heard on our left. We poured in upon them our canister shot as fast as possible, and the whole line from left to right became engaged. The smoke was very dense and no movements could be seen; but as soon as it arose, our infantry appeared to be slowly retreating and the Hessians slowly advancing, their officers urging them on with their hangers...

The troops continuing warmly engaged, Col. Johnson's regiment, coming up, threw in a heavy fire and compelled the Hessians to retreat. Upon this we advanced with a shout of victory. At the same time Auckland's corps gave way. We proceeded but a short distance before we came upon four pieces of brass cannon, closely surrounded with the dead and dying; at a few yards further we came upon two more. Advancing a little further, we were met by a fire from the British infantry, which proved very fatal to one of Col. Johnson's companies, in which were killed one sergeant, one corporal, fourteen privates – and about twenty were wounded.

They advanced with a quick step, firing as they came on. We returned them a brisk fire of canister shot, not allowing ourselves time even to sponge our pieces. In a short time they ceased firing and advanced upon us with trailed arms. At this juncture Arnold came up with a part of Brooks' regiment and gave them a most deadly fire, which soon caused them to face about and retreat with a quicker step than they advanced.

The firing had now principally ceased on our left, but was brisk in front and on the right. At this moment Arnold says to Col. Brooks, "Let us attack Balcarres' works."

Brooks replied, "No. Lord Auckland's detachment has retired there, we can't carry them."

"Well then, let us attack the Hessian lines."

Brook replies, "With all my heart."

We all wheeled to the right and advanced. No fire was received, except from the cannon, until we got within about eight rods, when we received a tremendous fire from the whole line. But a few of our men, however, fell. Still advancing, we received a second fire, in which a few of our men fell and Genl Arnold's horse fell under him and he himself was wounded. He cried out "Rush on, my brave boys!" after receiving the third fire, Brooks mounted their works, swung his sword, and the men rushed into their works. When we entered the works, we found Col. Bremen dead, surrounded with a *number of his companions, dead or wounded. We still pursued slowly, the fire, in the meantime decreasing. Nightfall now put an end to this day's bloody contest. During the day we had taken eight cannon and broken the center of the enemy's lines.*

We were ordered to rest until relieved from the camps. The gloom of the night, the groans and shrieks of the wounded and dying, and the horrors of the whole scene baffle all description. [20]

Ebenezer Mattoon

Captain George Pausch described the merciless sacrifices made from behind enemy lines.

At this junction, our left wing retreated in the greatest possible disorder, thereby causing a similar route among our German command, which was stationed behind the fence in the line of battle. They retreated – or to speak more plainly – they left their position without informing me, although I was but fifty paces in advance of them. Each man for himself, they made for the bushes. Without knowing it, I kept back the enemy for a while with my unprotected cannon loaded with shells. How long before this the infantry had left its position, I cannot tell, but I saw a great number advance towards our now open left wing within a distance of about 300 paces. I looked back towards the position still held, as I supposed, by our German infantry, under whose protection, I too, intended to retreat – but not a man was to be seen. They had all run across the road into the field and thence into the bushes, and had taken refuge behind the trees. Their right wing was thus in front of the house I have so often mentioned, but all was in disorder, though they still fought the enemy, which continued to advance.

In the mean time, on our right wing, there was stubborn fighting on both sides, our rear, meanwhile, being covered by a dense forest, which just before, had protected our right flank. The road by which we were to retreat lay through the woods and was already in the hands of the enemy, who accordingly intercepted us. Finding myself, therefore, finally in my first mentioned position – alone, isolated, and almost surrounded by the enemy, and with no way open but the one leading to the house where the two 12 pound cannon stood, dismounted and deserted – I had no alternative but to make my way along with great difficulty if I did not wish to be struck in a damned crooked road.

After reaching the house under the protection of a musketry fire – which, however, owing to the bushes, was fully as dangerous to

286

me as if the firing came from the enemy – I presently came across a little earthwork, 18 feet long by 5 feet high. This I at once made use of by posing my two cannon, one on the right and the other on the left, and began a fire alternately with balls and with shells, without, however, being able to discriminate in favor of our men who were in the bushes; for the enemy, without troubling them, charged savagely upon my cannon, hoping to dismount and silence them...

A brave English lieutenant of artillery, by the name of Schmidt, and a sergeant were the only two who were willing to serve the cannon longer. He came to me and asked me to let him have ten artillerymen and one subaltern from my detachment to serve these cannon. But it was impossible for me to grant his request, no matter how well disposed I might have been towards it. Two of my men had been shot dead; three or four were wounded; a number had straggled off and all of the infantry detailed for that purpose either gone to the devil or run away. Moreover, all I had left, for the serving of each cannon, were four or five men and one subaltern. A six-pound cannon, also, on account of its rapidity in firing, was more effectual than a twelve-pounder, with which only one-third the number of shots could be fired; and furthermore, I had no desire to silence my own cannon, which were still in my possession and thereby contribute to raise the honors of another corps. Three wagons of ammunition were fired away by my cannon, which became so heated that it was impossible for any man to lay his hands on them. In front, and also to the right and left of my guns, I had conquered, for myself and for those who were in the same terrain, a pretty comfortable fort. But this state of things lasted only a short time, the fire behind us coming nearer. Finally, our right wing was repulsed in the rear; its infantry, however, fortunately retreating in better order than our left wing had done.

I still could see, as far as the plain and clearing reached, the road, on which I had marched to this second position, open, and a chance, therefore, to retreat. Accordingly, myself, the artilleryman Hausemann, and two other artillerymen, hoping to save one of the cannon, dragged it towards this road. The piece of wood on the cannon made the work for us four men very difficult and, in fact, next to impossible. Finally, a subaltern followed with the other cannon and placed it on the carriage. We now brought up the other carriage, on which I quickly placed the remaining gun, and marched briskly along the road, hoping to meet a body of our infantry and with them make a stand. But this hope proved delusive and was totally dispelled; for some ran in one and others in another direction; and by the time that

287

I came within gunshot of the woods, I found the road occupied by the enemy. They came toward us on it; the bushes were full of them, they were hidden behind the trees; and bullets in plenty received us.

Seeing that all was irretrievably lost, and that it was impossible to save anything, I called to the few remaining men to save themselves. I myself took refuge through a fence, in a piece of dense underbrush on the right of the road, with the last ammunition wagon, which, with the help of a gunner, I saved with the horses. Here I met all the different nationalities of our division running pell-mell, among them Capt. Shoel, with whom there was not a single man left of the Hanau Regiment. In this confused retreat all made for our camp and our lines. The entrenchment of Breymann was furiously assailed; the camp in it set on fire and burned, and all the baggage horses and baggage captured by the enemy. The three 6-pound cannon of my brigade of artillery were also taken, the artillerymen, Wachler and Fintzell, killed, and artilleryman Wall (under whose command were the cannon) severely, and others slightly wounded. The enemy occupied this entrenchment and remained in it during the night. The approaching darkness put an end to further operations on the part of the Americans. [20]

With the Breymann Redoubt overrun, the Americans were able to diminish the British and force Burgoyne to order a full retreat into the Great Ravine as recalled by Digby.

Brigadier General Fraser was mortally wounded, which helped to turn the fate of the day. When General Burgoyne saw him fall, he seemed then to in the highest degree our disagreeable situation. He was the only person we could carry off with us. Our cannon were surrounded and taken – the men and horses all killed – which gave them additional spirits, and they rushed on with loud shouts when we drove them back a little way with so great loss to ourselves that it evidently appeared a retreat was the only thing left for us.

They still advanced upon our works under a severe fire of grapeshot, which in some measure stopped them by the great execution we saw made among their columns; during which another body of the enemy stormed the German lines after meeting with a most shameful resistance and took possession of all their camp and equipage, baggage, &c., &c., Colo. Breymann fell nobly at the head of the foreigners, and by his death blotted out part of the stain his countrymen so justly merited from that day's behavior.

On our retreating, which was pretty regular, considering how hard we were pressed by the enemy, General Burgoyne appeared greatly agitated as the danger to which the lines were exposed was of the most serious nature at that particular period... He said but little, well knowing we could defend the lines or fall in the attempt. Darkness interposed (I believe fortunately for us), which put an end to the action.

General Fraser was yet living, but not the least hopes of him. He that night asked if General Burgoyne's Army were not all cut to pieces, and being informed to the contrary, appeared for a moment pleased, but spoke no more. Capt. Wight (53rd Grenadiers) my captain, was shot in the bowels early in the action. In him I lost a sincere friend. He lay in that situation between the two fires and I have been since informed lived till the next day and was brought into their camp. Major Acland was wounded and taken prisoner with our quartermaster general and Major Williams of the artillery. Sir Francis Clarke fell, aid de camp to the General, with other principal officers. Our grenadier company, out of 20 men going out, left their captain and 16 men on the field.

Some here did not scruple to say General Burgoyne's manner of acting verified the rash stroke hinted at by General Gates in his orders of the 26th; but that was a harsh and severe insinuation, as I have since heard his intended design was to take post on a rising ground on the left of their camp – the 7th – with the detachment, thinking they would have acted on the offensive, but stood to their works, and on that night our main body was to move, so as to be prepared to storm their lines by daybreak of the 8th; and it appears by accounts since that Gen. Gates would have acted on the defensive, only for the advice of Brigadier General Arnold, who assured him from his knowledge of the troops a vigorous sally would inspire them with more courage than waiting behind their works for our attack, and also their knowledge of the woods contribute to ensure the plan he proposed.

During the night we were employed in moving our cannon, baggage, &c., nearer to the river. It was done with silence and fires were kept lighted to cause them not to suspect we had retired from our works where it was impossible for us to remain, as the German lines commanded them, and were then in possession of the enemy, who were bringing up cannon to bear on us at daybreak. It may easily be supposed we had no thought for sleep and some time before day we retreated nearer to the river. Our design of retreating to Ticonderoga then became public. [20]

Down in the Highlands on the **8th**, the defenders of Fort Constitution spared Sir Henry the trouble by torching it for him before fleeing. Considering his mission accomplished since he had no further orders from Howe to go farther, Clinton wrote to Burgoyne wishing him all the best, not knowing that he had just suffered the worst before headed back to New York, a day late and a directive short of helping Gentleman Johnny breakthrough to Albany. Not only did Clinton fail to show up for Burgoyne, but neither did his message as Thacher explained on the **14th** while at Albany.

October 14, 1777: It is the prevalent opinion here that by taking advantage of wind and tide, it is in the power of Sir Henry Clinton to convey his forces to this city within the spaces of five or six hours, and having arrived here, a march of about twenty miles will carry him without opposition to Stillwater, which must involve General Gates in inexpressible embarrassment and difficulty by placing him between two armies and thereby extricating Burgoyne from his perilous situation.

We have been trembling alive to this menacing prospect, but our fears are in a measure alleviated by the following singular incident. After the capture of Fort Montgomery, Sir Henry Clinton dispatched a messenger by the name of Daniel Taylor to Burgoyne with the intelligence; fortunately he was taken on his way as a spy and finding himself in a danger, he was seen to turn aside and take something from his pocket and swallow it. General George Clinton, into whose hands he had fallen, ordered a severe dose of emetic tartar to be administered. This produced the happiest effect as respects the prescriber; but it proved fatal to the patient. He discharged a small silver bullet, which being unscrewed, was found to enclose a letter from Sir Henry Clinton to Burgoyne. "Out of thine own mouth thou shalt be condemned." The spy was tried, convicted, and executed. The following is an exact copy of the letter enclosed:

To General Burgoyne

Fort Montgomery, October 8th
Dear General
Nous y voici and nothing now between us and Gates; I sincerely hope this little success of ours may facilitate your operations. In answer to your letter of 28th September by Captain Campbell, I shall only say I cannot order or even advise for reasons obvious. I heartily wish you success.

290

The **17th** was marked as a historic day as Burgoyne surrendered six thousand surviving troops to Gates, rendering the first decisive victory for America's quest for independence. For winning the first American victory in the war at Saratoga, Gates acquired and accepted the credit, the sword, and the glory for the battle that would go down in the history books as "the turning point of the Revolution." This didn't sit well with Arnold, who was for the moment deprived as being the "Hero of Saratoga" while he lay in a hospital bed in Albany alongside British Major John Dyke Acland. It was only after reports from several of Arnold's brothers in arms trickled in over time that credit was fully restored to him. One of those reports claimed, "Arnold exhibited upon this occasion all the impetuosity of his courage; he encouraged his men by voice and example." [41] Digby disclosed the sorrow felt by his comrades at the surrender.

October 17 – A day famous in the annals of America.

Gen. Burgoyne desired a meeting of all the officers early that morning, at which he entered into a detail of his manner of acting since he had the honor of commanding the Army; but he was too full to speak; Heaven only could tell his feelings at this time. He dwelled much on his orders to make the wished-for junction with General Clinton, and as to how his proceedings had turned out, we must (he said) be as good judges as himself. He then read over the Articles of Convention and informed us the terms were even easier than we could have expected from our situation, and concluded with assuring us he never would have accepted any terms, had we provisions enough, or the least hopes of our extricating ourselves any other way.

About 10 o'clock we marched out, according to treaty, with drums beating and the honors of war, but the drums seemed to have lost their former inspiriting sounds, and though we beat the Grenadiers march, which not long before was so animating, yet then it seemed by its last feeble efforts as if almost ashamed to be heard on such an occasion.

As to my own feelings, I cannot express them. Tears (though unmanly) forced their way, and if alone, I could have burst to give myself vent. I never shall forget the appearance of the troops on our marching past them; a dead silence universally reigned through their numerous columns, and even then they seemed struck with our situation and dare scarce lift up their eyes to view British troops in such a situation. I must say their decent behavior during the time (to us so greatly fallen) merited the utmost commendation and praise.

The meeting between Burgoyne and Gates was well worth seeing. He paid Burgoyne almost as much respect as if he was the conqueror; indeed, his noble air, though prisoner, seemed to command attention and respect from every person. A party of light dragoons were ordered as his guard, rather to protect his person from insults than any other cause.

Thus ended all our hopes of victory, glory, &c. Thus was Burgoyne's Army sacrificed to either the absurd opinions of a blundering ministerial power, the stupid inaction of a General (Howe), who, from his lethargic disposition, neglected every step he might have taken to assist their operations, or lastly, perhaps, his own misconduct in penetrating so far as to be unable to return, and though I must own my partiality to him is great, yet if he or the Army under his command are guilty, let them suffer to the utmost extent, and by an unlimited punishment in part blot out and erase, if possible, the crime charged to their account. [20]

After Arnold spent months hounding the delegates to restore the date of his rank over the juniors who were promoted before him, a letter from newly elected President Henry Laurens notified him that Congress had at last conceded on **November 29th**. With the help of his wealthy family, Laurens had received the best education in South Carolina before completing his studies in the art of enterprise in London to become one of the most leading merchants and plantation owners in Charleston. Although his short stature and dark complexion made him appear aggressive and arrogant, he was as fair and honest as any family man with a mind that was intuitive, ingenious, methodical, and industrious, yet his heart seemed self-satisfied, self-righteous, and sensitive. During the French and Indian War he served in the Assembly and in the militia. At the beginning stages of the Revolution, he served for six months in the Provincial Congress before becoming President of the Congress and the Council of Safety. He was then elected to the Continental Congress in January of the present year.

To General Arnold

York, Penn, 29th November 1777

Sir

In obedience to the order of Congress I now transmit to you a resolve by the House of this date intended to restore to you your rank

*in the Army – to which is subjoined a resolve of the 12th instant.
Confirming the recommendation of a Board of Officers for settling
rank & precedence. These you will find under this cover.*

*Permit me to assure you Sir I respect your character as a
citizen & soldier of the United States of America, that I rejoice at
your recovery from the dangerous wounds which you lately received
in the defense of your country, that I wish you perfect health & a
continued succession of honor, that I am with very great respect &
esteem &c.*

Henry Laurens [67]

Washington dispatched Arnold's commission on **January
20th, 1778**, explaining that the delay was nothing personal, just
business and that he looked forward to seeing him back on his feet
again.

To M General Arnold in Albany
Headquarters Valley Forge, 20 January, 1778
Dear Sir

*Enclosed you will receive a commission, by which you will
find, that you are restored to the rank you claim in the line of the
Army. This I transmit by direction of Congress, and in pursuance of
their resolution of the 29th of November. The situation of my papers
and the want of blank commissions prevented my doing it before. May
I venture to ask whether you are upon your legs again, and, if you are
not, may I flatter myself that you will be soon? There is none, who
wishes more sincerely for this event, than I do, or who will receive the
information with more pleasure. I shall expect a favorable account
upon the subject; and as soon as your situation will permit, I request
that you will repair to this Army, it being my earnest wish to have
your services in the ensuing campaign. In hopes of this, I have set you
down in an arrangement now under consideration, and for a
command, which I trust will be agreeable to yourself, and of great
advantage to the public.*

*I have nothing of importance to inform you of in the military
line that is new or interesting. The enemy still remains in possession
of Philadelphia, and have secured themselves by a strong chain of
redoubts, with entrenchments of communications from the Schuykill to
the Delaware. We, on our part, have taken a post on the west side of
the former about twenty miles from the city, and with much pains and
industry have got the troops tolerably well covered in huts. We have
to regret that we are not in more comfortable quarters, but these*

293

could not be found, unless we had retired to the towns in the more interior part of the State; the consequence of which would have been distress to the virtuous citizens of Philadelphia, who had fled tither for protection, and the exposure of a considerable tract of fertile country to ravage and ruin.
I am, Dear Sir, with great esteem and regard, &c. [68]
G. Washington

On **April 8**[th], Arnold sent a love letter to Betsy Deblois.

To Miss Betsy Deblois

April 8, 1778
Dear Madam,

Twenty times I have taken my pen to write to you and as often has my trembling hand refused to obey the dictates of my heart. A heart which has so often been calm and serene amidst the clashing of arms and all the din and horrors of war trembles with diffidence and the fear of giving offense when it attempts to address you on a subject so important to its happiness. Long have I struggled to efface your heavenly image from it. Neither time, absence, misfortunes, nor your cruel indifference have been able to efface the deep impression your charms have made, and will you doom a heart so true, so faithful, to languish in despair? Shall I expect no returns to the most sincere, ardent, and disinterested passion? Dear Betsy, suffer that heavenly bosom (which surely cannot know itself the cause of misfortune without a sympathetic pang) to expand with friendship at last and let me know my fate. if a happy one, no man will strive more to deserve it; if on the contrary I am doomed to despair, may latest breath will be to implore the blessing of heaven on the idol and only wish of my soul.

Adieu, Dear madam and believe me most sincerely,
Your devoted and humble servant,
B. A. [22]

Although she had responded to him requesting "to solicit no further," he was never one to take no for an answer and wrote back on the **26**[th].

To Miss Betsy Deblois

April 26, 1778
Dear Betsy,

Had I imagined my letter would have occasioned you a moment's uneasiness, I never should forgive myself for writing it. you entreat me to solicit no further for your affections. Consider, Dear Madam, when you urge impossibilities I cannot obey; as well might you wish me to exist without breathing as cease to love you and wish for a return of affection. As your entreaty does not amount to a positive injunction and you have not forbid me to hope, how can I decline soliciting your particular affections, on which the whole happiness of my life depends.

A union of hearts, I acknowledge, is necessary to happiness; but give me leave to observe that true and permanent happiness is seldom the effect of an alliance formed on romantic passion where fancy governs more than judgement.

Friendship and esteem, founded on the merit of the object, is the most certain basis to build a lasting happiness upon; and when there is a tender and ardent passion on one side, and friendship and esteem on the other, the heart must be callous to every tender sentiment if the taper of love is not lighted up at the flame, which a series of reciprocal kindness and attention will never suffer to expire.

If fame allows me any share of merit, I am in a great measure indebted for it to the pure and exhalted passion your charms have inspired me with, which cannot admit of an unworthy thought or action; a passion productive of good and injurious to no one you must approve and suffer me to indulge.

Dear Betsy, I have enclosed a letter to your Mama for your Papa and have presumed to request his sanction to my addresses. May I hope for your approbation? Let me beg of you to suffer your heart if possible to expand with a sensation more tender than friendship. Consider the consequences before you determine. Consult your own happiness, and if incompatible with mine, forget there is so unhappy a wretch; for let me perish if I would give you one moment's pain to procure the greatest felicity to myself. Whatever my fate may be, my most ardent wish is for your happiness.

I hope a line in answer will not be deemed the least infringement on the decorum due to your sex, which I wish you strictly to observe.

In the most anxious suspense, I am Dear Betsy, unalterably yours,

B. Arnold [22]

Although he poured out his heart to hers, the feelings weren't mutual, and he accepted the fact that this was one battle, which he could not win. On **May 1st**, he returned to his sister's home in New

Haven, where Army officers, members of the militia, cadets, citizens greeted him, along with a thirteen gun salute. On the 7th, Washington wrote to invite Arnold to his headquarters at Valley Forge to presented him with the honorable recognition that Arnold was worthy of and a new assignment.

To M General Arnold

May 7, 1778

Dear Sir

    A gentleman in France having very obligingly sent me three sets of epaulettes and sword-knots, two of which professedly to be distributed to any friends I should choose, I take the liberty of presenting them to you and
General Lincoln, as a testimony of my sincere regard and approbation of your conduct. I have been informed by a brigade major of General Huntington's of your intention of repairing to camp shortly; but not withstanding my wish to see you, I must beg that you will run no hazard by coming out too soon.

    I am sincerely and affectionately, your obedient, &c.,

G. Washington [68]

X
Philadelphia

Upon arriving at Valley Forge on the 16th, Washington informed Arnold that the British were planning to pull out of the capital city, and that he was to be appointed as the new Military Governor of Philadelphia on the 28th. This new position would prove to be a most difficult task for Arnold to serve two masters; they being the Supreme Executive Council of the State of Pennsylvania and the Continental Congress. After accepting his new assignment from the Commander-in-Chief, Arnold reaffirmed his pledge for the American cause in writing as required by the Resolve of Congress on February 3, 1778.

I, *Benedict Arnold, Major General,* do acknowledge the UNITED STATES of AMERICA to be free, independent, and sovereign states and declare that the people thereof owe no allegiance or obedience to George the Third, King of Great Britain; and I renounce, refuse, and abjure any allegiance or obedience to him; and I do swear that I will, to the utmost of my power, support, maintain, and defend the said United States of America with fidelity, according to the best of my skill and understanding.

Sworn before me this thirtieth day of May, 1778,
Artillery Park, Valley Forge
H. Knox, Brigadier General, Artillery [82]

On **June 4**th, Robert Skewell; the owner of a British vessel named *The Charming Nancy*, approached Arnold and requested a pass for himself, his ship, the skipper, William Moore, and her crew; William Constable, James Seagrove, and William Shirtliff. Skewell stated that the official reason for the pass was to move his ill wife and some personal belongings to a farm in Maryland along with loading supplies for the American Army. There was speculation that he was only trying to transport goods to sell in a merchant port and Arnold issued the pass based upon a share in the profits, but this was never proven. Passes were required because privateers were capturing ships and pirating their cargo coming out of Philadelphia after the British evacuation. Passes were also hard to come by, because Pennsylvania authorities considered merchants conducting business in British occupied Philadelphia as Tories. Although Arnold issued the pass, it was not honored by Samuel Ingersoll, the commander of the privateer vessel *Santippe*, who forced the ship into Egg Harbor, New Jersey for collection.

To whom concerned,

Valley Forge, 4 June 1778
Whereas Captain Robert Skewell Junior, merchant of the City of Philadelphia, in behalf of himself and company, has this day made information to me, that himself and company have a certain schooner called the Charming Nancy, New England built, about seventy-five tons berthen, now lying before the City of Philadelphia, which schooner William Moore is master, loaded with salt, linens, woolens, glass, loaf sugar, and bohea tea, nails, etc. consigned to William Shirtliff, supercargo on board; which property, they were of opinion, was not safe at Philadelphia, and as friends to their country, wished to have a protection for said vessel and cargo, that the same might be brought into some port in the United States of America.

In full confidence of their upright intentions, I do hereby grant said Robert Skewell Junior and company protection for said vessel and cargo. And said schooner is hereby permitted to sail into any of the ports of the United States of America, and all officers and soldiers of the Continental Army, and other persons, are hereby forbid to give any umbrage or molestation to the said Captain Moore, or the said vessel and cargo.

Given under my hand,
B. Arnold, M. Genl [36]

As Military Governor, Arnold's instructions were "to take every prudent step in your power to preserve tranquility and order in the city and give security to individuals of every class and description. Restraining, as far as possible, till the restoration of civil government, every species of persecution, insult or abuse, either from the soldiery to the inhabitants or among each other." [79] To do so, Washington directed Arnold to "adopt such measures as shall appear to you most effectual, and at the same time least offensive, for answering the views of Congress." [79] In anticipation of the British leaving Philadelphia, Congress issued an order to secure all items until inventoried by the Army upon their reoccupation.

In Congress. June 5, 1778.
Resolved, that, should the City of Philadelphia be evacuated by the enemy, it will be expedient and proper for the Commander-in-

298

Chief to take effectual care that no insult, plunder or injury of kind may be offered to the inhabitants of the said city. That, in order to prevent public or private injury, from the operations of ill disposed persons, the General be directed to take early and proper care to prevent the removal, transfer, or sale of any goods, wares, or merchandise in possession of the inhabitants of the said city, until the property of the same shall be ascertained by a joint committee, consisting of persons appointed by Congress, and of persons appointed by the Supreme Executive Council of the State of Pennsylvania. To wit, so far as to determine whether any, or what part thereof, may belong to the king of Great Britain and his subjects.

Extract from the minutes,
Charles Thompson, Secretary. [36]

The key person that Arnold would be working with to carry out these orders was one, Lieutenant Colonel Joseph Reed of the Pennsylvania Light Horse Militia, a local attorney who currently served as the vice-president to the council and as a delegate to Congress. Born the son of a wealthy merchant from Trenton, New Jersey, he was well educated at the College of New Jersey (now Princeton University) and the Middle Temple in London while attending Parliamentary debates regarding colonial matters. On his return to America, he set up a law practice in Trenton and accepted a position as the deputy secretary of New Jersey. After moving his law practice to Philadelphia, he became very active on the political scene establishing a correspondence with the newly appointed secretary of state for the colonies, Lord William Legge Dartmouth. Having a courteous, cosmopolitan, and capable manner, he later became a member of the Assembly, Committee of Correspondence, Chairman of the Committee of Safety, and President of the 2nd Provincial Congress. When the fuse for independence was ignited, he was appointed as a lieutenant colonel of militia prior to becoming a secretary for Washington and later as adjutant general, serving under him as an advisor at Long Island, Trenton, Princeton, Brandywine, Germantown, and Monmouth. Upon hearing of the official British evacuation of Philadelphia on the **18th**, Washington issued Arnold's orders to reoccupy the capital.

To M General Arnold

Given at Headquarters this 18th day of June 1778

Sir

You are immediately to proceed to Philadelphia, and take the command of the troops there. You will find the objects of your command specified in the enclosed copy of a resolution of Congress of the 5ᵗʰ instant. The means of executing the powers vested in you, I leave to your own judgement, not doubting that you will exercise them in the manner which shall be found most effectual, and, at the same time, most consistent with the rights of the citizens.

I have directed the quartermaster general, commissary general, and clothier general to send proper persons in their respective departments into the city, to take possession, for the use of the Army, of all public stores left in the city by the enemy, which may not properly fall into the description of the enclosed resolve. In the execution of this duty, they will act under your directions and with your assistance.

I have the honor to be, &c.,

G. Washington [36]

On the **19ᵗʰ**, a short time after the British abandoned the city, the American Army marched back in and regained its capital city to the roar of a thirteen-gun salute and the equal roar of thousands of cheering citizens. Major Alexander Clough headed the Third Dragoons into the city, which were followed by Reed and thirty of his militia. Arnold rode into the city by carriage and chose the William Penn Mansion, known as the "slate roof house" for its architectural cover, to be used as his new headquarters, just as Sir Henry Clinton had before him. Being drawn into the frenzy of victory, citizens gathered together in mobs and attempted to take back that which had been denied them during the past eight months of tyranny. When Reed confronted Arnold about the looting mobs, he produced his written orders from Washington and Congress and declared martial law for one week, thus closing all of the shops and offering Reed to post the order as a representative of the council. Restoring order in the city proved no easy task when many shop owners objected violently to Arnold's order to close the shops, even when he explained that he was just following the directions of Congress. The posting of this order was the first official task of Arnold's new aide-de-camp, thirty-six year old Major David Solebury Franks, a native of Montreal who had previously abandoned his father's loyalist beliefs to become a volunteer on Arnold's staff at Albany.

A Proclamation
By the honorable Major General Arnold,

300

Commander-in-Chief of the forces of the United States of
America,
in the City of Philadelphia.
June 19, 1778.

In order to protect the persons and property of the
inhabitants of this city from insult and injury, to secure the
public and private stores which the enemy may have left in the
city, and to prevent the disorder and confusion naturally
airing from want of government, his Excellency General
Washington, in compliance with the following resolution of
Congress, has thought proper to establish military law in this
city and suburbs, until the civil authority of the state can
resume the government thereof.

{Resolution of Congress June 5, 1778 cited.}

In order the more effectually to carry into execution the
above resolve, all persons having European, East or West
India goods, iron, leather, shoes, wines, and provisions of
every kind, beyond the necessary use of a private family, are
ordered to make return of the same to the town major, by
twelve o'clock tomorrow, specifying the quantity, and, as
nearly as they can judge, the amount of the same, in order
that the quartermaster, commissary, and clothier generals
may contract for such goods as are wanted for the use of the
Army, and until permission is given by the General, there be
no removal, transfer, or sale of goods, as it will be deemed a
breach of the above resolution of Congress, and such goods
will be seized and confiscated for the public use.

All persons having in their hands public stores or
effects the property of the subjects of the King of Great Britain
or their adherents, who have departed with them are to make
a like report by Monday noon next, under penalty of the
confiscation of their own effects; and any persons discovering
such concealed stores or effects, will be suitably rewarded.

Any persons harboring or concealing any officer,
soldier, or other person belonging to the enemy, or any
deserter from the Continental Army, will be severely punished,
unless they make immediate discovery to some officer of the
said Army.

Given at headquarters in the City of Philadelphia,
B. Arnold, Major Genl
By his Honor's command,
David S. Franks, Secretary. [36]

301

Arnold's presence in Philadelphia did not seem all that different to Reed in comparison to the occupation of the British before him. Arnold was prodigal in his personality, which Reed did not see to be politically correct in a city that was forced to withstand the enemy's seizure. One example was Arnold's extravagant furnishing of the Penn Mansion after the British had stripped it and left him nothing to cater his prominent guests with. On the **23rd**, without the consent of Reed, Arnold signed a secret buy and sell agreement with James Mease, clothier general of the Army and his assistant, William West. 'By purchasing goods and necessaries for the use of the Army, sundry articles not wanted for that purpose may be obtained. All such goods and merchandise which are or may be bought by the clothier general or persons appointed by him shall be sold for the joint equal benefit of the subscribers Arnold, Mease, and West and bought at their own risk.' [79] This translated into Mease and West buying clothes on public credit, selling the Army what it needed, selling the remainder to the public, and dividing the profit with Arnold. By applying the law of supply and demand, Arnold monopolized over other merchants whose shops were closed and charged exorbitant prices.

Another thorn in Reed's side was Arnold's decline of a request by Captain Charles Willson Peale and his Pennsylvania radicals to carry out the arrest of a long list of known enemy sympathizers. This did not sit well with the radical Reed who regarded this as an attempt to protect Tories. That thorn was imbedded deeper while at a gathering to celebrate the second **July 4th** anniversary of the Declaration of Independence at City Tavern, when Arnold fell in love and began a courtship with Peggy Shippen, a striking gray-eyed, blonde of eighteen, twenty years his junior, but equal in personality. Aside from being the youngest of her sisters, Hannah, Polly, and Sally, she was also the most dramatic daughter born to the British loyalist, Judge Edward IV and his wife Hannah. Arnold's character as a benefactor was demonstrated in a letter to Miss Mercy Scollay on the **15th**, regarding the children of Major General Joseph Warren, a Harvard physician and politician who was killed at Bunker Hill.

To Miss Scollay

July 15, 1778

Dear Madam

About three months ago I was informed that my late worthy friend General Warren, left his affairs unsettled, and that, after

302

paying his debts, a very small matter, if anything, would remain for the education of his children, who, to my great surprise, I find have been entirely neglected by the State. Permit me to beg your continuing your care of the daughter, and that you will at present take charge of the education of the son. I make no doubt that his relations will consent that he shall be under your care. My intention is to use my interest with Congress to provide for the family. If they decline it, I make no doubt of a handsome collection by private subscription. At all events, I will provide for them in a manner suitable to their birth and the grateful sentiments I shall ever feel for the memory of my friend. I have sent you by Mr. Hancock five hundred dollars for the present. I wish you to have Richard clothed handsomely and sent to the best school in Boston. Any expense you are at, please call on me for, and it shall be paid with thanks. [5]

Your obedient, honorable servant,

B. Arnold

Considering to find better prospects of profit on sea than on land, Arnold writes to Washington on the **19**[th] to request naval service.

To His Excellency General Washington

Philadelphia, July 19, 1778

Dear General

 I beg pardon for neglecting your Excellency's kind favor of the 11th instant. I should by no means have so long omitted writing had I not known Congress had transmitted every intelligence of consequence.

 I beg leave (though late) to present your Excellency my congratulatory compliments on the arrival of the French fleet & Minister and the pleasing prospect of our affairs.

 My wounds are in a fair way and less painful than usual, though there is little prospect of my being able to take the field for a considerable time; which consideration together with that of having been obliged entirely to neglect my private affairs since I have been in the service has induced me to wish to retire to public business unless an offer which my friends have mentioned should be made to me of the command of the Navy to which my being wounded would not be so great an objection, as it would remaining in the Army. I must beg leave to request your Excellency's sentiments respecting a command in the Navy; I am sensible of my inability and of the great hazard and fatigue attending the office; and that I should enjoy much greater

happiness in a retired life, still my wishes to serve my country have a greater weight with me than domestic happiness or ease.
I have the honor to be with the most profound respect & esteem,
Dear General,
your Excellency's most obedient humble servant,
B. Arnold [84]

Washington responds to Arnold on **August 3rd** explaining his lack of expertise in the ways of the water, but is pleased to hear that his leg is getting better and looks forward to having him back on the field.

To M General Arnold

Headquarters White Plains, August 3, 1778
Dear Sir
Your two agreeable favors of the 19th and 22nd ultimo came to hand, which I now have to acknowledge.

I am very happy to learn that your wounds are less painful and in so fair a way of doing well, the only drawback in the pleasure we receive is that the condition of your wounds is still such as not to admit of your active services in this campaign.

You will rest assured that I wish to see you in a situation where you can be of the greatest advantage and where abilities like yours may not be lost to the public; but I confess myself no competent judge in marine matters to offer advice on a subject so far out of my line, believe me though, that it is my desire that you may determine in this case in a manner most conducive to your health, honor, and interest.

I am, Dear Sir, &c., [24]
G. Washington

Arnold then invested in supporting an appeal for four Americans who had, in his eyes, a most inspiring cause. In **early September**, second mate Gideon Olmsted and three friends were captured by the British and forced to enlist as crew members of the trade ship *Active* for its journey from Jamaica to New York. When the ship reached the waters off Long Island on the **6th**, the men captured the ship from fourteen British officers and seamen. While en route to Chestnut Neck, the ship was attacked by privateers aboard the *Convention*, who forced it into Egg Harbor. Not believing that four men could overcome fourteen, a Pennsylvania jury awarded the privateers with the proceeds from the ship sold at auction. Feeling empathy towards men who acted in a valiant spirit comparable to his own, Arnold gambled in supporting their defense for an appeal in exchange for splitting the proceeds awarded to them. Yet after numerous proceedings, Pennsylvania upheld its ruling, leaving Arnold to feel as though he had been pirated by the jury members themselves. On the **22nd**, a New Jersey judge of admiralty "acquitted, released, and discharged" the *Charming Nancy* from capture by the *Santippe*. While on the **25th**, Arnold released his feelings for Peggy in a letter to her that sounded quite familiar.

To Miss Peggy Shippen

Sept. 25, 1778

Dear Peggy,

    Twenty times have I taken up my pen to write to you, and as often has my trembling hand refused to obey the dictates of my heart – a heart which, though calm and serene amidst the clashing of arms and all the din and horrors of war, trembles with diffidence and the fear of giving offense when it attempts to address you on a subject so important to its happiness. Dear Madame, your charms have lighted up a flame in my bosom which can never be extinguished; your heavenly image id too deeply impressed ever to be effaced.

    My Passion is not founded on personal charms only; that sweetness of disposition and goodness of heart, that sentiment and sensibility which so strongly mark the character of the lovely Miss P. Shippen, renders her amiable beyond expression and will ever retain the heart she has once captivated. On you alone my happiness depends and will you doom me to languish in despair? Shall I expect no return to the most sincere, ardent, and disinterested passion? Do you feel no pity in your gentle bosom for the man who would die to make you happy? May I presume to hope it is not impossible I may make a favorable impression on your heart? Friendship and esteem you acknowledge. Dear Peggy, suffer that heavenly bosom (which cannot know itself the cause of pain without a more sympathetic pang) to expand with a sensation more soft, more tender than friendship, which is the most certain basis to build a lasting happiness upon; and when there is a tender and ardent passion on one side and friendship and esteem on the other, the heart must be callous to every tender sentiment if the taper of love is not lighted up at the flame.

    I am sensible to your prudence and the affection you bear you're your amiable and tender parents forbids your giving encouragement to the addresses of any one with their approbation. Pardon me, Dear Madame, for disclosing a passion I could no longer confine in my tortured bosom. I have presumed to write to your Papa, and have requested his sanction to my addresses. Suffer me to hope for your approbation. Consider before you doom me to misery, which I have not deserved but by loving you too extravagantly. Consult your own happiness, and if incompatible, forget there is so unhappy a wretch; for may I perish if I would give you one moment's inquietude to purchase the greatest possible felicity to myself. Whatever my fate may be, my most ardent wish is for your happiness, and my last breath will be to implore the blessings of heaven on the idol and only wish of my soul.

Adieu, Dear Madame, and believe me unalterably, your sincere admirer and devoted humble servant,

B. Arnold [5]

In a letter to Peggy's father, Arnold acknowledged their political differences, but expressed hope for peace between the two nations.

To Judge Shippen

September, 1778

Your Honor,

My fortune is not large, though sufficient (not to depend upon my expectations) to make us both happy. I neither expect nor wish one with Miss Shippen. My public character is well known; my private one is, I hope, irreproachable. If I am happy in your approbation of my proposal of an alliance, I shall most willingly accede to any you may please to make consistent with the duty I owe to three lovely children. Our difference in political sentiments will, I hope, be no bar to my happiness. I flatter myself the time is at hand when out unhappy contest will be at an end, and peace and domestic happiness be restored to everyone. [5]

I am, &c.,

B. Arnold

On **October 3rd**, Arnold dispatched a regiment of militia to the shipping village of Egg Harbor, New Jersey, where the British destroyed several ships and houses. On the **5th**, Reed's secretary, Timothy Matlack, wrote a letter of complaint to Arnold regarding his aide, Major Franks. Between the time of the French and Indian War and the Revolution, Matlack was disowned by the Quakers for acquiring too much gambling debt before serving as a congressional assistant and storekeeper of military supplies. As one of the more spirited members in the militia, he wore his sword in the streets of Philadelphia and served in the operations around Trenton and Princeton. His dispute with Arnold was in defense of his son, Sergeant William Matlack, a Presbyterian lawyer and member of the local militia, who had been ordered by Franks to fetch a barber for him and later cursed him when the barber failed to show.

To Major General Arnold

Philadelphia, October 5, 1778

Sir

The militia sergeant who attended at your quarters on Sunday, complains that Major Franks, one of your aids, had given him orders to call his barber, which order was obeyed; that on the barber not appearing the order was repeated, and the sergeant, though hurt by both the order itself, and the manner of it, again obeyed; he also informs me, that he has, this morning, made you acquainted with this complaint, and that you had been pleased to say, that every order given by you or your aids is to be obeyed. This, I suppose, must intend every proper order.

The militia of the several states have, occasionally, rendered the great cause in which we are engaged such services, as must convince every man that it is of very great importance to treat those who are necessarily called out, in such manner as to make the duty as agreeable to them is consistent with the service to which they are called: For it is upon their will, more than upon the force of any law, that we are to depend for their assistance in the time of need. The severity of military discipline in such a case as that above mentioned, where no important end is to be answered by it, must make every free man feel. At a time when you were one of the militia of the state of which you are a citizen, what would have been your feelings, had an aid of your commanding officer ordered you to call his barber? From your feelings in such a case, it will be easy to judge of that of other men. Free men will be hardly brought to submit to such indignities; and if it is intended to have any of the respectable citizens of the state, in service in the militia, military discipline in such instances must be relaxed; but if it is an object to render the militia in the several states contemptible and useless, the continuance of such treatment will probably effect it. Military duty of every kind is rather disagreeable; and perhaps, to free men, garrison duty more disagreeable than any other. The sergeant above mentioned entered the service to discharge his duty, and as an example to other young men of the city, and not from necessity, in any sense of the word.

It appears to me a duty, which I owe to the public, to represent this matter to you in a respectful manner, in expectation that, from attachment to the public interest, you will give such orders as will prevent any further complaints of this kind, which is all the satisfaction sought after, either by the sergeant, who is my son, or

Sir, your most obedient humble servant,

T. Matlack, Esq. [36]

Arnold responded back on the **6ᵗʰ** explaining the duty of a soldier is to put his feelings aside as a citizen and follow the orders given to him.

To Timothy Matlack, Esq.

Philadelphia, Oct. 6, 1778

Sir

I am to acknowledge the receipt of your letter of yesterday, respecting the militia sergeant who complains of being ill-treated. No man has a higher sense of the rights of a citizen and free man than myself: they are dear to me, as I have fought and bled for them, and as it is my highest ambition and most ardent wish to resume the character of a free citizen, whenever the service of my country will permit. At the same time I beg leave to observe, that whenever necessity obliges the citizen to assume the character of a soldier, the former is entirely lost in the latter, and the respect due to a citizen is by no means to be paid to the soldier, any farther than his rank entitles him to it. This is evident from the necessity of military discipline, the basis of which is implicit obedience, and however the feelings of a citizen may be hurt, he has this consolation, that it is a sacrifice he pays to the safety of his country.

You are pleased to ask, "what my feelings would have been on a similar occasion?" They have been tried; I have served a whole campaign under the command of a gentleman, who was not known as a soldier until after I had been some time a brigadier: My feelings were hurt not only as a citizen, but more so as a soldier; they were however sacrificed to the interest of my country. The event proved unfortunate to me; but I have the satisfaction to think I rendered some service to my country.

I wish to make the duty as agreeable to the militia as is consistent with the good of the service, for which purpose military discipline has been greatly relaxed; was it executed with strictness, most of the militia, from their inattention, would feel the effects of it.

I cannot think (as you seem to imagine) any indignity is offered to the citizen, when he is called upon to do the duty of a soldier in the station he is in, which was the case of the sergeant, it is his duty to obey every order of my aids, not a breach of the laws or principles of the Constitution, as mine, without judging of the propriety of them; neither can I have any idea from the militia's being put on the same footing as the standing Army, they will refuse their assistance, as preservation is the first principle of human nature, theirs will ever induce them to turn out and defend their property.

These, Sir, are the sentiments of a soldier, a citizen, and of, Sir,
your most obedient humble servant,
B. Arnold [36]

Matlack responded back on the **10th** claiming that the order was one that should have been given to a menial servant and not a dutiful soldier. He added that if orders of a similar nature continue to be given, then he will remove his son from the militia and state his reason for doing so to the public.

To Major General Arnold
Philadelphia, October 10, 1778
Sir
I received your letter of the 6th instant; and it gives me real and great pleasure to be informed of your patriotic behavior in the case you mention. Such conduct is the effect of genuine spirit and true greatness of mind; but is very different from the case I stated. You obeyed, because the essential interest of your country was concerned, and a regard to your own fame required it; but the same principles, which induced this conduct, would have induced you to scorn at commands dictated by pride and insolence. I cannot bring myself to believe, that the respect due to the citizen is entirely lost when he takes upon himself the character of a soldier: I entertain a higher sense of the rights of citizens and free men.

If on the one hand, soldiers are bound implicitly to obey military orders, so, on the other hand, are officers accountable for the orders, which they give; and their propriety or impropriety often depends entirely on time and circumstance. Occasions may occur in which an officer may justify commands which expose a citizen to certain death; but I know of none which would justify a command to a citizen serving in the militia to clean his officers shoes. The necessity of implicit obedience on the part of the citizen, when in military service, is so far from being ground, on which to justify every

309

command which may be given, that it is the strongest possible reason, why an officer should be very cautious and circumspect in his orders; and it also lays the citizen under a necessity of calling officers to a strict account for the orders which they give. I will venture to say, that in a free government, implicit obedience will not be submitted to much longer than commanders use their authority with great prudence and discretion; and, if it be really necessary, commanders, who destroy it, by degrading and unnecessary orders, they will be accountable for the consequences. You say it is the duty of an orderly sergeant "to obey every order of your aids (not a breach of the laws or principles of the Constitution) as yours, without judging of the propriety of them." This sentiment must have dropped from your pen in a moment of haste; as it appears to me to be a sentiment improper to be entertained either by the citizen or soldier: For even common soldiers retain some right to judge of the propriety of the orders which they have obeyed; and to demand satisfaction in cases where improper or unnecessary orders have been given: and free men will judge for themselves and speak for themselves with decency and firmness when the occasion requires it. The calling of Major Franks' barber to dress his hair, was the office of a menial servant, not the duty of a soldier; and I still think it an indignity to a free citizen to be ordered to go on such an errand. Such commands cannot be mistaken for and obeyed as the orders of a wife and prudent General.

My letter to you was written for the single purpose of preventing orders being inadvertently given, which would offend a militia who have suffered greatly many ways; and I had a hope, that you would have thought it proper to have given some assurance that attention would have been paid to this, as it appears to me, necessary precaution; but I am not a little mortified to find the order, of which I complained, so fully justified and supported by you. If it is your intention, as commanding officer, to countenance orders of this kind, it is my duty as a father, to withdraw my son from a service in which commands are to be given him which to obey would lessen him in the esteem of the world; and I shall consider it as a duty which I owe to myself to acquaint my fellow citizens of my reason for so doing.

I am with sentiments of great respect, Sir,
your most obedient and very humble servant,
T. Matlack, Esq. [36]

On the **11th**, Skewell reported to Arnold that only a handful of militia had responded to Egg Harbor and he pleaded with him to save his cargo. Arnold agreed with one condition, that he would receive half of the profits from what was saved and sold. After Skewell accepted the terms, Arnold wrote to Washington complaining of the militia's failure to respond in force.

To His Excellency General Washington

Philadelphia, 11ᵗʰ Oct. 1778

Dear General

The want of news agreeable on entertaining, with indisposition, will I hope apologize to your Excellency for my long silence. The third instant I was informed that the enemy mediated an attack on little Egg Harbor, where there were several privateers and fifteen or twenty sail vessels, with a considerable quantity of European and West India goods. Col. Proctor's Regiment was ordered to march immediately for the defense of place & next day I sent one hundred Militia to reinforce him. Col. Proctor reached the neighborhood of Egg Harbor on the 7ᵗʰ, where he was joined by only fifty Militia, although they had been ordered only four or five days before. This force was not sufficient to oppose the enemy who appeared with a frigate, two sloops, two row galleys, and six flat bottomed boats & landed about five hundred men, burnt all the houses, eight or ten vessels, & did considerable other damage. Fortunately most of the valuable goods & part of the vessels were removed to the Forks, thirty miles above and were saved.

About this time Count Pulaski's Legion and some Militia arrived, when the enemy thought proper to embark, the last account from them was the 9ᵗʰ when they were making towards great Egg Harbor, with designs as was supposed, to destroy that place. Count Pulaski's Corps, Col. Proctor's Regiment, with some Militia were watching their motions.

I have no news to add worth notice, with the highest respect & return, I have the honor to be, Dear General, your Excellency's most obedient, humble servant, B. Arnold [84]

Arnold then responded to Matlack on the **12ᵗʰ**, stating that he will not be intimidated by the press.

To Timothy Matlack, Esq.

Philadelphia, October 12, 1778

Sir

By your letter of the 10th, I perceive that my sentiments are not clearly understood; but it is needless to discuss a subject, which will perhaps be determined more by the feelings than the reason of men. If the declaration that you will withdraw your son from the service and publish the reasons is intended as a threat, you have mistaken your object. I am not to be intimidated by a newspaper. To vindicate the rights of citizens, I became a soldier, and bear the marks upon me. I hope your candor will acquit me of the inconsistency of invading what I have fought and bled to defend. As I am earnestly desirous of closing this correspondence. I shall confine myself to what occasioned it. "An improper order" as you conceive, "given by Major Franks, my aid de camp, to the orderly sergeant, your son." Without examining into the propriety or impropriety of the order, about which we may differ, I perfectly agree with you, that the delivering of it in a haughty, imperious, or insolent manner, is blamable; and if the sergeant had so represented it to me at that time, he would have had justice. The affair is now out of my hands and lies between the sergeant and the major. If the latter hath behaved amiss, it is his duty to make reparation. I trust I never shall countenance pride or insolence to inferiors in him, or any other officer under my command. Let me add, that disputes, as to the rights of citizens and soldiers, in conjectures like the present, may be fatal to both.

I am, Sir, your most obedient humble servant,

B. Arnold [36]

Arnold was not willing to submit to more of his own personal financial losses and on the **22nd**, made several verbal requests to the quartermaster, Colonel John Mitchell, to give him twelve wagons in which he would pay "to remove property which was in imminent danger of falling into the hands of the enemy." [79] Although dutiful on the surface, resentment arose from the Pennsylvania Council when they discovered that they had not countersigned the original pass. Their ill feelings grew upon learning that the cargo was transported fifty miles into Philadelphia by twelve Army wagons to a store owned by a merchant named Stephen Collins, who sold the goods at high prices and split the profits with Arnold. On the **23rd** Washington explained to Arnold that all cannot be saved.

To M General Arnold

Headquarters Fredericksburg, October 23, 1778

Dear Sir

312

I was favored with your letter of the 11th instant. I am sorry at the destruction of property at Egg Harbor; but in attending to the general objects of war, we must at times submit to such losses or depend on the exertions of the militia for their prevention.

No doubt you have been informed of the progress of the enemy's embarkation at New York. The 19th and 20th instant about 120 sail of vessels including transports and ships of war put to sea with a considerable part of the garrison & stood eastward. Their destination still continues a matter of inquiry and whether they are to be followed by the garrison. However this latter must be ascertained in a very little time. [24]

I am, Dear Sir, your most humble servant,
G. Washington

During the month of **November**, Arnold and Matlack held a verbal sparring match by publishing articles against one another in the *Pennsylvania Packet*. In order to make up for the loss of his investments, both here in Philadelphia and in Quebec, Arnold considered making a switch from the Army to the Navy. Before the end of the month, he presented Congress with a plan to capture one of the British held Windward Islands in order to "seize and harass British shipping wherever we found it and create havoc with the British line of supply." [77] The privateer fleet would serve as a second Navy to the United States and operate out of New London, Connecticut with Arnold serving as the commodore. He cited his qualifications for the position to be his successful experience in building, sailing, and commanding war ships as he had done on Lake Champlain, while his desire for the command to be for the benefit of his leg injury. Members of Congress, now presided by Henry Laurens, agreed to study the plan, but over time, the members never committed themselves to the active pursuit of it. Reed was inaugurated as President of the Supreme Executive Council of Pennsylvania on **December 1st**, and put his political muscle to work. After learning that Arnold had lost his patience with a few of the board members and had challenged them to a duel, Washington writes to him on the **13th** warning that such behavior was no way to gain their support.

To M General Arnold

Headquarters Middlebrook, December 13, 1778

Dear Sir

Upon my arrival here I found your favor of the 5th. Your own

letter communicated the first hint that I ever received of any representations on reports made by the Board of War to Congress respecting you or your command in Philadelphia. the board some little time ago applied to me for a regiment or two to be stationed at Philadelphia and Trenton to do the town duties and guard the stores, alleging that the militia complained of the hardship of being turned out for these purposes. I have accordingly ordered down Colo. Hogan's regiment of North Carolina, which is as much as I can (with propriety) spare. I (have never heard, nor is it my) wish to be acquainted with the causes of the coolness between some gentlemen composing the Board of War and yourself. I most sincerely hope that they may never rise to such a height as to oblige either party to make a public matter of it, as I am under more apprehensions on account of our own dissentions than of the efforts of the enemy. [24]

I am with great regard, Dear Sir, yours &c.,
G. Washington

On **January 19, 1779**, Matlack wrote to Reed explaining his involvement with the wagons issued to Arnold.

To Hon. Joseph Reed, Esq.
President of the State of Pennsylvania
    Quartermaster General's Office, Philadelphia, January 19, 1779
Sir
    I this day received an order, signed by the secretary of the honorable council of this state, requesting I would give them information respecting a brigade of wagons under the conduct of Jesse Jordan, a wagon master from Chester County, the council having been informed that I sent them to Egg Harbor, to convey private property to this city. I shall at all times be ready to give your Excellency and the honorable council every information you think necessary for the good of the public, or this state in particular, which relates to my office, or the benefits of the department, as I have no desire to conceal any part of my conduct as a public officer, having conducted the benefits under my direction with integrity, and justice to the public. The following are the state of the facts required.
    In the month of October last, at the time the enemy had landed some troops at Egg Harbor, General Arnold desired I would furnish him with a brigade of teams, which he wanted to send to the Jerseys, and that he would pay the hire of them, they being wanted to remove property which was in imminent danger of falling into the hands of the enemy. I informed him, he should have the wagon master of the first brigade, who could be spared for public service, sent to him,

314

when he would give such orders as he pleased. Accordingly, about the 22nd of October, Mr. Jordan was sent to the General to receive his directions, having at that time sent forward a large supply for the Army, &c. when Jordan returned, he was desired to make out his account to General Arnold, to be paid. I do not know where the loading was stored, nor whose property it was, further than what is before mentioned. A greater number of Continental teams coming in than I expected, enabled me to comply with General Arnold's request, without any inconvenience to the service. if there is anything further, in which I can satisfy your Excellency and the council, I will wait on you at anytime with pleasure.

I have the honor to be with great respect, your Excellency's most obedient and most humble servant, John Mitchell, D.Q.M.G. [36]

On the **21st**, Matlack wrote on Reed's behalf requesting Arnold to "inform this board whether the property for which the said wagons were ordered was public or private. If the latter, to whom the same belonged; and farther to inform this board by virtue of what resolve of Congress, or other authority, public wagons of this state were sent to another state to do business merely of a private nature." [79] On the **25th**, Arnold responded on the wagons by recalling the facts from the quartermaster's office. In regards to his personal involvement, he claimed, "I shall only say that I am at all times ready to answer my public conduct to Congress or General Washington, to whom alone I am accountable." [79] Reed then protested to John Jay, the new President of Congress, demanding that Arnold be removed from command in Pennsylvania for a list of charges "involving a willful abuse of power and criminal acts." [4] Jay was an aristocrat raised from a wealthy merchant family in New York City and graduated from King's College (now Columbia University). He was more of a self-confident and self-satisfying man rather than one who was ambitious; uncommon characteristics for a lawyer. On the other hand he held strong reasoning powers, comprehensive views, enduring applications, and a firm mind, which yielded much success as a partner to Robert R. Livingston, Jr. and as a member of the Continental Congress. Although Congress was not willing to consider such a radical request without specific charges, the members did agree to appoint another special committee to investigate the matter. On the **30th**, Mitchell wrote to Arnold explaining Jordan's pay for the use of the wagons.

To Hon. Major General Arnold

January 30, 1779

Sir

Mr. Jordan is entitled to pay from the day he left home, and as he was not employed in public service, but sent to you on his arrival, it is but just he should be paid by the person who employed him; but if you order I should pay him any part of the time for hire of his teams, I will obey your order.

I have the honor to be, with respect, Sir, your most obedient, humble servant,

J. Mitchell [36]

On the **6ᵗʰ of February**, Arnold was notified of the charges by dispatch while meeting with Washington at Middlebrook, New Jersey. The Commander-in-Chief in turn advised Arnold to request a court martial. In a letter to Peggy on the **8ᵗʰ**, Arnold is grateful to be called back from a real estate trip to buy some property in Connecticut when he realizes that absence does make his heart grow fonder.

To Miss Peggy Shippen

Camp at Raritan, February 8ᵗʰ, 1779

My Dearest Life

Never did I so ardently long to see or hear from you as at this instant. I am all impatience and anxiety to know how you do; six days' absence, without hearing from my Dear Peggy, is intolerable. Heavens! What must I have suffered had I continued my journey – the loss of happiness for a few dirty acres. I can almost bless the villainous roads, and more villainous men, who oblige me to return. I am heartily tired with my journey and almost so with human nature. I daily discover so much baseness and ingratitude among mankind that I almost blush at being of the same species, and could quit the stage without regret was it not for some gentle, generous souls like my Dear Peggy, who still retain the lively impression of their Maker's image, and who, with smiles of grace and goodness, make all happy around them. Let me beg of you not to suffer the rude attacks on me to give you one moment's uneasiness; they can do me no injury. I am treated with the greatest politeness by General Washington and the officers of the Army, who bitterly execrate Mr. Reed and the council for their villainous attempt to injure me. They have advised me to proceed on my journey. The badness of the roads will not permit, was it possible to support an absence of four weeks, for in less time I could not accomplish it. the day after tomorrow I leave this, and hope to be made happy by your smiles on Friday evening; 'till then all nature smiles in vain; for you alone, heard, felt, and seen, possess my every thought, fill every sense and pant in every vein.

Clarkson will send an express to meet me at Bristol; make me happy by one line, to tell me you are so; please to present my best respects to your mamma and the family. My prayers and best wishes attend my Dear Peggy.

Adieu! And believe me, sincerely and affectionately thine,

B. Arnold [5]

On the **9ᵗʰ**, Reed had the eight charges printed in the *Pennsylvania Packet* newspaper and sent copies to Washington and the authorities of every state. In the council's opinion, Arnold's behavior was "oppressive to the faithful subjects of this state, unworthy of his rank and station, highly discouraging to those who have manifested their attachment to the liberties and interests of America, and disrespectful to the supreme executive authority." [79]

First – That while in the camp of General Washington at Valley Forge last spring, he gave permission to a vessel belonging to persons then voluntarily residing in this city with the enemy and of disaffected character. Then allowing them to come into a port of the United States without the knowledge of the authority of the state, or of the Commander-in-Chief, though then present. (Issuing a pass to the British sloop *The Charming Nancy* out of the Delaware without a countersignature from the council while other ships remained on restriction.)

Second – In having closed the shops and stores upon his arrival in the city, so as even to prevent officers of the Army from purchasing, while he privately made considerable purchases and sales for his own benefit, as is alleged and believed. (Closing Philadelphia businesses, thus forcing people to buy items from him.)

Third – In imposing menial offices upon the sons of free men of this state, when called forth by the desire of Congress to perform militia duty and when remonstrated to, hereupon justifying himself in writing, upon the ground of having power to do so. Thus when a citizen assumed the character of a soldier, the former was entirely lost in the latter and that it was the duty of the militia to obey every order of his and his aides without judging of the propriety of them. (Allowing

Franks to order petty duties, such as fetching a barber, upon the local free members in the militia.)

Fourth – For that, when a prize was brought into this port by the *Convention* brig of this state, any dispute that arose respecting the capture have had the great probability of being amicably adjusted between the claimants. Yet General Arnold interposed by an illegal and unworthy purchase of the suit at a low and inadequate price, as has been publicly charged by a reputable citizen. To which may in some degree be ascribed the delay of justice in the court of appeal and the dispute in which the state may probably be involved with Congress hereupon. (Interfering with the ruling made by a Pennsylvania court in regards to the capture of the *Active* for want of profit.)

Fifth – The appropriation of the wagons of this state when called forth upon a special emergency last autumn, for the transportation of private property and that of persons who voluntarily remained with the enemy last winter and were deemed disaffected to the interests and independence of America. (Using government property for private use when the cargo of the *Charming Nancy* was off-loaded when threatened by American fire.)

Sixth – In that Congress by a resolve of the 21st of August last, having given to the executive powers of every state an exclusive power to recommend persons desirous of going within the enemy's lines to the officer there commanding. General Arnold in order as may reasonably be inferred to elude the said resolve, wrote a letter as appears by comparison of hands and the declaration of the intended bearer, recommendatory for the above purpose and caused his aide-de-camp, Major Matthew Clarkson to sign the name. But the said device not taking effect through the vigilance of the officers at Elizabethtown. General Arnold, without disclosing any of the above circumstances applied to council for their permission, which was instantly refused. The connection, character, and situation of the party being well known and deemed utterly improper to be indulged with such permission, thereby violating the resolve of Congress and usurping the authority of this board. (Writing a letter to recommend a pass across the lines without proper authority.)

Seventh – This board having upon the complaint of several inhabitants of Chester County, through the late wagon-master general, requested of the said General Arnold to state the said transaction respecting the wagons, in order that they might satisfy the complainants. Or else explain the same without further trouble, received in return an indecent and disrespectful refusal of any satisfaction whatsoever. (Rudely disavowing to report the details of a transaction.)

Eighth – The discouragement and neglect manifested by General Arnold during his command to civil, military, and other characters that have adhered to the cause of their country with an entirely different conduct towards those of another character are too notorious to need proof or illustration. And if command has been as is generally believed to be supported by an expense of four or five thousand pounds per annum to the United States, we freely declare we shall very unwillingly pay any share of expenses thus incurred. (Showing favoritism to Tories over patriots.) [5]

The council called for the attorney general of Pennsylvania to prosecute him "for such illegal and oppressive conduct cognizable in the courts of law." [79] In addition, they refused to pay for any charges required by the Army or activate the militia unless absolutely necessary as long as Arnold remained in command in Philadelphia. Arnold met with Washington, who had requested a congressional inquiry, but Arnold felt that a military court martial would prove better to clear his name. On the 16th, Congress authorized William Paca of Maryland to preside over a public hearing committee regarding the charges. A descendant of a wealthy planter on Maryland's eastern shore, Paca graduated from Philadelphia College, studied law in Annapolis, attended the Middle Temple in London, and was admitted to the bar. He was elected as a member of the legislature, Committee of Correspondence, delegate to Congress, signer of the Declaration, and state senator. When the *Royal Gazette* had gotten wind of Arnold's legal troubles, it had publicized them in an article on the 17th, an article that Sir Henry Clinton read with a most keen interest.

General Arnold heretofore has been styled another Hannibal, but losing a leg in the service of Congress, the latter considering him unfit for any further exercise of his military talents, permit him thus to fall into the unmerciful fangs of the Executive Council of Pennsylvania. [79]

To add insult to Arnold's injury and to make a character statement of him, Matlack, disguised under the initials T. G., had John Brown's charges reprinted in the *Pennsylvania Packet* on the 27th. On

March 3rd, Clarkson and Franks swore before Judge Benjamin Paschall that Arnold made no purchases during the time that the shops were closed.

We do certify, that when the shops in this city were shut in June last, by order of Major General Arnold, in consequence of a resolution of Congress of the 4th June. We do not know of General Arnold's making any purchases of goods of any kind, directly or indirectly; and we have every reason to believe that no such purchases were made either by General Arnold or his agents, except a few trifling articles to furnish his table, and for his family's use, most of which were supplied him by the quartermaster or commissary. General Arnold's invoices, minute and account books being always open to our inspection, confirms us in our belief as mentioned above.

M. Clarkson, Aid de Camp,
David S. Franks, Aid de Camp.

On the third of March, 1779, personally appeared before me, the subscriber, one of the justices of the peace of the city and county of Philadelphia, M. Clarkson and David S. Franks; and being both duly sworn, do declare the above to be true, to the best of their knowledge.

Benjamin Paschall [36]

Arnold responded to Matlack's reprint of Brown's charges on the 4th stating, "Envy and malice are inexhaustible. Where they have not invention enough to frame new slanders, or the slanders newly framed are found totally inadequate to their purpose, they will call in the feeble aid of old ones." [79] On the 5th, Arnold presented his case to the committee, addressing each of the charges in defense of his duty, honor, and sovereignty. He affirmed that he had the authority to grant passes as Military Governor. He presented the affidavits from the crew of the *Active*, which proved his assistance in their appeal, yet neglected to mention his monetary motives. He submitted his communications with Matlack regarding the Franks issue and stated that the papers regarding the wagons were already submitted to Congress. He claimed, "on his honor as a gentleman," that he made no purchases while the shops were closed, but failed to notify the committee members that Franks and Mease were actually doing it for him. [77] He explained that all of his correspondence with the council was as respectful as he thought worthy. His final claim was that he had always been courteous to all patriots and loyalists. The committee cleared him from six of the eight charges, but recommended a court martial to decide the remaining two indictments.

Matlack himself admitted that it was doubtful that Arnold could have committed so many crimes in such short a time as initially charged. He then added, "but when I meet your carriage in the street, and think of the splendor in which you live and revel, of the settlement which it is said you have proposed in a certain case, and of the purchases you have made, and compare these things with the decent frugality necessarily used by other officers in the Army, it is impossible to avoid the question. From whence have these riches flowed if you did not plunder Montreal?" [79] On the 17th, Timothy Matlack wrote to Arnold requesting that the matter be taken care of between Arnold and himself, being that he had originally issued the order and that it was imposed upon a minor.

To Major General Arnold

Philadelphia, March 17th 1779

Sir

It appears to me proper to communicate to you, that I shall, on Saturday evening next, lay before a respectable number of citizens, the several letters which have passed between you and myself, relating to the orders delivered by one of your aids to my son. My intention is, to consult with them on the measures necessary to prevent effectually, a like insult being offered by you, to any other citizen of this state. I lay, by you, because it is estimated in your letter, of the 12th of October, that the matter lies between your major and my son; whereas the order being your order, and my son several years under age, I conceive it to lie between yourself and me.

And am, Sir, your very humble servant,

T. Matlack [36]

The council responded that same day stating that only the 1st, 2nd, 3rd, and 5th charges were triable by a court-martial. That being said, Arnold also wrote to John Jay, asking him to act with speed and expediency, for the sooner the issue was resolved, the better.

To Hon. John Jay, Esq.

Philadelphia, March 17, 1779

Sir

I did myself the honor of writing to you on the 12th to which I ask leave to refer. I am gratefully sensible of the attention, which

Congress paid to my request, in appointing a committee of their honorable body to esquire into the charges published against me by the President and Council of Pennsylvania; and having been informed, that the committee have finished their inquiry, and delivered in their report, I pray you, Sir, to recommend to Congress, to examine and decide thereon as soon as possible. I am sensible of the multiplicity of business before Congress, yet I flatter myself, that they will consider the cruel situation in which I am placed by the persecution of my enemies, and relieve me by a speedy decision.

As an individual, I trust I shall ever have spirit to be the guardian of my own honor; but as the servant of Congress, when attacked by a public body, I consider myself bound to make my appeal to that honorable body in whose service I have the honor to be; and whilst my conduct and the charges against me are under their consideration, I think it my duty to wait the issue, without noticing the many abusive misrepresentations and slanderous reports, which are daily circulated by a set of wretches beneath the noise of a gentleman and man of honor; yet permit me to say that these slanderers, employed and supported by persons in power and reputable stations, whilst my cause remains undetermined before Congress, consider themselves secure, and industriously spread their insinuations and false assertions through these United States, to poison the minds of my virtuous countrymen and fellow-citizens, and to prejudice them against a man whose life has ever been devoted to their service, and who looks on their good opinion and esteem, as the greatest reward and honor he can receive. This the circumstance, I cannot be charged with undue impatience for soliciting an immediate decision on the charges brought against me; and I flatter myself, that every member of that honorable body must have some idea of what I have suffered on this occasion, and that they will relieve me from a situation, the cruelty of which is beyond my power to express.

I have the honor to be with great respect and esteem, Sir,
your most obedient humble servant,
B. Arnold [36]

Arnold resigned his command in Philadelphia to Brigadier General James Hogun on the **19**[th] and then wrote to Washington stating that he would accept a command while expressing his ill feelings towards the council. Hogun was a native of Ireland who settled in North Carolina, where he served as a member of the Provincial Congress and organized a militia regiment, which he led in the battles of Brandywine and Germantown. Following the formation

322

of Continental units in his home state, he assisted in building the fortifications at West Point.

To His Excellency General Washington

March 19, 1779

Sir

As soon as my wounds will permit, I shall be happy to take a command in the line of the Army and at all times of rendering my country every service in my power. The final determination of the charges must make both the President and the council appear to the world in their true colors, as a set of unprincipled, malicious scoundrels, who have prostituted their honor and truth, for the purpose of gratifying their private resentment against an innocent person. [70]

I have the honor to be with great respect & esteem,
your Excellency's most obedient humble servant,
B. Arnold

When the treasury board maintained its insistence on having Arnold produce all receipts and vouchers of his expenses to be reimbursed, he mortgaged everything he had in order to purchase the ninety-six acre Mount Pleasant estate (Fairmount Park) on the banks of the Schuykill on the **22ⁿᵈ** for $70,000. Once described by John Adams as "the most elegant seat in Pennsylvania," for its grand views, Mount Pleasant was built in 1761 by the privateer, Captain John Macpherson. [77] Arnold used $25,000 of his credit, which he claimed to be owed to him by Congress for his reimbursements and back salary, and mortgaged the rest. Meanwhile, Reed battled with Congress long enough to overturn the Paca Report regarding the *Active*. After a long wait that ended on **April 3ʳᵈ**, Congress, in agreement with the Pennsylvania Council, resolved that Arnold should be tried on a total of four of the eight charges; issuing a pass to the *Charming Nancy*, the closing of the shops in Philadelphia, imposing menial duties on the militia, and the misuse of military wagons. The trial date was set for May 1ˢᵗ.

Saturday, April 3, 1779

Resolved, That his Excellency Joseph's Reed's letter to Congress of the 25 January, 1779, and General Arnold's of the 8ᵗʰ and 12ᵗʰ of February, and the resolves therein contained of the Executive Council of Pennsylvania, be, with the evidence which hath been collected and reported by the committee on those letters, transmitted to the

323

Commander-in-Chief; and that he be directed to appoint a court martial on the 1st, 2nd, 3rd, and 5th articles contained in the said resolves of the said Executive Council, the said articles only being cognizable by a court martial; and that the reference be notified to the Supreme Executive Council, and they be requested to furnish the evidence to the court martial. [28]

On the **8th**, while leaning on the arm of Franks, Arnold married Peggy in an Episcopalian ceremony conducted by Bishop William White of Christ Church in the library of her father's house. Born and raised in Philadelphia, White graduated from the College of Philadelphia (now University of Pennsylvania) and obtained his holy orders in England before becoming the first Protestant Episcopal bishop of Pennsylvania and a zealous supporter of the colonies during the Revolution. Following the ceremony instead of taking his bride through the threshold of his newly acquired mansion, Arnold was forced to move his family into a small house in Philadelphia owned by Peggy's father called the Master's House, sometimes also known as the Richard Penn Mansion, at the corner of Sixth and High Streets. With great reluctance, he was forced to rent out "Peggy's Palace" to the Spanish Ambassador in order to make his mortgage payments on his house in New Haven and farm in Connecticut after making several unsuccessful attempts at trying to sell them. Although they were happily married to each other, the local inhabitants did not welcome this union of an American officer and a tory. On the **14th**, Arnold wrote to Congress to inquire how he could be charged for so-called crimes for which there was no evidence.

To Hon. John Jay, Esq.

Philadelphia, April 14th, 1779

Sir

I find by a resolution of Congress of the third instant, that they have directed his Excellency General Washington to call a court martial on the 1st, 2nd, 3rd, and 5th charges contained in the resolves of the Executive Council of the State of Pennsylvania, of the 3rd of February, the said charges being only recognizable by a court-martial.

I cannot but resist my surprise, that a court martial should be ordered to try me for offences, some of which the committee of Congress in their report say, "there appears no evidence tending to prove the same, that the said charges are fully explained, and the appearances they carry of criminality fully obvious by clear unquestionable evidence." If Congress have been induced to take this measure for the public good, and to avoid a breach with this state, however hard my case may be, and however I am injured as an individual, I will suffer with pleasure, until a court martial can have an opportunity of doing me justice by acquitting me of these charges a second time.

As Congress have not decided on the 6th, 7th, and 8th charges, though their committee have acquitted me, I must now beg the favor of their decision on those charges: I ask it as a piece of justice due to a faithful and honest servant, and make no doubt of their immediately complying with my request.

I have the honor to be, Sir, your very humble servant,

B. Arnold [36]

Arnold wrote to Washington on the **18th** to protest the charges, but if there was to be a court-martial, he would like to get it over and with.

To His Excellency Genl Washington

Philadelphia, April 18, 1779

Dear Sir

Agreeably to your Excellency's advice to me when at camp, I requested Congress to appoint a committee to examine into the charges alleged against me by the President and the council of this state. My request was compiled with. The report of the committee I have taken the liberty to enclose. After perusing it, your Excellency will doubtless be surprised to find, that Congress have directed a court-martial to try me (among other charges) for some of those of which their committee have acquitted me in the fullest and clearest manner; and though this conduct may be necessary for the public interest, it is hard to reconcile it to the feelings of an individual, who is thereby injured.

Mr. Reed has by his address kept the affair in suspense for near two months, and at last obtained the foregoing resolution of Congress, and will, I make no doubt, use every artifice to delay the proceeding of a court-martial, as it is in his interest that the affair should remain in the dark; and the Congress, to avoid a breach with this State, have declined deciding on the report of their committee. I have no doubt of obtaining justice from a court-martial, as every officer in the Army must feel himself injured by the cruel and unprecedented treatment I have met with. I must earnestly entreat your Excellency that a court-martial may be directed to sit as soon as possible. If it can be done in this city, I shall esteem it a great favor, as my wounds make it extremely inconvenient for me to attend at camp, where it is very difficult to obtain the necessary accommodations for the recovery of them. It will also be extremely difficult, if not impracticable, to produce in camp the evidences, which are all in this city. But, should the service make it absolutely necessary that the court should be held at camp. I beg that an early day may be fixed for it as possible, and that the President and council of this state may have such notice, that the court may not be delayed for want of their evidence. Mine will be ready at the shortest notice. When your Excellency considers my sufferings, and the cruel situation I am in, your own humanity and feeling as a soldier will render everything I can say farther on the subject unnecessary. [68]

I by my best respects to Mrs. Washington and am with sentiments of perfect respect & esteem, Dear Sir, your Excellency's affectionate & most obedient humble servant,

B. Arnold

On the **20th**, Washington notified Arnold that he had scheduled his court martial.

To M General Arnold

Headquarters Middlebrook, April 20, 1779

Dear Sir

I have your favor of the 18th instant. I have, in obedience to the resolve of Congress, ordered a court martial to sit at this place on the 1st of May to try you on the 1st, 2nd, 3rd, and 5th charges exhibited against you by the Council of the State of Pennsylvania.

It would have given me great pleasure to have indulged you with a court at Philadelphia, but such is the weak state of the line in respect to General and field officers that it would have been impossible without entirely divesting the Army of officers of that rank.

I am, Sir, &c., [24]

G. Washington

On the **24th**, under the impression that Washington was wanting to rush through the matter, Reed threatened to refuse wagons to the Army again if it did not deem Arnold's misuse of them as a serious offense and then demanded an indefinite postponement to collect evidence and produce witnesses.

To His Excellency General Washington

Sir

Your Excellency's letter of the 20th instant has been laid before the board, informing us that a Court-Martial will be held at the camp on the 1st of May instant, "for the trial of General Arnold on the first, second, third, and fifth charges exhibited against him by the board."

We apprehend that there must have been some mistake in the mode of transmitting this business to your Excellency, as we never exhibited any other charge against General Arnold to Congress, than that of appropriating the wagons of the State to private uses, and that only that he might remain to answer. Nor do we think it by any means consistent with the duty we owe the State to be considered in the light of parties, as thereby we establish a principle, under which we may either submit silently to injuries and insults, or follow military courts into any part of the country, wherever the service may require to be.

The light in which we have ever considered ourselves, and which we wish to be considered by your Excellency, is as a public body, the representatives of free men of Pennsylvania, expressing our opinion of General Arnold's conduct, founded upon facts disclosed to us, and answering to our own knowledge, asking nothing of Congress but that he should not continue to command in this state. The history of this country affords many instances of this proceeding in the cases of oppressive Governors, and it is a right which we hold independent, and unaccountable to any other power. No one doubts the right of a public body to praise, and this shows very strongly they have a power to censure, it only operating as an opinion, unaccompanied with any punishment.

In the present instance, General Arnold refused to give any explanation of his conduct, though civilly requested, or ever offered to disprove the facts alleged; of course we were obliged to exercise our judgements upon the evidence and proofs we had. At the same time we perfectly approve the trial, being of opinion, that General Arnold's conduct deserves some military reprehension; and we doubt not the officers of the Army will impartially weigh the duty they owe to the country, as well as the person charged; and if the facts are proved, let the mitigating circumstances, if there are any, operate on the sentence, not the nature of the transaction. Such is the dependence of the Army upon the transportation of this state, that should the court martial treat it as a light and trivial matter, we fear it will not be practicable to draw forth wagons in the future, be the emergency what it may, and it will have very bad consequences.

327

We could have wished your Excellency had appointed a later day or we could have had earlier notice. Your letter is dated the 20th instant and was not received till the 22nd; and, considering the distance of some of the witnesses, we fear it will not be possible to give them notice, much less to procure their attendance, and we presume no ex parte testimony ought to be received by the court. Our view of the matter was, and it was so considered by the joint committees, that we should transmit the papers to your Excellency and inform you of the names of the witnesses to prove the several points; that then your Excellency, by your own authority or that of Congress, would have procured the attendance of the witnesses. Two officers of Congress, not in any respect under our control, are material witnesses, of which we informed Congress, requesting they might not proceed to Carolina till their testimony could be had. No notice was taken of it, and they set off about a week ago, and, as we have reason to think, with a view to be absent till the trial is over. Colonel Fitzgerald, who is also a material witness, we suppose is in Virginia.

As substantial justice, not a mere formality, is undoubtedly your Excellency's object on this occasion, we submit to your judgement whether a competent time for the attendance of those witnesses, at least, who are within reach, and the judgement of some previous points, will not make a further delay necessary. These points are, at whose expense and by whose procurement are the witnesses to be had; and whether the service will not admit of the sitting of the Court at some nearer point than camp. If that cannot be, we must rely upon your Excellency to give further directions for the accommodation of the persons who may attend in behalf of the prosecution. As the idea expressed in your Excellency's letter does not correspond with the resolve of Congress transmitted to us, and differs from that entertained by the Joint Committee of Congress, Council, and Assembly, in which it was expressly declared that this Board was not to be considered as a party, we trust the proceedings in this business will conform to this idea; otherwise, besides the inconvenience above mentioned, we shall be liable to a charge of inconsistency not well founded.

We are, Sir, with every sentiment of respect and regard,
Your most obedient, humble servants,
Joseph Reed

P. S. By the time this will reach your Excellency, there will remain but three days, so that we shall be glad to have as early an answer as possible; for we beg leave to assure you, that no other delay is sought but what is necessary to proceed to business with effect. 75.

Congress heard from Reed as well, who threatened them with succession if they were to renege on their decision to press for a court martial. Washington passed the bad news of the delay on to Arnold, yet omitted the reason.

To M General Arnold
                    Headquarters Middlebrook, April 26, 1779
Dear Sir
        I find myself under a necessity of postponing your trial to a later period than that for which I have notified your attendance. I send this information in a hurry, lest you set out before it might arrive, if delayed an hour of more leisure. In a future letter, I shall communicate my reasons and inform you of the time, which shall be finally appointed.
                                              I am, &c., [24]
                                              G. Washington

Washington revealed his reasons two days later on the **28**[th].

To M General Arnold
                    Headquarters Middlebrook, April 28, 1779
Dear Sir
        I informed you in a short line of the 26th *that your trial was postponed with a promise to explain the reason at another opportunity. I had received a letter from the council representing that the period appointed for the purpose and the previous notice given were too short to admit of the necessary witnesses being produced in time. One of the most material they inform me is in Virginia and two others in Carolina. The necessity of a free and full investigation both for the sake of public justice and for your own honor made it my duty to attend to this representation and defer the trial to a future day. I have therefore postponed it with this alternative, that it shall come on by the first day of July, if it be thought necessary to wait the arrival of the two gentlemen said to be in Carolina. Though the delay in your situation may be irksome, I am persuaded you will be of opinion with me that it is best on every principle to submit to it, rather than there should be the least appearance of precipitancy in the affair.* [24]
                            I am with great regard, Dear Sir, &c.,
                                              G. Washington

Arnold responded on **May 5th**, revealing that he knew that the council didn't really have a case and just wanted to drag out the issue as long as possible. He on the other hand, just wanted closure on the matter and exposed a audacious attitude to make his point.

To His Excellency General Washington

May 5, 1779

Dear General

I have been honored with your Excellency's two letters of the 26th and 28th of April, and am extremely sorry that it should be thought there was a necessity of postponing my trial to so late a period as June or July, for no other reason than the council of this state 'representing that the period appointed for the purpose, and the previous notice given, were too short to admit of the necessary evidence being produced in time.' From a candid view of the charges and of the whole proceedings against me contained in the papers transmitted to your Excellency, you must be fully persuaded that I have been unjustly accused, and that I have been refused justice from Congress on the report of their committee. From a knowledge of my public conduct, since I have been in the Army, no man is better qualified to judge whether I have merited the treatment I have received.

If your Excellency thinks me a criminal, for Heaven's sake let me be immediately tried, and if found guilty, executed. I want no favor; I only ask justice. If this is denied me by your Excellency, I have nowhere to seek it but from the candid public, before whom I shall be under the necessity of laying the whole matter. Let me beg of you, Sir, to consider that a set of artful, unprincipled men in office may represent the most innocent actions and, by raising the public clamor against your Excellency, place you in the same situation I am in. Having made every sacrifice of fortune and blood, and become a cripple in the service of my country, I little expected to meet the ungrateful returns I have received from my countrymen; but as Congress have stamped ingratitude as a current coin, I must take it. I wish your Excellency, for your long and eminent services, may not be paid in the same coin. I have nothing left but the little reputation I have gained in the Army. Delay in the present case is worse than death; and, when it is considered, that the President and council have had three months to produce their evidence, I cannot suppose the ordering of court-martial to determine the matter immediately in the least precipitating it, as in justice it ought to have been determined

long since. The President and council wish to put it off until the campaign opens, considering undoubtedly that the service will then prevent the court-martial from sitting, and cause the trial to be postponed until the end of the campaign. I must therefore entreat, that the court may be ordered to sit as soon as possible, and, if the court find sufficient reasons, they will of course adjourn to a longer time.
[68]

Not doubting but my request will be granted,
I have the honor to be with the highest respect and esteem,
your Excellency's most obedient humble servant,
B. Arnold

With the pressures of war, debt, humiliation, and marriage upon him, Arnold seemed vulnerable, and **early in May**, that vulnerability was tested. He received a visit from British Lieutenant Christopher Hele, a recent parolee who had been charged with delivering a manifesto and proclamation of peace to Congress from the British Peace Commissioners. The letter was written by a former friend of Washington's, now the commander of the Loyal American Regiment, Colonel Beverly Robinson, and its intentions was to recruit America's greatest craftsman in the art of war. Born into a prominent Virginia family in 1722, Robinson had served in the French and Indian War before marrying the wealthy Susanna Philipse and becoming one of the most prosperous landowners in the state of New York. Siding with Britain as a loyalist for the duration of the Revolution, his shrewd nature proved to be a valuable asset as an agent in the secret service by providing information on the people and places in the Hudson Valley. Following his distinctive conduct during the attack on Fort Montgomery, he requested a meeting with Major General Israel Putnam with the intentions of persuading him to return his allegiance to the legal government. Although this meeting with Putnam never took place, he made a similar offer to Arnold, an offer that Arnold simply couldn't refuse.

To Major General Arnold

May 1779

Sir

Among the Americans who have joined the Rebel standard, there are very many good citizens whose only object has been the happiness of their country. Such men will not be influenced by motives of private interest to abandon the cause they have espoused.

331

They are now offered everything, which can render the colonies really happy; and this is the only compensation worthy of their virtue.

The American colonies shall have their Parliament, composed of two chambers, with all its members of American birth. Those of the upper house shall have titles and rank similar to those of the house of peers in England. All their laws, and particularly such as relate to money matters, shall be the production of this assembly, with the concurrence of a viceroy. Commerce, in every part of the globe subject to British sway, shall be as free to the people of the thirteen colonies as to the English in Europe. They will enjoy, in every sense of the phrase, the blessings of good government. They shall be sustained, in time of need, by all the power necessary to uphold them, without being themselves exposed to the dangers or subjected to the expenses that are always inseparable from the condition of a state.

Such are the terms proffered by England at the very moment when she is displaying extraordinary efforts to conquer the obedience of her colonies. Shall America remain, without limitation of time, a scene of desolation? Or are you desirous of enjoying peace and all the blessings of her train? Shall your provinces, as in former days, flourish under the protection of the most powerful nation of the world? Or will you forever pursue that shadow of liberty, which still escapes from your hand, even when in the act of grasping it? And how soon would that very liberty, once obtained, turn into lewdness, if it not be under the safeguard of a great European power? Will you rely upon the guarantee of France? They among you whom she has seduced may assure you that her assistance will be generous and disinterested and that she will never exact from you a slavish obedience. They are frantic with joy at the alliance already established and promise you that Spain will immediately follow the example of France. Are they ignorant that each of these states has an equal interest in keeping you under and will combine to accomplish their end? Thousands of men have perished; immense resources have been exhausted; and yet, since that fatal alliance the dispute has become more embittered than ever. Everything urges us to put a conclusion to dissentions not less detrimental to the victors than to the vanquished. As desirable as peace is, it cannot be negotiated and agreed upon between us as between two independent powers; it is necessary that a decisive advantage should put Britain in a condition to dictate the terms of reconciliation. It is her interest as well as her policy to make these as advantageous to one side as the other. It is at the same time advisable to arrive at it without any unnecessary waste of that blood of which we are already as sparing as though it were again our own.

There is no one but, General Arnold who can surmount obstacles so great as these. A man of so much courage will never despair of the republic, even when every door to a reconciliation seems sealed. Render then, brave General, this important service to your country. The colonies cannot sustain much longer the unequal strife. Your troops are perishing in misery. They are badly armed, half-naked, and crying for bread. The efforts of Congress are futile against the exhaustion of the people. Your fields are untilled, trade languishes, learning dies. The neglected education of a whole generation is an irreparable loss to society. Your youth, torn by thousands from their rustic pursuits or useful employment are mown down by war. Such as survive have lost the vigor of their prime, or are maimed in battle. The greater part of these, bring back to their families the idleness and the corrupt manners of the camp. Let us put an end to so many calamities. You and ourselves have the same origin, the same language, and the same laws. We are inaccessible in our island and you, the masters of a vast and futile territory, have no other neighbors than the people of our loyal colonies. We posses rich establishments in every quarter of the globe and reign over the fairest portions of Hindostan. The ocean is our home and we pass across it as a monarch traversing his dominions. From the northern to the southern pole, from the east to the west, our vessels find everywhere a neighboring harbor belonging to Great Britain. So many islands, so many countries acknowledging our sway, are all ruled by a uniform system that bears on every feature the stamp of liberty, yet is as well adapted to the genius of different nations and of various climates.

While the Continental powers ruin themselves by war and are exhausted in erecting the ramparts that separate them from each other, our bulwarks are our ships. They enrich us; they protect us; they provide us as readily with the means of invading our enemies as of supporting our friends. Beware then, of breaking forever the links and ties of a friendship whose benefits are proven by the experience of a hundred and fifty years. Time gives to human institutions a strength which what is new can only attain, in its turn, by the lapse of ages. Royalty itself experiences the need of this useful prestige and the race that has reigned over us for sixty years has been illustrious for ten centuries.

United in equality, we will rule the universe, we will hold it bound, not by arms and violence, but by the ties of commerce – the lightest and most gentle bonds that human kind can wear. [5]

I am, Sir, &c.,
Beverly Robinson, Colonel
Loyalist King's American Regiment

With no more patience to bear, Arnold called on Joseph Stansbury, an intelligent, optimistic, and energetic, twenty-nine-year-old local merchant, who held a neutral point of view regarding the international political scene. Arnold had first met him when he purchased his dining room set from him for the slate roof house. Stansbury recalled after the war, "About the month of June 1779, General Arnold sent for me and, after some general conversation, opened his political sentiments respecting the war carrying on between Great Britain and America, declaring his abhorrence of a separation of the latter from the former as a measure that would be ruinous to both. General Arnold then communicated to me, under a solemn obligation of secrecy, his intention of opening his services to the Commander-in-Chief of the British forces in any way that would most effectually restore the former government and destroy the usurped authority of Congress, either by immediately joining the British Army or cooperating on some concealed plan with Sir Henry Clinton. I went secretly to New York with a tender of his services to Sir Henry Clinton." [79] After reading Arnold's panic attack, Washington wrote to him on the 7ᵗʰ to announce his new trial date, but he was too late, for Arnold had already turned from a hero to a spy.

To M Genl Arnold

Headquarters Middlebrook, May 7, 1779
Dear Sir
I have the pleasure to inform you that the time of your trial is now finally fixed on the first day of June. If something very extraordinary does not intervene to prevent it, it will certainly come on then as I am truly desirous that it may have as speedy a decision as a regard to propriety will permit.

I am, Dear Sir, &c., [24]
G. Washington

To keep his identity a secret, Arnold chose the code name of Gustavus Monk. The first name was adopted from Adolphus Gustavus, a Swedish military hero known for his war on Catholics and his hatred for the French. The second name was inspired from George Monk, who changed sides to restore monarchy during the

334

Civil War of Great Britain a century before and was honored with a dukedom and a handsome reward from the King. On Monday the 10th, Stansbury traveled to New York City and met his counterpart, Reverend Doctor Jonathan Odell, at his Wall Street home. A graduate of the College of New Jersey (now Princeton University), Odell had studied medicine and served as a surgeon in the British Army before returning to England and becoming an ordained priest. Upon returning to Burlington, New Jersey, he served both as a man of the cloth and the cleaver. With the outbreak of the war, he staunchly supported the British and published many of his poetic yet satirical thoughts in newspapers, which brought about his being placed on parole. After escaping to New York City, the grand jury of Burlington County ordered him to be placed under arrest and questioned for treason, but he remained safe within the confines of the British lines. When Stansbury arrived, Odell escorted him to the white brick mansion that served as British headquarters at 1 Broadway to meet with an aspiring officer, who was given the recent assignment of military intelligence in his Majesty's secret service, twenty-nine year old, Captain John Andre`.

He was born to a Swiss father and English mother in London on May 2, 1751, and grew up in a family of merchants. He studied at Geneva, Switzerland and was adorned with the arts of music, drama, drawing, and poetry. During the summer of '69 while visiting the Lichfield home of his poetic friend, Anna Seward, he met and fell in love with a beautiful, blue-eyed blond named Honora Sneyd. His devotion was so deep for her that her captured her radiance in a pair of miniature portraits, giving one to Anna and keeping one for himself. He had asked her to marry him, but her father desired him to save up for such an expenditure, which he did in the family shipping trade. As his London business kept him separated from her, his absence did not make her heart grow fonder. Convinced that her lack of writing to him was brought on by her bout with tuberculosis, he continued to write to her often and with affection for over a year.

When he came home for Christmas in 1770, he got the feeling that the chemistry between them had diminished. He later learned that the reason lay with the addition of one other element to the mix, Richard Lovell Edgeworth; elegant in looks, eloquent in speech, and eminent in wealth. Perhaps being a merchant wasn't good enough for her, so Andre` set out in search of military greatness by purchasing a second lieutenant's commission in the British Army on March 4, 1771 and joined the Royal English Fusiliers. After serving on a special mission in Germany from '72 to '73 he was ordered to America and stopped by Lichfield to pay his respects to his former, only to learn that she had, on a recent occasion, accepted the hand of Edgeworth. Following an unknown delay, he arrived in America in September of 1774 at the port of Philadelphia before sailing north to Montreal, Canada, where he served at Fort Chambly. Five months after Arnold had captured Ticonderoga, American forces under Major James Livingston captured Fort Chambly on October 18th. Upon being taken captive, Andre` had already adopted some spy skills, which he revealed in a letter to a friend

I have been taken prisoner by the Americans, and stripped of everything except the picture of Honora, which I concealed in my mouth. Preserving that, I yet think myself fortunate. [41]

On the morning of November 3rd, Andre` along with 600 of his comrades headed south as prisoners. In the spring of 1776, he was kept at a home owned by a Mrs. Ramsey located at the corner of Locust Alley and South Hanover Street in Carlisle, Pennsylvania. At the end of the year he was exchanged for American POWs and reported to his new commander, Sir William Howe in New York City. During his time in captivity, he kept a journal of the people, places, and things along the way. This valuable intelligence impressed Howe so much that on January 18, 1777, Andre` was promoted Captain of the 26th Regiment and served as aide de camp to General Charles Grey during the British occupation of Philadelphia. It was here that he met and socialized with the family of Peggy Shippen and took a fancy to her friend, Peggy Chew. As an ambitious, industrious, talented, and engaging young officer, Andre` also did his share of entertaining the locals during the drab winter months of '77 – '78 when he and his comrades revived an old theater to display their acting talents, putting on as many as thirteen plays. He later organized a lavish event held on May 8th in honor of Sir William Howe at the home of Joseph Wharton. Embellished with costumes and competitions, dinner and dancing, pomp and circumstance, the extravaganza was dubbed the "Mischianza." In June, Andre` made his exit with the British as Arnold made his entrance with the Americans. During the summer and fall of 1778, he served in the battles of Monmouth, Brandywine, and Germantown, which won him a promotion to the rank of Major on October 23rd and an assignment as Sir Henry Clinton's Adjutant General. While serving at his headquarters in New York, Andre` had introduced some Shakespearean work that had never been seen before in the Theater Royal on John Street. With a character that embraced both military abilities and social graces, Andre` was in the truest sense an officer and a gentleman. After receiving Arnold's response to Robinson's invitation, Andre` advised Clinton to take advantage of the opportunity while they can.

To His Excellency Sir Henry Clinton
New York Island, the 10ᵗʰ May 1779
Sir
The matter I mentioned this morning to your Excellency may be so important that I have thought on it afresh here and written the enclosed, as I felt much more forcibly than you could do the kind of confusion such sudden proposals created when one must deliberate and determine at once. The man must return in order not to be missed, Laird has a sloop & whaleboat at his orders. Capt. Chiniry is desired to recommend him to the armed vessel at Princes Bay and a confidential person is to be his coxswain at night.

I hope, Sir, you will think a sufficient foundation is laid and all done which the time would admit of it. The enclosed is just what he has already verbally and I take the liberty of requesting you to transmit it if it meets with your Excellency's approval. Not finding myself very well, I, in consequence of your indulgence, on these occasions came into the Country.

I have the honor to be, with the utmost respect and fidelity, Sir, your most obedient & most humble servant,
John Andre`
P. S. I trouble your Excellency to seal the enclosure as well as Mr. Odell's note. [79]

Clinton then assigned him to the task of communicating with and qualifying Arnold's offer to serve the crown and was given the code names of John Anderson and Joseph Andrews. The two had responded back to Stansbury later that afternoon, making the point that they would be willing to buy Arnold's offer on the condition that they make a significant gain of the enemy's logistics. Messages were kept secret by way of code using a series of numbers to correspond with pages, lines, and words. Another method was the use of invisible ink, which was revealed by heat or acid and having the envelope marked with the letter A for acid or F for fire. A third option was the use of a mask, which worked as a stencil to only reveal hidden messages within a letter of general interest. In the case of Arnold's absence, communication with Andre' could be made through Peggy, who had met Andre's acquaintance in Philadelphia, prior to Arnold's arrival as Military Governor.

To Joseph Stansbury

May 10, 1779

Sir

Although I think we understood each other clearly this morning and nothing was omitted which I could have to say on the subject; it is, or may be, of too much importance not to take further pains that all may be perfectly well comprehended.

On our part we meet Monk's overtures with full reliance on his honorable intentions and disclose to him with the strongest assurance of our sincerity, that no thought is entertained of abandoning the point we have in view. That on the contrary, powerful means are expected for accomplishing our end. We likewise assure him that in the very first instance of receiving the tidings or good offices we expect from him, our liberality will be evinced, that in case any partial but important blow should by any means be struck or aimed upon the strength of just and pointed information & cooperation, rewards equal at least to what such service can be estimated at, will be given, but should the abilities and zeal of that able and enterprising gentlemen amount to the seizing an obnoxious band of men, to the delivering into our power or enabling us to attack to advantage and by judicious assistance completely to defeat a numerous body, then would the generosity of the nation exceed even his most sanguine hopes and in the expectation of this he may rely on that honor he now trusts in his present advances. Should his manifest efforts be foiled and after every zealous attempt, flight be at length necessary the cause in which he suffers will hold itself bound to indemnify him for his losses and receive him with the honor his conduct deserves. His own judgement will point out the services required, but for his satisfaction we give the following hints.

Councils of: contents of dispatches from foreign abettors, original dispatches and papers which might be seized and sent to us, channels through which such dispatches pass, and hints for securing them. Number and position of troops, whence and what reinforcements are expected and when. Influencing persons of rank with the same favorable disposition in their several commands in different quarters. Conferring the means of a blow of importance. Fomenting any party which when risen to a height might perhaps easily be drawn into a desire of accommodation rather than submit to an odious yoke. The locations of current and new-forming magazines. To interest himself in procuring an exchange of prisoners for the honor of America. The other channel you mentioned to me this morning through which a communication was formerly held must be kept unacquainted with this and with regard to it the same may be said as with regard to Monk that liberal acknowledgements will infallibly attend suspicious services.

You will leave me a long book similar to yours. Three numbers make a word, the 1st is the page, the 2nd is the line, and the 3rd is the word. A comma is placed between each word when only the first letter of the line is wanted in order to compose a word not in the book; the number representing the word will be -/-. In writings to be discovered by a process, F is fire, A is acid. In general information, as to the complexion of affairs, an old woman's health may be the subject.

The lady might write to me at the same time with one of her intimates. She will guess whom I mean, the latter remaining ignorant of interlining and sending the letter. I will write myself to the friend to give occasion for a reply. This will come by a flag of truce, exchange officer & every messenger remaining ignorant of what they are charged with. The letters may talk of mischianza (entertainment) & other nonsense. You will take your mysterious notes from this letter and burn it or rather leave it sealed with me. [79]

I am, &c.,
John Anderson

On the **14th**, Arnold wrote a thank-you note to Washington for resetting his day in court.

To His Excellency General Washington
Philadelphia, May 14th 1779
Dear Sir
Yesterday I had the honor to receive your Excellency's favor of the 7th instant, informing me that the time of my trial was finally fixed on the 1st day of June; which I am very happy to hear, as nothing can be more disagreeable than the cruel situation I am in at present, not only as my character will continue to suffer until I am acquitted by a court-martial, but as it effectually prevents my joining the Army, which I wish to do as soon as my wounds will permit; and to render my country every service in my power at this critical time; for, though I have been ungratefully treated, I do not consider it as from my countrymen in general, but from a set of men, who void of principle, are governed entirely by private interest.

339

The interest I have in the welfare and happiness of my country, which I have made ever evident when in my power, will I hope always overcome my personal resentment for any injury I can possibly receive from individuals. [68]

I have the honor to be with the most perfect respect and esteem, your Excellency's most obedient humble servant,

B. Arnold

Arnold then wrote to William Paca to submit a copy of the committee report to Congress for his court martial.

To Hon. William Paca, Esq.

Philadelphia, May 14th, 1779

Dear Sir

As you are the chairman of the committee on my letter to Congress, respecting the report of the committee and letters of the President and council of this state, I must request the favor of your endeavoring to have your report made to Congress as soon as possible, and of knowing when that will probably be, as my trial is positively fixed to the first day of June. If the report is not made in a few days, I shall be deprived of the benefit of those papers, which I conceive to be my right, and absolutely necessary to obtain justice of the court martial.

I am with great esteem, Dear Sir, your most obedient servant,

B. Arnold [36]

Paca had followed up on the **15th**, but to Arnold's horror, he was not able to submit the report, thus leaving Arnold with a significant lack of support..

To Major General Arnold

May 15, 1779

Dear Sir

As Congress cannot comply with your request, the committee can make no report that will be of any service to you. You cannot have a copy of the report you refer to, nor of the letters which passed between the committees, because, on the late conference and accommodation between Congress and the State of Pennsylvania, those proceedings are to cease, and not to be brought again into view or discussion. The whole of the evidence, which relates to the charges on which you are to be tried, is transmitted to General Washington, with the charges, and there is nothing kept back, which you could avail yourself of in your defense. As to the resolutions of the report acquitting you of particular charges, they were founded, you know, on ex parte hearing. The committee were obliges to finish the report, and as the Executive Council, from some difference between their committee and the committee of Congress, would not produce the evidence in support of those charges, the committee took up the evidence offered on your part, and passed the resolutions of acquittal; but the Executive Council and Congress having settled the misunderstandings between the committees, and Congress not having decided upon the report, and the said Executive Council having offered to produce the evidence before a court martial, the resolutions of the committee can have no operation whatever: when we therefore come to report on your late application, we must report, that your application cannot be complied with.

I am, Sir, your obedient humble servant,

W. Paca [36]

Washington also wrote to express his regrets on the previous delay and his wishes to prevent any more.

To M General Arnold

Headquarters Middlebrook, May 15, 1779

Dear Sir

I have received your favor of the 5ᵗʰ instant and read it with no small concern. I feel my situation truly delicate and embarrassing, on the one side your anxiety, very natural in such circumstances, and the convenience of the Army strongly urges me to bring the affair to a speedy conclusion; on the other, the pointed representations of the state on the subject of witnesses and the impropriety of precipitating a trial so important in itself to leave me no choice. I beg you to be convinced I do not indulge any sentiments unfavorable to you; while my duty obliges me and I am sure you wish me to avoid even the resemblance of partiality. I cautiously suspend my judgement 'till the result of a full and fair trial shall determine the merits of the prosecution.

In the meantime I entreat you to realize the motives which impel me to delay and the consequences of an appearance of precipitancy both to yourself and to me. I am told by a public body that the most important witnesses are at such a distance as to require considerable time to produce them. The charges are of a serious and interesting nature and demand the freest investigation. I could not answer it to the public were I not to allow the time deemed necessary for the purpose. The interpretation that might otherwise be given to my conduct needs no comment; an acquittal, should that be the event of the trial, would in this case be no acquittal. If you consider the relation in which you stand to the Army, it will suggest an additional reason for not being hasty.

I have not yet received an answer from the council respecting the alternative mentioned in my last. I have since written to the President, enclosing a letter for you, appointing the first of June which I requested him to forward in case that period should not be thought too soon. It is my fixed intention that the trial at the latest shall come on the first of July and I shall endeavor to let it meet with no interruption from military operations. I sincerely wish it may with propriety take place before. I write to the council by this opportunity. Believe me my Dear Sir that I have no other object in view than to act in such a manner, as when all the circumstances of my conduct are known will convince the world and yourself of my strict impartiality.

I am, Dear Sir, yours, &c., [24]

G. Washington

On the morning of the **21**[st], the Board of War heard Arnold's testimony regarding the expenses that he incurred during the Canadian campaign. Later that afternoon, Arnold had appointed Stansbury to serve as his private secretary for him in order to hide his own handwriting if it was ever discovered. Arnold's first spy strategy was to choose Baily's Dictionary as a medium of code words for their correspondence rather than Blackstone's Commentary, which he found to be too bulky.

To John Andre', Esquire

May 1779

Sir

To write with dispatch, G(eneral) A(rnold) had made use of Baily's. This I have paged for him, beginning at A. Each side is numbered and contains 927 pages. He adds 1 to each number of the page, of the column, and of the line, the first word of which is always used too. Zoroaster will be 928.2.2 and not 927.1.1. Tide is 838.3.2 and not 837.2.1. When he would express a number, so (11,000). He depends on me for conveying, which is dangerous. He goes to camp next week, from thence he will write to you. His signature will be AG or a name beginning with A. [79]

I am, &c.,

Joseph Stansbury

On **May 23rd**, Arnold explained what he could and could not deliver by giving a preliminary logistics report. In his report, Arnold gave up Charleston, South Carolina to the British who seized it a year later. Stansbury acted as secretary in case the letters were ever discovered.

To M--- J--- A---

May 23rd, 1779

Sir

Our friend S(tansbury) *acquaints me that the proposals made by him in my name are agreeable to S*(ir): *H*(enry): *C*(linton): *and that he engages to answer my warmest expectations for any services rendered. As I esteem the interest of America and Great Britain inseparable S: H: may depend on my exertions and intelligence: It will be impossible to cooperate unless there is a mutual confidence. S: H: shall be convinced on every occasion that his is not misplaced. Gen: W*(ashington): *and the Army move to the North River as soon as forage can be obtained. C*(ongress) *have given up Chs Town if attempted. They are in want of arms, ammunition, and men to defend it. 3 or 4 thousand militia is the most that can be mustered to fight on any Emergency. Seizing papers is impossible. Their contents can be known from a member of Congress. 4 months since the French Minister required Congress to vest their Agents with powers to negotiate peace with Britain. The time is elapsed in disputing if they shall demand independence with their original terms or insist on the addition of Newfoundland. No decision, no measure taken to prevent the depreciation of money, no foreign loan obtained. France refused to become surety, no encouragement from Spain. The French fleet has conditional orders to return to this continent. They depend on great part of their provision from hence a transport originally a 64 and a foreign 28 guns and daily expected here for provision. I will cooperate when an opportunity offers and as life and every thing is at stake I will expect some certainty my property here secure and a revenue equivalent to the risk and service done I cannot promise success; I will deserve it. Inform me what I may expect, could I know S. H. intentions he should never be at a loss for intelligence I shall expect a particular answer through our friend S.*

Madam Ar(nold) *presents you her particular compliments.* [79]

I am, &c.,

Gustavus

On the **31ˢᵗ**, Odell received the shock of his life when he read one of Stansbury's letters to Andre` while trying to salvage it after getting wet from the rain. He apologized for peeking at the confidential contents and shunned any involvement unless of course Andre` wanted him.

On His Majesty's Service, Capt. Andre`
Aid de Camp at Headquarters

New York, May 31, 1779

My Dear Sir

I am mortified to death – having just received (what I had been so anxiously expecting) a letter from S and, by a private mark agreed between us, perceiving it contained an invisible page for you, I assessed it by the fire, when to my inexpressible vexation, I found that the paper, having by some accident got damp on the way, had spread the solution in such a manner as to make the writing all one indistinguishable blot, out of which not the half of any one line can be made legible. I shall use every diligence to forward a letter to him and to instruct him how to guard against the like accident in future, and hope it will not be long before I shall receive a return. The ostensible page of this letter is dated the 21ˢᵗ instant, which I take it for granted must have been before he could have received my last, to which I am in hourly expectation of receiving an answer; and as my friend cannot but be aware of the precarious chances in conveying letters, I flatter myself that the substance of the one I have received will be repeated with additions in the one I expect. The moment I have the good fortune to get it I shall forward it to you and beg leave to ask whether it would not be proper on your part to instruct me in the channel through which I can most speedily and safely convey my letters to you. For the conveyance of this I took the liberty of applying to Capt. Smith the secretary, but did not find that he seemed so perfectly possessed as I expected with the means of speedy conveyance.

There is one point of delicacy in my situation, which I must take liberty to mention – I must not disassemble with you that my friend uses with me the same cipher which you fixed on for your own correspondence, and therefore, without your permission, I am doubtful whether it may not be improper for me to assess such papers as I have reason to conclude are intended rather for your own perusal than mine. I should not have taken the liberty in the present case, but I confess that my joy on getting the letter was such that before I had made the reflection, I had already flown to the fire with my paper, and, as it has turned out, I am glad to have spared you the vexation of a useless trouble. As toasted paper becomes too brittle to bear folding, if you think proper to confide so far in my discretion, I shall make it a rule to assess and carefully transcribe such passages as may come to me for your perusal. Though the receipt of this letter is unfortunately of no other use, yet in one view it gives me pleasure, as from its date it appears that our friend, though we waited long for its arrival, was not negligent nor tardy in beginning his expected correspondence.

Permit the Parson to conclude with his earnest prayers for your health, safety, and glory; may our General have the happiness, by his triumphs, to make us forget all past misfortunes.

I am, as you see, devoutly and most affectionately yours,

Jonathan Odell [79]

On **June 1st**, officers gathered together in Raritan, New Jersey to commence Arnold's long awaited court martial, but the proceedings soon broke up when it was learned that British forces under Clinton and Andre` took Stony Point and Verplank's Point. On the **2nd**, Washington expressed his regrets for yet another delay, but there *was* a war going on.

To M General Arnold

Headquarter, June 2, 1779

Dear Sir

I am sorry to inform you that the situation of affairs will not permit a court martial to proceed on your trial at this time. The movements of the enemy make it indispensably necessary, that the Army should at least advance towards the North River with all practicable expedition and require that the officers appointed to compose the court should be with their several commands. The following is a copy of the opinion of the General officers upon the occasion, who were convened yesterday evening to consider some points, which I judged it material to submit to them respecting your trial, in consequence of a letter from the judge-advocate.

'His Excellency the Commander-in-Chief having received intelligence that the enemy had moved out in full force from New York to Kingsbridge and towards the White Plains, and, during our deliberations on the points submitted by the foregoing state, a letter from Colonel Thomas Clarke, dated at Paramus the 31st ultimo, at seven o'clock P. M., advising that the enemy were at Teller's Point with forty-six sail, six of which were very large, and a number of flat

345

boats, and that they had landed a party of men on the other side of the North River, and a party on this side of the Slote; we are of opinion, upon the question being propounded, that the situation of affairs renders it necessary to postpone the consideration of the matter so submitted to us, and that the meeting of the members nominated to compose the said court-martial be deferred, till the Commander-in-Chief shall judge the circumstances of the service will better admit it.'

It is still a matter of greater concern that it is impossible for me to fix the time when the court will sit as it must depend upon the enemy's operations. Whenever these will permit, you shall be informed of the day and you may rest assured there shall be no delay but such as proceeds from necessity and the exigency of the public service.

I am, Dear Sir, &c., [68]

G. Washington

It appears that Andre` did take Odell into his secret circle as is revealed in a follow up letter of the **9<sup>th</sup>**, when Odell wrote to Stansbury and explained that his previous letter was damaged, but to continue communications in order to maintain Andre`'s confidence.

To Joseph Stansbury

June 9th 1779

Dear Sir

I lately wrote you by express to inform you that yours of May 21 had been injured by some accident of weather and was not legible; if you mean in earnest and with advantage to carry on the commercial plan, you must not delay the expected remittances. Both your credit and mine will suffer greatly if you do. Let us leave affairs of State to politicians while we attend to our little matters of trade and commerce; for thus our correspondence, though secret, will be harmless and we shall have no cause to repent our choice. I have yours from Gravell's of May 26 and for the present desire you to stick to your Oxford Interpreter.

Lothario (Andre`) is impatient: convince him of your sincerity and you may rely upon it that your most sanguine hopes will be surpassed. Now is the time for profitable speculation, while the multitude are idly debating about the fate of our paper, which we may appreciate if we will. Adieu, - let me hear from you soon and to the purpose. [79]

I am, Sir, &c.,

J. O.

On the same day Stansbury informed Odell that his first message was received and has already contributed to Andre`'s plan.

To Jonathan Odell

June 9th 1779

Sir

About three this afternoon I received your request of a copy of the invoice of the French cargo (letter), *which got damaged in its passage. The original is either mislaid or destroyed, and as I have written you several letters lately, which must reach your hands on a similar commercial subject, it is the less necessary. However it is at present out of my reach, as well as the invoice* (dictionary) *the prices of which you quote in yours just received. You know the antipathy or rather fear which I have of thunder, and I have sought a shelter here, where the tall trees and high buildings* (committees), *which surround and make my dwelling rather dangerous in stormy weather, are not to be met with. I have some time since forwarded to Mr. Andrews* (Andre`) *a plan of trade which will, I hope, be to the satisfaction of the concerned. Mr. A. G.* (General Arnold) *is at present out of town on private business. I shall endeavor to keep up our mercantile communications and interest you in anything that bids fair to quit cost. I asked your opinion lately on a passage in Blackstone's Commentaries, whether you perfectly understood me I know not, but should be glad to have you joined me in opinion that my critique on that celebrated author was at least defensible. I want to have a Baily's Dictionary – having left mine in the hurry-scurry of moving last winter twelvemonth. If it is the same edition with yours it will be more to my satisfaction. Naval and military matters are very dry and unsatisfactory to my turn. Paliwole will become Pacoli, which is shorter and more intelligible.* [79]

I am, Sir, &c.,
Joseph Stansbury

Prior to receiving Arnold's preliminary logistics report, Andre` wrote to him on behalf of Clinton stating that they wanted the necessary intelligence in order to arrest enough men and ammunition to put an end to the war. Such a place as Charleston or West Point would suffice if the British were in a position to capture Arnold's command on the march near Stony Point, or by pirating the shipping trade by intercepting incoming or outgoing supplies.

To Gustavus Monk

June 1779

Sir

The most essential services for resting this country from ruin and oppression would be in revealing the counsels of its rulers so as to counteract them and in affording an opportunity to defeat the Army. Generous terms would follow our success and ample rewards and honors would be the portion of the distinguished characters, which would contribute to so great an end.

The operation of the former of these services is slow, but has its importance and must be attended to. Dispatches to and from foreign courts, original papers, intimation of channels through which intelligence passes, and are the objects chiefly to be attended to, but, the most brilliant and effectual blow finally to complete the overthrow of the present abominable power would be the destruction of the Army. This may be effected by a grand stroke or by successive severe blows, here follow hints for both.

I should style a partial blow the taking possession of a considerable seaport and defeating the troops assigned to the defense of the province. Thus, so as to be able to make progress through it drive away or disarm the disaffected. By curbing the trade and displaying at the same time our gallantry and leniency, give a spring to the just indignation of the suffering people and induce them to return to their allegiance. Could you obtain the command in Carolina? The rest you must understand.

A surprise of a considerable body of men or the means pointed out of ambushing them, crossing upon their march, etc. Such a body might be collected and put in motion in consequence of operations on our part and the most effectual ones for that purpose you might suggest such as our threatening a magazine, a port in the sound, &c.

The intercepting a convoyed fleet to or from France or the West Indies might be effected by means of proper intelligence.

Magazines or barracks might be burnt and on certain occasions all the guns of a fort or field artillery spiked.

As to a general project against the whole Army, could anything take place on the West side of the north river? We should be glad of your sentiments on that head.

Here are our ideas for movements to the eastward. A considerable corps shall march into New England. The consequence will be that W(ashington) will cross the north river and hasten to the points attacked. He would possibly be preceded by a picked corps similar to that in Jersey under General Lee, which would have orders to harass, attack, awe the country, etc. could you command that corps, it might be concerted where and when it should be surprised, defeated, or obliged to negotiate. Complete information might be received concerning the main body, its baggage, its means of supply, &c., convoys might be intercepted, magazines burnt, boats on the north river seized, & the passage back prevented by a re-embarkation of the corps to the eastward or by the cooperation of troops from New York.

A chain of connivance must be very artfully laid to multiply difficulties & baffle resources. Under the circumstances, W(ashington) might be attacked, or be left to disperse from want of supplies. At such an hour when the most boisterous spirits were with the Army and everyone intent on its fate the seizing the Congress would decide the business. You must observe that our Navy would not be idle during this time & that a small corps attending a few ships of war might either be assisting in bringing off the C (Congress): or in increasing the general confusion be descents on the coast... [79]

I am, &c.,
John Anderson

In **mid-June**, when Clinton learned that Arnold did not hold a present command, he sent instructions for him to accept one of significant size, for he was willing to pay a bigger price for a bigger prize.

To Gustavus Monk

June 1779

Sir
I have your letter of the 23rd May: one in cipher received before was injured by the damp and not legible. Some messages through S(tansbury). will have shown my wish to hear from you and that in a tone consonant to the enlarged plan upon which S: H: C: is taught to expect your concurrence. With the same candor which you will experience when engaged in any operation concerted with H(is). E(xcellency). wishes to apprize you that he cannot reveal his intentions as to the present campaign nor can he find the necessity of such a discovery or that a want of a proper degree of confidence is to be inferred from his not making it. He informs you with the strictest truth that the war is to be prosecuted with vigor and that no thought is entertained of giving up the dependency of America, much less of harkening to such a claim as you have been told the Congress affect to debate upon. He begs you that you proposed your assistance for the

delivery of your country. You must know where the present power is vulnerable, and the conspicuous commands with which you might be vested may enable us at one shining stroke, from which both riches and honor would be derived. To accelerate the ruin to which the usurped authority is verging and to put a speedy end to the miseries of our fellow creatures. Join the Army, accept a command, be surprised, and be cut off; these things may happen in the course of maneuver, nor you be censured or suspected. A complete service of this nature involving a corps of five or six thousand men would be rewarded with twice as many thousand guineas. The method would be arranged by my meeting you as flag of truce or otherwise as soon as you come near us. It is service of this nature or intelligence having evidently led to such strokes, which S H C looks for. It is such as these that he pledges himself, shall be rewarded beyond your warmest expectations. The color of the times favors them and your abilities and firmness justify his hopes of success. In the meantime, your influence might be generously as well as profitably employed in procuring the exchange of General Burgoyne's Army. It could be urged by none with more propriety, nor would you be sorry to see this act of justice superbly added to the shining revolution that you may perhaps be instrumental in effecting.

A. [79]

In a letter of **July 11th**, Stansbury, identifying himself as Jonathan Stevens, wrote to Andre` stating that Arnold wanted a financial guarantee, win, lose, or draw and included a complete logistics report of the entire Continental Army to back up his proof as a partner.

To John Anderson, Esq. near Woodbridge

11. 7. 79

Sir

I delivered Gustavas your letter, yet it is not equal to his expectations. He expects to have your promise that he shall be indemnified for any loss he may sustain in case of detection. And whether this contest is finished by sword or by treaty, that 10,000 pounds shall be engaged to him for his services, which shall be faithfully devoted to your interest.

I received a letter from Mr. Cox requesting an answer to many particulars: what follows I gathered: what follows I gathered from Gustavus & must be considered as his own.

Washington's Army now with him is ten thousand effectives. Could be joined by militia from 4 to 6 or 8 thousand, that depending on where the scene of action lay. Plenty of everything at camp. Supplied from everywhere. Route various accordingly. No magazines. Sullivan commands 5 thousand regulars, are now sixty miles above Wyoming. Detroit the object, usual route. 6 or 8 field pieces. Plenty of provisions carried on 15 hundred-pack horses. Whether likely to succeed you must be the best judge. Gates is at Providence with 15 hundred regulars, design to guard that place, has power to call out the militia if wanted. Heath is at Boston. Lincoln has 3 thousand regulars & 5 hundred militia, not likely to collect any Army of consequence, the militia do not turn out with agility. 23 to 24 thousand the whole force of the Continental Army. I have written fully on the paper money already. There re 10 or 11 frigates from 24 to 36 guns & they will all be cruising soon. Two of them are out to the eastward, two expected from England with a cartel of 6 or 7 hundred prisoners exchanged with France. Four are in or near our ports. The forts in our rivers are in a batter state than ever before. No heavy cannon, garrison small, no stores being supplied from this town occasionally. D'Estaing coming here this summer depends on the British admiral. We know nothing about it. So far Gustavus...

I am your most obedient servant,
Jonathan Stevens [79]

In order to rejoin the Army and implement Andre`'s proposal of taking a fall, Arnold, on the **13th**, asked Washington to reset his trial date.

To His Excellency General Washington
Philadelphia July 13th, 1779
Dear Sir
I have been anxiously waiting for a long time in expectation that the situation of the Army would admit the court-martial to proceed on my trial. As a part of the British Army are gone down the North River, I hope the time is now arrived. If it can be done without prejudice to the service, I beg your Excellency to appoint as early as early a day as possible. The cruel situation I am in will apologize for my pressing the matter. My wounds are so far recovered, that I can walk with ease and I will soon be able to ride on horseback. If there is no probability of the court's meeting soon, I must request the favor to know it, in which case I shall beg the Congress a few month's absence on my private affairs. [68]

I have the honor to be with great respect and esteem,
your Excellency's most obedient humble servant,
B. Arnold

In the predawn hours of **July 16th**, three columns of American Light Infantry recaptured Stony Point under the leadership of Brigadier General Anthony Wayne. Born in Easton, Pennsylvania, Wayne had been educated at the Philadelphia Academy and became a land surveyor and tanner before being elected as a Whig member of the Pennsylvania Convention, Assembly, and Committee of Safety. His previous private study of the art of war prepared him well to raise a regiment of troops and received a colonel's commission when the time came to do some artwork on the British. He then applied his brush at Three Rivers, Brandywine, Germantown, Monmouth, and presently at Stony Point, where he captured the garrison by climbing up the steep, rocky cliffs from the river in the dark of night and silently surprised the British troops with unloaded muskets and fixed bayonets. This tactic was a form of payback for the same silent approach that had been applied on him two years previously by Major General Sir Charles Grey. It has been said that there is a fine line between crazy and creative; for the courage that he inspired within his men, "Mad" Anthony Wayne was certifiably creative. Having lost control of the west side of the river in that area, the British soon abandoned Fort Lafayette directly across from it on the east side. On the **20th**, Washington wrote back to Arnold stating that the court schedule was out of his hands until hunting season was over.

To M General Arnold

Headquarters West Point
July 20th, 1779

Dear Sir

I have received your favor of the 13th instant. The situation of affairs would not permit a court-martial to sit, since you were at Middlebrook. You may be assured it is not my wish to delay your trial a single moment. At the same time you must be sensible, that I cannot fix with precision on any day, during the more active part of the campaign, for it to come on. The movements of the enemy will govern ours, and, if a day were proposed, a disappointment might take place, as it did before. If, however, there should be a time, when appearances promise that the enemy will remain inactive, I will appoint a day, of which you shall be notified. At present there is no such prospect. I am happy to hear that your wounds are so far recovered; and I hope they continue to mend, till you are perfectly well.

I am, Dear Sir, &c., [68]

G. Washington

At the end of July, Andre` wrote to Arnold asking him to establish his abilities before agreeing on a price.

To Gustavus Monk

July 1779

Sir

I am sorry any hesitation should still remain as I think we have said all that the prudence with which our liberality must be tempered will admit. I can only add that as such sums as are held forth must be in some degree accounted for, real advantage must appear to have arisen from the expenditure or a generous effort must have been made.

We are thankful for the information transmitted and hope you will continue to give it as frequently as possible as possible. Permit me to prescribe an accurate plan of West Point, with the new roads, New Windsor, Constitution (Island) and an account of what vessels, gun boats, or galleys are in the North River or may be shortly built there and the weight and metal they carry. The Army brigade with the commanding officers of Corps in the form commonly called the Order of Battle. Sketches or descriptions of harbors to the eastward which might be attacked and where stores and shipping might be destroyed.

The only method of completing conviction on both sides of the generous inventions of each and making arrangements for important operations is by a meeting. Would you assume a command and enable me to see you I am convinced a conversation of a few minutes would satisfy you entirely and I trust would give us equal cause to be pleased. In any concerted plan, which may not be carried into execution before that time Gen: Philips coming here on parole would be an exceeding good opportunity for further explanations. He is S: H: C's: firm friend and a man of strict honor, but neither to him or any person can we give the smallest hint without your permission; which we do not mean to ask unless you are perfectly willing to grant it. But above all Sir, let us not lose time or contract our views which on our part have become sanguine from the excessive strain of your overtures, and which we cannot think you would on your side confine to general intelligence whilst so much greater things may be done and advantages in proportion as much greater can be reaped. [79]

I am, &c.,
John Anderson

Negotiations soon came to a sticking point when Arnold stated that he wanted to know their price before making a commitment.

To John Anderson Esq. near Brunswick

July 1779

Sir

 I have had an interview with ------ (Arnold) who showed me your letter and remarked that it contained no reply to the terms mentioned in my last. Though he could not doubt your honor yet there was no assurance given that his property in this Country should be indemnified from any loss that might attend unfortunate discovery: however severely he wished to serve his Country in accelerating the settlement of this unhappy contest, yet he should hold himself unjust to his family to hazard his all on the occasion and part with a certainty (potentially at least) for an uncertainty. He hopes to join the Army in about three weeks when he will, if possible, contrive an interview. He will make a point of seeing Genl Philips if he comes here and may perhaps open himself to that gentleman; at same time he depends on your honor that nothing ever transpires to his disadvantage. I wished him to put pen to paper himself, but he said he had told me his sentiments and confided in me to represent them, which I have done with fidelity.

 In the course of the conversation, he asked me if I knew that Sir Henry was going home and Lord C---- (Cornwallis) was to have the command. He said he had nothing to communicate at present that could be of service. he had not the plan of West Point, being only in Genl Washington's hands and the engineers who made the draught. It had many new works and he could when there make a drawing of it easily. The number of men and the commanding officers were shifting daily. The commanding officer of a wing today being ordered perhaps to some post tomorrow. The harbors &c. to the eastward he thought you may well be acquainted with and also knew where the vessels stores &c. lay at Boston, Newburyport, Salem, &c. That the convention had been for 4 weeks and was yet waiting to carry Mr. Girard home who was detained by Congress not having come to any definitive terms to offer G. Britain. That four frigates were ordered to cruise off Newfoundland, about a thousand men on board, the fleet gone against Penobscot (Maine).

I am sensible I have been tedious & have not leisure at this
late hour to throw it into better order or smaller compass. Saturday
3 AM [79]

I am, Sir, &c.,
Jonathan Stevens

On **August 16th**, Andre` wrote an open letter to Peggy, offering to supply her with millinery materials, while making a direct and covert connection for writing to Arnold.

To Margaret Arnold

Headquarters New York, the 16th Aug. 1779

Madame

Major Giles is so good as to take charge of this letter, which is meant to solicit your remembrance, and to assure you that my respect for you and the fair circle in which I had the honor of becoming acquainted with you, remains unimpaired by distance or political broils. It would make me very happy to become useful to you here. You know the mischianza made me a complete milliner. Should you not have received supplies for your fullest equipment from that department, I shall be glad to enter into the whole detail of capwire, needles, gauze, &c., and, to the best of my abilities, render you in these trifle services from which I hope you would infer a zeal to be further employed. I beg you would present my best respect to your sisters, to the Miss Chews, and to Mrs. Shippen and Mrs. Chew.

I have the honor to be, with the greatest regard, madam, your most obedient and most humble servant,
John Andre` [79]

On **October 4th**, Arnold had come to the aide of James Wilson; an attorney who had defended hundreds of loyalists prosecuted by Reed. The Scottish born Wilson had immigrated to America to study law and after his admittance to the bar, began his practice in Pennsylvania before authoring several pamphlets against the acts of Parliament. Although he was in no rush to go to war, his voice against British tyranny garnered him as a member of the Provincial meeting of deputies, Provincial Convention, Continental Congress, and signer of the Declaration. Another client of Wilson's that was unpopular among the people was Robert Morris. Known as the "Financier of the Revolution," Morris had immigrated to America from Liverpool, England and utilized his bold and shrewd entrepreneurial energy to work his way up in a Philadelphia counting house, which held the leading position in colonial trade through both wars of the period. Given his position as a merchant, he proved to be a vital member of the council of safety in personally arranging for the procurement of vessels, munitions, and naval armament. Although he was elected to the 1ˢᵗ Continental Congress, he notably became one of the last signers of the Declaration of Independence. As chairman of the Secret Committee of Trade and active member of the Committee of Secret Correspondence and the Marine Committee, he served as the chief commercial and financial agent to Congress. Public dissention towards him arose from accusations of his raising prices by hoarding grain that was really in reserve for our allies in the French Army.

Wilson and Morris had "fortified" themselves inside Wilson's house with Captain George Campbell, Colonel Stephen Chambers, and thirty of his Republicans in his home at Third and Walnut Streets while 200 of Reed's radicals gathered outside with an equal amount of angry residents. Campbell appeared in a third story window shouting down at the crowd and waving a pistol. Someone fired a shot at him, which he returned and dropped a few members of the mob before he was killed by a return volley. The others blazed away into the crowd and drove them back for the moment until the front door was rushed and battered down. An exchange of fire erupted in the staircase that killed Chambers before the crowd could be repelled out of the house and the door was barricaded with furniture. Arnold rushed towards the commotion upon hearing the gunshots and was bombarded with stones and insults from the mob.

Reed arrived just as Arnold brandished his pistols when backed up against a wall. "What are you doing here, General?" cried Reed, "You have no more voice in the military affairs of this city." [77] "You've raised a riot, Reed," Arnold shouted, "and now you have no power to quell it." [77] Upon the arrival of Continental troops a short time later, Reed ordered everyone inside and outside of the house arrested. Arnold, Wilson, Morris, and the Republicans were released once they posted bail. The militia mob of Radicals was released soon afterwards when Reed sought out and won amnesty for them. Allan McLane recalled the events in his journal.

I was standing on the front steps of my house on Walnut Street and observed Colonel Grayson beckoning me from the door of the war office. I went to him and he told me he was glad I had not left the city, for that he had great apprehensions that several of our most respectable citizens, then assembled at Mr. Wilson's house, would be massacred, as they were determined to defend themselves against the armed mob that had assembled on the commons this morning and were moving down Second Street, expecting to find Mr. Wilson and his friends at the city tavern, but they were within pistol shot of the war office. I listened to the sound of the drum and fife, could distinctly hear the sound on Second Street, and in a few minutes observed the front of those in arms appeared on Walnut Street, moving up the street; by this time the front of the mob was near Dock Street, on Walnut Street.

The colonel asked me if I knew those in front of the armed men; I answered I thought the leader was Captain Faulkner, a militia officer. The colonel proposed that we should meet and persuade them to turn up Dock to Third Street, which we did attempt. I introduced Colonel Grayson to Captain Faulkner as a member of the Board of War. Grayson addressed him and expressed his fears as to the consequences of attacking Mr. Wilson or his house; their object was to support the constitution, the laws, and the Committee of Trade. The laboring part of the city had become desperate from the high price of the necessaries of life.

The halt in front brought a great press from the rear; two men, Pickering and Bonham, ran up to the front, armed with muskets and bayonets fixed, and inquired the cause of the halt, at the same time ordered Faulkner to move up Walnut Street. Grayson addressed Bonham and I addressed Pickering, who answered me with the threat of a bayonet, sometimes bringing himself in the attitude of a charge of trailed arms. Captain Faulkner and Mr. John Haverstadt interfered, to pacify Pickering and Bonham. Then word was given to pass up Walnut Street. By this time the press of the mob was so great that it was difficult to keep our feet and we were crowded among the citizen prisoners, which they had taken into custody in their march through the city. Colonel Grayson and myself linked arms and determined to clear ourselves from the press when we reached the war office.

As we passed my house, I saw my wife and Mrs. Forrest at the window of the second story. The moment she saw me in the crowd she screamed out and fainted. It was impossible then to escape. We were then within pistol shot of Wilson's house. I saw Captain Campbell of Colonel Hazen's regiment of the Continental Army, at one of the upper windows at Wilson's house; heard him distinctly call out to those in arms to pass on. Musketry was immediately discharged from the street and from the house, the mob gave way and fled in all directions, and left Grayson and myself under the eaves of the house

357

on Third Street, exposed to the fire of those in the street at a distance. We concluded we would run into Wilson's garden, but there we found ourselves exposed to the fire of both the mob in the neighbor's yard as well as those of Wilson's friends in the house.

In a few minutes we were discovered by General Mifflin, who recognized us as officers of the Continental Army, and ordered one of the doors of the back building to be opened; at this moment several persons in the house became much alarmed and jumped out of the second-story windows. The back door of the house was immediately opened and we entered. General Mifflin and Thompson met us on the lower floor and requested us to follow them upstairs, observing that Mr. Wilson and his friends were about retiring to the upper rooms, which we did. When I reached the third story, I looked out of one of the windows on Third Street, looked up Third Street, could see no person in the street nearer than Dock Street, where the mob had dragged a field piece. I looked down Third Street and saw a number of desperate looking men in their shirt sleeves coming out of Pear Street, moving towards Wilson's house, armed with bars of iron and large hammers, and in a minute reached the house and began to force the doors and windows; they presently made a breach on Third Street, but on entering the house they received a fire from the staircases and cellar windows, which dropped several of them, the others broke and dispersed, leaving their wounded in the house. Some of Wilson's friends ran downstairs, shut the doors, and barricaded them...

In a few minutes, Governor Reed, with a detachment of the first troops of City horse, appeared. Wilson and his friends in the house sallied out. I moved with them and the first person I recognized in the street was Governor Reed, who called upon me, by name, to aid in seizing the rioters. [20]

In an official statement, Peale issued a detailed account of the attack on "Fort Wilson" and the events preceding it.

The rapidity of the depreciation of the Continental money was at this period such that those who retained it a few days could not purchase near the value which they had given for it.

This being a grievance greatly felt by those who had been most active in favor of the Revolution, and among them those who had on every occasion rendered their personal service in the militia, many of whom thought that this continual depreciation of their favorite paper was brought about by the machinations of their internal enemies. Very few indeed could trace the real or principal cause to its true source, namely that of too great a quantity being issued and put into circulation. Taxation being too slow to obtain the necessary supply for the support of an Army, Congress were continually obliged to be issuing more, although there was already so much in use as to have totally banished gold and silver in common dealings.

At the meeting of the militia of Philadelphia on the commons in 1779, a number of those active Whigs whose zeal would carry them any length in their favorite cause, and those tempers had now become soured by the many insults they had met with from the Tories, assembled at Burns' Tavern and after they had come to some resolutions, more passionate than judicious, that of sending away the wives and children of those men who had gone with British, or were within the British lines, was adopted.

After these zealots had formed this design, they then began to devise the mode of carrying it into execution, and proposed to put themselves under some commander, and accordingly sent a messenger to request Captain Peale to attend them. But so soon as he was made acquainted with the business, he told them that he could not approve of the measure, as it would in the practice be found a dangerous and difficult undertaking; that the taking of women and children from their homes would cause much affliction and grief; that, when seen, the humanity of their fellow citizens would be roused into an opposition to such a measure; that such attempts must of course fail. But all his arguments were in vain; they could not see these difficulties with a determined band. He then told them that the danger in case of a failure in such an attempt would be eminent to the commander of such a party. The reply was that General Washington could not take his command without running some risks and that they in this undertaking would sacrifice their lives or effect it.

Captain Peale was at last obliged to refuse, and made the excuse that he was applied to by some of his friends to stand as a candidate at the then approaching election for members of the General Assembly; after which all further entreaty ceased, and he left them, and did not hear anything further of their proceedings until the Thursday following, when he received a notice that desired him, with Col. Bull, Major Boyd, and Dr. Hutchinson, to meet the militia on the Monday following at Mrs. Burns' tavern on the common. Those persons so noticed having consulted together; all of them disapproved of the violent proceedings of the militia. Dr. Hutchinson said he would not attend the meeting; Peale and the other gentlemen conceived that they as good citizens were in duty bound to go and use endeavors to restrain, as far as they might be able, any violent and improper proceedings, and, in duty to themselves, at least to demonstrate in a public manner against having any part in the business. After further consideration, Dr. Hutchinson agreed to meet them; Col. Bull, being dangerously ill, could not attend.

Accordingly on that memorable Monday, Dr. Hutchinson, Major Boyd and Captain Peale went to Mrs. Burns' tavern (where great numbers of the militia had already assembled), and they did use every argument in their power to prevent any further proceedings in that vain and dangerous undertaking. They represented the difficulty of selecting such characters as all could agree to be obnoxious amongst such a body of the people; that in such an attempt they must infallibly differ as to the object – of course no good purpose could be answered.

Among the militia were many Germans, whose attachment to the American cause was such that they disregarded every danger, and whose resentment at this time was most violently established against all Tories. They only looked straight forward, regardless of consequences. In short, to reason with a multitude of devoted patriots assembled on such an occasion was in vain; and after Peale found all that could be said availed naught, he left them and went to his home, and afterwards to the President's, General Reed, whom he found was preparing to go out in order to prevent mischief, which he said was to be feared from the tidings that brought him. Captain Peale immediately returned to his home, where he had not long been before he heard the firing of small arms. He then began to think that he ought to prepare himself by getting his firearms in order, in case he should be under the necessity of making use of them; for no man could now know where the affair would end; and finding his wife and family very easy, he determined to stay within his own doors for the present time. Shortly that tragic scene was ended and very fortunately no more lives were lost.

The militia having taken two men who they conceived were inimical to the American cause, they were parading them up Walnut Street, and when they had got opposite James Wilson, Esq.'s house at the corner of third Street, where a considerable number of gentlemen to the number of about thirty had collected and had armed themselves, amongst them Captain Campbell, commander of an invalid corps, this unfortunate person hoisted a window with a pistol in his hand, and some conversation having passed between him and the passing militia, a firing began, and poor Campbell was killed; a Negro boy at some distance from the house was also killed, and four or five persons badly wounded. The militia had now become highly

360

aggravated and had just broke into the house, and most probably would have killed everyone assembled within those walls; but very fortunately for them, General Reed with a number of the light horse appeared at this fortunate juncture and dispersed the militia. Numbers of them were taken and committed to the common jail and a guard placed to prevent a rescue.

The next morning the officers of the militia and numbers of the people assembled at the Court House in Market Street and the minds of the citizens generally seemed to be much distressed. The militia of Germantown were beginning to assemble and General Reed had sent Mr. Matlack, the Secretary f the Council, to the officers of the militia, then assembled in Market Street, as above mentioned, to endeavor to keep them waiting until he could address the militia of Germantown, after which he would be with them. Peale, hearing of this meeting at the Court House, went there and found that the officers were exceedingly warm and full of resentment that any of the militia should be kept in durance in the jail; they appeared to be ripe for undertaking the release of prisoners and all Mr. Matlack's arguments, perhaps, would have been insufficient to keep them much longer from being active. [20]

At the same time another mob harassed Arnold on his way home from a meeting of Republicans at Grays Ferry. Once again, he had to draw his pistols and threaten to shoot two men who attempted to approach him. Once inside, he complained to Congress, asking newly elected President Samuel Huntington for an order of protection. Huntington was a self-educated lawyer from Arnold's hometown of Norwich, Connecticut, who served as a member of the General Assembly, Committee for the Colony's Defense, Court Judge, signer of the Declaration, and four-year member of Congress.

To His Excellency Samuel Huntington, Esq.
President of Congress
                                    Philadelphia, Oct. 6th 1779
Sir
     A mob of lawless ruffians have attacked me in the street and threaten my life, now I am in my own house, for defending myself when attacked. As there is no protection to be expected from the authority of the state for an honest man, I am under the necessity of requesting Congress to order me a guard of Continental troops. This request I presume will not be denied to a man, who has so often fought and bled in the defense of his country.

I have the honor to be with great respect, Sir,
your most obedient humble servant,
B. Arnold
N. B. I believe 20 men with a good officer sufficient. [14]

Not wanting to get involved, Huntington responded to Arnold's plea on that same day and directed him to consult with Reed on the matter.

To Major General Arnold

In Congress, Oct. 6th 1779
Sir
The enclose act contains the answer of Congress to your letter of this day, which I communicated immediately upon the receipt of it.
I am, &c.,
S. H.
President [67]

Wednesday, October 6, 1779
...On motion of Mr. Morris, seconded by Mr. Gerry,
Ordered, That the President inform General Arnold that his application ought to be made to the Executive Authority of the state of Pennsylvania in whose disposition to protect every honest citizen Congress have full confidence, and highly disapprove of every individual to the contrary. [26]

Reed at last dispatched a squad of guards, who responded in a very relaxed manner. On the **13th**, Peggy gave her regards to Andre`.

To Captain Andre`

Philadelphia, October 13th 1779
Mrs. Arnold presents her best respects to Capt. Andre`, is much obliged to him for his very polite and friendly offer of being serviceable to her. Major Giles was so obliging as to promise to procure what trifles Mrs. Arnold wanted in the millinery way, or she would with pleasure have accepted of it. Mrs. Arnold begs leave to assure Captain Andre` that her friendship and esteem for him is not impaired by time or accident. The ladies to whom Capt. A. wished to be remembered are well and present their compliments to him.
Mrs. Arnold 7.

On **October 23rd**, at the young age of twenty-three, Andre' was appointed as Clinton's Deputy Adjutant General of the British Army and promoted to the rank of major. After several further delays, Washington was at last able to afford the officers necessary to convene for Arnold's hearing at Norris' Tavern, a.k.a. Dickerson's Tavern, in Morristown, New Jersey as called for in his announcements of **December 22nd**.

> *General Orders*
> *Headquarters Morristown*
> *Wednesday, December 22, 1779*
> *Parole Gillbralter.*   *Countersigns Goa, Goree.*
> *The General Court-Martial whereof Maj. General How is President is to sit tomorrow morning at ten o'clock at Norris' Tavern. Lieut. Col. Comt. Weisenfels is appointed a member of the Court; vice Colonel Hazen and Colonel Jackson, vice Col. Humpton absent on command.* [24]

The next morning at ten o'clock, the **23rd**, as ordered, Major General Robert Howe of North Carolina presided over the court while Brigadier General Henry Knox of Massachusetts served as vice-chairman and Colonel John Laurance managed the prosecution as Judge Advocate General of the Continental Army. Howe was a wealthy planter who was educated in England and served in the French and Indian War. After becoming a delegate in the Colonial Congress, he was denounced by the Governor for forming and training local militia. In the present conflict, he was credited with extracting British forces out of Norfolk, Virginia. Laurence was born and raised in England until the age of thirteen when he immigrated to New York. Following his admittance to the bar he was commissioned in the Army and took part in the invasion of Canada. In 1776 he was appointed aide-de-camp to Major General Alexander McDougall and in 1777 he was appointed judge advocate general.

Board members included Brigadier Generals William Maxwell and Mordecai Gist. Maxwell, better known as "Scotch Willie" for his bold Irish burr rather than his being quite fond of the drink, was a tall and strong, red faced man of forty-seven. After immigrating to America, he spent his youth working on his parents farm in New Jersey, before serving in the French and Indian War. At the start of the Revolution, he became a member of the New Jersey Provincial Congress and Chairman of the Committee of Safety before receiving his commission as a colonel. Although he lost a devastating battle at Three Rivers in Canada, his bravery granted him a promotion to brigadier in which he led troops at Brandywine, Germantown, and Monmouth. Gist had been a merchant trader in Baltimore and captain of a volunteer military group prior to the war. While in command of the Maryland 1st Brigade, this ardent patriot of admirable ethics had fought gallantly at Long Island and Germantown. Colonel Elias Dayton of the 3rd New Jersey was an open, generous, and sincere man who had served in the French and Indian War, on the Committee of Safety, and held a physical resemblance to Washington. During the Revolution he rebuilt Fort Stanwix, constructed Fort Dayton, and had served with distinction at Bound Brook, Staten Island, Brandywine, Germantown, and Monmouth.

Among the other officers included were Colonels Philip Burr Bradley; John Gunby of the 7th Maryland; Josias Carvil Hall of the 4th Maryland; Henry Jackson; Henry Sherburne from Rhode Island; Oliver Spencer from New Jersey; Philip Van Cortlandt from Westchester County, who fought alongside Arnold at Saratoga; and Lieutenant Colonel Weisenfels. The twelve officers sat at a long wooden table as split logs burned in the fireplace to warm the chilled winter air. The witnesses heard during the trial were: Timothy and William Matlack; Franks, twenty-three year old Lieutenant Colonel Alexander Hamilton, aide to Washington; Deputy Quartermaster General, Colonel John Mitchell; and John Hall, assistant to Mitchell. Hamilton, of Scottish decent, was a slender and energetic young man of average height with reddish-brown hair, fair-toned skin, and deep blue eyes. In his love for learning, he attended preliminary studies in Elizabethtown, New Jersey before enrolling as a student at King's College (now Columbia University). His expansive knowledge on British and American government, influenced his decision to bail out of higher education in order to bear arms against British oppression. In forming and commanding a volunteer company at the start of the war, he made an influential impression on Nathanael Greene, who in turn introduced him to George Washington. Being fluent in French and proficient in writing, he was appointed as Washington secretary and aide de camp at the young age of twenty after displaying his leadership abilities in the battles of Long Island, White Plains, Trenton, and Princeton. In addition to his administrative duties, Hamilton proved to be a trusted advisor to the Commander-in-Chief, submitting reports of problems and potential solutions for America's military machine as well as being a remarkable representative for him with his charm, grace, and manners.

On **January 21, 1780** acting as his own defense council, Arnold presented his opening statement expressing his loyalty and sacrifices in answering his country's call to war and found it insulting to be called to answer libelous accusations.

"Mr. President and gentlemen of this honorable court; I appear before you to answer charges brought against me by the late Supreme Executive Council of the Commonwealth of Pennsylvania. It is disagreeable to be accused, but when an accusation is made, I feel that it is a great source of consolation to have an opportunity of being tried by gentlemen. Of whose delicate and refined sensations of honor will lead them to entertain similar sentiments concerning those who accuse unjustly and those who are justly accused. In the former case, your feelings revolt against the conduct of the prosecutors; in the latter, against those who are deserved objects of a prosecution. Whether those feelings will be directed against me or against those whose charges have brought me before you, will be known by your just and impartial determination of this cause.

"When the present necessary war against Great Britain commenced, I was in easy circumstances and enjoyed a fair prospect of improving them. I was happy in domestic connections and blessed with a rising family who claimed my care and attention. The liberties of my country were in danger. The voice of my country called upon all her faithful sons to join in her defense. With cheerfulness I obeyed the call. I sacrificed domestic ease and happiness to the service of my country and in her service have I sacrificed a great part of a handsome fortune. I was one of the first that appeared in the field and from that time to the present hour have not abandoned her service.

"When one is charged with practices which his soul abhors and which conscious innocence tells him he has never committed, an honest indignation will draw from him expressions in his own favor, which on other occasions might be ascribed to an ostentatious turn of mind. The part, which I have acted in the American cause, has been acknowledged by our friends and by our enemies to have been far from an indifferent one. My time, my fortune, and my person have been devoted to my country in this war. And if the sentiments of those who are supreme in the United States in civil and military matters are allowed to have any weight, then my time, my fortune, and my person have not been devoted in vain. You will indulge me, gentlemen, while I lay before you some honorable testimonies, which Congress and the Commander-in-Chief of the armies of the United States have been pleased to give of my conduct. The place where I now stand justifies me in producing them." [36]

Arnold then asked to read complimentary citations to the court from Washington, which the court honored. He then followed with a question of honor. "If the testimonies have any foundation in truth, and I believe the authority of those who gave them will be thought at least equal to that of those who have spoke, and wrote, and published concerning me in a very different manner, is it probable that after having acquired some little reputation, and after having gained the favorable reputation of those, whose favorable opinion it is an honor to gain, I should all at once sink into a course of conduct equally unworthy of a patriot and a soldier? No pains have been spared, no artifice has been left untried to persuade the public that this has been the case. Uncommon attention has been employed in propagating suspicions, invectives, and slanders to the prejudice of my character. The presses of Philadelphia have groaned under the libels against me, charges have been published, and officially transmitted to the different states, and to many parts of Europe, as I am informed, before they were regularly exhibited, and long before I had an opportunity of refuting them; and indeed every method that men ingeniously wicked could invent, has been practiced to blast and destroy my character. Such a vile prostitution of power, and such instances of glaring tyranny and injustice, I believe are unprecedented in the annuls of any free people. I have long and impatiently waited for an opportunity of vindicating my reputation, and have frequently applied for it; but the situation of affairs at the beginning and during the continuance of the campaign, necessarily, and against the General's inclination, prevented it, until now. But now it is happily arrived, and I have the most ardent hopes of being able to avail myself of it, by satisfying you and through your sentence, by satisfying the world, that my conduct and character have been most unwarrantably traduced, and that the charges brought against me are false, malicious, and scandalous." [36]

The first charge was for issuing a pass to the *Charming Nancy* to leave the port of Chestnut Neck (Egg Harbor), New Jersey. Arnold explained that his decision was issued based on the owner's claim that its cargo was for the use of the citizens of the United States, which seemed to him most praiseworthy and he had felt obliged to further it. In addition, he pointed out how easy it was to mistake the loyalties of Philadelphians at that time and although Reed was not present to respond, Arnold made a verbal attack on him labeling him a political opportunist for insinuating that he and the council had to act for Washington.

"The permission was given on the fourth day of June, 1778, when though I had no formal instructions from the General to take the command in Philadelphia, I had intimations given me that I should be fixed upon for that appointment. The gentleman who applied for the protection in behalf of himself and company, was not then residing in the city with the enemy; he had taken the oath of allegiance to the State of Pennsylvania, required by its laws, as appeared by a certificate which he produced to me. What his political character, and those of the others, in whose behalf he applied to me, was, I pretend not to ascertain; nor do I mean to become their advocate, any further than the justice due to an injured character requires. I think it has been clearly proved by the testimony of several gentlemen, (not parties in this matter) that the general character of those gentlemen was unexceptionable, some of them had taken an active part in favor of these states; and the tenor of their conduct since, will I presume justify a favorable opinion of them. It is enough for me to show that their intentions with regard to this vessel and cargo seemed to be upright, and that the design of saving them for the use of the citizens of the United States, appeared to be worthy of praise, instead of a reprimand. This appears evident from the depositions of Mr. Collins, Mr. Beveridge, and Colonel Proctor.

"Why the protection is viewed an indignity to the authority of the state of Pennsylvania, I own I cannot discover. The President and the council of that state were then in Lancaster; the pass to the vessel was to 'sail into any of the ports of the United States of America.' To sail into the port of Philadelphia was not the object; the vessel was there already. If there was an encroachment upon the authority of any state, it must have been some other than the state of Pennsylvania. The vessel sailed into one of the ports of New Jersey; the government of that state, though far from being insensible to its honor, has never complained of their indignity offered to it by my protection; a jury of that state acquitted the vessel by their verdict; and the judge of admiralty of that state confirmed the verdict by his decree, which is in evidence before this honorable court.

"It is part of this charge that the permission was granted without the knowledge of the Commander-in-Chief, though then present. I think it peculiarly unfortunate that the armies of the United States have a gentleman at their head, who knows so little about his own honor, or regards it so little, as to lay the President and Council of Pennsylvania under the necessity of stepping forth in his defense. The General is invested with power and he possesses spirit to check and to punish every instance of disrespect shown to his authority, but he will not prostitute his power by exerting it upon a trifling occasion; far less will he pervert it when no occasion is given at all.

"His Excellency knew, and you, gentlemen, well know, it has been customary for General officers of the Army to grant passes, protections for persons and property, to the inhabitants of the United States, who appeared friendly to the same. The utility of the measure, which was evident in the present case, without any precedent, I conceive to be a sufficient justification. The protection was designed only to prevent the soldiery from plundering the vessel and cargo, coming from the enemy, that proper authority might take notice of the matter. I must beg leave to mention a resolution of Congress in point. I do not recollect the date. It was, however, previous to the pass. That honorable body therein promise, to all persons in the enemy's service, for their encouragement and reward, all vessels and cargoes that they shall seize upon, in possession of the enemy, and bring into any of the United States. If such reward is given to our enemies, can it be esteemed criminal to protect the property of the citizens of the United States, when coming from the enemy. Certainly not. At the time the protection was given, I had no doubt of the right or propriety of giving it. I am now confirmed in my opinion, and that the resolution of Congress I have mentioned, warrants the measure. But, if strictly considering the matter, it shall be thought that I exceeded my power, by granting the protection, I hope his Excellency General Washington, and this honorable court, will do me the justice to believe, that it was not out of any disrespect to his authority, but an error in judgement, as I was convinced at the time I had a right to grant the pass; and had I refused, I should have thought myself guilty." [36]

In response to the second charge, he read his orders from Washington and Congress along with the proclamation from Reed to close the shops. "The resolution of Congress 'directs me to take early and proper care to prevent the removal, transfer, or sale of any goods, wares, or merchandise, in the possession of the inhabitants of the city, until the property of the same shall be ascertained by a joint committee, consisting of persons appointed by Congress, and of persons appointed by the Supreme Executive Council of Pennsylvania.' My instructions from the General mention, 'that I will find the objects of my command specified in the resolution of Congress, and that the means of executing the powers vested in me were left to my own judgement.' How could I better prevent the removal, transfer, or sale of any goods, wares, and merchandise in the possession of the inhabitants of the city than by shutting the shops and stores? If the officers of the Army were prevented from purchasing, it was because the sale of any goods was directed by Congress to be prevented, in which the sale of goods to officers was necessarily included; and it was in order (as is stated in the proclamation) that the quartermaster, commissary, and clothier generals might contract for such goods, as were wanted for the use of the Army.

"What I have already mentioned, renders it surprising that shutting the shops and stores should be made a charge against me by any man, or body of men; what I am going to mention, renders it peculiarly surprising that this charge should be made against me by the gentleman, who is now President of the State of Pennsylvania. It is in evidence before this honorable court, that this very gentleman proposed to one of my aids, that he, even before my arrival in town, should publish an order to prevent the selling of any goods or merchandise; that this very gentleman was urgent to have this done; that this very gentleman, after my arrival in town, drew up a proclamation for that purpose, which was presented to me. The same gentleman now exhibits the same measure as an article of accusation against me.

"The last part of this charge is a serious nature indeed: it is that, while I prohibited others from purchasing, I privately made considerable purchases for my own benefit, as is alleged and believed. If this part of the charge is true, I stand confessed, in the presence of this honorable court, the vilest of men; I stand stigmatized with indelible disgrace, the disgrace of having abused an appointment of high trust and importance, to accomplish the meanest and most unworthy purposes: the blood I have spent in defense of my country will be insufficient to obliterate the stain. But if this part of the charge is void of the truth; if it has not even the semblance of truth, what shall I say of my accusers? What epithets will characterize their conduct, the sentence of this honorable court will soon determine.

"It is 'alleged and believed' that I privately made considerable purchases for my own benefit. I am not conversant in the study of jurisprudence; but I have always understood, that public charges ought to have some other foundation to rest upon, than mere unsupported 'allegation and belief.' Who allege and believe this accusation? None, I trust, but the President and Council of Pennsylvania; because, I trust, none else would allege and believe anything tending to ruin a character, without sufficient evidence. Where is the evidence of this accusation? I call upon my accusers to produce it: I call upon them to produce it, under the pain of being held forth to the world, and to posterity, upon the proceedings of this court, as public defamers and murderers of reputation.

"They have indeed produced the evidence of a certain Colonel Fitzgerald, to prove that he saw an anonymous paper in the hands of Major Franks, one of my aids. I shall take no notice of the paper he alludes to, as it cannot be deemed a proof, or admitted as evidence; but the manner of his procuring a fight of the paper, I cannot help taking notice of: lodging in the same house with Major Franks, in his absence, Colonel Fitzgerald's curiosity prompted him to examine Major Franks' papers, when he stumbled upon a secret too big for him to keep. Was not this a gross violation of the confidence subsisting between gentlemen? But what shall I say of the use this gentleman made of his secret? I will not say it was a disgrace to the character of a soldier and gentleman. I will leave it to the gentleman's own feelings, which (if he is not callous) will say more to him that I can possibly do on the subject. In the nature of things, it is impossible for me to prove, by positive and direct evidence, the negative side of a charge: but I have done all that in the nature of things is possible. On the honor of a gentleman and soldier, I declare to gentlemen and soldiers, that the charge is false.

"My aids de camp were acquainted with my transactions, and had access to my papers: my invoice, my minutes, and account books were always open to their inspection. Could I have made considerable purchases without their knowledge? And yet did they not know of my making any purchases of goods of any kind, directly or indirectly; and they had every reason to think, that no such purchases were made, either by me or my agents, except a few trifling articles to furnish my table, and for my family's use; most of which were supplied me by the quartermaster, commissary, and clothier generals. If I made considerable purchases, considerable sales must have been made to me by some person in Philadelphia. Why are not these persons produced? Have my prosecutors so little power and influence in that city, as to be unable to furnish evidence of the truth?" [36]

To the accusation that he had imposed menial duties on the sons of Pennsylvania free men instead of servants, Arnold countercharged that it was nothing more than gossip to alienate the militia from him. "With respect to the third charge of the Supreme Council of the State of Pennsylvania, I think it necessary to make some observations on it, because it is evidently calculated, by a false coloring of a trifling and innocent transaction, to subject me to prejudice of the free men of the states, and particularly of the Militia of the state of Pennsylvania.

"I am charged 'with imposing menial offices upon the sons of free men of this state, when called forth by desire of Congress to perform militia duty; and when demonstrated to thereupon, justifying myself in writing, upon the ground of having the power so to do. The letters, which are in evidence before this honorable court, which passed between Mr. Secretary Matlack and myself, will explain the sole transaction, upon which this general accusation is founded.

"By what strained construction the sentiments which I have expressed, that when a citizen assumes the character of a soldier, the former was entirely lost in the latter, should be extended to a justification of myself, on the mere principal of power is somewhat extraordinary. My opinion in this matter is confirmed, not only by the sentiments of many of the most enlightened patrons of liberty in this and other countries, but sanctified by the militia law of several free states, both in Europe and America, particularly Switzerland and the state of New York, where (if I am not mistaken) the militia of the latter, when called forth into Continental service, are subjected to the same rules of discipline, with the troops of the United States; the character and conduct of that militia prove the policy of this principle. My ambition is to deserve the good opinion of the militia of these states, not only because I respect their character and their exertions, but because their confidence in me may prove beneficial to the general cause of America: but having no local politics to bias my voice or my conduct, I leave it to others to wriggle themselves into a temporary popularity, by assassinating the reputation of innocent persons, and endeavoring to render odious a principle, the maintenance of which is essential to the good discipline of the militia, and consequently to the safety of these states. I flatter myself the time is not far off, when, by the glorious establishment of our independence, I shall again return into the mass of citizens: 'tis a period I look forward to with anxiety; I shall then cheerfully submit as a citizen, to be governed by the same principle of subordination, which has been tortured into a wanton exertion of arbitrary power. "This insinuation comes, in my opinion, with an ill grace from the state of Pennsylvania, in whose more immediate defense I sacrificed my feelings as a soldier, when I conceived them incompatible with the duties of a citizen and the welfare of that state.

"By a resolution of Congress, I found myself superseded (in consequence of a new mode of appointment of General officers) by several who were my juniors in service; those who know the feelings of an officer, must judge what my sensations were at this apparent mark of neglect. I repaired to the City of Philadelphia in the month of May 1777, in order either to attain a restoration of my rank, or the permission to resign my commission; during this interval, the van of General Howe's Army advanced, by a rapid march, to Somerset Courthouse, with a view (as was then generally supposed) to penetrate to the City of Philadelphia.

"Notwithstanding I had been superseded, and my feelings as an officer were wounded, yet, on finding the state was in imminent danger from the designs of the enemy, I sacrificed those feelings, and with alacrity put myself at the head of the militia, who were collected to oppose the enemy, determined to exert myself for the benefit of the public, although I conceived myself injured by their representatives. How far the good countenance of the militia under my command operated, in deterring General Howe from marching to the city of Philadelphia, I will not pretend to say; certain it is, he altered his route. What returns I have met with from the state of Pennsylvania, I leave to themselves to judge, in the cool hour of reflection, (notwithstanding the frenzy of party and the pains so industriously taken to support a clamor against me) must sooner or later arise." [36]

Arnold concluded his statement with a reading of the letter from Matlack to him on March 17th 1779.

With regard to the *Active*, Arnold pointed out that this was a matter for the civil courts and that the grand jury dismissed the indictment for the unlawful act of maintaining a suit for lack of evidence. "The fourth charge is evidently triable only in a court of common law, I should not therefore notice it at present, did it not add to the torrent defamation which has been poured forth against me, and which, if not checked, may leave upon the minds of fellow soldiers and citizens, disagreeable impressions, even though I should be acquitted of the charges which are sensible by the law martial. I therefore beg leave to lay before the court, a certified copy of an indictment preferred against me for this supposed offense, in behalf of the commonwealth of Pennsylvania, with the jurors return." [36] Arnold then presented the papers regarding the *Active* to the court.

"Notwithstanding all the influence of the ruling powers of Pennsylvania, which must be well known by several of the honorable court; the unexampled method adopted by the council to prejudice the minds of the citizens against me, previous to a trial, and the daily slander invented and industriously circulated to prevent the popular heat from subsiding, the impartiality and good sense of a body of free men of the City of Philadelphia, were impregnable to all the arts made use of to poison the fountain of justice. And here I cannot but congratulate my countrymen upon the glorious effects of the exertions we have made, to establish the liberties ourselves, and posterity, upon the firm basis of equal laws. Had it not been for the grand bulwark against the tyranny of rulers, the trial by peers, it is easy to foresee, from the spirit of those who have been my accusers, what must have been my fate. When I reflect on this circumstance, I contemplate, with a grateful pleasure, the fears I have received in defense of a system of government, the excellence of which, though frequently before the subject of my speculation, is now brought home to my feelings.

"It is difficult to account for the extraordinary mode pursued by the State of Pennsylvania, to damn my reputation, and for the abrasive manner with which I was persecuted, on any other principle, than one, by which states, as well as individuals, are too often tempted to commit the most flagrant acts of injustice, I mean interest. The sloop *Active*, which was the object of the suit, which I was accused of unlawfully maintaining, was taken by part of the crew of the vessel, who were Americans, whose role upon the rest, and after having confined the captain and others, were bringing her into port. In this situation, she was boarded by a vessel belonging to the State of Pennsylvania, and brought in, and afterwards libeled as a prize taken by themselves. The original captors, who were (some of them) born in Connecticut, my native country, with whose connections I was acquainted, applied to me for my assistance in obtaining them justice. I assisted them both with my advice, my time, and my purse; and though three fourths of the vessel and cargo were, by the lower court of admiralty for the State of Pennsylvania, adjudged to the state captors, this sentence was, by a unanimous opinion of a court of appeals, reversed and adjudged to those whom I patronized, as appears by their decree, which I beg to read, with their report to Congress, and the resolutions of Congress thereupon." [36] Arnold then read the findings of the appeals court and Congress. "This, gentlemen, is my cardinal guilt; hence proceeds the vengeance of an interested government against me; hence the pain and anxiety I have suffered, in feeling the fair fabric of reputation, which I have been with so much danger and toil raising since the present war, undermined by those, whose posterity (as well as themselves) will feel the blessed effects of my efforts, in conjunction with you and others, in refusing them from a tyranny of the most cruel and debasing nature." [36]

As for his use of public wagons for private property, Arnold had admitted requesting them and paying for them. He explained that the wagons were idle at the time and the property that required their use was in danger of falling into enemy hands, to which he felt it was his duty to save. A copy of a disposition by the wagon master, Jesse Jordan was read before the court. In his statement, Jordan admitted that he had received an order from the quartermaster, Colonel Mitchell to report to General Arnold for orders. At Arnold's headquarters, Jordan received orders from Franks to proceed to Egg Harbor with twelve wagons, report to Captain Moore, and return to Philadelphia. Moore directed him to load up sugar, tea, coffee, swivel guns, nails, cloths, linens, and other articles from the ship were then delivered to Stephen Collins in Philadelphia. When Jordan applied for his pay from Mitchell, he was informed that his order should not be made out to the United States, but to General Arnold and that he should collect his pay from him. When Jordan made the request to Arnold, he told him to return at a later time. Arnold reported to Mitchell that he was willing to pay for the time that the wagons left Philadelphia until their return and asked Mitchell to pay for the initial days when the wagons were dispatched to Philadelphia. Mitchell declined Arnold's offer and the matter then went before the council when they discovered that the property that was transported was private and not public.

When Mitchell's minute book was produced for the court, it showed that the original entry of October 22, 1778 for Jordan's wagon was altered from "gone to Egg Harbor by order of General Arnold" to "went to Egg harbor by direction of General Arnold" and that the October 30, 1778 entry of the arrival to Egg Harbor had been obliterated. When questioned by the council as to the reason for the alteration, Arnold answered that the entry was made as a mistake by a clerk and adjusted without Arnold's knowledge.

"With respect to the fifth charge, of appropriating wagons of the State of Pennsylvania, when called forth upon a special emergency, last autumn, to the transportation of private property. The evidence relative to that transaction, before the court, will, I doubt not, justify my conduct in their opinion. It has been clearly proved by the testimony of Colonel Mitchell and Major Franks, that the wagons were supplied by the deputy quartermaster general upon a private request, and not considered as in the public service, when employed. Suppose application had been made to me, for wagons, during my command in the City of Philadelphia, for removing property belonging to private persons, which was in danger of falling into the hands of the enemy, and I found the same could be done without injury to the public, should I be justified in refusing the public assistance? Certainly not. Does then the criminality consist in removing the property, because I was interested in it? Had the supplies for the Continental Army been obstructed by this transaction, or had I endeavored to make it a public charge, my conduct would certainly have been blame worthy; but as it evidently appears, that neither the one or the other was the case, I flatter myself that my conduct, instead of being condemned by this honorable court, will be approved, and that an honorable acquittal will follow from the facts I have proved.

"What shall I say of the conduct of the President and the Council of Pennsylvania, respecting the wagons? They first charge me with employing public wagons to remove private property, insinuating, that the wagon master was refused payment for the hire of his wagons, and that I intended to defraud the public. It would have been but candid had they informed the public, that Jesse Jordan the wagon master had not been refused payment for the hire of his wagons, but that by their influence and advice, he had been prevented calling on me for his pay, that they might have some pretence for insinuating an action and this charge against me.

"In the next instance, they wrote, or caused to be wrote, a letter to Jesse Jordan, directing him to make out the account of the hire of his wagons, assuring him that if he charged eighty pounds for the hire of each wagon, (more than double the first account which he had presented to me) they did not doubt of his recovering the whole sum, and directed him to send his account to the attorney general, who had orders to commence an action against me for the same, which he accordingly did; and there is now an action against me, depending in one of the courts of Pennsylvania, for upwards of eleven hundred pounds, for the hire of those wagons. It is not very extraordinary that I should be accused and tried before this honorable court, for employing public wagons, and at the same time, and by the same persons, be prosecuted in a civil court of Pennsylvania, for employing the same wagons as private property." [36]

Arnold explained to the court that the pass that he ordered for a tory was only done after an official request had been made from Brigadier General William Maxwell. "As to the sixth charge, professing, that by my recommendatory letter to General Maxwell, to grant a pass to Miss Levy to go to New York, I had violated the resolve of Congress, and undermined the authority of the State of Pennsylvania. To attempt a serious refutation, would be as ridiculous as the charge itself. Let the letter written on this occasion speak for itself. I kept no copy of it, but well remember the purpose." [36]

To General Maxwell

Philadelphia, October 3, 1778

Sir

The bearer, Miss Levy, is a young woman of good character who has an aged parent that is blind, and entirely supported by her. She wishes to obtain a pass to go into New York, to receive a sum of money, which the British officers owed her when they left Philadelphia. The loss of which will greatly distress the family. I will be answerable for her conduct, if permitted to go in, which will much oblige, Sir,

Your most obedient humble servant,

Arnold had admitted to showing disrespect to the council for refusing to furnish it with additional information on his use of the public wagons. "As to the seventh charge, of an indecent and disrespectful behavior to the Council of Pennsylvania. True it is, I refused to obey an arbitrary mandate (to render to them an account of my conduct) calculated to incriminate myself. They complain, that by my refusal their dignity is wounded. Had I obeyed, soldiers and citizens might justly have said, that I had betrayed their rights, and wounded their dignity. The very demand was an insult to common sense. I beg to observe, that no one has greater respect than myself for the civil authority, and no one is more convinced of the necessity of supporting it. But when public bodies of men show themselves actuated by passions of anger, or envy, and apply their efforts to sap the character of an individual, and to render his situation miserable, they must not think it extraordinary, if they aren't treated with all the deference which they think their due.

"It is the dignity with which an office is executed, much more than the name, that can ever secure respect and obedience from a free people, and true dignity consists in exercising power with wisdom, justice, and moderation. Had I experienced this, and had any unguarded expressions escaped my pen in my letters to the President and Council of Pennsylvania, I would cheerfully, in a cooler hour of reflection, have made an acknowledgement; but they have thought proper to take vengeance for themselves: I shall therefore leave it to the impartial public of America to judge between us." [36]

In regards to the final charge of favoring Tories in Philadelphia, while neglecting the claims of patriots, the Supreme Executive Council closed with the following observation for having a lack of proof. "That the discouragement and neglect manifested by General Arnold to civil, military, and other characters, who have adhered to the cause of their country, with an entire different conduct to those of another character, are too notorious to need proof or illustration." [36] Nevertheless, Arnold responded. "I am not sensible, Mr. President, of having neglected any gentlemen, either in the civil or military line, who have adhered to the cause of their country, and who have put it into my power to take notice of them; with respect to the gentlemen in the civil line and Army, I can appeal to the candor of Congress and to the Army, as scarcely a day passed but many of both were entertained by me; they are the best judges of my company and conduct.

"With respect to attention to those of an opposite character, I have paid none but such, as in my situation, as was justifiable on the principles of common humanity and politeness. The President and Council of Pennsylvania will pardon me, if I cannot divest myself of humanity, merely out of compliance to them. It is enough for me, Mr. President, to contend with men in the field; I have not yet learned to carry on warfare against women, or to consider every man as disaffected to our glorious cause, who, from an opposition in sentiment to those in power in the State of Pennsylvania, may, by the clamor of party be styled a tory: it is well known that this hateful appeal has, in that state been applied by some, indiscriminately, to several of illustrious character, both in the civil and military line.

"On this occasion I think I may be allowed to say, without vanity, that my conduct, from the earliest period of the war to the present time, has been steady and uniform. I have ever obeyed the calls of my country and stepped forth in her defense in every hour of danger, when many were deserting her cause, which appeared desperate: I have often bled in it; the marks that I bear, are sufficient evidence of my conduct. The impartial public will judge of my services and whether the returns that I have met with are not tainted with the basest ingratitude. Conscious of my own innocence and the unworthy methods taken to injure me, I can with boldness say to my persecutors in general, and to the chief of them in particular, that in the hour of danger, when the affairs of America wore a gloomy aspect, when our illustrious General was retreating through New Jersey with a handful of men, I did not propose to my associates basely to quit the General and sacrifice the cause of my country to my personal safety, by going over to the enemy and making my peace. I can say that I never basked in the sunshine of my General's favor, and courted him to his face, when I was at the same time treating him, with the greatest disrespect and vilifying his character when absent. This is more than a ruling member of the Council of the State of Pennsylvania can say, as is alleged and believed.

"Before I conclude, I beg leave to read before this honorable court a report of the committee of inquiry of Congress, on the charges published against me by the Council of Pennsylvania, with several letters I did myself the honor to write to Congress, and a letter from their committee in answer: I do not presume to offer these as evidence, but as they show the anxiety I had to have my conduct investigated, and the reluctance of my accusers to bring matters to an issue, I think it incumbent on me as an officer, to lay them before you."

"I have now gone through all the charges exhibited against me; and have given to each such an answer as I thought it deserved. Are they all, or any of them supported by truth and evidence? Or rather, does not each of them appear to this honorable court to be totally destitute of every semblance of a foundation in fact? And yet baseless as they themselves are, they were intended to support a fabric with the weight of which attempts were made to crush my reputation and fortunes: I allude to the preliminary resolution of the council, containing severe but general criticism upon my character and conduct; criticism of such a serious and important nature, that they themselves were sensible, the public would not think them justified in making them, unless upon the most questionable grounds. Let them now be measured by their own standard. Had they unquestionable grounds to go upon? Why then, in opposition to every principle of candor and justice, in opposition to their own ideas of candor and justice, did they make and publish resolutions containing censures of such a high import against me?

"An artful appearance of tenderness, and regard for my services, by which the council members are pleased to say, I formerly distinguished myself, is held forth in the introduction to their charges. Did they mean by this to pour balsam or to pour poison into my wounds? I leave it to this court and to the world to judge, whether they intended it to balance the demerits they then urged against me by my former good conduct as far as it would go; or whether they designed it as a sting to their charges, by persuading the public that my demerits were so enormous that even the greatest and most unaffected tenderness for my character, would not excuse them in continuing silent any longer.

"If in the course of my defense I have taken up the time of the court longer than they expected, they will, I trust, impute it to the nature of the accusations against me. Many of which, though not immediately before you as charges, were alleged as facts and were of such a complexion as to render it necessary to make some observations upon them; because they were evidently calculated to raise a prejudice against me, not only among the people at large, but in the minds of those who were to be my judges. I have looked forward with pleasing anxiety to the present day when, by the judgement of my fellow soldiers, I shall (I doubt not) stand honorably acquitted of all the charges brought against me and again share with them the glories and dangers of this just war." [36]

Five days later on the **26th**, his premonition of an acquittal from the board had come to light.

Having considered the several charges against General Arnold, the evidence produced on the trial, and his defense, are of opinion, with respect to the first charge, that he gave permission for a vessel to leave a port in possession of the enemy, to enter into a port in the United States, which permission, circumstanced as he was, they are clearly of opinion he had no right to give, being a breach of article 5th, section 18th of the rules and articles of war. Respecting the second charge, that although it has been fully proved, that the shops and stores were shut by General Arnold's orders on his arrival in Philadelphia, they are of opinion, that he was justifiable in the order by the resolution of Congress of the 5th of June, 1778, and his Excellency the Commander-in-Chief's instructions of the 18th of June 1778: and with respect to the latter part of the same charge, the making considerable purchases while the shops and stores were shut, they are clearly of opinion, that it is entirely unsupported, and they do fully acquit General Arnold of it. They do acquit General Arnold of the third charge. Respecting the fourth charge, it appears to the court that General Arnold made application to the deputy quartermaster general, to supply him with wagons to remove property in imminent danger from the enemy; that the wagons were supplied to him by the deputy quartermaster general on this application, which had been drawn from the state of Pennsylvania for the public service; and it also appears, that General Arnold intended this application as a private request, and that he had no design of employing the wagons otherwise than at his own private expense, nor of defrauding the public, nor injuring or impeding the public service; but considering the delicacy attending the high station in which the General acted, and that requests from him might operate as commands, they are of opinion, the request was imprudent and improper, and that, therefore, it ought not have been made. The court in consequence of their determinations respecting the first and last charges exhibited against

Major General Arnold, do sentence him to receive a reprimand from his Excellency the Commander-in-Chief.
Robert Howe, Major General, President
John Laurance, judge advocate [36]

On **February 12th**, Congress approved the court's verdict, but did not communicate its approval to Washington for several weeks. Obligatory pressures mounted from the threat of losing his home and Peggy's baby coming due, to financial pressures as lenders refused to lend and the financial board refused to bend, Arnold wrote to obtain a loan from the Chevalier de la Luzerne, the new French Minister. In his position, Luzerne was in charge of purchasing supplies for French troops with borrowed funds in Philadelphia, which he did successfully by being friendly, tolerant, wise, and well regarded by both pro and anti-French Americans.

To The Chevalier de la Luzerne

Sir,
It is animosity of the government of Pennsylvania that has ruined me and how can such a body be resisted when it suits it to accuse? Of what avail in this case is the solitary protest of an innocent individual against the clamors and calumnies of the band of panders and parasites that swell the train of power? But what better can be expected from those who administer our affairs? I admonish you that things must continue to grow worse as long as the reins are allowed to remain in such unskillful hands. It is of consequence to you as the Minister of France to attend to this matter. I have shed my blood for my country and she is ungrateful. The disorder, which the war has occasioned in my private affairs, may force me into retirement. I will abandon a profession more burdensome than lucrative, if I cannot borrow a sum equal to the amount of my debts. The bounty of your sovereign would be more agreeable to me than any other. It concerns your interest that an American General should be secured to you by the ties of gratitude and I promise you mine without swerving from my duty as an American. [71]
I am, Sir, &c.,
B. Arnold

La Luzerne met with Arnold and agreed to the loan, but with one condition, that Arnold would make a public report of the loan, to which he could not accept. Soon after the discovery of Arnold's treason, some letters were discovered in Peggy's apartment and brought to the Minister, who consigned them to the flames without having read them. The following letter was dramatically recollected by the Minister's secretary, Francois de Barbe`-Marbois.

"I wish to meet the confidence you show me with frankness and reason. You desire a service from me which would be easy for me to perform, but which would degrade us both. When the Minister of a foreign power gives, or if you will, lends money, it is usually for the purpose of corrupting those who receive it. And converting them into the mere creatures of the sovereign whom he represents, or rather, he corrupts without persuading, he buys and does not secure.

But the alliance formed between the King and the United States is the work of justice and the soundest policy, goodwill and reciprocal interests are its vital principles. My true glory is the mission with which I am entrusted is to accomplish it without intrigue or cabal, without parade or intricacy or negotiation; without secret practices; by power only of the conditions of the alliance. Hitherto. I have asked nothing of Congress which they have not immediately done or granted; their foresight has indeed, often anticipated my requests. There is not one of my official measures that the whole world may not know.

Judge then, if I ought to render you a mysterious service, you, one of the most illustrious men of the United States, and whose military abilities make, as it were, part of the public estate. What have you to offer us as an equivalent for this largess, that would justify us before posterity, for having thus tarnished the immortal glory, which the independence of your country promises to the French nation, and to her wise and generous monarch. I will gratify your wishes, nevertheless, if you can after receiving my presents, openly acknowledge them; but I easily comprehend that this avowal is not meditated. There remains for me but one observation to make concerning the state of your pecuniary affairs; it is that your friends will be eager to secure you as soon as you adopt a system of order and economy. Of this you may be assured.

But before you leave me, I wish to give you a proof of my friendship a thousand times more precious than the gold, which I deny. I wish to point out to you the means of perpetuating the fame you have already acquired, and which you will infallibly lose by pursuing the course you are now taking." [71]

Following his response from Luzerne, Arnold petitioned Congress again for a settlement of his accounts, which in turn gave them to a five-member committee to audit. On the 14th, the committee declared the task "impracticable with that accuracy and attention which the nature of them demand." [80] In addition, it was recommended that the accounts be returned to the Board of Treasury where "the business of liquidating accounts is now carried on in a regular manner." [80] On the following day, Congress accepted the committee's recommendation and ordered the accounts to be delivered back to the Board. Arnold protested the order stating that the Board was motivated by "private resentment or undue influence," but Congress refused to back down and the controversy continued. [80] Since he had lost out on making money with the *Charming Nancy* and the *Active*, Arnold tried to get into the privateering business himself. On **March 6th**, Arnold informed Washington that the Admiralty Board had considered him for a naval command, but in truth they hadn't.

To His Excellency General Washington

Philadelphia, 6 March, 1780

Dear Sir

I am requested by the board of admiralty to inform your Excellency that they have in contemplation an expedition with several of their frigates, which will require three or four hundred land forces to act in conjunction and who may act as Marines when on board, which will obviate the great difficulty of procuring men for their ships. They wish to be informed if the men can be spared from the Army. They will be wanted to embark (probably at New London) by the middle of April, for an expedition of about two months. If seamen can be drafted, they will be much preferable to other troops.

From the injury I have received in my leg and the great stiffness in my ankle, my surgeons are of opinion it will not be prudent for me to take a command in the Army for some time to come. As I wish to render my country every service in my power, I have offered the Board to take the command of the expedition, provided it is agreeable to your Excellency and the men can be spared from the Army; in which case, I shall soon have the honor of laying the plan before your Excellency and believe you will think it an object of importance.

I have just received a letter from Major Clarkson, dated Charleston, January 30th, who writes me, that "the fleet which sailed from New York in December, are certainly arrived and arriving at

Savannah; their force uncertain, but very large." Two of our frigates have captured a brigantine, with clothing and two sloops with dragoons of Lord Cathcart's legion, who have saved only two horses of forty-five. The fleet were dispersed in a few days after they sailed and greatly injured by several storms.

I suppose your Excellency will receive particular information from Congress.

I have the honor to be, with great respect and esteem, your Excellency's affectionate and obedient humble servant,
Benedict Arnold [70]

When Arnold hadn't heard back from Washington regarding his sanction for sea duty, he asked him again on the **20th**, this time citing medical reasons for the request.

To His Excellency General Washington

March 20, 1780

Dear Sir

The foregoing is a copy of a letter I did myself the honor of writing your Excellency, which went by express the day it was wrote, from Colonel Mitchell's office. As a fortnight has elapsed (2 weeks), *and I have not been favored with an answer, I conclude the letter has miscarried; I therefore take the liberty of sending a copy. If the service will not admit a draft of men from the Army, the expedition must, of course, be declined, as there is not the least probability of manning the ships without; in which case, I must request of Your Excellency a leave of absence for the ensuing summer or until my wounds are so well as to admit my riding and walking with some degree of ease and, of course, being able to take the command of a division in the Army.*

Your Excellency will believe I should not ask this indulgence, could I, with justice to myself or country, take a command in the condition I am at present. My surgeons flatter me that a voyage to sea and bathing frequently in salt water will be of great service in strengthening my leg and relaxing the muscles, which are greatly contracted, and thereby rendering it more useful.

Mrs. Arnold yesterday presented me with a son. She joins me in best respects to Mrs. Washington.

I have the honor to be, very sincerely and affectionately, your Excellency's most obedient and very humble servant,
Benedict Arnold [70]

On the **22nd**, Arnold reported the decision of the court in a letter to Silas Deane.

To Silas Deane

March 22, 1780

Sir

I believe you will be equally surprised with me when you find the court martial having fully acquitted me of the charge of employing public wagons, or defrauding the public, or of injuring or impeding the public service. Yet in their next sentence say, 'as requests from him might operate as commands,' I ought to receive a reprimand. For what? Not for doing wrong, but because I might have done wrong; or rather, because evil might follow the good that I did! [79]

...I have proposed to the Board of Admiralty an expedition, which will require three or four hundred land forces to act in conjunction with the ships. the matter rests with General Washington. If men can be spared and my plan takes place, you will hear from me soon. If it should not, I propose going to Boston with the intention to take the command of a private ship. [70]

I am, &c.,

B. Arnold

To bring the true light to Washington, the Admiralty Board wrote to him on the **23rd**, explaining that the naval project had been abandoned. On the **28th**, prior to Washington receiving word from the board, he granted Arnold his requested leave-of-absence and sent his regards on the birth of his son on the 19th.

To M General Arnold

Morristown, 28 March, 1780

Dear Sir

In a letter to the Board of Admiralty I communicated my sentiments respecting the subject of your letter. I observed to the Board; "With respect to the troops, that, from the detachment lately sent to the southward, and the great decrease of our force besides, occasioned by the daily expiration of the men's enlistments, it appears to me that none can be spared from the Army, consistently with prudence or policy. But should the Board finally determine on the proposed enterprise, and the troops be essential to its success, that under the circumstances of the Army I have stated, I should not think myself authorized to send them, without the concurrence and direction of Congress." This will show you the footing on which I found myself obliged to place the business. As to the second point, should the enterprise be undertaken, so far as my concurrence may be considered necessary, I shall have no objection to your going on the command.

With regard to a leave of absence from the Army during the ensuing summer, should it be found inexpedient to go into the proposed enterprise, and under the representation of your health, you have my permission, though it was my wish and expectation to see you in the field; but, provided your views extend to a voyage, leave for this purpose must be obtained from the Congress, as I have in no instance whatever ventured to grant a furlough to any place not within the united States. I hope you will find the experiments you propose, to answer your expectations, and that you may soon experience a situation for actual service. Let me congratulate you on the late happy event. Mrs. Washington joins me in presenting her wishes for Mrs. Arnold on the occasion.

I am, &c., [68]
G. Washington

On **April 6th**, the Commander-in-Chief delivered the official order from Congress in the form of a reprimand for abusing public trust.

To M General Arnold

April 6, 1780
Dear Sir

The Commander-in-Chief would have been much happier on an occasion of bestowing a commendation on an officer who has rendered such distinguished service to his country as Major General Arnold. But in the present case a sense of duty and a regard to candor oblige him to declare that he considers his conduct in the instance of his issuance of the permit, as peculiarly reprehensible, both in a civil and military view, and in the affair of the wagons as imprudent and improper. [24]

As I am with great respect, Dear Sir, your most obedient servant,
G. Washington

Washington then wrote a consoling letter to Arnold off the record offering to help him to reestablish his reputation.

To M General Arnold

386

Sir

Our profession is the purest of all. Even the shadow of a fault tarnishes the luster of our finest achievements. The least indiscretion may rob us of the public favor, so hard to be acquired. I reprimand you for having forgotten that, in proportion as you have rendered yourself formidable to our enemies; you should have been guarded and temperate in your deportment towards your fellow citizens. Exhibit anew those noble qualities, which have placed you on the list of our most valued commanders. I will myself furnish you, as far as it may be in my power, with opportunities for regaining the esteem of your country. [5]

As I am with great respect, Dear Sir, your most obedient

servant,

G. Washington

The Board of Treasury reported to Congress on **April 27**[th], claiming that according to their best calculations, Arnold owed a balance of one thousand pounds or $3,333.00. This of course he objected to in a letter to Congress on **May 10**[th], which they responded to on the same day, telling him to "put it in writing."

Wednesday, May 10, 1780

A letter of this day from Major General B. Arnold was read, informing that "on examining the report of the Board of Treasury on his public accounts, he finds himself under the necessity of appealing to the honorable Congress and requesting favor of that honorable body to point out the method of proceeding in appeals from the Board of Treasury and to be informed when he can be heard on the subject of appeal."

Ordered, That Major General Arnold be informed he is at liberty to state in writing any objections he may have to the report of the Board of treasury on his accounts, and to lay them before Congress. [26]

XI
West Point

With this insult on top of injury first from Congress and then from Washington, Arnold planted various seeds to position himself for what he considered to be the ultimate payback. In a meeting with General Schuyler, who had arrived as a recent New York delegate to Congress, he laid out his medical as well as military reasons to command West Point. Arnold followed this up with a letter to each of the New York Assembly delegates. On March 29th, Clinton and Andre` acted on Arnold's intel regarding Charleston by initiating a siege that lasted until **May 12**[th] when the city fell and surrendered 5,000 troops under Lincoln, who had taken over Arnold's troops at the second battle of Saratoga. While the two of them were in the southern region, Arnold corresponded with the Hessian Lieutenant General Wilhelm von Knyphausen and Captain George Beckwith. Knyphausen was a brave and skillful German Commander-in-Chief who had previously served in the Prussian Army during the Seven Years' War. This thin, grim, silent, and sharp-featured officer of medium height always carried himself in a strict military manner, and expected the utmost discipline from his troops. While in his early sixties, he led his men in the assault on Fort Washington and fought side by side with them in the thickest part of the battle to victory, thus renaming the garrison, Fort Knyphausen. In his reply to Arnold, he stated that he would accept communications and forward them to Clinton, but would not take responsibility for negotiating the terms of the agreement.

To Mr. Moore

Sir

The affair in agitation is of so important a nature that General Knyphausen does not think himself authorized to give an answer to it in its full extent; and the more so as the matter is already known to the Commander-in-Chief. The General will therefore take the first opportunity of communicating the transaction to Sir Henry Clinton, and in the meantime will feel happy in cultivating the connection and in giving Mr. Moore every testimony of his regard, from the persuasion, which the General entertains of his righteousness and sincerity. Any trifling expenditures which may be made in the channel of communication, previous to a full answer from Sir Henry, will be readily reimbursed.

An officer will give Mr. Moore the meeting, which he solicits, whenever the practicability of it can be pointed out. In the meantime, two rings are procured which are exactly alike and one of them is sent by his friend, with whom a mode of correspondence by cipher is likewise settled. [79]

W. K.

Knyphausen in turn made notes on Arnold's correspondence.

Memo

A Mr. Moore had made proposals to ----- (Clinton) previous to his departure from hence, relative to himself, the proposals were declined at first from particular circumstances; but offers were then made, which Mr. Moore had now accepted of, provided that assurances are given to him of certain indemnifications, for himself and family, in cases of emergency; the indemnifications required are as follows: first the loss of his private fortune 5,000 pounds sterling; ye debt due to him by the community of 5,000 pounds sterling to be made good, or whatever part is lost, & to have a new raised battalion here upon the common footing – to be supplied with money from time to time as circumstances may require; Mr. Moore is now at P. (Philadelphia) & waits there for a few days; he intends going to C. (Connecticut) and to return in three or four weeks to camp – where he is to remain in a military line: he wishes to have a conference with a military officer – he offers to take decisive part in case of an Emergency – or in view of attack on B. (Boston), P. (Philadelphia), or any other place; he declared were it not for his family, he would without ceremony have thrown himself into the protection of the King's Army;

This to go no further here; it may be communicated to S. H. C. (Sir Henry Clinton) with the particulars of the indemnification required; in addition to promises made him formerly on which he relies to fix upon a particular token, place of meeting, cipher & channel of communication, permission for a few articles. [79]

When Arnold had not heard from Schuyler, he wrote a follow up letter on the **25th**.

To General Schuyler

May 25, 1780

Dear Sir

I have not had the pleasure of receiving a line from you since you arrived at camp, and know not who is to have the command at the north river. If General Heath joins the Army, as I am informed he intends, that post will of course, I suppose, fall under his command, unless some other arrangement is more agreeable to him. When I requested leave of absence of his Excellency General Washington for the summer, it was under the idea that it would be a very inactive campaign, and that my services would be of little consequence, as my wounds made it very painful for me to walk or ride. The prospect now seems to be altered, and there is a probability of an active campaign; in which, though, attended with pain and difficulty, I wish to render my country every service in my power, and with the advice of my friends am determined to join the Army; of which I beg you will do me the favor to acquaint his Excellency General Washington, that I may be included in any arrangement that may be made. A violent cold, which has confined me for some days, will prevent my setting out for camp for some days longer. [79]

I am your most humble servant,
B. Arnold

The seed took root, for Schuyler met with Washington at Morristown giving his endorsement of Arnold for the command at West Point. Following the conference he wrote to Arnold.

To General Arnold

June 2, 1780

My Dear Sir

The letter which I did myself the pleasure to write you on the 11th of May, you had not received when yours of the 25th was written. In that I advised you that I had conversed with the General on the subject, which passed between us before I left Philadelphia, that he appeared undecided on the occasion, I believe because no arrangement was made, for he expressed himself with regard to you in terms such as the friends whose love you could wish. When I received yours of the 25th of May, I read it to him. He was much engaged. Next day he requested to know the contents again. I put it into his hands. He expressed a desire to know whatever was agreeable to you, dwelt on your abilities, your merits, your sufferings, and on the well-earned claims you have on your country, and intimated that as soon as his arrangements for the campaign should take place, he would properly consider you. I believe you will have an alternative proposed, either to take charge of an important post with an honorable command, or your station in the field. Your reputation, my Dear Sir, so established, your honorable scars put it decidedly in your power to take either. A state, which has full confidence in you, will wish to see its banner entrusted to you. If the command at West Point is offered, it will be honorable; if a division in the field, you must judge whether you can support the fatigues, circumstances as you are. Mrs. Schuyler proposes a jaunt to Philadelphia; if she goes I shall accompany her and have the pleasure of seeing you. She joins me in every friendly wish; please to make my respects to your lady and her amiable sisters.

Believe me, with the most affectionate regard and esteem, yours, most sincerely, &c., &c., Philip Schuyler [67]

On **June 4th**, Washington sent Arnold some misinformation to throw the British off from New York and head to Canada in order to allow the Americans to retake the city in their absence. Yet, Washington refrained from telling Arnold the real plan.

To M General Arnold

Morristown, 4 June, 1780

Dear Sir

Enclosed you will find a draft of a proclamation addressed to the inhabitants of Canada. You will be pleased to put this into the hands of a printer, whose secrecy and discretion may be depended on, and desire him to strike off a proof sheet with the utmost dispatch, which you will send to me for correction. We shall want at least five hundred copies. The importance of this business will sufficiently impress you with the necessity of transacting it with every possible degree of caution. The printer is to be particularly charged not on any account to reserve a copy himself, or suffer one to get abroad.

With great regard, I am, &c., [68]
G. Washington

The ploy worked, for on **June 7th**, Arnold gave Beckwith a false logistics update along with his itinerary and followed up his request for an official interview.

To Captain Beckwith

Philadelphia, June 7, 1780

Sir

I have receive from the Commander-in-Chief a proclamation in order to have a number of copies printed, the purpose of which, will be transmitted to you by J: S: to whom I have communicated it.

The Minister of France this day assured me that the French troops destined for Canada amount to eight thousand.

The 8ᵗʰ instant I propose going to camp, will be at Morristown the 12ᵗʰ, King's Ferry the 16ᵗʰ, & New Haven the 20ᵗʰ, and return to camp by the 4ᵗʰ of July. If I meet a person in my mensuration, who has the token agreed upon, you may expect every intelligence in my power, which will probably be of consequence.

When fully authorized by Sir Henry Clinton to treat, I wish to have a conference with one of your officers in whom we can place a mutual confidence.

The American Army intended to cooperate with the French will probably go up Connecticut River to number four and cross the country to St. John's. [79]

I am, &c.,
Mr. Moore

Upon arriving at Morristown on the **12ᵗʰ**, Arnold followed up with an alert to Beckwith with news of the allied fleet to arrive in New England, which Washington revealed in his council of war at Morristown. Little did Arnold know that this was a scheme set up by Washington and the French, to draw the British out of New York and recapture it. Washington also wanted the capital moved out of Philadelphia, because it was a sieve for intelligence, yet unbeknownst to him, Arnold was the aperture.

To Captain George Beckwith

Morristown, June 12, 1780

Sir

Six French ships of the line, several frigates and a number of transports with six thousand troops are expected at Rhode Island in two or three weeks to act under General Washington. It is probable three or four thousand rebels will be embanked with them and proceed up the St. Lawrence to Quebec. While the Marquis de Lafayette with two or three thousand will go from the Connecticut River to St. John's and Montreal. Governor Trumbull is laying up flour and pork at the Connecticut River for the French. The drafts when completed will make General Washington twenty thousand. But some state are so dilatory, he does not expect strong reinforcements before August. [79]

I am, &c.,
Mr. Moore

Following the council, Arnold made mention of his desire to be at West Point, but Washington did not think that would suit his greatest fighting General because it would have been covered by the main Army, and would only require the care of invalids and a small garrison of militia. Being the ultimate optimist, Arnold jumped the gun and told Beckwith that West Point was in his pocket.

To Captain George Beckwith

Morristown, June 12, 1780

Sir

    Mr. Moore expects to have the command of West Point offered to him on his return. Troops and provisions wanting there. Only 1500 men. Little flour, and none to be had but from Pennsylvania, whence they have required 10,000 barrels. Mr. Moore thinks it would be a good stroke to get between General Washington and West Point. [79]

J. S.

The British referred to West Point as the "Gibraltar of America," for the rock on which the fort stood and its purpose, to defend the Hudson Highlands. [54] The Highlands were considered by Washington to be the "Key to the Continent," because of the rich natural resources that it held and a river to transport them. [54] The defense of the Hudson River was set up by way of a chain supported by logs that stretched across the river. The chain was placed in a strategic location between two ninety-degree angle turns that sat only 500 feet apart at the edge of the fort. In addition, an assembly of batteries erected at high and low altitudes on both sides of the river could strike any ship attempting to attack the fort. On the 16th, Arnold furnished Beckwith with a logistics report of the fort.

To Captain George Beckwith

Fishkill, June 16, 1780

Sir

    I called on General Howe at West Point, which I never saw before and was greatly disappointed both in the works & garrison. There is only fifteen hundred soldiers, which will not man half the works, but General Clinton's Brigade of twelve hundred men are ordered to join the garrison and are on their march from Albany. It is hoped that they will arrive before the English can make an attack,

394

which it is thought they have in contemplation. This place has been greatly neglected. General Howe tells me that there is not ten days provision for the garrison. A quantity is on the way from Connecticut and soon expected, but if the English were to cut off the communication with Pennsylvania, they would be distressed for flour, which is not to be procured in this part of the country. It is surprising a post of so much importance should be so totally neglected. The works appear to me, most wretchedly planned to answer the purpose designed; to maintain the post and stop the passage of the river. The point is on a low piece of ground comparatively to the chain of hills, which lie back of it. The highest called Rocky Hill, which commands all the other works is about a half a mile from Fort Putnam, which is strong. On Rocky Hill, there is a small redoubt to hold two hundred men and two six pounders pointed on the other works. The wall is six feet thick and defenseless on the back. I am told the English may land three miles below and have a good road to bring up heavy cannon to Rocky Hill. This redoubt is wretchedly executed, only seven or ten feet high and might be taken by assault by a handful of men. I am convinced the boom or chain thrown across the river to stop the shipping cannot be depended upon. A single ship, large and heavy-loaded with a strong wind and tide would break the chain. The Committee of Congress have made requisition to the different states, which if compiled with will enable us to act offensively this summer and to some purpose. [79]

I am, &c.,
Mr. Moore

To Arnold's relief, Clinton returned to New York on the 17th. On the 22nd, Congressman Robert R. Livingston, with all due respects to Washington, sent his letter of recommendation for Arnold to succeed Howe as the commander of West Point. Livingston, a brother-in-law to the late Major General Richard Montgomery, had graduated from Kings College, (now Columbia University) and studied law, as did his father and grandfather of the same name and was accepted to the bar before becoming a primary member of the Continental Congress.

To His Excellency General Washington

Trenton, 22 June, 1780
Dear Sir
My anxiety for the supplies of the Army has brought me to this place, in order that I might satisfy myself as to the quantity on hand

395

and the means of forwarding them. General Knox has communicated to me your Excellency's orders on this subject. Nothing short of them would, I am fully persuaded, be of sufficient force to produce the desired effect; and the knowledge of them will, in a great measure, render the execution of them unnecessary. Impressed with this idea, I have been long laboring to bring Congress to assume the power, which will enable them to call forth the resources of the States, but unhappily without effect. However, I hope much from their pressing and reiterated demands.

What principally introduced me to trouble your Excellency at this time is an apprehension which I, in common with other gentlemen, entertain of the propriety of leaving the command at West Point in the hands of General Howe. Having no personal acquaintance with him, I can have no prejudices, but the gentlemen from the southward by no means speak so favorably at him as I could wish. But in this, I conceive, that as of yet he has no opportunity of acquiring a military character. But confidence, which is so necessary to inspire courage, especially in militia, will, I fear, be wanting in him. If I might presume so far, I should beg leave to submit it to your Excellency, whether this post might not be most safely confided to General Arnold, whose courage is undoubted, who is the favorite of our militia, and who will agree perfectly with our Governor.

Your Excellency will not consider this as designed to convey the most distant reflection on General Howe, of whom I know nothing but by report, which may very possibly be ill grounded; but, if the most distant doubt remains, in a matter of so much moment, I conceive it should be removed. I make no other apology for the liberty I take, than the motive that suggests it, which has before now induced your Excellency to pardon an interference in matters to which I was no more competent than the present.

This hasty letter is written while the express waits, whom I am willing to detain longer than while I declare the respect and esteem with which I am, your Excellency's most obedient and humble servant, Robert R. Livingston [70]

On the **29th**, Washington responded to Livingston's endorsement of placing Arnold at West Point.

To Robert R. Livingston

Ramapo, June 29, 1780

Dear Sir

I have the honor to receive your favor of the 22nd from Trenton and thank you for the aid you have been pleased to afford in getting the provisions and stores removed from that place; happily for us, the transportation is in a better train and in a greater forwardness than I had reason a few days ago to expect it would be at this time. I am under no apprehension now of danger to the post at West Point on the score either of provisions, strength of the works, or garrison. I am sorry however to find there are apprehensions on account of the Commandant and that my knowledge of him does not enable me to form any decisive judgement of his fitness to command, but as Genl McDougall and Baron Steuben (men of approved bravery) are both with him and the main Army is in supporting distance, I confess I have no fear on the ground of what I presume is suspected. To remove him therefore under these circumstances and at this period must be too severe a wound to the feelings of any officer to be given but in cases of real necessity. When a general arrangement is gone into and a disposition made for the campaign, I can with propriety, and certainly shall bring General Howe into the line of the Army and place the gentleman you have named at that post if the operations of the campaign are such as to render it expedient to leave an officer of his rank in that command. If the States mean to put the Army in a condition to adopt any offensive plan, the period cannot be far off when this measure must take place.

Your sentiments, my Dear Sir, upon this occasion required no apology and advice of my friends I receive at all times as a proof of their friendship and am thankful when they are offered.

I am so well persuaded of the safety of West Point and of the necessity of easing the Militia as much as possible, and of husbanding our provisions and stores, that I have dismissed all the Militia that were called in for the defense of the posts on the North River. [24]

With the greatest esteem & regard,
I have the honor to be your most humble servant,
G. Washington

After one month had passed with no word from Beckwith, Arnold had Stansbury follow up on **July 7th**.

To Captain Beckwith

July 7, 1780

Mr. M. requests a very explicit answer to his letter of June 7th and that some method may be fallen on to obtain an interview with Major General Philips or some other proper officer, as nothing *further can be done without it. on the arrival of the French troops, New York is the object, if an Army can be raised which is thought to equal the attempt. The Canada expedition is a secondary object in case the other fails. Genl Washington will throw a detachment over the North River when the French fleet arrives at Newport, but not before. The garrisons of Stony Pt. And Verplank's have orders to withdraw on the appearance of the enemy in force & not risk a defense. There are in each; fifty men, one 12 pounder & two howitzers. The stores are already removed from them. Two or three persons in whom you confide as spies on General Howe are in his pay & often give him important intelligence. He thinks General Philips might come out to negotiate an exchange of prisoners or his own for Lincoln. He begs you would write to him only by such channels as may be fully depended on. He is to take the command of W. P. immediately on the fleet's arrival or at any rate in the course of this month. He has a drawing of the works on both sides of the river done by the French engineer & thinks he could settle matters with a proper officer that you might take it without loss, and also lay down a plan of communication whereby you should be informed of everything projected at headquarters. 7.*

J. S.

Being the ultimate optimist, Arnold accepted Washington's idea as a guarantee when Livingston had shared it with him. After still no response from Beckwith by the **11th**, Arnold, desperate for a meeting, wrote directly to Andre` to conclude their business at hand, adding that he would like to be paid 10,000 pounds now and another 10,000 upon delivery.

To Mr. John Anderson, Merchant

July 11th, 1780

Sir

   A mutual confidence between us is wanting, the persons we have employed have deceived us, or we have been unfortunate in our negotiation, in which on both sides we are deeply interested. If the first, then it is here that our correspondence ought to end. If the second, then an opportunity offers itself of relieving any abuse. If the latter, a stricter attention and proper regard to the interests of both parties may remedy the misfortune.

   To my letter of the 7th June, I have received no answer I then referred you to our mutual friend S for the particulars of a conversation which I thought interesting, a few days since I imparted *to him some matters of still greater importance. The bearer is charged with others, and is instructed to fix on a plan of safe conveyance and operation. My stock in trade is 10,000 pounds sterling, with near an equal sum of outstanding debts, an equal sum I expect will be put into stock and the profits arising be equally divided. I have advanced several sums already, and risked still greater without any profit. It is now become necessary for me to know the risk I run in case of a loss. I expect you will pay into the hands of the bearer one thousand guineas to be vested in goods suitable for our market on receipt of which I will transmit to you their full value, in good French bills drawn on sight or at a short time for other advances, you shall have good sterling bills well endorsed.*

I wish for a personal conference with Captain B or some one of the co-partnership. This I apprehend may very easily be brought about if you have any regard for your own interest or my safety by no means trust to any conveyance that is not known and approved or proved you may be deceived with false friends. Mention no names, write me in cipher and through some medium a clear, explicit, and confidential answer. In cipher will enable us to cooperate to mutual advantage or end this correspondence to the mutual safety of all concerned, as I make no doubt the strictest honor will be observed.

I am, Sir, your obedient & humble servant,

J Moore [79]

Confident that he would succeed, Arnold wrote to Andre` on the **12th** claiming that he already had the rock in hand.

To Mr. John Anderson, Merchant

July 12th, 1780

Sir

I have received no answer to my letter, or any verbal message. I expect soon to command W(est) P(oint) and most seriously wish an interview with some intelligent officer in whom a mutual confidence could be placed. The necessity is evident to arrange and to cooperate. An officer might be taken prisoner near that post and permitted to return on parole, or some officer on parole sent out to effect an exchange. I have accepted the command at W(est) P(oint) as a post in which I can render the most essential services and which will be in my disposal. The mass of the people are heartily tired of the war and wish to be on their former footing. They are promised great events from this year's exertion. If disappointed, you have only to preserve and the contest will soon be at an end. The present struggles are like the pangs of a dying man, violent but of a short duration.

As life and fortune are risked by serving His Majesty, it is necessary that the latter shall be secured as well as the emoluments I give up, and a compensation for services agreed on, and a sum advanced for that purpose which I have mentioned in a letter which accompanies this, which Sir Henry will not, I believe think unreasonable.

I am, Sir, your humble servant,
J. Moore [79]

As Clinton was maneuvering to take the Point, Washington was doing the same to take Manhattan. The first phase of Washington's plan was complete when he received notice from Major General William Heath, who announced the arrival of French warships at Newport, Rhode Island under General Jean Baptiste Rochambeau and Admiral Chevalier de Ternay in an attempt to draw British forces out of New York. Prior to the Revolution, Heath was a farmer, militiaman, and politician in his home state of Massachusetts, where he served as a member of the Provincial Congress and Committee of Safety. While his unit saw no action during the French and Indian War, he was an avid student in the art of war, reading all that he could on military history. Although knowledgeable in the science, he was not aggressive in the field, a trait that was proven when his decision to delay an attack on Fort Independence in New York brought about a British rout, which labeled him a disgrace not only by his men, but by Washington as well. Born of an ancient and honorable family in 1725, Rochambeau had served in a number of European campaigns before succeeding his father as the Governor in his hometown of Vendome, France. Ternay was a tough and determined fifty-eight-year-old veteran of the French and Indian War.

To His Excellency General Washington

Newport, 12 July, 1780

Dear General

I arrived here the night last and this morning had the honor of congratulating Monsieur le Compte de Rochambeau and Monsieur le Chevalier de Ternay on their safe arrival in this harbor. The fleet consist of seven sail of the line; the Duc de Burgogne, of eighty guns; Le Neptune and Le Conquerant, of seventy-four; Le Jason, L'Eville, L'Ardent, and Le Province, of sixty four, mounts forty guns; two

*frigates and two bombs with about five thousand land forces and one
thousand Marines…*

I have the honor to be, with the greatest respect,

William Heath [70]

On the **13th**, Andre` at long last acknowledged Arnold's report
on the present condition of West Point and its value, but failed to
make any mention of payment.

Gustavus Monk

July 13, 1780

Sir,

H(is) *E*(xcellency) *S*(ir) *H*(enry) *C*(linton) *is much obliged to
you for the useful intelligence you have transmitted to him. It
corresponds with other information and gives him full conviction of
your desire to assist him. He had hoped to communicate with you in a
very satisfactory manner, but is disappointed. His Excellency hopes
that you still keep in view the project of essentially cooperating with
him. He thinks that having the command at W P would afford the best
opportunities for it and would willingly know from you some scheme
for effecting a service of importance there. The General could point
out such plausible measures as would ward off all blame or suspicion
and be very eligible at the juncture of an attack upon Canada. An
interview between you and a person is absolutely necessary. Your
visiting Elizabethtown or some place near us, which a flag of truce
could reach and where you might be supposed to be detained by
sickness is the expedient, which strikes S H C as a practicable one.
The General trusts that in the same confidence in which you
communicate with him you will rely on his promise that upon effectual
cooperation you shall experience the full measure of the national
obligation & His Excellency will in the meantime give you in such
manner as you may require it an ample stipend.* [79]

I am, &c.,

John Anderson

Arnold replied to Andre` on the **15th**, explaining that his price
of 20,000 pounds must precede his promise.

To John Anderson, Merchant

July 15th, 1780

Sir

401

Two days since I received a letter without date or signature, informing me that S H was obliged to me for the intelligence communicated and that he placed a full confidence in the sincerity of my intentions. On the 13th instant I addressed a letter to you expressing my sentiments and expectations, that the following preliminaries be settled previous to cooperating. First, that Sir Henry Clinton secure to me my property, valued at ten thousand pounds sterling, to be paid to me or my heirs in case of loss, and as soon as that shall happen. A hundred pounds per annum to be secured to me for life, in lieu of the pay and emoluments I give up, for my services as they shall deserve. If I point out a plan of cooperation by which Sir Henry shall possess himself of West Point, the garrison, stores, etc., twenty thousand pounds sterling I think will be a cheap purchase for an object of so much importance. At the same time I request a thousand pounds to be paid to my agent. I expect a full and explicit answer. The 20th I set off for W P. A personal interview with an officer that you can confide in is absolutely necessary to plan matters. In the meantime I shall communicate to our mutual friend S, all the intelligence in my power until I have the pleasure of your answer. [79]

I am, &c.,
J. Moore

On the **17th**, Arnold wrote to Congress asking for four months advance pay in expectation of a field command.

To the Hon. Congress,

July 17, 1780

Gentlemen

I am under the necessity of informing Congress that there is due to me upwards of four years pay; and to request that honorable body that they will give orders that I may receive four months' pay in coin or paper equivalent, to enable me to purchase horses, camp equipment, etc., that I may be enabled to take the field, which I am called upon by his Excellency General George Washington to do immediately. [79]

I am your humble servant,
B. Arnold

On the **21st**, in expectation of this, Congress advanced him four months pay in the amount of $25,000. On the same day, Heath notified Washington that he had sighted the British fleet.

To His Excellency General Washington

Newport, 10 o'clock P. M., 21 July, 1780

Dear General

This afternoon fifteen or sixteen British ships of war have made their appearance off this harbor to the eastward of Block Island. More than half of them, I think, are ships of the line. From appearances, at sunset, they intended to come to under Block Island.

Admiral Graves has probably joined Admiral Arbuthnot and their design is to block up the fleet of Monsieur le Chevalier de Ternay, and, if possible, intercept the expected second division of the French fleet. I thought it my duty to give immediate notice to your Excellency and beg leave to submit the expediency of some small cruisers being immediately sent from the Delaware, to cruise for the French fleet and direct them to a place of safety. I have written to the council and Navy Board at Boston and proposed the same in case the fleet should take the eastern coast. I have mentioned this to his Excellency General Rochambeau, who was so much pleased with it that he requested I would write, for that he should leave it wholly with me...

I have the honor to be, with the greatest respect,
your Excellency's most obedient servant,
William Heath [70]

After several months of negotiation and impatience by Arnold, he agreed to sell the plans of West Point for 20,000 pounds of British sterling and a General's commission in the Royal Army. On the **24th**, after several months of negotiation, Andre` agreed to pay Arnold 20,000 pounds of British sterling and a General's commission in the Royal Army in exchange for the fortification plans of West Point, but also noted that there is no "A" for effort, only for accomplishment.

To Mr. Moore

July 24, 1780

Sir

West Point derives its importance from the nature of the operations of our enemy. Yet should we throw your means possess ourselves of 3,000 men and its artillery and stores which the magazine of provision for the Army which may probably be there the sum even of 20,000 pounds should be paid to you. You must not suppose that in case of detection or failure that your efforts being known you would be left a victim, but services done are the terms on which we promise rewards; in these you see we are profuse; we

403

conceive them proportioned to your risk. As to an absolute promise of indemnification to the amount of 10,000 pounds and annuity of 500 whether services are performed or not, it can never be made. Your intelligence we prize and will freely recompense it 200 pounds shall be lodged in your agents hands as you desire & 300 more are at your disposal. [79]

I am, &c.,

J Anderson

This letter was included in one from Odell to Stansbury on the same day emphasizing the delivery of compensation and offering that Andre` himself was willing to meet with Arnold.

To J. Carleton

July 24, 1780

Dear Sir

Yours of the 7th was answered yesterday; and after that answer was dispatched I received one of the 15th enclosing one of the same date from Mr. Moore to Mr. Anderson and another of the 18th from yourself. I have this morning had the honor of a conversation with the Commander-in-Chief on the subject. In addition to what is stated in the enclosed to Mr. Moore, his Excellency authorizes me to repeat in the strongest terms the assurances so often given to your partner: that he is in earnest and will to the extent of his ability cooperate with us. He shall not in any possible event have cause to complain, and essential services shall be even profusely rewarded far beyond the stipulated indemnification, etc. But indemnification as a preliminary is what Sir Henry thinks highly unreasonable. However, he has not the smallest doubt but that everything may be settled to mutual satisfaction when the projected interview takes place at West Point. From whence it is expected Mr. Moore will take occasion (upon entering on his command there) to correspond with Sir Henry by flag of truce. Mr. Anderson is willing himself to effect the meeting either in the way proposed or in whatever manner may at the time appear most eligible. As to the speculation you propose on your own account, His Excellency has no other objection than that the plan is inconvenient especially in the absence of the Admiral. He permits me to assure you that he will do justice to your zeal and attention in transacting the business of the House in trusted to your care, and will reward your services in full proportion to their value & importance.
[79]

I am, &c.,

On the **27**[th], Washington notified General Rochambeau of the French Army in Rhode Island that Clinton had taken the bait from the planted letter to the Canadians and was headed his way.

To Comte de Rochambeau

Headquarters, July 27, 1780, 10 o'clock P. M.

Sir

I had the honor of addressing your Excellency this morning. I have just received advice from New York confirming our accounts hitherto of an embarkation to proceed up the Sound to Rhode Island. It is said to consist of the principal part of the enemy's Army commanded by General Clinton in person and was to have sailed this morning from White Stone a few miles on the east side of Hell gate. Thirty-six pieces of heavy cannon of different caliber with two mortars provided with shells and carcasses are also said to have been embarked.

The Army is already under marching orders and will without delay be put in motion towards New York to endeavor to take advantage of General Clinton's absence or at least to embarrass and precipitate his movements. [24]

I have the honor to be with perfect consideration and attachment, Sir,

your most obedient & humble servant,

G. Washington

When his reinforcements for New York failed to arrive by the **30**[th], and his intelligence from Arnold proved that he should not trust Washington, Clinton decided to abandoned his plans for Newport. On the **31**[st], Arnold reported to Washington just above Stony Point. While the Commander-in-Chief supervised the Army's crossing of the river, Arnold asked if he had thought of anything for him. Washington answered, "Yes, you are to command the left wing, the post of honor." [5] Although Washington expected him to say a word of thanks or expressing pleasure to this announcement, Arnold, in shock, never opened his mouth, but Hamilton, who was present at that moment later recalled that Arnold's face seemed to turn red out of anger or embarrassment. Washington, who was puzzled by this reaction or the lack of one, asked Arnold to ride to his headquarters at nearby Peekskill and wait for him there. Upon arriving at headquarters, Arnold vented his stress to Washington's chief of staff, Colonel Tench Tilghman. Here he claimed that his leg was so bad that he could not last very long on horseback while in charge of a wing, but that only a stationary command such as West Point would suit him. Tilghman noticed that while he was ranting about his leg, he spent his time waiting for Washington limping back and forth on it at a nervous pace. Born in Talbot County in Maryland, Tilghman was a graduate from the College, Academy, and Charitable School of Philadelphia (now University of Pennsylvania). With the approach of war, he liquidated his business and was appointed as secretary and treasurer to the Continental Congress Commissioners to the Iroquois at Albany before serving under the Commander-in-Chief. At Washington's return, Tilghman informed him of Arnold's disturbing behavior, which moved Washington to patiently debate the issue with Arnold, explaining that his talents were best applied in the field, but Arnold refused to give in and reclaimed his need for a rear-area assignment on account of his injury. Washington agreed to think the matter over and notify Arnold of his decision. The next day, **August 1st**, General orders from Washington confirmed his decision that Arnold was headed where he belonged, in the field.

General Orders
Headquarters Peekskill, Tuesday, August 1, 1780
Parole Copenhagen. Countersigns K., F.
Watchword Discipline.
... The following will be the order of battle for the present. The right wing commanded by Major General Greene will consist of two divisions in the first line and one division in the second line.
1st Line Right Wing
  Right: 1st and 2nd Pennsylvania brigades will compose one division commanded by Major St. Clair.
  Left: New Jersey and New York brigades will compose one division commanded by Major General Lord Stirling.
2nd Line Right Wing
  1st and 2nd Connecticut brigades will compose one division commanded by the eldest Brigadier.
The left wing commanded by Major General Arnold will consist of two divisions in the first line and one division in the second line.
1st Line Left Wing
  Right: 1st and second Massachusetts brigades will compose one division commanded by Major General Howe.
  Left: Stark's and Poor's brigades will compose one division commanded by Major General McDougall.
2nd Line Left Wing

3rd and 4th Massachusetts brigades will compose one division commanded by Maj. Genl B. de Steuben. [24]

Peggy also reacted to the news of her husband's assignment, but in a more dramatic sense. According to Robert Morris of Philadelphia, while she was dining at his house one evening, "a friend of the family came in and congratulated Mrs. Arnold on a report that her husband was appointed to a different but more honorable command," than West Point. "The information affected her so much as to produce hysteric fits. Efforts were made to convince her that the General had been selected for a preferable station. These explanations, however, to the astonishment of all present produced no effect." [79] Upon receiving word of Clinton's sudden change in direction, Heath communicated the news to the Commander-in-Chief, which reached him on the **3rd**.

To His Excellency General Washington

Newport, 31 July, 1780

Dear General

In consequence of intelligence, received yesterday morning from the westward, that the fleet of transports, which were lately in the Sound and supposed to be coming this way, had sailed towards New York, General Count de Rochambeau expressed his pleasure that the militia, which had arrived and were on their march for his support, except those detached for three months, should return home, I immediately communicated it to them...

I have the honor to be, with the greatest respect,

your Excellency's most obedient servant,

William Heath [70]

As Washington had told Arnold earlier, that the movements of the enemy would dictate theirs, so it did here. When Washington learned that the boys were back in town, he decided to bring the Army back across the river and bestow Arnold with the command of West Point.

General Orders

Headquarters Peekskill

Thursday, August 3, 1780

Parole Hopkinton.   Countersigns Hull, Here.

Watchwork Hark!

The Army having moved to the present ground in consequence of the enemy's dispositions to make a combined attack upon our allies at Rhode Island, for the purposes of taking such advantages as their absence from New York might afford or obliging them to relinquish their intended expedition; and the latter having apparently taken place, probably in consequence of the movement on our part, the Army will re-cross the river tomorrow to prosecute the original plan of the campaign... 37.

Given under my hand,
G. Washington

To M General Arnold
Headquarters at Peekskill, August 3, 1780
Sir
You are to proceed to West Point and take the command of that post and its dependencies in which all are included from Fishkill to King's Ferry. The Corps of infantry and cavalry advanced towards the enemy's lines on the east side of the river will also be under your orders and will take directions from you. You will endeavor to obtain every intelligence of the enemy's motions. The garrison of West Point is to consist of the Militia of New Hampshire and Massachusetts. As soon as the number from those States amounts to twelve hundred, the New York Militia under the command of Colonel Malcolm, are to join the main Army on the west side of the river. When the number from Massachusetts Bay alone shall amount to fifteen hundred rank and file, the Militia of New Hampshire will also march to the main Army. Colonel James Livingston's regiment is, till further orders, to garrison the redoubts at Stony and Verplank's Point.

Claverack upon the North River is appointed for the place of rendezvous of the Militia of New Hampshire and Massachusetts, from whence you will have them brought down as fast as they arrive. A supply of provision will be necessary at that place, which you will order from time to time as there may be occasion.

You will endeavor to have the works at West Point carried on as expeditiously as possible by the garrison under the direction and superintendence of the engineers. The stores carefully preserved with the provision safely deposited and often inspected, particularly the salted meat. A certain quantity of provision has been constantly kept in each work to be ready against a sudden attack. Where there are bomb proofs, they serve for magazines; but in the smaller works there are none. You will have places erected sufficiently tight to preserve the provision from damage and pillage.

You will, as soon as possible, obtain and transmit an accurate return of the militia which have come in, and inform me regularly of their increase. Should any levies, from the State of New York or those to the eastward of it, intended for the Continental Army arrive at West Point, you will immediately forward them to the lines to which they respectively belong. The difficulties we shall certainly experience on the score of provisions render the utmost economy highly necessary. You will therefore attend frequently to the daily issues and by comparing them with your returns, will be able to check any impositions.

I am, &c.,

G. Washington [24]

XII
Garrison

On **August 5th** Arnold took over Robert Howe's headquarters at the Beverly Robinson House across the river just to the south of West Point in an area now known as Garrison. This was the same Beverly Robinson who introduced Arnold into the concept of conspiring against his country. The location of the house also put Arnold in a well-placed position to escape when the attack on the fort was initiated. In a letter to Howe, who held the previous command of West Point, Arnold justified his choice of residence and put in a request for the names of undercover operatives.

To Major General Howe
Robinson House in the Highlands, August 5, 1780
Sir
...I have not been on the point since I came here; I shall carefully inspect both sides of the river and take quarters where I think myself free from danger and in a condition to render the greatest service. At present I apprehend no danger in these quarters, which are the most convenient for an invalid. The safety of this post and garrison in a great measure depends on having good intelligence of the movements and designs of the enemy, and you have been fortunate in the agents you have employed for that purpose. I must request to be informed who they are, as I wish to employ them for the same purpose. I will engage upon honor to make no discovery of them to any person breathing. [79]
I am, Sir, your obedient humble servant,
B. Arnold

Howe declined to reveal the names of his agents, but did recommend a loyalist attorney from Haverstraw named Joshua Hett Smith. Born in New York City, Smith was an active Whig who had served in the Provincial Congress and the local militia. Howe had described him as a gentleman in whom confidence might be placed and whose aid would be valuable in securing important news of the enemy's plans. Arnold had met Smith two years before in Philadelphia, but did not divulge this to Howe and sent the lawyer a letter requesting his assistance. Arnold also attempted to secure the names of spies in New York while at Washington's headquarters from the twenty-two year-old, red-haired Frenchman, Major General Marquis de Lafayette. A wealthy orphan when he was just thirteen

411

and yearning to follow in his family's tradition of serving in the military, Lafayette enlisted in the King's Musketeers as a shy and awkward fourteen-year-old. Upon hearing of America's rebellion against England, he was attracted to the idea of aiding them in their quest for liberty in order to satisfy his own desire of avenging his father's death and country's humiliation in the Seven Years' War. Following the announcement of the Declaration of Independence, he made his way to America and volunteered for service in Philadelphia. Although insensitive and egocentric, his naïve optimism and ambition inspired Washington to adopt him onto his staff. Christened by a leg wound at the battle of Brandywine, he later fought at Monmouth and Newport, and proved to be a valuable liaison officer for Washington in meetings with the French admiral Charles Hector Theodat, Comte d'Estaing and Rochambeau as well as successfully attaining further support of the French government in the American cause. Born in 1729, d'Estaing was appointed colonel of a regiment at the young age of sixteen and later fought in the Seven Years' War during which the brave, handsome, and energetic naval officer was twice imprisoned. Although Arnold explained that intelligence might reach him with more expedition at West Point, Lafayette objected to the proposal upon the principle that he was bound in honor and conscience not to reveal the names of his agents to anyone. Unbeknownst to Arnold's true plans for the post, Washington aided in his treachery by instructing him to remove any unnecessary personnel from the fort.

To Major General Arnold, West Point
Headquarters Peekskill, 5 August, 1780
Dear Sir
Enclosed is a letter, which I received this day from Colonel Malcolm. His observations may perhaps be of use to you. He was a considerable time in command at the post, and is well acquainted with what relates to its security. It would be well to make inquiry into the cases of the number of persons, who are confined in the fort. Some of them may have been committed on frivolous occasions, and no charges, that can be supported, left against them. If so, they had better be discharged than kept. Some of the others may be usefully employed, in the way Colonel Malcolm mentions. The quartermaster general expects some camp kettles shortly. He will, if possible, spare some of the militia. I imagine they are what are principally wanting. In the mean time, they must endeavor to make a shift with the few cooking utensils they have. I believe the matter of changing the

officers of the light infantry companies has been settled between Governor Clinton and the Baron.

I am, Dear Sir, &c., [68]

G. Washington

Washington then added more ammunition to Arnold's arsenal of treason by revealing how to obtain a plan of the fortifications in a letter on the **6**[th].

To M General Arnold

Headquarters Peekskill, August 6, 1780

Sir

Colonel Kosciuszko having permission to join the southern Army, Major Villefranche has directions to repair to West Point and take upon him the superintendence of the works. You will, I am persuaded, find this gentleman fully acquainted with the business and I doubt not but he will give general satisfaction to those with whom he will be immediately concerned in the execution of the works.

I am, Sir, your most obedient servant,

G. Washington

P. S. If General Howe has not left you a plan of the works, Major Villefranche will be able to furnish you with one. [24]

On the **8**[th], perhaps planning an escape route when the British took the fort or an access route for Andre' to meet him, Arnold asked Washington for a map of the area on the other side of the river from West Point.

To His Excellency General Washington

Headquarters Robinson's House, August 8, 1780

Dear Sir

I wish your Excellency would be kind enough to order Mr. Erskine to send me a map of the country from this place to New York, particularly on the east side of the River, which would be very useful to me.

The officers in general from the State of Massachusetts Bay have never been in the service before, and are extremely ignorant of their duty, which throws everything into confusion and in case of an attack on the post, from their inexperience, I believe little dependence can be placed on them, the troops are good and well armed, would it not be better Sir to continue a part of the whole of the New York Brigade at this post whose officers (particularly Col. Malcolm) well acquainted with the duty and can be depended on, and the troops have in general bad arms & few bayonets.

I am convinced that the Massachusetts or Hampshire troops will be better in the field from this circumstance in their arms.

Major Villefranche has surveyed the works at West Point and informs me that there is a vast deal to do to complete them, that large quantities of materials, such as timber, plank, boards, stone, &c., will be wanted, part of the materials are at different places near this post, but I do not find that there are any teams or forage in the department, and at present there is no prospect of any being furnished.

I am sorry to trouble your Excellency with so long a list of grievances and am very respectfully, your Excellency's most obedient and obliged humble servant, B. Arnold [84]

During his tenure at the fort, Arnold took slow and meticulous steps in repairing the fortifications in order to weaken them. In addition, he dispatched troops off the post for sentry duty, artillery assignments, prisoner escort, removing cannon barrels from carriages for repair, sunken gunboat retrieval, and firewood detail as far as Fishkill. In addition, when regular troops were rotated out, they were replaced with untrained and undisciplined militia. On the 11th, Washington had learned that a large formation of British troops might be headed for the Highlands. He ordered Arnold to make-ready for their arrival and for the arrival of a new quartermaster general, Colonel Timothy Pickering. After graduating from Harvard, Pickering had studied law and was admitted to the bar, but didn't engage in a full-time practice. After being commissioned a lieutenant of militia, following the French and Indian War, this outspoken, self-righteous, serious, and firm- minded patriot drafted several notices and petitions in support of the revolutionary movement. Just twelve days prior to the battle of Lexington, he was elected as a colonel in the Continental Army and marched at the head of 300 men to cut off the British retreat from there. As a devout student of military history and tactics, he published an illustrated manual entitled, "An Easy Plan of Discipline for a Militia," which emphasized simplicity and maneuverability of troops achieved through means of leading by example of respect and devotion. He also emphasized that the reasons behind tactics and strategies should be explained to the men so that they may better understand their benefits. This guiding light for leadership was used throughout the Army until it was replaced by Baron von Steuben's manual. In his hometown of Salem,

Massachusetts, he demonstrated his ambitious and industrious integrity by accepting a commission as a selectman, town clerk, justice of the peace, judge of the maritime court, and representative to the general court. Following this he was granted the appointment of adjutant general to Washington and became a member of the board of war. While in the field he served at the battles of Brandywine and Germantown and called things as he saw them with no holds barred.

To M General Arnold

Headquarters Orangetown, 11 August, 1780

Dear Sir

I have received intelligence, that the British troops, who lately returned from the eastward and debarked upon Long Island, have orders to embark again. I cannot suppose, that they mean again to go towards Rhode Island; neither can I think, that, in the present situation of matters, they can expect any success from an attempt upon West Point; but, in order that we may run no risk, I shall write to Colonel Malcolm, directing him to halt in the neighborhood of Haverstraw till further orders. He will from thence be within supporting distance of the posts, should a serious move up the river take place. You will also detain all of the Militia of Massachusetts and New Hampshire, who may come in, until we receive more certain intelligence of the views and intentions of the enemy. you will put all your posts upon their guard. They can be affected by nothing but a surprise, while this Army is so near them.

We shall have occasion to throw up some small works at Dobbs Ferry, to secure the intended communication at that place; and, in order that we may be enabled to finish them in the most expeditious manner, you will be pleased to order sixty of Colonel Baldwin's artificers to come immediately down here.

Colonel Hay writes, that he shall be able to lay up some stock of hay at Fishkill, provided orders are given, that none shall be issued while grass or pasture is to be had, except upon such occasions as you, or the deputy quartermaster general at that post, shall think proper. This measure appears to be necessary; and you will, therefore, be pleased to give orders to have it carried into execution. A new quartermaster general (Colonel Pickering) is appointed. Whether he will be supplied with the means of procuring what is necessary in the department, or whether the new system is calculated to produce them, is yet to be known. In the mean time, you can only proceed in working up the materials, which you find on hand.

I am, &c., [68]

On the **12th**, after making a logistics inquiry to Washington, Arnold uses Colonel Udny Hay as a scapegoat to transfer men out of the fortress and the new quartermaster for failing to supply it with the proper means.

To His Excellency General Washington

> *Headquarters Robinson's House, August 12, 1780*

Dear Sir

I am this instant favored with your Excellency's letter of yesterday, on the 10th I received advice from Colonel Sheldon that the enemy were embarking troops & heavy artillery at White Stone and New York, which I thought would justify me in detaining the New York Militia, until I received an answer to my letter of the 8th especially as very few of the Massachusetts & New Hampshire Militia have come in since that time & I am informed that two thousand of them have been ordered to Rhode Island, and the officers present are of opinion that very few more will join this garrison unless those ordered here which are said to be gone to Rhode Island.

By enclosed returns your Excellency will see that the Massachusetts & New Hampshire Militia amount to only 1918 rank and file, 405 of which are in command which leaves 1433 in garrison, and Colonel Hay has requested 200 men to cut firewood and make brick for the use of the garrison next winter. He informs me that the wood must be transported a considerable distance by water; that the vessels employed are so badly found with cables, anchors, and sails that they cannot ply after the middle of October. I find on inquiry that the wood is destroyed in the vicinity of the garrison, and unless a stock is laid in this fall they will be put to the greatest difficulty for fuel next winter. Colonel Hay is of opinion that with 200 men he can furnish a sufficient quantity for the garrison next winter. I wish your Excellency's directions in this matter.

The New York levies under Colonel Malcolm will march from this post tomorrow for Haverstraw. I have ordered the remainder of the rum requested by Colonel Stewart to be forwarded on immediately. 80 of Col. Baldwin's artificers will be drafted and sent immediately to the main Army. The order which your Excellency mentions respecting forage shall be strictly attended to.

I think it requires very little dissertation to foresee that a change in the Quartermaster's Department in the middle of a campaign will throw the whole into confusion & be attended with more fatal consequences than any abuses which are said to exist in the Department. If materials are not furnished to complete the redoubts and works on the Point this fall, they will in a great measure be defenseless this winter, in a ruinous condition by spring, and a great part of the work which is done will be totally lost & to be done over again. With such men and materials as I have, I will do all that can be done.

Enclosed is a letter from Genl Parsons to Genl Howe, requesting a flag, which he requests for Capt. Benedict to go to New York. I beg your Excellency's instructions on this matter and on flags in general.

I have the honor to be most respectfully,
your Excellency's most obedient and very humble servant,
B. Arnold [84]

As the war raged on, the recession was starting to be felt by others under the service of Congress. On the 3rd, the General officers in the Army had asked for a raise in pay, but the only response from Philadelphia was to forego their finances, reach deep down into their patriotic souls, and feel the intangible benefits of their cause.

Saturday, August 12, 1780
Resolved, That the said General Officers be informed that Congress have at no time been unmindful of the military virtues which have distinguished the Army of the United states through the course of this war; and that it has been constantly one of the principle objects of their care, not only to provide for the health and comfort of the Army, but to gratify their reasonable desires as far as the public urgencies would admit:

That patience and self-denial, fortitude and perseverance, and the cheerful sacrifice of time, health, and fortune are necessary virtues which both the citizen and the soldier are called to exercise while struggling for the liberties of their country. This moderation, frugality, and temperance must be among the chief supports, as well as the brightest ornaments of that kind of civil government which is wisely instituted by the several states in this union. [26]

After painting such a bleak picture of the condition of the fort, Washington concurred with Arnold on the 13th.

To M General Arnold
Headquarters Orangetown, 13 August, 1780

Dear Sir

I have received your favor of yesterday. The providing of wood in season for the garrison is so essential a matter that you will be pleased to furnish Colonel Hay with the men required. I expect that those men, who were detained at Rhode Island while there was an expedition of General Clinton, will soon come forward. Colonel Sheldon may be directed to send down a flag with Captain Benedict and Mr. Stevens. If the former can obtain liberty to be admitted into New York, I have no objection to his going. The general directions, which have been given respecting flags, have been as follows; To discourage the frequent use of them as much as possible; to permit no persons, inhabitants of the States, to go into New York without permission in writing from the respective Governors, except in such a case as that of Captain Benedict, who shows good cause for going; and always to grant flags upon the application of the Governors of the neighboring States...

I am, Dear Sir, &c., [68]
G. Washington

On the **13th**, Smith accepted Arnold's request for intelligence and made a request of his own.

To Major General Arnold

Belmont White House, Aug, 13ᵗʰ 1780

Dear General

Soon after I had the pleasure of your company I made the inquiries for the bedding agreeable to your request by sending one of my domestic servants to the person who had offered to sell them to me, being unable to stir from home myself by reason of the complaint I had when you were here, but was sorry to be informed they were sold. The person sent to us a bed asking to sell if that could be serviceable. I begin to gain strength and am under engagement to visit his Excellency and Genl Howe, the beds were in the neighborhood of the present headquarters. I propose fulfilling these engagements early in the week and you may rest assured I shall endeavor to procure them for you and shall at all times be happy to render any service to a gentleman whose character I revere.

The source of General Howe's information was various and seldom confined any length of time for any particular person for obvious reasons. The principal person was lately was Captain Lawrence, whose mode of procuring intelligence can better be mentioned to you shown committed to paper, an opportunity of doing which I shall embrace as soon as the flurry of invoice will admit of my taking him from his command and introducing him to you at Robinson's, a circumstance in which I anticipate much pleasure. Capt. Lawrence is in your command, but I believe at present very actively employed.

I think it may be depended upon from accounts below that Rodney is in a woeful predicament and that he has presumptuously ordered Arbuthnot to join him in the West Indies or the British fleet and Islands must be sacrificed. If so the Yorkers say Graves, whom the latter commands, must go likewise. Sir Henry concentrates his force as much as possible and no person is permitted to use the common ferryboats from the Country. But a signal is given from Paulus Hook and a special boat is sent over. They are damned cautious who they suffice to come in or out since Genl Washington has drawn down. They have evacuated the blockhouse at Fort Lee and still continue to fortify New York. He is covering every apprehension of a formidable attack. I think should any appreciation look towards West Point, I shall receive the earliest intelligence in which case expect an express or even if it should affect your command remotely. The enemy are arming everything that can carry in sail more for show than annoyance. Col. Malcolm who I am told is at West Point can furnish you with an accurate list of the homes of all the well-affected on the lines near Kings Bridge taken some time since by an officer under his command, remarkable for his address in sifting characters. You will find great use in procuring a copy.

Should Mrs. Arnold pay you a visit, 'tis more than probable she will take this house in which case I shall be happy should she make my house a stage until your barge can meet her at the ferry. Every civility in my power to render this Country respectable good be heartily at her service.

The Governor of this state desired Genl Howe, when in your command, to grant permits to such women to pass into New York whose husbands and relatives were there, provided they did not return. This was sound policy as so many mouths from us to feed and landed the enemy with them. Besides the objects of our war is not to disrespect women and children. There are a couple of women who are in this predicament with children who are in a starving condition here and I think their friends in the City if they were there might relieve them. Motives of humanity induces me to beg if consistent that you would transmit them a pass. Their names are below. I would be happy to hear from you on this subject.

I am, Dear Genl in haste with lively esteem, yours &c.,

Catherine John } 5 children
Elizabeth Gerard } 3 children [84]

On the **14th**, Howe responded in a similar manner as Lafayette had, claiming that his two best men "are persons of character and property who cannot without utter ruin get out of the enemy's power and yet, devoted to America, have agreed to serve in a way they do not like but which is the only way they can at present serve her in." [79] In a strange order of events, it wasn't until the **15th**, that Hay's official petition for firewood was sent to Arnold, even though he notified Washington of it three days before.

To Major General Arnold

August 15, 1780

Sir

I beg to leave mention the necessity of adopting some certain plan by which a quantity of wood may immediately be cut for and be conveyed to the garrison at West Point. When you view the distance from which that article must be brought by land if not laid in before the river shuts, you will be fully convinced of the necessity of procuring an immediate and as far as possible, a full supply. I would otherwise observe that there are but very few vessels in this river that have either sails or cables fit for the fall; of consequence the conveyance of wood as well as forage and provisions must become very precarious. [79]

I am, &c.,
Udny Hay

On the **16th**, prior to receiving Smith's letter, Arnold wrote a follow up to Howe to get the name of his agent.

To Major General Howe

August 16, 1780

Sir

You have my honor that I will not be solicitous about the real name of Mr. Williams and you may pledge my faith to him that if accident should disclose to me his real name I will not discover it. I will take proper precautions that no gentleman of my family open any letters addressed to me as private. [79]

I am, &c.,
B. Arnold

As Arnold was stripping the garrison of men, he was also stockpiling it with supplies for the British as revealed in a letter to the new quartermaster general, Colonel Timothy Pickering.

To Col. Pickering, Q.M.G.
Headquarters Robinson House, August 16, 1780
Dear Sir
His Excellency Genl Washington has advised me of your appointments to the Q.M.G. department, I have therefore taken the earliest opportunity to transmit to you a return of the stores, &c. in the Q.M. magazine in this poverty struck place, and to inform you of our wants that you may take proper and speedy measures to supply them.

From the returns you will find that everything is wanting so that it will be unnecessary for me to enumerate the articles. Those that are in more immediate want are horses for ten horse teams. Ten wagons without which the necessary repairs & works to be done on the redoubts must be affected. They are also wanted for the purpose of repairing the old & raise up new barracks, sore storehouses & a provost, all which are exercising by warrant. The barracks here will not contain more than eight hundred men or any kind of camp equipment, there is not a tent at West Point and it is with great difficulty that one can be made to cover the troops, who are in general exposed to the inclemency of the weather. Ten thousand Albany Rounds at least will be wanted & a large quantity of provisions, without these supplies the garrison will be in a wretched, uncomfortable situation next winter, the works in a void & by next spring defenseless condition and great part that is done will be to do over again. The magazines of every house of stores is the Q.M. Department in this district I am with an entirely empty you will therefore be enrolled to make an estimate of the articles and quarters wanted, which I make no doubt you are enabled to supply immediately.

I am with great regard, Dear Sir, Your obedient servant,
B. Arnold [84]

Along with his offer to serve the General, Smith asked for Arnold's assistance in helping some lovely young ladies and their children get down to New York. Arnold was always willing to help a damsel in distress, especially if she would be willing to do him the favor of dropping off a letter for him while she was down there. But in order to prevent a repeat of his "Philadelphia Story," Arnold made an inquiry to Governor George Clinton on the **17th** regarding the issuance of passes. Clinton had served in the French and Indian War with his father, Charles, and brother, James, before practicing law and becoming a member of the Assembly and a delegate to Congress. As a man of vigor and courage, he served as a brigadier general during the attack on Fort Montgomery, made by his older brother Sir Henry in October of 1777, but the devastating loss proved him to be deficient in military ability and he was re-elected as Governor.

To His Excellency Governor Clinton
Headquarters Robinson's House, August 17, 1780
Dear Sir
Joshua Smith, Esquire, of Haverstraw, in a letter of the 13th, applied to me for permits for two women, the one named Catherine John, with five children, and the other Eliza Gerard, with three children, to pass within the enemy's lines.

He informs me that they and their children are in a starving condition here, and that they have friends with the enemy, who, if they were there, might relieve them.

Sentiments of humanity would induce me to give them permits, if it not be inconsistent with the policy and laws of the state. I shall, therefore, be very happy to receive your Excellency's advice on this subject, as well as what line of conduct you wish to be observed, with respect to such inhabitants of this state as may in future apply to me for permits and flags to go to New York.

I beg your answer on the subject and am,
with sentiments of great regard and esteem,
your Excellency's most obedient and very humble servant,
B. Arnold [33]

Feeling the constrains of a lack of manpower, Colonel John Lamb, now serving as the 2nd Artillery commander at West Point, had protested Arnold's actions in a letter to him on the **18th**.

To Major General Arnold
West Point, August 18, 1780
Dear General
I mentioned to Major Franks yesterday that two hundred men from the Massachusetts Brigade were sent to Fishkill previous to your arrival. What occasion there is for such a guard at that place I cannot possibly conceive. Half the number will be sufficient.

If such drafts as are called for are made from the garrison, we shall neither be able to finish the works that are incomplete nor in a situation to defend those that are finished. Captain Hubbell will explain to you the reasons why the men ordered for cutting firewood are still here. They are waiting your further orders respecting them.

I am, respectfully, Dear General, your obedient servant,

John Lamb [39]

On the **19**[th], Major Jean Villefranche, the French engineer who had been sent by Washington to inspect the great chain across the river, had reported to Franks that new logs should be installed under the chain as soon as possible in order to keep it afloat. On the **22**[nd], Arnold applied to Governor Clinton of New York to send teams to draw the great chain out of the river. On the record this was for the sole purpose of making the necessary repairs on the chain, but his real reason was to clear the way for the British to attack. When he learned that the teams were not available, he wrote another complaint to Pickering.

To Timothy Pickering, Quartermaster General

August 22, 1780

Sir

I am informed that the middle part of the chain is sinking and in a dangerous situation, on account of the logs, which it has hitherto floated on, being water-soaked. Unless this be speedily remedied it will be out of our power to raise it but with great expense of time and trouble; the new timber cannot be hauled for want of teams, of which we have not half sufficient for the daily necessities of the garrison. [79]

I am, &c.,

B. Arnold, Major General

On the same day, Governor George responded to Arnold's inquiry regarding passes, stating that they were up to his discretion, having command of the area.

To the Honorable Major General Arnold

Poughkeepsie, August 22, 1780

Dear Sir

I have received your favor of the 17th *instant. The practice hitherto pursued in granting passes to any of the inhabitants of this State applying to go within the enemy's lines, has been by application in the first instance to the person administering the government for his consent, which being obtained, the commanding officer of the department has granted his pass for them to proceed. This has prevented, on one hand, impositions which have been often attempted by persons no ways meriting indulgences or worthy of confidence; on the other, a communication with the enemy at improper seasons, and, if agreeable to you, is the mode I wish to be pursued.*

With respect to flags, few pass, and none are ever granted by the authority of the State, without previously consulting the officer commanding the department.

I am with the highest esteem and respect, Dear Sir,
your most obedient servant,
Geo. Clinton [33]

When Arnold learned Washington's real plan to take New York while Sir Henry was off chasing ghosts in Rhode Island, he sent word of the trap off in time for the General to cancel his marching orders. When he received word that Congress denied pay raises for General officers, he tried to organize a protest. On the 23rd, he wrote to Greene proposing that a committee of 1,000 or 1,500 men of all ranks within the Army should be sent to Congress "to present a spirited but decent memorial setting forth their claims requesting immediate justice as far as the public are able. This measure I think would be attended with happy consequences to the country; for if justice is not done to the Army their necessities will occasion them to disband, and the country will of course be left to the ravages to the enemy." [79] In another letter to Major General Samuel Holden Parsons on the 27th, he dissented that the resolutions were, "founded on principles of genuine congressional virtue, magnanimity, benevolence, patriotism, and justice. I hope they meet with a proper reception by all who are interested in them. The insult added to injury is too pointed to pass unnoticed." [79] Parsons, originally from Lyme, Connecticut, grew up in Newburyport, Massachusetts, graduated from Harvard, and settled back in his hometown of Lyme to study law and begin a practice. He was elected to the General Assembly at the young age of twenty-five and later served as a King's attorney and a member of the Committee of Correspondence before becoming a colonel in the 6th Connecticut when the battle with Britain had begun. Accompanying Ethan Allen, he participated in the attack on Fort Ticonderoga and following his promotion to brigadier, he led his troops in the battle of Long Island as an intelligent and conscientious officer.

Soon thereafter, Stansbury declined to continue as a messenger of the tedious and dangerous correspondence and recommended Andre` to deal in a direct manner with Arnold and be done with it. Arnold then realized that a face-to-face meeting must be arranged in order to work out particulars, exchange vital data, establish reassurance, and seal the deal. Arnold soon found his a courier when one arrived with a letter from Major General Samuel Holden Parsons asking for a pass to allow a friend to travel to New York.

To Major General Arnold

Redding, August 28, 1780

Dear General

The bearer, William Heron, awaits upon you to request a flag for the purpose of securing a debt due him; the probability of effecting it he will convince you of. Mr. Heron is a neighbor of mine for whose integrity and firm attachment to the cause of the country I will hold myself answerable. If it will not consist with the present circumstances of the Army, I shall be much obliged to you to grant him the favor he requests. I am certain he will conduct with strict honor every matter he undertakes.

I am your obedient servant,

S. H. Parsons [30]

On the **30**[th], Arnold asked Heron to deliver a letter in person that Arnold had resealed. Heron agreed, but unbeknownst to Arnold, this former schoolteacher and surveyor from Ireland, now a member of the Connecticut Assembly, was also a British spy. Equally enough and unbeknownst to Heron, Arnold was a traitor. Being a good spy, (smart, shrewd, fluid, and flattering), Heron grew suspicious of Arnold's letter because it was sealed twice. As Parsons had mentioned in his letter, Heron did conduct himself with strict honor, for instead of delivering it, he handed it over to Parsons when he returned to Connecticut. Parsons thought it to be nothing more than a mere reference to a commercial deal and placed it in his desk drawer.

To Mr. John Anderson, Merchant

August 30, 1780

Sir

On the 24th *instant, I received a note from you without date in answer to mine of the 7*[th] *of July. Also a letter from your house of the 24*[th] *of July in answer to mine of the 15*[th]*, with a note from Mr. B-----*

of the 30ᵗʰ July; with an extract of a letter from Mr. J. Osborn of the 24ᵗʰ. I have paid particular attention to the contents of the several letters. Had they arrived earlier, you should have had my answer sooner. A variety of circumstances has prevented my writing you before, I expect to do it very fully in a few days and to procure you an interview with Mr. M(oor)e when you will be able to settle your commercial plan I hope agreeable to all parties. Mr. M(oor)e assures me that he is still of opinion that his first proposal is by no means unreasonable and makes no doubt when he has a conference with you that you will close with it. He expects when you meet that you will be fully authorized from your house that the risks and profit of the co-partnership may be fully and clearly understood.

A speculation might at this time be easily made to some advantage with ready money, but there is not the quantity of goods at market, which your partner seems to suppose and the number of speculators below, I think will be against your making an immediate purchase. I apprehend goods will be in greater plenty and much cheaper in the course of the season; both dry and wet are much wanted and in demand at this juncture. Some quantities are expected in this part of the Country soon.

Mr. M(oor)e flatters himself that in the course of ten days he will have the pleasure of seeing you. He requests me to advise you that he has ordered a draw on you in favor of our mutual friend S(tansbur)y for 300 pounds which you will charge on account of the tobacco. I am in behalf of Mr. M(oor)e and Co.,

Sir, your obedient humble servant,
Gustavus [30]

In a letter of the 31ˢᵗ from Clinton to Lord George Germain, Secretary of State for the Colonies, Andre` had been recommended to the full rank of Adjutant General. On **September 1ˢᵗ**, Arnold made a follow up inquiry to Colonel Elisha Sheldon from Connecticut regarding a double spy named Elijah Hunter to act as a potential messenger.

To Colonel Elisha Sheldon
Headquarters Robinson's House, September 1, 1780
Sir
I wish to be informed if the person you mentioned to me is returned from his excursion. On considering the matter I am conceived that material intelligence might be procured through the channel I mentioned.

I am with sentiments of the most sincere regard and esteem, Dear Sir,
your most humble servant,
B. A. [33]

On the **2nd**, Washington notified Arnold of a possible attack by the British and to prepare the defenses.

To M General Arnold
> *Headquarters Liberty Pole, Bergen County, September 2, 1780*
Dear Sir
> *Having received intelligence that the enemy are in preparation for (some important) movement, I thought it advisable that you should be apprised of it. because it is uncertain (if the information should prove true) whether their object will be an attack on the main Army or an attempt on the posts in the Highlands. I wish you therefore to put the latter in the most defensible state, which is possible.*
> *Orders are already given for the two state regiments of Connecticut to form a junction with Colonel Sheldon and in case the enemy should make demonstrations of a serious attack of the fortifications on the north river, you will immediately call this force to your relief, collect all your detachments, and withdraw the garrisons from the posts at King's Ferry. At the same time removing all the stores from thence. For this and other purposes you will be pleased without delay to order sixty (of the largest flat) boats to that place with five men each to be ready to act as circumstances may require.*
[24]
> *I am, Dear Sir, your most obedient & very humble servant,*
> *G. Washington*

When Arnold failed to hear back from Andre`, he sent another letter of the same by way of Mrs. Mary McCarthy, who held a pass from Governor Clinton allowing her to travel from Quebec to New York on the **4th**.

To Lieutenant Isaac Barber
> *Headquarters Robinson's House, September 4, 1780*
Sir
> *You are to proceed in a barge with a flag, one sergeant, and seven privates to Fort Washington or other British post on the river, taking with you Mary McCarthy and her two children, late of Quebec,*

427

who have my permission to enter the British lines, where you are to
leave them and return without delay. [79]

Given under my hand,
B. Arnold

In the letter, Arnold informed Andre` of **Plan A**: that he would meet him at Dobbs Ferry on Monday the 11th at noon, that he requested Colonel Elisha Sheldon to serve as an escort, that he should be notified upon his arrival, that the meeting was for the interest of the public good, and that it was signed 'Gustavus' for security purposes. Arnold then gave orders to thirty-two year old Colonel James Livingston of the 2nd Canadian Regiment, who commanded at Verplank's and Stony Points, to "clear out" in case the British ascend up the river, giving them the least amount of resistance to take West Point.

To Colonel Livingston at King's Ferry
Headquarters Robinson's House, September 4, 1780
Dear Sir
His Excellency General Washington informs me that he is apprehensive that the enemy intend to attack on the posts in the Highlands. When that matter is ascertained and they appear in force, it is his intention to have Stony and Verplank's Points evacuated and the cannon royals and stores removed to this place, for which purpose I have by his orders sent down sixty flat-bottomed boats with five men in each under the command of Captain John Denny, of the bateaumen, who has orders to put himself under your command and follow your directions. Whenever the enemy appear in force near your post, and it is clearly demonstrated to you that they intend an attack on these posts, you will immediately embark all the troops, stores, cannon, &c., at King's Ferry and come with them to West Point. This measure is not to be taken precipitately or on any slight alarm; nor neglected so long as to risk anything or render it difficult to execute. As you are on the spot you will be the best judge of the time proper to execute it.

Perhaps n any movement of the enemy up the river it will be prudent to remove the stores to the landing, or put them in the boats, to be ready, so that no time may be lost in case the movement of the enemy should be rapid.

I am, Dear Sir, your obedient servant,
B. Arnold [33]

Andre`, wanting to close the long, drawn out deal as well, accepted his offer.

To Gustavus Monk

September 1780

Sir

The method would be arranged by my meeting you as flag of truce or otherwise as soon as you come near us. It is service of this nature, or intelligence having evidently led to such strokes, which S. H. C. looks for. It is such as these that he pledges himself and shall be rewarded beyond your warmest expectations. The color of the times favors them, your abilities, and firmness justify his hopes of success. In the meantime your influence might be generously, as well as profitably, employed in procuring the exchange of General Burgoyne's Army. It could be urged by none with more propriety, nor would you be sorry to see this act of justice superbly added to the shining revolution that you may perhaps be instrumental in effecting. [79]

I am, &c.,

John Anderson

On Wednesday the **6**[th], Washington held a council of war with his Generals at his headquarters at Tappan where he asked several questions in regards to a potential British attack on West Point, but Arnold was not present to answer. On Thursday the **7**[th], Arnold wrote a letter of introduction to Colonel Elisha Sheldon of the 2nd Dragoons, who was in charge of the forces watching the enemy's lines.

To Colonel Sheldon

Robinson House, 7 September

Sir

...I am sorry the person you refer to is not returned. I wish to see him as soon as he does, as I am in hopes through him to open a channel of intelligence that may be depended upon...

Since I saw you, I have had an opportunity of transmitting a letter to the person in New York of whom I made mention, and am in expectation of procuring a meeting at your quarters. If I can bring this matter about, as I hope, I shall open a channel of intelligence that will be regular and to be depended upon. [33]

I am with great respect & esteem, Dear Sir,

your obedient humble servant,

B. Arnold

Andre` also wrote a follow up letter to Sheldon, but the letter raised suspicion, because Sheldon never received Arnold's preceding letter, having been intercepted along with the memory of their previous conversation.

To Colonel Sheldon

September 7, 1780

Sir

I am told my name is made known to you, and that I may hope your indulgence in permitting me to meet a friend near your outpost. I will endeavor to obtain permission to go out with a flag, which will be sent to Dobbs Ferry on Monday next, the 11th, at twelve o'clock, when I shall be happy to meet Mr. G---. Should I not be allowed to go, the officer who is to command the escort, between and myself no distinction need be made, can speak on the affair. Let me entreat you Sir to favor a matter so interesting to the parties concerned & which is of so private a nature that the public cannot on either side be injured by it. I shall be happy on my part in doing any act of kindness to you in a family or property concern of a similar nature. I trust I shall not be detained; but, should any old grudge be a cause for it, I shall rather risk that than neglect the business in question, or assume a mysterious character to carry on an innocent affair and, as friends have advised, get to your lines by stealth. [79]

I am your most humble servant,

John Anderson

On the same day, Washington approved Arnold's "defense plan."

To M General Arnold

Headquarters Bergen County, September 7, 1780

Dear Sir

I have received your favor of the 5th enclosing your instructions to Col. Livingston, which perfectly comprehend my ideas of the rule of conduct, which is to be observed should the enemy come up the river in force. I hear nothing further of any extraordinary preparations, but our precautions should be continued, because if they do operate against you, it will be rapidly...

I am, &c.,

G. Washington

P. S. There are eight men of Colonel Putnam's Regiment, who were employed as bargemen by General Howe and left at West Point. You will be pleased to send them down to join their Regiment. [84]

On the 8th day, Arnold did not rest, but rather repeated his resentment towards Congress in a letter to Parsons along with a request to get his "mail" through.

To General Parsons
> *Headquarters Robinson's House, September 8, 1780*
Dear Sir
> *Your favor of the 5th instant I received yesterday and am very sorry to hear you are unwell. I hope soon to have the pleasure of seeing you here in perfect health.*
> *For some movements of the enemy the General was apprehensive they mediated an attack on his Army or their posts, which occasioned his order to you to take the command of the troops on the lines. General Schuyler, who was here two days since, informs me his fears on this head have subsided.*
> *Your observations on the resolutions of Congress I think perfectly just. I believe the Army in general are fully convinced that their wish and intention is to disgust and disband us in detail as soon as they can; their contracted politics and little souls will not suffer them to admire or reward the virtues they cannot imitate. I believe the officers will unite (as soon as they know the final resolution of Congress respecting the remonstrance) in some spirited measures, to do themselves justice. I recommended sending a small committee of a thousand or fifteen hundred men of all ranks in the Army to Congress to present a spirited but decent memorial setting forth their claims, and requesting immediate justice as far as the public are able. This measure I think would be attended with happy consequences to the Country; for if justice is not done to the Army their necessities will of course be left to the ravages of the enemy.*
> *I suppose by this time you have heard of the unhappy fate of our southern Army, who – if their danger has not been exaggerated by the fears of the doughty General* (Gates) *– are most probably departed, if not totally cut off, and the Southern States left entirely defenseless.*
> *A lady of my acquaintance had some trifling articles purchased for her in New York by Colonel Webb and Major Giles. By her desire, I have some little time since requested Sheldon to endeavor to get them out by one of his flags, which he promised to do,*

431

and gives me encouragement of their being sent out. They will be in a box or small trunk, if they come out when you are on the lines, I beg the favor of you to take care of them and send them to me. I am told there is a General order prohibiting any goods being purchased and brought out of New York, but as the goods were brought many months before the order was issued, I do not conceive they come under the intentions or spirit of it. However, I would not wish my name to be mentioned in the matter, as it may give occasion for scandal.

> *I am, with kind regards, your obedient servant,*
> *B. Arnold* [33]

In order to prevent any suspicion, Arnold then had his secretary, Colonel Richard Varick, take a letter for him written to Washington regarding the movement of troops to show both of them that he was respecting the chain of command.

To His Excellency General Washington
> *Headquarters Robinson's House, September 8, 1780*
Dear Sir
> *I do myself the favor to enclose your Excellency copy of a letter from Colonel Hay of the 5th instant. In answer to his letter I informed him that our force on the lines was already inadequate to the duty required to be done in that quarter and that I did not think it prudent to withdraw the two companies of Malcolm's Brigade without first advising with your Excellency on this subject; and that I should inform him of the result as soon as I was favored with your orders. I shall therefore be happy to receive your Excellencies directions as to this matter by the returning express.*

> *I have the honor to be, with every sentiment of regard and respect,*
> *your Excellency's most obedient and very humble servant,*
> *R. V. for B. A.* [33]

Sheldon notified Arnold of Anderson's letter on Saturday the 9th.

To Major General Arnold
> *Lower Salem, 9 September*
Dear Sir
> *Enclosed I send you a letter which I received last evening from New York, signed John Anderson. If this is the person you mentioned in your favor of yesterday, he must have had his information by your letter, as I never heard his name mentioned before I received this*

letter. I hope you will not fail meeting him at Dobbs Ferry; if you cannot meet him yourself, pray send some person that you can confide in. I am so much out of health that I shall not be able to ride that distance in one day. [1]

I am, &c.,

John Jameson

Arnold then responded to Sheldon on Sunday the **10**th, before spending a social evening at Smith's house, where he wrote a private reprimand to Andre`.

To Colonel Sheldon

Headquarters Robinson's House, September 10, 1780

Dear Sir

    I received last night your favor of yesterday. You judge right. I wrote Mr. Anderson on the 3rd instant, requesting him to meet me at your quarters and informed him that I had hinted the matter to you and that you would send any letter to me or inform me of his arrival. I did not mention his name in my letter to you, as I thought it unnecessary. I was obliged to write with great caution to him. My letter was signed Gustavus, to prevent any discovery in case it fell into the hands of the enemy. as you are unwell and I want to go to Verplank's Point to give directions in some matters there, I am determined to go as far as Dobbs Ferry and meet the flag. If Mr. Anderson should not be permitted to come out with the flag, and should find means to come to your quarters, I ask that you send an express to let me know, and send two or three horsemen to conduct him on his way to meet me, as it is difficult for me to ride so far. If your health will permit, I wish you to come with him. I am convinced of his inclination to serve the public; and if he has received my letter and in consequence thereof should come to your quarters, I make no doubt to fix on a mode of intelligence that will answer my wishes. If General Parsons has arrived, I wish you to show him my letter and tell him that my request is to have Mr. Anderson escorted to me. I have promised him your protection and that he shall return in safety. Please write me, by return of the express, through what channel you received Mr. Anderson's letter, and if your emissary has returned.

I am your obedient servant,

B. Arnold [1]

To Mr. John Anderson

Sept. 10, 1780

Dear Sir

I have received your letter of the 7ᵗʰ instant with your signature directed to Colonel Sheldon. From the tenor of your letter, I suspect my letter to you of the 7ᵗʰ instant has been interrupted and the answer dictated by the enemy in hopes of drawing you into a snare, for I cannot suppose you would be so imprudent as to trust a British officer, commanding a flag with our private concerns although of a commercial nature, you must be sensible that my situation will not permit my meeting or having any private interview with such an officer. You must therefore be convinced that it will be necessary for you to come or send some person you can confide in to Colonel Sheldon's quarters, to whom I have written requesting him to send a pilot with you to meet me which he has promised to do and will perhaps come himself. By no means hint to him or any other person your intentions in coming out as it may prevent our speculation, which can be of no consequence to any one but our selves.

If I have been mistaken and the letter directed to Colonel Sheldon was written by you, then I do by all means advise you to follow the plan that you propose of getting to our lines by stealth. If you can do it without danger on your side, I will engage you shall be perfectly safe here.

I am, Dear Sir, your obedient humble servant,
Gustavus [79]

On the morning of Monday the **11ᵗʰ**, Clinton wrote a holographed letter to Andre` sending him up the river.

To Major Andre`

11 Sept. 1780

Dear Andre`

Col. Robinson will probably go with the flag himself, as you are with him at the fore post, you may as well be of the party. You will find me on your return at Genl Knyphausen's.

Faithfully yours,
H. Clinton [79]

Bearing a flag from Clinton's headquarters, Robinson and Andre` rode horseback up to the north end of Manhattan, across the King's Bridge at Spuyten Duyvil, and boarded the *Vulture*, which sailed them up the Hudson to Dobbs Ferry. At about the same time, Arnold set out to meet Andre` from Smith's house. To cover this particular mission, Arnold wrote to Washington stating that he was performing some security exercises, while at the same time depleting the security of the fort.

To His Excellency General Washington
Dobbs Ferry, 11 September 1780
Dear Sir
Yesterday I had the honor to receive your Excellency's favor of the 7th and am very happy to hear such favorable accounts from the southward. I hope our affairs in that quarter will soon wear a more pleasing aspect than ever.

Colonel Sheldon complains to me that his horses are much worn down; and the inhabitants of Westchester complain that the country is not sufficiently guarded against the enemy. I have, therefore, sent Colonel Hay fifty men from West Point, as more eligible from taking them from the lines. Mr. Stephens informs me that there are one hundred hogsheads of rum at Springfield, but that teams cannot be procured to bring it on.

I came here this morning to establish signals to be observed in case the enemy come up the river. To give some directions respecting the guard boats, and to have a beacon fixed upon the mountain about five miles South of King's Ferry, which will be necessary to alarm the country. The one fixed there formerly has been destroyed.

There are some cannon at West Point, which are of little service, except for signal guns. I propose sending two of them to Colonel Gouvion, for that purpose, if agreeable to your Excellency. A supply of cattle, for some days, had arrived at West Point before I left it. I am informed that considerable numbers have been crossed at King's Ferry. I am in hopes the Army will be better supplied in future.

I have the honor to be, &c.,
Benedict Arnold [33]

When Arnold arrived at Haverstraw, he met up with Smith, who had inquired if there was any impropriety in inquiring the purpose of a series of flags that he had noticed passing back and forth along the bank assuming that if they were for an exchange of prisoners by cartel. Arnold responded that the business of the flags would be explained in a short time. Some time after Arnold had departed the shore with his eight bargemen; he came within sight of a British gunboat that was patrolling the area. Unaware of the nature of Arnold's meeting; the gunboat fired upon his barge, only missing it by inches, and chased it back to the western shore. Although no damage was done to the barge, Arnold barely escaped with his life before he reached the blockhouse at Sneden's Landing. Here he stayed for almost nine hours until sunset when he returned to the Smith House to meet Peggy and their new son, who had just traveled up from Philadelphia. Expecting the arrival of Gustavus at any moment, Andre` and Robinson waited in the blockhouse at Dobbs Ferry until sundown, but to no avail. Disappointed, they embarked onto the *Vulture* and headed back to New York. **Strike one.** On the **12th**, Arnold notified Washington that he had received his copy of the situation report, but would need more time to reflect on it, thus buying himself time to act on his true intentions. In addition, he secured the bargemen from the fort for his own use in case he needed to get out of Dodge in a hurry.

To His Excellency General Washington
              Headquarters Robinson House, 12 September 1780
Dear Sir

Last night, I had the honor to receive your Excellency's favor of yesterday, enclosing a copy of a council of war, held the 6th. I will endeavor agreeably to your Excellency's request, to transmit my opinion on the matters submitted, by the time required. I sincerely wish the situation of our affairs would admit my giving it with more decision than I am able to do at present.

The order, contained in the postscript of your Excellency's letter of the 7th, to send the eight bargemen of Colonel Putnam's regiment to join their regiment, I conceive to be on a supposition of their being idle at West Point. I beg leave to observe, that they are now employed as my bargemen; that all the militia oarsmen had, previous to the receipt of the order, been drafted and sent to different commands at King's Ferry and elsewhere, so that it is out of my power to procure a proper crew for my barge; for which reasons I have thought proper to detain them until I receive your Excellency's further orders on the subject.

I take the liberty of enclosing extracts of a letter from Colonel Hay, of the 9th, respecting flour, &c. I sincerely wish he may succeed in his endeavors to procure flour (of which I am doubtful) in the quantities he has requested, as I believe the requisition larger than (when all others are answered) the State can comply with.

About thirty bateau men, mentioned in Colonel Hay's letter, were sent down with Captain Denny to King's Ferry. As, in case of an evacuation of these posts, Colonel Livingston's garrison, with the troops sent down, will be sufficient to man the bateau, I think it will be best to order the bateau men to be sent to Fishkill. Your

Excellency's general orders of the 28ᵗʰ and 30ᵗʰ ultimo, from the Adjutant General, were received last evening and published in my orders of the day. [33]

I have the honor to be,
with the highest sentiments of regard & esteem,
your Excellency's affectionate & obedient humble servant,
Benedict Arnold

That same day in a letter to Greene, Arnold gloats about the retreat of Gates and suggests taking out Congress for failing to feed its troops properly.

To Major General Greene
Headquarters Robinson's House, September 12, 1780
Dear Sir
Your favor of the 7ᵗʰ conveying to me an account of our misfortunes to the southward was delivered to me on the 8ᵗʰ.

I am happy to find that General Gates' information was so ill founded. It is an unfortunate piece of business to that hero and may possibly blot his escutcheon with indelible infamy. It may not be right to censure characters at a distance, but I cannot avoid remarking that his conduct on this occasion has in no ways disappointed my expectations or predictions on frequent occasions, and not withstanding the suggestions of his friends that he had not retreated to the borders of Virginia, he must have been at a great distance and pretty secure from danger, as he had no advice of the retreat of the Maryland troops for at least four days.

Yours of the 8ᵗʰ by Captain Vanderhorst and Lieutenant McCall were delivered to me by those gentlemen on the 9ᵗʰ. I have endeavored to render their situations pleasing to them during their stay with me, which respect I shall always be happy to pay to any gentleman who entitles himself to your introduction and recommendation.

It is a matter much to be lamented that our Army is permitted to starve in a land of plenty. There is a fault somewhere; it ought to be traced up to its authors and if it was preferred they ought to be capitally punished. This is in my opinion the only measure left to procure a regular supply to the Army in the future.

Where shall I procure papers for the garrison, as well as my own office? No returns can be made till a supply is sent. Colonel Pickering in a letter of the 28ᵗʰ informs me that he had not yet received the stores into his hands or money to purchase any with.

With sentiments of the most sincere regard and affection,
I am, Dear Sir, your most obedient servant,
B. A. [33]

When Robinson returned to the area on Wednesday the 13th, Livingston wrote to Arnold with suspicions in mind.

Colonel Beverly Robinson has come to Tarrytown in a barge under pretense of a flag, but I think it more probable to reconnoiter the country. [79]

Livingston asked Arnold if he should send a force "to give them a check" to verify their intentions. [79] Arnold responded on the same day with advice that would clear the field so that he could meet with Andre`.

We ought to be exceedingly cautious how we venture small parties as low down as Tarrytown. I am well informed that the enemy generally comes out in force. [79]

In order to prevent getting shot at again, Arnold decided that it would be best if Andre` came to him and developed two new plans to meet him, one by land, the other by sea. To help establish a secure land passage for Andre` to take if he should choose to do so, Arnold wrote to twenty-six year old Major Benjamin Tallmadge of the 2nd Dragoons in command at North Castle. Born in Brookhaven, Connecticut, Tallmadge graduated from Yale as a tall and muscular young man with polished manners and a generous heart who served as superintendent of Wethersfield High School before entering the Revolution as a lieutenant and adjutant at the end of '76. Following his appointment to Washington's secret service, he fought in the battles of Long Island, White Plains, Brandywine, Germantown, and Monmouth.

To Major Tallmadge

September 13, 1780

Sir

If Mr. John Anderson, a person I expect from New York, should come to your quarters, I have to request that you will give him an escort of two horsemen, to bring him on his way to this place, and send an express to me, that I may meet him. If your business will permit, I wish you to come with him. [33]

I am, &c.,
B. Arnold, Major General

Arnold then made up a story to Sheldon, claiming that Anderson failed to appear.

To Colonel Sheldon
     Headquarters Robinson's House, September 13, 1780
Dear Sir
  Your favor of the 12th is now before me. A variety of circumstances confirm my suspicions that my letter to Mr. Anderson was intercepted by the enemy, and unanswered. I was at the Block House at Dobbs Ferry on Monday, agreeable to the mode pointed out in the letter and remained there till three o'clock in the afternoon; but saw no flag.
  I am sorry to hear that Mr. Hunter can furnish you with no material intelligence.
  It gives me pain to know your situation is aspersed and vilified by a person of Mr. Stoddard's character. I shall be happy to know of his being baffled in any unjust attempt of that kind.
      I am, with affectionate wishes,
      your very obedient and very humble servant,
        B. A. [33]

To insure that Andre` wouldn't be fired upon as he had been on the 10th, Arnold sent a request to Lamb to secure the riverbank.

To Col. Lamb
     Headquarters Robinson's House, Sept. 13, 1780
Dear Sir
  Two nine or twelve pounders are wanted in the redoubts at Dobbs Ferry, for the purpose of signal guns, as well as to keep off the enemy's boats, who come up almost every day and insult the post. You will therefore please to inform me by the bearer, whether there are none of the stocked pieces of those calibers, which are of no great service here; and that may answer the purpose mentioned at King's Ferry. The twelves will be most eligible, if to be spared.
          I am, &c.,
          B. Arnold [39]

On Thursday the **14th**, Arnold gave Washington his requested opinion from the council of war, which stretched from vague to confound to pessimistic, all in an attempt to persuade him to take no action at all, because change was in the air.

To His Excellency General Washington

September 14, 1780

Sir

In answer to your Excellency's questions, proposed to the Council of General Officers on the 6th instant, I beg leave to observe that, from the uncertainty of the arrival of the second division of the French fleet, as well as of their force, and from the fluctuating situation of our affairs, which may be totally changed in a short time, by a variety of circumstances which may happen, it appears to me extremely difficult to determine, with any degree of precision, the line of conduct proper to be observed.

If the second division of the French fleet may be soon expected, and their force, of which I am ignorant, will give us a decided superiority over the enemy as well by land as sea, I am of opinion every necessary preparation and disposition should be made to attack New York, provided we have a sufficiency of ammunition and military stores, and there is a prospect of the Army (when collected) being supplied with provision (the former I much doubt). But if there is not good reason to suppose the second division of the French fleet, with a force superior to that of the enemy, will arrive in the course of a month, I am of opinion no offensive operations can, with prudence, be undertaken this fall against New York; in which case, it is possible the enemy will detail a part of their force in New York to join those in South Carolina, or to cooperate with those in Virginia or Maryland.

I am, therefore, of opinion, that the Pennsylvania line, which I suppose to amount to twenty-five hundred or three thousand men, should hold themselves in readiness to march; and if the same division of the French fleet does not arrive by the first of October, that then the Pennsylvania line should march to the relief of the Southern States, who, with the aid of so formidable a regular force here, if they do their duty, will be able to repel the enemy in that quarter; and, if the French fleet should arrive too late to operate against New York, South Carolina may be an object worthy of their attention.

Without a decided superiority by sea, I am of opinion no offensive operations against the enemy can, with prudence, be undertaken this fall; and, it is to be hoped, that the States, by this time, are convinced of the necessity of immediately raising an Army during the war, and that they will, without loss of time, take future measures for that purpose. I should suppose the Pennsylvania line might be replaced by some of the troops at Rhode Island, before the time is expired for which the militia are called out.

I have the honor to be with the highest respects, your Excellency's most obedient and very humble servant,

B. Arnold [33]

Plan B. Arnold arrived at Smith's house later that morning and flattered him with expressions of the highest confidence and regard to help Arnold meet a person of consequence from New York with valuable intelligence from the enemy. He then persuaded Smith to obtain a boat and an oarsman to row down the river to Dobbs Ferry on the night of the 20th, retrieve a gentleman named Anderson from the *Vulture,* and deliver him to Smith's house, where he would meet with him on the following day. Arnold wrote to Andre` on the morning of Friday the **15th** before leaving for his headquarters and offered him an alternative plan if he chose to pursue it.

To Mr. John Anderson

Sept. 15, 1780

Dear Sir

On the 11th at noon agreeable to your request, I attempted to go to Dobbs Ferry, but was prevented by the armed boats of the enemy who fired several times upon us and continued opposite the ferry until sunset. The forgoing letter was intended as a caution to you not to mention your business to Colonel Sheldon or any other persons. I have no confident, I find I have made one too many already, which has prevented several profitable speculations.

Lieutenant Colonel Jameson commands the lines in the room of Colonel Sheldon. If you think proper to pursue your former plan, you will be perfectly safe in coming to his quarters or those of Major Tallmadge of his regiment. Either of those gentlemen will immediately send an escort with you to meet me. **(Plan C.)** *If you have any objection to this plan, I will send a person in whom you may confide to meet you at Dobbs Ferry on Wednesday the 20th between 11 & 12 o'clock at night, who will conduct you to a place of safety by water where I will meet you. It will be necessary for you to be disguised and if the enemy's boats are there, it will favor my plan, as the person is not suspected by them. If I do not hear from you before you may depend upon the person being punctual at the place before mentioned.*

My partner of whom I hinted in a former letter (Washington) *has 10,000 pounds cash in hand ready for a speculation* (10,000 ready troops) *if any should offer which appears profitable. I have about 1,000 pounds on hand* (troops at West Point) *and can collect 1,500 more in two or three days. Add to this, I have some credit. From these hints you can judge of the purchase* (capture) *that can be made. I cannot be more explicit at present. Meet me if possible. You may rest assured that if there is no danger in passing your lines, you will be perfectly safe where I propose the meeting; of which you shall be informed on Wednesday evening if you think it proper to be at Dobbs Ferry.*

Adieu and be assured of the friendship of,

Gustavus [79]

Plan D. Later, Arnold received his last letter from Washington, written the previous day, revealing his itinerary to have Arnold escort him to Peekskill, where he would depart to meet with Rochambeau and Ternay in Hartford, Connecticut, and then see Arnold back at Robinson's. This intelligence inspired yet another opportunity to take the fort if he were able to capture the commander.

To M General Arnold

Headquarters Bergen County, 14ᵗʰ September, 1780

Dear Sir

I have received your favors of the 11ᵗʰ and 12ᵗʰ instant. I have no objection to your sending down the two pieces of cannon to Colonel Gouvion. Under the circumstances you mention, you may detain the men of Colonel Putnam's regiment, who are serving as bargemen to you; and, if you can with convenience withdraw the bateau men, sent down to King's Ferry, it will be a measure entirely agreeable to me. I hope Colonel Hay's plans for obtaining a supply of flour from the State of New York, and his application to the people of the grants, will both meet with success. He is a faithful and indefatigable officer.

I am, Dear Sir, your most obedient and humble servant,

G. Washington

P. S. I shall be at Peekskill on Sunday evening on my way to Hartford, (Connecticut) *to meet the French Admiral* (Ternay) *and General* (Rochambeau). *You will be pleased to send down a guard of a captain and 50 at that time, and direct the quartermaster to have a night's forage for about 40 horses. You will keep this to yourself, as I want to make my journey a secret.* [33]

But Arnold did not keep it to himself, instead he rushed a message of the trip to Andre`, considering that the arrest of Washington would assure the attainment of West Point.

To John Anderson

September 15, 1780

Sir

General Washington will be at King's Ferry Sunday evening next on his way to Hartford, where he is to meet the French Admiral and then will lodge at Peekskill. [79]

Gustavus

On Saturday the **16**[th], prior to receiving Arnold's last letter to him, Robinson boarded the sixteen gun *Vulture* in New York and sailed up the Hudson to Croton under a flag of truce to observe the Rebel troops cross the river while Washington was at Hartford. Its covert mission was for Robinson to find out why the meeting at Dobbs Ferry had failed to take place on Monday and arrange for another one. In order to inform his counterpart of his visit, Robinson wrote a feigning letter to General Putnam in care of Arnold, announcing that he had arrived in the highlands and wished to have a conference with him regarding a private affair. Knowing that Putnam was in fact not in the area, he asked if Arnold would be willing to see him if the General was not available and included a ciphered message regarding their previous appointment.

To Gustavus Monk

September 16, 1780

Sir

I have been greatly disappointed in not seeing Mr. Smith at the time appointed, being very anxious to conclude our business, which is very necessary should be done without delay. [38]

I am, &c.,
Beverly Robinson

Wanting to keep the fort strong, Washington instructed Arnold to have Lamb use smaller guns for smaller tasks.

To Colonel Lamb

Headquarters Robinson's House, September 16, 1780

Dear Sir

443

Having received his Excellency's approbation of my proposal to send two pieces of artillery to the officer commanding at Dobbs Ferry, I am to request that you will order two of the stocked nine-pounders with their apparatus complete, and fifty rounds round shot, and a few shots of grape to each, to be put on board one or two bateaus and sent down under care of a proper officer and party, to the officer commanding at Dobbs Ferry.

I am with sincere regard and esteem, Dear Sir, your obedient servant,

B. A. [33]

In order to buy himself more time to put his offensive plan into action before Washington could effect a defensive one, Arnold promised to see him in person regarding that very issue. It was also the last letter that Arnold would submit to his Commander-in-Chief as an American soldier.

To His Excellency General Washington

Headquarters Robinson's House, September 16, 1780

Dear Sir

Last evening I was honored with Your Excellency's favor of the 14ᵗʰ.

I have given orders for the guard requested, as also to the quarter-master to furnish forage at Mr. Birdsall's for the number of horses mentioned in your Excellency's letter.

My answer to the questions proposed by your Excellency relative to the council of war I will do myself the honor to deliver in person.

I am, with sentiments of the most profound respect and esteem,

your Excellency's most obedient servant,

B. Arnold [33]

On the afternoon of Sunday the **17ᵗʰ**, Arnold had invited Smith, his wife, and their two nephews to the house for a visit on their way to Fishkill. Other guests included the Army surgeon and Harvard graduate, Dr. William Eustis, who treated casualties at Bunker Hill and in his hometown of Cambridge; Colonel Return Jonathan Meigs, who commanded Fort Meigs with the 6ᵗʰ Connecticut at West Point, and Colonel Lamb, who donned a patch over one eye from an injury sustained at Quebec. Prior to their arrival, Arnold reminded Franks that the two of them would be riding to the Smith House to meet with Washington for dinner before accompanying him to Peekskill, where he would leave for Hartford. Varick interjected by warning Arnold not to have anything to do with that "snake in the grass Smith," because he was a "damn tory." [33] After Smith arrived with his family, a message was delivered during lunch to Arnold from Robinson reporting aboard the British sloop *Vulture*, now off Teller's Point at Croton. Robinson's letter explained that he was very anxious to make terms for the recovery of his estates (making the exchange with Arnold), and that he was authorized to propose through his medium, some preliminary grounds for an accommodation between Great Britain and America.

To Major General Arnold
               On board the Vulture, off Tellers Pt., September 17, 1780
Sir
       Having heard that Genl. Putnam is at the Highlands on a visit to you, I have obtained Sir Henry Clinton's leave to come up in this ship to endeavor to have an interview with him. As I understand, you command in the Highlands and make your headquarters at my house, to which I am persuaded that I could be so happy as to see you. But for prudential reasons I dare not explain the matter further until I have some assurances that it shall be secret if not granted. I did intend in order to have your answer immediately to have sent this by my servant, James Coburn with a flag to you, but thinking he might be stopped at Verplank's Point, I leave it to the officer commanding there, desiring it may be forwarded to you as soon as possible. [79]
                                                            I am, Sir, &c.,
                                                            Beverly Robinson

Plan E. Arnold pondered the proximity the vessel being just six miles south of Washington's scheduled landing at Peekskill and the potential of having Robinson on board. He remarked to his guests that Robinson wanted to see him, which brought about a great protest from Lamb, who thought it improper of Robinson, a tory, to ask for a conference with an American officer. Fearing that a meeting might raise suspicions, he suggested that Arnold show the letter to Washington later that afternoon. Arnold agreed. After Smith left, Varick expressed a warning to Arnold regarding his guest as a spy and suggesting that he not associate with him. Arnold brushed his concerns aside claiming that he would never put Smith in a position to hurt either him or the country.

Arnold and Franks crossed the river to land at King's Ferry and rode to Smith's house to meet with Washington, Knox, Lafayette, along with their aides, Hamilton, Captains Samuel Shaw and James McHenry for their dinner meeting. At twenty-one, Shaw hailed from Boston, working in his father's counting house before receiving a second lieutenant's commission in the artillery at the start of the Revolution in which he served with intelligence, activity, and bravery at Trenton, Princeton, Brandywine, Germantown, and Monmouth. After immigrating to the colonies from his native Ireland, McHenry attended the Newark Academy in Delaware to seek out his poetic abilities, but in finding too few of them, he moved to Philadelphia to study medicine under Dr. Benjamin Rush. Once the shooting had begun between England and America, McHenry immediately offered his skillful hands as a staff member in a military hospital in Cambridge and as a surgeon in the field where he was taken prisoner during the fall of Fort Washington. Following his release from captivity, he served as the "Senior Surgeon of the Flying Hospital at Valley Forge, where he was soon appointed as a secretary to Washington before being recently transferred to Lafayette.

Afterwards, the officers set out for Peekskill and crossed the Hudson on Arnold's barge with nineteen guards. During the trip, Arnold shared the letter that he had received from Robinson, requesting a meeting with him regarding the use of his home, but Washington declined the request on the grounds that it was a civil matter, not a military one and that it would be improper for an officer to be present at a meeting with a loyalist and recommended that a representative be sent instead. **Strike two.** Washington then commented on the *Vulture's* proximity to the fortifications while viewing it through a telescope, but Arnold assured him that the river was safe and handed over his report of the fortifications at West Point as promised. A French squadron under the great sixty-eight year old naval tactician, Count de Guichen was expected each day to appear on the coast, but was not to be found upon this crossing. Recalling Robinson's request to meet with Arnold, Lafayette had turned to him and joked, "General Arnold, since you have a correspondence with the enemy, you must ascertain as soon as possible what has become of Guichen." [69] Arnold, who was noticed to be uneasy and emotional, abruptly demanded to know what he meant by that remark, but then took account of his emotions and regained his composure. Lafayette looked at him with both surprise and confusion, and before he could reply, the boat reached the dock and the officers disembarked onto the shore. The party spent a peaceful night in Peekskill, for Clinton was not able to respond to the kidnapping conspiracy in time. **Strike**

three. On the morning of Monday the **18**[th], Arnold responded to Robinson's request.

To Colonel Beverly Robinson

September 18, 1780

Sir

I have received a letter from you of yesterday's date, with one for General Putnam, and have consulted with his Excellency General Washington on the subject of them, who is of opinion, that any application respecting your private affairs in this country ought to be made to the civil authority of this State, as they are entirely out of the line of the military. However willing I may be to oblige Colonel Robinson on any other occasion, it is not in my power to do it in this instance. General Putnam left this place some days since. I have, therefore, agreeably to your request, returned the letter addressed to him.

If you have any other proposals to make, of a public nature, of which I can officially take notice, you may depend on it, that the greatest secrecy shall be observed, if required, as no person except his Excellency General Washington shall be made acquainted with them. The bearer, Captain Archibald, will take particular care of your letters and deliver them to me in his own hand.

I am, Sir, &c.,

B. Arnold [79]

Upon his departure for Connecticut, Washington announced that he would return in one week to spend the night at Arnold's headquarters and inspect the fortifications at West Point. Arnold inquired as to the precise day of his return, to which Washington pondered and answered, five days. With that, he and his entourage headed out for Hartford, without incident. **Plan F.** While en route back to his headquarters, Arnold considered the possibility of having Washington captured during his upcoming visit to the Robinson House as Peggy served him an endless feast. He then hastened back to his headquarters and wrote to Robinson to explain the dilemma along with the new opportunity. To introduce Smith as the person with whom Andre` could confide, Arnold addressed the envelope to Joshua's brother William, with a note stating that Robinson may view the contents.

To Beverly Robinson

September 18, 1780

Sir

I parted with his Excellency General Washington this morning, who advised me to avoid seeing you, as it would occasion suspicions in the minds of some people, which might operate to my injury. His reasons appear to me well founded, but I was of a different opinion for I could not see you at present. I shall send a person to Dobbs Ferry or on board the Vulture on Wednesday night the 20th *and furnish him with a boat and a flag of truce. You may depend on his secrecy and honor, and that your business of whatever nature shall be kept a profound secret. If it is a matter in which I can officially act, I will do everything in my power to oblige you, consistent with my duty. To avoid censure, this matter must be conducted with the greatest secrecy. I think it will be advisable for the Vulture to remain where she is until the time mentioned. I have enclosed a letter for a gentleman in New York* (Andre`) *from one in the country* (Arnold) *on private business, which I beg the favor of you to forward, and make no doubt he will be permitted to come at the time mentioned.*

I am, Sir, &c.,

B. Arnold

I expect his Excellency General Washington to lodge here on Saturday night next, and will lay before him any matters you wish to communicate. [79]

In the same envelope, Arnold included a confirmation letter to Andre` stating that he will be met by boat in Dobbs Ferry on the 20th.

To John Anderson

September 18, 1780

Sir

I will send a person in whom you can confide by water to meet you at Dobbs Ferry at the landing on Wednesday the 20th *instant who will conduct you to a place of safety where I will meet you. It will be necessary for you to be disguised, and if the enemy boats are there, it will favor my plan, as the person is not suspected by them. If I do not hear from you before you may depend upon the persons being punctual at the place above mentioned.* [38]

I am, &c.,

Gustavus

Arnold then rode to Smith's house and mentioned that he had received another flag of truce from Robinson offering an interview

448

"to be more explanatory of propositions to produce a general peace if acceded to by Congress." [66] He added that this would "happily terminate the expense of blood and treasure that were ruinous to both countries, in the prosecution of a war without an object." [66] He went on to claim that he was tired of the war and the disrespect from members of Congress and Pennsylvania for not appreciating his services. Gesturing to his leg he said, "Here I am after having fought the battles of my country and find myself with a ruined constitution and a useless limb. Where am I to seek compensation for the damages I've sustained at the end of this war?" [38] Smith inquired as to whether he proposed the invitation to Washington, but Arnold explained that he had gone to New England to confer with Rochambeau and revealed his detestation of the French alliance. Believing that they projected "a dishonest national character and elaborating on his point by ridiculing the impropriety and inconsistency of an absolute monarch being the ally of a people contending for freedom, who kept his own subjects in absolute slavery." [66] He considered the union between the two nations to be unnatural and non-enduring, because the coalition was not made until France saw that Americans were able to defend themselves, which would only add to their own national honor and glory. On the morning of Tuesday the 19th, Arnold returned to his quarters and Smith rode north to visit his family, whom he had sent off to Fishkill for a vacation with other relatives in order for Arnold to have use of his house. Meanwhile, Robinson acknowledged Arnold's message and agreed to talk to him at a better time.

To General Arnold

Vulture, off tellers Point, 19 September, 1780

Sir

I am favored with yours by Captain Archibald, and am sorry I have missed the opportunity of seeing General Putnam, and that it is not thought proper to allow me to see you, my business being entirely of a private nature, only concerning myself, and no ways affecting public matters of either side. I was induced to make the application to you in hopes of meeting with a favorable reception from a gentleman of your character. But I have not the least reason to expect any civility from the civil authority of this State; neither am I at all disposed to ask any favor from them.

Had I known General Washington was with you, I should certainly have made my application to him, as I flatter myself I should be allowed every reasonable indulgence from him. I beg my best respects may be presented to him. I can have nothing further to say to you at present, but must wait a more favorable opportunity of doing something for my family.

I return you my thanks for your polite letter and civil expressions to me,

and am, &c., [68]

Beverly Robinson

Arnold wrote to Livingston to take away all boats in the river to clear it for the arrival of the British.

To Colonel James Livingston

Headquarters Robinson's House, September 19, 1780

Dear Sir

I am advised by Captain Archibald, who is returned with a flag from the Vulture British man-of-war, that the Captain thereof had informed him he had since his coming up the river taken up forty flat-bottom boats which have driven down from your posts above you past your water-guards. Captain Archibald also informs me that a number are lying on shore between your posts and Teller's Point. You will please to order those within your power to be immediately collected, drawn on shore and properly secured, and pointedly enjoin the most proper attention and vigilance with respect to the boats remaining at your posts and that may hereafter drive down from the posts north of you, and punish any neglect of, or inattention to, your orders in this respect in an exemplary manner.

I am also informed that the two pieces of artillery, which I ordered to be sent from this post to Dobbs Ferry, were put on board a sloop instead of bateaus. As it is probable the boat will not be able to go down while any of the enemy's armed vessels remain in the river, I think it advisable to put them in bateaus and send them down to the commanding officer at Dobbs Ferry the very first favorable opportunity.

His Excellency informs me that Colonel Spencer's regiment is on its march to reinforce your post. As soon as that arrives you will send an equal number of the troops who were detached from hence in the bateaus, to this post without delay.

I am, Dear Sir, with sentiment of esteem, your obedient servant,

B. A. [33]

Arnold then sent a message to New York with the help of two tory women whom he had issued passes for.

By the Honorable Benedict Arnold, Esquire,
Major General in the Army of the United States,
commanding in a separate department.
Permission is granted to Messengers Nathaniel Garrison,
Thomas Bullas, Jacob Sharpstone, and Isaac Filkins to proceed in
four wagons with two horses each, with a flag, by the shortest route
from the post to the nearest British post at King's Bridge; taking with
them Mary Ham, wife of Frederick Ham, with three children, the
eldest seven years old; Lucy German, wife of Isaac German, and one
child eight years old; Mary Munger, wife of ------ Munger, and her
child, three years old; Sarah Munger, wife of ------ Munger, and her
child, two years old; and Elizabeth German, wife of ------ German,
with her two children, the eldest seven years old; who have my leave
to pass into the British lines where they the said Garrison, Bullas,
Sharpstone, and Filkins are to leave them and return with their horses
and wagons without delay.
Given under my hand at Headquarters Robinson's House
September 19, 1780
By the General's command,
R. V.
Secretary [33]

In the evening, Clinton held a banquet as a parting compliment
to Andre` at the Kip Mansion in New York now the corner of Second
Avenue and Thirty-fourth Street. During the course of the celebration,
the band played the favorite dinner air, "The Roast Beef of England"
and many of his fellow officers sang popular drinking songs between
toasts in his honor. Clinton made the final toast claiming, "A word in
addition, gentlemen, if you please. The major leaves the city on duty
tonight, which will most likely terminate in making plain John
Andre`, Sir John Andre`, for success must crown his efforts." [63] Just
after dinner, Clinton conferred in private with Andre` to give him
three explicit instructions; do not change your dress as proposed by
General Arnold, do not go within the American posts, and do not
carry any communications.

451

XIII
Haverstraw

On the cloudy morning of Wednesday the 20th, Andre` left New York for Dobbs Ferry on horseback, yet it wasn't until he arrived that he learned that the *Vulture* had moved up to Croton, about ten miles beyond the British lines. To secure his safe arrival, Andre` arranged for a gunboat to take him up the river to the sloop and embarked at around seven in the evening, greeted by Robinson and Captain Andrew Sutherland. Earlier that morning, some Americans had raised a white flag on the eastern shore and Sutherland sent out a boat assuming that Arnold was trying to send a message. To his surprise, Sutherland soon learned the first rule of spec war; never assume, for as the boat approached the shore, the Americans fired their muskets on it and drove it back to the *Vulture*. Although Clinton had sent orders along with Andre` for Sutherland to pull the sloop back to Dobbs Ferry, Arnold had requested him to remain at Tellers Point in order to send a trusted emissary that evening. The three officers on board conferred and concluded to stay, but little did they know that they were sitting in harm's way. That very afternoon, a skeptical message from Lamb had accompanied some ammunition that Livingston had requested to shoo off the Vulture.

To Colonel Livingston

West Point, 20th Sept. 1780

Sir

I have sent you the ammunition you requested, but at the same time, I wish there may be not a wanton waste of it, as we have little to spare.

Firing at a ship with a four pounder is in my opinion a waste of powder; as the damage she will sustain is not equal to the expense. Whenever applications are made for ammunition, they must be made through the commanding officer of artillery at the post where it is wanted.

I am, Sir, your obedient servant,
John Lamb [39]

Smith had stopped back to the Robinson House as Arnold had requested and was issued a pass to obtain a light boat for the night from Major Edward Kierse, the quartermaster at Verplank's Point.

Headquarters Robinson House, September 20, 1780

Permission is given to Joshua Smith, Esquire, a gentleman, Mr. John Anderson, who is with him, and his two servants, to pass the guards near King's Ferry at all times.

B. Arnold, M Genl. [59]

Smith verbalized the impropriety of conducting a flag at night, deeming it unprecedented, but Arnold overruled his objection with the assurances that it was properly understood on board the *Vulture,* and that the business was of a nature not to be generally known for the present among the citizens. Smith agreed to help without much enthusiasm and met his cousin, Colonel James Livingston at Fort Lafayette in Verplank. The fort consisted of a stone redoubt and a square wooden tower to observe the southern gate to the highlands. Smith presented his pass and was informed that Kierse was across the river at Stony Point. Once there, Kierse explained that no boats were available. He then forged on to ask the local residents for one and by sundown, came upon a tenant farmer named Samuel Cahoon while gathering his cows. Samuel was unable to help him with a boat or the oars, but had agreed to deliver a letter to Arnold after Smith urged him to take on the "great business." [66] Meanwhile as the night passed, Andre` paced the deck of the sloop for a time until he felt the uneasiness of raising potential suspicion with the sailors, which forced him to go below. **Strike four.** When he awoke on the morning of Thursday the **21**[st], Andre` feigned illness in order to attempt another meeting later that night and wrote an open letter to Clinton explaining his ailment as the reason for his postponement.

To His Excellency Sir Henry Clinton

21st *Sept. 1780*

Sir

As the tide was favorable on my arrival at the sloop yesterday, I determined to be myself the bearer of your Excellency's letters as far as the Vulture. I have suffered for it, having caught a very bad cold, and had so violent a return of a disorder in my stomach, which had attacked me a few days ago, that Captain Sutherland and Colonel Robinson insist on my remaining on board till I am better. I hope tomorrow to get down again.

I have the honor, &c.,
John Andre` [79]

An enclosed letter to Clinton explained the real reason for Andre`'s delay being that Arnold still hadn't shown up.

To His Excellency Sir Henry Clinton
On board the Vulture, 21ˢᵗ Sept. 1780
Sir
    I got on board the Vulture at about seven o'clock last evening; and after considering upon the answer given by Colonel Robinson, that he would remain on board, and hoped that I should be up. We thought it most natural to expect man I sent into the country here, and therefore did not think of going to the ferry. Nobody has appeared. This is the second excursion I have made without an obvious reason, and Colonel Robinson both times of the party. A third would infallibly fix suspicious. I have therefore thought it best to remain here on pretence of sickness as my enclosed letter will feign and try further expedients. Yesterday the pretence of a flag of truce was made to draw people from the Vulture on shore. The boat was fired upon in violation of the customs of war. Capt. Sutherland with great propriety means to send a flag to complain of this to General Arnold. A boat from the Vulture had very nearly taken him on the 11ᵗʰ and pursued him close to the shore. I shall favor him with a newspaper containing the Carolina News, which I brought with me from New York, for Anderson to whom it is addressed on board the Vulture.
I have the honor, &c.,
John Andre [79]

    Andre˙ then acted as a secretary for Sutherland in a letter to Livingston, complaining of the violation of a flag of truce the day before when the boat was fired upon. When shown the letter, Arnold recognized Andre˙'s handwriting and realized that he was aboard the vessel.

To Major General Arnold
Vulture off Teller's Point, Sept. 21, 1780
Sir
    I consider it as my duty to complain of any violation of the laws of arms and I am satisfied that I now do it where I cannot fail to meet redress. It is therefore with reluctance, I give you the concern to know that a flag of truce having been shown yesterday on Teller's Point. I sent a boat towards the shore presuming some communication was thereby solicited. The boat's crew on approaching received a fire from several armed men who until then had been concealed. Fortunately none of my people were hurt, but the

455

treacherous intentions of those who fired are not vindicated from that
circumstance.

I have the honor to be Sir,
your most obedient and most humble servant,
A. Sutherland [79]

Robinson also expressed his disappointment to Arnold for failing to appear a second time.

To Major General Arnold

Sept. 21, 1780

Sir

I have been greatly disappointed in not seeing Mr. Smith at the time appointed, being very anxious to conclude our business, which is very necessary should be done without delay. I can now make a final settlement with him, as my partner (André`) *upon receipt of the letter I forwarded to him yesterday immediately set off from New York and arrived here last night. If Mr. Smith will come here we will attend him to any convenient and safe place.* [79]

I am, Sir, &c.,
Beverly Robinson

After riding through the night, Samuel arrived at the Robinson House early in the morning, delivered the letter (stating that Smith had not succeeded) to one of Arnold's aides, and told that he did not need to wait for an answer. **Plan G.** Enraged, Arnold decided to secure a boat himself and set out in search of Kierse. Upon finding him and requesting a boat, he and was again informed that none were yet available. Arnold left orders that as soon as one was available, it was to be sent right off to Hay's Landing at Minisceongo Creek, and to "let Mr. Smith or himself know by express, for Mr. Smith was going for intelligence of some importance." [38] He added that the guards were to be notified that Smith had permission to pass anytime of the day or night. Arnold found Smith back at the house when he returned and once again encouraged him to secure oarsmen for the evening.

Smith set out and encountered Samuel and brought him back to Arnold who asked him to go with Mr. Smith apiece that night. Samuel said that he could not go, because he was fatigued from having been up the night before delivering the message to Arnold. Arnold said that if he was a friend of his country then he should do his best. When Samuel asked where they were going, Arnold answered, to the ship in the river to retrieve a man that he wanted to see very much. Samuel asked what the meeting was about, but Arnold said that he could not say until morning. Samuel then raised concerns about making the trip at night adding that he was always willing to render any service to the General when he could do it with propriety and would not object to going with a flag in the morning. Arnold replied that the morning would to be too late, that there was a gentleman on board the vessel whom he must see that night and must be brought to shore. Arnold continued by saying that the business at hand was of utmost importance to the country and that if Samuel was a friend to his country, then he would not hesitate a moment to comply with the request. Samuel stated that he felt that a night errand was risky and irregular, but Arnold assured him that the matter was not a secret, yet well known to the officers and the guard boats who knew the countersign and would allow passage to the boat that has been provided by Major Kierse. When Samuel asked why the trip could not wait until morning, Arnold informed him that he did not want the meeting to be generally known to the inhabitants, for it would defeat the whole object of the plan. Samuel then countered that he could not manage the boat such a distance by himself, but Smith made the simple suggestion to fetch his brother, Joseph, to assist him with the task. Samuel agreed and left for his home, but returned without his brother, explaining that he had spoken to his wife who forbade him to go. Arnold sprang from his seat and smashed his fist on the table threatening that he would have both brothers arrested as disaffected men, to which Samuel, having no choice, agreed and descended the stairs escorted by Smith.

When the two brothers returned, Smith met them outside the house. Joseph then raised the same concerns, as did his brother before regarding the time of the trip, the river guard, and the reason for going. Smith repeated the same responses that Arnold had given to Samuel earlier, stating that he had a pass from General Arnold for a private meeting of general business with a gentleman on shore and if anything should come against either one of them, he would represent them as legal council. Smith went inside to bring Arnold out to speak to Joseph as he continued to have reservations about going. Arnold came outside and repeated what he had said to his brother earlier and added that he would pay them fifty weight of flour as an added inducement for their cooperation. He then took their silence as an acceptance and suggested to Joseph that he ride down to the ferry and see if the boat had arrived yet, but Joseph refused out of arrogance and told Smith to send his servant instead. Arnold returned to the inside of the house as Smith's servant rode down the road by horse and met a messenger on the road with a dispatch stating that the boat had arrived. Not knowing this, the Cahoons decided to decline the General's request for a midnight river run, but didn't know how to tell him. When the servant returned with the message, they realized that they better cancel the arrangement now. Joseph approached the porch and Smith summoned him in to see Arnold who was seated at a desk. Joseph sat down and Arnold announced that the boat had arrived and that they will be making the trip that evening. Joseph explained to Arnold that he and his brother felt that it was too late and that they would rather make the trip in the morning. Arnold stood up to tower over him and told him that he had to be back at his headquarters by ten the next morning and that if he refused to help his country then he would place him under arrest. The intimidation was brief, but effective, and Joseph concurred to make the trip. Arnold then asked Smith to call for Samuel and poured a drink for the four of them to seal the deal and calm their nerves.

Well after dark, the four men emerged from the house with Arnold speaking in a hush tone to Smith, cautioning him to instruct the boatmen to say nothing to the sailors on board the ship. He then approached the brothers and instructed them to take sheepskins to muffle the oars to avoid detection by the American water patrols. This brought about an alarm to Samuel who exclaimed that if the business was of an honest nature as Arnold declared it to be, then he saw no need to disguise their approach and row to the vessel in the middle of the night. Arnold then assured them that he had command of the country for sixty miles around West Point and had given countersign to the guard boats so that they would have no trouble in passing the patrols. Smith then thrust a sheepskin into each of the brothers' hands without saying a word. The three then set out for Hay's Landing located a mile to the east and boarded a boat to retrieve a man named Anderson, shoving off at about midnight.

With muted oars under a dark sky, they forded the three-mile span to the *Vulture*. As they approached the sloop a voice bellowed out asking where they were from and where they were going. Smith called back from the tiller, "from King's Ferry to Dobbs Ferry." [38] The officer then barked an order followed by a threat, "spring your luff and come alongside, you son of a sea cook, or I'll deaden your headway before you can say your prayers." [63] "Coming up alongside," Smith exclaimed as they positioned themselves parallel with the sloop to enable Smith to climb up a rope ladder to the deck above. [66] The officer questioned his business and how he could presume to come on board his Majesty's ship under color of flag of truce at night. He responded that he was so authorized by his papers, which he requested to be presented to Captain Sutherland and Colonel Robinson. The officer yelled at him threatening to hang him from the nearest yardarm to which Smith replied that the officer would be answerable for his being delayed. Soon afterwards a boy came on deck and reported, "The Captain orders the man below." [66] Smith was then escorted into a cabin where he met Sutherland and Robinson and presented his pass along with Arnold's letter for Anderson.

> *Headquarters Robinson House, Sept. 21, 1780*
> *Permission is granted to Joshua Smith Esq., to go to Dobbs Ferry with three men and a servant to carry some letters of a private nature for gentlemen in New York, and to return immediately. He has permission to go at such hours and times as the tide and his business suits.* [79]
>
> *B. Arnold, M Genl*

To John Anderson
> *September 21ˢᵗ 1780*

Sir
> *This will be delivered to you by a Mr. Smith, who will conduct you to a place of safety. Neither Mr. Smith nor any other person shall be made acquainted with your proposals. If they are of such a nature that I can officially take notice of them, I shall do it with pleasure. If not you shall be permitted to return immediately. I take it for granted Colonel Robinson will not propose anything that is not for the interest of the United States as well as himself.*
>
> *I am, Sir, &c.,*
> *B. Arnold* [79]

Robinson perused the letters from Arnold as Smith related his rude reception on deck to Sutherland, who compensated him with pleasant civility. Robinson then handed the letter to Sutherland, excused himself, and left to get Anderson, who was asleep. Smith passed the time conversing with Sutherland who lay ill on his bunk reading Arnold's letters. When Robinson returned, Andre' had donned a long, navy blue cape over his uniform and after receiving

459

Sutherland's acknowledgement to go ashore, Andre` followed Smith down the rope ladder to the boat waiting below while the oarsmen held it steady. Seeing that only two men were rowing the boat, Robinson offered to have the boat towed by an armed barge, but Smith made a strong objection, deeming that to be an infringement of the flag. As the Cahoon brothers rowed against the tide of the river, Andre` was growing closer and closer to his fateful rendezvous with Arnold that forever changed the tide of history.

At close to two o 'clock in the morning of the **22nd**, the boat's keel met pebbled sand near Kierse Dock at the foot of Long Cove Mountain. Smith's servant then escorted Smith up the river road to a clump of fir trees where Arnold was waiting. Arnold raised his lantern, acknowledged him, and directed him to bring Anderson up to the meeting site and then to wait with the Cahoons at the boat. Smith was both mortified and displeased with this direction, thinking that he would be attending the meeting after all of the pains taken and sacrifices made to bring the meeting about. Arnold repeated the order, to which Smith turned away from the insult and walked back down the hill.

The details of the meeting can only be speculated, but it could not have gotten off to a good start when Arnold learned that Andre` was only commissioned to promise him 6,000 pounds sterling. Arnold must have been angered because of all the time that he spent to negotiate that he would be paid half of the 20,000 pounds sterling up front as a down payment for his services, risk, and the potential loss that he would sustain in case a his plans were discovered and he were forced to take refuge in New York. Andre` stated that he was convinced of the reasonableness and assured him though he would use his influence with Sir Henry to allow the sum proposed to which he had no doubt that he would agree. The two then discussed the benefits and dilemmas of attacking the fort while Washington was in the post, but decided that it would be best attempted if Arnold was in command at the time. Arnold displayed six papers containing information on the troops, ordnance, artillery orders, and fortifications. The only thing that he did not have was a map. With these plans in hand, Arnold would have explained the details of each area while Andre` brought up the problems that he foresaw in his own attack plan and the two worked out solutions to overcome them. After two or three hours of their meeting, they hadn't noticed the coming of dawn being under the trees, but Smith had made his way up the hill to warn them of it. Andre` made his way to the riverbank, but the Cahoon brothers stated that they were too tired to make another trip against the tide, which had changed during the meeting, and having concluded that with time and tide against them, they were sure to be seen. A historical marker for the treason site can be found 100 feet south of Riverside Avenue along the Hook Mountain State Park trail in Haverstraw.

Artillery Orders:
The following disposition of the corps is to take place is case of an alarm.

Capt. Daniels with his Company repair to Fort Putnam,
detach an officer with 12 men to Wyllys Redoubt,
a non-commissioned officer with 3 men to Webb Redoubt,
and the like number to Redoubt No. 4.

Captain Thomas and Company to repair to Fort Arnold.

Captain Simmons and Company to remain at the North and South Redoubts at the east side of the river until further orders.

Lieut. Barber with 20 men of Captain Jackson's Company will repair to Constitution Island; the remainder of the company with Lieut. Masons will repair to Arnold.

Capt. Lieut. George and Lieut. Blake with 20 men of Capt. Treadwell's Company will repair to Redoubt No. 1 & 2, the remainder of the company will be sent to Fort Arnold.

Late Jones' Company with Lieut. Fisk to repair to the South Battery.

The Chain Battery, Sherburne's Redoubt, and the brass field pieces will be manned from Fort Arnold. As occasion may require.

The commissary and conductor of military stores will in turn wait upon the commanding officer of artillery for orders.

The artillery officers in the garrison, (agreeable to former orders) will repair to Fort Arnold and there receive further orders from the commanding officer of artillery, S. Bauman, Major Commt. Artillery.

Estimate of the forces at West Point and its dependencies, Sept. 13th 1780

A brigade of Massachusetts Militia & two regiments of rank & file New Hampshire Inclusive of 166 Bateaus Men at Verplank's and Stony Points.	*992*
On command & extra service at Fishkill, New Windsor, etc, etc who may be called in occasionally.	*852*
3 regiments of Connecticut Militia under the Command of Colonel Wells on the lines near N. Castle.	*488*
A detachment of New York levies on the lines.	*115*
Militia	*2,447*
Colonel Lamb's Regiment	*167*
Colonel Livingston at Verplank & Stony Pts.	*80*
Continental	*247*
Colonel Sheldon's Dragoons on the lines, ½ Mounted	*142*
Bateau Men and Artificers	*250*
Total	*3,086*

Estimate of the number of men necessary to man the works at West Point & in the vicinity, Sept. 1780.

Fort Arnold	*620*
Fort Putnam	*450*
Fort Webb	*140*
Fort Wyllys	*140*
Reboubt No. 1	*150*
Redoubt No. 2	*150*
Redoubt No. 3	*120*
Redoubt No. 4.	*100*
Redoubt No. 5	*130*
Redoubt No. 6	*110*
Redoubt No. 7	*78*
North Redoubt	*120*
South Redoubt	*130*
Total	*2,438*

Villefranche, Engineer
(The artillery men are not included in the above estimate.)

Return of Ordnance in the Forts & Batteries at West Point and its dependencies, Sept. 5th, 1780.

S. Bauman, Major Comdt. Of Artillery

Forts

Arnold	Garrison Carriage	– 1 Iron 24 lb., 6 / 18 lb.
	Stocked Carriage	– 1 Iron 12 lb.
	Travelling Carriage	– 1 Brass 4 lb., 3 Iron 3 lb.
	Mortars	– 5 Brass 10", 5 / 5", 1 / 4"
Putnam	Garrison Carriage	– 5 Iron 18 lb., 2 / 12 lb.
	Travelling Carriage	– 2 Brass 5 lb., 1 / 4 lb.
	Mortars	– 4 Brass 5"
V. Pt / S. Pt	Travelling Carriage	– 1 Iron 18 lb.
	Stocked Carriage	– 2 Iron 12 lb.
	Mortars	– 2 Brass 5", 1 / 4"
	Howitzers	– 1 Iron 8"
Con. Isl.	Garrison Carriage	– 4 Iron 12 lb., 1 / 9 lb., 5 / 6 lb.

Batteries

South	Garrison Carriage	– 4 Iron 18 lb., 1 / 12 lb.
Chain	Garrison Carriage	– 1 Iron 12 lb.
	Stocked Carriage	– 2 Iron 12 lb.
Lanthorn	Garrison Carriage	– 2 Iron 9 lb.

Redoubts

No. 1	Garrison Carriage	– 1 Iron 12 lb., 4 / 9 lb.
No. 2	Garrison Carriage	– 2 Iron 9 lb.
No. 4	Garrison Carriage	– 2 Iron 6 lb.
Meigs	Garrison Carriage	– 1 Iron 6 lb.
	Travelling Carriage	– 1 Iron 4 lb.
North	Garrison Carriage	– 3 Iron 18 lb., 3 / 12 lb.
Sherman	Garrison Carriage	– 2 Iron 6 lb.
	Stocked Carriage	– 3 Iron 6 lb.
South	Garrison Carriage	– 1 Iron 12 lb., 4 / 6 lb.
Webb	Garrison Carriage	– 1 Iron 12 lb., 1 / 4 lb.
	Stocked Carriage	– 2 Iron 6 lb.
Wyllys	Travelling Carriage	– 2 Iron 18 lb., 3 / 3 lb.

Fort Arnold - built of dry fascines, wood in a ruinous condition, incomplete, and subject to take fire from explosive shells.

Fort Putnam – The stone is wanting great repairs, the wall on the east side broke down and rebuilding from the foundation at the west and south sides have been a spiked barricade on the west side broke in many places. The east side is open, two bomb proofs, a provision magazine, and a slight wooden barrack. A commanding piece of ground lies 500 yards west between the fort and Redoubt No. 4, Rocky Hill.

Fort Webb – Built of facings and wood, a slight work, very dry and liable to be set on fire as the approaches are very easy, without defenses save a slight spiked barricade.

Fort Wyllys – Built of stone 5 feet high and 15 feet thick, the work above plank is filled with earth 9 feet thick. No bomb proofs among the batteries within the fort.

Redoubt No. 1 – On the south side, wood is 9 feet thick, the west, north, and east sides are 4 feet thick. No cannon in the works, a slight and single abattis, no ditch or picket. Cannon on two batteries, no bomb proofs.

Redoubt No. 2 – The same as No. 1, no bomb proofs.

Redoubt No. 3 – A slight wood work 3 feet thick, very dry, no bomb proofs, a single abattis, easily set on fire, no cannon.

Redoubt No. 4 – A wooden work about 10 feet high and 4 or 5 feet thick, the west side faced with a stone wall 8 feet high and 4 feet thick. No bomb proof, two six pounders, a slight abattis, a commanding piece of ground 500 yards west

North Redoubt – On the east side of the river built of stone 4 feet high, above the stone, wood filled in with earth, very dry, no ditch, a bomb proof, three batteries without the fort, a poor abattis, a rifling piece of ground 500 yards south of the approaches under cover to within 20 yards. The work easily fired with faggots dipped in pitch etc.

South Redoubt – Much the same as the north, a commanding piece of ground 500 yards due east, 3 batteries without the fort.

At a Council of War, held in Camp Bergen County,
Sept. 6th, 1780   Present – The Commander-in-Chief
The Commander-in-Chief states to the council, that since he
had the honor of laying before the General officers, at Morristown,
the 6th of June last, a general view of our circumstances, several
important events have occurred, which have materially changed the
prospects of the campaign.

That the success expected from France, instead of coming out
in one body and producing a naval superiority in these seas, has been
divided into two divisions. The first of which only consisting of seven
ships of the line, one forty-four and three smaller frigates, with five
thousand land forces, had arrived at Rhode Island.

That a reinforcement of six ships of the line from England
having reinforced the enemy, has made their naval force in these seas
amount to nine sails of the line. Two fifties, two forty-fours, and a
number of smaller frigates, a force completely superior to that of our
allies and which has in conference held them blocked up in the harbor
of Rhode Island till then 29th. Ultimately at which period the British
fleet disappeared and in no advice of them has since been received.

That accounts received by the alliance frigate, which left
France in July, announces the second division to be confined in Breft
with several other ships by a British fleet of thirty-two sails of the line
and a fleet of the allies of thirty-six or thirty-eight ships of the line
ready to put to sea from Cadiz to relieve the Port of Breft.

The most of the states in their answers to the requisitions
made of them, give the strongest assurances of doing every thing in
their power to furnish the men and supplies required for the expected
cooperation. The effect of which, however, has been far short of our
expectations, for not much above one third of the levies demanded for
the Continental Battalions, nor above the same proportion of militia
have been assembled, and the supplies have been so inadequate that
there was a necessity for dismissing all the militia, whose immediate
services could be dispensed with to lessen our consumption,
notwithstanding which the troops now in the field are severely
suffering for want of provision.

That the Army at this post and in the vicinity in operating
force consists of 10,400 Continental troops and about 400 militia,
besides which is a regiment of Continental Troops of about 500 at
Rhode island left there for the assistance of our allies, against any
attempt of the enemy that way and two Connecticut State Regiments
amounting to 800 at North Castle.

467

That the times of service for which the levies are engaged will expire on the first of January, which if not replaced, allowing for the usual casualties, will reduce the Continental Army to less than 6,000 men.

That since the state to the council above referred to, the enemy have brought a detachment of about 3,000 men from Charleston to New York, which makes the present operating force in this quarter between ten and eleven thousand men.

That the enemies force now in the southern states has not been lately ascertained by any distinct accounts, but the General supposes that it cannot be less than 7,000 (of which about 2,000 are in Savannah) in this estimate, the decrease by the casualties of the climate is supposed to be equal to the increase of force derived from the disaffected.

That added to the loss of Charleston and its garrison accounts of a recent misfortune are just arrived from Major General Gates, giving advice of a general action, which happened on the 16th of August near Camden, in which the Army under his command met with a total defeat and in all probability the whole of the Continental Troops and a considerable part of the militia would be cut off.

That the State of Virginia has been sometime exerting itself to raise a body of 3,000 troops to serve till the end of December 1781, but how far it has succeeded is not known.

That Maryland had resolved to raise 2,000 men of which a sufficient number to compose one battalion was to have come to this Army. The remainder to recruit the Maryland Line, but in consequence of the latest advice, an order has been sent to march the whole southward.

That the enemy's force in Canada, Halifax, St. Augustine, and at Penobscot, remains much the same as stated in the preceding council.

That there is still reason to believe the Court of France will prosecute its original intention of giving effectual succor to this country as soon as circumstances will permit; and it is hoped the second division will certainly arrive in the course of the fall.

That a fleet greatly superior to that of the enemy in the West Indies and a formidable land force had failed sometime since from Martinique to make a combined attack upon the Island of Jamaica, that there is a possibility of a reinforcement from this quarter also to the fleet of our ally at Rhode Island.

The Commander-in-Chief having thus given the council a full view of our present situation and future prospects, requests the opinion of each member in writing, what plan it will be advisable to pursue, to what objects our attention ought to be directed in the course of this fall and winter, taking into consideration the alternative of having or not having a naval superiority, whether any offensive operations can be immediately undertaken and against what point, what ought to be our immediate preparations and dispositions, particularly whether we can afford or ought to fend any reinforcements from this Army to the southern states, and to what amount the General requests to be favored with these opinions by the 10th instant at farthest. [3]

Having agreed to return to the sloop on the following evening, the officers mounted their horses and made their way to Smith's house, about six miles away during the early morning hours of Friday the 22nd. Arnold sent Smith to return the boat to the dock at Crom Island in Minesceongo Creek with the Cahoons. Along the road, a sentry challenged Arnold and Andre` with a password, which Arnold countered with the proper response, "Congress," and they continued on. [1] Andre`'s nervous tension was well justified for he now realized that he was behind enemy lines.

Just as the two officers arrived at the Smith House, cannon fire echoed through the Hudson Valley. They turned to see a puff of smoke from coming Teller's Point. Under the command of Livingston, two local militiamen named John Peterson and George Sherwood had fired upon the sloop for over staying her welcome. The *Vulture* returned fire and within moments a ship to shore battle had ensued. At the dock, Smith and the Cahoons watched with indignation as they realized that had they returned to the sloop, they would have fall victim to the bombardment. Arnold and Andre` also watched with the same astonishment from the porch of the Smith House before Arnold rushed Andre` inside the house to an upstairs bedroom with a window that provided a clear view of the engagement.

Arnold met Smith and the Cahoons in the back yard when they returned and sent the Cahoons home, then asked Smith to serve breakfast in the upstairs bedroom. While inside, Andre` removed his cloak, revealing his British uniform, as Arnold used the daylight to once again point out the details of the fortifications. When Smith entered with breakfast, his expression showed a mix of confusion and surprise as he gazed upon Andre`'s attire. In haste, Arnold explained that it was borrowed from a friend who was a military acquaintance and worn out of harmless vanity. An explanation which Smith accepted. Feeling uneasy that things were not going according to plan, Andre` passed up the offer for breakfast as he and Arnold watched the battle for ninety minutes. Just when they thought things couldn't get any worse, they did, between seven and eight o'clock the tide rose, enabling the *Vulture* to fill her sails and retreat down river out of Andre`'s sight and grasp. **Strike 5.** As delay is the deadliest form of denial, Andre`'s failure to return to the ship in time, stripped him of his sanctuary. Unbeknownst to them, the sloop had only gone down as far as Ossining on the other side of the Croton peninsula. The *Vulture's* log gave an assessment of the damage done to both sides.

"The standing and running rigging shot away in many places, two of the iron stantions on the gangway broke by their shot, several of their shells broke over us and many of the pieces dropped on board." [54]

This was the toughest shot that Arnold had taken, because Lamb had borrowed the money to build this artillery unit from him. He then instructed Andre` to destroy the papers in the event that any accident should befall him. Andre` agreed and explained that he would have them tied to a string and a stone once he got into the boat. Arnold then explained that he would not be able to return by boat, but would have to return by land. Andre` argued, but Arnold reminded him that he had already been fired upon in daylight and assured him that more patrol boats would be out that evening after the skirmish. After a moment of silent contemplation, Andre` accepted the idea, feeling stripped of any other option available to him. Arnold then directed him to conceal the papers in his stocking and would make arrangements for Smith to escort him across the river by ferry and continue on by horseback. Arnold placed each of the six papers into an envelope and handed them to Andre` who inserted three into his right sock and three into his left. **Plan H.** Arnold then instructed Smith to escort Anderson to White Plains in order to meet a man to transact some other public business. A historical marker for the "Treason House" can be found along Route 9W in front of the Helen Hayes Hospital in Haverstraw. A historical marker honoring Sherwood and Peterson can be found on a boulder between the river and the pavilion in Croton Point Park.

XIV
Yorktown

After breakfast, Arnold wrote out permission slips for Smith and Anderson.

Headquarters Robinson House, Sep. 22, 1780
Joshua Smith Esq. has permission to pass the guards to the White Plains, & to return, being on public business by my direction.

B. Arnold, M General

Headquarters Robinson House, Sep. 22, 1780
Permit Mr. John Anderson to pass the guards to the White Plains or below if he chooses, he being on public business by my direction.

B. Arnold, M. General[5]

While analyzing the situation to anticipate further problems, Arnold realized that it would be impossible for Anderson to travel through Northern Westchester to White Plains in a British uniform and that it would be imperative for him to change his clothing. Arnold gave Andre` a black horse with a white star on its forehead and a Continental Army brand on its shoulder. He then asked Smith to lend Anderson a coat for the trip. Being of the same size, Smith agreed and gave him a purple cloak along with a black bowler-type beaver hat with a wide brim. Andre` shed his uniform coat and donned cloak given to him over his own blue cloak. Smith placed Andre`'s hat and coat in a bedroom closet. The delay was one fear factor, but it only added to his concern about breaking the three distinct orders given to him upon his departure by Sir Henry Clinton: do not change your dress, do not place yourself within the American posts, and do not carry any communications.

As Smith accompanied Arnold to his barge at Stony Point, Arnold recommended that he and Anderson make a nighttime passage, but left it up to Smith's discretion as to what route he would return him to White Plains. When Varick realized that Arnold wasn't coming home the prior evening, he shared his suspicions with Franks that his absence was further proof that Smith was not a man of loyal character. They referred to him as an "avaricious man who surely had some commercial plan in agitation with some people in New York under the sanction of his own command and through the rascal

Smith." [33] When they shared their concerns with Arnold's wife, she pleaded that he would never do anything dishonorable, but would influence him to stop seeing Smith. In private, the two officers pledged to each other that they would leave him if their doubts were confirmed.

Andre`, wanting to get the mission over with, spent a nervous morning trying to convince his host to row him to the sloop now, but Smith was more concerned about the gun boats that were sure to be on their guard. Although visitors stopped at the house throughout the day, Andre` avoided any contact. After a short dinner at sundown, the two set out with Smith's servant for Stony Point about two and a half miles away. As they approached the area, Smith questioned Andre` about Anthony Wayne's capture of the fort, but Andre` declined to answer under the stress of the moment. Just before arriving, they chanced upon Major John Burrowes who had charge of the guard of the lower end of Haverstraw. Smith made small talk with him, which only added to the stress felt by Andre`, but soon excused himself to attend to business that he had to take care of, and rode off.

As a sentry challenged them at the ferry entrance, both men displayed their passes and leaned down to present them. After the guard waved them on, the two men dismounted and walked their horses down the path to the dock. Upon seeing Smith, some of Livingston's officers and the ferrymen hailed him to come and share a drink with them. Smith approached and entered the tent and did so while passing a minute of time with Captains William Jameson and William Cooley. Andre` took a seat near the bow of the boat, a blank stare written on his face. When Smith approached the boat, he again made animated conversation with the crew as he offered them "something to revive their spirits" if they made haste in the crossing. [38] The ferrymen; Cornelius Lambert, Lambert Lambert, William Van Wart, and Benjamin Acker nodded a vigorous agreement along with their coxswain, Henry Lambert and made swift strokes towards the other shore.

Upon arriving at the King's Ferry landing at Verplank's Point, Smith paid Henry Lambert eight dollars and then stepped into Livingston's tent at Fort Lafayette just off the dock. Livingston looked up and asked him where he was going and Smith explained that he was on his way to the Robinson House adding that he would also be seeing the Governor at Poughkeepsie. Livingston asked him to

474

deliver a dispatch to Arnold and George Clinton along with offering him supper and a drink. Smith declined explaining that his companion had urgent business to get on with and had to catch up with him on the Ferry Road. Livingston wished him well and Smith departed, receiving his horse from his servant. A historical marker for King's Ferry can be found at the foot of Broadway in Verplank.

Andre`, Smith, and his servant continued onward through the dark to the Post Road, which led into the area of Lent's Cove through Peekskill to the Crompond Road and rode unchallenged until they reached the area of Crompond, about eight miles east of the river where they encountered a small patrol of Westchester militia. A sentry called out, "who goes there?" to which Smith called out, "friends." [38] He dismounted, handed his reins to Andre`, and asked for the commanding officer. Captain Ebenezer Boyd of the 3rd Westchester Militia emerged from his guardhouse and had inquired as to who they were, where they lived, and why were they traveling at night. Smith introduced himself and his fellow traveler, Mr. Anderson. He explained that he lived in the white house on the other side of King's Ferry, and that he and his companion had passes from General Arnold to pass the guards. Boyd then asked him what time they crossed the river, what there destination was, and how far they intended to travel that night. Smith replied that they had been ferried over at dusk and had hoped to stop at the home of Major Joseph Strang, whom he described as a staunch friend to the cause of his country, who would treat them well and render every aide in his power that tended to promote the welfare of America. Boyd informed him that the major was not at home and that it would be an inconvenience to seek lodging from his wife who was assured to be asleep. Smith remarked that he then might try his friend Lieutenant Colonel Gilbert Drake, but Boyd remarked that he had moved to Salem. Boyd asked to see the passes and stepped inside to examine them in the light, which brought Andre` to show a sense of uneasiness, but Smith assured him that Arnold's passes were certain to protect them.

Boyd emerged from the house moments later satisfied with the passes and returned them, but insisted upon knowing the nature of the business that would propel them to travel through the night. Smith told him that he was the brother of Chief Justice William Smith in New York and that he and his companion were in General Arnold's employ to meet a man at White Plains and obtain some intelligence from the British Army as soon as possible. Boyd warned him of the troubled conditions between the lines and that travel by night was dangerous for cowboys from the British posts and local bandits had infested the roads below the Croton River. He then explained that the cowboys and bandits had driven off cattle and taken some farmers prisoner adding that the trio had little chance of defending themselves against the two parties as he had heard some shots fired a short time before they arrived. He then urged them to return to the Andreas Miller House in Yorktown, which was located about a third of a mile East of Crompond Road on Old Crompond Road, and get an early start in the morning. Smith discussed the situation to Andre` who was eager to continue on, but Smith convinced him that if they did not stop for the night, they might be intercepted.

When they arrived at the Miller House, Smith knocked a number of times until Andreas appeared, heard Smith's plea for refuge, and accepted them inside. The two men were brought to a guest bedroom that held a single bed as Miller explained that he could provide sleeping accommodations, but no food for cowboys had raided his farm leaving him with barely enough to feed his wife and children. There was no rest for the weary as Smith recalled the remains of that evening, saying, "I was often disturbed with the restless motions, and uneasiness of mind exhibited by my bedfellow, who on observing the first approach of day, summoned my servant in the barn to prepare the horses for our departure." [66]

XV
Tarrytown

After extending a few dollars gratuity to their host, Andre`, Smith, and his servant set out again on the morning of Saturday the 23rd of September 1780, under an ominous gathering of clouds in the sky. Further on down the road, a sentry halted them at Crompond Corners, where the Somerstown and Salem Road branched from the highway leading to Pines Bridge, the present location of Crompond Road and Hallocks Mill Road. Smith presented the passes to assistant deputy commissary, Captain Ebenezer Foote, a man in his early twenties, who was stationed at the site of Mead's Tavern and asked him where troops were posted on the lines. Foote informed him that the only soldiers on duty were the Second Continental Dragoons at Wright's Mill. Smith asked for directions and was directed to proceed to a fork located one half mile beyond Pines Bridge and take the left road to the mills, for the other road led to Sing Sing and Tarrytown.

The three men continued on and stopped to have breakfast at the home of Isaac and Sarah Underhill, near Cat Hill in the Pines Bridge area of Yorktown. When they finished their meal, Smith paid Mrs. Underhill and the three prepared to depart. A historical marker for the Isaac Underhill House can be found at the intersection of Hanover Street and California Road in Yorktown Heights. Andre` appeared to feel better after a breakfast of corn mush because he rode with cheerful serenity, entertaining Smith and his servant with his knowledge of the history of New York and America, which he referred to as the residuary legatee of the British government. He lamented the causes which gave birth to and continued the war, and said if there was a correspondent temper on the part of the Americans, with the prevailing spirit of the British ministry, peace was an event not far distant. It was here, just fifteen miles north of White Plains that Smith notified Andre` that they were now beyond the American outposts and that he would accompany him no farther, but would visit family up north in Fishkill. Andre` asked Smith for some money to which Smith gave him eight Continental dollars after dividing the amount in his pocket and a rough map of the area south of Pines Bridge, which he folded and slipped into his boot. Andre` offered Smith his gold watch as a keepsake, but Smith declined the gift, and instead, gave him a message to deliver to his brother William.

Smith headed back toward Peekskill and then turned north through Continental Village and onward to the Robinson House, where he informed Arnold of the progress that had been made. Arnold was well pleased that the plan had at last been completed and offered Smith to join him for the noonday meal. When a servant informed Peggy that they had run out of butter, Arnold exclaimed, "Bless me! I had forgot the olive oil I bought in Philadelphia. It will do very well with salt fish." [33] When Franks complimented the General on its taste, Arnold insisted that it should, for it cost eighty dollars. Smith replied, "eighty pence," referring to the declined value of the continental dollar. [33] Varick snapped, "That is not true, Mr. Smith!" [33] The officers argued with the attorney at length until Peggy asked them all to drop the matter. Varick, feeling ill all of a sudden, excused himself and entered his room.

When Smith left following dinner, Arnold entered Varick's room with Franks and reprimanded him for his behavior against his guest proclaiming, "If I had asked the devil himself to dine with me, the gentlemen of his family should be civil to him." [33] Franks responded with a sharp tone, cursing Smith, exclaiming that, "If he was not at the General's table, then I would have thrown the bottle at him and would thereafter treat him as a rascal." [33] He continued, stating that he had observed that Arnold had viewed every part of his conduct with an eye of prejudice and thus begged Arnold to discharge him from his family. He then left headquarters in a huff to travel to Newburgh on business, while Varick remained behind cursing Smith as a "damned rascal, a scoundrel, and a spy and my reason for affronting him was because I thought him so." [33] He then added that his advice to Arnold had proceeded from a regard to Arnold's reputation, which Arnold had repeated in confidentiality that he wished to stand well in this state, and which Varick had very often told Arnold that he would suffer by an improper intimacy with Smith. Arnold responded that he was "always willing to be advised by the gentlemen of his family but, by God, would not be dictated by them; that he thought that he possessed as much prudence as the gentlemen of his family." [33]

Later, Varick received a letter from Lieutenant Colonel Benson of Governor Clinton's staff responding to an inquiry by Varick regarding Smith's character, which Benson reported, was not a favorable one. He showed the letter to Arnold as proof of his reservations and declared Arnold's past conduct and language

478

towards him as unwarranted, that he felt that Arnold did not place confidence in his advice, and that he could no longer act within his capacity with propriety. Thinking that he had concluded his private matter with Smith, Arnold responded by giving Varick the assurance of his full confidence in him, a conviction of the integrity of his conduct, an agreement to his opinion of Smith's character, admitting to treating him with cavalier language, and declaring that he would never associate with Smith again.

Andre' continued on down the road that is now Saw Mill River Road (Route 100), crossed over the Pines Bridge, turned South on the present Seven Bridges Road and Quaker Street (Route 120), then traveled to Underhill's Corners and approached the house of Stevenson Thorne at the intersection of Kipp Street. Seeing a boy on top of a woodpile, he asked his way to Tarrytown to which the boy jumped off and sought out his father inside. Thorne emerged from the house, approached the horseman, and instructed Andre' to continue west down Kipp Street to Hardscrabble Road. Andre' obliged and carried on until he reached the house of Sylvanus Brundage on Hardscrabble Road just north of Pleasantville Road to water his horse. After a short break, he rode down Bedford Road (Route 117) through Rossell's Corners a.k.a. McKeel's Corners and turned down Old Saw Mill River Road to Hawthorne and stopped again at Sergeant Staats Hammond's House on present day Route 100 C, to get himself a drink of water from fourteen and twelve year old David and Sally Hammond, who were playing at a well. While Sally fetched the water, Andre' asked David if any scouts were to be seen along the road to White Plains. David said that there were. After quenching his thirst, he thanked Sally for the water, gave her a sixpence and then thanked David for holding his horse and asked "How far is it to Tarrytown?" [59] "Four miles," replied the boy. [59] "I did not think it was so far," said Andre'. [59] With a tip of his hat, he turned and headed back to the corners and turned west on Bedford Road to what is now Route 448 to Tarrytown Heights.

Unbeknownst to him, seven members of the 1st Westchester Militia in their early twenties named Sergeant John Paulding, James Romer, Isaac See, Isaac Van Wart, Abraham Williams, and Sergeant John Yerkes had convened at Yerkes' Tavern in North Salem. At the tavern, they set off on a scouting mission in the retrieval of cattle that were stolen by the British. After passing the house of Joseph Benedict, they were joined by twenty-five year old David Williams from Tarrytown who had served under Montgomery in Canada. Setting out in a southwest direction, they spent the night sleeping in John Andrews' hay barn in Pleasantville. Continuing on to Tarrytown, they stopped at the house of James Romer where Fanny Romer fixed them breakfast and a basket dinner. Afterwards, Paulding made a stop at the home of Isaac Reed to borrow a pack of playing cards. The men then split up into two groups with Paulding, Isaac Van Wart, and David Williams to cover the Post Road along the river to New York, while the others covered the old Bedford Road on Davis Hill to the northeast.

A short time later and just five miles north of his objective, Andre` was reading his map as he crossed over a small bridge spanning Clark's Kill, now called Andre` Brook, and chanced upon Van Wart playing sentry at the base of a hill, while Paulding and Williams played cards under a tulip tree. Van Wart announced, "Here's a horseman coming," to which they stood up, grabbed their muskets, and blocked the road, pointing their weapons in his general direction. [21] Andre` noticed that Paulding, who stood taller than the other two, was wearing a red faced green coat and a green fatigue hat of a Hessian soldier, which he had used as a disguise to escape from a British prison one week earlier. Thinking that these men were loyalists, Andre` stuffed the map back into his boot and announced; "Gentlemen, I hope you belong to our party." [21] "What party" asked Paulding. [21] "The lower party," replied Andre`. [21] Paulding noticed the white topped chamois boots that Andre` wore and replied, "We do." [21] "Thank God! I am once more among friends. I am a British officer," he announced as he pulled his timepiece from his pocket adding, "to show you that I am a (British) gentleman, here is my gold watch." [21] Paulding then exclaimed, "We are Americans." [21] When Andre` sensed that the men were not really loyalists as he had presumed, but rebels, he then chuckled with a charming smile while blushing and exclaimed, "God bless my soul, a man must do anything to get along." [21] Paulding asked, "What is your name?" to which Andre` replied, "John Anderson." [1] He handed Arnold's pass to Paulding and added, "I have been up in the country on particular business and would not wish to be detained a single moment." [21] Paulding read each word aloud and then ordered Andre` to "stand." [21] Andre` proclaimed, "Gentlemen, you had best let me go or you will bring yourselves in trouble, for by your stopping me, you will detain the General's business." [21] Paulding responded, "We care not for that," and took him down from his horse. [21] Paulding asked him his name to which he replied John Anderson, referring to the pass. "Damn Arnold's pass," Van Wart shouted, "Where is your money?" [60] "I have none about me," replied Andre`. [60] "You a British officer and no money?" Van Wart challenged, "Let's search him." [60]

Williams removed some fence rails to allow Paulding and Van Wart to escort him into the woods and then replaced the rails to avoid any suspicion from other passersby. "I hope you will not be offended and we do not mean to take anything from you," Paulding explained, "but there are many bad people going along the road, and I do not know if perhaps you might be one." [69] While gathered around a whitewood tree, Van Wart ordered him to undress, he obeyed by handing each article of clothing to Williams who gave them a thorough search. The trio retrieved his gold watch and eight Continental dollars, which seemed to satisfy them and bring a wry smile to Andre`'s face until Williams ordered him, "Take off your boots." [69] Andre`'s expression melted. He swallowed, removed one boot, and handed it to Williams, who searched it. Finding nothing inside, he handed it back to Andre`, but when he raised his foot to put his boot back on, one member of the trio noticed a bulge in the bottom of his sock. Williams ordered him to remove his sock, which he did with hesitation and revealed three papers hidden inside. Paulding, being the only one able to read, perused the papers in his hands and exclaimed, "My God," raising his eyes to Andre`, "he's a spy." [22] Upon searching the other sock, they found three more papers. "Where did you get these papers?" inquired Paulding. [1] "Of a man at Pine's Bridge, a stranger to me," Andre` said shaking. [1] "What would you be willing to give us if we let you go," Williams asked. [1] "Any sum you want," Andre` pleaded. [1] Williams asked him, "A hundred guineas, with the horse, and your watch?" [1] "Yes, and the money shall be sent here if you want," Andre` replied. [1] "Will you not give more?" asked Williams. [1] "Yes," said Andre` with a nervous smile, "any quantity of dry goods." [1] Paulding studied the papers and then suggested that he be taken to the nearest outpost. [1] Van Wart and Williams looked at each other for a moment in silent consideration until one of them offered, "Well, a bird in the hand is worth two in the bush." [1] **Strike 6.** A historical marker and monument to Andre`'s captors can be found along Route 9 just north of the Tarrytown Library.

XVI
North Castle

Andre` was put back on his horse and followed by his three musket toting captors close behind him. It literally rained on Andre`'s parade as steady drizzle formed while the trio escorted him up the trail and met with the four other cowboys. While declaring what part of the prize each would claim, Andre` noticed their thirst for money and offered that if they took him to Kingsbridge, they would be paid in a handsome way. The cowboys were quick to retort that if they were to be drawn in by that, then he would be sure to have them arrested and lose their money. Andre` offered that they hold him under guard while one of them went to the British lines and procured as much as one thousand guineas. After several minutes of debating, the trio felt that their chances of reward were better with their own officers than with the British and decided to proceed onward. As they departed their comrades, Yerkes called out to Andre`, not to make any attempt to escape, for if he did, he was a dead man. With a solemn voice, Andre` said, "I would to God that you had blown my brains out when you stopped me." [21] Having forgotten their lunch amidst the excitement of the capture, the group returned to the Romer House for a brief stop where Paulding announced, "Take care what you say, Aunt Fanny; I believe we have a British officer with us." [1] The four then forged on along Nepperhan Road (Saw Mill River Parkway), making stops at Reed Tavern, also known as the Landrine House, near the lakes in East Tarrytown; the Foshay House along Lakeview Avenue below Kensico; and the Rueben Wright House at Kensico for brief meals of bread and milk. Andre` was offered, yet replied, "Oh madam, it is all very good, but indeed I cannot eat." [1]

Andre' was then transported east to the John Robbins House at Wright's Mill at the present site of the Kensico Reservoir, where the party expected to see Lieutenant Colonel John Jameson of the 2nd Dragoons, but he was not to be found. The group continued on up present day Route 22 and by late afternoon, found Jameson at Sands' Mill at the intersection of High Street, Cox Avenue, and Greenway Road in North Castle, who rewarded the three captors with Andre`'s watch and horse for their loyalty. Suspecting that the papers were stolen, he then ordered Lieutenant Solomon Allen to deliver the prisoner to Arnold with a report of his capture, but the papers found on him would be retained. Andre` pleaded to have the papers sent along with him to Arnold, but Jameson refused. **Strike 7.** A historical marker and monument for Wright's Mill can be found along Route 22 on the western side of the Kensico Reservoir in North Castle. A historical marker and monument for Sand's Mill can be found at the intersection of High Street, Cox Avenue, and Greenway Road in North Castle.

A four-man escort mounted up and headed northwest up the present Route 128 to Route 117, and Route 133 to Crow Hill Road, before crossing the Pines Bridge and retracing Andre`'s steps through Yorktown along Crompond Road until reaching Locust Avenue, which lead into Continental Village towards the Robinson House. Andre` in the center of the column, his arms bound behind him with a strap being held by a soldier while Allen followed up the rear. Meanwhile, a messenger was sent from Sand's Mill to intercept Washington at Danbury, who was returning from a meeting with French Admiral Ternay and General Rochambeau in Hartford, Connecticut. Instead of retaining the papers found on Andre`, Jameson sent them to Washington for clarification.

To His Excellency General Washington

North Castle, Sept. 23rd 1780

Dear Sir

Enclosed you will receive a parcel of papers taken from a certain John Anderson who has a pass signed by General Arnold. I have sent the prisoner to General Arnold. He is very desirous of the papers and everything being sent with him, but as I think they are of a very dangerous tendency, I thought it more proper your Excellency should see them. [79]

I am, &c.,

John Jameson

When Tallmadge, on scouting duty, arrived at North Castle late that night and learned that Andre` was heading south toward the enemy lines when he was captured, he offered up to his superior that he ought to recall the guard and have the prisoner brought back at once. Jameson argued that it was his duty to obey General Arnold's orders, but Tallmadge offered to accept the responsibility as the area officer in charge of intelligence. His experience in the field of espionage raised his intuition to consider the possibility of Arnold's involvement after receiving a letter from him to expect Anderson. It wasn't until Tallmadge offered a safe method in which to retrieve the party that Jameson agreed to do so, but insisted upon continuing his report to Arnold.

To Lieutenant Allen

North Castle, Sept 23ʳᵈ 1780

Sir

For some circumstances I have just heard, I have reason to fear that a party of the enemy are above and as I would not have Anderson retaken or get away. I desire that you would proceed to lower Salem with him & deliver him to Captain Hoogland. You will leave the guard with Captain Hoogland except one man whom you may take along. You may proceed on to West Point and deliver the letter to General Arnold. You may also show him this, so that he may know the reason why the prisoner is not sent on. You will please to return as soon as you can do your business.

I am in haste, Dear Sir, &c.,

John Jameson [79]

Andre`'s spirits must have taken a significant downturn as the column turned about face and marched away from Arnold's headquarters, for he realized that although his mission had been compromised, he may have just missed his only opportunity to escape.

485

XVII
South Salem

Allen returned the prisoner as ordered and in the early morning hours of Sunday the 24th, he set out again with a revised report to Arnold. Andre` shamed Jameson for disobeying a direct order from a superior, but Jameson wanted assurance that neither the papers nor Arnold's loyalty had been stolen. Allen then set out to deliver a revised report to Arnold. In observing Andre`'s behavior, Tallmadge noticed that he turned on his heel as he paced the floor and notified Jameson of his suspicions that "he had been bred to arms." [75] He then escorted Andre` along with twenty dragoons over Coman's Hill, through Bedford and Cross River to the Jacob Gilbert House in South Salem, which served as Colonel Sheldon's headquarters. Upon arriving tired, hungry, dirty, and miserable, Andre` was delivered to Lieutenant Joshua King of the 2nd Dragoons, who shared breakfast with him and offered the services of his barber, which he was grateful to accept. When the barber uncovered the prisoner's scarf, he discovered that his neck was full of powder, which made King realize that this was no ordinary person. Andre` had requested permission to take the bed while his shirt and scarf might be washed, but King stated that it was needless, for a shirt was at his service, which he again accepted with graces.

Upon learning that the papers found on him had been forwarded to Washington, Andre' realized that it would be in his best interest to concede the truth. Admiring the yard outside the window with a gesture of his hand, Andre' asked King if he might be permitted to walk the property with him. The Lieutenant accepted and summoned his guard for security. While strolling the grounds, Andre` claimed that he must make a confidant of someone and knew not a more proper person than King, as he appeared to befriend a stranger in distress. His host accepted the plea and to his astonishment, Andre` confessed, "Lieutenant King, I am not John Anderson, an American agent, I am Major John Andre`, Adjutant General of the British Army." [1] Andre` went on boasting of his career and the details of his recent mission, which impressed King. Afterwards, he asked to be favored with a pen, ink, and paper along with a request to write a letter to Washington and Sir Henry Clinton in order to explain his circumstances along with a letter to a friend for a clean set of clothes, which Tallmadge granted.

To His Excellency General Washington

Salem, September 24ᵗʰ, 1780

Sir

What I have as yet concerning myself was in the justifiable attempt to be extricated. I beg your Excellency will be persuaded that no alteration in the temper of my mind, or apprehension for my safety, induces me to take the step of addressing you. But that it is to rescue myself from an impression of having assumed a mean character for treacherous purposes or self-interest; a conduct incompatible with the principles that activate me, as well as with my condition in life. It is to vindicate my fame that I speak, and not to solicit security. The person in your possession is Major John Andre`, Adjutant General of the British Army.

The influence of one commander in the Army of his adversary is an advantage taken in war. A correspondence for this purpose I held, as confidential with his Excellency Sir Henry Clinton. To favor it, I agreed to meet upon ground not within the posts of either Army, a person who was to give me intelligence. I came up in the Vulture man-of-war for this effect, and was fetched by a boat from the ship to the beach. Being here, I was told that the approach of day would prevent my return, and that I must be concealed until the next night. I was in my regimentals and had fairly risked my person.

Against my stipulations, my intention, and without my knowledge beforehand, I was conducted within one of your posts. Your Excellency may conceive my sensation on this occasion, and must imagine how much more must I have been affected by a refusal to re-conduct me back the next night as I had been brought. Thus becoming a prisoner, I had to concert my escape. I quitted my uniform, and was passed another way in the night, without the American posts, to neutral ground, and informed I was beyond all armed parties, and left to press for New York. I was taken at Tarrytown by some volunteers. Thus, as I have had the honor to relate, I was betrayed into the vile condition of an enemy in disguise within your posts.

Having avowed myself a British officer, I have nothing to reveal but what relates to myself, which is true on the honor of an officer and a gentleman. The request I have to make to your Excellency, and I am conscious I address myself well, is that in any rigor policy may dictate. A decency of conduct may mark that, though unfortunate, I am branded with nothing dishonorable, as no motive could be mine but the service of my King, and, as I was involuntary an imposter.

Another request I have is that I may be permitted to write an open letter to Sir Henry Clinton and another to a friend for fresh clothes and linen. I take the liberty to mention the condition of some gentlemen at Charleston, who being either on parole or under protection, were engaged in a conspiracy against us. Though their situation is not similar, they are objects who may be set in exchange for me, or are persons whom the treatment I receive might affect. It is no less Sir, in a confidence of the generosity of your mind, than on account of your superior station, that I have chosen to importune you with this letter.

> *I have the honor to be with great respect, Sir,*
> *your Excellency's most obedient and humble servant,*
> *John Andre`, Adjutant General* [3]

Andre` handed the open letter to Tallmadge, who perused it and reacted with shock when he discovered that although his premonition was correct, he did not think that he would be of such high rank. Meanwhile, the messenger who was sent to deliver the report to Washington had missed him and so returned to North Castle. It was then that word had reached the outpost that Washington and his officers had moved on to Fishkill and stopped at the Brinkerhoff House for dinner with Dr. McKnight and Brigadier General John Morin Scott that evening, and would be meeting with Arnold at his headquarters the next day. As it so happened, Smith had also joined them for dinner at Brinkerhoff's along with the Chevalier de La Luzerne. Washington shared a story or two about his trip to Hartford, which greeted him with the honors of a thirteen-gun salute and the pageantry of the French troops. Smith on the other hand did not have much to talk about; the only exciting bit of news he had to share was a cannonade that he watched from his house with Arnold two days before. A skirmish so effective that it was able to force the enemy ship *Vulture* down river from her anchorage at Teller's Point. The two couriers with messages for Arnold and Washington had stopped their pursuit due to a downpour of rain with the approach of nightfall. After failing to see the return of Andre` to the *Vulture* by Sunday evening, Robinson sent off a report to Clinton of the previous days events along with notification that Sutherland was requesting backup from Admiral Sir George Rodney. Born in 1718, Rodney had enlisted in the Royal Navy at age fourteen with an endorsement from his godfather, King George I, and through his own personal courage and professional skill, he rose to the rank of admiral. As a suave gambler and a handsome romantic, he was elected to the House of Commons and appointed commander of the port of Portsmouth, England. Here he organized press gangs that arrested any able-bodied man on the street or on a ship without an official exception and pressed him into becoming an able-bodied seaman for the King. Following the capture of a Spanish fleet at Gibraltar and three engagements with the French in Barbados, he arrived in New York on his way to engage the French fleet under Ternay at Newport, Rhode Island.

To Sir Henry Clinton

Vulture off Sing-Sing, Sept. 24ᵗʰ, 1780

Sir

Major Andre` acquainted you last Thursday morning of his arrival on board the Vulture the evening before and that no person appeared on Wednesday night as was promised in the letters I sent to you. This disappointment made us greatly at a loss what step to take next, but on Wednesday morning a man appeared with a white flag upon which Captain Sutherland sent a boat to take him off. As soon as the boat got near the shore, the people called to him to come into the water and they would take him up. He answered that he had 3 or 4 companions on the hill standing sentry & he would run up and call them. Immediately 10 or 12-armed men came down, sheltered themselves behind the rocks and fired at the boat. The gun boat was then sent to drive them off, they kept up a fire on the boats for some hours, but did no kind of mischief or hurt to any of our people. Major Andre` and myself proposed to Captain Sutherland to send a flag to General Arnold remonstrating against such a scandalous & unjust behavior as firing under the sanction of a flag.

I took this opportunity of writing a second letter to Arnold and said 'I have been greatly disappointed in not seeing Mr. Smith at the time appointed, being very anxious to conclude our business which is very necessary and should be done without delay. I can now make a final settlement with him as my partner upon the receipt of the letter that I forwarded to him yesterday immediately set off from New York & arrived here last night. If Mr. Smith will come here, we will attend him to any convenient & safe place." This letter & Captain Sutherland's flag met Arnold at or near Smith's house about 12 o'clock that night.

Mr. Smith came on board with two men & brought me the following letter from Arnold. 'This will be delivered to you by Mr. Smith who will conduct you to a place of safety. Neither Mr. Smith or any other person shall be made acquainted with your proposals if they are of such a nature that I can officially take notice of them I shall do it with pleasure. If not, you shall be permitted to return immediately. I take it for granted that Colonel Robinson will not propose anything that is not for the interest of the United States as well as himself. I am & signed B. Arnold.'

Mr. Smith had a paper from Arnold in the nature of a flag for himself, one man & two servants to go down by water to Dobbs Ferry for the purpose of forwarding some letters to New York on private business. He had a second paper as a pass to bring with him two servants and a gentleman Mr. John Anderson. He had a third small scrap of paper on which was wrote nothing more than Gustavus to John Anderson.

Upon considering all these matters, Major Andre` thought that it was best for him to go alone as both our names were not mentioned in any one of the papers and it appeared to him, as indeed it did to me, that Arnold wished to see him. I therefore submitted to be left behind, and Major Andre` went off with Smith between 12 & 1 o'clock Thursday night. Smith told me that Arnold would be about one o'clock at a place called the old trough or road, a little above DeNoyells with a spare horse to carry him to his house. It is with the greatest concern that I must now acquaint your Excellency that we have not heard the least account of him since he left the ship.

You will remember, Sir, that Arnold in his first letter to me desired the Vulture might continue her station at Teller's Point for a few days. This induced us to think that we might lay there with the greatest safety and be unmolested. But on Thursday night, they brought down on Teller's Point; one six-pounder & a howitzer, entrenched themselves on the very point & at daylight Friday morning began a very hot fire on us from both which continued two hours, and would have been longer but luckily their magazine blew up.

It was near high water, and the tide very slack and no wind filled the sail, so that it was impossible, though every exertion was made with auxiliary boats to get the ship turned out of their reach sooner. Six shot hulled us, one between wind and water; many others struck the sails and rigging, and boats on deck. Two shells hit us, one full on the quarterdeck, another near the main shrouds. Captain Sutherland is the only person hurt, and he very slightly on the nose by a splinter.

Captain Sutherland has wrote to Sir George Rodney desiring to have a galley or some other reinforcement if it should be necessary for us to continue here any time longer. I hope to have your

Excellency's further instructions what to do. I shall do everything in my power to come at some knowledge of Major Andre`.

I am your Excellency's most obedient and humble servant,

Bev: Robinson [79]

XVIII
Putnam

On the morning of Monday the 25th, Washington, led by his 50 horse security force, set out for his meeting with Arnold, but decided to inspect the North and South Redoubts while he was in the area. Lafayette made a comment to Washington when he noticed Washington heading down a narrow road that led towards the river. "General, you are going in the wrong direction; you know that Mrs. Arnold is waiting breakfast for us and that road will take us out of our way." [69] Washington chided, "Ah, Marquis, I know you young men are all in love with Mrs. Arnold and wish to get where she is as soon as possible. You may go and take your breakfast with her, and tell her not to wait for me. I must ride down and examine the redoubts on this side of the river, and will be there in a short time." [5] McHenry and Shaw then set off for Robinson House at a full gallop. A historical marker for the North Redoubt can be found along Travis Corners Road just west of the Walter Hoving Home in Garrison. A historical marker for the South Redoubt can be found along Route 403 just east of the Hamilton Fish Memorial Library in Garrison. Peggy greeted the young officers upon their arrival and then went upstairs to feed her son. Arnold joined them at the breakfast table and made polite conversation until Allen arrived to deliver Jameson's report to Arnold, which he read to himself.

To Major General Arnold

North Castle, 23rd September 1780

Sir

I have sent Lieutenant Allen with a certain John Anderson taken while going to New York. He has a passport signed with your name and a parcel of papers taken from under his stockings, which I think, is a very dangerous tendency. The papers I have sent to General Washington. They contain the number of men at West Point and its dependencies; the number of cannon etc.; the different pieces of ground that command each fort; & what distance they are from the different forts; the situation of each fort, and which may be set on fire with bombs and carcasses, and which are out of repair; the speech of General Washington to the Council of War held the sixth of this month; the situation of our armies in general &c., &c.

I am, with regard, &c.,

John Jameson [79]

Keeping a poker face, Arnold excused himself, walked to the foyer with Allen, and instructed him not to mention the message to anyone, but to wait for an answer. He limped out to the porch and called out to his servant, "A horse! Any one – even if a wagon horse, and inform the barge crew to stand by." [80] Stepping back inside, he ascended the stairs and entered his bedroom to explain to his wife that all was lost for them, Andre` had been captured, he must flee before Washington arrived, and she must burn all letters of evidence. Her only response at the moment was to faint. Arnold caught her, placed her on the bed, and summoned a servant to get her a cold cloth for her head. When Washington's servant arrived to announce that, "His Excellency is nigh at hand," Franks went upstairs to notify Arnold, who nodded an acknowledgement while concealing his anxiety. [79]

When Arnold returned downstairs, he told Franks that Mrs. Arnold was in need of Dr. Eustis, for she was ill and to inform Washington that he had gone to West Point and would return in a bout an hour. Upon making a hasty exit from the house and discovering that no horse was awaiting him, he mounted up on the one belonging to Allen and charged down the path towards Robinson's Landing. Once there, he vaulted off the animal, jumped aboard the stern of his barge, and drew his sword. "Down river," he exclaimed, "and be quick about it, for I'll give two gallons of rum if you can get me to Stony Point and back in time to meet General Washington." [2] The coxswain, James Larvey, did as ordered, thus providing Arnold a narrow escape. Historical markers for the Robinson House and Arnold's Flight can be found along the east and west sides of Route 9D, midway between the Bear Mountain Bridge and Route 403 in Garrison.

Soon afterwards, Washington arrived at the Robinson House at around 10:30 A.M. and was greeted by Major Franks, who explained that Arnold was called upon to West Point at once, expressed his regrets for his unavoidable absence, and would return in about an one hour. He then informed the General that both Mrs. Arnold and Colonel Varick were ill and indisposed. Washington consumed a quick breakfast and was given a brief greeting by Varick, who soon returned to bed to rest his illness. Following the meal, Washington decided to meet up with Arnold at the fort rather than to wait for him and crossed the river with Knox and Lafayette. Seeing the approach of a barge, Colonel Lamb came down the rocky ridge to meet it at the landing and was surprised to see Washington and not

Arnold. Lamb apologized and explained that if he had been expecting such visitors, then he would have been prepared to receive them in a proper manner. He then asked the General to excuse him for being taken by surprise, displaying his apparent neglect, and for not having put the garrison into a suitable condition for a military inspection and review. "How is this, Sir," inquired Washington, "is not General Arnold here?" [69] "No, Sir," Lamb answered, "he has not been here in two days, nor have I heard from him in that time." [69] Lafayette and Knox exchanged glances giving each other a puzzled look, feeling that something was awry. "This is extraordinary", replied Washington, "we were told that he had crossed the river and that we should find him here. However, our visit must not be in vain. Since we have come, although unexpectedly, we must look round a little and see in what state things are with you." [69] For two hours Washington viewed the fortifications becoming more disappointed with each one. The eastern wall of Fort Putnam had fallen, its *chevaux de frise* (spiked barricade) broken in many places, half-empty magazines, rusted wheels, shoddy barracks, crumbling parapets, and a sinking chain, held together at the center with a rope. When Washington inquired as to the reason for the deterioration, Colonel Lamb, Majors Jean Villefranche and Sebastian Bauman explained that it was due to a shortage of men and supplies along with an extended list of other projects, which Arnold introduced.

As Arnold passed Verplank's Point, he spotted the *Vulture* on the eastern shore, directed the barge crew to the vessel, tied a handkerchief to his cane, and raised it high, signaling Livingston that he was delivering a flag, which prevented him from being stopped by a patrol boat. Once on board the *Vulture*, he introduced himself to Robinson, informed him of Andre''s arrest, and called down to his barge crew in an attempt to recruit them. "My lads, I have quitted the rebel Army and joined the standard of his Britannic Majesty. If you will join me, I shall make sergeants and corporals of you all, and for you Larvey, I will do something more." [5] "No, Sir," Larvey replied, "one coat is enough for me to wear at a time." [5] Two of the crew agreed to stay while the rest were taken to New York as prisoners where they were given parole by Clinton. Arnold then explained the events of the past day to Robinson before the two of them both wrote to Washington, explaining the actions of Andre'. Leaving their letters at the blockhouse, the *Vulture* sailed South for New York at approximately 3:00 P.M.

About noontime as Varick lay on his bed, Franks appeared outside his window and notified him of "a report that one Anderson was taken as a spy on the lines and that a militia officer had brought letters to Arnold and that he had been enjoined in secrecy by Arnold." [33] The two officers were hesitant to announce their suspicions, yet at the same time, afraid to remain silent as suspects. Later Peggy had called for Varick and when he entered her room to check on her, she asked trembling, "Colonel Varick, have you ordered my child to be killed?" then fell on her knees and prayed at his feet while pleading for her baby's life. [33] Eustis had arrived and entered the room with Franks to carry her into her bed. Sensing that she was suffering from a fever, they tried to calm her by stating that her husband would soon return, but she cried out in response, "No, General Arnold will never return. He is gone. He is gone forever, there, there, there," as she pointed to the ceiling, "the spirits have carried him up there, they have put hot irons on his head." [33] When she learned that Washington had returned without her husband, she cried that "a hot iron has been put upon her head and no one but General Washington could take it off." [33] Dr. Eustis left the room with Varick and Franks and asked where Arnold had gone. The officers reported that he had gone over to West Point to which he begged for God's sake to send for him or the woman would die.

Washington, accompanied by Lamb and Villefranche, crossed back over the river on Lamb's barge, the *Bennington*, and returned to the Robinson House at about 4 o'clock. As he stepped off, Hamilton approached him and spoke a few words in a low tone before entering the house with him and conversing in a private room. During the General's absence across the river, Jameson's second messenger had arrived at Arnold's headquarters to deliver his report to Washington. Inside the bulky packet, the General discovered Jameson's note, Anderson's pass, a logistics report on West Point, along with a listing of ordinance, a chart detailing the arrangement of artillery, an order of operations in case of attack, and a copy of Washington's minutes of the council of war dated September 6th. He recognized Arnold's handwriting and questioned himself as to how they could have ended up in the hands of an unknown, so close to the enemy lines. Washington's thoughts then went from unsure to shock when he read Andre`'s letter to him, which revealed the whole ugly truth.

Washington called Knox and Lafayette into a small room, closed the door behind them, and summed up the situation declaring,

"Arnold has betrayed us, whom can we trust now?" [63] Realizing that Arnold had somehow been warned, Washington dispatched Hamilton and McHenry to Verplank's Point to try to intercept him, but ordered them to bring him back unharmed. He then ordered Lamb to dispatch ten boats to Nelson's Point, now Garrison's Landing, which he did.

To Col. Wade

Headquarters Robinson's House, 25th Sept, 1780

Dear Sir

Immediately on receipt of this, send ten boats properly manned to Nelson's Point, where they are to remain till further orders. You will pay particular attention to this matter, as it is indispensably necessary.

I am, Dear Sir, your obedient servant,
John Lamb,
Col. Commandant [1]

By now, Peggy was running around in hysterics, tearing at her nightgown, and talking like a madwoman by shouting accusations that the officers were plotting to kill her child. They summoned Washington to see if he could bring any serenity to her, but when the officers introduced him, she reacted with horror, raving one moment and melting into tears the next. Looking up at him from a cowered position in the corner, she clutched her baby, and cried out, "No, that is not General Washington, that is the man who is going to assist Colonel Varick in killing my child." [79] She writhed, her eyes frozen open, and in flailing her free arm, her garment dropped from her shoulder, exposing it. Blushing out of embarrassment for her sake, Washington turned on his heel and strode out of the room.

Not knowing whom he could trust until Arnold was captured and interrogated, Washington concealed his emotions and issued orders that no one was to leave. He then called his officers to dinner by saying, "Come gentlemen, as Mrs. Arnold is unwell, and the General is absent, let us sit down without ceremony." [41] Afterwards he asked Varick to join him outside for a private discussion. While the two men strolled along the grounds, Washington disclosed that he had the most indubitable proofs of Arnold's treachery and perfidy. Varick, both shocked and embarrassed, apologized for not discovering proof of his suspicions earlier. Washington explained that he had not the least cause of suspicion of either he or Franks, but that his duty as an officer made it necessary to inform him that he must consider himself a prisoner to which Varick accepted without protest. Varick then described the few details of Arnold's dealings with Anderson and Smith before Washington followed up with a similar conference outside with Franks, who consented as well. Varick recalled the events during his Court of inquiry held five weeks later. "Mrs. Arnold called for me and when I waited on her I found from her language and conduct that she was in great pain and had lost her reason, but could not divine the cause. Some time before dinner (the hour I do not know, but I think just before his Excellency General Washington returned from West Point), Mrs. Arnold recovering her reason in some measure, complained to me that she was left without a friend. I attempted to soothe her by saying she had many friends, enumerating Major Franks and myself, and that General Arnold would be there soon. On my mentioning his name, she replied in great agony: 'Oh, no, no! He is gone, gone, forever!' I soon left the room, found his Excellency had returned, and that Arnold had not been at West Point; and then recollecting Franks' declaration while I lay in bed, and his unaccountable and long absence, and Captain Hoogland's having come with dispatches to his Excellency, and evading answers to my inquiries with respect to Anderson's being taken, I mentioned to Franks that I was very apprehensive of his having destroyed himself or gone off, and in very few minutes after, we mentioned our fears to Dr. Eustis in confidence, lest we might be deceived and our reputations ruined forever.

We were anxious to advise the General of our suspicions, but fearful of doing it in a direct manner, when Mrs. Arnold's request to see him, to ask for relief, soon furnished us with the opportunity and I waited on his Excellency into her room accordingly.

Soon after and just before dinner, I communicated my suspicions to Colonel Lamb in confidence, and it was not till after dinner that his Excellency communicated Arnold's perfidy and treachery to us." [33]

When Hamilton arrived at Verplank's Point, he learned that Arnold had passed by earlier on his barge and then dispatched two letters; one for Washington and one for Peggy. Realizing that Arnold had made a successful escape to the British, Hamilton sent an express to Washington announcing that he would activate the local forces.

To His Excellency General Washington
Verplank's Point, September 25, 1780
Dear Sir

You will see by the enclosed that we are too late. Arnold went by water to the Vulture. I shall write to General Green advising him that without making a bustle, to be in readiness to march and even to detach a brigade this way. Although I do not believe the project will go on, it is possible Arnold has made such dispositions with the garrison as may tempt the enemy in West Point's present weakness to make the stroke this night and it seems prudent to be providing against it. I shall endeavor to find Meigs and request him to march to the garrison and shall make some arrangements here. I hope Your Excellency will approve these steps, as there may be no time to be lost.

I am, your most obedient & humble,
A. Hamilton

P. S. The Vulture is gone down to New York. [74]

To Major General Greene

Verplank's Point, 25th Sept. 1780

Sir

There has just been unfolded from this place a scene of the blackest treason. Arnold has fled to the enemy. Andre` the British Adjutant General is in our possession as a spy. This capture unraveled the mystery. West Point was to have been the sacrifice. All the dispositions have been made for the purpose and 'tis possible, though not probable, tonight may see the execution. The wind is fair. I came here in pursuit of Arnold but was too late. I advise your putting the Army under marching orders and detaching a brigade this way.

I am, with great regard, your obedient servant,
Alexander Hamilton, Aid de Camp [74]

Just before 7:00 that evening, Washington received the letters from Hamilton, Arnold, and Robinson.

To His Excellency General Washington

Vulture sloop of war, Sept. 25th 1780

Sir

The heart, which is conscious of its own rectitude, cannot contemplate to palliate a step, which the world may censure as wrong. I have ever acted from a principle of love to my Country, since the commencement of the present unhappy contest between Great Britain and the Colonies. The same principal of love to my Country actuates my present conduct, however it may appear inconsistent to the world, which very seldom judges right of any man's actions. I have no favor to ask for myself. I have too often experienced the ingratitude of my Country to attempt it. But, from the known humanity of your Excellency, I am induced to ask your protection for Mrs. Arnold from every insult and injury that a mistaken vengeance of my Country may expose her to. It ought to fall only on me; she is as good and innocent as an angel, and is incapable of doing wrong. I beg she may be permitted to return to her friends in Philadelphia, or come to me, as she may choose. From your Excellency I have no fears on her account, but she may suffer from the mistaken fury of the Country. I have to request that the enclosed letter may be delivered to Mrs. Arnold, and that she be permitted to write to me.

P.S. In justice to the gentlemen of my family, Colonel Varick and Major Franks, I think myself in honor bound to declare that they, as well as Joshua Smith, Esq. are totally ignorant of any transactions of mine that they had reason to believe were injurious to the public.

I am your most obedient and most humble servant,
Benedict Arnold [5]

To His Excellency General Washington
Vulture, off Singsing, Sept. 25, 1780
Sir

I am this moment informed that Major Andre`, Adjutant General of his Majesty's Army in America, is detained as a prisoner by the Army under your command. It is therefore incumbent on me to inform you of the manner of his falling into your hands. He went up with a flag at the request of a General Arnold, on public business with him, and had his permit to return by land to New York. Under these circumstances Major Andre` cannot be detained by you, without the greatest violation of flags, and contrary to the custom and usage of all nations. I imagine you will see this matter in the same point of view as I do, I must desire you will order him to be set at liberty and allowed to return immediately. Every step Major Andre` took was by the advice and direction of General Arnold, even that of taking a feigned name, and of course he is not liable to censure for it.

I am, Sir, not forgetting our former acquaintance,
your very humble servant,
Beverly Robinson,
Colonel, Loyal Americans [1]

Expecting a possible enemy advance that evening, Washington engaged in restoring the defenses at West Point. He ordered Hamilton to locate Meigs and have him mobilize his 6th

Connecticut Regiment towards the fortress with half of them covering the North and South Redoubts and then sent out orders to all commanders in the Hudson Highlands. His first concern was to cover the fort and asked, "Who has the immediate command?" [1] The reply was Wade, to which he responded, "He is a true man; I am satisfied." [1]

To Col. Wade at West Point
                    Headquarters Robinson House, September 25, 1780
Sir
        General Arnold is gone to the enemy. I have just received a line from him, enclosing one to Mrs. Arnold, dated on board the Vulture. From this circumstance, and Colonel Lamb's being detached on some business, the command of the garrison for the present devolves upon you. I request you will be as vigilant as possible, and as the enemy may have it in contemplation to attempt some enterprise, even tonight against these posts. I wish you to make, immediately after receipt of this, the best disposition you can of your force, so as to have a proportion of men in each work on the west side of the river. You will see or hear from me further tomorrow.
                    I am, Sir, your most obedient servant,
                                    G. Washington [24]

To Lt. Col. Gray
                    Headquarters Robinson's House,
                    September 25, 1780, 7 o'clock P. M.
Sir
        From some intelligence I have received, I think it necessary that the regiment at present under your command should march without a moment's delay. You will therefore I request on receipt of this, put it in motion and with one half you will occupy the North and Middle redoubts on the heights above this place as soon as possible. The other half of the regiment will proceed on to the landing place above Mandeville's near the old Connecticut encampment and will cross the river immediately after their arrival.
                    I am, Sir, with great regard, &c.,
                                    G. Washington [24]

To Col. John Lamb of the Artillery
                    Headquarters Robinson's House,
                    September 25, 1780, 7 o'clock P. M.
Sir

It is my wish to see Colonel James Livingston tonight and I write him by you on the occasion. In his absence you will take command of the posts at Stony and Verplank's Point, till further orders.

I am, Sir, your most obedient servant,
G. Washington [24]

To Col. James Livingston

Headquarters Robinson's House
September 25, 1780, 7 o'clock P. M.

Sir

I wish to see you here immediately and request that you will come without the least delay.

I am, &c.,
G. Washington [24]

To Lt. Col. John Jameson

Headquarters Robinson's House
September 25, 1780, 7 o'clock P. M.

Sir

I wish every precaution and attention to be paid to prevent Major Andre` from making his escape. He will without doubt make it if possible, and in order that he may not have it in his power, you will send him under care of such a party and so many officers as to protect him from the least opportunity of doing it.

That he may be less liable to be recaptured by the enemy, who will no doubt make every effort to regain him. He had better be conducted to this place by some upper road rather than by the route through Crompond. I would not wish Mr. Andre` to be treated with insult, but he does not appear to stand upon the footing of a common prisoner of war. Therefore he is not entitled to the usual indulgences they receive, and is to be most closely and narrowly watched to insure that Andre` must not escape.

General Arnold before I arrived here went off today to the enemy and is on board the Vulture Sloop of War.

I am, Sir, your most obedient servant,
G. Washington [24]

To M General Greene at Tappan

Headquarters Robinson's House
September 25, 1780, ½ after 7 o'clock P. M.

Dear Sir

I request that you will put the division on the left in motion as soon as possible with orders to proceed to King's Ferry where (or before) they will be met by further orders. The division will come on light, leaving their heavy baggage to follow. You will also hold on the shortest notice. Transactions of a most interesting nature and such will astonish you that have been just discovered.

I am, Dear Sir, &c.,
G. Washington [24]

To Major Low

Headquarters Robinson's House
September 25, 1780, ½ after 7 o'clock P. M.

Sir

You will be pleased to march early tomorrow morning with all the militia under your command and proceed to the landing opposite West Point. You will send an officer on to this place by which you will receive further orders.

Colonel Gouvion, the bearer of this, will apply to you for an officer and a small party of men. These you will furnish.

I am, &c.,
G. Washington [24]

To the Officer Commanding the Woodcutting Party

Headquarters Robinson's House
September 25, 1780, ½ after 7 o'clock P. M.

Sir

I request that you will, on receipt of this, march with the wood cutting detachment under your command to Fishkill where you will remain until further orders.

I am, &c.,
G. Washington [24]

To William M. Betts

Headquarters Robinson's House
September 25, 1780, ½ after 7 o'clock

Sir

It is my wish from some matters which have just occurred, to call the militia employed in cutting wood to Fishkill, where they will receive further orders. The enclosed is to the officer, who commands the detachment, on the subject, which you will forward by express.

I am, &c.,
G. Washington [24]

By the grace of God, the attack never came. At about midnight, a small contingent of Massachusetts's militiamen approached and surrounded the Hay House in Fishkill under the leadership of thirty-three year old Lieutenant Colonel Jean Baptiste Gouvion, one of four French engineers who helped to build the fortifications at West Point and Verplank's Point. Sound asleep, Smith and his wife were jolted awake when the door to the bedchamber burst open revealing the light from a lantern followed by Gouvion who ordered him to dress right now and accompany him to General Washington. He was then escorted out to the main room where hot coals glowed in the fireplace. While gathering warmth and his wits, he leaned toward his brother-in-law seated next to him and asked why he was being arrested. Hay explained that the reasons encircled around a trip that he had made to the British sloop *Vulture*. Smith admitted to the voyage to retrieve a man named Robinson to meet with Arnold, but a man named John Anderson was met instead. Arnold had then asked him to shelter the man, loan him a coat and deliver him into Westchester. Hay decided to accompany the escort to get a full report. Smith verbalized his anger, to be treated in such a vile fashion after his service to his country. On the way to Robinson House, the party could see activity buzzing about at West Point; arming cannon, manning the forts, and otherwise preparing for battle.

Jameson received Washington's letter around midnight as well and escorted Andre` in the rain along with Tallmadge, Captains Jeronemus Hoogland and Jedediah Rogers, Lieutenant King, and 100 dragoons. The troops traveled over Long Pond Mountain, up Oscaleta Road west of Lake Waccabuc, through North Salem up Hawley Mountain Road, along Grant Road, Bogtown Road, Mills Road, Titicus River Road into Purdys, up Old Route 22 into Croton Falls, along Croton Falls Road into Mahopac, and down Route 6N into Mahopac Falls, where they stopped to rest at the home of Major James Cox, later known as the Odell-Johnson House, at the Red Mills. Andre` entered the house and upon seeing a baby laying in her cradle, leaned down and in a gentle voice said, "Happy childhood, we know its pleasures but once. I wish I were as innocent as you." [1] The troops then continued southwest along Route 6N through the Shrub Oak plains, turning north onto Locust Avenue, over Gray's Hill, past St. Peter's Church before stopping for a brief rest at the Hollman House in North Peekskill. This house was just down the road from where Andre`'s original escort to Arnold was turned around near St.

Peter's Church. From there they marched towards Garrison over Gallows Hill Road, Old West Point Road, and up Route 403, where they turned south on Route 9D and arrived at the Robinson House at daybreak. Historical markers for Andre''s journey can be found along Route 6N at the intersections of Potter Road and Archer Road in Mahopac. A historical marker for the Red Mills can be found at the intersection of Route 6N and Hill Street in Mahopac Falls.

Smith and the Massachusetts militiamen arrived at the Robinson House before dawn as Washington stepped outside for a moment to glare at the captive, reflecting on the dinner they shared just a few nights ago, before stepping back inside. Smith was then escorted into a back room and seated before Washington entered with Lafayette, Knox, Hamilton and Lieutenant Colonel Robert Hanson Harrison. Smith demanded an explanation for his being taken and conducted to headquarters in so humiliating a manner. Washington responded that he was charged with the blackest treason against the United States and he was authorized by Congress to hang him in haste as a traitor. The General added that nothing could save him other than a full confession including the names of his accomplices. Smith retorted that he had done nothing of a public nature to justify a charge of treason, but was done by direction of General Arnold who could prove that what he said was true. If there was any fault to be found then it was to be found with General Arnold. "Sir", Washington exploded, "do you know that Arnold has fled and that Mr. Anderson, whom you piloted through our lines, proves to be Major John Andre`, the Adjutant General of the British Army, who is now our prisoner! I expect him here under guard of one-hundred horse to meet his fate as a spy, and," – extending his long arm and pointing a finger to a tree outside the window —"unless you confess who were your accomplices, I shall suspend you both on that tree." [38]

Smith's face flushed red, then grew pale as he realized the depth of the situation. He gathered himself enough to call upon Almighty God to bear witness to the integrity of his heart, and in terse, clipped tones professed his ignorance of Arnold's desertion and denied knowledge that he had been conducting negotiations with the enemy against the country. He insisted that nothing would have induced him to assist Arnold, but the perfect conviction that he was acting for the good of the nation. Washington listened without interruption before urging Smith to confess of his accomplices, that the evidence he possessed of Smith being a party, was sufficient to take away his life. Being the lawyer that he was, Smith responded like one. "As a citizen I do not conceive myself amenable to a military jurisdiction. I well recollect that when you came forward from Philadelphia to take the command of the Army at the camp at Cambridge, the Provincial Congress of New York addressed you for the purpose of preserving the rights of citizenship. You replied that when you assumed the character of a soldier, you did not forget that of the citizen. That you looked forward with pleasure to that auspicious period, when the rights of your country were being secured, you might retire to the sweets of peaceful tranquility under the protection of the law. I therefore cannot conceive that any simple recommendatory resolve of Congress, to which you just alluded, could abrogate a fundamental clause in the constitution of the state, of which I was a member. And which had for the benefit of the subject, established the right of trial by jury in all cases, whatever they may be. That it was a violation of that right, which Congress had assigned, amongst others, for their separation from Great Britain, and which had given birth to the present war." [38]

Washington asked Smith if he had brought a British officer named John Anderson from the sloop *Vulture*, to which Smith admitted that he did. He then asked if he knew that Anderson was actually Major John Andre`, Adjutant General of the British Army, to which Smith admitted he did not. Washington then ordered Smith to give him an account of everything he knew of Arnold's transaction and relate his own actions for the previous days. Smith recalled his participation with Arnold and Howe who had employed him as a confidential agent and that Arnold had led him to believe that a very important line of communication had been opened with Colonel Beverly Robinson, from whom he expected information of great importance for the country. He explained that Arnold ordered a boat and a pair of oarsman to be rowed to the sloop to deliver a message to Robinson and then to return him to meet with Arnold at Haverstraw. He then elaborated on the point that Anderson was sent to conduct the business for Robinson who met with Arnold in private and after a time, the three men returned to the house and the oarsmen returned the boat. The next morning Arnold asked him to give Anderson a cloak to wear for a night ride by ferry and horse to White Plains for he did not want their meeting to be of a public knowledge. They set out that evening as instructed, crossed over to King's Ferry, traveled to lodge at Crompond, and ate breakfast in Yorktown the next morning before parting at Pines Bridge. He then went north to meet with his cousin at Fishkill and stopped to dine with Arnold along the way before spending the following days with his cousin until his abrupt awakening when he was taken into custody early this morning.

The officers then interrogated him asking detailed questions regarding the events of the past week. Why did he undertake the business? He answered at Arnold's request. Did he not protest the impropriety of going on board a British ship to obtain intelligence? No. Did he consider himself under sanction of a flag of truce at night? Yes, with the assurance from Arnold that the ship would accept his pass and he did not want the business to be known to the local inhabitants. Did he bring on shore a British officer under the assumed name of John Anderson? Yes. Did he know that Anderson was the Adjutant General of the British Army and that his real name was John Andre`? No, he did not know anyone named Andre`. How was Anderson dressed? Wearing a dark cloak. Where did he change his uniform? At the house. Why did he give him a merchant's coat to wear? Arnold explained that the uniform was worn out of vanity. Did he know of any of the conversations between Arnold and Andre`? No. Why did Andre` not return to the sloop? The time and tide prevented it. What did Arnold reveal about the reason for the meeting? Arnold had led him to believe that a very important line of communication had been opened with Colonel Beverly Robinson, from whom he expected information of great importance to the country. All throughout the inquiry he remained with his statements that he had just revealed, but Washington was still not satisfied. He then ordered Harrison to send for Andre`'s uniform coat at the Smith House, which would serve as evidence. In a letter to his brother Thomas at Haverstraw, Smith requested to retrieve the coat and deliver it to Captain Patrick Carnes who was staying with him.

To Thomas Smith, Esq. of Haverstraw
Robinson House, September 25, 1780
Dear Brother
I am here a prisoner, and am therefore unable to attend in person. I would be obliged to you if you would deliver to Captain Carnes of Lee's Dragoons, a British uniform coat, which you will find in one of the drawers in the room upstairs, I would be happy to see you. Remember me to your family.
I am, affectionately yours,
Joshua H. Smith [21]

With the arrival of William Duer, a former delegate to Congress and presently the official commissioner for detecting conspiracies in the State of New York, Washington asked Smith if he had any written correspondence that could prove the nature of his association with Arnold. Smith acknowledged the request and instructed Duer to where he could find a key to his desk at the White House and the letters that he had exchanged with Arnold. Duer, an aristocrat by birth, had attended school at Eton in England and served in the British Army before immigrating to New York just prior to the war. A number of his appointments include: member of the Provincial Congress, adjutant general of troops with the rank of colonel, member of the Committee of Public Safety, delegate to the Continental Congress, and a member of the Board of War. Just after sunrise on the 26th, Washington wrote a very difficult letter to Congressional President John Hancock in Philadelphia, informing him of Arnold's treason.

To the President of Congress
> *Headquarters Robinson's House in the Highlands*
> *September 26, 1780*

Sir,

 I have the honor to inform Congress that I arrived here yesterday about twelve o'clock, on my return from Hartford. Some hours previous to my arrival, Major General Arnold went from his quarters, which were this place, and, as it was supposed, over the river to the garrison at West Point, where I proceeded myself, in order to visit the post. I found General Arnold had not been there during the day; and, on my return to his quarters, he was still absent. In the meantime, a packet had arrived from Lieutenant Colonel Jameson, announcing the capture of a John Anderson, who was endeavoring to go to New York, with several papers, all in the handwriting of General Arnold. This was also accompanied with a letter from the prisoner, avowing himself to be Major John Andre`, Adjutant General to the British Army, relating the manner of his capture, and endeavoring to show that he did not come under the description of a spy. From these several circumstances, and information that the General seemed to be thrown into some degree of agitation, on receiving a letter a little time before he went from his quarters. I was led to conclude immediately that he had heard of Major Andre`'s captivity, and that he would, if possible, escape to the enemy; and accordingly took such measures as appeared the most probable to apprehend him. But he had embarked in a barge, and *proceeded down the river, under a flag, to the Vulture ship of War, which lay at some miles below Stony and Verplank's Points. He wrote me a letter after he got on board. Major Andre` is not yet arrived, but I hope he is secure, and that he will be here today. I have been, and am taking precautions, which I trust will prove effectual, to prevent the important consequences which this conduct, on the part of General Arnold, was intended to produce. I do not know the party that took Major Andre`, but it is said that it consisted only of a few militia, who acted in such a manner upon the occasion, as does them the highest honor, and proves them to be men of great virtue. As soon as I know their names, I shall take pleasure in transmitting them to Congress. I have taken such measures with respect to the gentlemen of General Arnold's family, as prudence dictated. But, from everything that has hitherto come to my knowledge, I have the greatest reason to believe they are perfectly innocent. I early secured Joshua H. Smith, the person mentioned in the close of General Arnold's letter, and find him to have had considerable share in the business.* [24]

I have the honor to be, with most perfect respect,
your Excellency's most obedient humble servant,
G. Washington

To Governor Clinton
Headquarters Robinson's House, September 26, 1780
Dear Sir

I arrived here yesterday on my return from an interview with the French General and Admiral and have been witness to a scene of treason as shocking as it was unexpected. General Arnold from every circumstance had entered into a plot for sacrificing West Point. He had an interview with the British Adjutant General last week at Joshua Smith's where the plan was concerted; by an extraordinary concurrence of incidents, Andre` was taken on his return with several papers in Arnold's handwriting that proved the treason. The latter unluckily got notice of it before I did, went immediately down the river & got on board the Vulture, which brought up Andre` and proceeded to New York.

I found the post in the most critical position and have been taking measures to give it security, which I hope will be tonight effectual.

With the greatest respect, and regard,
I have the honor to be your most obedient humble servant,
G. Washington

509

P. S. Smith is also in our possession and has confessed facts sufficient to establish his guilt. [24]

Washington then got himself a good lawyer, one who had served as Arnold's prosecutor just nine months earlier, Colonel John Laurance, judge advocate general of the Continental Army.

To John Laurance, Esq.
Judge Advocate
> *Headquarters Robinson's House in the Highlands*
> *September 26, 1780*
Sir
> *You will have heard, probably before the receipt of this, that Major General Arnold has gone to New York, and that the Adjutant General of the British Army and Mr. Joshua Smith who were concerned with him in measures which occasioned his flight are both in our hands. I am desirous of seeing you without loss of time, in consequence of these events, and request that you will proceed to headquarters, wherever they my be, without delay.*
> *I am, Dear Sir, with regard of esteem, your most obedient servant,*
> *George Washington* [33]

That same morning, Hamilton finished a letter to his fiancée, Elizabeth Schuyler, the General's daughter, in which he describes his shock towards Arnold and sympathies towards Peggy.

To Elizabeth Schuyler
> *Sept. 25 (26), 1780*
My Dear Elizabeth
> *In the midst of my letter, I was interrupted by a scene that shocked me more than anything I have met with – the discovery of a treason of the deepest dye. The object was to sacrifice West Point. General Arnold had sold himself to Andre` for this purpose. The latter came but in disguise and in returning to New York was detected. Arnold hearing of it immediately fled to the enemy. I went in pursuit of him, but was much too late, and I could hardly regret the disappointment, when on my return, I saw an amiable woman frantic with distress for the loss of a husband she tenderly loved – a traitor to his country and to his fame, a disgrace to his connections. It was the most affecting scene I ever was witness to. She for a considerable time entirely lost her senses. The General went up to see her and she upraided him with being in a plot to murder her child; one moment*

510

she raved; another she melted into tears; sometimes she pressed her infant to her bosom and lamented its fate occasioned by the imprudence of its father in a manner that would have pierced insensibility itself. All the sweetness of beauty, all the loveliness of innocence, all the tenderness of a wife and all the fondness of a mother showed themselves in her appearance and conduct. We have every reason to believe she was entirely unacquainted with the plan, and that her first knowledge of it was when Arnold went to tell her he must banish himself from his Country and from her forever. She instantly fell into a convulsion and he left her in that situation.

This morning she is more composed. I paid her a visit and endeavored to sooth her by every method in my power, though you may imagine she is not easily to be consoled. Added to her other distresses, she is very apprehensive of her country will fall upon her (who is only unfortunate) for the guilt of her husband. I have tried to persuade her, her apprehensions are ill founded; but she has too many proofs of the illiberality of the state to which she belongs to be convinced. She received us in bed, with every circumstance that could interest our sympathy. Her sufferings were so eloquent that I wished myself her brother, to have a right to become her defender. As it is, I have entreated her to enable me to give her proofs of my friendship.

Could I forgive Arnold for sacrificing his honor, reputation, and duty? I could not forgive him for acting a part that must have forfeited the esteem of so fine a woman. At present she almost forgets his crime in his misfortune and her horror at the guilt of the traitor is lost in her love of the man. But a virtuous mind cannot long esteem a base one, and time will make her despise, if it cannot make her hate.

Indeed my angelic Betsey, I would not for the world, do anything that would hazard your esteem. 'Tis to me a jewel of inestimable price & I think you may rely I shall never make you blush.

I thank you for all the goodness of which your letters are expressive, and I entreat you my lovely girl to believe that my tenderness for you every day increases and that no time or circumstances can abate it. I quarrel with the hours that they do not fly more rapidly and give us to each other. [74]

I remain, Dear Betsey, your affectionate,
Alexander

Soon afterwards, Andre` arrived at the Robinson House and Smith was transferred by Lieutenant Samuel Shepard to the provost guard room in Fort Putnam located atop Mount Independence, on the high ground of West Point. Andre` was then interrogated in much the same fashion as Smith and afterwards transferred to Fort Putnam and held in the north cell looking east, where he was under the care of Captain Ebenezer Smith of the 13th Massachusetts. Major General Nathaneal Greene issued the address of the day to the Army, which stirred their spirits into a new sense of patriotism.

General Orders
Headquarters Orangetown
Tuesday, September 26, 1780
Parole Smallwood.   Countersigns Gist, Marion.
Watchword Intrepid.

...Treason of the blackest dye was yesterday discovered. General Arnold, who commanded at West Point, lost to every sentiment of honor, of public and private obligation, was about to deliver up that important post into the hands of the enemy. Such an event must have given the American cause a dangerous, if not a fatal wound; but the treason has been timely discovered, to prevent the fatal misfortune. The Providential train of circumstances, which led to it, affords the most convincing proof that the liberties of America are the objects of divine protection. At the same time that the treason is to be regretted, the General cannot help congratulating the Army on the happy discovery. Our enemies, despairing of carrying their point by force, are practicing every base art, to effect by bribery and corruption what they cannot accomplish in a manly way. Great honor is due to the American Army that this is the first instance of treason of the kind, where many were have been expected from the nature of the dispute. The brightest ornament in the character of the American soldiers is their having been proof against all the arts and seductions of an insidious Army. Arnold has made his escape to the enemy, but Major Andre`, the Adjutant General in the British Army, who came out as a spy, is our prisoner. His Excellency the Commander-in-Chief has arrived at West Point from Hartford, and is no doubt taking proper measures to unravel fully so hellish a plot. [24]

Greene later reflected on the treason and characterized Arnold in a dark light befitting the traitor. "Since the fall of Lucifer, nothing has equaled the fall of Arnold. His military reputation in Europe and America was flattering to the vanity of the first General of the age. He will now sink as low as he had been high before; and as the devil made war upon heaven after his fall, so I expect Arnold will upon America. Should he ever fall into our hands, he will be a sweet sacrifice." [38] When Arnold and Robinson arrived in New York,

Arnold made a report to inform Clinton of the circumstances regarding the mission and the major.

To His Excellency Sir Henry Clinton

New York, 26ᵗʰ September 1780

Sir

In answer to your Excellency's message respecting your Adjutant General, Major Andre`, and desiring my idea of the reasons why he is detained, being under my passports. I have the honor to inform you, Sir, that I apprehend a few hours must return Major Andre` to your Excellency's orders. As that Officer is assuredly under the protection of a flag of truce sent by me to him for the purpose of a conversation, which I requested to hold with him relating to myself, and which I wished to communicate through that officer, to your Excellency.

I commanded at the time at West Point, had an undoubted right to send my flag of truce for Major Andre`, who came to me under that protection, and having held my conversation with him, I delivered him confidential papers in my own hand writing to deliver to your Excellency. Thinking it more proper he should return by land, I directed him to make use of the feigned name of John Anderson; under which he had by my directions come on shore and gave him my passports to pass my lines to the White Plains on his way to New York. All which I then had a right to do, being in the actual service of America, under the orders of General Washington and Commanding General at West Point and its dependencies. This officer therefore cannot fail of being immediately sent to New York, as he was invited to a conversation with me, for which I sent him a flag of truce, and finally gave him passports for his safe return to your Excellency. All of which I had a right to do, being in the actual service of America, under the orders of General Washington, and commanding General at West Point and its dependencies.

I have the honor to be
your Excellency's most obedient and very humble servant,
B. Arnold [79]

Clinton then wrote to Washington requesting Andre`'s release being under a flag of truce.

To His Excellency General Washington

New York, September 26, 1780

Sir

I have been informed that the King's Adjutant General in America has been stopped under Major General Arnold's passports and is detained a prisoner in your Excellency's Army. I have the honor to inform you, Sir, that I permitted Major Andre` to go to Major General Arnold at the particular request of that General officer. You will perceive Sir, by the enclosed paper, that a flag of truce was sent to receive Major Andre` and passports granted for his return. I therefore can have no doubt but your Excellency will immediately direct that this officer has permission to return to my orders at New York.

I have the honor to be
Your Excellency's most obedient and most humble servant,
H. Clinton [79]

On the morning of Wednesday the **27ᵗʰ**, Franks escorted Peggy to Philadelphia in a solemn state of silence while Washington dispatched follow up orders to Greene to prepare for the arrival of prisoners and Wade for the possible onslaught of attack.

To M General Greene
Headquarters Robinson's House, September 27, 1780
Dear Sir
I have concluded to send Major Andre` of the British Army and Mr. Joshua Smith who has had a great hand in carrying on the business between him and Arnold to camp tomorrow. They will be under an escort of horse and I wish you to have separate houses in camp ready for their reception, in which they may be kept perfectly secure and also strong trusty guards threefold officered that a part may be constantly in the rooms with them. They have not been permitted to be together and must be still kept apart. I would wish the room for Mr. Andre` to be a decent one and that he may be treated with civility. But that he may be so guarded as to preclude a possibility of his escaping, which he will certainly attempt to effect if it shall seem practical in the most distant degree. Smith must also be as carefully secured and not treated with severity. I intend to return tomorrow and hope to have the pleasure of seeing you in the course of the day. You may keep these several matters secret. I write to Mr. Tilghman.

I am, Dear Sir, &c., [24]
G. Washington

To the Officer Commanding at West Point and its dependencies

Sept. 27, 1780

Sir
　　You will immediately make a distribution of the troops under your command to the special post that the whole may be in a state of defiance at the shortest notice. You will also have each work supplied with ten days provision, wood, water, and stores and keep up constantly that supply – and you will take every other precaution for the security of the post. The enemy will have acquired from General Arnold a perfect knowledge of the defenses, and will be able to take their measures with the utmost precision. This makes it essential our vigilance and care should be redoubled for its preservation. You will do everything in your power to gain information of the enemy's designs and give me intelligence as early as possible of any movement against you.

　　A party of militia who have been employed cutting wood and another as guards to the stores at Fishkill, that have been called in are to return to their destination.

　　Colonel Gouvion will remain a few days at this post to adjust in the necessary arrangements.

Given at Headquarters Robinson's House,
G. Washington [24]

　　Jameson wrote an apology to Washington, claiming that he was only following protocol.

To His Excellency General Washington
North Castle, 27 September 1780
Sir
　　This will be delivered to you by John Paulding, one of the young men that took Major Andre`, and who nobly refused any sum of money that he should demand. The other two young men that were in company with him are not yet found; as soon as they arrive, they shall be sent on...

　　I am very sorry that I wrote to General Arnold. I did not think of a British ship being up the river, and expected that, if he was the man he has since turned out to be, he would come down to the troops in this quarter, in which case I should have secured him. I mentioned my intention to Major Tallmadge and some others of the field officers, all of whom were clearly of opinion that it would be right, until I could hear from your Excellency...[33]

Your Excellency's most obedient & very humble servant,
John Jameson

XIX
Tappan

On the morning of Thursday the **28**th, Varick requested a Court of Inquiry to declare his innocence in the Arnold-Andre` affair, which Washington granted without question. Across the river at West Point, a large escort of dragoons accompanied Andre` in the front of the column followed by Smith in the rear to the landing where Tallmadge commanded the two barges that transported the prisoners down river to Stony Point. Along the way, Tallmadge inquired to Andre`, who was seated in the stern of the first barge, if he was to partake in the attack, had his mission been a success. Andre` assented, pointing out a table of land on the western shore where he would have landed at the head of a selected corps. He then elaborated on the plot by explaining an approach to the rear of Fort Putnam with little resistance. When Tallmadge asked what his reward was to be for his victory, Andre` replied that military glory was all that he sought with the appreciation from his General and his King.

Andre` then asked Tallmadge his opinion as to the result of his capture to which Tallmadge responded, "I had a much loved classmate in Yale College by the name of Nathan Hale, who entered into the Army in 1775. Immediately after the battle of Long Island, General Washington wanted information respecting the strength, position, and probable movements of the enemy. Captain Hale tendered his services, went over to Brooklyn, and was taken just as he was passing the outposts of the enemy on his return. Do you remember the sequel of this story?" [5] "Yes," said Andre`, "he was hanged as a spy. But you surely do not consider his case and mine alike?" [5] Tallmadge replied, "Yes, precisely similar, and similar will be your fate." [5] Shortly before the battle of Harlem Heights, Washington had requested a volunteer from Knowlton's Rangers for an intelligence mission within enemy lines. Captain Nathan Hale from Connecticut stepped forward and offered his services, explaining to a concerned friend, "I wish to be useful, and every kind of service, necessary to the public good, becomes honorable by being necessary." [86] Dressed in civilian attire, he set out on the 12th of September 1776, gathered the information, and headed back to camp, but was captured just short of the American lines on the 21st. Being that he was out of uniform, with incriminating papers, and within enemy territory, Sir William Howe sentenced him to be hanged without a trial. At the gallows, he claimed his patriotism by declaring, "I regret that I only have one life to give for my country." [86]

The barges continued down to the Stony Point landing, where the prisoners were transferred to horses to complete the journey to Tappan. As they approached Haverstraw, Smith had asked Tallmadge permission to stop at his house for a moment to retrieve papers to use for his defense. The request was approved, but when he entered, Smith's face was washed over with shock as he saw that the house had been ransacked. He asked to speak to his brother, Thomas, in private, but his request was denied and he was ordered back on his horse. The group then continued on heading south down Route 9W through Haverstraw and turned southwest along Route 202 before heading south again on Route 45 into New Hempstead. Here they arrived at Judge John Coe's Tavern opposite the Kakiat Presbyterian Church for a noontime meal. After their meal, they traveled eastward along New Hempstead Road to New City, then south down Little Tor Road, east along Germounds Road, south down Strawtown Road, east along West Nyack Road, and south down Western Highway through Blauvelt and Orangeburg. At dusk, the group arrived at the De Wint House in Tappan where Washington set up a new headquarters. After Tallmadge received his orders from the Commander-in-Chief, the two prisoners were then escorted to their makeshift prison cells. Andre` was confined in the storeroom at Casparus Mabie's Stone Tavern and Smith detained in a small room inside the Dutch Reformed Church. Many of the villagers gathered and greeted them with insults as others rushed to nail together a coffin for each of them, which they paraded in front of the windows of the captors holding sites. A historical marker, monument, and visitor's center for the De Wint House can be found at the intersection of Oak Tree Road and Livingston Street in Tappan. Adjutant General, Colonel Alexander Scammell, who had fought at Arnold's side at Saratoga, issued an order to the guards in charge of Andre`.

Major Andre`, the prisoner under your guard, is not only an officer of distinction in the British Army, but a man of infinite artfulness and address, who will leave no means unattempted to make his escape and avoid the ignominious death which awaits him. You are therefore, in addition to your sentries, to keep two officers constantly in the room with him, with there swords drawn whilst the other officers who are out of the room are constantly to keep walking the entry and round the sentries to see that they are alert. [1]

Inside the church, Nathaniel Greene presided over the historic espionage hearing with fourteen other officers on the morning of Friday the 29th. Seated in order of rank alongside Greene at a long table were Secretary Alexander Hamilton along with Major Generals; Robert Howe, Marquis de Lafayette, Arthur St. Claire, William Alexander (Lord Stirling), and Baron Von Steuben. Brigadier Generals included James Clinton, John Glover, Edward Hand, Jedidiah Huntington, Henry Knox, Samuel Holden Parsons, John Paterson, and John Stark.

Born to a noble family in Magdeburg, Prussia in 1730, von Steuben had served in the First Silesian War with his father at the young age of fourteen before he was appointed as an aide to Frederick the Great during the Seven Years' War. Speaking not a word of English yet having a referral from both Benjamin Franklin and Silas Deane, he came to America in the third year of the Revolution. After reviewing the American troops, he decided that they needed a little organizational guidance and demonstrated the drill maneuvers that he had learned flawlessly in the Prussian Army. Slowly but surely, with as much cursing and swearing in German and French that he could muster through his translator, he made noticeable progress in drilling the American troops, which paid victorious dividends at Monmouth, where he served as Washington's inspector general. The successful results following the implementation of his leadership inspired the production of a written structure of troop formations and functions. This developed into a drill manual that he wrote in French and had translated into English entitled, "Regulations for the Order and Discipline of the Troops of the United States," otherwise known as the "blue book." The publication of this manual recognized him as "the first teacher of the American Army" and granted him the appointment of serving as Washington's representative to Congress on matters of reorganizing the Army.

James Clinton was the younger brother to Sir Henry and older brother to Governor George, who all fought in the French and Indian War. He served as a delegate to the New York Provincial Congress, marched under Montgomery to assault Quebec, and was wounded during the battle of Fort Montgomery. Hand was a former surgeon who served with Washington at the battles of Long Island, White

Plains, Trenton, and Princeton. In the eyes of his troops he was a strict disciplinarian, but in the eyes of Washington he was highly regarded for his energy, zeal, daring horsemanship, and military ability. Huntington was a Harvard graduate from Arnold's hometown of Norwich, Connecticut who had fought alongside him at Ridgefield. After graduating from Yale, Paterson taught, practiced law, and was a justice of the peace in his hometown of New Britain, Connecticut. After settling in Massachusetts, he served as a member of the Provincial Congress and was commissioned as a colonel following word of the battle at Lexington. As a man of commanding presence, being over six feet tall with an athletic build, he led his minutemen into Boston and directed them to build a redoubt at Charlestown near Prospect Hill, which they defended during the battle of Bunker Hill. Following the disastrous battle of the Cedars, his regiment participated in the battles of Trenton, Princeton, Monmouth, and Saratoga, where he narrowly escaped death himself when he had his horse shot under him by a cannonball.

Tallmadge entered the church followed by six armed guards accompanying Andre`, who was brought before a small table with a chair in the center of the room, wearing the same clothes when he was captured. He gave a slight bow to Greene who was in the middle of the row of officers arranged by seniority and sat down. Greene, whose tall frame and stocky build held a strong presence, acknowledged Colonel John Laurance, who acknowledged him in return as he rose from a table set off to the side to read the order from Washington.

To a Board of General Officers convened at Tappan
Headquarters Tappan, Sept. 29, 1780
Gentlemen
   Major Andre`, Adjutant General to the British Army will be brought before you for examination. He came within our lines in the night, on an interview with Major General Arnold, in an assumed character, and was taken within our lines in a disguised habit, with a pass under a feigned name, and with the enclosed papers concealed upon his person. After a careful examination, you will be pleased as speedily as possible, to report a precise state of the Andre` case, together with your opinion of the light in which he ought to be considered, and the penalty that ought to be inflicted. The Judge Advocate, John Laurance who will attend to assist in the examination, has sundry other papers relative to this matter, which he will lay before the board.

I have the honor to be, gentlemen,
your most obedient, humble servant,
G. Washington [3]

Laurance announced that he would begin with a reading of Andre`'s letter to Washington explaining the preceding events. When he asked Andre` to identify the letter, Andre` acknowledged it to be the same. At the conclusion of the letter, Greene challenged Andre` by summarizing the final paragraph to be a threat of retaliation on innocent soldiers in British hands depending upon the officer's verdict of him, adding that Andre` wished to be recognized as an officer and a gentleman and denying to have acted in a mean character. Greene then leaned forward and questioned Andre` of the contradiction, but was interrupted by Laurance who suggested that the questioning of the prisoner be delayed until after his presentation of the evidence and Andre` has had a chance for a full reply, having brought a written statement. Greene then sat back in his chair and acknowledged Laurance to proceed. Laurance then continued, stating that the prisoner was granted the request to write to His Excellency General Washington and Sir Henry Clinton along with a letter to a friend for want of clean clothes. He then pointed out that in those letters he came on shore from the *Vulture* sloop of war in a boat that carried no flag. He also brought attention to the fact that he was wearing a surtout coat over his regimentals, and that he wore a surtout coat knowing that he was within our posts when he was taken.

Stark directed the first question regarding the evidence to Andre`, asking why in his letter to Washington he avoided naming Arnold as his American conspirator, but rather referred to him as "a person who was to give me intelligence." Andre` explained that the letter was written the day following his capture while he was being held at an American militia outpost. At the moment, he had no idea as to whether Arnold had been exposed or was even subjected, if he was in custody or still at large. He withheld his identity in order to buy time for him to extricate himself and allow a chance for their original design to succeed. Stark acknowledged that the plan made sense, but did not understand why he made such a rapid confession to his true identity, which may not have been penetrated for many days. Andre` stated that as he explains in his letter, he wished to protect his honor as an officer and a gentleman, because he was not in disguise by choice, but rather was betrayed into that vile condition by circumstances.

Laurance then laid before Andre` and the board, the papers found on him when he was taken, which he acknowledged. Laurance noted that three of the letters to be in the handwriting of Arnold who was in command at West Point and described their contents.

-A pass from Major General Benedict Arnold to a Mr. John Anderson, which Andre` acknowledged to be the name he assumed.

-Estimate of men to man the works at West Point.

-Remarks on works at West Point.

-Copy of a state of matters laid before a council of war, by his Excellency General Washington, September 6, 1780.

-An estimate of forces at West Point and its dependencies reported by Major Villefranche dated September 1780.

-A return of ordinance at West Point dated September 1780 and artillery orders dated September 5, 1780, both reported by Major Bauman.

-Andre`'s letter to Colonel Sheldon on September 7, 1780.

After the officers perused the documents, Laurance requested that the board hear Andre`'s testimony, which Greene acknowledged.

"I had left New York on the 20th and boarded the *Vulture* in expectation of meeting Arnold later that evening. Arnold did not arrive as scheduled, but on the following evening a boat with a gentleman and two hands came on board in order to fetch Mr. Anderson on shore and if too late to bring me back to lodge me until the next night in a place of safety. I went into the boat and spoke with Arnold. I got on horseback with him to proceed to the gentleman's house and on the way passed a guard I did not expect to see, having Sir Henry Clinton's directions not to go within the enemy's post, or to quit my own dress. In the morning, Arnold quitted me, he himself made me put the papers I bore between my stockings and foot. Whilst he did it, he expressed a wish in case of any accident befalling me, that they should be destroyed in which I said of course if that be the case as when I went into the boat I should have them tied about with a string and a stone. Before we parted, some mention had been made of my crossing the river and going by another route, but I objected much against it and thought it was settled that in the way I came I was also to return. In the morning I came with the gentleman as far as within two and a half miles of Pines Bridge, where he said he must part with me as the cowboys infested the road thenceforward. I was now near 30 miles from King's Bridge and left to the chance of passing that space undiscovered. I got to the neighborhood of Tarrytown, which was far beyond the points described as dangerous, when I was taken by three volunteers. Not being satisfied with my pass, the trio riffled me, and finding papers, made me a prisoner. It was only when I was challenged by a sentry that I found myself within the enemy's posts and changed my dress to concert my escape." [38]

When interrogated about his conception of his coming on shore under the sanction of a flag, Andre` responded that it was impossible for him to suppose he came on shore under that sanction; for if that were the case, he would be certain to have returned under it. Greene asked him "When you landed, did you consider yourself acting as a British officer, or as a private individual?" to which Andre` responded, "As a British officer." [1] When shown the letter written from John Anderson to Sheldon, of the 7th saying that he would meet Gustavus at Dobbs Ferry, he acknowledged that it was he who had written it. Although he claimed that it served as proof that he did not intend to come within the American lines, he added that he did not see himself as an ordinary spy, though a chain of accidents had made him act and look like one. He was assigned to a hard duty on behalf of his King and Country and if he had failed, then he believed that he had failed as a soldier and was entitled to be dealt with as a soldier fallen into the enemy's hands.

When he was dismissed from the courtroom, the following letters were laid before the board and read:
-Arnold's letter of the 25th to Washington from the sloop,
-Robinson's letter of the 25th to Washington from the sloop,
-Arnold's letter of the 26th to Clinton upon arriving in New York,
-Clinton's letter of the 26th to Washington from New York.
The common theme from these letters claimed that Andre` had come ashore under a flag and acted under Arnold's orders, therefore not qualifying him as a spy.

When Andre` was returned to his holding cell, he passed the time by writing letters, sketching a self-portrait, and sketching a picture of his trip across the river from the *Vulture*. Later that afternoon, a court of line officers was assembled to hear the case of Smith with Colonel Henry Jackson presiding. While in concession, the officers came to agree that Andre` was guilty, but could not agree on a form of execution, as six proposed hanging while the other six proposed a firing squad. Greene made the final decision for hanging and the officers each signed the report. Andre`, who was returned to face the officers and hear their verdict, amazed his captors with the gallant statement, "I am prepared for any fate to which an honest seal for my King's service may have devoted me. This assemblage of officers has treated me with every mark of indulgence. If ever I felt any prejudice against the Americans, this present experience must obliterate them." [3] Scammell read the findings aloud to Andre`.

The board of General officers appointed to examine into the case of Major Andre` report:

First, That he came onshore from the Vulture sloop of war in the night of the twenty-first of September instant on an interview with General Arnold, in a private and secret manner.

Secondly, That he changed his dress within the American lines, and under a feigned name and in a disguised habit. That he passed the fortifications at Stony and Verplank's Points, the evening of the twenty-second of September instant, at Tarrytown in a disguised habit, being then on his way to New York; and when taken, he had in his possession several papers, which contained intelligence for the enemy.

The board having maturely considered these facts, do also report to his Excellency General Washington, that Major Andre`, Adjutant General of the British Army, ought to be considered as a spy from the enemy, and that agreeable to the law and usage of nations it is our opinion that he is to suffer death. [76]

Each of the officers had signed the report along with their official rank and submitted its official report the Commander-in-Chief. A historical marker for the Trial of Andre` can be found across from the cemetery on Greenbush Road in Tappan. After hearing no response from the Americans, the British Commandant of New York, Lieutenant General James Robertson, wrote to Washington, echoing the previous claims made by Clinton that Andre` was being held illegally. Born in Newbigging, Scotland in 1717, Robertson was a veteran of the French and Indian War whose ambition enabled him to rise through the ranks from private to general in which he became a wise and well respected leader at Bunker Hill, the Boston siege, Long Island, and Manhattan.

To His Excellency General Washington

New York, 29ᵗʰ September, 1780

Sir

Persuaded that you are inclined rather to promote than to prevent the civilities and acts of humanity which the rules of war permit between civilized nations, I find no difficulty in representing to you, that several letters and messages sent from here have been disregarded, are unanswered, and the flags of truce that carried them, detained. As I have ever treated flags of truce with civility and respect, I have a right to hope that you will order my complaint to be immediately redressed. Major Andre`, who visited an officer commanding in a district, at his own desire, and acted in every circumstance agreeable to his direction, I find is detained a prisoner; my friendship for him leads me to fear he may suffer some inconvenience for want of necessaries; I wish to be allowed to send him a few, and I shall take it as a favor if you will be pleased to permit his servant to deliver them.

In Sir Henry Clinton's absence it becomes a part of my duty to make this representation and request. [1]

I am, Sir, your Excellency's most obedient humble servant,
James Robertson
Lt. General

In his cell, with a full display of emotion, Andre` confided to Hamilton. "I foresee my fate and though I pretend not to play the hero or to be indifferent about life, yet I am reconciled to whatever may happen, conscious that misfortune, not guilt has brought it upon me. There is only one thing that disturbs my tranquility. Sir Henry Clinton has been too good to me; he has been lavish of his kindness. I am bound to him by too many obligations, and love him too well, to bear the thought that he should reproach himself or others should reproach him on the supposition of my having conceived myself obliged by his instructions to run the risk I did. I would not for the world leave a sting in his mind that should embitter his future days." [74] He was then overcome with emotion and burst into tears confessing, "I am in a deplorable state, just about to be launched into the presence of my God. I wish to be permitted to assure him that I did not act under this impression, but submitted to a necessity imposed upon me, as contrary to my own inclination as to his orders." [74] After regaining his composure, he asked Hamilton the favor of forwarding a letter to Clinton. As a courtesy from one officer to another, along with feeling a certain sense of sympathy for him, regardless of his stature as an enemy, he agreed to deliver it personally.

To His Excellency Sir Henry Clinton

525

Tappan, Sept. 29, 1780

Sir

    Your Excellency is doubtless already apprised of the manner in which I was taken and possibly of the serious light in which my conduct is considered and the rigorous determination that is impending. I wish to remove from your breast any suspicion that I could imagine I was bound by Your Excellency's orders to expose myself to what has happened. The events of my coming within an enemy's posts and of changing my dress, which led me to my present situation, were contrary to my own intentions, as they were to your orders, and the circuitous route which I took to return was imposed without alternative upon me. I am perfectly tranquil within my mind, and prepared for any fate to which an honest zeal for my King's service may have devoted me. In addressing myself to Your Excellency on this occasion, the force of all my obligations to you, and of the attachment and gratitude I bear you, occurs to me. With all the warmth of my heart, I give you thanks for Your Excellency's profuse kindness to me, and I send you the most earnest wishes for your welfare, which a faithful, affectionate, and respectful attendant can frame. I have a mother and three sisters to whom the value of my commission would be an object, as the loss of Grenada has much affected their income; it is needless to be more explicit on this subject: I am persuaded of Your Excellency's goodness. I receive the greatest attention from his Excellency General Washington, and from every person under whose charge I happen to be placed.

    I have the honor to be with the most respectful attachment,
Your Excellency's most obedient and most humble servant
John Andre`, Adj. General [3]

On the morning of Saturday the **30th**, Washington wrote out his official response to the board's report.

To a Board of General Officers Convened at Tappan
    Headquarters, September 30th, 1780
Gentlemen
    The Commander-in-Chief approves of the opinion of the board of General officers respecting Major Andre` and orders that the execution of Major Andre` take place tomorrow at 5:00 P.M.
    I am your obedient servant,
George Washington,
General of the Armies [1]

When the officers' report reached New York, Arnold wrote a letter to Washington pleading for the release of Andre` as a prisoner of war.

To His Excellency General Washington

Sept. 30, 1780

Dear Sir

I apprehend that a few hours must return Major Andre` to your Excellency's orders. As that officer is assuredly under the protection of a flag of truce sent by me to him for the purpose of a conversation which I requested to hold with him relating to myself and which I wished to communicate through that officer to your Excellency. Thinking it more proper that he should return by land, I directed him to make use of the feigned name of John Anderson, under which he had by my directions come on shore. I then gave him my passports to pass my lines to the White Plains on his way to New York. [79]

I am, Sir, &c.,

B. Arnold

Along with this letter, Arnold had sent his regards to Lamb by way of the messenger to which Lamb replied, "Tell General Arnold that the acquaintance between us is forgotten; and that if he were to be hanged tomorrow, I would go barefooted to witness his execution." [39] Washington chose to respond not to Arnold's request for Andre`'s release, but rather to Robertson's request for his effects.

To Lieut. General Robertson

Tappan, September 30, 1780

Sir

I have just received your letter of the 29th. Any delay, which may have attended your flags, has proceeded from accident and the peculiar circumstances of the occasion – not from intentional neglect or violation. The letter that admitted of an answer, has received one as early as it could be given with propriety, transmitted by a flag this morning. As to messages, I am uninformed of any that have been sent.

The necessaries for Major Andre` will be delivered to him, agreeable to your request. [24]

I am, Sir, your most obedient humble servant,

G. Washington

In the meantime, Harrison sent the official order for Smith's trial to Laurance.

To a Board of Officers Convened at Tappan
Headquarters, September 30ᵗʰ, 1780
Gentlemen
You will prosecute before the court martial now sitting Joshua H. Smith, Esquire, an inhabitant of the State of New York, on the following charges:
First – For going on board the Vulture, sloop of war, belonging to the enemy, on the night of the 21ˢᵗ of this month, in a private manner, and bringing on shore from the said vessel, Major Andre`, Adjutant General of the British Army.
Secondly – For secreting the said Major Andre` in his house near our post at Stony Point, for furnishing him with clothes to disguise himself, and for passing with him by our posts at Stony and Verplank's Points, so disguised, and under a feigned name. Also for conducting him in his way to New York in a disguised habit, and under a feigned name with intelligence for the enemy.
Thirdly – For acting as a spy in procuring intelligence for the enemy.
Fourthly – For aiding and assisting Benedict Arnold, late a Major General in our service, in a combination with the enemy, to take, kill, and seize such of the loyal citizens or soldiers of these United States, as were in garrison at West Point and its dependencies.
I am your most obedient and most humble servant,
G. Washington [38]

Upon the commencement of his hearing, Smith responded in the same manner as he did to Washington, on the night of his arrest. "I object to the legality or propriety of being tried by a military tribunal. As a citizen, I conceive myself only amenable to the civil authority to the state to which I belong. That which has established the right of trial by jury in the constitution recently adopted. Thus determining the liberties of the subjects within the state and has ordained the right of trial by jury in all cases wherein it had been formerly used in the Colony of New York should be and remain inviolate forever." [66] The court responded according the law. "Mr. Smith, you are being tried by a resolve of Congress, passed in the year 1777. This law authorizes the Commander-in-Chief of the Army to hear and try by a court martial, any citizens of the United States, who should harbor or secret any of the subjects or soldiers of the King of Great Britain. If knowledge of the above proves instrumental in conveying intelligence to the enemy, and if found guilty, those involved should be condemned and executed as a traitor, assassin, and spy." [66] Smith rebutted that the law was unconstitutional because it made the military paramount to the civil authority, which would destroy the principle of liberty, the prominent reason assigned by Congress for their separation from Great Britain as inscribed in the Declaration of Independence. The court then took a brief recess to consider the objection and upon their return, read the charges that related him to Arnold and Andre`. Smith then rebutted the connection of the charges, concerned that proof of one would support another, and requested that the charges be consolidated into one general accusation.

The court withdrew a second time to deliberate this new issue. After a brief recess, the general court-martial reconvened and concurred that it did not possess jurisdiction to try him on the first three charges, but did have authority to try him on the fourth. The fourth charge was read to him, which Smith replied, "not guilty," and the court asked for the evidence of the prosecution. [66] Laurance, acting as the counsel for the prosecution, summoned the Cahoon brothers, who gave the first witness testimony regarding their activities with Smith, Arnold, and Andre`. They were followed with testimonies from the ferrymen and the captors. Washington wrote a report of the situation to Clinton declaring that Andre` did not act according to the rules of war.

To His Excellency Sir Henry Clinton
Headquarters, September 30, 1780
Sir
In answer to your Excellency's letter of the 26th, which I have had the honor to receive, I am to inform you that Major Andre` was taken under such circumstances as would have justified the most summary proceedings against him. I determined however to refer his case to the examination and decision of a Board of General Officers; who have, on his free & voluntary confession and letters reported.
First, that he came on shore from the Vulture Sloop of War in the night of 21st September last on an interview with General Arnold in a private and secret manner.
Secondly, that he changed his dress within our lines and under a feigned name, and in a disguised habit passed our works at Stony and Verplank's Points, the evening of the 22nd September last. He was taken the morning of the 23rd of September last at Tarrytown in a

529

disguised habit, being then on his way to New York, and when taken he had in his possession several papers, which contained intelligence for the enemy.

The board having maturely considered these facts, do also report to his Excellency General Washington that Major Andre`, Adjutant General to the British Army ought to be considered as a spy from the enemy. And that, agreeable to the Law and Usage of Nations, it is in their opinion he ought to suffer death. From these proceedings it is evident major Andre` was employed in the execution of measures very foreign to the objects of flags of truce, and such as they were never meant to authorize or countenance in the most distant degree, and this gentleman confessed with the greatest candor in the course of his examination that it was impossible for him to suppose he came on shore under the sanction of a flag. [3]

I have the honor to be
your Excellency's most obedient & humble servant,
G. Washington [3]

After receiving the officers' report, Clinton extended an invitation to have Lieutenant Governor Andrew Elliot and Chief Justice William Smith meet with Washington to discuss the matter. Smith just happened to be Joshua's sixty-two-year-old brother, who had graduated from Yale, studied law under William Livingston, married Janet Livingston, was an active Whig, and published a number of titles on the history of New York.

To His Excellency General Washington

New York, Sept. 30, 1780

Sir

From your Excellency's letter, I am persuaded by the Board of General Officers, to whom you referred the case of Major Andre`, cannot have been rightly informed of all the circumstances on which a judgement ought to be formed. I think it of the highest moment to humanity that your Excellency should be perfectly apprized of the state of this matter, before you proceed to put that judgement in execution.

For this reason I shall send His Excellency Lieutenant General James C. Robertson, and two other gentlemen, to give you a true state of facts, and to declare to you my sentiments and resolution. They will set out tomorrow as early as the wind and tide will permit, and will wait near Dobbs Ferry for your permission and safe conduct, to meet your Excellency, or such persons as you may appoint, to converse with them on this subject.

*I have the honor to be
your Excellency's most obedient and most humble servant,
H. Clinton
P. S. The Honorable Andrew Elliott, Esq., Lieutenant Governor, and the Honorable William Smith, (brother of Joshua) Chief Justice of this province, will attend His Excellency Lieutenant General Robertson.* [3]

Upon receiving this communication, Washington chose to postpone the execution until the next day. Considering the desire of the British to negotiate in person, Lafayette proposed the intriguing idea of trading Andre` for Arnold. Washington himself could not have endorsed the idea, but in a disguised letter to Clinton, Hamilton had asked him to consider the concept.

To General Sir Henry Clinton

Sept. 30. 80.

Sir

It has so happened in the course of events, that Major John Andre` Adjutant General of your Army has fallen into our hands. He was captured in such a way as will according to the laws of war justly affect his life. Though an enemy, his virtues and his accomplishments are admired. Perhaps he might be released for General Arnold, delivered up without restriction or condition, which is the prevailing wish. Major Andre`'s character and situation seem to demand this of your justice and friendship. Arnold appears to have been the guilty author of the mischief and ought more properly to be the victim. As there is great reason to believe he meditated a double treachery, and had arranged the interview in such a manner that if discovered in the first instance, he might have it in his power to sacrifice Major Andre` to his own safety.

*I have the honor to be,
A. B.
No time is to be lost.* [79]

On Sunday **October 1st**, Varick wrote a narrative of the events in the form of a letter to his sister.

*Robinson's House, Sunday Morning, October 1, 1780
Read this to yourself.*

My Dear Jane

I now set myself down to my pen and paper to give you a small detail of the most painful scenery and the black secret transactions of my late bosom friend and social companion, but now the abominably perfidious and treacherous parricide, the late Major General Benedict Arnold, of infamous memory, whose thirst after the accursed treasure of British gold has at one stroke blotted out,   and   as with a sponge wiped away, the memory of illustrious actions and signal services rendered his country on diverse occasions, and stamped his character with all that infamy can call her own.

You have no doubt heard the particulars; they are too tedious for my weak memory and trembling hand to recount; when I see my friends I will satisfy them on this head. Let me only inform you that I lay sick in my bed on Monday morning, 25th September about 10 o'clock; Arnold received advice by two letters that Major Andre`, Adjutant General of the British Army, was taken with sundry papers in Arnold's handwriting, and without waiting to see General Washington, who was within one mile of us, I am informed he called for a horse, bid the officer who brought the letters to be silent, went upstairs and took leave (I suppose) of his more than amiable wife, left her in a swoon and rode off to the lands, telling Major Franks to advise General Washington that he was gone on some business to West Point, and would return in an hour; and rowed down the river with his barge crew and passed King's Ferry as a flag and went on board the vulture, a British man-of-war. This infamous business had been carried on by Joshua H. Smith, brother of Billy Smith, Esquire, now in New York, who with Andre`, have, I hope, shared their proper fate.

General Washington came here and was informed, as Arnold had told Franks, and he to me. I then rose from my bed, dressed and paid my respects to the General, the Marquis, General Knox, &c., but my fever obliged me to retire again. When the General had breakfasted, he went to West Point in expectation of meeting Arnold there, and about an hour thereafter Mrs. Arnold (good woman) inquired how I was from the housekeeper and bid her go and see (that amiable lady had the Sunday evening before spent an hour at my bedside while I lay in a high fever, made tea for me, and paid me the utmost attention in my illness. No sooner had the housekeeper turned her back but Mrs. Arnold pursued her raving (sick), mad to see him, with her hair disheveled and flowing about her neck; her morning gown with few other clothes remained on her, too few to be seen even

532

by a gentleman of the family, much less by strangers. I heard a shriek to me and sprang from my bed, ran upstairs, and there met the miserable lady, raving distracted, she seized me by the hand with this, to me distressing, address and a wild look; "Colonel Varick, have you ordered my child to be killed?" judge you of my feelings at such a question, from this most amiable and distressed of her sex, whom I most valued. She fell on her knees at my feet with prayers and entreaties to spare her innocent babe. A scene too shocking for my feelings, in a state of body and nerves thus so weakened by indisposition and a burning fever, I attempted to raise her up, but in vain. Major Franks and Dr. Eustis soon arrived, and we carried her on the bed, raving mad. I must stop this detail till I see you. I know no cause for all this.

When she seemed a little composed she burst again into pitiable tears and exclaimed to me, alone on her bed with her, that she had not a friend left here. I told her she had Franks and me, and General Arnold would soon be home from West Point with General Washington. She exclaimed, "No, General Arnold will never return, he is gone; he is gone forever, there, there, there, the spirits have carried him up there, they have put hot irons on his head;" pointing that he was gone up to the ceiling. This alarmed me much. I felt apprehensive of something more than ordinary having occasioned her hysterics and utter frenzy. Soon after General Washington returned from West Point without Arnold; this convinced me all was not right. She soon after told there was a hot iron on her head and no one but General Washington could take it off, and wanted to see the General. I waited on his Excellency, informed him of all matters, and Mrs. Arnold's request. I attended him to her bedside and told her there was General Washington. She said no, it was not. The General assured her he was, but she exclaimed no, that is not General Washington; that is the man who is going to assist Colonel Varick in killing my child. She repeated the same sad story about General Arnold. Poor distressed, unhappy, frantic, and miserable lady.

The next day, 26th, she recovered a little and remembered nothing of what happened on the 25th. On the 27th she left us, escorted by Major Franks, for Philadelphia, by leave of his Excellency.

General Washington had by this time, 2nd, indubitable proofs of the infamous practices of Arnold. It was now four o'clock of the 25th and we sat down to dinner in a strange manner; I had a high fever, but officiated at the head of the table. Franks attended also when Mrs. Arnold's affairs would permit. Dull appetites surrounded a *plentiful table. His Excellency behaved with his usual sociability and politeness to me. The matter was certain.*

After dinner some time his Excellency called to me to take my hat and walk out with him, which I did. He thus declared he had the most indubitable proofs of Arnold's treachery and perfidy. I told him I was sorry for it, and he said he had not the least cause of suspicion of Major Franks or myself, but that his duty as an officer made it necessary to inform me that I must consider myself a prisoner, in which I, as politely as I could, acquiesced. It was what I expected. I then told him the little all I knew... [33]

I am, &c.,
Richard

At Tappan, Smith was taken ill and asked to postpone the proceedings of his trial until the following morning, which the court accepted. On the shore of Dobbs Ferry, General Greene attempted a compromise aboard the *HMS Greyhound* with Robertson. Upon departing the *Greyhound* at noontime, Greene ordered Robertson to disembark alone and gave him a firm greeting by stating, "Let us understand our position; I meet you only as a private gentleman, not as an officer, for the case of an acknowledged spy admits of no discussion." [1] Greene shared a letter with Robertson that Andre` had written to Washington earlier that morning asking for a death with honor and pointed out that it amounted to a full confession with no mention of a flag. Robertson handed over a letter from Arnold to be given to Washington, also asking for Andre` to be spared which Greene opened and read.

To His Excellency General Washington

New York, October 1, 1780
Sir

The polite attention shown by your Excellency and the gentlemen of your family to Mrs. Arnold when in distress, demand my grateful acknowledgements and thanks, which I beg leave to present.

From your Excellency's letter to Sir Henry Clinton, I find a Board of General Officers have given it as their opinion that Major Andre` comes under the description of a spy. My good opinion of the candor and justice of these gentlemen leads me to believe, that if they had been made fully acquainted with every circumstance respecting Major Andre`, they would by no means have considered him in the light of a spy, or even of a prisoner. In justice to him, I think it my duty to declare that he came from on board the Vulture at my *particular request by a flag sent on purpose for him by Joshua Smith Esquire, who had permission to go to Dobbs Ferry to carry letters, and for other purposes not mentioned and return. This was done as a blind to the spy boats. Mr. Smith at the same time had my private instructions to go on board the Vulture, and bring on shore Col. Robinson, or Mr. John Anderson, which was the name I had requested Major Andre` to assume. At the same time I desired Mr. Smith to inform him, that he should have my protection, and a safe passport to return in the same boat as soon as our business was completed. As several accidents intervened to prevent his being sent on board, I gave him my passport to return by land. Major Andre` came on shore in his uniform, which with much reluctance at my particular and pressing resistance, he exchanged for another coat. I furnished him with a horse & a saddle, & pointed out the route by which he was to return. And as commanding officer in the department, I had an undoubted right to transact all these matters, which if wrong, Major Andre` ought by no means suffer for them.*

But if after this just and candid representation of Major Andre`'s case, the board of General officers adhere to their former opinion, I shall suppose it dictated by passion and resentment. If that gentleman should suffer the severity of their sentence, then I shall think myself bound by every tie of duty and honor to retaliate on such unhappy persons of your Army as may fall within my power. In so doing, I expect that the respect due to flags and the Law of Nations may be better understood and observed.

I have further to observe that forty of the principal inhabitants of South Carolina have justly forfeited their lives, which have hitherto been spared by the clemency of his Excellency Sir Henry Clinton. For his Excellency cannot in justice extend his mercy to them any longer, if Major Andre` suffers which in all probability will open a scene of blood, at which humanity will revolt.

Suffer me to entreat your Excellency for your own and the honor of humanity, and the love you have of justice, that you suffer not an unjust sentence to touch the life of Major Andre`. But if this warning should be disregarded, and he should suffer, I call Heaven and Earth to witness that your Excellency will be justly answerable for the torrent of blood that may be spilled in consequence.

I have the honor to be, with due respect, your Excellency's most obedient and very humble servant,

B. Arnold [3]

Instead of folding it back up, Greene was contempt to let it fall to the ground at Robertson's feet. When he returned on board the sloop, Robertson sent an express to Clinton.

To His Excellency Sir Henry Clinton

> *Greyhound Schooner, Flag of Truce,*
> *off Dobbs Ferry, Oct. 1, 1780*

Sir

> *On coming to anchor here, I sent Captain Murray on shore, who soon returned with notice that General Greene was ready to meet me, but would not admit a conference with the other two gentlemen.*
> *I paid my compliments to his character, and expressed the satisfaction I had in treating with him in the cause of my friend, the two armies and humanity. He said he could not treat me as an officer – that Mr. Washington had permitted him to meet me as a gentlemen, but the case of an acknowledged spy admitted no opportunity of discussion. I said that knowledge of the facts was necessary to direct a General's judgement; that in whatever character I was received, I hoped that he would represent what I said candidly to Mr. Washington. I laid before him the facts and Arnold's assertion of Mr. Andre`'s being under a flag of truce and disguised by his order. He showed me a low-spirited letter of Andre`'s saying that he had not language that admits it to be criminal. I told him that Andre` stated facts with truth, but reasoned ill upon them; that whether a flag was flying or not, was of no moment. He landed and acted as directed by their General. He said they would believe Andre` in preference to Arnold.*
> *Greene said one thing would satisfy them – they expected if Andre` was set free, Arnold should be given up. This I answered with a look that only threw Greene into confusion. I am persuaded Andre` will not be hurt.*

> *Believe me, Sir,*
> *I am your most obedient and most humble servant,*
> *James Robertson* [79]

Upon hearing of the unofficial offer being made by his former comrades, Arnold offered to trade fates with Andre`. As prisoner's could be returned to their own Army's, deserters could not, so Clinton declined the proposal stating, "Your offer, Sir, does you great honor, but if Andre` were my own brother, I could not consent to it." [1] As a gesture of gratitude to his assigned hosts, Andre` handed over his self-portrait sketch to twenty year old Ensign Jabez H. Tomlinson, an officer of the guard. Soon afterwards, Captain William Allen was relieved by Captain John Hughes and Major Tallmadge upon the arrival of Andre`'s servant, Peter Laune, who was authorized to come to Tappan and deliver up the major's dress uniform. Upon donning his colors, Andre` then passed the time making amiable conversation with Tallmadge and Hughes, offering them to partake of a drink to cheer their crestfallen spirits. "Come let us take a glass of wine. It only makes me feel worse to see your feelings hurt." [1] Unbeknownst to him, less than a half mile to the West, a large crude gallows was being constructed for his execution made of two-forked apple trees with a third laid across. When the only response from New York was Arnold's resignation from the Continental Army, Washington concluded that the negotiations were over and the order for Andre`'s execution was to be carried out at noon on the very next day.

To His Excellency General Washington

New York, October 1, 1780

Sir

I take this opportunity to inform your Excellency that I consider myself no longer acting under the commission of Congress: Their last to me being among my papers at West Point, you, Sir, will make such use of it as you think proper.

At the same time, I beg leave to assure your Excellency that my attachment to the true interest of my country is invariable, and that I am actuated by the same principle which has ever been the governing rule of my conduct, in this unhappy contest.

I have the honor to be very respectfully,
your Excellency's most obedient & humble servant,
B. Arnold [3]

Laurance informed Andre` that evening that the negotiations for an exchange had failed and that he was sentenced for execution the following day at noon. Andre`, now hearing the reality of the situation, accepted it in a calm and solemn manner stating, "I avow no guilt, but I am reconciled to my fate." [1]. In a conversation with Hamilton, he claimed that since it was his lot to die, then he should have a choice in the manner and asked to write to Washington, requesting that he be shot like a gentleman instead of being hung as a spy. To this favor, Hamilton also granted.

To His Excellency General Washington

Tappan, October 1, 1780

Sir

Buoyed above the terror of death by the consciousness of a life devoted to honorable pursuits, and stained with no action that can give me remorse. I trust that the request I make to Your Excellency at this serious period, and which is to soften my last moments, will not be rejected. The sympathy toward a soldier will surely induce Your Excellency and the military tribunal to adapt the mode of my death to the feelings of a man of honor. Let me hope Sir, I shall experience the operations of these feelings within your breast by being informed that I am not to die on the gibbet.

I have the honor to be,
your Excellency's most obedient and most humble servant,
John Andre`,
Adj. Genl to the British Army [3]

After hearing no word of refusal from Washington and assuming that his request had been accepted, Andre` wrote to a friend claiming that he was willing to take a bullet for peace.

To Lieut. Col. William Crosbie, 22nd Regiment, New York

October 1, 1780
Dear Sir

The manner in which I am to die at first gave me some slight uneasiness; but I instantly recollected that it is the crime alone that makes any mode of punishment dishonorable – and I could not think an attempt to put an end to a civil war, and to stop the effusion of human blood, a crime. [1]

I have the honor to be, &c.,
John Andre`

Smith's trial continued on the morning of Monday the 2nd with the testimony of the ferrymen who transported Smith and Andre` from Stony Point to Verplank's Point. Colonel Livingston from King's Ferry then gave his testimony along with the three militiamen who captured Andre`, Lieutenant Colonels Harrison and Hamilton from the headquarters staff, and a second calling on Samuel Cahoon. That morning, Scammell announced to Andre` that his execution was set for high noon.

To Major Andre`

Oct 2nd
Sir

His Excellency General Washington has fixed the hour at 12 o'clock this day.

> *I am, Sir, your most obedient servant,*
> *A. Scammell, Adj.* [1]

Greene sent Robertson word that Washington's opinion of the situation was unchanged.

To Lieut. Genl Robertson

> *Camp, Tappan, 2 October*

Sir

Agreeably to your request, I communicated to General Washington the substance of your conversation, with all the particulars, as far as my memory served me. It made no alteration in his opinion and determination. I need say no more, after what you have already been informed.

> *I have the honor to be with respect, your Excellency's &c.,*
> *Nath Greene* [79]

Upon receiving notification from Greene that Washington had not been moved, Robertson tried again.

To His Excellency General Washington

> *Greyhound Schooner, Flag of Truce, Dobbs Ferry, Oct. 2,*
> *1780*

Sir

A note I had received from General Greene leaves me in doubt if his memory had served him, to relate to you with exactness the substance of the conversation that had passed between him and myself on the subject of Major Andre`. If an affair of so much consequence to my friend, to the two armies, and humanity, I would leave no possibility of a misunderstanding, and therefore take the liberty to repeat the substance of what I said to General Greene.

I offered to prove by the evidence of Colonel Robinson and the officers of the Vulture, that Major Andre` went on shore at General Arnold's desire, in a boat sent for him with a flag of truce; that he not only came ashore with the knowledge and under the protection of the General who commanded in the district, but that he took no step while on shore but by direction of General Arnold, as will appear by the enclosed letter from him to your Excellency delivered the previous day.

Under these circumstances I could not, and hoped you would not, consider Major Andre` a spy, for any improper phrase in his letter to you.

The facts he relates correspond with the evidence I offer; but he admits a conclusion that does not follow. The change of clothes and name was ordered by General Arnold, under whose direction he necessarily was, while within his command.

As General Greene and I did not agree in opinion, I wished that disinterested gentlemen of knowledge of the law of war and nations, might be asked their opinion on the subject; and mentioned Monsieur Knyphausen and General Rochambault.

I related that a Colonel Robinson had been delivered to Sir Henry Clinton as a spy, and undoubtedly was such; but that it being signified to him that you were desirous that this man should be exchanged, he had him ordered to be exchanged.

I wished that an intercourse of such civilities as the rules of war might admit of, might take off many of its horrors. I admitted that Major Andre` had a great share of Sir Henry Clinton's esteem, and that he would be infinitely obliged by his liberation; and that if he was permitted to return with me, I would engage to have any person you would be pleased to name, set at liberty. I added that Sir Henry Clinton had never put to death any person for a breach of the rules of war, though he had, and now has, many in his power. Under the present circumstances, much good might arise from humanity, much ill from want of it. If that could give any weight, I beg leave to add, that your favorable treatment of Major Andre` will be a favor I should be ever intent to return to any you hold dear. My memory does not retain with the exactness I could wish, the words of the letter General Greene showed me from Major Andre` to your Excellency. For Sir Henry Clinton's satisfaction, I beg you will order a copy of it to be sent to me at New York. [79]

I have the honor to be
your Excellency's most obedient and most humble servant,
J. Robertson

As the sun lit the morning sky, Andre`'s aide brought him tea and had asked, "Can I do anything else?" [3] "No Peter," replied Andre`, "You have done well, you have done well." [22] He consumed his last meal, which had been sent to him from the General's table each day, shaved, and dressed into his regimentals with the assistance of his aide, who became overcome with grief, to which Andre` snapped, "Leave me until you can show yourself more manly." [3]

When he concluded his personal preparations, with a sense of cheer Andre' informed his guards, "I am ready at any moment, gentlemen, to wait on you." [3] While it was still somewhat early, about ten o'clock, he continued to make polite conversation with his guardsmen inquiring of their military careers and their families. At Washington's headquarters as the noon hour approached, the Commander-in-Chief ordered the window shutters to be closed so that he and his staff would not be in sight of the hill where a large crowd had gathered. The sound of fife and drum could be heard off in the distance, growing louder as it drew closer and then ceased when it reached the tavern. Andre' rose from his chair, looked out the window, and announced that his escort had arrived. In noticing the large crowd that had gathered he smiled and added that they shall not be without a sufficient audience. Scammell entered the room and asked him if he was ready, to which he replied in the affirmative, placing his tricorn hat on his head. Scammell then turned and exited the room followed by the prisoner and his guards. A historical marker can be found in front of *The Old 76 House* on Main Street in Tappan, which still operates as a restaurant today.

Andre' was lead out onto the porch where he was flanked by Captains John Hughes and Ebenezer Smith on his right; and Captains Samuel Bowman and John Van Dyke on his left. The officers fell in place of the detachment of 500 dragoons in a formation of four abreast. Ahead of him, marched the fife and drum corps while a black coffin atop a two-horse baggage cart brought up the rear. Scammell raised his hand to signal the band to begin and the procession to proceed. Deputy Adjutant General, John Glover, serving as the officer of the day, led the column ahead of his aides, two colonels and two majors. The weather was summer-like as the cadence filled the air with the tune of 'The Bluebird' as he was marched up the Old Tappan Road. He displayed a complacent smile as he strode along and gestured with a bow to the board of officers that convicted him, which was returned with the same respect. At one point he complimented the officers that escorted him stating, "I am very much surprised to find your troops under such good discipline and your music is excellent." [21] Thacher recalled the procession in his journal.

I was so near during the solemn march to the fatal spot, as to observe every movement and to participate in every emotion the melancholy scene was calculated to produce. Melancholy and gloom pervaded all ranks and the scene was affectingly awful. The eyes of

541

*the immense multitude were fixed on him who, rising superior to the
fears of death, appeared as if conscious of the dignified deportment
he displayed. Not a murmur or a sigh ever escaped him and the
civilities and attentions bestowed on him were politely acknowledged.*
[76]

Dr. James Thacher

A historical marker for the Andre` Monument can be found at
the intersection of Old Tappan Road and Andre` Hill in Tappan. As
the column turned South off the Old Tappan Road, the fifers then
played the customary funeral dirge, "Roslin Castle." [2] When he came
in sight of the gallows, he stopped all of a sudden started backward.
The captain of the guard questioned the sudden change in his
behavior, "Why this emotion, Sir?" [3] Andre` implored, "Must I die in
this manner? I am reconciled to my fate, but not to the mode." [3] The
captain responded to his orders stating, "It is unavoidable, Sir," for
Washington had thought it best not to notify Andre` of his decision. [3]
The two battalions of infantrymen formed a hollow square to hold
back the immense multitude that had come to witness the deed, his
captors among them. A monument to the execution site can be found
at the top of Andre` Hill.

At the gallows, Andre` eyed an open grave dug nearby,
regained his composure, and said, "How hard is my fate, but it will
soon be over." [3] While waiting for the formation to assemble, Andre`
stood next to the wagon, his head down, rolling a pebble around on
the ground under his boot and uttered a choking sound. He resumed
the position of attention as Glover read the death sentence and
announced, "Major Andre` you will please get on the wagon." [38]
With his face pale and breathing shallow, he placed his hands on the
tailboard of the wagon and tried to spring up, but failed. Taking a
deep breath, he placed one knee on the wagon, climbed up, stepped
upon the coffin, placed his hands on his hips, raised his head in sight
of the noose before him, and strode the length of the casket to the
noose. Stopping just before it, he turned on his heels, removed his hat
and placed it on the coffin. He then removed his white neckcloth,
thrust it into his pocket, and pulled open the collar of his ruffled shirt
with his forefinger.

Strickland, a tory from Ramapo Valley, had gained his
freedom by acting as hangman, covering his face with black grease
and dirt in order to conceal his identity. He then made an awkward

542

attempt to place the noose over Andre`'s head, but was brushed aside with a sharp command by the condemned man, "Take off your black hands!" [21] Andre` then grasped the noose himself, slipped it over his head and drew it close above his right ear. While Strickland tied the rope to the cross pole, Andre` drew a handkerchief from his pocket, folded it into a flat strip, and tied it across his eyes. Scammell then called out to him, "Major Andre` if you have anything you wish to say, you have the opportunity, for you have but a short time to live." [63] Andre` gave him a slight bow, took in a breath, and exclaimed, "I have nothing more to say gentlemen but this, you all bear me witness that I meet my fate as a brave man." [3] Glover then called out, "His arms must be tied." [59] Andre` raised the handkerchief that covered his eyes, reached into his other pocket to remove another handkerchief, rolled it, and extended it in the direction of Strickland, before returning the handkerchief over his eyes. Strickland took the handkerchief and tied it just above his elbows. Taking a full breath, he murmured, "It will be but a momentary pang." [3] Strickland climbed down off the wagon and placed himself to the side of the horse team and wagon. Glover directed his eyes towards Andre` and raised a drawn sword, which glinted in the light of the sun. When his eyes met Strickland's, he lowered the sword, and Strickland led the horses forward. Andre`'s body swung in a great arc, which drew a gasp from the crowd. As the momentum subsided, his body twitched for a minute before surrendering to expiration.

Clinton had made one last written attempt to convince Washington of the legalities of the matter on the 4th, but before it was delivered, Andre`'s servant had returned to New York to inform him that he was gone. That same day, Congress declared to strip Arnold from the record... in the literal sense.

Wednesday, October 4, 1780
Resolved, That the Board of War be and hereby are directed to erase from the register of the names of the officers of the Army of the United States, the name of Benedict Arnold. [26]

When Arnold heard on the 5th, he swore to Washington that he would avenge any harm that his family might suffer.

To His Excellency General Washington
New York, October 5, 1780
Sir

The wanton execution of a gallant British officer in cold blood may be only the prelude to further butcheries on the same ill-fated occasion. Necessity compelled me to leave behind me in your camp a wife and offspring that are endeared to me by every sacred tie. If any violence be offered to them, remember I will revenge their wrongs in a deluge of American blood.

B. Arnold [1]

Three years to the day of his most revered gallantry, Arnold publicly attempted to justify his treachery, but nobody bought it.

To the Inhabitants of America

New York, Oct. 7th, 1780

I should forfeit even in my own opinion, the place I have so long held in yours, if I could be indifferent to your approval and silent on the motives which have induced me to join the king's arms.

A very few words, however, shall suffice upon a subject so personal, for to the thousands who suffer under the tyranny of the rulers in the revolted provinces, as well as to the great multitude who have long wished for its defeat, this instance of my conduct can want no vindication, as to that class of men who are criminally prolonging the war from sinister views, at the expense of the public interest, I prefer their hostility to their applause. I am only, therefore, concerned in this address to explain myself to such of my countrymen as want abilities or opportunities to detect the trickery by which they are duped.

Having fought by your side when the love of our country activated our arms, I shall expect from your justice and sincerity, what your deceivers, with more art and less honesty, will find it inconsistent with their own views to admit.

When I quitted domestic happiness for the perils of the field, I conceived the rights of my country in danger, and that duty and honor called me to her defense. A remedy of grievances was my only object and aim; however, I agreed in a step which I thought hastened the declaration of Independence; to justify the measure many plausible reasons were urged, which could no longer exist. When Great Britain, with the open arms of a parent, offered to embrace us as children and grant the wished for remedy.

And now that her worst enemies are in her own bosom, I should change my principles, if I conspired with their designs. Yourselves being judges, was the war the less just because fellow subjects were considered as our foes? You have felt the torture in which we raised our arms against a brother, God incline the guilty protractors of these unnatural dissentions to resign their ambition and cease from their delusions in compassion to kindred blood.

I anticipate your question: was not the war a defensive one until the French joined in the combination? I answer, that I thought so. You will add, was it not afterwards necessary till the separation of the British empire was complete? By no means; in contending for the welfare of my country, I am free to declare my opinion, that had this end been attained, all strife should have ceased.

I lamented therefore the political tyranny and injustice, which with a sovereign contempt of the People of America, studiously neglected to take their collective sentiments of the British proposals of peace. And to negotiate under a suspension of arms, for an adjustment of differences, as a dangerous sacrifice of the great interest of this country to the partial views of a proud, ancient, and crafty foe. I had my suspicions of some imperfections in our councils, on proposals prior to the parliamentary commission of 1778; but having then less to do in the cabinet than the field (I will not pronounce dogmatically as some may, and perhaps justly, that Congress have veiled them from the public eye), I continued to be guided in the negligent confidence of a soldier. But the whole world saw, and all America confessed, the overtures of the second commission exceeded our wishes and expectations. If there was any suspicion of the national liberality, it arose from its excess.

Do any believe that we were at that time really entangled by an alliance with France? Unfortunate deception! And thus they have been duped by a virtuous gullibility, in the incautious moments of unrestrained passion, to give up their fidelity to serve a nation counting both the will and the power to protect us, and aiming at the destruction both of the mother country and the provinces. In the simplicity of common sense, for I pretend to no deceptive reasoning, did the pretended treaty with the Court of Versailles amount to more than an overture to America? Certainly not, because no authority had been given by the people to conclude it, nor to this very hour have they authorized its ratification, the Articles of Confederation remain still unsigned.

In the firm persuasion, therefore, that the private judgement of any individual citizen of this country is as free from all conventional restraints since, as before the insidious offers of France. I preferred those from Great Britain, thinking it infinitely wiser and safer to cast my confidence upon her justice and generosity, than to trust a monarchy too feeble to establish your independence. So perilous to her distant dominions, the enemy of the Protestant faith, and fraudulently avowing an affection for the liberties of mankind, while she holds her native sons in subservience and chains.

I affect no disguise, and therefore frankly declare that in these principles, I had determined to retain my arms and command for an opportunity to surrender them to Great Britain, and in contriving the measures for a purpose, in my opinion, as grateful as it would have been beneficial to my country; I was only solicitous to accomplish an event of decisive importance, and to prevent, as much as possible in the execution of it, the effusion of blood.

With the highest satisfaction I bear testimony to my old fellow soldiers and citizens, that I find solid ground to rely upon the clemency of our sovereign and abundant conviction that it is the generous intention of Great Britain, not only to have the rights and privileges of the colonies unimpaired, together with their perpetual exemption from taxation, but to add such further benefits as may consist with the common prosperity of the empire. In short, I fought for much less than the parent country is as willing to grant to her colonies, as they can be to receive or enjoy.

Some may think I continued in the struggle of those unhappy days too long, and others that I quitted it too soon. To the first I reply, that I did not see with their eyes, nor perhaps had so favorable a situation to look from, and that to one common master I am willing to stand or fall. In behalf of the candid among the latter, some of whom I believe serve blindly but honestly in the ranks I have left, I pray to God to give them all the lights requisite to their own safety before it is too late; and with respect to that kind of critics whose hostility to me originates in their hatred to the principles, by which I am now led to devote my life to the reunion of the British Empire, as the best and only means to dry up the streams of misery that have deluged this country, they may be assured that, conscious of the integrity of my intentions, I shall treat their malice and accusations with contempt and neglect. [5]

On that very same day, Washington in turn justified his actions and requested that Congress recognize the three captors as compatriots.

To the President of Congress

Paramus, 7 October

Sir

I have the honor to enclose to Congress a copy of the proceedings of a board of General officers in the case of Major Andre`, adjutant general to the British Army.

This officer was executed in pursuance of the opinion of the Board on Monday the 2nd instant, at twelve o'clock, at our late camp at Tappan. He acted with great candor, from the time he avowed himself after his capture, until he was executed. Congress will perceive by copy of a letter I received from him on the 1st instant, that it was his desire to be shot; but the practice and usage of war, circumstanced as he was, were against the indulgence.

I have now the pleasure to communicate the names of the three persons who captured Major Andre` and who refused to release him, notwithstanding the most earnest importunities and assurances of a liberal reward, on his part. Their conduct merits our warmest esteem; and I beg leave to add that I think the public will do well to make them a handsome gratuity. They have prevented, in all probability, our suffering one of the severest strokes that could have been mediated against us. Their names are John Paulding, David Williams, and Isaac Van Wart.

I have the honor, &c., &c.,
G. Washington [1]

On the **8th**, Clinton released a report to his Majesty's military.

General Orders of October 8, 1780
The Commander-in-Chief does with infinite regret inform the Army of the death of the adjutant general, Major Andre`.

The unfortunate fate of this officer calls upon the Commander-in-Chief to declare his opinion that he ever considered Major Andre` as a gentlemen as well as in the line of his military profession of the highest integrity and honor, and incapable of any base action or unworthy conduct.

Major Andre`'s death is severely felt by the Commander-in-Chief, as it assuredly will be by the Army, and must prove a real loss to His Majesty's service. [1]

I am your most humble servant,
H. Clinton

On the **11th**, Hamilton wrote his report of the Arnold-Andre` conspiracy to Lieutenant Colonel John Laurens, the son of Henry Laurens. Born on the family's wealthy estate in Charleston, South Carolina, John attended school in Geneva, Switzerland and London,

England, where he studied law. Coming home to America in the third year of the war, this romantic and impulsive twenty-three-year-old volunteered as an aide to Washington, serving as a secretary and a translator. He fought valiantly at Brandywine, Monmouth, Newport, Savannah, and was wounded at Germantown. He was recently released as a prisoner in the Charleston siege.

To Lieutenant Colonel John Laurens
Preakness, New Jersey, October 11, 1780
Sir
Since my return from Hartford, my Dear Laurens, my mind has been too little at ease to permit me to write to you sooner. It has been wholly occupied by the affecting and tragic consequences of Arnold's treason. My feelings were never put to so severe a trial. You will no doubt have heard the principal facts before this reaches you; but there are particulars, to which my situation gave me access, that cannot have come to your knowledge from public report, which I am persuaded you will find interesting.

From several circumstances, the project seems to have originated with Arnold himself and to have been long premeditated. The first overture is traced back to some time in June last. It was conveyed in a letter to Col. Robinson; the substance of which was, that the ingratitude he had experienced from his Country, concurring, with other causes, had entirely changed his principles, that he now only sought to restore himself to the favor of his King, by some signal proof of his repentance, and would be happy to open a correspondence with Sir Henry Clinton for that purpose. About this period he made a journey to Connecticut, on his return from which to Philadelphia, he solicited the command of West Point; alleging that the effects of his wound had disqualified him for the active duties of the field. The sacrifice of this important post was the atonement he intended to make. General Washington hesitated the less to gratify an officer who had rendered such eminent services, as he was convinced the post might be safely trusted to one, who had given so many distinguished specimens of his bravery.

In the beginning of August, he joined the Army and renewed his application. The enemy, at this juncture, had embarked the greatest part of their force on an expedition to Rhode Island; and our Army was in motion to compel them to relinquish the enterprise or to attack New York in its weakened state. The General offered Arnold the left wing of the Army; which he declined on the pretext already mentioned, but not without visible embarrassment. He certainly might have executed the duties of such a temporary command, and it was expected from his enterprising temper, that he would gladly have embraced so splendid an opportunity. But he did not choose to be diverted a moment from his favorite object, probably from an apprehension, that some different disposition might have taken place, which would have excluded him. The extreme solicitude he discovered to get possession of the post would have led to a suspicion of treachery, had it been possible from his past conduct to have supposed him capable of it.

The correspondence thus begun was carried on between Arnold and Major Andre` Adjutant General to the British Army on behalf of Sir Henry Clinton, under feigned signatures and in a mercantile disguise. In an intercepted letter of Arnold which lately fell into our hands he proposes an interview, "to settle the risks and profits of the co-partnership"; and in the same style of metaphor, intimates an expected augmentation of the garrison, and speaks of it as the means of extending their traffic. It appears by another letter that Andre` was to have met him on the lines, under the sanction of a flag in the character of Mr. John Anderson, but some cause or other, not known, prevented this interview.

The 20th of last month Robinson and Andre` went up the river in the Vulture Sloop of War. Robinson sent a flag to Arnold with two letters; one to General Putnam enclosed in another to himself; proposing and interview with Putnam, or in his absence, with Arnold, to adjust some private concerns. The one to General Putnam was evidently meant as a cover to the other, in case by accident, the letters should have fallen under the inspection of a third person.

General Washington crossed the river on his way to Hartford the day these dispatches arrived. Arnold conceiving he must have heard of the flag, thought it necessary for the sake of appearances, to submit the letters to him and ask his opinion of the proprietary of complying with the request. The General with his usual caution, though without the least surmise of the design, dissuaded him from it, and addressed to the civil authority. This reference fortunately deranged the plan and was the first link in a chain of events that led to the detection. The interview could no longer take place in the form of a flag, but was obliged to be managed in a secret manner.

Arnold employed one Smith to go on board the Vulture the night of the 22nd to bring Andre` on shore with a pass for Mr. John Anderson. Andre` came ashore accordingly and was conducted within a picket of ours to the house of Smith, where Arnold and he remained together in close conference all that night and the day following. At

549

daylight in the morning, the commanding officer at King's Ferry, without the privity of Arnold moved a couple of pieces of cannon to a point opposite to where the Vulture lay and obliged her to take a more remote station. This event, or some lurking distrust, made the boatmen refuse to convey the two passengers back, and disconcerted Arnold so much, that by one of those strokes of infatuation, which often confound the schemes of men conscious of guilt, he insisted on Andre`'s exchanging his uniform for a disguise, and returning in a mode different from that in which he came. Andre` who had been undesignedly brought within our posts in the first instance remonstrated warmly against this new and dangerous expedient. But Arnold persisting in declaring it impossible for him to return as he came, he at length reluctantly yielded to his direction. Smith furnished the disguise, and in the evening passed King's Ferry with him and proceeded to Crompond where they were stopped the remainder of the night (at the instance of a militia officer) to avoid being suspected by him. The next morning they resumed their journey, Smith accompanying Andre` a little beyond Pine's Bridge, where he left him.

He had reached Tarrytown, when he was taken up by three militiamen, who rushed out of the woods and seized his horse. At this critical moment his presence of mind forsook him. Instead of producing his pass which would have extricated him from our parties and could have done him no harm with his own, he asked the militiamen if they were of the upper or lower party, distinctive appellations known among the enemy's refugee corps. The militiamen replied they were of the lower party; upon which he told them he was a British officer and pressed them not to detain him, as he was upon urgent business. This confession removed all doubt and it was in vain he afterwards produced his pass. He was instantly forced off to place of greater security; where after a careful search there were found concealed in the feet of his stocking several papers of importance delivered to him by Arnold; among these were a plan of the fortifications of West Point, a memorial from the Engineer on the attack and defense of the place, returns of the garrison, cannon and stores, & a copy of the minutes of a council of war held by General Washington a few weeks before. The prisoner at first was inadvertently ordered to Arnold; but on recollection, while still on the way, he was countermanded, and sent to Old Salem. The papers were enclosed in a letter to General Washington, which having taken a route different from the one he returned by, made a circuit, that afforded leisure for another letter, though an ill-judged delicacy

550

written to Arnold with information of Anderson's capture, to get to him an hour before General Washington's arrival at his quarters, time enough to elude the fate that awaited him. He went down the river in his barge to the Vulture with such precipitate confusion that he did not take with him a single paper useful to the enemy. on the first notice of the affair he was perused, but much too late to be overtaken.

Arnold, a moment before his setting out, went into Mrs. Arnold's apartment and informed her that some transactions had just come to light, which must forever banish him from his Country. She fell into a swoon at this declaration; and he left her in it to consult his own safety, "till the servants alarmed by her cries came to her relief. She remained frantic all day, accusing everyone who approached her with an intention to murder her child (an infant in her arms) and exhibiting every other mark of the most genuine and agonizing distress. Exhausted by the fatigue and tumult of her spirits, her frenzy subsided towards evening and she sunk into all the sadness of affliction. It was impossible not to have been touched with her situation; everything affected into female tears, or in the misfortunes of beauty, everything pathetic in the wounded tenderness of a wife, or in the apprehensive fondness of a mother, and, 'till I have reason to change the opinion, I will add, everything amiable in suffering innocence conspired to make her an object of sympathy to all who were present. She experienced the most delicate attentions and every friendly office 'till her departure for Philadelphia.

There was some color for imagining it was a part of the plan to betray the General into the hands of the enemy. Arnold was very anxious to ascertain from him the precise day of his return and the enemy's movements seem to have corresponded to this point. But if it really was the case, it was very imprudent. The success must have depended on surprise, and as the officers at the advanced posts were not in the secret, their measures might have given the alarm, and General Washington taking the command of the post might have rendered the whole scheme abortive. Arnold it is true had so dispersed the garrison as to have made a defense difficult, but not impracticable; and the acquisition of West Point was of such magnitude to the enemy, that it would have been unwise to connect it with any other object however great which might make the obtaining it precarious.

Andre' was without loss of time conducted to the headquarters of the Army, where he was immediately brought before a board of General officers, to prevent all possibility of misrepresentation or

551

criticism on the part of the enemy. the Board reported, that he ought to be considered as a spy and according to the laws and usages of nations to suffer death; which was executed two days after.

Never perhaps did any man suffer death with more justice, or deserve it less. The first step he took after his capture was to write a letter to General Washington conceived in terms of dignity without insolence and apology without meanness. The scope of it was to vindicate himself from the imputation of having assumed a mean character for treacherous or interested purposes; asserting that he had been involuntarily an imposter, that contrary to his intentions, which was to meet a person for intelligence on neutral ground, he had been betrayed within our posts and forced into the vile condition of an enemy in disguise, soliciting only that to whatever rigor policy might devote him a decency of treatment might be observed, due to a person who though unfortunate had been guilty of nothing dishonorable. His request was granted in its full extent, for in the whole progress of the affair, he was treated with the most scrupulous delicacy. When brought before the Board of Officers, he met with every mark of indulgence and was required to answer no interrogatory, which could even embarrass his feelings. On his part, while he carefully concealed everything that might involve others, he frankly confessed all the facts relating to himself; and upon his confession without the trouble of examining a witness, the Board made their report. The members of it were not more impressed with the candor and firmness mixed with a becoming sensibility, which he displayed than he was penetrated with their liberality and politeness. He acknowledged the generosity of the behavior towards him, in every respect, but particularly in this, in the strongest terms of manly gratitude. In a conversation with a gentlemen who visited him after his trial, he said he flattered himself he had never been ignorant; but if there were any remains of prejudice in his mind, his present experience must obliterate them.

In one of my visits to him (and I saw him several times during his confinement) he begged me to be the bearer of a request to the General for permission to send an open letter to Sir Henry Clinton. "I foresee my fate (said he) and though I pretend not to play the hero or to be indifferent about life; yet I am reconciled to whatever may happen, conscious that misfortune, not guilt, has brought it upon me. There is only one thing that disturbs my tranquility – Sir Henry Clinton has been too good to me; he has been lavish of his kindness. I am bound to him by too many obligations and love him too well to bear the thought, that he should reproach himself, or that others should reproach him on the supposition of my having conceived *myself by his instructions to run the risk I did. I would not for the world leave a sting in his mind that should embitter his future days."* He could scarce finish the sentence, bursting into tears, in spite of his efforts to suppress them, and with difficulty collected himself enough afterwards to add, *"I wish to be permitted to assure him, I did not act under this impression, but submitted to a necessity imposed upon me as contrary to my own inclination to his orders."* His request was readily complied with, and he wrote the letter annexed, and with which I dare say, you will be as much pleased as I am both for the diction and sentiment.

There was something singularly interesting in the character and fortunes of Andre`. To an excellent understanding well improved by education and travel, he united a peculiar elegance of mind and manners, and the advantage of a pleasing person. 'Tis said he possessed a proficiency on poetry, music, and painting, his knowledge appeared without ostentation and embellished by a distrust that rarely accompanies so many talents and accomplishments, which left you to suppose more than appeared. His sentiments were elevated and inspired esteem. They had a softness that reconciled affection. His oration was handsome; his address easy, polite and insinuating. By his merit he had acquired the unlimited confidence of his General and was making a rapid progress in military rank and reputation. But in the height of his career, flushed with new hope from the execution of a project the most beneficial to his party that could be devised, he was at once precipitated from the summit of prosperity and saw all the expectations of his ambition blasted and himself ruined.

The character I have given of him is drawn partly from what I saw of him myself and partly from information. I am aware that a man of real merit is never seen in so favorable a light, as through the medium of adversity. The clouds that surround him are shades that set off his good qualities. Misfortune cuts down the little vanities, that in prosperous times served as so many spots in his virtues; and gives a tone of humility that makes his worth more amiable. His spectators who enjoy a happier lot are less prone to detract from it, through envy, and are more disposed by compassion to give him the credit he deserves and perhaps even to magnify it.

I speak not of Andre`'s conduct in the affair as a philosopher, but as a man of the world. The authorized maxims and practices of war are the satire of human nature. They countenance almost every species of seduction as well as violence; and the General that can make most traitors in the Army of his adversary id frequently most applauded. On this scale we acquit Andre`, while we could not but *condemn him, if we were to examine his conduct by the sober rules of philosophy and moral rectitude. It is however a blemish in his fame, that he once intended to prostitute a flag; about this a man of nice honor ought to have had a scruple, but the temptation was great; let his misfortunes cast a veil over his error.*

When his sentence was announced to him, he remarked that since it was his lot to die there was still a choice in the mode, which would make a material difference to his feelings, and he would be happy, if possible, to be indulged with a professional death. He made a second application by letter in concise, but persuasive terms. It was thought this indulgence being incompatible with the customs of war could not be granted and it was therefore determined in both cases to evade an answer to spare him the sensations, which a certain knowledge of the intended mode would inflict.

In going to the place of execution, he bowed familiarly as he went along to all those with whom he had been acquainted in his confinement. A smile of complacency expressed the serene fortitude of his mind. Arrived at the fatal spot, he asked with some emotion, must I die in this manner? He was told it had been unavoidable. "I am reconciled to my fate (said he) but not to the mode." Soon however recollecting himself, he added, "it will be but a momentary pang," and springing up upon the cart performed the last offices to himself with a composure that excited the admiration and melted the hearts of the beholders. Upon being told the final moment was at hand and asked if he had anything to say, he answered: "nothing but to request you will witness to the world, that I die like a brave man." Among the extra ordinary circumstances that attended him, in the midst of his enemies, he died universally esteemed and universally regretted.

Several letters from Sir Henry Clinton and others were received in the course of the affair, feebly attempting to prove that Andre` came out under the protection f a flag, with a passport from a General officer in actual service, and consequently could not be justly detained. Clinton sent a deputation composed of Lt. General Robertson, Mr. Elliott, and Mr. William Smith to represent as he said, the true state of Major Andre`'s case. General Greene met Robertson & had a conversation with him, in which he reiterated the pretence of a flag, urged Andre`'s release as a personal favor to Sir Henry Clinton, and offered any friend of ours in their power in exchange. Nothing could have been more frivolous than the plea, which was used. The fact was that besides the time, manner, object of the interview, change of dress, and other circumstances, there was not a single formality customary with flags and the passport was not to

Major Andre`, but to John Anderson. But had there been, on the contrary, all the formalities, it would be an abuse of language to say that the sanction of a flag for corrupting an officer to betray his trust ought to be respected. So unjustifiable a purpose would not only destroy its validity, but make it an aggravation. Andre` himself has answered the argument by ridiculing and exploding the idea in his examination before the board of officers. It was a weakness to urge it. there was in truth no way of saving him. Arnold or he must have been the victim; the former was out of our power.

It was by some suspected, Arnold had taken his measures in such a manner, that if the interview had been discovered in the act, it might have been in his power to sacrifice Andre` to his own security. This surmise of double treachery made them imagine Clinton might be induced to give up Arnold for Andre`, and a gentleman took occasion to suggest this expedient to the latter, as a thing that might be proposed to him. He declined it. the moment he had been capable of so much frailty, I should have ceased to esteem him.

The infamy of Arnold's conduct previous to his desertion is only equaled by his baseness since. Besides the folly of writing to Sir Henry Clinton; assuring him that Andre` had acted under a passport from him and according to his directions, while commanding officer at a post, and that therefore he did not doubt he would be immediately sent in; he had the audacity to write to General Washington, in the same spirit, with the addition of a menace of retaliation, if the sentence should be carried into execution. He has since acted the farce of sending in his resignation. This man is in every sense despicable. Added to the scene of dishonesty and prostitution during his command at Philadelphia, which the late seizure of his papers has unfolded; the history of his command at West Point is a history of little, as well as great, villainies. He practiced every dirty art of embezzlement; and even stooped to connections with the suppliers of the garrison to defraud the public.

To his conduct, that of the captors of Andre` forms a striking contrast. He tempted them with the offer of his watch, his horse, and any sum of money they should name. They rejected his offers with indignation; and that gold that could seduce a man high in the esteem and confidence of his country, who had the remembrance of past exploits; the motives of present reputation and future glory to cloak his integrity, had no charm for three simple peasants, leaning only on their virtue and an honest sense of their duty. While Arnold is handed down with abomination to future times, posterity will repeat with reverence the names of Van Wert, Paulding, and Williams!

I congratulate you my friend on our happy escape from the mischief with which this treason was big. It is a new comment on the value of an honest man and if it were possible, would endear you to me more than ever.

Adieu,

A. H. [74]

On the same day, Sir Henry Clinton gave a full explanation of Andre`'s demise to Lord George Germain, which included a confirmation from General Sir Frederick Haldimand to hijack the Hudson and assume control of the colonies. Born in Switzerland in 1718, Haldimand distinguished himself in the attack on Ticonderoga during the French and Indian War and succeeded Carleton as governor and commander-in-chief of Canada back in '78.

To His Lordship George Germain

New York, October 11, 1780

My Lord

About eighteen months since, I had some reason to conceive that the American Major General Arnold was desirous of quitting the Rebel service and joining the cause of Great Britain. A secret correspondence which I conceived to be from this officer, which expressed a displeasure at the alliance between America and France, engaged me to pursue every means of ascertaining the identity of the person who was thus opening himself to me, and from whom I had had on every occasion received, during the whole of our correspondence, most material intelligence. I was not at first, however, spirited in my ideas of General Arnold's consequence, as he was said to be then in a sort of disgrace, had been tried before a court martial, and not likely to be employed; and, whatever merit this officer might have had, his situation, such as I understood it then to be, made him less an object of attention. I apprehended that without employment he might be of more use to me in corresponding than by joining me.

In the course of our communication, information was given me that he should certainly be again employed in the American service, with an offer of surrendering himself under every possible advantage to His Majesty's arms. The correspondence was continued up to July 1780, when Major General Arnold obtained the command of all the Rebel forts in the Highlands, garrisoned with near 4,000 men. And it seemed to me, by the correspondence in question, that it was certainly that officer who made the offers under the description I have given.

The getting possession of these posts with their garrisons, cannon, stores, vessels, gunboats, &c., &c., appeared to me an object of the highest importance, which must be attended with the best consequences to His Majesty's service – among others that of opening the navigation of the North River and the communication, in a certain degree, with Albany, as appears by the enclosed copy of a letter from General Haldimand to me.

The very particular situation of the campaign at this period will mark of what great import such an event would prove. A French fleet and a considerable land force had arrived at Rhode Island. Mr. Washington had very much augmented his army, and was drawing additional strength to it daily by every strained exertion upon the country and the militia of it. There was great reason, from information, to suppose that an attempt was intended upon New York, that Mr. Washington with his Army was to have moved upon King's Bridge and Morris Heights while a Corps threatened – perhaps attacked – Staten Island, at the same time that the French would have invaded Long Island and have moved upon New York by that inroad. To have pursued these plans, large magazines of every nature must have been formed by the Rebels and it is beyond doubt that the principal Rebel depot must have been made at West Point and its dependent forts.

From this description, which I have reason to believe just, will be seen of what great consequence would be the encouraging and closing in with a plan of such infinite effect, if carried into execution, toward the success of the campaign, and that it was to be pursued at every risk and expense. My idea of putting into execution this concerted plan with General Arnold with most efficiency was to have deferred it till Mr. Washington, cooperating with the French, moved upon this place to invest it, and till the Rebel magazines should have been collected and formed in their several depots, particularly that at West Point. General Arnold surrendering himself, the forts, and garrisons at this instant of time would have given every advantage, which could have been desired. Mr. Washington must have instantly retired from King's Bridge and the French troops upon Long Island would have been consequently left unsupported and probably would have fallen into our hands. The consequent advantage of so great an event I need not explain.

I had prepared for this serious purpose and for the movements which would have attended upon it everything which my reflection could suggest as necessary upon the occasions, and there were vessels properly manned and of a particular draft of water ready to

557

have improved the designed stroke to the utmost. The important news from South Carolina of Lord Cornwallis having defeated Mr. Gates' Army arrived here the latter end of August, and I watched the effect it might have upon Mr. Washington's Army. But he did not in the least alter his positions, or send a man to the southward, from whence I was led to imagine this place was still his object – in which, indeed, I was confirmed by intelligence from General Arnold.

At this point Sir George Rodney arrived with a fleet at New York, which made it highly probable that Mr. Washington would lay aside all thoughts against this place. It became, therefore, proper for me no longer to defer the execution of a project which, from the situation of the Rebel Army and its chief (then about West Point), would be derived such considerable advantages, nor to lose so fair an opportunity as was presented, and under so good a mask as an expedition to the Chesapeake, which every person imagined would of course take place. Under this feint, therefore, I prepared for a movement up the North River. I laid my plan before Sir George Rodney and Lieutenant General Knyphausen, when Sir George – with that zeal for His Majesty's service which marks his character – most handsomely promised to give me every naval assistance in his power.

It became at this instant necessary that the secret correspondence under feigned names which had been so long carried on should be rendered into certainty, both as to the person being Major General Arnold, commanding at West Point, and that, in the manner in which he was to surrender himself, the forts, and troops to me, it should be so conducted under a concerted plan between us as the King's troops sent upon this expedition should be under no risk of surprise or counterplot. And I was determined not to make the attempt but under such perfect security.

I knew the ground on which the forts were placed and the continuous country tolerably well, having been there in 1777, and had received many hints respecting both from General Arnold. But it was certainly necessary that a meeting should be held with that officer for settling the whole of the plan. My reasons as I have described will, I take for granted, prove the propriety of such a measure on my part. General Arnold also has his reasons, which must be so very obvious as to make it unnecessary for me to explain them.

Many projects for a meeting were formed, and in consequence several appointments made, in all which General Arnold seemed extremely desirous that some person who had my particular confidence might be sent to him – some man, as he described in writing, of his own measure. I had thought of a person under this *immediate description, who would have cheerfully undertaken it but that his peculiar situation at the time (from which I could not then release him) precluded him from engaging in it. general Arnold finally insisted that the person sent to confer with him should be the Adjutant General, Major Andre`, who indeed had been the person on my part who managed and carried on the secret correspondence.*

A meeting was proposed to be held at a particular place and on neutral ground, on a fixed day and hour. The parties accordingly were on their way to the rendezvous, but an unlikely accident prevented the conference. A gunboat which had been up the river, falling down to the usual station, very near met that in which General Arnold was, who with difficulty escaped, and was in some risk of his life. This necessarily put off the matter for some days. The correspondence was obliged to be renewed and another appointment made to meet at the same spot as first proposed.

The appointment took place, though not exactly as intended, as appears by the narrative which I have the honor to transmit herewith to Your Lordship; and it proved a most unfortunate one respecting the general plan, and a most fatal one to the adjutant general, Major Andre` - who was taken prisoner, tried by a board of Rebel general officers, and condemned by their sentence to suffer death, which sentence was confirmed and ordered to be put into execution upon this unhappy gentleman by the Rebel General Washington. Major General Arnold received intelligence of Major Andre`'s being taken just in time to allow him to make his escape, which he did with great difficulty and danger, being pursued by land and by water.

Thus ended the proposed plan of a project from which I had conceived such great hopes and from whence I imagined would be derived such great consequences. The particulars respecting the ill-fated ending of this serious – I may say great – affair shall be detailed in a narrative wherein all papers and letters connected with it will be inserted. As this very commendable step of General Arnold is likely to produce great and good consequences, I have thought it right to appoint him colonel of a regiment, with the rank of brigadier general of provincial forces. I must beg leave to refer Your Lordship to him for other particulars and information.

The unexpected and melancholy turn in which my negotiations with General Arnold took, with respect to my Adjutant General, has filled my mind with the deepest concern. He was an active, intelligent, and useful officer, and a young gentleman who promised to be an honor to his country as well as an ornament to his profession.

Therefore, as he has fallen a sacrifice to his great zeal for the King's service, I judged it right to consent to his wish that his company, which he purchased, may be sold for the benefit of his mother and sisters. But I trust, My Lord, that Your Lordship will think Major Andre''s misfortune still calls for some further support to his family, and I beg leave to make it my humble request that you will have the goodness to recommend them in the strongest manner to the King for some beneficial and distinguishing mark of His Majesty's favor. [85]

I am, &c.,

Sir Henry Clinton

Washington also wrote to John Laurens on the **13**[th] and reflected on the excruciating events of just a few weeks ago.

To Lieut. Col. John Laurens

Headquarters Passaic Falls, October 13, 1780

My Dear Laurens

Your friendly and affectionate letter of the 4th *came to my hands on the 10*[th] *and would have been acknowledged yesterday by the Baron de Steuben, but for some important business I was preparing for Congress.*

In no instance since the commencement of the war has the interposition of Providence appeared more conspicuous than in the rescue of the post and garrison of West Point from Arnold's villainous perfidy. How far he meant to involve me in the catastrophe of this place does not appear by any indubitable evidence, and I am rather inclined to think he did not wish to hazard the more important object of his treachery by attempting to combine two events, the lesser of which might have marred the greater. A combination of extraordinary circumstances. An unaccountable deprivation of presence of mind in a man of the first abilities, and the virtuous conduct of three Militia men, threw the Adjutant General of the British forces in America (with full proofs of Arnold's treachery) into our hands; and but for the extraordinary folly, or the bewildered conception of Lt. Col. Jameson, who seemed lost in astonishment and not to have known what he was doing I should as certainly have got Arnold. Andre' has met his fate, and with that, fortitude, which was to be expected from an accomplished man and gallant officer. But I am mistaken if at this time, Arnold is undergoing the torments of a mental hell. He wants feeling! From some traits of his character which have lately come to my knowledge, he seems to have been so hired in villainy, and so lost to all sense of honor and shame that while his faculties will enable

560

him to continue his selfish pursuits, there will be no time for
remorse...

Your sincere friend, [24]
G. Washington

Various other versions of the preceding events were later portrayed in a poetic style to recall the patriotism of Paulding, as written here and sung to the tune of "Bonny Boy."

The Ballad of Major Andre`

Come all ye brave Americans, and unto me give ear,
I'll sing you now a ditty, that will give your spirits cheer,
Concerning a young gentleman, whose age was twenty-two;
He fought for North America, his heart was just and true.

They took him from his dwelling, and did him close confine,
They cast him into prison, and kept him there a time;
But he being something valiant, resolved not long to stay,
He set himself at liberty, and soon did run away.

And when that he had returned, home to his own country,
There was a plan contriving, to undo America,
Plotted by General Arnold, and his bold British crew,
Who thought to shed our innocent blood, and America subdue.

He with a scouting party, went down to Tarrytown,
Where they met a British officer, a man of high renown;
Who said unto these gentlemen "You're of the British cheer,
I trust that you can tell me if there is danger near?"

Then up spoke this young hero, John Paulding was his name;
"Oh tell us where you're going, Sir, and also whence you came?"
"I bear the British flag, Sir, I've a pass to go this way,
I'm on an expedition, I have no time to stay."

Then round him came this company, and bade him to dismount;
"Come tell us where you're going, give us a strict account;
For now we are resolved, that you shall not pass by."
On a strict examination, they found he was a spy!

He begged for his liberty, he pled for his discharge,
And oftentimes he told them, if they'd set him at large,
"Here's all the gold and silver, I have laid up in store,
And when I reach the city, I will send you ten times more."

"We scorn your gold and silver, you have laid up in store,
And when you reach the city, you need not send us more."
He saw that his conspiracy, would soon be brought to light,
He begged for pen and paper, and asked for to write.

The story came to Arnold, commanding at the Fort:
He called for the *Vulture*, and sailed for New York;
Now Arnold to New York has gone, a-fighting for his King,
And left poor Major Andre`, on the gallows for to swing.

Andre` was executed, he booked both meek and mild,
Around on the spectators, most pleasantly he smiled;
It moved each eye to pity, and every heart there bled,
And everyone wished him released, and Arnold in his stead.

He was a man of honor, in Britain he was born,
To die upon the gallows, most highly he did scorn:
And now his life has reached its end, so young and blooming still,
In Tappan's quiet countryside, he sleeps upon the hill.

A bumper to John Paulding! Now let your voices sound,
Fill up your flowing glasses, and drink his health around;
Also to those young gentleman, who bore him company,
Success to North America, ye sons of liberty! [50]

Meanwhile on the **20th**, Arnold made a public attempt to publicly recruit his former comrades.

New York, October 20, 1780
By
Brigadier General Arnold
A Proclamation
To the officers and soldiers of the Continental Army who have the real interest of their Country at heart, and who are determined to be no longer the tools and dupes of Congress or of France.

Having reason to believe that the principals I have avowed, in my address to ye public of the 7th instant, animated ye greatest part of this continent, I rejoice in the opportunity I have of inviting you to join his Majesty's Arms.

His Excellency Sir Henry Clinton has authorized me to raise a corps of cavalry and infantry, who are to be clothed, subsisted and paid as the other corps are in the British service, and those who bring in horses, arms, or attire, are to be paid their value, or have liberty to sell them. To every non-commissioned officer and private, a bounty of three guineas will be given, and as the Commander-in-Chief is pleased to allow me to nominate the officers, I shall with infinite satisfaction embrace this opportunity of advancing men whose valor I have witnessed, and whose principles are favorable to a union with Britain and true American liberty.

The rank they obtain in the King's service will bear a proportion to their former rank and ye number of men they bring with them.

It is expected that a Lieutenant Colonel of Cavalry will bring with him or recruit in a reasonable time – 75 men. Major of Horse, 50 men; Lieut. Col. of Infantry, 75 men; Captain of Horse, 30 men; Major of Infantry, 50 men; Lieut. of Horse, 15 men; Captain of Infantry, 30 men; Cornet of Horse, 12 men; Lieutenant of Infantry, 15 men; Sergeant of Horse, 6 men; Ensign of Infantry, 12 men; Sergeant of Infantry, 6 men.

N. B. Each field officer will have a company. Great as this encouragement must appear to such as have suffered every distress, of want, of pain, hunger, and nakedness from the neglect, contempt, and corruption of Congress, they are nothing to the motives which I expect will influence the brave and generous minds I hope to have the honor to command, and I wish to have a chosen band of Americans to ye attainment of peace, liberty, and safety (that first object in taking the field) and with them to share in the glory of rescuing our native

Country from the grasping hand of France, as well as from the ambitious and interested views of a desperate party among ourselves, who, in listening to French overtures, and rejecting those from Great Britain, have brought ye Colonies to ye very brink of destruction.

Friends, fellow soldiers, and citizens, arouse and judge for yourselves – reflect on what you have lost – consider to what you are reduced, and by your courage repel the ruin that still threatens you.

Your Country once was happy and had the proposed peace been embraced, your last two years of misery had been spent in peace and plenty, and repairing the desolation of a quarrel that would have set ye interest of Great Britain and America in its true light, and cemented their friendship; whereas you are now the prey of greed, the scorn of your enemies, and ye pity of your friends.

You were promised liberty by ye leaders of your affairs, but is there an individual in ye enjoyment of it, saving your oppressors? Who among you dare speak or write what he thinks against the tyranny which has robbed you of your property, imprisons your persons, drags you to ye field of battle, and is daily deluging your Country with your blood.

You were flattered with independence as preferable to a redress of grievances, and for that shadow, instead of real felicity, are sunk into all ye wretchedness of poverty by the greed of your own rulers. Already are you disqualified to support ye pride of character they taught you to aim at, and must inevitably shorten belong to one or other of the great powers, their folly and wickedness have drawn into conflict. Happy for you that you may still become the fellow subject of Great Britain, if you nobly disdain to be vassals of France.

What is America but a land of widows, beggars, and orphans? And should the Parent Nation cease her exertion to deliver you, what security remains to you for the enjoyment of ye consolations of that religion for which your fathers braved the ocean, ye heathen, and ye wilderness? Do you know that the eye which guides this pen lately saw your mean and profligate Congress at mass for the soul of a Roman Catholic in Purgatory, and participating in the rights of a church against whose anti-Christian corruption your pious ancestors would have witnessed with their blood.

As to you who have been soldiers in the Continental Army, can you at this day want evidence that the funds of your Country are exhausted, or that the managers have applied them to their own private uses? In either case you surely can continue no longer in their service with honor or advantage; yet you have hitherto been their supporters of that cruelty, which, with an equal indifference to your, as well as to the labor and blood of others, is devouring a Country, which ye moment you quit their Colors, will be redeemed from their tyranny.

But what need of arguments to such as feel infinitely more misery than language can express? I therefore only add my promise of ye most affectionate welcome and attention to all who are disposed to join me in the measures necessary to close the scene of our afflictions, which intolerable as they are, must continue to increase until we have the wisdom (shown of late by Ireland) in being contented with ye liberality of the Parent Country, who still offers her protection, with ye immediate restoration of our ancient privileges, civil and sacred, and a perpetual exemption from all taxes, but such as we shall think fit to impose on ourselves.

B. Arnold [5]

XX
New York

Washington had also devised a plan to capture Arnold and bring him to a justice more deserving than that given to Andre' by summoning twenty-four year old Major Henry Lee to his headquarters. Better known as "Light Horse Harry," Lee was an adventurous and whimsical Federalist from Virginia who joined the Revolution right out of the College of New Jersey. Displaying soldierly qualities from the start, he was taken into Washington's confidence and reconnaissance. Being a dashing and capable cavalry officer, his elite troops known as "Lee's Legion" made a surprise attack at Paulus Hook, New Jersey and captured 160 enemy troops with minimal casualties in which he was awarded a medal from Congress.

To Major Lee

October 13, 1780

Dear Sir

I am very glad your letter of this date has given strength to my conviction of the innocence of the gentleman, who was the subject of your inquiry. I wish to see you on a particular piece of business. If the day is fair and nothing of consequence intervenes, I will be at the Marquis' quarters by ten o'clock tomorrow. If this should not happen, I shall be glad to see you at headquarters.

I am, Dear Sir, your obedient servant,

G. Washington [40]

When Lee arrived, Washington announced the result of his meditations. "I have sent for you, in the expectation that you have in your Corps individuals capable and willing to undertake an indispensable, delicate, and hazardous project. Whoever comes forward on this occasion, will lay me under great obligations personally; and, in behalf of the United States, I will reward him amply. No time is to be lost; he must proceed if possible, this night. My object is to probe to the bottom the afflicting intelligence contained in the papers you have just read, to seize Arnold, and, by getting him, to save Andre'. They are all connected. While my emissary is engaged in preparing means for the seizure of Arnold, the guilt of others can be traced; and the timely delivery of Arnold to me will possibly put it into my power to restore the amiable and unfortunate Andre' to his friends. My instructions are ready, in which you will find my express orders that Arnold is not to be hurt; but that he be permitted to escape if to be prevented only by killing him, as his public punishment is the sole object in view. This you cannot too forcibly press upon whomsoever may engage in the enterprise; and this fail not to do. With my instructions are two letters, to be delivered as ordered, and here are some guineas for expenses." [40]

Upon returning to camp on the **16**[th], Lee called upon twenty-three year old Sergeant Major John Champe from London County in Virginia. Lee chose Champe as the man for the job because he thought him to be non-imposing, dignified, thoughtful, quiet, courageous, and persevering; the perfect spy. His mission, if he would choose to accept it, was to feign a desertion, escape to New York, appear friendly to the enemy, and join Arnold's command. Champe accepted with eagerness, claiming that no soldier exceeded him in respect and affection for the Commander-in-Chief. His only concerns were not of the danger and difficulty of the task, but of the disgrace of desertion, to which Lee assured him that no request by the Commander-in-Chief could be considered to be desertion. Lee also revealed that he was honored to be called upon by his Excellency to select a soldier from his own corps who was ready, willing, and capable to execute a project so tempting to the brave and would feel mortified if he was forced to ask the General to seek an agent to execute this bold and important enterprise elsewhere. Champe committed himself to the task and took notes in code regarding the directions for the plan. With the assistance of an accomplice for Champe, Lee wrote out a very attractive offer to Washington on the **20**[th].

To His Excellency General Washington

(October 20th)

Dear General

I have engaged two persons to undertake the accomplishment of your Excellency's wishes. In my negotiation I have said little or nothing concerning your Excellency as I presumed it would operate disagreeably, should the issue prove disastrous. The chief of the two persons is a sergeant in my cavalry. To him I have promised promotion, the other is an inhabitant of Newark; I have experience of his fidelity and his connections with the enemy render him, with his personal qualifications, very fit for the business. To this man I have engaged one hundred guineas, five hundred acres of land, and three Negroes. I gave him the promise of three Negroes, because he is engaged in aiding me to destroy the refugees at Bergen Point. Success there puts it in my power to reward him according to compact. If nothing is done, he is to receive an additional sum of money. The outlines of the scheme, which I have recommended, are, that the sergeant should join General Arnold as a deserter from us, should engage in his corps now raising, and should contrive to insinuate himself in some menial or military birth about the General's person; that a correspondence should be kept up with the man in Newark by the latter's visiting the former every two days; and that, when the favorable moment arrives they should seize the prize in the night, gag him, and bring him across to Bergen Woods.

If your Excellency approves of what is done, the Sergeant will desert from us tomorrow. A few guineas will be necessary for him. I have advised that no third person be admitted into the virtuous conspiracy, as two appear to me adequate to the execution of it.

The sergeant is a very promising youth of uncommon tact and invincible perseverance. His connections and his service in the Army from the beginning of the war, assure me that he will be faithful. I have instructed him not to return till he receives direction from me, but to continue his attempts however unfavorable the prospects may appear at first. I have excited his thirst for fame by impressing on his mind, the virtue and glory of the act.

I have the honor to be, &c., [68]
Henry Lee

Washington accepted Lee's nominee, yet with explicit instructions.

To Major Lee
Headquarters, October 20, 1780
Dear Sir
The plan proposed for taking A_____, the outlines of which are communicated in your letter which was this moment put into my hands without a date, has every mark of a good one. I therefore leave the whole to the guidance of your own judgement, with the express stipulation and pointed injunction, that he is brought to me alive. No circumstances whatever shall obtain my consent to his being put to death. The idea, which would accompany such an event, would be that ruffians had been hired to assassinate him. My aim is to make a public example of him; and this should be strongly impressed upon those who are employed to bring him off. I send you five guineas, but I am not satisfied of the propriety of the sergeant's appearing with

569

much specie. The sergeant must be very circumspect, too much zeal may create suspicion; and too much pertinacity may defeat the project. The most inviolable secrecy must be observed on all hands. The interviews between the party should be managed with much caution and seeming indifference or else the frequency of their meetings may betray the design and involve bad consequences. But I am persuaded you will place every matter in a proper point of view to the conductors of this interesting business and therefore I shall only add that I am, Dear Sir, your obedient & affectionate servant,

G. Washington [40]

Champe engaged himself in the task on the night of the **20**ᵗʰ by acting out the part of a deserter in a chase scene. He was witnessed by a patrol that challenged where he was going, but his only response was to show them the rear end of his horse as he raced off towards Paulus Hook. The Officer of the Day, Captain Patrick Carnes reported the desertion to Lee, who bought time to continue the secret mission by ordering all men to be accounted for. When Champe was identified as missing, Lee added to the delay by summoning Cornet William Middleton to play the part of bounty hunter, but having to lead by example and do his duty, wrote the standard written order for such a case. "Pursue as far as you can with safety, Sergeant Champe, who is suspected of deserting to the enemy, and has taken the road leading to Paulus Hook. Bring him alive, that he may suffer in the presence of the Army; but kill him if he resists, or escapes after being taken." [40] The guards followed his horse's tracks that were identified by a special stamp on the shoe and enhanced by a recent fall of rain and pursued him through the streets of Bergen until dawn when he caught sight of a pair of British galley tenders in the bay. He charged towards the waterfront, leaped from his horse, trudged through the marsh, and called out to the ships, which soon sent out a boat and snatched him up. When Middleton returned with Champe's horse and a depressed expression, Lee feared that the sergeant had been killed in the hunt, but was relieved when he learned of his escape. On the **21**ˢᵗ, Lee notified Washington that the first phase of the operation was a success.

To His Excellency General Washington

October 21ˢᵗ, 1780

Dear Sir

I have just returned from Newark, where I completed the business your Excellency committed to me. The virtuous sergeant deserted last night. I saw the two in Newark this day. This night they go to New York.

Desertion among us is a perfect stranger. My officers are very attentive, and some of them men of nice discernment. This leads me to apprehend they will discover that the sergeant is on some secret command. Lest the example may operate on the soldiers, the captains will probably inform their troops of the conclusion. From the soldiers, the same sentiments may reach the people.

To prevent this, I wish your Excellency would order me to move to a forage country; this is very scarce of hay. I can send two troops, including the one to which the deserter belongs, to an abundant neighborhood back of the Mountain Meeting House, where they will be safe, and ready for any operation. One troop can remain with me here, which number is adequate to the common duties. Sir Henry Clinton is still in New York. Report says Arnold sailed with the fleet, though this is not credible. [68]

I have the honor to be with the most perfect respect,
your Excellency's obedient servant,
Henry Lee

Upon his arrival in New York, Champe was sent to see Sir Henry Clinton who treated him with kindness and questioned him with intent. How many troops were as disaffected by the war as he was? Could more be persuaded? Could any officers pick up where Arnold left off? Champe performed as expected throughout the interrogation, giving him the most vague but convincing answers. To show his appreciation for his "loyalty to the Crown", Clinton awarded Champe with a couple of guineas for deserting and recommended him to a new commander in the British ranks, who was anxious to procure American recruits, Benedict Arnold. By chance, Champe met Arnold in the street and claimed that the Arnold's example had inspired him, which impressed the traitor enough to appoint him in his American Legion at his current rank. In a letter to Washington on the 25th, Lee reported phase two complete.

To His Excellency General Washington
Light Camp, 25 October, 1780
Dear General

My friend got safe into New York. He was before Sir Henry Clinton and passed all the forms of the garrison. He accidentally met Col. Arnold in the street, which has paved a natural way for further acquaintance. The party entertains high hopes of success. I fear their patience will be exhausted; therefore am of opinion it ought to be impressed on their minds at every meeting. I informed Mr. Baldwin that I was under orders to march south; that I would see him tomorrow, and send on some officer from you, who should transact the business on your Excellency's part in case of my departure. I also promised him ten or twelve guineas. I was induced to do this, because I apprehended he would fail in his attentions, unless he received some part of his promised reward. On hearing from your Excellency I shall be able tomorrow to ascertain with Mr. Baldwin the next interview, the time, the place, and the person. The time and place I will communicate to my successor. Should I leave this Army, I entreat your Excellency's attention to my Sergeant, and should be happy if he could be sent on to me.

I beg leave to thank your Excellency for the confidence and friendship you have been pleased to give me since I became a soldier. I flatter myself I shall enjoy a continuation of it though absent, and that I shall be called on to perform any service private or public you may wish to execute, convenient to my local situation, and not superior to my ability or station. I sincerely pray for your health, happiness, and success. May you never again experience a second base desertion and may you live to put an end to a war, which you have hitherto conducted happily, amidst s many and so great difficulties. [68]

I have the honor to be, with the highest respect & esteem,
your Excellency's most obedient servant,
Henry Lee

While serving as the highest-ranking non-commissioned officer in Arnold's headquarters at 3 Broadway, Champe had access to Arnold's townhouse as well, which enabled him to make a mental record of the General's schedule. The American mole made his daily observations of Arnold and noticed that it was his custom to return home every night around midnight and walk through his garden to use the necessary before retiring. Champe then made arrangements with his counterparts to put the mission into motion. The plan was to kidnap Arnold on his way back from the garden, remove three fence posts that gave access to an adjourning alley, and pass him through, bound and gagged to a pathway that ran down to the river where a boat would be waiting. If they were ever challenged by anyone, they would have referred to Arnold as a drunken soldier whom they were escorting to the guardhouse. He wrote to Lee stating that his arresting band was ready and to have a party of dragoons meet him at Hoboken in order to deliver up Arnold on the night of **December 11th**. As fate would have it, on the morning of the 11th, Arnold moved his quarters to another part of the city and had his legion including Champe, ordered to board transport ships and make their way down to Virginia. Later that night, Lee's dragoons waited in the woods as instructed, but to no avail, the mission literally headed south. Champe then escaped from the British when they landed at Petersburgh, Virginia and rejoined Lee. The poetic account is as follows:

Sergeant Champe.
A Ballad of the Revolution.

Come sheathe your swords, my gallant boys, and listen to the story,
How Sergeant Champe, one gloomy night, set off to catch the tory.

You see the General had got mad, to think his plans were thwarted,
And swore by all, both good and bad, that Arnold should be carted.

So unto Lee he sent a line, and told him all his sorrow,
And said that he must start the hunt, before the coming morrow.

Lee found a sergeant in his camp, made up of bone and muscle,
Who never knew fear, and many a year, with Tories had a tussle.

Bold Champe when mounted on old Rip,
all buttoned up from weather,
Snag out "goodbye", cracked off his whip,
and soon was in the heather.

He galloped on towards Paulus Hook, improving every instant,
Until a patrol, wide-awake, descried him in the distance.

On coming up the guard called out, and asked him where he's going,
To which he answered with his spur, and left him in the mowing.

The bushes passed him like the wind, and pebbles flew asunder,
The guard was left far, far behind, all mixed with mud and wonder.

Lee's troops paraded, all alive, although 'twas one the morning,
And counting over a dozen or more, one sergeant was found wanting.

A little hero, full of spunk, but not so full of judgement,
Pressed Major Lee to let him go, with the bravest of his regiment.

Lee summoned Cornet Middleton, expressed what was urgent,
And gave him orders how to go, to catch the rambling sergeant.

Then forty troopers, more or less, set off across the meader,
'Bout thirty-nine went jogging on, a-following their leader.

At early morn a-down a hill, they saw the sergeant sliding,
So fast he went, it was not ken't, whether he rode or riding.

None looked back, but on they spurred, a-gaining every minute,
To see them go, 'twould done you good, you'd thought old Satan in it.

The sergeant missed 'em, by good luck, and took another tracing,
He turned his horse from Paulus Hook, Elizabethtown facing.

It was the custom of Sir Hal, to send the galleys cruising,
And so it happened just then, that two were at Van Deusen's.

Straight unto these the sergeant went, and left old Rip, a-standing,
Awaiting for the blown cornet, at Squire Van Deusen's landing.

The troopers didn't gallop home, but rested from their labors,
And some 'tis said took gingerbread, and cider from their neighbors.

'Twas just at eve the troopers reached, the camp the left that morning,
Champe's empty saddle, unto Lee, gave an unwelcome warning.

"If Champe has suffered, 'tis my fault",
so thought the generous major:
"I would not have his garment touched, for millions on a wager!"

The cornet told him all he knew, excepting of the cider,
The troopers, all, spurred very well, but Champe was the best rider.

And so it happened that brave Champe, unto Sir Hal deserted,
Deceiving him, and you and me, and into York was flirted.

He saw base Arnold in his camp, surrounded by the legion,
And told him of the recent prank, that threw him in that region,

Then Arnold grinned and rubbed his hands,
and almost choked with pleasure,
Not thinking Champe was all the while, a "taking of his measure".

"Come now," says he, "my bold soldier, as you're within our borders,
let's drink our fill, old care to kill, tomorrow you'll have orders."

Full soon the British fleet set sail, say, wasn't that a pity?
For thus it was brave Sergeant Champe, was taken from the city.

To southern climes the shipping flew, and anchored in Virginia,
When Champe escaped and joined his friends among the picinnini.

Base Arnold's head, by luck, was saved, poor Andre` was gibbeted,
Arnold's to blame for Andre`'s fame, and Andre`'s to be pitied. [40]

Smith's trial had lasted for sixteen days and on **October 26th**, he was found not guilty of knowing the conspiracy between Arnold and Andre`. Back in Philadelphia on the **27th**, the Supreme Executive Council of Pennsylvania adopted a resolution to evict Peggy, not just from the city, but from the entire state.

Philadelphia, Friday, Oct. 27, 1780
The Council taking into consideration the case of Margaret Arnold (the wife of Benedict Arnold, an attainted traitor, with the enemy at New York), whose residence in this city has become dangerous to the public safety; and this board being desirous, as much as possible, to prevent any correspondence and intercourse being carried on with persons of disaffected character in this State and the enemy at New York, and especially with the said Benedict Arnold, therefore, Resolved, That the said Margaret Arnold depart this State within fourteen days from the date hereof, and that she do not return again during the continuance of the present war. [5]

On **November 3rd**, as proceedings commenced for Varick's Court of Inquiry, Congress had put out a resolution to give recognition to his captors.

Friday, November 3, 1780
Whereas Congress have received information that John Paulding, David Williams, and Isaac Van Wart, three young

volunteer militiamen of the State of New York, did on the 23rd day of September last, intercept Major John Andre`, Adjutant General of the British Army, on his return from the American lines in the character of a spy. Notwithstanding the large bribes offered them for his release, nobly disdaining to sacrifice their country for the sake of gold, secured and conveyed him to the commanding officer of the district, whereby the dangerous and traitorous conspiracy of Benedict Arnold was brought to light, the insidious designs of the enemy baffled, and the United States rescued from impending danger:

Resolved, That Congress have a high sense of the virtuous and patriotic conduct of John Paulding, David Williams, and Isaac Van Wart.

In testimony whereof,

Ordered, That each of them receive annually, two hundred dollars in specie, or an equivalent in the current money of these states during life. That the Board of War be directed to procure each of them a silver medal, on one side of which shall be a shield with this inscription, 'Fidelity', and on the other, the following motto, 'Vincit amor patrioe'. And forward them to the Commander-in-Chief, who is requested to present the same with a copy of this resolution and the thanks of Congress for their fidelity and the eminent service they have rendered their country. [26]

Washington later honored each of the three captors at the Post Hannock House near Verplank's Point and offered them all a captaincy in the Army, which they declined. In addition to receiving an annual pension, they were also granted 500 acres of land. Van Wart chose a farm at Mount Pleasant, Paulding opted for Van Cortlandtville (Cortlandt Manor) near Peekskill and Williams settled first in Eastchester then upstate in Broome. A historical marker for the Post Hannock House can be found along Kings Ferry Road on the eastern side of Lake Meahagh in Verplank.

Upon his death, Paulding was buried in St. Peter's Church Cemetery in Van Cortlandtville on February 18, 1818 and eulogized by Isaac Van Wart. In his honor twenty West Point cadets gave him a three-volley salute. Among the cadets stood eighteen year old, George Washington Tallmadge, whose father Benjamin had snatched Andre` from his inevitable escape. A decade later on May 1, 1828, Van Wart passed on and was buried in the Dutch Reformed Church Cemetery in Elmsford, New York along with the same military honors and a similar obelisk was dedicated on June 11, 1829. In 1876, a monument to the captors was erected in the Old Stone Fort in Schoharie. David Williams survived to be honored at several events marking the fiftieth anniversary of Andre''s arrest before joining his fellow captors nine months later on August 2, 1831 and was put to his final rest in the Old Stone Fort. When the initial report of Andre''s execution reached England, the King memorialized him as a national hero in Westminster Abbey where he was later buried in 1821. A historical marker for Paulding's birthplace can be found along Old Saw Mill River Road in Hawthorne. A monument for Paulding can be found just outside the old St. Peter's Church within Hillside Cemetery in Cortlandt Manor. A historical marker for Van Wart's burial site can be found along Route 9A between Main and Van Wart Streets in Elmsford.

An inscribed monument in memory of Andre' was erected in 1880 upon his execution site.

Here died, October 2, 1780
Major John Andre' of the British Army,
who, entering the American lines,
on a secret mission to Benedict Arnold
for the surrender of West Point,
was taken prisoner, tried, and condemned as a spy.
His death,
though according to the stern code of war,
moved even his enemies to pity;
and both armies mourned the fate
of one so young and brave.
In 1821 his remains were removed to
Westminster Abbey.
A hundred years after the execution
this stone was placed above the spot where he lay,
by a citizen of the United States against which he fought,
not to perpetuate the record of strife,
but in token of those better feelings
which have since united two nations,
one in race, in language, and in religion,
in the hope that the friendly understanding
will never be broken.

Arthur Penrhyn Stanley,
Dean of Westminster

He was more unfortunate than criminal.

George Washington

Sunt lachrymae rerum et mentem mortalia tangunt.

Aeneid, Book 1., line 462 [1]

The Latin verse reads: Even here the tear of pity springs and hearts are touched by many things. [1]

After hearing several letters of endorsement from his brothers in arms and a display of all correspondence with Arnold, Varick was cleared of any suspicion of conspiracy to commit treason. On the evening of **October 23, 1786**, while in a conversation with William Henry Drayton and Ralph Izard, Washington recalled Arnold's treason and gave the following account in the presence of his private secretary, Tobias Lear.

"I confess I had a good opinion of Arnold before his treachery was brought to light; had that not been the case, I should have had some reason to suspect him sooner, for when he commanded in Philadelphia, the Marquis Lafayette brought accounts from France of the armament which was to be sent to cooperate with us in the ensuing campaign. Soon after this was known, Arnold pretended to have some private business to transact in Connecticut and on his way there he called at my quarters, and in the course of conversation expressed a desire of quitting Philadelphia and joining the Army the ensuing campaign. I told him that it was probable we should have a very active one and that if his wound and state of health would permit, I should be extremely glad of his services with Army. He replied that he did not think his wound would permit him to take a very active part; but still he persisted in his desire of being with the Army.

"He went on to Connecticut and on his return called again upon me. He renewed his request of being with me in the next campaign and I made him the same answer I had done before. He again repeated that he did not think his wound would permit him to do active duty and intimated a desire to have the command at West Point. I told him I did not think that would suit him, as I should leave none in the garrison but invalids, because it would be entirely covered by the main Army. The subject was dropped at the time and he returned to Philadelphia. It then appeared somewhat strange to me that a man of Arnold's known activity and enterprise should be desirous of taking so inactive a part. I however thought no more of the matter.

"When the French troops arrived at Rhode Island, I had intelligence from New York that General Clinton intended to make an attack upon them before they could get themselves settled and fortified. In consequence of that, I was determined to attack New York, which would be left much exposed by his drawing off the British troops; and accordingly formed my line of battle, and moved down with the whole Army to King's Ferry, which we passed. Arnold came to camp at that time, and having no command, and consequently no quarters (all the houses thereabouts being occupied by the Army), he was obliged to seek lodgings at some distance from the camp. While the Army was crossing at King's Ferry, I was going to see the last detachment over and met Arnold, who asked me if I had thought of anything for him. I told him that he was to have the command of the light troops, which was a post of honor, and which his rank indeed entitled him to. Upon this information his countenance changed and he appeared to be quite fallen; and instead of thanking me or expressing any pleasure at the appointment, never opened his mouth. I desired him to go on to my quarters and get something to refresh himself, and I would meet him there soon. He did so.

"Upon his arrival there, he found Col. Tilghman, whom he took a one side and mentioning what I had told him, seemed to express great uneasiness as it − as his leg, he said, would not permit him to be long on horse back; and intimated a great desire to have the command at West Point. When I returned to my quarters, Col. Tilghman informed me of what had passed. I made no reply to it − but his behavior struck me as strange and unaccountable. In the course of that night however, I received information from New York that General Clinton had altered his plan and was debarking his troops. This information obliged me otherwise to alter my disposition and return to my former station, where I could better cover the country. I then determined to comply with Arnold's desire and accordingly gave him the command of West Point.

"Things remained in this situation about a fortnight, when I wrote to the Count Rochambeau desiring to meet him at some intermediate place (as we could neither of us be long enough from our respective commands to visit the other), in order to lay the plan for the siege of Yorktown and proposed Hartford, where I accordingly went and met the Count. On my return I met the Chevalier Luzerne towards evening, within about 15 miles of West Point (on his way to join the Count at Rhode Island), which I intended to reach that night, but he insisted upon turning back with me to the next public house; where, in politeness to him, I could not but stay all night, determining, however, to get to West Point to breakfast early. I sent off my baggage and desired Colonel Hamilton to go forward and inform General Arnold that I would breakfast with him.

"Soon after he arrived at Arnold's quarters, a letter was delivered to Arnold which threw him into the greatest confusion. He told Colonel Hamilton that something required his immediate attendance at the garrison, which was on the opposite side of the river to his quarters; and immediately ordered a horse to take him to the river, and the barge, which he kept to cross, to be ready; and desired Major Franks, his aid, to inform me when I should arrive that he was gone over the river and would return immediately.

"When I got to his quarters and did not find him there, I desired Major Franks to order me some breakfast; and as I intended to visit the fortifications I would see General Arnold there. After I have breakfasted, I went over the river and inquiring for Arnold, the commanding officer told me that he had not been there, I likewise inquired at the several redoubts, but no one could give me any information where he was. The impropriety of his conduct when he knew I was to be there struck me very forcibly and my mind misgave me; but I had not the least idea of the real cause.

"When I returned to Arnold's quarters about two hours after and told Colonel Hamilton that I had not seen him, he gave me a packet which had just arrived from Col. Jameson, which immediately brought the matter to light. I ordered Colonel Hamilton to mount his horse and proceed with the greatest dispatch to a post on the river about eight miles below, in order to stop the barge if she had not passed; but it was too late.

"It seems that the letter Arnold received which threw him in such confusion was from Col. Jameson, informing him that Andre' was taken and that the papers found upon him were in his possession. Col. Jameson, when Andre' was taken with these papers, could not believe that Arnold was a traitor, but rather thought it an imposition of the British in order to destroy our confidence in Arnold. He, however, immediately on their being taken, dispatched an express after me, ordering him to ride night and day till he came up with me. The express went the lower road, which was the road by which I had gone to Connecticut, expecting that I would return by the same route and that he would meet me; but before he had proceeded far, he was informed that I was returning by the upper road. He then cut across the country and followed in my track till I arrived at West Point. He arrived about two hours after and brought the above packet.

"When Arnold got down to the barge, he ordered his men, who were very clever fellows and some of the better sort of soldiery, to proceed immediately on board the *Vulture* sloop of war, as a flag, which was lying down the river; saying that they must be very expeditious, as he must return in a short time to meet me and promised them two gallons of rum if they would exert themselves. They did accordingly; but when they got on board the *Vulture*, instead of their two gallons of rum, he ordered the coxswain to be called down into the cabin and informed him that he and his men must consider themselves as prisoners. The coxswain was very much astonished and told him that they came on board under the sanction of a flag. He answered that that was nothing to the purpose; they were prisoners. But the Captain of the *Vulture* had more generosity than this pitiful scoundrel and told the coxswain that he would take his parole for going on shore to get cloths and whatever else was wanted for himself and his companions. He accordingly came, got his clothes and returned on board. When they got to New York, General Clinton, ashamed of so low and mean an action, set them all at liberty." [20]

Arnold went on to serve as a brigadier general in the British Army. Following one invasion in Petersburg, Virginia, in May of 1781, he posed a question to a captured American officer, "What would be my fate if *I* should be taken prisoner?" [5] The captain responded, "They will cut off that shortened leg of yours wounded at Saratoga, and bury it with all the honors of war, and hang the rest of you on a gibbet." [5] After conducting further raids in his home state of Connecticut, he returned to Britain with his family in 1782 and acted as a military advisor until the war was lost to the Americans. He was then outcast by the government for being a failure to the British and a traitor to the Americans. He, whose family name is derived from an old English word meaning, honor, had destined himself to change it to be synonymous with treason. For his failure, he died broken and friendless in June of 1801, to be buried in St. Mary's Church in Battersea. Just nine months later, America gave birth to a National Military Academy at West Point, which proudly bears the motto, "Duty, Honor, Country."

Many people wonder why we were saved from this conspiracy. Some say that it was a stroke of luck while others say that it was a cast of fate. I happen to agree with General Washington, who believed that it was something greater; something that he had called, "the interposition of Providence." [24]

581

John Andre` *Engraving by W. G. Jackman* [14]

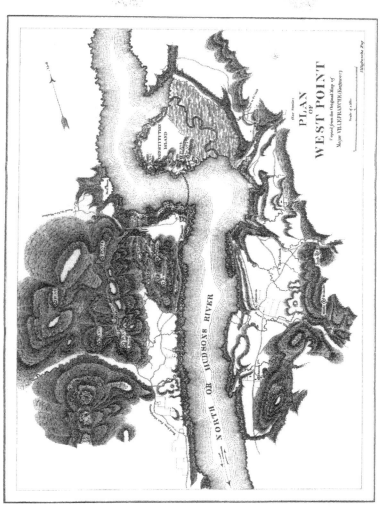

The Gibraltar of America. [12]

Arnold & Andre Rendezvous

Arnold Seals Andre's Fate

Courtesy of Library of Congress Prints & Photographs Division
Catalog Number LCUSZ62-2433

Head Quarters Robinsons
House Sep.r 22d.1780

Permit Mr. John Anderson to pass the
Guards to the White Plains, or below
if He Chuses. He being on Public
Business by my Direction

B, Arnold M Genl

Arnold's Pass [28]

Andre' ambushed. *Harper's Weekly – October 2, 1880* [28]

Andre` discovered as a spy. [28]

Arnold escapes. [28]

Andre' sentenced to death. [28]

Self-sketch of Andre` awaiting execution. [28]

Andre` executed. [28]

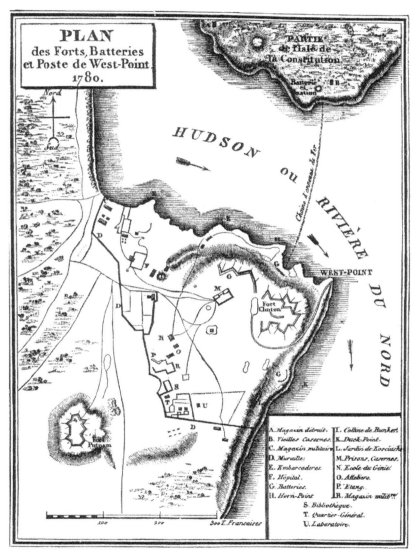

The Key to the Continent is Saved. [28]

And the rest is history. [16]

Bibliography

[1]
Abbatt, William. (1899).
The Crisis of the Revolution.
Harrison, NY: Harbor Hill Books.

[2]
Aimone, Alan C. (March 1976 – Vol. 34 No. 4).
John Andre`: Daring Dandy of the British Army.
West Point, NY: Assembly.

[3]
Andre`, John. (September 29, 1780).
Proceedings of a board of General Officers, held by order of His
Excellency General Washington, Commander in Chief of the Army of
the United States of America. Philadelphia, PA: Francis Baily.

[4]
Arnold, Benedict. (1779).
Proceedings of the Supreme Executive Council of the State of
Pennsylvania in the case of Major General Arnold.
Philadelphia: Hall and Sellers.

[5]
Arnold, Isaac N. (1880).
The Life of Benedict Arnold.
Chicago: Jansen, McClurg & Company.

[6]
Bakeless, John. (1998).
Turncoats, Traitors, & Heroes.
New York: Da Capo Press.

[7]
Beach, James Caleb. (1980).
Year of the Patriots.
Tarrytown, NY: Tri-village Bicentennial Committee.

[8]
Beliles, Mark A., McDowell, Stephen K. (1989).
America's Providential History.
Charlottesville, VA: Providence Foundation.

[9]
Benson, Egbert. (1817).
Vindication of the Captors of Major Andre'.
New York: Kirk and Mercein.

[10]
Blanco, Richard L. 1993.
The American Revolution: 1775 – 1783: An Encyclopedia.
New York: Garland Publishing, Inc.

[11]
Boatner, Mark Mayo. (1975).
Encyclopedia of the American Revolution.
New York: David McKay Company.

[12]
Boynton, Edward C. (1864).
History of West Point and its Military Importance during the American Revolution.
New York: D. Van Nostrand.

[13]
Bratton, John R. (2002).
The Gondola *Philadelphia* & the Battle of Lake Champlain.
College Station, TX: Texas A&M University.

[14]
Burnett, Edmund C. (1963).
Letters of Members of the Continental Congress.
Gloucester, MA: Peter Smith.

[15]
Butler, John P. (1978).
Index: The Papers of the Continental Congress: 1774 – 1789 (5 volumes). (Microfilm).
Washington, D. C.: U. S. Government Printing Office.

[16]
Cirker, Hayward and Blanche. (1967).
Dictionary of American Portraits.
New York: Dover Publications, Inc.

[17]
Clark, Stephen. (2003).
Following Their Footsteps.
Shapleigh, ME: Clark Books.

[18]
Clark, William Bell; Morgan, William James. (1964 - 1980).
Naval Documents of the American Revolution.
Washington, D. C.: U. S. Government Printing Office.

[19]
Coburn, Frank Warren. (1970).
The Battle of April 19, 1775.
Port Washington, NY: Kennikat Press.

[20]
Commager, Henry Steele, and Morris, Richard B. (1967).
The Spirit of Seventy-Six: The Story of the American Revolution.
as told by participants.
New York: Harper & Row.

[21]
Dawson, Henry B. (1866).
Papers Concerning the Capture of Major John Andre`.
Yonkers, NY: The Gazette.

[22]
Decker, Malcolm. (1932).
Benedict Arnold: Son of the Havens.
New York: Antiquarian Press, Ltd.

[23]
Dykman, Jackson O. (1889).
The Last Twelve Days of Major Andre`.
Mount Vernon, New York: Magazine of American History.

[24]
Fitzpatrick, John C. (1937).
The Writings of George Washington. (38 Volumes).
Washington D.C.: United States Government Printing Office.

[25]
Force, Peter. (1972).
American Archives. (9 Volumes).
New York: Johnson Reprint Company.

[26]
Ford, Worthington Chauncey. (1968).
Journals of the Continental Congress. (34 volumes)
New York: Johnson Reprint Corp.

[27]
Freeman, Douglas Southall. (1952).
George Washington: A Biography.
New York: Charles Scribner's Sons.

[28]
French, Allen. (1928).
The Taking of Ticonderoga in 1775.
Cambridge, MA: Harvard University Press.

[29]
Grafton, John. (1975).
The American Revolution: A Picture Sourcebook.
New York: Dover Publications.

[30]
Hall, Charles S. (1905).
Life and Letters of Samuel Holden Parsons.
Binghamton, NY: Otseningo Publishing Co.

[31]
Hamilton, Edward P. (1964).
Fort Ticonderoga: Key to a Continent.
Boston: Little, Brown and Company.

[32]
Hand, Julianna Free. (1980).
The Westchester Treasure Hunt Tour.
Croton on Hudson, NY: Julianna Free Hand.

[33]
Hart, Albert Bushnell. (1907).
The Varick Court of Inquiry.
Cambridge, MA: H. O. Houghton and Company.

[34]
Hatch, Robert McConnell. (1986).
Major John Andre`: A Gallant in Spy's Clothing.
Boston, MA: Houghton Mifflin Company.

[35]
Heitman, Francis B. (1914).
Historical register of Officers of the Continental Army during the War of the Revolution – April, 1775 to December, 1783.
Washington, D. C.: The Rare Book Shop Publishing Company, Inc.

[36]
Hoffman, Francis. (1865).
Proceedings of a General Court-Martial for the trial of Major General Arnold with an introduction, notes, and index.
New York: J. Munsell.

[37]
Ketchum, Richard M. (1997).
Saratoga: Turning Point of America's Revolutionary War.
New York: Henry Holt and Company.

[38]
Koke, Richard J. (1973).
Accomplice in Treason: Joshua Hett Smith and the Arnold Conspiracy.
New York: The New York Historical Society.

[39]
Leake, Isaac Q. (1857).
Memoir of the Life and Times of General John Lamb.
Glendale, NY: Benchmark Publishing Company Inc.

[40]
Lee, Henry. (1864).
Champe's Adventure.
New York: Office of the Rebellion Record.

[41]
Lossing, Benson J. (1851).
The Pictorial Field Book of the Revolution.
New York: Harper Brothers.

[42]
Lossing, Benson J. (1860).
The Life and Times of Philip Schuyler.
New York: Sheldon and Company.

[43]
Lundeberg, Philip K. (1995).
The Gunboat *Philadelphia* and the Defense of Lake Champlain in 1776.
Vergennes, VT: Lake Champlain Maritime Museum.

[44]
Luzader, John. (2002).
Decision on the Hudson: The Battles of Saratoga.
Fort Washington, PA: Eastern National.

[45]
Mahan, Alfred Thayer. (1913).
The Major Operations of the Navies in the War of Independence.
Boston: Little, Brown, and Company.

[46]
Malone, Dumas. (1933).
Dictionary of American Biography (11 volumes).
New York: Charles Scribner's Sons.

[47]
Martin, James Kirby. (1997).
Benedict Arnold: Revolutionary Hero: An American Warrior Reconsidered.
New York: New York University Press.

[48]
Massachusetts Provincial Congress. (1838).
The Journals of Each Provincial Congress of Massachusetts in 1774 and 1775,
and the Committee of Safety.
Boston: Dutton and Wentworth.

[49]
Mintz, Max M. (1990).
The Generals of Saratoga.
New Haven, CT: Yale University Press.

[50]
Moore, Frank. (1860).
Diary of the American Revolution.
New York: C. Scribner.

[51]
Moore, Howard Parker. (1949).
A Life of General John Stark of New Hampshire.
Boston: Spaulding-Moss Company.

[52]
Morrissey, Brendan. (2000).
Saratoga 1777: Turning Point of a Revolution.
Oxford, UK: Osprey Publishing.

[53]
Nickerson, Hoffman. (1928).
The Turning Point of the Revolution.
Boston: Houghton Mifflin.

[54]
Palmer, Dave Richard. (1969).
The River and the Rock.
New York: Greenwood Publishing Corporation.

[55]
Randall, Willard Sterne. (1990).
Benedict Arnold: Patriot and Traitor.
New York: William Morrow and Company, Inc.

[56]
Richardson, C. Benjamin. (1857).
The Historical Magazine.
Boston: The Historical Magazine.

[57]
Roberts, Kenneth. (1938).
March to Quebec.
New York: Doubleday, Doran & Company, Inc.

[58]
Sanford, Harry E. and Kern, Michael J. (1976).
American Revolutionary History in North Castle.
North Castle, NY: North Castle Bicentennial Committee and
Historical Society.

[59]
Sargent, Winthrop. (1861).
The Life and Career of Major John Andre`.
Boston: Ticknor and Fields.

[60]
Scheer, George F. and Rankin, Hugh F. (1957).
Rebels and Redcoats.
New York: The World Publishing Company.

[61]
Scott, John Albert. (1927).
Fort Stanwix and Oriskany.
Rome, NY: Rome Sentinel Company.

[62]
Senter, Dr. Isaac. (1969).
The Journal of Isaac Senter.
New York: Arno Books.

[63]
Sherwin, Oscar. (1931).
Benedict Arnold: Patriot and Traitor.
New York: The Century Co.

[64]
Shonnard, Frederic and Spooner, W. W. (1900).
History of Westchester County.
New York: The New York History Co.

[65]
Smith, George. (1917).
The Dictionary of National Biography (22 volumes).
London: Oxford University Press.

[66]
Smith, Joshua Hett. (1808).
An Authentic Narrative of the Causes which led to the Death of Major Andre`.
London: Mathews and Leigh.

[67]
Smith, Paul H. (1981).
Letters of Delegates to Congress.
Washington, DC: U. S. Government Printing Office.

[68]
Sparks, Jared. (1838).
The Writings of George Washington: Being his Correspondence, Addresses, Messages, and other Papers, Official, and Private, Selected and Published from the Original Manuscripts; with a Life of the Author, Notes and Illustrations. (12 Volumes).
Boston: Ferdinand Andrews.

[69]
Sparks, Jared. (1848).
The Library of American Biography: The Life and Treason of Benedict Arnold.
New York: Harper & Brothers, Publishers.

[70]
Sparks, Jared. (1853).
Correspondence of the American Revolution: Letters to Washington. (4 Volumes).
Boston: Little, Brown and Company.

[71]
Sullivan, Edward Dean. (1932).
Benedict Arnold: Military Racketeer.
New York: The Vanguard Press.

[72]
Swanson, Susan Cochran and Fuller, Elizabeth Greene. (1982).
Westchester County, A Pictorial History.
Norfolk, VA: The Donning Company.

[73]
Sweetman, Jack. (1998).
Great American Naval Battles.
Annapolis, MD: Naval Institute Press.

[74]
Syrett, Harold C. (1961).
The Papers of Alexander Hamilton.
New York: Columbia University Press.

[75]
Tallmadge, Benjamin. (1858).
Memoirs of Major Benjamin Tallmadge.
New York: Thomas Holman.

[76]
Thacher, James. (1969).
Military Journal of the American Revolution.
Hartford, CT: Hurlbut, Williams & Company.

[77]
Thompson, Ray. (1975).
Benedict Arnold in Philadelphia.
Fort Washington, PA: Bicentennial Press.

[78]
Tillotson, Harry Stanton. (1948).
The Beloved Spy.
Caldwell, Idaho: The Caxton Printers, Ltd.

[79]
Van Doren, Carl. (1941).
Secret History of the American Revolution.
New York: The Viking Press.

[80]
Wallace, Willard M. (1954).
Traitorous Hero: The Life and Fortunes of Benedict Arnold.
New York: Harper & Brothers Publishers.

[81]
Walsh, John Evangelist. (2001).
The Execution of Major John Andre.
New York: Palgrave.

[82]
Washington, George. (Spring 1778).
Oaths subscribed by Washington and his principal officers at Valley Forge.
West Point, NY: Special Collections.

[83]
Washington, George. (September 27, 1780).
Letter to the Officer Commanding at West Point and its Dependencies.
West Point, NY: Special Collections.

[84]
Washington, George. (1741-1799).
George Washington Papers – Series 4 – loc.gov – Electronic Resources.
Washington, D. C.: Library of Congress.

[85]
Willcox, William B. (1954).
The American Rebellion: Sir Henry Clinton's Narrative of his Campaigns, 1775 – 1782, with an Appendix of Original Documents.
New Haven: Yale University Press.

[86]
Wilson, James Grant and Fiske, John. (1887).
Appleton's Cyclopedia of American Biography. (10 volumes)
New York: D. Appleton and Company.

[87]
Winsor, Justin. (1887).
Narrative and Critical History of America.
New York: Houghton, Mifflin and Company.

[88]
Wood, W. J. (1990).
Battles of the Revolutionary War: 1775 – 1781.
Chapel Hill, NC: Algonquin Books.

Index

Articles of Confederation: 545
Atwater, Dr. David: 234
Augusta, ME: 75
Babcock, CPT Elisha: 63
Balcarres, LTC Alexander Lindsay: 268, 281, 282, 285
Balcarres Redoubt – NY: 268, 282, 285
Baldwin, COL Jeduthan: 259, 415, 416
Barbe`-Marbois, Francois: 382
Barber, LT Isaac R.: 427, 462
Barber's Wheat Field – NY: 267
Barker, LT John: 12
Battersea, UK: 581
Bauman, MAJ Sebastian: 462, 465, 495, 522
Beckwith, CPT George: 389, 392-394, 397, 398
Beecher, John: 5
Beecher House – CT: 5
Bemis, Jotham: 259,
Bemis Heights – NY: 259, 262, 272
Benedict, Joseph: 479
Bennington, VT: 21, 25, 249, 252, 261, 268
Bennington: 496
Bethel, CT: 228, 232
Bigelow, MAJ Timothy: 68, 76, 167
Blakeslee, Tilley: 5
Blauvelt, NY: 518
Boles, Peter: 4, 5
Boston, MA: 5-8, 10, 11, 16, 18, 24, 40, 47, 49, 68, 85, 117, 123, 130, 137, 143, 146, 156, 179, 209, 214, 216, 218, 220, 223, 239, 252, 262, 281, 303, 351, 354, 385, 390, 403, 446, 520, 524
Boston: 159, 169
Botsford, ENS Clemens: 174, 176
Boyd, CPT Ebenezer: 475, 476
Bradley, Anar: 234
Bradley, COL Philip Burr: 364
Brandywine, PA: 299, 322, 336, 352, 364, 412, 415, 438, 446, 548
Brant, Joseph: 251
Bray, Asa: 283
Breed's Hill – MA: 146
Breymann, LTC Heinrich: 266, 268, 282, 288
Breymann Redoubt – NY: 268, 282, 288
Briggs, William: 198
Brinkerhoff House – NY: 489

Bristol, RI: 208, 211, 212, 241, 243, 317
Britannia: 74
Broad Bay: 74
Brookhaven, CT: 438
Brooks, LTC John: 254, 255, 279, 280, 282, 285
Broome, NY: 576
Brown, LTC John: 7, 8, 15, 17, 21, 24, 26, 31-33, 35, 41, 42, 46, 48,
58, 63, 64, 116-118, 154, 224, 230, 239, 247, 250, 261, 276, 319, 320
Browne, Montfort: 230
Brundage, Sylvanus: 479
Brundage House – NY: 479
Brunswick, NJ: 213, 215, 242-244, 354
Brunswick: 177
Bull, Epap: 24
Bull, COL Thomas: 240, 244, 359, 360
Bullas, Thomas: 451
Bunker Hill – MA: 67, 207, 223, 252, 254, 262, 302, 444, 520, 524
Burgoyne, GN John: 10, 129, 130, 141, 192, 195, 196, 199, 205, 245-
247, 249-252, 255, 256, 259-263, 265-269, 274, 275, 277, 278, 281,
282, 288-292, 350, 429
Burns' Tavern – PA: 359, 360
Burrowes, MAJ John: 474
Bush, ENS John: 176
Button Bay – VT: 190
Cadwalader, BG John: 209, 211
Cahoon, Joseph: 457, 458, 460, 461, 470, 529
Cahoon, Samuel: 454, 456-458, 460, 461, 470, 529, 538
Calderwood, LT James: 171, 172, 182
Cambridge, MA: 11, 12, 15-17, 27-30, 33-35, 38, 42, 44, 46, 50, 59,
64, 68, 67, 70, 73, 92, 93, 110, 114, 126, 130, 162, 223, 252, 255,
264, 444, 446, 506
Campbell, LTC Donald (Royal Army): 275
Campbell, COL Donald (Continental Army): 99, 102, 116, 118
Campbell, CPT George: 290, 356, 357, 360
Canassadaga, NY: 136
Canterbury, CT: 1, 2
Carleton, GN Sir Guy: 20, 49, 51, 52, 66, 82, 91, 94, 104, 106, 108,
109, 112, 113, 124, 128, 129, 146, 150, 184, 187, 187, 190, 192, 194,
195, 197-199, 205, 268, 556
Carleton, LTC Thomas: 185
Carleton: 177, 184-186, 189, 190, 193, 196-198
Carlisle, PA: 336

Carnegy, Patrick: 186
Carnes, CPT Patrick: 507, 570
Carroll, Charles: 123, 124
Castleton, VT: 18, 25, 59
Caughnawaga, NY: 51, 134, 137
Caughnawaga Indians: 133
Cedar Point – CT: 227, 232
Cedars, The – NY: 131, 132, 135, 136, 251, 520
Chambers, COL Stephen: 356
Chambly, QC: 32, 39, 43, 52, 53, 87, 112, 128, 130, 131, 135, 137, 138, 140, 144, 147, 159, 336
Champe, SGM John: 568, 570-575
Charleston, SC: 221, 292, 343, 347, 383, 389, 468, 489, 547, 548
Charlestown, MA: 520
Charming Nancy: 297, 298, 305, 317, 318, 323, 366, 383
Chase, Samuel: 123, 124, 171, 172
Chaudiere Pond – QC: 76, 78, 80, 81, 86
Chaudiere River – QC: 78, 79, 82, 83
Cheeseman, CPT Jacob: 97, 99, 116
Chestnut Neck, NJ: 304, 366
Chew, Peggy: 336, 355
Chimney Point – VT: 190
Church, Dr. Benjamin: 16, 17, 67
Churchill Papers: 265
Cilley, COL Joseph: 262, 263, 278
City Tavern – PA: 302, 357
Clark, Jonas: 11
Clark's Kill – NY: 480
Clarke, Sir Francis: 282, 289
Clarke, COL Thomas: 345
Clarkson, MAJ Matthew: 260, 318, 320, 377, 383
Claverack, NY: 408
Clinton, GOV George: 207, 261, 275-277, 290, 413, 422-424, 427, 478, 509
Clinton, GN Sir Henry: 207, 208, 267, 273, 275, 276, 290, 291, 300, 319, 334, 336, 337, 345, 347, 349, 363, 389, 390, 393-395, 400, 402, 405, 407, 418, 424, 426, 434, 445, 446, 451, 453-455, 473, 475, 487, 488-490, 495, 509, 513, 514, 521-525, 529-531, 534-536, 540, 543, 547-549, 552, 554-556, 560, 563, 571, 579, 581
Clinton, BG James: 109, 111, 275, 277, 394, 519
Clough, MAJ Alexander: 300
Coburn, James: 445

DeBlois, Betsy: 218, 294
De Haas, COL John: 136
Delaware Bay – DE: 240
Delaware River – NJ/PA: 141, 241-243, 259, 261, 293, 317, 403
Denny, CPT John: 428, 436
Deschambault, QC: 131, 132
De Wint House – NY: 518
Dickerson's Tavern – NJ: 363
Digby, LT William: 203, 264, 288, 291
Dobbs Ferry, NY: 415, 428, 430, 433-436, 439, 441-444, 448, 450, 453, 458, 459, 491, 523, 530, 534-536, 539
Don, LT John: 263
Douglas, CPT Charles: 147, 194
Douglass, CPT Asa: 25
Douglass, CDE William: 114, 119, 123-126
Drake, LTC Gilbert: 475
Duer, William: 63, 508
Dunbarton, NH: 223
Dunn, CPT Isaac Budd: 178, 180
Dutch Reformed Church – NY: 518-520
Eagle: 74
Eastchester, NY: 576
Egg Harbor, NJ: 298, 304, 306, 310, 311, 313, 314, 366, 374, 375
Elizabethtown, NJ: 318, 364, 401, 574
Elliott, Andrew: 530, 531, 554
Elmsford, NY: 576, 577
Enos, LTC Roger: 68, 76, 80-82, 84, 86, 92
Enterprise: 132, 159, 169, 185, 190
Erskine, BG Sir William: 230
Estaing, Charles Hector Theodat, Comte d': 351, 412
Eustis, Dr. William: 444, 494, 496, 498, 533
Fairmount Park – PA: 323
Feltham, LT Jocelyn: 19, 23, 49, 51
Ferris Bay – VT: 190
Filkins, Isaac: 451
Fishkill, NY: 394, 408, 414, 415, 422, 436, 444, 449, 463, 477, 489, 503, 504, 507, 515
Fisk, LT Squire: 462
Fitzgerald, COL John: 328, 370
Flemington, NJ: 240, 241
Foggland Ferry – RI: 211, 212
Foote, CPT Ebenezer: 477

Fredericksburg, NY: 312
Freeman, John: 262
Freeman's Farm – NY: 262-264, 267, 278
French and Indian War: 3, 10, 13, 15, 17, 19, 20, 28, 39, 51, 66, 67, 68, 69, 86, 123, 126, 128, 136, 140, 143, 146, 152, 156, 209, 216, 217, 222, 223, 243, 247, 250-252, 260, 292, 331, 363, 364, 400, 422, 519, 524, 556
Gage, GN Thomas: 10, 16, 18, 30, 33, 49
Gansevoort, COL Peter: 250, 251, 253, 256, 257
Gardiner, ME: 75
Garrison, Nathaniel: 451
Garrison, NY: 411
Gates, MG Horatio: 140-142, 145, 146, 148-153, 156, 158, 160, 161, 164-171, 174-182, 187, 190, 191, 194, 195, 196, 203, 224, 250-254, 259-264, 268, 269, 271-275, 277-281, 283, 284, 289-292, 351, 431, 437, 468, 558
George III: 39, 40, 146, 297
George, CPT LT John: 462
Germain, Lord George Sackville: 10, 194, 426, 556
German, Elizabeth: 451
German, Isaac: 451
German, Lucy: 451
German Flats – NY: 199, 252, 253
Germantown, PA: 299, 322, 336, 352, 361, 364, 415, 438, 446, 548
Gerry, Elbridge: 362
Gilbert, Jacob: 487
Gilbert House – NY: 487
Gist, BG Mordecai: 363, 364
Glover, BG John: 249, 260, 270, 282, 519, 541, 542, 543
Gorham, Timothy: 234
Gouvion, COL Jean Baptiste: 435, 442, 503, 504, 515
Gray, LTC Ebenezer: 501
Grays Ferry – PA: 361
Grayson, COL William: 356, 357
Green Mountain Boys: 17, 18, 20, 21, 24, 41, 252
Greene, LTC Christopher: 69, 82, 85, 99
Greene, MG Nathanael: 222, 224, 364, 406, 424, 437, 499, 502, 512, 514, 519-523, 534, 536, 539, 540, 554
Greer, MAJ David: 172, 174
Grey, MG Sir Charles: 266, 267, 336, 352
Greyhound: 534, 536, 539
Guichen, Luc Urbain de Bouexic, Comte de: 446

Gunby, COL John: 364
Gustavus, Adolphus: 334
Hadden, LT James: 192, 263
Hagan, Francis: 169
Haldimand, MG Sir Frederick: 556, 557
Hale, Sir Matthew: 67
Hale, Nathan: 517
Halifax, NS: 126, 468
Hall, COL Josias Carvil: 364
Halstead, John: 113
Ham, Frederick: 451
Ham, Mary: 451
Hamilton, LTC Alexander: 364, 405, 446, 496-500, 505, 510, 519, 525, 531, 537, 538, 547, 580
Hamilton, BG James: 262
Hammond, David: 479
Hammond, Sally: 479
Hammond, SGT Staats: 479
Hammond House – NY: 479
Hanna: 74
Hancock, John: 17, 114, 117, 119, 124, 148, 149, 155, 161, 170, 201, 223, 235, 245, 246, 260, 271, 273, 303, 508
Hand, BG Edward: 519
Harlem Heights – NY: 223, 517
Harrison, LTC Robert Hanson: 505, 507, 528, 538
Hartford, CT: 17, 24, 37, 38, 39, 41, 42, 46, 63, 442, 443, 444, 447, 484, 489, 508, 512, 548, 549, 579
Hartley, LTC Thomas: 150, 151, 164, 165, 173, 181, 183
Harvard University – MA: 6, 16, 47, 117, 123, 179, 239, 262, 302, 414, 424, 444, 520
Haverstadt, John: 357
Haverstraw, NY: 411, 415, 416, 422, 435, 461, 471, 474, 506, 507, 518
Hawley, CPT David: 169, 178, 185
Hawthorne, NY: 479, 577
Hay, COL Udny: 259, 415, 416, 418, 420, 432, 435, 436, 442
Hay House – NY: 504
Hazen, COL Moses: 128, 129, 133, 137, 138, 154, 156, 157, 159, 170, 172, 357, 363
Heath, MG William: 209, 351, 391, 400-403, 407
Hele, LT Christopher: 331
Hendricks, CPT William: 68, 100, 102, 104

Henry, PVT John Joseph: 84, 99, 103
Henshaw, COL Joseph: 41, 42, 46, 47, 55
Herkimer, BG Nicholas: 251
Herkimer, NY: 251, 252
Heron, William: 425
Hinman, COL Benjamin: 46, 55, 56, 58, 62-64
Hogun, BG James: 322
Hoit, Winthrop: 39, 40, 51
Hollman House – NY: 504
Holt, John: 58, 59
Hoogland, CPT Jeronemus: 485, 498, 504
Houghton: 74
Howe, MG Robert: 363, 381, 394-398, 406, 411, 413, 417-419, 431, 506, 519
Howe, Sir William: 146, 147, 150, 183, 205, 214, 222, 249, 266, 267, 290, 292, 336, 372, 517
Howlands Ferry – RI: 212
Hubbardton, VT: 245, 268
Hudson River – NY/NJ: 7, 141, 146, 227, 230, 237, 245, 259, 261, 266, 267, 275, 394, 434, 443, 446, 556,
Hughes, CPT John: 537, 541
Hunter, Elijah: 426, 439
Huntington, BG Jedediah: 229, 233, 296, 519, 520
Huntington, Samuel: 361, 362
Huntington, NY: 233
Hunt's Tavern – CT: 13
Hunter: 87
Inflexible: 177, 184-186, 189, 190, 198
Ingersoll, Samuel: 298
Isle Au Noix, QC (Nut Island): 52, 136, 144, 150, 174, 182, 192
Isle Aux Tetes, NY: 160, 174
Isle La Motte, VT: 172-174, 176-178, 180, 192
Isle Perot, NY: 133
Jackson, COL Henry: 363, 364, 523
Jameson, LTC John: 433, 441, 483-485, 487, 493, 496, 502, 504, 508, 515, 560, 580
Jameson, CPT William: 474
Jay, John: 315, 321, 324
Jordan, Jesse: 314-316, 374-376
Kakiat Presbyterian Church – NY: 518
Keeler Tavern – CT: 229
Kennebec River – ME: 68, 70, 75-77, 79

Kensico – NY: 483
Kierse, MAJ Edward: 453, 454, 456, 457
King, Absalom: 1
King, LT Joshua: 487, 504
King's Ferry – NY: 393, 408, 427, 428, 435, 436, 439, 442, 443, 445, 454, 458, 474, 475, 503, 506, 532, 538, 550, 579
Kip Mansion – NY: 451
Knox, BG Henry: 126, 127, 218, 297, 363, 396, 445, 494-496, 505, 519, 532
Knox, Dr. Robert: 184
Knyphausen, LTG Wilhelm von: 389, 390, 434, 558
Kosciuszko, COL Thaddeus: 259, 413
La Chine, QC: 132, 133, 136
Lafayette, MG Marquis de: 393, 411, 412, 420, 445, 446, 493, 494-496, 505, 519, 531, 578
Lake Champlain – NY/VT: 3, 7, 18, 35, 40, 45, 46, 48, 54, 55, 56, 60, 62, 64, 127, 130, 135, 139, 141, 144, 147, 148, 150, 154, 159, 160, 164, 169, 170, 190, 192, 197-199, 201, 254, 313
Lake George – NY: 3, 43-46, 56, 64, 139, 141, 152, 261
Lake Megantic, QC: 82
Lamb, COL John: 98, 100, 103, 105, 116, 127, 228, 229, 233, 234, 422, 423, 439, 443-445, 453, 463, 471, 494-498, 501, 527
Lambert, Cornelius: 474
Lambert, Henry: 474
Lambert, Lambert: 474
Lancaster, PA: 69, 367
Landrine House – NY: 483
Lathrop, Dr. Daniel: 2-4
Lattimer, COL Jonathan: 262, 281
Laune, Peter: 537, 540
Laurance, COL John: 363, 381, 510, 520-522, 528, 529, 537
Laurens, Henry: 292, 293, 313, 547
Laurens, LTC John: 547, 548, 560
Leamington, UK: 1
Learned, BG Ebenezer: 222, 248, 251, 259, 263, 264, 269, 270, 274, 278, 280-282, 284
Lebanon, CT: 47, 251
Lechmere's Point – MA: 11
Lee, MG Charles: 112, 121, 348
Lee, MAJ Henry: 507, 567-574
Lee, Richard Henry: 219
Lee: 159, 171, 186

Morris Heights – NY: 557
Morristown, NJ: 210, 212, 213, 215, 217, 219, 223, 237, 245, 363, 385, 391-394, 467
Mount Defiance – NY: 245, 261
Mount Pleasant – NY: 576
Mount Pleasant Estate – PA: 323, 324
Munger, Mary: 451
Munger, Sarah: 451
Murphy, Timothy: 281
Natanis: 76, 85, 103
Neilson, John: 261
Neilson House – NY: 261
New Britain, CT: 520
New City, NY: 528
New England Chronicle: 30, 59
New Haven, CT: 4, 5, 32, 48, 55, 154, 231, 233, 234, 296, 324, 393
New Haven: 159, 169
New Hempstead, NY: 518
New Jersey: 159
New London, CT: 207, 211, 281, 313, 383
New Windsor, NY: 276, 353, 463
New York: 159, 169, 188, 189
New York Gazette: 3
New York Journal: 58
New York Packet: 116
Newbury, CT: 228
Newark, DE: 446
Newark, NJ: 198, 568-571
Newburyport, MA: 68, 70, 74, 75, 354, 424
Newport, RI: 1, 208, 211, 212, 214, 220, 222, 398, 400, 403, 405, 407, 412, 490, 548
Nicoll, COL Isaac: 199
Ninham, CPT Abraham: 39, 40
Nixon, BG John: 248, 280, 284
Norridgewock, ME: 76, 77, 80
Norris's Tavern – NJ: 363
North Castle, NY: 438, 467, 483-485, 489, 493, 515
North Salem, NY: 475, 479, 504
Norwich, CT: 1-4, 281, 361, 520
Odell, Dr. Jonathan: 335, 337, 344-347, 404
Odell-Johnson House – NY: 504
Olmsted, Gideon: 304

Orangeburg, NY: 518
Orangetown, NY: 415, 417, 512
Oriskany, NY: 251, 254, 255
Ossining, NY: 470
Oswald, LTC Eleazer: 32, 48, 53, 66, 99, 106, 109, 233
Oswego, NY: 250
Oxford, MA: 251
Paca, William: 319, 323, 340, 341
Paramus, NJ: 345, 546
Parker, CPT John: 10, 12
Parker, CPT Sir Peter: 221, 222
Parsons, MG Samuel Holden: 417, 424, 425, 431, 433, 519
Paschall, Benjamin: 320
Passaic, NJ: 560
Paterson, BG John: 270, 282, 519, 520
Paulding, SGT John: 479-481, 483, 515, 547, 555, 561, 562, 575-577
Paulet River – VT: 64
Pausch, CPT George: 190, 286
Peale, CPT Charles Willson: 302, 358-361
Peekskill, NY: 228, 230, 237, 242, 250, 275, 405-408, 412, 413, 442-446, 475, 478, 504, 576
Pell, Joshua, Jr.: 186
Pellew, Mid. Edward: 186
Penn, Richard – PA: 324
Penn, William: 300
Penn Mansion – PA: 300, 302, 324
Pennsylvania Gazette: 123, 199
Pennsylvania Packet: 313, 317, 319
Percy, Lord Hugh: 214, 215
Peterson, John: 470, 471
Phelps, CPT Elisha: 36, 37, 48
Phelps, CPT Noah: 24
Philadelphia: 159, 169, 187, 188, 200
Phillips, MG William: 245, 262, 263, 266, 278
Pickering, COL Timothy: 414, 415, 421, 423, 437
Pines Bridge – NY: 477, 479, 481, 484, 506, 522, 550
Pitcairn, MAJ John: 10-12
Pittsfield, MA: 7, 17, 24, 26, 224
Plattsburgh, NY: 174
Pleasantville, NY: 480
Point Aux Trembles, QC: 89-91, 94, 129
Point Levi, QC: 82, 86, 87, 89, 92, 93, 129

Robbins, John: 483
Robbins House – NY: 483
Robertson, LTG James C.: 524, 525, 527, 530, 531, 534, 536, 539, 540, 554
Robinson, COL Beverly: 331, 334, 337, 411, 434, 436, 438, 443, 445-450, 453-456, 459, 460, 489, 491, 492, 495, 549, 500, 504, 506, 507, 512, 523, 535, 539, 540, 548, 549
Robinson House – NY: 411, 413, 416, 419, 421, 422, 426-429, 431-433, 436, 437, 439, 442-444, 447, 450, 451, 453, 456, 459, 473, 474, 478, 484, 493, 494, 496, 497, 501-505, 507-511, 514, 515, 531
Rochambeau, GN Jean Baptiste Donatien de Vimeure: 400, 403, 405, 407, 412, 442, 449, 484, 579
Rodney, ADM Sir George Brydges: 419, 489, 491, 558
Rogers, CPT Jedediah: 504
Rogers, MAJ Robert: 180, 223
Rogers' Rangers: 180, 223, 252
Romans, COL Bernard: 24, 28, 29, 32, 33, 41
Rome, NY: 247, 250
Romer, Fanny: 480, 483
Romer, James: 479, 480
Romer House – NY: 480, 483
Royal Gazette: 319
Royal Savage: 135, 159, 163, 169, 175, 178, 184-188, 192, 193, 196, 202, 238
Sabatis: 85
St. Clair, MG Arthur: 155, 195, 216, 245, 250, 262, 406, 519
St. George's Key, BWI: 5
St. John's, QC: 29, 32, 33, 35-37, 39, 40, 43, 47, 52, 53, 63, 66, 81, 87, 95-98, 112, 116, 128, 132, 137-140, 143, 144, 147, 150, 171, 174, 176, 183, 192, 393
St. Lawrence River – QC: 7, 79, 85-87, 89, 91, 94, 95, 119, 126, 147, 393
St. Leger, BG Barry: 250, 251, 253-256
St. Mary's Church – UK: 581
St. Peter's Church – NY: 504, 505, 576, 577
Salem, MA: 354, 414
Santippe: 298, 305
Saratoga, NY: 261, 291, 364, 389, 518, 520, 581
Saratoga Lake – NY: 245
Savannah, GA: 384, 468, 548
Scammell, COL Alexander: 262, 263, 266, 269, 518, 519, 524, 538, 539, 541, 543

Supreme Executive Council of Pennsylvania: 297, 299, 300, 312-331, 338, 340, 341, 342, 361, 365, 367-371, 373, 375, 377-379, 575
Sutherland, CPT Andrew: 453-456, 459, 460, 489-491
Swallow: 74
Swift, COL Heman: 169
Sword's Farm – NY: 261
Tallmadge, MAJ Benjamin: 438, 441, 484, 487, 489, 504, 515, 517, 518, 520, 537, 576
Tarrytown, NY: 228, 275, 438, 477, 479-481, 483, 488, 523, 524, 529, 550, 561
Taylor, Daniel: 290
Teller's Point – NY: 345, 445, 449, 450, 453, 455, 470, 489, 491
Ten Broeck, BG Abraham: 248
Ternay, ADM Charles Louis d'Arsac, Chevalier de: 400, 403, 442, 484, 490
Thatcher, CPT John: 169
The Old 76 House – NY: 541
Thomas, MG John: 126, 127, 130, 131
Thompson, Charles: 299
Thompson, BG William: 143, 162
Thorne, Stevenson: 479
Thorne House – NY: 479
Three Rivers (Trois Rivieres) – QC: 52, 104, 109, 112, 130, 137, 143, 216, 249, 268, 281, 352, 364
Thunderer: 177, 184, 186, 187
Tilghman, COL Tench: 405, 406, 514, 579
Tohickon, PA: 240
Tomlinson, ENS Jabez H.: 536
Treadwell, CPT William: 462
Trenton, NJ: 208, 209, 216-218, 223, 252, 260, 261, 299, 307, 314, 364, 395, 397, 446, 520
Trenton, RI: 241, 244
Trumbull, COL John: 179-181, 183
Trumbull, Jonathan: 47, 48, 62, 169, 207, 208, 215, 261, 393
Trumbull: 179, 181, 183, 184, 188, 190
Tryon, MG William: 227, 230, 231
Tryon, NY: 199, 227, 252
Uncas, Benjamin: 2
Underhill, Isaac: 477
Underhill, Sarah: 477
Underhill House – NY: 477
University of Pennsylvania – PA: 168, 209, 324, 406

Valcour Island, NY: 174, 176-178, 180-182, 184, 186, 188, 192, 193, 197, 201, 202, 204, 205, 264
Valley Forge, PA: 293, 296, 297, 298, 317, 446
Van Cortlandt, COL Philip: 262, 263, 364
Van Schaick's Island – NY: 259
Van Wart, Isaac: 479-481, 547, 575, 576, 577
Van Wart, William: 474
Vanschaak's Island – NY: 269
Varick, COL Richard: 158, 260, 269, 272, 274, 432, 444, 445, 473, 478, 479, 494, 496-498, 500, 517, 531, 533, 575, 578
Verplank, NY: 275, 345, 398, 408, 428, 433, 445, 453, 454, 463, 474, 475, 495, 497-499, 502, 504, 509, 524, 528, 529, 538, 576
Villefranche, MAJ Jean: 415, 416, 425, 466, 497, 498, 524
Vulture: 434, 436, 441, 443, 445, 446, 448-450, 453-455, 458, 470, 488-491, 495, 499-502, 504, 506, 509, 521-524, 528, 529, 532, 534, 535, 539, 549-551, 562, 581
Wade, COL Nathaniel: 497, 501, 514
Wakefield, CPT Ebenezer: 283, 284
Warner, COL Seth: 21, 23, 25, 59, 115, 175, 179, 181, 249, 252
Warren, Joseph MG: 302
Washington: 159, 183, 184, 187, 188, 189, 194, 197-200
Waterbury, BG David: 152, 167, 169, 174, 180, 182-184, 188, 189, 194, 195, 197, 199, 201-203, 205
Waterman, Hannah: 1
Watertown, MA: 23, 30, 34, 41, 48, 218
Waterville, ME: 75
Wayne, BG Anthony: 267, 352, 474
Webb, COL Charles: 46, 277, 431, 462, 464-466
Weisenfels, LTC Frederick: 363, 364
Wells, COL Levi: 463
West, William: 302
West Point, NY: 267, 275, 323, 347, 352-354, 389, 391, 392, 394-398, 401-404, 406-409, 411-415, 419-422, 428, 429, 431, 435, 436, 442-444, 446, 447, 453, 458, 463-466, 485, 493, 494, 496, 498-501, 503-505, 509-514, 517, 522, 528, 532, 533, 537, 548, 550, 551, 555, 557, 558, 560, 576-581
Westminster Abbey – UK: 577
Whitcomb, LT Benjamin: 171, 174-176, 178
White, William: 324
White Plains, NY: 209, 228, 254, 261, 304, 345, 364, 438, 471, 473, 475, 477, 479, 506, 513, 520, 527
Whitehall, NY: 135

Whitestone, NY: 230
Wigglesworth, COL Edward: 179, 180, 182-184, 188, 204
Wilkinson, COL James: 140, 259, 260, 264, 277-279
Willett, LTC Marinus: 250, 253
Williams, Abraham: 479
Williams, David: 479-481, 547, 555, 575-577
Williamstown, VT: 64
Willsborough, NY: 171, 189, 194
Wilson, James: 355-358, 360
Windmill Point – NY: 171, 187, 190
Winchester, VA: 68
Wise, John: 5
Woedtke, BG Frederick William, Baron de: 148, 162
Wolfe's Cove – QC: 88, 94
Wood, John: 77
Woodhull, Nathaniel: 123
Wooster, BG David: 13, 55, 98, 103, 106, 108, 109, 111, 112, 115, 119, 122, 128, 130, 139, 228, 229, 231, 232
Wright, Rueben: 483
Wright House – NY: 483
Wright's Mill – NY: 477, 483, 484
Wynkoop, CPT Jacobus: 114, 119, 123, 124-127, 130, 153, 163, 164, 166-170
Yale University – CT: 2, 7, 13, 67, 123, 228, 438, 517, 520, 530
Yates, Abraham: 19, 20
Yerkes, SGT John: 479, 483
Yerkes' Tavern – NY: 479
York, PA: 267

For many, Benedict Arnold is considered to be both a Hero and a Spy.

From the beginning of America's quest for independence, Arnold valiantly performs his duty in honor of his country by pursuing life, liberty, and those who threaten it. He recaptures Fort Ticonderoga from the British; leads an Army through the wilderness of Maine; takes a bullet while attacking Quebec; stops the British naval forces on Lake Champlain; repels 2,000 British regulars with only 500 Militiamen at Ridgefield; and takes another bullet while defeating their land forces at Saratoga. Claimed by George Washington to be his "greatest fighting general," he is a true patriot to say the least, but, in his quest for glory, he initiates some political battles along the way. A lengthy investigation of his reimbursements brings about verbal skirmishes with members of Congress resulting in the delay of his back pay and promotion. Anxious to regain his luxurious lifestyle, war or no war, he indulges in private business ventures while serving as Military Governor of Philadelphia. His unethical activities bring about a court martial by the state of Pennsylvania, charging him with abuse of public trust. These insults to his reputation on top of his injury sustained while defending his country leaves Arnold screaming for vengeance. Driven by power, greed, and an overbearing ego, he accepts an offer from the British that he cannot refuse; pay and recognition for his services. Shortly before the deed is done, his plan unravels and he escapes just moments before George Washington arrives to discover his treachery.

This is the story that saved the states,
for if the British had captured West Point,
America would have lost its War of Independence.

The true account of seven attempts
to bring down one Nation under God.

Read the book. See the sights. Feel the history.

Mr. Lea has adapted **A Hero and a Spy** into a screenplay and is currently producing a biography and screenplay on the life of John Paul Jones.

Printed in Great Britain
by Amazon

75308460R00364